W9-BHR-663

BOTTOM LINE YEAR BOOK 2009

BY THE EDITORS OF

Bottom Line
PERSONAL

www.BottomLineSecrets.com

Contents

5 • NATURAL HEALTH

6 • VERY PERSONAL

PART TWO: YOUR MONEY

7 • MONEY COACH

8 • INSURANCE SOLUTIONS

9 • TAX TIME

13 • ESTATE PLANNING NOW

PART FOUR: YOUR LEISURE

14 • TRAVEL GUIDE

15 • JUST FOR FUN

16 • HIT THE ROAD

1

Health News

Medical Symptoms Never To Ignore...or Else

Millions of people ignore the symptom that they should pay attention to right away. They think a high fever will decrease or stomach pain will go away—but symptoms such as these can be signs of dangerous, even life-threatening, conditions. *Here are symptoms that should never be ignored...*

ABDOMINAL PAIN

Severe abdominal pain often is a symptom of a medical crisis. *Possibly happening...*

- **Appendicitis.**
- **Gallbladder problems.**
- **Diverticulitis** (an infection of the wall of the intestines).
- **Aortic aneurysm** (a weakened or bulging area in the aorta, the primary vessel that feeds blood to the body).

- **Tumor.**

Urgent: If the pain doesn't go away within five minutes, call 911 or have someone drive you to the emergency room (ER).

If you wait too long: While most of these conditions can be resolved quickly with immediate surgery, waiting can make this problem worse.

Example: Appendicitis can become a ruptured appendix—and instead of going home the day after your surgery, you may end up in the intensive care unit.

SHORTNESS OF BREATH

If you begin to have trouble breathing, you could have...

- **Chronic Obstructive Pulmonary Disease (COPD),** such as emphysema.

Maurice A. Ramirez, DO, an emergency room doctor at Pasco Regional Medical Center, Dade City, Florida. He is a specialist in emergency and disaster medicine and founding chair of the American Board of Disaster Medicine. Dr. Ramirez supervised triage at Louis Armstrong New Orleans International Airport in the days immediately following Hurricane Katrina.

• **Congestive heart failure**—this means the heart does not pump strongly enough to keep blood from backing up into the lungs.

• **Heart attack.**

• **Asthma attack or anaphylaxis** (throat constriction caused by a severe allergic reaction).

• **Pneumonia.**

Urgent: If you are slightly short of breath—you can still speak a sentence without having to stop and take another breath—you can drive yourself or ask someone to drive you to the ER unless you also have chest pain (see the next page).

If you are huffing and puffing, turning blue and/or cannot finish a sentence without taking another breath—what ER doctors call "one-sentence dyspnea"—you are in severe trouble. And "four-word dyspnea"—you can't speak just four words without needing a breath—is extremely dangerous, and you should be on a ventilator. In either case, call 911 immediately.

If you wait too long: Depending on the condition, there could be damage to the heart and possible death from lack of oxygen.

HIGH FEVER

A fever is cause for concern if it is higher than 103°F and is accompanied by a stiff neck, severe headache and/or a rash. *Possibly happening…*

• **Meningitis.**

• **Rocky Mountain spotted fever.**

• **Pneumonia.**

Urgent: Go to the ER fast.

If you wait too long: Serious infection can lead to shock (when the body's circulatory system fails to maintain adequate blood flow).

If you have pneumonia and wait more than four hours to have the high fever treated, you are more likely to die of pneumonia.

HIVES ALL OVER

You suddenly have itchy, red bumps over much of your body. This may be accompanied by difficulty breathing…pale, cool and clammy skin…or a weak or rapid pulse.

You could be having an allergic reaction to an insect bite or sting, a food or other type of allergen.

Urgent: Go to the ER, and don't leave without a prescription for *epinephrine* (EpiPen). Cases of

"hives all over" often will spontaneously recur during the next month—even if you are not exposed to the allergen again—getting worse each time. The epinephrine can short-circuit a severe allergic reaction.

Caution: Once you use your EpiPen, don't assume that the problem is gone. Go to the ER immediately.

If you wait too long: Anaphylactic shock, a life-threatening drop in blood pressure that also can result in difficulty breathing, dizziness and/or loss of consciousness.

SUDDEN VISION OR HEARING LOSS

If you're suddenly blind in one or both eyes and/or deaf in one or both ears, this could be a stroke.

Urgent: Call 911.

If you wait too long: Loss of vision and/or hearing, as well as other stroke damage, possibly leading to death.

DIFFICULTY MOVING OR SPEAKING

If you can't move part of your body, and/or you start slurring words, possibilities include…

• **Stroke,** caused by a clot blocking an artery to the brain.

• **Ruptured cerebral aneurysm** (enlarged area of a blood vessel in the brain).

• **Brain tumor.**

• **Tumor or bone chip in the spinal canal,** pressing on a nerve.

Urgent: Call 911, even if your paralysis or slurred speech goes away. A temporary disconnection between your brain and the rest of your body is always cause for concern.

If you wait too long: If you don't receive treatment for a stroke within six hours, your odds of future disability are 50%. If you are treated within three hours, there is a 70% chance of full recovery.

An undiagnosed tumor can damage the brain. An undiagnosed impediment in the spinal canal can destroy the nerve, causing permanent loss of function, even paralysis.

CHEST PAIN

Most people know that chest pain is a dangerous sign—and yet people with chest pain typically wait six hours before going to the ER.

Then it's often too late to receive treatments that can stop or reverse damage to the heart, brain and other vital organs. *Possibly happening...*

- **Heart attack.**
- **Pulmonary embolism** (a blood clot in a lung artery).
- **Ruptured aortic aneurysm** (a tear in the body's largest artery).

Urgent: If you have chest pain for more than five minutes, call 911. Do not drive to the ER or ask someone to drive you. You need emergency care in an ambulance.

If you wait too long: Heart muscle can die, causing permanent heart damage or death...a partial aortic tear can develop into a full tear, causing a stroke.

New Ways to Prevent a Stroke from America's Leading Specialist

Larry B. Goldstein, MD, a professor of medicine and director of the Duke Center for Cerebrovascular Disease and the Duke Stroke Center at Duke University Medical Center, Durham, North Carolina. He was the chairman of the committee that prepared the American Stroke Association's 2006 Primary Stroke Prevention Guidelines and is a former chair of the American Stroke Association and the Stroke Council of the American Heart Association.

Most people worry more about having a heart attack than a stroke. Heart attacks are more common, but even what may seem like a mild stroke can have serious consequences, leaving you with functional deficits that affect everyday life. Stroke is the third-leading cause of death in the US—and 15% to 30% of patients who have a stroke are permanently disabled.

Latest strategies: The American Stroke Association's guidelines include both well-known preventive measures (such as regular exercise) and measures that have only recently come to light.

Example: Premenopausal women who suffer from migraines have about twice the risk for stroke as those who do not have migraines

(although the absolute risk of stroke for women with migraines is small). It's not known if treating migraines decreases stroke risk—but these patients need to be especially careful about controlling other risk factors for stroke.

Important steps everyone can take...

MANAGE BLOOD PRESSURE

Hypertension (high blood pressure) is the single most important treatable stroke risk factor. It increases the risk of both types of stroke—ischemic, in which a clot blocks circulation to the brain, and hemorrhagic, when a blood vessel in the brain leaks or ruptures.

Because hypertension does not cause symptoms in most individuals, millions of Americans who have it do not know it. Among those who have been diagnosed, less than half manage hypertension successfully.

Good news: For every 10-point reduction in systolic pressure (the upper number) and five-point reduction in diastolic pressure (lower number), the risk of stroke drops by about 30%.

What to do: Get your blood pressure checked. A reading below 120/80 is preferred for stroke prevention. Patients who have had a prior stroke or a transient ischemic attack (TIA, sometimes it's referred to as a "ministroke," which generally causes symptoms for an hour or less) should always take steps to lower their blood pressure. Available data suggest that those who have had a stroke and have blood pressure below 120/80 benefit from lowering pressure further.

Most patients can significantly decrease blood pressure with changes in lifestyle, such as losing weight, exercising more and consuming less salt. If the numbers still are elevated—140/90 is the threshold for hypertension—patients should be treated with antihypertensive drugs.

CHECK YOUR HEART'S RHYTHM

Atrial fibrillation is an irregular rhythm in the upper chambers (atria) of the heart. It prevents blood from circulating efficiently, which makes clots more likely, increasing the risk of ischemic stroke.

Some patients with atrial fibrillation have no symptoms. But, those who have symptoms may experience palpitations, confusion, light-headedness or shortness of breath.

What to do: Check your wrist pulse. See a doctor if the rhythm seems irregular.

Atrial fibrillation often can be treated with a daily aspirin to reduce clotting. Patients with additional stroke risk factors, including those who have had a prior stroke or a TIA, have a higher risk. They may require *warfarin* (Coumadin), a more potent anticlotting drug. There is no evidence that treating the rhythm problem itself decreases stroke risk.

CONTROL CHOLESTEROL

Patients who have high cholesterol—over 240 milligrams per deciliter (mg/dL)—have an increased risk of ischemic stroke. The Asia Pacific Cohort Studies Collaboration, which looked at more than 352,000 people, found a 25% increase in ischemic stroke rates for every 38.7 mg/dL increase in cholesterol.

What to do: Most people can significantly improve cholesterol with regular exercise and a healthy diet—less saturated fat, more fiber, etc.

Patients with existing heart disease, or those who have had a prior stroke or a TIA, should talk to their doctors about cholesterol-lowering statin drugs. The use of statins can decrease the risk of stroke in some patients who have seemingly "normal" cholesterol levels.

DON'T IGNORE SNORING

Loud snoring may be a sign of sleep apnea, in which breathing intermittently stops and starts during sleep. Moderate-to-severe sleep apnea can increase blood pressure, worsen atrial fibrillation and increase stroke risk.

What to do: Any person with apnea symptoms—loud snores or snorts, gasping for breath, daytime fatigue and morning headaches—needs to be evaluated by a sleep specialist. Talk to your primary care provider about sleep specialists in your area.

AVOID SECONDHAND SMOKE

People who smoke have approximately twice the risk for ischemic stroke as nonsmokers, and two to four times the risk for hemorrhagic stroke. Smoking is believed to contribute to at least 12% of all stroke deaths.

Secondhand danger: Exposure to environmental (secondhand) cigarette smoke is nearly as dangerous as actively smoking. People who are exposed to secondhand smoke regularly are 50% more likely to suffer a stroke than unexposed nonsmokers.

What to do: If you smoke, talk to your doctor about the behavioral and pharmacological treatments for smoking cessation. Also, try to avoid secondhand smoke whenever possible.

EAT MORE FRUITS AND VEGETABLES

The average American diet is high in sodium and low in potassium—two factors that can increase blood pressure and risk of stroke. A diet that's high in fruits and vegetables (and relatively low in saturated fat) naturally increases potassium and lowers sodium.

Data from the Nurses' Health Study and the Health Professionals' Follow-up Study indicate that each daily serving of fruits and vegetables can reduce the risk of ischemic stroke by 6%.

What to do: Eat a minimum of three servings of fruits and vegetables daily—but the more produce you eat, the lower your risk of stroke.

ASK ABOUT ASPIRIN FOR WOMEN

Low-dose aspirin therapy is not typically recommended for stroke prevention in men, but it does make a difference in women—particularly those with an elevated stroke risk, for whom the benefits of aspirin can outweigh the potential side effects (such as gastrointestinal distress).

What to do: Women who are at high risk for stroke should discuss aspirin therapy with their doctors. The recommended dose is 81 milligrams (mg) daily.

More from Dr. Larry Goldstein...

Stroke Warning Signs

One treatment for ischemic stroke is a drug called *tissue plasminogen activator* (tPA)—but it has to be given within three hours of the onset of symptoms to be effective.

Unfortunately, about half of American adults can't name a single stroke symptom. It is common for patients to ignore mild symptoms and fail to get to an emergency room in time.

What to do: Call 911 immediately if you or someone you are with exhibits any of the following symptoms...

• **Sudden unexplained weakness,** tingling or numbness in the face, arm or leg—usually on just one side.

• **Sudden difficulty talking** or understanding words.

• **Sudden changes in vision,** such as blurred or decreased vision.

• **Sudden and severe headache,** sometimes with nausea/vomiting.

• **Sudden dizziness** or difficulty with walking/coordination.

Improved Stroke Detection

Researchers studied 356 people who received a magnetic resonance imaging (MRI) or a computed tomography (CT) scan after suffering stroke-like symptoms, such as slurred speech or weakness on one side of the body.

Conclusion: Physicians accurately diagnosed strokes 83% of the time when patients received an MRI scan, compared with merely 26% of the time when CT scans were given.

Reason: MRI scans can detect changes within minutes after the onset of a stroke...a CT scan may not be accurate until hours later.

Julio A. Chalela, MD, medical director, Neuroscience Intensive Care Unit, Medical University of South Carolina, Charleston.

Daytime Dozing Danger

In one recent finding, people in their 70s who dozed a lot during the day had more than four times the risk of having a stroke than those who didn't doze. They also had a higher risk for heart attack and other cardiovascular problems. People in their 70s who dozed moderately had a 2.5-fold increased stroke risk.

Self-defense: If you're dozing a lot during the day, tell your doctor.

Bernadette Boden-Albala, PhD, assistant professor of sociomedical sciences at Columbia College of Physicians and Surgeons, New York City.

Migraines Raise Stroke Risk

In one study of 1,000 women, those who had migraine headaches at least twice a year preceded by visual auras (bright flashing dots, blind spots or distorted vision) had a 50% greater risk for ischemic stroke (caused by a blood clot) than women who did not have migraines.

If you suffer from migraines with aura: Ask your doctor to monitor your stroke risk.

Leah R. MacClellan, PhD, former researcher, University of Maryland School of Medicine, Baltimore.

The Ultimate Cholesterol Profile: Dramatically Decrease Heart Attack Or Stroke Risk

Michael D. Ozner, MD, medical director of Wellness & Prevention at Baptist Health South Florida and past-chairman of the American Heart Association of Miami. He is the author of *The Miami Mediterranean Diet* (Cambridge House). Dr. Ozner's Web site is *www.cardiacoz.com*.

For years, physicians have performed routine cholesterol tests to help identify people at risk for a heart attack or stroke.

Problem: Conventional cholesterol tests that provide basic readings—such as total cholesterol ...HDL "good" cholesterol...and LDL "bad" cholesterol levels—identify only 40% of people at risk for cardiovascular disease.

Each year, about 830,000 Americans die of heart attack or sudden cardiac death (abrupt loss of heart function). Unfortunately, for the majority of people, heart attack or sudden cardiac death is the initial symptom for heart disease. A test that more accurately predicts heart disease risks could prevent many of these deaths.

New strategy: Expanded lipid testing identifies up to 90% of patients at risk for heart disease, according to researchers at Duke University.

LDL ALONE IS NOT ENOUGH

LDL is the form of cholesterol that's most closely linked to cardiovascular disease. Yet the long-running Framingham Heart Study has reported that 80% of patients who suffered a heart attack had the same LDL levels as those who did not have a heart attack.

Reason: Risk is determined not only by the level of LDL cholesterol measured by a blood test, but also by the size of the LDL particles.

Example: Two patients could both have normal LDL readings of 98 milligrams per deciliter (mg/dL). The patient with a higher percentage of small LDL particles is more likely to have a heart attack or stroke than the patient with more of the large LDL particles.

LDL SUBCLASSES

Expanded lipid testing includes a variety of LDL subclasses.

Most important…

• **Lp(a) is a very small, dense form of LDL.** Lp(a) particles readily penetrate the endothelium (the artery lining) and enter the artery wall itself, causing deadly inflammation and atherosclerosis (fatty buildup in the arteries). In fact, patients with elevated Lp(a) are up to 10 times more likely to have a heart attack than those with lower levels.

Treatment: Initial treatment for patients with elevated Lp(a) focuses on decreasing their LDL levels, then addressing Lp(a) levels. Niacin (vitamin B-3) can lower LDL and Lp(a) levels and increase HDL. Patients with high Lp(a) also may need to take the triglyceride-lowering drug *fenofibrate* (Tricor), which can help reduce Lp(a) levels.

• **IDL stands for intermediate-density lipoprotein** (a form of protein combined with lipids). It's a midsized particle that's more likely to cause atherosclerosis than an equal amount of LDL.

Treatment: A cholesterol-decreasing statin drug, such as *atorvastatin* (Lipitor) or *simvastatin* (Zocor), used in combination with niacin.

• **Size pattern.** Pattern A means that a patient has a high percentage of large particles, which are desirable. Pattern B indicates a higher percentage of dangerous small particles.

A patient with Pattern B is up to six times more likely to suffer a heart attack than a patient with Pattern A.

Treatment: Usually a statin drug, combined with niacin and/or fenofibrate.

• **Total number of particles.** The higher the number of LDL particles, the higher the risk for cardiovascular disease. That's because a greater amount increases the likelihood that particles will penetrate the endothelium and travel to the artery wall.

Treatment: Typically, a statin drug.

HDL SUBCLASSES

The HDL form of cholesterol is protective because it helps to remove LDL from arterial walls. Like LDL, it can be subdivided into different particle sizes.

Most important…

• **HDL-2.** These are the larger HDL particles. They transport LDL out of the arterial wall and into the liver for disposal. These particles have antioxidant/anti-inflammatory effects.

Treatment: Niacin increases total HDL as well as HDL-2.

• **HDL-3.** Like HDL-2, these particles lower LDL and can help prevent the dangerous oxidation of cholesterol that's already present in artery walls. However, HDL-3 is smaller than HDL-2 and may not be quite as protective.

Treatment: Niacin helps to increase the size of HDL particles, changing them from HDL-3 to HDL-2 particles.

ARE THESE TESTS FOR YOU?

All patients with cardiovascular risk factors, such as hypertension…diabetes…family history of heart attack or stroke…or smoking, should ask their doctors about getting expanded lipid testing. This testing is not necessary for people with no known risk factors for cardiovascular disease, but it could help uncover hidden risks in such individuals.

Expanded lipid testing costs about the same as the older cholesterol tests and may be covered by insurance, depending on the patient's medical history.

Even if it is not covered, this type of testing, which costs about $100,* on average, is far less expensive than the cost of being treated for a heart attack or stroke.

*Price subject to change.

Women Less Likely to Control Cholesterol

In an overview of 194 health-care plans, researchers found that women were significantly less likely than men to maintain their LDL "bad" cholesterol at the recommended levels (below 100 milligrams per deciliter [mg/dL] for healthy women and below 70 mg/dL for women with heart disease or other risk factors).

Theory: Women and their health-care providers underestimate risk for high cholesterol.

If you are a woman, ask your doctor to check your cholesterol. If it is high, ask how you can lower LDL levels through diet, exercise and/or other medication.

Ileana Piña, MD, professor of medicine, Case Western Reserve University, Cleveland.

More Accurate Blood Pressure Readings

Researchers who followed 1,766 adults found that morning blood pressure measurement, taken at home, more accurately indicates stroke risk than a reading taken in the doctor's office.

Theory: Morning blood pressure is less affected by stress or diet.

Self-defense: Take your blood pressure within an hour of waking but after you use the toilet. (A full bladder can raise blood pressure.)

At-home blood pressure devices can be purchased at most drugstores for $30 to $100.*

Kei Asayama, MD, PhD, senior research officer, Tohoku University, Sendai, Japan.

*Prices subject to change.

Heart Disease and RLS

Restless leg syndrome (or RLS) may indicate heart disease risk.

Recent study: People with RLS were studied in a sleep laboratory. During leg movement episodes, their systolic blood pressure (the upper number) was found to increase by an average of 20 points, while diastolic blood pressure rose an average of 11 points. Episodes occurred frequently—as often as every 40 seconds—causing frequent surges in blood pressure. The study authors warn that this repetitive rise in blood pressure could be harmful to the cardiovascular system, particularly in severe cases of RLS, the elderly and patients with a long history of this syndrome.

Further studies are required to confirm the negative impact of such blood pressure changes. If you have RLS, consult your doctor.

Paola Lanfranchi, MD, MSc, University of Montreal Sacré-Coeur Hospital, Montreal.

Often-Overlooked Heart Disease Risk

When researchers measured the levels of triglycerides (a type of blood fat) in 13,953 men, those with high initial levels were four times more likely to develop heart disease five years later than those with low levels.

Theory: Elevated triglyceride levels are closely linked to a sedentary lifestyle and obesity, which are well-known heart disease risk factors.

When you have a routine cholesterol test: Be sure to ask about your triglyceride levels.

Amir Tirosh, MD, PhD, an attending physician, department of internal medicine at Sheba Medical Center, Tel-Hashomer, Israel.

Diabetes Risk For Women

The risk of dying from heart disease associated with diabetes is 50% greater for women than for men. Women with diabetes also have a nearly threefold greater risk for fatal heart disease than women without diabetes.

Self-defense: Speak with your doctor about ways to treat blood pressure and cholesterol as well as diabetes.

Mark Woodward, PhD, director of the epidemiology and biostatistics division at The George Institute for International Health, University of Sydney in Camperdown, Australia, and leader of a study of 450,000 people, presented at the Second International Conference on Women, Heart Disease, and Stroke.

Flu Linked to Heart Attacks

A recent study discovered a 33% spike in fatal heart attacks during influenza outbreaks. When you have the flu, your white blood cells release enzymes that inflame and damage coronary arteries. As the artery walls heal, a clot can form.

Self-defense: Get a flu shot this year, especially if you're at higher-than-normal risk for a heart attack (e.g., you have high cholesterol, high triglyceride levels or high blood pressure, or you are overweight).

Mohammad Madjid, MD, senior research scientist at the Texas Heart Institute, Houston.

Migraines May Predict Future Heart Attacks

When 20,084 men were followed for 15.7 years, the researchers found that migraine sufferers were 42% more likely to have a heart attack than people who did not experience migraines. Previous studies have found a similar link in women.

Theory: The mechanism that brings on migraines may be associated with an increased cardiovascular risk.

If you suffer from migraines: Ask your doctor to check your heart disease risk factors, such as cholesterol and blood pressure levels.

Tobias Kurth, MD, ScD, assistant professor of medicine, Harvard Medical School, Boston.

Panic Attacks Increase Risk for Heart Attack And Stroke

Panic attacks are characterized by sudden fear and anxiety, sweating, shortness of breath, choking sensation, chills and chest pain.

Recent finding: Older women who had one or more panic attacks in the past six months had four times more risk for a heart attack within the next six months than women who had no panic attacks...and three times more risk for stroke.

Self-defense: If you are having panic attacks, see your doctor.

Jordan Smoller, MD, ScD, associate professor of psychiatry at Harvard Medical School, and director of the psychiatric genetics program in mood and anxiety disorders, Massachusetts General Hospital, both in Boston, and leader of a study of 3,369 women, published in *Archives of General Psychiatry.*

Ibuprofen and Heart Attack Risk

In one recent study, 18,523 osteoarthritis patients took the COX-2 inhibitor *lumiracoxib* (the prescription painkiller expected to undergo FDA review soon) or the over-the-counter pain reliever *ibuprofen* (Advil). Some of the patients also took low-dose aspirin daily. Patients at high cardiovascular risk who took low-dose aspirin and ibuprofen were nine times as likely to suffer cardiovascular events one year after the study as patients taking lumiracoxib and aspirin.

Theory: Ibuprofen interferes with the blood-thinning properties of aspirin.

Self-defense: Do not use ibuprofen if you are taking aspirin for your heart.

Michael Farkouh, MD, associate professor of medicine, Mount Sinai Cardiovascular Institute, New York City.

Viagra May Reduce Heart Attack Damage

According to one recent study, post–heart attack use of *sildenafil* (Viagra) or *vardenafil* (Levitra) can cut heart injury by almost 50%.

Theory: Erectile dysfunction (ED) drugs help cardiac muscle cells remain functional.

However: ED drugs should not be used to protect the heart until more research is done. Recent research used an animal model to simulate heart attack injury in the laboratory.

George Vetrovec, MD, cardiology chair, Virginia Commonwealth University Pauley Heart Center, Richmond.

Latest Research: Half Of Angioplasties May Not Be Needed

Richard A. Stein, MD, director of preventive cardiology at Beth Israel Medical Center and professor of clinical medicine at the Albert Einstein College of Medicine, both in New York City. He is also the author of *Outliving Heart Disease* (Newmarket) and a recipient of the National Institutes of Health's (NIH) Preventive Cardiology Academic Award.

Most Americans who die each year from heart disease have atherosclerosis, fatty deposits (plaques) in their arteries that restrict blood flow to the heart. Many cardiologists routinely recommend angioplasty (inflating a small balloon inside of an artery), usually with stenting (inserting a wire mesh tube), to remove or flatten the plaques.

Newest research: *The New England Journal of Medicine* recently published a study that found that at the close of five years, angioplasty with stenting was no better than medication (such as cholesterol-lowering statins and beta-blockers to control heart rate), plus lifestyle modifications, for nonemergency heart patients. Based on these findings, some experts estimate that at least half of the 1.2 million angioplasties performed in the US each year may be unnecessary.

Surprising: The clots that cause most heart attacks usually develop in areas with only minor plaques—not in the severely clogged areas that look so threatening on imaging tests. That's why preventing clots (by treating plaques) is actually preferable to restoring "normal" circulation to diseased arteries with an invasive procedure.

A BETTER APPROACH

Angioplasty with stenting as well as bypass surgery (grafting healthy veins from other parts of the body) can curb symptoms and prolong life when used appropriately (see "Surgical Options" on page 11).

However, researchers have found that the incidence of heart attacks in some nonemergency patients could be reduced by as much as 70% by combining nonsurgical "medical management," such as that used to lower cholesterol and blood pressure, with changes in diet and other lifestyle factors. The steps required to achieve this level of risk reduction are easy to follow—the key is simply to do all of them.

People who smoke should most certainly give up cigarettes. It's also important to address stress and depression—taking care of how you feel is critical to taking care of your heart. Most people know by now to eat salmon or other cold-water fish. The Harvard Physicians' Health Study found that people who eat fish once or twice weekly have a significant reduction in the number of cardiovascular events, including heart attacks.

Anyone who is at risk for heart disease (due to family history, high blood pressure or diabetes, for example) or has a history of heart disease also should be aware that…

•**Statins do more than lower cholesterol.** This class of cholesterol-lowering medications—

lovastatin (Mevacor), *simvastatin* (Zocor), *atorvastatin* (Lipitor), etc.—has revolutionized both the prevention and treatment of heart disease. These drugs can reduce heart attack risk by up to one-third…and they're just as effective for primary prevention (preventing a first heart attack) as for secondary prevention (preventing a heart attack in patients who already have had one).

Recent finding: Statins may reduce the size of arterial plaques. When LDL "bad" cholesterol is decreased to extremely low levels (below 70 milligrams per deciliter [mg/dL]), plaques cease growing or even shrink. But this isn't the only benefit. Statins also prevent plaques from getting larger…convert plaques from vulnerable (likely to rupture and cause clots) to stable (less likely to rupture and cause clots)…and reduce damaging inflammation in the blood vessels.

Suggested: An LDL reading below 100 mg/dL in patients with heart disease…or 130 mg/dL or lower in patients without heart disease. Every patient with elevated LDL should ask his/her doctor if he should take a statin. (Red yeast rice, a dietary supplement that has the same active ingredient as statins, can be taken as an alternative to statins.)

• **Not paying attention to HDL "good" cholesterol is dangerous.** Doctors tend to focus on reducing their patients' LDL levels because there are many treatment options—and each point reduction can reduce the heart attack risk by 1%. However, HDL cholesterol may be even more important. For every point increase in HDL, heart attack risk drops by 2% to 3%. HDL should be 40 mg/dL or higher in men…or 50 mg/dL or higher in women.

Suggested: Taken in high doses (more than 1.5 g daily), the B vitamin niacin can increase HDL levels by 50% or more. Unfortunately, niacin at these doses frequently causes side effects, primarily itching and/or facial flushing. A slow-release form, such as Niaspan, taken at bedtime, can make side effects less troublesome. Taking a baby aspirin one hour before taking niacin also reduces side effects.

Also helpful: Regular exercise can raise HDL by about 10%. People who stop smoking also will experience a slight increase in HDL.

• **The definition of high blood pressure has changed.** High blood pressure is one of the major risk factors for heart disease. Your blood pressure should be checked by your doctor at least once a year.

If it is elevated—now described as 120/80 or above, rather than above 140/90—work with a doctor to reduce it through diet, exercise and/or medication.

• **Low-dose aspirin is all that is needed.** Aspirin reduces the risk for a first heart attack by about 20%, and the risk for a second by about 25%. In patients who also have high blood pressure, it can reduce the risk for a stroke by about 35%.

Suggested: A low-dose (81-mg) aspirin daily. Higher doses are no more effective in most patients and are more likely to cause stomach upset and/or bleeding. Aspirin treatment is not recommended for women age 65 or younger who do not have heart-disease symptoms, such as chest pain (angina) during exertion. In this group, the risk for bleeding outweighs the heart-protective benefits.

Talk to your doctor before beginning daily aspirin therapy.

• **Fruits and vegetables are more powerful than most people realize.** Eating nine daily servings (one-half cup each) can reduce the risk for a heart attack by as much as 30%. Fruits and vegetables contain antioxidants, which curb inflammation, and fiber, which helps to lower cholesterol.

Best: A Mediterranean-style diet, which consists mainly of plant foods…moderate amounts of fish and poultry…and olive oil instead of butter or other saturated fats. People who adhere to this diet can decrease heart disease risk by 50% or more.

For more information on the Mediterranean diet, go to *www.oldwayspt.org*, the Web site of the Oldways Preservation Trust, a nonprofit food issues advocacy group.

• **Drinking wine really does help.** There's been so much talk about the heart-protective benefits of wine (red or white) that some people think it's hype. But it is true that small amounts of wine (five to 10 ounces daily for men…and five ounces daily for women) are good for the heart. Beer and spirits, in small amounts, also can be beneficial. People who drink moderately can reduce their risk for a first or second heart attack by 7% to 10%.

• **Burning up calories is more important than the type of exercise you do.** Exercise increases blood flow through the coronary arteries. The rushing blood stimulates cells lining the blood vessels (endothelial cells) and makes them more resistant to plaque buildups.

The Harvard Alumni Study looked at exercise in terms of calories burned, rather than the type or duration of exercise. Men who burned 3,000 calories a week by performing moderate-intensity exercise had the lowest incidence of heart disease. (Women should aim to burn 2,500 calories weekly.) This can be achieved by walking briskly for about 45 to 60 minutes most days of the week.

More from Dr. Richard Stein...

Surgical Options

There *are* instances when angioplasty with stenting or bypass surgery is usually necessary. They include when the patient has severe blockages in all three coronary arteries...when the heart muscle is damaged (often because of a previous heart attack)...when there are blockages in two coronary arteries...or when there's a blockage of more than 50% in the left main coronary artery.

In addition, these procedures can be lifesaving if a patient is in the early stages of a heart attack or has pre–heart attack symptoms, such as worsening chest pain and/or elevated levels of certain blood enzymes.

Heart Surgery Breakthrough

A new heart surgery technique will allow doctors to replace heart valves without opening a patient's chest. For the aortic valve only, stents with collapsible valves folded inside are inserted through a leg artery and passed up into the heart. Clinical trials are under way.

Robert O. Bonow, MD, heart-valve specialist, Max & Lilly Goldberg Distinguished Professor at Northwestern University's Feinberg School of Medicine, Chicago.

---

iPods and Pacemakers

When an Apple iPod is held two inches away from the chest of someone wearing a pacemaker, electromagnetic interference can occur in 10 seconds, causing rapid heartbeats.

Self-defense: If you have a pacemaker, don't put your iPod in a chest pocket or hold it anywhere near the pacemaker.

Krit Jongnarangsin, MD, assistant professor, division of cardiovascular medicine, University of Michigan, Ann Arbor, and senior author of a study of 100 pacemaker wearers, presented at a Heart Rhythm Society meeting.

Aspirin Update: Less Is More

Charles Campbell, MD, director of the Coronary Care Unit at the University of Kentucky's Gill Heart Institute and an assistant professor of medicine, Lexington. Dr. Campbell was lead author of an article on aspirin in the May 2007 *Journal of the American Medical Association.*

One out of every five Americans takes aspirin regularly to prevent heart attack and stroke.

That is no surprise. Studies show that taking aspirin daily can lower your heart attack risk by 33% and reduce your combined risk for heart attack, stroke and cardiovascular death by 15%.

Despite these well-established cardiovascular benefits, doctors disagree on the optimal dose of aspirin—about 60% advise one 81-milligram (mg) dose daily (often referred to as "low-dose" or baby aspirin), while about 35% recommend one 325 mg daily (a standard-sized tablet).

What's new: At the University of Kentucky, researchers analyzed 11 major clinical trials comparing different aspirin doses in 10,000 patients with cardiovascular disease (CVD) and reported that 75 mg to 81 mg daily prevents heart attacks and strokes as well as higher-dose (325 mg) aspirin—in some cases, even better—with fewer reports of gastrointestinal bleeding.

HOW ASPIRIN WORKS

Aspirin helps guard against heart attack and stroke by inhibiting the effects of *cyclooxygenase-1* (COX-1), the enzyme that blood platelets require for coagulation (clotting). Aspirin's effect on this enzyme helps prevent the formation of clots that might choke off oxygen to the heart or brain.

Aspirin also inhibits *cyclooxygenase-2* (COX-2), a related enzyme that helps regulate pain and inflammation, such as that caused by arthritis. However, aspirin is a much more effective blood thinner than anti-inflammatory—it typically requires eight times as much of the drug to relieve pain and swelling as it does to reduce heart attack and stroke risk.

My advice: Enteric-coated aspirin should not be used to protect against heart attack or stroke, as it has not been well studied for this purpose. The coating might permit aspirin to pass undigested through the stomach, possibly limiting its clot-inhibiting powers.

WHO SHOULD TAKE ASPIRIN?

Due to the risk for gastrointestinal bleeding and other side effects, aspirin should be used only by people who need it.

My advice: If you have a 10% or greater risk of having a heart attack within 10 years, consult your doctor about aspirin therapy. To learn your heart attack risk, ask your doctor or go to the Web site of the American Heart Association (*www.americanheart.org/riskassessment*).

If you're a man over age 40 or a woman over age 50 with atherosclerosis (fatty buildup in the arteries)...high cholesterol (defined as 200 milligrams per deciliter [mg/dL] or higher)...diabetes ...or a first-degree relative (parent and/or sibling) who has heart disease, you're among those who may benefit from aspirin therapy. Do not begin aspirin therapy without consulting your doctor. A previous heart attack or stroke also means that you should be sure to discuss aspirin therapy with your doctor.

HEART ATTACK PROTECTION

Aspirin can be a lifesaver if taken during— and for up to 30 days following—a heart attack, reducing your risk of dying by up to 23%.

My advice: If you think you are having a heart attack, first call 911, then chew 325 mg of aspirin immediately to help prevent the worsening of blood clots.

Caution: Aspirin should be avoided by people who are allergic to it and by those who have a bleeding disorder or asthma that is exacerbated by aspirin.

Important: Chewing 325 mg of aspirin (or four baby aspirin) before swallowing it can cut the absorption time from 60 minutes for an aspirin swallowed whole to 15 to 20 minutes. It's best not to use enteric-coated aspirin for heart attack symptoms—the coating prevents rapid absorption in the stomach.

Caution: Do not take aspirin if you believe you are having a stroke. Testing is necessary to determine whether a suspected stroke is caused by a blood clot or bleeding, the latter of which could be worsened by aspirin.

ASPIRIN RESISTANCE

Not everyone who takes aspirin experiences a reduction in heart attack and stroke risk. What's more, none of the dozen or so "aspirin-resistance" blood tests that measure a person's platelet response to aspirin has been particularly reliable, according to research done to date.

My advice: Skip the aspirin-resistance tests, and ask your doctor about taking 81 mg of aspirin daily if you are at increased risk for heart attack or stroke.

IBUPROFEN AND ASPIRIN

A study done by University of Pennsylvania researchers showed that *ibuprofen* (Advil) can block aspirin's blood clot–fighting activity—especially if the ibuprofen is taken before the aspirin and/or multiple times daily. Short-term use of ibuprofen (for a couple of days or less) is unlikely to interfere significantly with aspirin.

My advice: If you are relying on aspirin to prevent a heart attack or stroke, avoid long-term ibuprofen use. If you have arthritis or another chronic, painful condition, talk with your physician about taking supplements of *glucosamine* (promotes cartilage formation) and *chondroitin sulfate* (promotes cartilage elasticity)...using *acetaminophen* (Tylenol) at the dosage prescribed by your doctor...or getting local steroid injections.

ASPIRIN'S OTHER BENEFITS

Research suggests that aspirin may also...

•**Prevent adult-onset asthma.** Among the 22,000 men enrolled in the Physicians' Health Study, those who took 325 mg of aspirin daily for nearly five years were 22% less likely to develop asthma than those who took a placebo.

•**Reduce the risk for enlarged prostate by up to 50%,** possibly by fighting urinary tract inflammation, according to a recent Mayo Clinic study.

•**Curb cancer risks.** Of 22,507 postmenopausal women participating in the Iowa Women's Health Study, those who took aspirin once weekly were 16% less likely to develop cancer during a 12-year period than nonaspirin users. Other studies suggest that regular aspirin use may reduce the risks for skin, prostate, pancreatic and breast malignancies.

•**Improve longevity.** Aspirin may be a good preventive medicine overall. Cleveland Clinic researchers who followed 6,174 adults for three years found that those taking aspirin daily were 33% less likely to die during that period, with the largest benefits realized by people who were age 60 or older, unfit and/or diagnosed with a preexisting coronary artery disease.

Acetaminophen Alert

*A*cetaminophen can become toxic in overweight people. Obesity can cause changes in liver enzymes that make the liver vulnerable to the painkiller's effects.

Self-defense: Use as little as possible for pain relief. Do not exceed eight 500-milligram (mg) pills during 24 hours. Consider switching to a product without acetaminophen, such as Motrin or Aleve.

George Corcoran, PhD, professor and chair of pharmaceutical sciences, Wayne State University, Detroit.

Caffeine/Acetaminophen Warning

*C*ombining a large amount of *acetaminophen* and caffeine could cause liver damage and perhaps death. The interaction could occur from drinking caffeinated beverages while taking acetaminophen and also by taking large amounts (higher than recommended dosages) of medications that combine the two for the treatment of various ailments, including migraines, menstrual discomfort, arthritis, etc.

Best: While taking acetaminophen, limit caffeine intake to less than 10 cups per day, including energy drinks and strong coffee.

At a higher risk: People who are chronic drinkers of alcohol (daily consumption for two weeks or longer of the equivalent of six pints of beer, three one-and-one-half-ounce servings of hard liquor or four four-ounce servings of wine) or who take certain antiepileptic medications or St.-John's-wort (an herbal supplement) should discuss with their physicians how much acetaminophen is safe to use.

Sid Nelson, PhD, dean and professor of medicinal chemistry, University of Washington School of Pharmacy, Seattle.

Depression Linked To Diabetes

*R*esearchers followed 4,681 subjects (average age 73) for 10 years, screening them annually for signs of depression. People with a high number of depression symptoms were 50% to 60% more likely to develop type 2 diabetes than those who were not depressed.

Theory: Depressed people may be more vulnerable to diabetes because they typically have high levels of the stress hormone cortisol, which can reduce insulin sensitivity (the body's ability to respond to insulin).

If you have been diagnosed with depression: Ask your doctor to test you for diabetes.

Mercedes R. Carnethon, PhD, assistant professor of preventive medicine at Feinberg School of Medicine, Northwestern University, Chicago.

Diabetes and Hip Fracture Risk

In an analysis of 16 studies involving 836,941 people, researchers found that subjects with diabetes were 70% more likely to fracture a hip than nondiabetics. The reason has not yet been determined.

If you have diabetes: Ask your doctor if you should have an annual bone density test.

Mohsen Janghorbani, PhD, professor of epidemiology, School of Public Health, Isfahan University of Medical Sciences, Isfahan, Iran.

Diabetes Drug Danger

Two diabetes drugs may have dangerous side effects.

Recent research: Avandia (*rosiglitazone*) increased risk of heart attack (a clot blocking the blood supply to the heart) by up to 43%. Avandia and Actos (*pioglitazone*) were linked to increased risk of heart failure (when the heart is unable to pump properly).

These newer drugs are no more effective than older diabetes medications, such as Glucophage (*metformin*).

Caution: Do not stop taking any medication without consulting your physician.

Larry Deeb, MD, president for medicine and science, American Diabetes Association, Tallahassee, Florida, *www. diabetes.org.*

Better Insulin Therapy

During a five-year study, researchers tracked 1,300 diabetes patients who received insulin therapy using either syringes to inject insulin extracted from a vial…or the insulin pens, which contain a needle and a premeasured dose of the drug. The group with insulin pens had average annual health-care expenses about $17,000 lower than those who used syringes (due to lower total hospital costs, for example, and fewer trips to emergency rooms).

Theory: When using an insulin pen, there is less risk of getting an incorrect dose.

If you use a syringe for insulin therapy: Ask your doctor if switching to an insulin pen would be appropriate for you.

Rajesh Balkrishnan, PhD, professor of pharmacy, Ohio State University, Columbus.

Researchers Discover New Skin Cancer Risks: Simple Steps Could Save Your Life

Barney Kenet, MD, assistant attending dermatologist at Weill Medical College of Cornell University in New York City, and the founder and president of the American Melanoma Foundation in San Diego. He is also a coauthor of *Saving Your Skin: Prevention, Early Detection, and Treatment of Melanoma and Other Skin Cancers* (Four Walls Eight Windows).

Even though skin cancer is the most common form of cancer in the US, few people consistently follow the steps to adequately protect their bodies.

Think about it—Have you ever had a severe sunburn? Do you inspect your skin every month? Are the tops of your ears always protected when you spend time in the sun?

Virtually everyone falls short on occasion. But there are simple ways that everyone (regardless of age) can decrease skin cancer risk, including some new recommendations based on the latest research. *What you must know…*

BETTER THAN SUNSCREEN

Skin cancer most often results from exposure to ultraviolet (UV) radiation from the sun or tanning booths. UV exposure that is chronic—or intense, intermittent exposure—can harm cellular DNA, setting the stage for skin cancer.

What you may not know: Just one or two blistering sunburns can double lifetime melanoma risk—especially if the sunburn occurs before age 18, when the body's cells divide more rapidly than they do in adulthood.

Latest development: Recent research published in *The Lancet* indicates that wearing a hat and clothes, which can block harmful UV rays, is a more effective strategy than using sunscreen—a practice that many people rely upon too heavily in an effort to maximize time spent in the sun.

Scrupulous self-protection is especially important if you are fair-skinned and burn easily (turn red after 10 minutes of unprotected sun exposure)…have more than 100 moles…and/or have a history of skin cancer yourself or in a parent, child or sibling. All of these factors increase your skin cancer risk.

A recent finding: Cancers of the scalp account for only about 2% of all skin cancer cases, but they can be particularly deadly, according to a study of bald men recently published in *Dermatologic Surgery*.

Self-defense: Wear hats that have a two- to three-inch brim all the way around. Whenever possible, also wear a long-sleeved shirt and long pants. Tightly woven, thick fabric—such as denim—offers more protection than loosely woven cotton or linen.

Clothing that is made out of a sun-protective fabric helps as well. Such clothing is available from Coolibar (800-926-6509, *www.coolibar.com*) and from Sun Precautions (800-882-7860, *www.sunprecautions.com*).

Also, SunGuard, a laundry additive that contains a UV protectant, can be used when washing your clothes. It is available at most grocery stores and from the manufacturer (866-871-3157, *www.sunguardsunprotection.com*).

BE SMART WITH SUNSCREEN

If you must expose your skin to the sun, sunscreen provides the best protection—if it's used properly.

What you may not know: Sunscreen with a high sun-protection factor (SPF) does not give significantly greater or longer-lasting protection than sunscreen with an SPF of 15. An SPF 45 sunscreen, for example, blocks just 3% to 4% more UV rays than an SPF 15 product and should be applied just as often. For most people, an SPF 15 is adequate. The sunscreen should be labeled as "broad spectrum"—meaning it blocks both ultraviolet A (UVA) and ultraviolet B (UVB) rays.

Self-defense: Cover all exposed parts of your body with sunscreen anytime you expect to be in the sun—particularly when the sun's rays are strongest (typically, 10 am to 3 pm during summer months). Many people do not use enough sunscreen—apply a thin layer on all exposed areas. For maximum protection, apply sunscreen 30 minutes before going out…and reapply every few hours—it is removed by perspiration, swimming or by contact with any surface. (Even with sunscreen use, most people are able to produce adequate amounts of vitamin D, which requires only 15 minutes of sun exposure to the face and hands three times weekly.)

Development: Anthelios SX, a rich moisturizing cream containing a sunscreen that has long been available in Europe, was approved by the FDA in 2006. This contains *ecamsule* (Mexoryl SX), an ingredient that absorbs some UV rays that can pass through other sunscreens. Anthelios, which is available from the manufacturer, La Roche-Posay (800-560-1803 or *www.anthelios.com*), is expensive ($29 for 3.4 ounces compared to $10 for a typical eight-ounce bottle of a traditional sunscreen product*).

For more complete protection at less cost, use a sunblock that contains titanium dioxide—this blocks UV rays, rather than absorbing them, as most sunscreens do. Apply enough so that the sunblock remains slightly white on the skin.

A HIDDEN DANGER

UV light can penetrate most types of glass—and increase a person's risk for skin cancer.

Latest development: According to a recent study, the incidence of skin cancer on the left side of the body—the side that gets the most sun while driving—increases with driving time.

*Prices subject to change.

Children who sit in the back seat for long periods are also at risk.

Self-defense: Have car windows coated with a UV-protective film (look under "glass tinting" or "glass coatings" in your *Yellow Pages*). If you spend time near windows in your home or office, try to avoid long periods of direct sunlight or use blinds or shades.

ACT QUICKLY

With melanoma, early detection is a matter of life and death. Some evidence suggests that melanoma deaths could be reduced by more than 60% if everyone simply performed monthly skin exams.

While confined to the epidermis (the outermost layer of skin), melanoma is nearly 100% curable. For thicker lesions, the five-year survival rate is 50% to 60%.

To detect melanoma, people have traditionally been told to remember "A, B, C and D" in looking for moles, spots and freckles that…are Asymmetric (the two halves don't match)…have an irregular Border (the edges are scalloped or uneven)…show variation in Color (rather than uniform throughout)…and are large in Diameter (more than 6 millimeters [mm]—the size of a pencil eraser).

Latest development: Now there's an "E"— for Evolving. New research shows that change in appearance, itching or tenderness was the most striking characteristic of many early melanomas —particularly a highly aggressive type.

Basal cell carcinomas will typically appear as pearly bumps or as flat, scaly areas, sometimes with many blood vessels visible. And, squamous cell carcinomas typically are scaly, red, irregular patches. Both types bleed easily.

What you may not know: Skin cancer can develop in parts of the body that are not exposed to the sun, such as between the toes or the buttocks.

Self-defense: Perform a monthly self-exam of your skin, using a mirror to inspect hard-to-see parts of your body. Part your hair in sections and inspect each area. Consult a dermatologist about any spots, moles or freckles that look suspicious—and get an annual full-body exam by a dermatologist.

For the most accurate skin exam: Consult a dermatologist who has been trained to use *epiluminescence microscopy* (ELM), a technique that allows a doctor to spot difficult-to-find skin cancers with a small, handheld device.

What you may not know: Many prescription drugs—including some antibiotics, diuretics, antidepressants—and over-the-counter nonsteroidal anti-inflammatory drugs, such as *naproxen* (Aleve) and *ibuprofen* (Advil), can make your skin more vulnerable to damage from the sun.

Self-defense: If you take one of these drugs, ask your doctor for sun-protection strategies.

An Unusual Sign of Lung Cancer

Knee arthritis could be the first sign of lung cancer in heavy smokers.

A recent finding: Middle-aged males who had smoked more than 15 cigarettes per day for at least 20 years and who experienced arthritic knee inflammation, but no other arthritis symptoms, were more likely to have previously undiagnosed non-small cell lung cancer. In all cases studied, the cancer, which is difficult to treat as it progresses, was in an early stage and was operable—and after the cancerous tissue was removed, the knee symptoms decreased.

Self-defense: If you are a heavy smoker with isolated pain in your knee, see your doctor.

Fabrizio Cantini, MD, director, consultant in internal medicine and rheumatology, Hospital of Prato, Tuscany, Italy, and leader of a study of 296 patients with arthritic knee inflammation, published in *Annals of the Rheumatic Diseases*.

Cigarette Smoke Is Dangerous Outdoors, Too

In one recent finding, someone sitting within a few feet of a cigarette at an outdoor restaurant inhaled as much pollution as he/she would in a smoky tavern for a similar period.

Self-defense: Do not sit near smokers even when outside.

Neil Klepeis, PhD, department of civil and environmental engineering, Stanford University, and leader of a study financed by the state of California and Flight Attendant Medical Research Institute, published in *Journal of the Air & Waste Management Association.*

Talc Slows Tumors

Household talcum powder helps to increase the body's production of *endostatin*, a hormone that inhibits the blood vessels that promote the growth of lung tumors. When talc is blown through a scope into the chest cavity, it slows tumor growth. More research is needed.

University of Florida, Gainesville, *www.ufl.edu.*

Gum Disease Raises Pancreatic Cancer Risk

In a 16-year study of 51,529 men, those with gum disease were 63% more likely to develop pancreatic cancer than men with healthy gums.

A theory: The body's immune response to gum disease triggers inflammation throughout the body, which may lead to pancreatic cancer.

To decrease risk for pancreatic cancer: Practice good oral hygiene—brush twice a day, floss at least once daily and see your dentist every six months.

Dominique S. Michaud, ScD, assistant professor of epidemiology, Harvard School of Public Health, Boston.

Lifesaving Surgery Underused

Pancreatic cancer surgery is not used enough, even though it may extend survival. Nearly 40% of patients with early stage pancreatic cancer are not offered surgery, even though the five-year survival rate is 25% higher for patients who have the operation. Called the Whipple procedure, this surgery takes about eight hours and removes most or all of the pancreas, part of the intestine, the gallbladder and part of a bile duct. After surgery treatment includes chemotherapy and radiation therapy. Risk of death from surgery has fallen from 25% to 3% in major cancer centers that perform this surgery frequently.

Mark Talamonti, MD, a cancer surgeon at Northwestern Memorial Hospital and chief of surgical oncology at Northwestern University Medical School, both in Chicago. He was leader of a study of 9,559 pancreatic cancer patients, published in *Annals of Surgery.*

 # Asthma/ Cancer Link

A recent finding showed that asthmatic adults age 55 and older have a 50% greater risk of developing cancer than adults without asthma. The reason for this association is unknown.

If you have asthma: Eat a healthful diet and exercise for at least 30 minutes on most days... maintain good asthma control...and undergo a full physical exam annually.

Richard E. Ruffin, MD, professor of medicine at the Queen Elizabeth Hospital Campus, University of Adelaide, Woodville, Australia.

An Antibiotic That Fights Cancer

Siomycin A, a little-known antibiotic that has shown immunosuppressant qualities when used in mice, targets a gene needed for cancer cell proliferation. In laboratory studies, siomycin

17

A inhibits the gene without affecting other cell functions.

Result: Tumor cells die instead of proliferating. More research is needed before human trials can begin.

Andrei Gartel, PhD, assistant professor of medicine and of microbiology and immunology, University of Illinois at Chicago College of Medicine.

Aspirin Combats Cancer

In a recent study, people who took aspirin daily were 16% less likely to get any type of cancer than people who didn't take it. But aspirin has known disadvantages, such as increased risk of bleeding and gastrointestinal side effects.

Best: Talk to your doctor about the benefits and risks of aspirin.

Aditya Bardia, MD, MPH, a researcher at Mayo Clinic, Rochester, Minnesota, and leader of an analysis of data on 22,500 postmenopausal women, published in *Journal of the National Cancer Institute.*

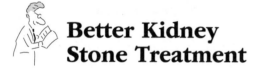 # Better Kidney Stone Treatment

Researchers recently reviewed nine studies involving 693 adults treated for kidney stone disease.

Result: Patients given calcium channel blockers, such as *nifedipine* (Procardia), used to treat heart disease...or alpha-blockers, such as *tamsulosin* (Flomax), typically prescribed for enlarged prostate, had a 65% greater chance of passing their kidney stones than those not given these drugs.

Theory: These medications relax the ureters (muscular tubes that push the urine from the kidneys to the bladder), easing stone passage.

If you have kidney stones: Ask your doctor about trying one of these drugs.

Brent K. Hollenbeck, MD, assistant professor of urology, department of urology, University of Michigan, Ann Arbor.

Don't Suffer with Chronic Heartburn

Philip E. Jaffe, MD, gastroenterologist, Gastroenterology Center of Connecticut, Hamden, *www.gastrocenter. org,* and associate clinical professor, Yale School of Medicine, New Haven, Connecticut. Dr. Jaffe is a spokesperson for the American College of Gastroenterology.

Almost everyone experiences occasional heartburn—that burning sensation in the chest caused when stomach acid washes back (or refluxes) into the esophagus. For millions of Americans, however, heartburn signals a much more serious condition called *gastroesophageal reflux disease* (GERD).

With GERD, the lower esophageal sphincter—the valve that holds gastric juices down in the stomach—becomes chronically leaky, as the result of obesity, certain types of medications or a hiatal hernia.

Result: Acid reflux occurs more frequently (even daily) than with occasional heartburn.

About 7% to 10% of the US population may have GERD—and this puts them at risk for serious esophageal damage from repeated acid exposure, including buildup of scar tissue (affecting swallowing)...esophageal ulcers and/or bleeding ...and Barrett's esophagus, a precancerous condition that, left untreated, can develop into esophageal cancer. Risk for severe esophageal damage, including Barrett's esophagus, increases with age.

SIGNS OF GERD

GERD-related acid reflux usually occurs after eating or while lying down. The most common symptom is a burning or stabbing sensation radiating up the chest toward the neck, sometimes accompanied by bitter regurgitation. *Get checked for GERD if...*

• **You have heartburn once per week or more,** and it's not responding well to over-the-counter (OTC) antacids.

• **You have heartburn less than once a week,** but it has continued for several months or gotten worse, despite taking OTC drugs.

• **You wake up during the night due to heartburn.**

• **Your heartburn is accompanied by...**

• Difficulty swallowing, or a feeling that food is stuck in your esophagus.

• Vomiting of blood…or having black, tar-like stools—both signs of esophageal bleeding.

• Difficulty breathing.

• A chronically sore or hoarse throat.

• A persistent cough.

DIAGNOSTIC TESTS

To determine how much reflux you are experiencing, your doctor may perform the following tests…

• **pH monitoring.** In wired pH monitoring, a very thin wire is inserted into the esophagus to measure acid exposure over 24 hours.

Problem: Though the wire does not usually cause discomfort, the patient does feel its presence, and that can change eating, sleeping and activity patterns, resulting in an imperfect record of typical acid reflux. There is no such sensation with a newer technology, the Bravo wireless pH capsule, in which tiny capsules are attached to the esophagus and stomach, where they transmit acid exposure data to a receiver on the patient's waist.

• **Combined esophageal impedance/pH monitoring.** Some patients may be refluxing nonacidic material, such as bile (an alkaline fluid that aids in the digestion of fats), which pH monitoring alone won't detect. This state-of-the-art approach uses a wire probe to measure acid flow and the movement of gas and liquid into the esophagus over a 24-hour period—providing an accurate record of all reflux. As this is a "wired" system, there remains the potential that patients may alter activities because they notice the wire.

• **Endoscopy.** If symptoms indicate possible corrosive damage to the esophagus—present in half of GERD cases—your doctor may insert an endoscope through the mouth to obtain a visual image of the esophagus.

LIFESTYLE FIX

Lifestyle modifications are often very effective in helping eliminate reflux symptoms—even if you are also taking an acid-suppressing medication. *Such changes include…*

• **Avoiding lying down for two hours after eating.**

• **Not eating within two hours of your bedtime.**

• **Being wary of foods and beverages that relax the lower esophageal sphincter,** including greasy or fatty foods, chocolate, mint, coffee and alcohol.

• **Minimizing nighttime reflux by raising the head of your bed or mattress four to six inches.**

Losing weight can also help. A recent analysis found that, compared with people who have a body mass index (BMI) of 25 or lower (considered a healthy weight), those with a BMI of more than 30 were twice as likely to have GERD.

To determine BMI: Use the calculator at the Department of Health and Human Services Web site (*www.nhlbisupport.com/bmi*).

GERD MEDICATIONS

People who suffer occasional heartburn may be able to relieve it with OTC antacids—alkaline compounds, such as Maalox, Mylanta, Rolaids, Tums, Alka Seltzer and Pepto-Bismol, which all chemically neutralize stomach acidity. *However, OTC antacids aren't strong enough for the severe acid reflux associated with GERD, which is treated with acid-suppressing medication…*

• **Proton pump inhibitors (PPIs).** PPIs are the main treatment used for moderate-to-severe GERD. Available in tablet, capsule or powdered form, they shut down enzymes responsible for the production of gastric acid—reducing stomach acid by up to 99%. They effectively relieve acid reflux symptoms and also allow damaged esophageal tissue to heal. For GERD patients, the PPIs can seem like a miracle, and in most cases, they don't interfere with digestion and the absorption of nutrients.

FDA-approved PPIs: Omeprazole (Prilosec, Losec, Rapinex, Zegerid), *lansoprazole* (Prevacid), *esomeprazole* (Nexium), *pantoprazole* (Protonix) and *rabeprazole* (Aciphex).

Omeprazole is also available without a prescription as Prilosec OTC. All are equally effective at relieving GERD symptoms and promoting esophageal healing, although individuals may respond better to one drug or another. They work best when taken 30 minutes before eating.

Cost: About $5 per capsule for brand-name prescription drugs, and just $2 per capsule for generics.* Potential side effects can include head-ache, diarrhea, abdominal pain, constipation, nausea and gas.

Typically, PPIs are given in therapeutic doses for up to eight weeks until the esophagus has healed. They may then be taken as needed or continued indefinitely at the lower maintenance dose, depending on a number of factors, including the severity of symptoms and the ability of the patient to control what provokes his/her acid reflux.

• **H2 receptor antagonists.** H2 blockers will also suppress acid secretion—although not as well as PPIs—by blocking the action of histamines (chemicals that stimulate the stomach's acid-producing cells). The four FDA-approved H2 blockers include *cimetidine* (Tagamet), *ranitidine* (Zantac), *famotidine* (Pepcid) and *nizatidine* (Axid).

In the 1980s, H2 blockers were the primary treatment for GERD. They've been replaced by PPIs in treating severe GERD cases.

Reason: H2 blockers are less effective at relieving severe reflux symptoms and are not as effective at promoting the healing of damaged esophageal tissue.

• **H2 blockers.** Sold over the counter as Tagamet HB, Zantac 75 and Zantac 150, and Pepcid AC (as well as the prescription Axid), they tend to cost less than PPIs and are popular for treating heartburn. They may also be used to treat mild cases of GERD.

All H2 blockers appear to be equally effective. Like PPIs, they work best when taken before a meal.

Cost: From five cents to $1 per capsule or tablet for brand-name OTC drugs. Potential side effects include headache, abdominal pain, diarrhea, nausea, gas and dizziness.

*Prices subject to change.

Ulcer Protection

There is a new treatment for ulcer-causing bacteria. The traditional treatment—a triple therapy of two antibiotics with a proton pump inhibitor (PPI) drug, such as *omeprazole* (Prilosec)—eradicates 80% of bacteria.

A recent finding: Sequential treatment—in which a different PPI/antibiotic combination is used after the traditional treatment—eradicates more than 90% of bacteria.

Better: Ask your physician about using *bismuth subsalicylate* (Pepto-Bismol) instead of a PPI. Pepto-Bismol soothes the stomach and prolongs the effects of the other medications.

Andrew L. Rubman, ND, director of Southbury Clinic for Traditional Medicines in Southbury, Connecticut, and associate professor of clinical medicine, College of Naturopathic Medicine in Bridgeport, Connecticut.

Arthritis Breakthroughs: Latest Treatments for Pain and Stiffness

Joan M. Bathon, MD, professor of medicine at Johns Hopkins School of Medicine, and director at The Johns Hopkins Arthritis Center, both in Baltimore. She is a recipient of the Mary Betty Stevens Award for Excellence in Clinical Research from the Maryland Chapter of the American College of Physicians.

Too many arthritis sufferers try one or two treatment options and then stop looking for a better way.

This is a big mistake: Doctors now have a wide variety of pain treatments at their disposal for arthritis patients, ranging from simple *acetaminophen* (Tylenol) to a highly targeted injection of *cortisone* and *hyaluronic acid*. For many arthritis pain sufferers, some combination of the treatments can provide more relief than they are getting now.

BEST PAIN MEDICATIONS

For mild arthritis, the recommended pain reliever is still acetaminophen, a fairly effective analgesic that carries no risk of gastrointestinal (GI) side effects. This treatment may be supervised by your primary care physician.

More than half of all patients with moderate to severe arthritis need more relief than acetaminophen can offer. If this is true for you, you're better off seeking treatment from a rheumatologist or an orthopedist, who may start with an X-ray or MRI to see how much the arthritis has progressed—and to rule out other joint ailments, such as bursitis or tendonitis.

The primary treatment for moderate arthritis pain and joint inflammation is usually a traditional nonsteroidal anti-inflammatory medication (NSAID). There are now many different traditional NSAIDs that could be prescribed for arthritis. They include *ibuprofen* (Advil, Mediprin, Motrin, Motrin IB, Nuprin), *naproxen* (Aleve, Anaprox, Naprelan, Naprosyn), *oxaprozin* (Daypro), *nabumetone* (Relafen), *piroxicam* (Feldene), *indomethacin* (Indocin), *etodolac* (Lodine) as well as *ketoprofen* (Orudis).

These drugs have gone through many trials that have concluded that there is no difference in effectiveness. But people react differently to different traditional NSAIDs, so there is a bit of trial and error involved to find which is most effective at relieving arthritis symptoms and is best tolerated by the patient. Two to three weeks is usually time enough to gauge a drug's effectiveness in a given patient.

Also, generally there has been no difference observed in the tendency of various traditional NSAIDs to cause GI complications—ulcers and bleeding—although some studies suggest that ibuprofen may be gentler on the GI tract than the others. Symptoms can be minimized by taking the drugs with food.

Traditional NSAIDs cause more complications when they are used regularly for a long period (over months and years, rather than just for a couple of weeks at a time when symptoms flare up) or are used at higher doses. Chronic users of traditional NSAIDs should always be carefully monitored by their doctors. Chronic use has also been linked to a slight rise in blood pressure in some people, and a slight increase in risk of cardiovascular events, such as heart attack and stroke.

COX-2 INHIBITORS

There's a great deal of interest in another variety of NSAIDs called COX-2 selective inhibitors. These drugs inhibit the activity of the COX-2 enzyme, which is involved in the inflammatory process, without affecting enzymes involved in GI function—theoretically reducing the risk of side effects. The only COX-2 inhibitor now available is *celecoxib* (Celebrex). Two other COX-2 inhibitors, *rofecoxib* (Vioxx) and *valdecoxib* (Bextra), were withdrawn from the market in 2004 and 2005, respectively, after being linked to an increased risk for heart attacks and strokes. Research into other new COX-2 inhibitors is continuing.

The effectiveness of Celebrex appears to be equivalent to that of traditional NSAIDs. Studies have found somewhat reduced risk for GI complications, but studies over the past three years have also found some increased risk for heart attacks and strokes at higher doses, compared with a placebo. For this reason, doctors are now cautious about prescribing Celebrex to people with high blood pressure or other risk factors for heart attack or stroke.

Costs for standard arthritis treatment do vary considerably—from inexpensive for ibuprofen, to about $40 a month for generic Daypro (*oxaprozin*) and up to about $110 a month for Celebrex at its lowest recommended arthritis dosage.*

GLUCOSAMINE

A major study recently found that daily doses of a combination of two nutritional supplements, glucosamine (1,500 milligrams [mg] per day) and chondroitin sulfate (1,200 mg/day), reduced arthritis pain levels somewhat in people who had moderate to severe pain. The treatment had no effect on people with mild arthritis pain. Neither glucosamine nor chondroitin had any effect when taken separately.

INJECTION TREATMENTS

If NSAIDs no longer provide enough arthritis pain relief, then your doctor may recommend injecting the affected joint with a corticosteroid such as cortisone, which can assuage pain and inflammation for up to two months. Because the cortisone injections can trigger cartilage damage if given too frequently, judicious use is recommended—no more than every three or four months.

Alternatively, the doctor may inject the joint with a hyaluronic acid preparation to lubricate the joint, allowing it to function more normally. This treatment is most often used for arthritis of the knee, since that joint injury is the most likely to lead to disability. Preparations approved for injection into the knee include Euflexxa, Hyalgan, Orthovisc, Supartz and Synvisc. Treatment

*Prices subject to change.

typically consists of a series of injections over several weeks.

Caution: It takes a very experienced practitioner to make the injection in the correct spot, especially in the deep hip joint—in that case the injection is typically done by a radiologist using an X-ray, to avoid hitting a nerve or major blood vessel. Use only a professional very experienced in administering hyaluronic acid injections. This treatment is relatively safe, with few side effects, although it can cause pain at the site of the injection. A rare complication of any injection into a joint is infection.

OTHER TREATMENTS

A range of herbal and dietary supplements—not to mention copper bracelets—are also advertised to relieve arthritis symptoms. But, most of these approaches have not been scientifically studied to prove whether they work. *A few options are worth considering, however…*

• **Exercise.** While it will not prevent arthritis progression, it will help strengthen the muscles around arthritic joints and keep the joints functional. Aerobic exercise can add strength to leg muscles and benefit the heart. Regular aerobic exercise involves low-impact activities, such as swimming, walking or working out on an elliptical trainer. Weight lifting is also beneficial, especially to the arms and legs, although it does not necessarily benefit the heart. Consult with a physical therapist first, to learn how to protect your joints by keeping them slightly flexed during your workouts. You run the risk of damaging your joints if you use incorrect form.

• **Electrical stimulation.** A device called BioniCare, which applies electrical stimulation to arthritic joints, is being studied. Some people report that it seems to help arthritis symptoms.

More information: www.bionicare.com or call 800-444-1456.

• **Magnet therapy** has been promoted as an arthritis treatment, the theory being that exposure to a magnetic field—by sleeping on a mattress cover that has magnets embedded in it, for example—can help to stimulate healing electrical activity in the affected joints. While no human studies have shown any benefits to date, some studies of arthritic mice found that those with magnets in their cages did experience less pain

than those without. Studies need to be done on humans who have arthritis before recommendations can be made.

More from Dr. Joan Bathon…

New Studies, New Hope

Currently, there is only one known way to slow osteoarthritis progression, and that is to lose weight—obesity has been clearly linked to increased risk for arthritis in the hips and in the knees.

Another possibility: Avoid repetitive movements which stress the knees, such as bending, squatting, kneeling…avoid contact sports, such as football, and sports in which falls are frequent …and avoid direct trauma to your joints, which also increases arthritis risk.

New studies: Researchers are now exploring drugs that inhibit *interleukin-1* (a chemical involved in inflammation and in the breakdown of cartilage) as well as drugs such as *metalloprotease inhibitors*, which inhibit enzymes that degrade cartilage.

One new National Institutes of Health study, called the Osteoarthritis Initiative, may get us to the finish line faster. This study will follow 5,000 people who have arthritis of the knee or risk factors for it, and gather all kinds of data—including regular MRIs of their knees as well as urine and blood workups. The hope is to identify arthritis progression benchmarks, which will help researchers determine more quickly which drugs are working and which aren't. It currently takes up to four years to tell whether an arthritis drug is effective, this includes the time to recruit patients to study for drug versus placebo treatment and for analysis.

Cola Caution

Cola can increase the risk of bone fractures in women.

Recent finding: Women age 30 to 87 who drank one can or glass of cola per day—either diet, regular or decaffeinated—had significantly decreased bone mineral density, compared with women who didn't drink cola.

Possible reason for low bone density: Cola contains caffeine and phosphoric acid, both of which may be harmful to bone health.

Scientists found no correlation between bone density and other types of soft drinks, and cola consumption had no adverse effect on men. Low bone density increases risk of bone fractures.

Katherine Tucker, MD, director, nutritional epidemiology program, Tufts University, Boston, and lead author of a study of 1,413 women and 1,125 men, published in *The American Journal of Clinical Nutrition.*

Antidepressants Increase Fracture Risk

Researchers tracked the health of 5,008 men and women for five years.

Outcome: The 137 participants who reported daily use of *selective serotonin reuptake inhibitor* (SSRI) antidepressants, including *citalopram* (Celexa) or *fluoxetine* (Prozac), were two times as likely to suffer bone fractures during the five-year period as those who did not take SSRIs.

Theory: SSRIs alter the action of serotonin, a brain chemical that's believed to influence bone formation.

If you take an SSRI: Ask your doctor if you should have periodic bone-density scans.

David Goltzman, MD, professor of medicine, McGill University, Montreal, Canada.

New Bone Density Drug

A new drug boosts bone density and reduces risk of fractures in postmenopausal women with osteoporosis. *Zoledronic acid* (Reclast) is administered once each year by an intravenous infusion. In one study, risk for vertebral fractures was decreased by 71%...risk for hip fractures by 40%. Short-term side effects include fever and flu-like symptoms. Zoledronic acid can be particularly beneficial for people who can't take oral bisphosphonates to strengthen bone.

Dennis M. Black, PhD, professor in residence, department of epidemiology and biostatistics, University of California, San Francisco, and author of a three-year study published in *The New England Journal of Medicine.*

Heartburn Drug Warning

Long-term daily use of proton-pump inhibitors (PPIs), such as Nexium (*esomeprazole*), Prevacid (*lansoprazole*) and Prilosec (*omeprazole*), increased hip fracture risk by up to 265% in one recent study.

Self-defense: Discuss the drug's benefits and risks with your physician. If a proton-pump inhibitor is needed to control gastroesophageal reflux disease (GERD) or other acid-related illness, use the lowest effective dose and make sure that your calcium intake is adequate.

Yu-Xiao Yang, MD, assistant professor of medicine and epidemiology, Center for Clinical Biology and Statistics, University of Pennsylvania School of Medicine in Philadelphia. He is coauthor of a study of 13,556 people with hip fractures, published in *The Journal of the American Medical Association.*

Migraines Linked To Vision Loss

Migraines may be linked to vision loss later in life. Preliminary research indicates that people who have migraines are more likely to develop retinopathy, a problem with the blood supply to the retina of the eye. This may mean that an underlying vascular problem causes both the headaches and the retinopathy.

Helpful: If you get migraines, inform your eye-care specialist and have regular checkups.

Kathryn Rose, PhD, research assistant professor, department of epidemiology, School of Public Health, University of North Carolina at Chapel Hill, and lead author of a study of migraines and retinopathy in nearly 11,000 people, published in *Neurology.*

Nonsurgical Nose Job

Nonsurgical nose jobs are quick, relatively inexpensive and effective for smaller bumps, dents and irregularities. A doctor injects an FDA-approved cosmetic filler called *Radiesse* into the nose to contour it and hide bumps. This procedure takes only about 15 minutes. The patient remains awake during the procedure so he/she can guide the doctor while looking in a mirror.

Cost: $800 to $1,500, compared with $15,000 for a surgical nose job.*

The effects last about a year.

Cameron K. Rokhsar, MD, assistant professor of dermatology at Albert Einstein Medical College, New York City, *www.cosmeticlaserskinsurgery.com*.

*Prices subject to change.

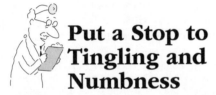

Put a Stop to Tingling and Numbness

Eva L. Feldman, MD, PhD, Russell N. DeJong Professor of Neurology and director of the Juvenile Diabetes Research Foundation Center for the Study of Complications in Diabetes and the Amyotrophic Lateral Sclerosis (ALS) Clinic at the University of Michigan in Ann Arbor.

If you experience persistent and/or painful tingling, numbness or weakness in your feet or hands, don't just shrug it off as a minor complaint.

Peripheral neuropathy is a nerve disorder that affects 15 million to 20 million Americans—and often it is one of the initial signals of a serious medical condition. For example, 60% to 70% of diabetics have peripheral nerve disease.

THE HIDDEN CULPRIT

The majority of people who have neuropathy have an underlying disease that affects multiple nerves. *Main causes...*

•**Diabetes** (or prediabetes, a precursor to diabetes) is the most common cause of peripheral neuropathy. Although it is not known exactly how diabetes triggers neuropathy, it is thought that episodes of elevated blood sugar (glucose) can overwhelm mitochondria (the power plants inside cells that convert glucose to energy), resulting in accumulations of molecules (such as free radicals) that damage nerve cells.

Red flag: Persistent foot pain and/or numbness is often the first symptom of diabetes. If you experience these symptoms, see your doctor right away.

•**Autoimmune diseases** (such as lupus and rheumatoid arthritis) can lead to peripheral neuropathy. That's because the body's immune system attacks the layers of tissue, known as myelin sheath, that wrap around peripheral nerves.

•**Medications can trigger toxic neuropathy**—in particular the chemotherapeutic drugs used to treat cancer. Other drugs that can cause peripheral neuropathy include certain antibiotics, such as *nitrofurantoin* (Macrodantin) and *metronidazole* (Flagyl). An exposure to workplace or environmental heavy metals, such as arsenic and mercury, also can cause neuropathy.

•**Vitamin deficiencies**—particularly a deficiency of vitamin B-12—could lead to a form of neuropathy most prevalent in older adults. These people are particularly at risk because they are more likely to have insufficient levels of intrinsic factor, a substance secreted in the stomach that's required for vitamin B-12 absorption.

GETTING THE RIGHT DIAGNOSIS

Neuropathy usually can be diagnosed in the doctor's office with a complete medical history, blood work and the following tests...

•**Pinprick.** The doctor will very lightly touch the patient's bare foot in several places with a pin. A patient with neuropathy—particularly if it's caused by diabetes—might not feel the pin.

•**Tuning fork.** Neuropathy patients may not feel the vibrations when it's held against the big toe.

•**Reflex tests.** Rapping the ankle, knee or another affected body part with a small rubber hammer helps determine whether muscles are responding properly to nerve signals.

In addition, the doctor might perform an electromyography (a test of electrical activity in the muscles) and/or a nerve conduction study, in which electrodes are placed on the patient's skin and nerves are stimulated via an electrical pulse.

The test measures the speed at which the nerves carry electrical signals.

BEST TREATMENT OPTIONS

Because neuropathy is almost always a symptom of another condition, the main goal is to identify and treat the underlying problem. Once that's achieved, the nerves will gradually start to heal—and the neuropathy will usually improve significantly—and even disappear.

For example, patients who have prediabetes or diabetes who achieve good blood sugar control—with diet, regular exercise and/or the use of medication—often will see a complete reversal of neuropathy within one year.

Nerves that are severely damaged or entirely dead—as a result of chemotherapy, for example—may continue to cause pain or other symptoms indefinitely.

Most effective pain treatments...

•***Pregabalin* (Lyrica) or *gabapentin* (Neurontin)** are used for treating diabetic neuropathy. Both drugs were originally developed for the prevention of epileptic seizures. Taken orally, the drugs are thought to work by affecting electrical activity in the brain and inhibiting pain sensations. Both drugs reduce pain by 20% to 30% in most patients.

Main side effects: Dizziness, sleepiness and/or peripheral edema (swollen ankles).

•***Duloxetine* (Cymbalta),** an antidepressant, was approved by the FDA in 2004 for treating diabetic neuropathy—even in patients who aren't depressed. This medication can increase levels of the brain chemicals serotonin and norepinephrine, which appear to work, in part, by increasing feelings of well-being. Like pregabalin and gabapentin, it decreases pain by 20% to 30% in most patients.

Main side effects: Nausea, dry mouth and/or constipation.

•**Opioid analgesics,** such as *dextromethorphan* (Neurodex), *oxycodone* (OxyContin) and codeine, are all very effective painkillers. These drugs commonly cause sedation (and also pose a risk for addiction), so they are recommended only for patients with severe pain that does not respond to the therapies described above.

Main side effects: Nausea, sleepiness and/or dependency.

•**Nondrug therapies,** such as acupuncture and transcutaneous electrical nerve stimulation (TENS), are often used with or without medication. Many patients report that acupuncture helps relieve the pain related to neuropathy.

TENS, which involves small electrical signals transmitted through the skin, appears to block pain signals. In patients who respond to TENS treatment (typically performed by physical therapists), it can reduce pain by 50% to 70%.

For more information on peripheral neuropathy, contact the Neuropathy Association at 212-692-0662, *www.neuropathy.org*.

Relief for Numb Hands and Feet

Medication relieves numb hands and feet. In a new study, 40 adults (mostly women) with Raynaud's disease (blood vessel constriction that causes numb hands and feet) took 10 milligrams (mg) of *vardenafil* (Levitra), an erectile dysfunction drug, twice daily for two weeks. In 70% of participants, symptoms improved.

Theory: The drug relaxes blood vessels, allowing for better blood flow.

If you have Raynaud's: Ask your doctor about trying vardenafil.

Stephan Rosenkranz, MD, associate professor of medicine, department of cardiology, University of Cologne, Germany.

Head Off Epilepsy

The main ingredient in many dandruff shampoos, *zinc pyrithione*, calms overstimulated nerve cells in the head, making it a possible future treatment for seizures. Research is needed.

John Hopkins Medical Institutions, Baltimore, Maryland, *www.hopkinsmedicine.org*

Meds and Mental Decline

Stomach-acid medications can lead to mental decline. Mental decline can range from mild confusion to severe dementia.

Recent finding: People who used prescription and over-the-counter H2 blockers, such as Axid, Pepcid, Tagamet and Zantac, for more than two years were nearly two-and-a-half times more likely to develop cognitive difficulties than people who had not used them.

Self-defense: Talk to your doctor about safer alternatives.

Malaz Boustani, MD, MPH, a geriatrician at Indiana University School of Medicine, Indianapolis, and leader of a study of 1,558 people, published in *Journal of the American Geriatrics Society.*

Estrogen/Alzheimer's Link

Estrogen is linked to Alzheimer's disease in older men.

Background: Men typically do have lower levels of the hormone estrogen than women. However, after menopause women have lower estrogen levels than men of the same age.

Recent study: Over an average of six years, researchers evaluated hormone levels and cognitive function in 2,974 men ages 71 to 93.

Result: The risk for Alzheimer's rose with increasing levels of estrogen.

Theory: The production of estrogen involves aromatase, an enzyme that, in some cases, may serve as a marker for Alzheimer's.

Previous research discovered a similar link in women. More studies are needed.

Mirjam I. Geerlings, PhD, associate professor, University Medical Center Utrecht, the Netherlands.

 # A Statin Bonus

A bonus for people taking cholesterol drugs is protection against Alzheimer's disease.

Recent finding: Patients who took the statin medicine Zocor (*simvastatin*) for at least seven months had a 54% reduction in the incidence of Alzheimer's and a 49% reduction in the occurrence of Parkinson's. The study showed no significant reductions among the participants who had Lipitor (*atorvastatin*) or Mevacor (*lovastatin*).

Self-defense: If you have a family history of either disease, ask your doctor about Zocor.

Benjamin Wolozin, MD, PhD, a professor of pharmacology, Boston University School of Medicine, and lead author of an analysis of data on 1,684,810 patients, published in *BioMed Central (BMC) Medicine.*

Little-Known Warning Sign of Alzheimer's Disease

In a recent finding, older people with mild difficulty recognizing scents, such as cinnamon and lemon, were 50% more likely to develop cognitive impairment within five years, compared with people whose odor recognition was intact. This impairment often precedes the development of Alzheimer's.

Robert S. Wilson, PhD, department of neuropsychology at Rush Alzheimer's Disease Center, Rush University Medical Center in Chicago, and author of a study of 589 people, ages 55 to 100, published in *Archives of General Psychiatry.*

New Alzheimer's Blood Test

Researchers have developed a new blood test which is designed to detect changes in 18 blood proteins that may predict Alzheimer's disease up to six years before diagnosis. The test, which is about 90% accurate, may eventually be available as a diagnostic tool.

Stanford University School of Medicine, Stanford, California, *www.med.stanford.edu.*

Alzheimer's Preventive?

In a novel approach to Alzheimer's, a bacterial virus (*phage*) is introduced through the nose, goes to the brain and dissolves disease-causing plaques. Mice given the phage for one year had 80% fewer plaques than untreated mice.

American Friends of Tel Aviv University at *www.aftau. org.*

Mold and Mood

European researchers have now found a link between moldy homes and depression. It is possible that mold toxins affect the brain and/or nervous system...or that mold causes other health problems that impair mental health.

Brown University in Providence, Rhode Island, *www. brown.edu.*

Testosterone for Depression?

In two recent studies that looked at a total of 1,050 men with low levels of the hormone testosterone, those who received testosterone replacement therapy for three years, on average, had a 70% improvement in scores on a standard test used to diagnose depression.

Theory: Hypogonadism (or low testosterone) can impact mood and result in depression—as well as fatigue, joint and muscle aches, and erectile dysfunction, all conditions that can, in turn, lead to depression.

Self-defense: If you are a man who experiences any or all of these symptoms, ask your doctor to assess your symptoms and check your testosterone level via blood tests. If you are diagnosed with hypogonadism, ask if testosterone replacement therapy is appropriate.

Caution: Men with prostate cancer, liver disease or high hematocrit (the volume of red cells in the blood) should not receive testosterone replacement therapy.

Lawrence Komer, MD, medical director, Masters Men's Clinic, Burlington, Ontario.

New Treatment for Depression

Depression sufferers may benefit from sleep apnea treatment.

Recent finding: When sleep apnea is controlled with continuous positive airway pressure (CPAP) treatment, the symptoms of depression may be alleviated. This is the standard treatment for sleep apnea—the patient wears a specially designed mask which keeps airways open so that he/she can breathe normally.

Note: It is possible that the symptoms of depression are misinterpreted and are in fact due to sleep apnea...or that obstructive sleep apnea may produce depression.

Daniel J. Schwartz, MD, director, Sleep Center at University Community Hospital Medical Center in Tampa, Florida.

Beware of the Other Killer "Superbug"

Carolyn Gould, MD, a medical epidemiologist and infectious-disease specialist in the division of health-care quality promotion at the Centers for Disease Control and Prevention (CDC) and an assistant professor of medicine at Emory University, both in Atlanta. Her research interests include the prevention of antibiotic resistance and health-care-associated infections.

With all the recent media attention, most people now have heard of *methicillin-resistant Staphylococcus aureus,* often called MRSA, a bacteria that is one of the nation's top threats to public health. Less well-known, but of similar concern to infectious-disease experts, is *Clostridium difficile* (C. difficile), a potentially deadly organism that's spreading fast.

In the US, the number of hospital discharges in which C. difficile was listed as the diagnosis doubled between 2000 and 2003, with a disproportionate increase in cases involving elderly patients—perhaps due to their generally weakened immunity. Over a recent five-year period, it is estimated that C. difficile was responsible for about 20,000 deaths.

FUELED BY ANTIBIOTICS

C. difficile bacteria can be found in stool (animal and human) and on many surfaces. Up to 3% of all healthy Americans are colonized with C. difficile—that is, they have the bacterium in their intestinal tract, but don't get sick from it. By comparison, 20% to 40% of patients in hospitals may be colonized with C. difficile.

Main risk: The use of antibiotics. The vast majority of patients infected with C. difficile are either taking—or have recently taken—antibiotics, and most acquire the infection in the hospital. One problem with antibiotics is that they not only kill disease-causing germs but also the beneficial organisms in the intestine, which normally prevent C. difficile from proliferating.

Once C. difficile multiplies, it produces highly virulent toxins that cause inflammation and damage cells in the lining of the large intestine. The newer "superstrains" of the bacterium are thought to produce up to 20 times more of these toxins than the usual strains.

Result: Watery, frequently violent diarrhea…severe intestinal cramping…blood or pus in the stools…and sometimes life-threatening colitis (inflammation of the colon).

Important: If you get diarrhea that is prolonged (more than two to three days) and/or severe, do not ignore it. See a doctor immediately. You should assume that it might be caused by C. difficile if you've taken antibiotics in the last few months, have recently been discharged from the hospital or have cared for someone with C. difficile.

Caution: The most widely used test for C. difficile, a stool test, is about 70% to 90% sensitive—some patients who test negative for the organism are later found to be infected.

A colonoscopy (examination of the colon using a long tube with a camera attached) could be performed to check for pseudomembranes, patches of inflammatory cells that are characteristic of C. difficile infection.

DIFFICULT TO ERADICATE

Unlike many disease-causing bacteria, C. difficile produces spores. These hardy, heat-resistant forms allow the bacterium to survive in a dormant form for months or even years in the intestinal tract…and on surfaces, such as floors and doorknobs, for weeks.

People acquire C. difficile from ingesting the spores, which resist the acidity of the stomach and germinate in the small intestine. Disruption of the normal flora (bacteria) of the colon—typically through exposure to antibiotics—allows C. difficile to flourish.

Those who are exposed to the spores could get infected—and, even when they do not have symptoms, can pass the infection on to others. This is a serious problem in nursing homes and hospitals, where people tend to have weakened immune systems and often take antibiotics. In these settings, C. difficile typically is spread via the hands of contaminated health-care workers or through exposure to contaminated surfaces.

The treatment: Two antibiotics, *metronidazole* (Flagyl) and *vancomycin* (Vancocin), appear to be equally effective in treating mild-to-moderate infections caused by C. difficile.

Doctors usually start treatment with metronidazole—it's much cheaper than vancomycin and may be less likely to lead to antibiotic-resistant organisms in the colon. For a serious infection, however, vancomycin considered better.

BEST PREVENTION STRATEGIES

There's some evidence that people who take antacids, including the proton-pump inhibitors, such as *esomeprazole* (Nexium), and H2 blockers, such as *ranitidine* (Zantac), have a higher risk for C. difficile—possibly because antacids decrease stomach acid, thereby making it easier for the bacterium to survive and germinate in the intestine. However, antacid use alone is unlikely to increase C. difficile risk significantly unless the patient is taking antibiotics and/or is hospitalized. *Effective ways to guard against C. difficile infection…*

• **Avoid unnecessary antibiotics.** Since active C. difficile infection is almost always associated with antibiotic use, patients can decrease their risk by taking antibiotics only when they're truly necessary. Do not ask your doctor for antibiotics when you have a viral illness, such as a cold or flu.

Important: Doctors are just as likely to prescribe antibiotics unnecessarily as patients are to ask for them. If your doctor recommends an antibiotic, ask what it's for...if he/she is sure that you have a bacterial (rather than a viral) illness ...and if it's possible that the condition will improve on its own without using antibiotics.

•**Ask for a culture.** If you need an antibiotic, ask your doctor to perform a culture (whenever possible) to target the drug to the infection. Virtually all antibiotics have been implicated in C. difficile infection, but the infection is more common in patients who take broad-spectrum antibiotics, such as *fluoroquinolone* and *cephalosporin* antibiotics, that have a greater tendency to disrupt the colon's normal flora.

•**Wash your hands frequently**—particularly when you're in the hospital—or if you're caring for someone infected with C. difficile. Use warm water and regular soap, and wash for at least 15 seconds to remove spores.

•**Decontaminate.** If you have been infected with C. difficile—or you are caring for someone who has had it—disinfect surfaces daily. Hospital rooms, especially bathrooms and frequently touched surfaces, are also commonly contaminated with C. difficile.

Tuberculosis Danger?

Tuberculosis (TB) has been in the news, but the risk for contracting it in the US is very low—new cases number only about 13,000 to 14,000 every year—and there are far fewer cases of the antibiotic-resistant form of the disease.

The only way that you can get TB is by breathing in bacteria from someone with active TB who has coughed or sneezed. Individuals with latent, or inactive, TB cannot spread the disease.

All new cases must be reported to state health departments. Officials then conduct "contact investigations" to determine who might have been exposed to the TB bacteria and who should be tested.

Treatment for tuberculosis includes multiple antibiotics taken for six months or longer. Treatment for the antibiotic-resistant form of tuberculosis can require 18 to 24 months of antibiotic medications, as well as surgery to remove damaged lung tissue.

Philip LoBue, MD, associate director for science, division of tuberculosis elimination, Centers for Disease Control and Prevention, Atlanta.

New Masks Filter Germs

The first respirators for public health emergencies have now been approved by the FDA. The over-the-counter respirators—called the 3M Respirator 8612F (cone-shaped) and 8670F (flat fold)—fit tightly over the nose and mouth and are designed to filter out at least 95% of airborne germs. These masks could be used during a flu pandemic or biological terrorist attack but do not replace standard infection-control steps, such as avoiding crowds. The respirators are now available at drugstores and on-line.

Sheila Murphey, MD, branch chief of infection, FDA Center for Devices and Radiological Health, Washington, DC.

Pneumonia Protection

Researchers analyzed 17,393 adults (median age 72) in the hospital with community-acquired pneumonia (a bacterial pneumonia that often follows a viral respiratory infection, such as influenza).

Result: Patients who had received the most current flu vaccine prior to hospitalization were one-third less likely to die while in the hospital than those who had not been vaccinated.

Theory: The flu vaccine reduces one's risk of getting life-threatening bacterial pneumonia.

Self-defense: If you are age 50 or older, or have a chronic health problem, such as lung disease or diabetes, ask your doctor about getting an annual flu shot in the fall.

Jennifer Daley, MD, chief medical officer, Tenet Healthcare Corporation, Dallas.

Before You Use the Microwave to Reheat...

Microwaves heat food unevenly, leaving cold pockets where bacteria can thrive. Several studies have shown that this can lead to food poisoning. One study showed that of 30 people who reheated roast pork that had been left unrefrigerated for many hours during a picnic, 10 who reheated the pork in a microwave contracted salmonella—compared with none out of 20 who reheated the pork using a conventional oven or skillet.

Self-defense: Use a microwave only to reheat meat that has been thoroughly cooked and properly stored. Also, do not cook previously uncooked meat in a microwave oven.

Bradford Gessner, MD, director, Maternal-Child Health Epidemiology Unit, Alaska Division of Public Health in Anchorage.

Caffeine Watch

When researchers analyzed the caffeine content of 131 soft drinks (national brands and store brands), caffeine levels varied widely from 4.9 milligrams (mg) of caffeine to 74 mg per 12 ounces, with store-brand sodas generally having lower levels of caffeine than national brands.

For example, a 12-ounce can of Coca-Cola contained 33.9 mg of caffeine, compared to 12.7 mg in a 12-ounce can of Walmart's Sam's Cola. And, citrus-flavored drinks, like Mountain Dew (54.8 mg per 12 ounces), generally contained more caffeine than other types of soda.

If you are watching your caffeine intake because of a heart arrhythmia, anxiety disorder or urinary frequency problem, opt to drink a non-caffeinated beverage, such as seltzer.

Leonard Bell, PhD, professor, department of nutrition and food science, Auburn University, Auburn, Alabama.

Is Microwave Popcorn Safe?

Some reports indicate that there may be cause for concern regarding microwave popcorn. The potential hazard was initially believed to affect only workers in microwave popcorn plants. An exposure to high concentrations of *diacetyl* (the compound that gives microwave popcorn its buttery smell and flavor) led to a severe form of lung disease, known in these workers as "popcorn lung," which causes progressive and disabling shortness of breath. Several workers required lung transplants, while other workers died. Workers exposed to smaller concentrations of diacetyl developed less severe symptoms.

Now, a case of popcorn lung has been reported in a consumer who ate microwave popcorn daily. We require more research to tell whether typical consumers are at risk. However, animal studies do suggest that diacetyl is toxic under specific conditions. Some manufacturers are now eliminating diacetyl from their microwave popcorn products. Until more research is completed, you may want to prepare popcorn on the stove or with an air popper.

Neil Schachter, MD, professor of pulmonary medicine, Mount Sinai Medical Center, New York City.

The Health Benefits Of Seafood

The health benefits of seafood far outweigh the risks from toxins. People who eat one to two servings of fish per week—especially types of fish high in omega-3 fatty acids, such as salmon, herring and mackerel—reduce risk for death from heart attacks by 36% and lower the risk for death from any cause by 17%. Talk to your doctor about the risks and benefits of fish.

Dariusch Mozaffarian, MD, assistant professor, department of epidemiology, Harvard Medical School, Harvard School of Public Health, Boston, and leader of a study on seafood published in *The Journal of the American Medical Association.*

2

Medical Insider

How Not to Be Misdiagnosed

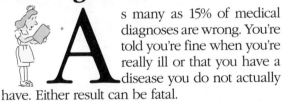

As many as 15% of medical diagnoses are wrong. You're told you're fine when you're really ill or that you have a disease you do not actually have. Either result can be fatal.

In one study reported in *Annals of Internal Medicine*, doctors at Harvard School of Public Health analyzed more than 300 incorrect diagnoses. They found that 59% of these misdiagnoses seriously harmed the patient in some way, and of those, 30% were the cause of death.

In the study, the most commonly overlooked of diagnoses were breast and colorectal cancers, fractures and infections. These probably were reported most often because they are all common problems that have significant negative consequences if missed.

Other health problems not caught were those having vague symptoms—such as fatigue—that make it difficult for the doctor to quickly arrive at a precise diagnosis. Diseases in this category include multiple sclerosis, thyroid diseases and certain cancers.

Here's how to help your physician make the correct diagnosis...

TELL YOUR STORY WELL

Doctors are medical detectives. They decipher clues from evidence, such as a physical exam or laboratory tests. Much of that evidence is rooted in your medical history—the story you tell your doctor about your health. Don't try to diagnose yourself. Simply tell your story clearly, completely and accurately.

Include the following...

•**Timing.** When did the problem start? How long has it been going on?

Mark Graber, MD, associate chair of the department of medicine at Stony Brook University, New York, and chief of medicine at Veteran's Administration Hospital in Northport, New York. Dr. Graber is widely recognized as a leading authority on diagnostic errors in medicine, and his scientific papers on the topic have appeared in *Archives of Internal Medicine, Academic Medicine* and other journals.

• **Symptoms.** Describe all your symptoms in detail. For example, is the pain localized or general...mild or severe...intermittent or constant? What seems to make your symptoms better or worse—eating, activity, time of day?

• **Tests.** Explain the tests that have been done and the results.

• **Treatments.** Which treatments have you tried? Did they help?

Trap: A nurse or health technician may interview you before you see the doctor. Do not assume that he/she will relay your story to the doctor completely. Instead, let the doctor hear all of the information firsthand.

KEEP CAREFUL RECORDS

Maintain your own medical records by writing down relevant facts about your condition. Include test results, an accurate list of all current medications (prescription and over-the-counter) and supplements, reports from specialists and hospital admissions. Bring your records to every doctor's visit. Even if you're seeing the same physician, it's not unusual for your records to be unavailable for one reason or another.

If you're seeing a new doctor, even one within the same health-care system, do not assume that he will get your medical records. Confidentiality rules make it difficult to move records from one doctor to another.

GET TEST RESULTS

Ask for your test results. No news might not be good news. Perhaps the doctor is out of town or sick, and your results are sitting in the office—this can be dangerous if you have a life-threatening disease. Know when test results are due. If you don't receive them on time, call the doctor's office.

Even better: Ask your doctor if the lab can send the results to you as well as to the doctor.

KNOW WHAT'S NEXT

A doctor might say, "I'm pretty sure this is what you have." At that point, ask what is likely to happen to you next if his diagnosis is right. If what the doctor expects to happen does not happen, the diagnosis may be wrong.

Example: A longtime smoker catches a cold, and the cough persists for two weeks after the other symptoms have disappeared. The

doctor might say, "I think you have bronchitis, which should resolve itself over the next two to three weeks. If not, get back to me." If the cough persists, the patient could have another more serious problem, such as heart failure or lung cancer.

ENCOURAGE YOUR DOCTOR TO THINK BROADLY

Experts who study misdiagnosis are fond of the following joke—What is the most commonly missed fracture?

Answer: The second fracture.

In other words, when a doctor finds a fracture or some other type of health problem, he may stop looking. This type of error has been dubbed satisficing—the doctor feels satisfied by finding one problem and stops looking for other problems. Satisficing is a common error. To help prevent it, ask your doctor, "What else do you think this could be?"

GET A SECOND OPINION

Give your primary care physician the first opportunity to diagnose and treat your problem, but if symptoms persist, you might want to get a second opinion. Ask your primary care physician for a recommendation.

Help everyone involved in your care to know what the other providers are thinking and planning. Don't assume that health professionals are coordinating your care behind the scenes—they probably aren't. You are the most reliable person for that job.

Where to Get Help with Medical Decisions

Albert G. Mulley, MD, chief of the general medicine division and director of the Medical Practices Evaluation Center at Massachusetts General Hospital in Boston. Dr. Mulley is also an associate professor of medicine and of health policy at Harvard Medical School and cofounder of the Foundation for Informed Medical Decision Making, *www.fimdm.org*, also in Boston.

S ome hospitals and physicians offer decision aids (interactive Web sites, DVDs and booklets) that give the pros and cons of different treatment approaches. There are more than 500 decision aids currently available, covering a wide range of topics, including cancer, heart disease and diabetes.

In a study of people with severe back pain caused by a ruptured disk, patients who watched a video that explained the possible risks and benefits of surgery were 30% less likely to choose surgery than patients who had simply discussed the operation with their surgeons.

Ask your doctor if he/she can provide a decision aid or tell you where you can get one. *Good resources…*

• **Center for Shared Decision Making,** part of Dartmouth-Hitchcock Medical Center, 603-650-5578, *www.hitchcock.org/dept/csdm.*

• **Foundation for Informed Medical Decision Making,** 617-367-2000, *www.fimdm.org.*

• **Patient Decision Aids,** from the Ottawa Health Research Institute, *www.ohri.ca/decision aid/.*

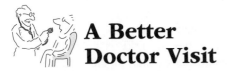 # A Better Doctor Visit

Doctors who try to bond with patients may spend too much time talking about themselves instead of focusing on the patient.

A recent finding: 96% of doctors' personal disclosures during examinations did not benefit the patients or establish greater rapport—and in some cases, these disclosures caused the doctor to lose his/her focus on the patient.

Self-defense: State your agenda (just one to three items) at the beginning of your time with the doctor so that you share responsibility for getting through it. If your doctor starts talking about himself in a way that is not relevant to your condition, ask him to refocus on you and your concerns.

Susan H. McDaniel, PhD, psychologist and associate chairwoman, department of family medicine, University of Rochester, Minnesota, and the leader of a study of 100 primary care doctors, published in *Archives of Internal Medicine.*

How to Check Out Your Doctor

Charles B. Inlander, a consumer advocate and healthcare consultant located in Fogelsville, Pennsylvania. He was the founding president of the nonprofit People's Medical Society, the consumer advocacy organization credited with key improvements in the quality of US health care in the 1980s and 1990s, and is the author of 20 books, including *Take This Book to the Hospital with You: A Consumer Guide to Surviving Your Hospital Stay* (St. Martin's).

Studies indicate that people looking for a new doctor generally ask a friend or family member for a recommendation before using other resources of information. But while a friend or relative's experience with a doctor can be helpful, neither person is likely to know the background information that is necessary to make a really informed choice. In the not-too-distant past, it was practically impossible for the average patient to find information about a physician's professional credentials. Today, there are a variety of ways to easily research these facts. *To learn more about your current doctor(s) or a new one you may be considering…*

• **Use the Internet.** The Internet has become the single greatest source for researching physicians, but many people do not know where to start. There are several Web sites—many of them available at no charge—that give basic data on just about every licensed doctor. For example, I recommend *www.findadoc.com,* developed by doctors and computer programmers, because it allows you to quickly look up a doctor and find out where he/she trained, whether he is board certified and the typical time spent in the waiting room. Another Web site, *www.healthgrades. com,* is similar but provides even more information on a doctor, including any malpractice judgments or disciplinary actions taken by a state licensing board. However, a report on a doctor costs $29.95.* And you can get most of the same information—at zero cost—*by using the sources listed below…*

• To find out about board certification, the American Board of Medical Specialties (or ABMS), which represents medical boards that have the strictest physician specialty requirements, hosts an

*Price subject to change.

excellent Web site at *www.abms.org*. It offers free verification of a doctor's board-certification status. Or you can call the ABMS at 866-275-2267.

•To learn about disciplinary measures taken against doctors, state medical licensing boards are usually the best resource. The American Medical Association's Internet site provides direct links to each state board at *www.ama-assn.org/ama/pub/category/2645.html*. You also can call a local or county court and ask the clerk of the court about any medical malpractice cases that have been filed against a local physician. Most noncourt sources of information about malpractice, such as state licensing boards or physician-rating Web sites, include only judgments—not settlements or cases filed.

•**Ask a nurse.** Nurses are wonderful—but underutilized—resources for information and insight about local doctors. If you know a nurse, ask for input on your doctor or one you're considering using.

•**Interview before choosing.** When selecting a new primary care doctor or specialist, set up an interview appointment. Ask about anything that your research has uncovered or any other points you would like to know about a doctor's background or experience. Most insurance plans will cover the cost of this visit.

More from Charles Inlander...

Is the Doctor Who Is Treating You a Novice?

You may have heard that July is not the best month to be admitted to a hospital because that's the month that new interns (doctors who have just graduated from medical school) join the staff. Over the years, medical experts have pooh-poohed that admonition, insisting that the quality of medical care does not suffer when new interns arrive at hospitals. But that's not the finding of a recent multi-institution study. This research found that not only are first-year interns more prone to mistakes than more experienced physicians, but so are all residents (the general term for doctors, including interns, who have been assigned to a hospital for advanced training in a medical specialty following four years of medical school).

The errors that these doctors in specialty training programs make, including misdiagnoses, not ordering necessary medical tests, etc., stem not only from their lack of judgment and technical competence, but also from inadequate supervision by senior physicians, who should review the doctors' diagnoses, test orders and treatment recommendations.

How to protect yourself or a loved one from such mistakes...

•**Know who is treating you.** After one year of training at a hospital, an intern is generally referred to as a "resident" or "resident physician." Residencies can last from two to five or more years, depending on the specialty in which the doctor is training. For example, internal medicine residencies average three years, while surgical residencies can last five or more years.

Self-defense: Always ask the doctor who is treating you in the hospital or emergency room whether he/she is a resident. If so, ask to see a senior physician (who always should be present or on call) to confirm the diagnosis or suggested treatment.

•**Don't be afraid to ask for a specialist's opinion.** Several months ago, I accompanied a female family member who was experiencing unexpected vaginal bleeding to her local emergency room. A resident was the first to see her and, after examining her, he told us he thought the problem was a minor irritation. He was about to discharge her with a recommendation to see her gynecologist later in the week when we asked to see the gynecologist on call. This doctor arrived about a half hour later. He immediately ordered a biopsy and imaging scans and within four hours determined that she had a growth in her uterus. Within a day, it was determined to be cancerous and surgery was quickly scheduled.

Self-defense: Do not be afraid to ask for a board-certified specialist to deal with your suspected or known problem.

•**Be on the lookout for fatigue.** Residents are often on call for 24 hours or more at a time, and many are dead tired from overwork and lack of sleep.

Self-defense: Whether you are in the emergency room or an inpatient at a hospital, don't be hesitant to ask how long any resident who is treating you has been on call or on duty. If it is more than 12 hours, ask for a second opinion on any medical advice this doctor gives you.

Charles Inlander on medical tests...

Do You Really Need That Medical Test?

A recent study found that an adult American's chances of having an unnecessary medical test at his/her next checkup is at least 43%. And a recent report in *The New England Journal of Medicine* suggested that up to 2% of all cancer cases come from overexposure to radiation from too many diagnostic computed tomography (or CT) scans. These reports—and many more like them—have raised a red flag about the overuse of unnecessary and/or risky testing. Of course you should not use any of these reports as an excuse for not having a test that might save your life, but it is important to understand why a test is being recommended.

QUESTIONS TO ASK YOUR DOCTOR

•**Do I really need the test?** This seems like an obvious question, but many people fail to ask it. The federal guidelines advise against such common medical tests as urinalysis, electrocardiograms (ECGs) and even routine chest X-rays unless you have symptoms that may be related to the urinary tract, heart or lungs, respectively. Yet one or more of those tests is often ordered for patients during annual checkups even though they have no associated symptoms. After asking your doctor to explain why he wants you to have a particular test, find out if he suspects a specific problem—and, if so, whether other follow-up tests may be necessary.

•**What are the risks associated with the test?** Many medical tests have some level of risk. For example, a CT scan of the stomach exposes a person to 50 times more radiation than a conventional stomach X-ray. The more radiation you have over a lifetime, the higher your risk for some types of cancer, including malignancies of the lungs and liver. If you're having a biopsy of the prostate gland, you should know that the procedure can cause infection or bleeding into the urethra or bladder. When asking your doctor about the risks associated with each test, find out whether there are less risky alternatives to the test that is being proposed. For example, one possible alternative to a prostate biopsy is a new special color-prostate sonogram (or ultra-

sound). Let your doctor know if you have had negative effects from any previous tests, such as bleeding or infections.

Helpful: Tell your doctor if you have had exposure to other CT scans or X-rays in the past.

QUESTIONS TO ASK YOURSELF

•**Are my fears preventing me from getting a necessary test?** While medical tests are not always comfortable, it's important to weigh the potential discomfort and/or risks against the benefits provided. For example, a recent report has shown that fewer women are getting mammograms than in years before. It cited the pain and discomfort associated with the test as the probable reason. Yet mammograms have been shown to be the primary reason that breast cancer deaths have declined in the US. Do not let your fear of the possible discomfort and/or risks associated with a medical test cloud your assessment of its benefits.

•**Do I have all the facts?** If you ask the right questions, do a little research and weigh the test's risks against its benefits, you can trust that the decision you and your doctor make will be the right one.

Better Biopsy

There are two parts to a biopsy—taking the specimen and reading it. Choose a physician you trust to take the specimen—and ask him/her where it will be interpreted. The lab should be accredited by the College of American Pathologists (800-323-4040, *www.cap.org*), and the physician should be certified by the American Board of Medical Specialties (866-275-2267, *www.abms.org*). Patients usually have no control over who reads the results, but your insurer may insist that the specimen go to a specific lab.

Self-defense: If the reading is abnormal, consider obtaining a second reading by a different pathologist.

Thomas M. Wheeler, MD, chairman, department of pathology, and professor of pathology and urology, Baylor College of Medicine, Houston.

What to Drink Before a CT Scan

Drink milk before a CT scan, instead of barium sulfate. People preparing for a CT scan traditionally have been given barium sulfate to drink so that the scan produces clear images of the intestinal walls. A new study shows that whole milk is almost as effective at producing clear images as barium sulfate—and it's cheaper and tastes better. Ask your doctor.

Lisa Shah-Patel, MD, resident, department of radiology, St. Luke's-Roosevelt Hospital in New York City, and leader of a study of 179 adult patients, presented at a meeting of the Radiological Society of North America.

What Doctors Should Ask About—but Usually Don't

Lars Osterberg, MD, a clinical assistant professor of medicine at Stanford University School of Medicine in Stanford, California, and chief of general internal medicine at the VA Palo Alto Health Care System in Palo Alto, California. He wrote a recent article on medication compliance for *The New England Journal of Medicine*.

Medication compliance means taking all of your prescription drugs as directed by your doctor—at the right times…in the right dosages…every day you are supposed to, for as long as necessary. In other words, it means following the instructions precisely. This sounds easy, right? Not necessarily.

Example: Longstanding research shows that about 125,000 Americans die each year because they do not take their heart medication properly.

Nearly one-third of people who are prescribed drugs don't even fill their original prescriptions. *Among people who do, compliance rates follow the "rule of sixths"…*

• **⅙ are virtually perfect in compliance.**

• **⅙ are pretty good,** but sometimes take the drug at the wrong time of day.

• **⅙ miss a day of medication on occasion.**

• **⅙ take "drug holidays"** (they discontinue medication for three or more days) three or four times per year.

• **⅙ take drug holidays once a month or more,** and frequently skip their medication for one to two days.

• **⅙ don't comply much at all…**but tell their doctors that they do.

WHY SO MUCH RESISTANCE?

There are a variety of reasons why people do not take their medication as it is prescribed. Unfortunately, many doctors don't ask about compliance, and patients usually don't bring up the topic on their own.

Important: Even if your doctor doesn't ask, be sure to discuss any problems you may be having adhering to the drug regimen you have been prescribed.

If you're having trouble sticking to your medication schedule, follow up with your doctor or his/her nurse by phone or e-mail between appointments.

Another option is to keep a medication log to take to the doctor—this will give you the feeling that you are preparing for an appointment every day. Make note of any side effects or problems you're having with adhering to the medication regimen.

The main reasons (listed alphabetically) that people don't take their medication and my advice for correcting the problem…

• **Apathy.** Some people lose interest in their health and, as a result, stop taking a prescribed medication.

Solution: Schedule an appointment to see your doctor. Your apathy may be a sign of depression. This is a relatively common secondary disorder among people faced with a serious or painful illness. Your physician usually can prescribe an antidepressant, which may improve both your mental outlook and your medication compliance.

• **Conscious omission.** When a doctor prescribes medication, some people feel compelled to defy authority or assert their independence.

Solution: Rather than waging an emotional rebellion, remember who stands to gain from medication compliance—if you don't take the drug, only you will be hurt…not the doctor.

•**Cost.** The medication is too expensive.

Solutions: Ask your doctor if there is a generic version of your medication…or if another, less expensive medication could be substituted. Another option is pill splitting. For some medications, the cost is the same, regardless of the dose—for example, a 5 milligram (mg) pill could cost the same as one that is 10 mg. By buying the higher dose and cutting the pills in half, you get twice the bang for your buck. Pill-splitting devices are available in drugstores for less than $10.* Not all medications can be split—ask your pharmacist.

•**Denial.** When taking medications for a "silent" disease, such as high blood pressure, some people disregard the diagnosis, thinking that if they were really sick, they would feel bad.

Solution: Ask your doctor what the risks are in not taking the medication. For example, even if you do know that a medication helps reduce blood pressure, you may need to be reminded that your risk for stroke and heart attack is increased if your blood pressure is not controlled effectively.

•**Fear.** Some people think that all prescription drugs—or a particular prescription drug—will hurt them.

Solution: If you are concerned about potential side effects of prescription drugs and prefer "natural" or herbal treatments, discuss this with your doctor. He may be able to recommend a dietary supplement or to allay your fears concerning the medication.

•**Feeling better.** Once the immediate health problem improves, many people cut down or stop taking the prescribed medication.

Solution: Realize that doctors prescribe medication according to specific dosing schedules so that the medication builds up in the bloodstream. If you stop taking an antibiotic, for example, you may not eliminate all the bacteria causing an infection. "Drug holidays" should be avoided, because skipping days may cause fluctuations in the blood levels of medication, which can make the drug less effective.

•**Forgetfulness.** Memory problems, as well as having other priorities, cause many people to miss taking medication.

*Prices subject to change.

Solutions: Count doses in advance and store them in a compartmentalized pill storage box. One- or two-week containers are now available at most supermarkets and drugstores.

It also helps to put medication in a place where you are most likely to see it. For example, if you take it in the morning, store the medication near your coffee mug or in the utensil drawer. If the medication must be refrigerated, place a reminder note near your mug or in the utensil drawer.

People who own cell phones, personal digital assistants or computers with an alarm feature can set these devices to ring at the same time every day. Pocket-sized alarms used solely as a reminder to take medication are now available in drugstores for about $6 to $10.

•**Lifestyle.** Travel, inconsistent work or home hours, or a generally busy schedule can interfere with medication compliance.

Solution: Keep your medication stored in a pill box and leave it where you will be sure to see it—such as on a bedside table—whether you're at home or traveling.

•**Side effects.** Nausea, headache, drowsiness and upset stomach occur with many drugs.

Solution: Your physician usually can change the prescription, give suggestions about other ways to take the medication—for example, with food—or prescribe an additional drug to counteract the side effects.

The Perils of "Underprescribing"

Rebecca Shannonhouse, editor of *Bottom Line/Health*, Boardroom Inc., 281 Tresser Blvd., Stamford, Connecticut 06901.

Researchers have long known that many people—especially elderly adults—often take prescription drugs that are ineffective, unnecessary or otherwise inappropriate.

Now: A recent review of the medical records of 196 older patients confirmed the overuse of some drugs—but also found that 64% were not taking a drug that would have been appropriate, such as aspirin to help prevent a heart attack.

Reason: Many older patients take a dozen or more drugs for different conditions, which is a lot to discuss in a brief office visit, explains Michael Steinman, MD, lead author of the recent review study and a staff physician at San Francisco VA Medical Center. A doctor will necessarily focus in on the most pressing issues, and may neglect (or forget) to talk about secondary concerns, such as high blood pressure, constipation or pain.

Yet underprescribing is potentially as risky as taking the wrong drug or an incorrect dose. *To prevent the misuse of prescription drugs...*

• **Ask your doctor whether you need a separate appointment to review your medications** if you take multiple drugs.

• **Never stop treating a condition simply because of a single drug's cost,** side effects, etc. There are usually drug alternatives that can circumvent these concerns.

• **If you take drugs for chronic conditions,** such as high blood pressure or diabetes, discuss with your doctor at least twice a year whether any of these medications can be discontinued—or if there are additional (or different) drugs you should be taking.

More from Rebecca Shannonhouse...

The Power of Placebos

The placebo response—obtaining therapeutic effects from an inactive substance, such as a sugar pill—is a well-known phenomenon. In one recent study of 466 Chicago internists, 45% said they had prescribed a placebo at some time during their clinical practice. Yet the placebo response is generally thought to be short-acting... and most effective for subjective conditions, such as the perception of pain. Now research shows that greater benefits may be possible.

New finding: When researchers interviewed 84 hotel maids (who are much more active than most Americans are), 67% did not perceive their work as exercise. The researchers then took the maids' physical measurements, including blood pressure and body weight, and separated them into two groups—one group was informed how many calories they actually burned during daily activities, while the second group did not have this information.

Result: One month later, maids in the "informed" grouping, unlike their counterparts, had experienced a 10% drop in blood pressure and a two- to four-pound decline in body weight, on average—even though their daily activity levels stayed constant.

This study suggests that the mind and body are more intimately related than scientists had previously thought, explains Ellen J. Langer, PhD, a Harvard psychologist and lead researcher of the study. Perceiving the daily activity as exercise produced benefits that didn't occur with the activity alone.

Advice from Dr. Langer: The next time you are making fitness or other health-related goals, consider putting the placebo effect to work—believe that you will succeed, and you might just have a better chance.

Generic Drug Dangers: More Side Effects...Less Effective?

Joe Graedon, a pharmacologist, and Teresa Graedon, PhD, consumer advocates who specialize in health issues related to medicines, herbs and vitamins. Their syndicated newspaper column "The People's Pharmacy" is widely distributed in the US and abroad, and they cohost an award-winning radio talk show. The Graedons are the coauthors of many books, including *Best Choices from The People's Pharmacy* (Rodale).

Generic drugs cost 30% to 80% less than their brand-name counterparts, but most people do feel safe taking them because the FDA requires that both types of medications provide the same active ingredients and level of effectiveness.

Development: In 2006 a survey found that about 25% of 300 physicians throughout the US don't believe that generics are chemically identical to brand-name drugs...nearly one in five believe that generics are less safe...and more than one in four believe that generics cause more side effects.

So what's the truth about generic drugs?

WHAT PATIENTS SAY

Since 1976, when our book *The People's Pharmacy* was originally published as a consumer guide to drug and health information, thousands of patients have contacted us about their experiences with medications.

In the last few years, we have received hundreds of letters and e-mails—most of them complaints—regarding generic drugs, including pain relief drugs, antidepressants and blood pressure medicines. The number of such complaints has increased dramatically in that time.

What we have learned: Some patients who switch from a brand-name to a generic report a decline in drug effectiveness—for example, blood pressure that isn't controlled as well or a worsening of depression. Others report having a rash or other types of allergic reactions, probably due to one of the inactive "filler" ingredients in generic drugs. There also seem to be problems with the timed-release mechanism of some generics.

Example: A manufacturer's timed-release generic formulation might release too much of a medicine too quickly (known as "dose dumping"). This might explain the side effects that some people experience when they take a generic drug, but not the brand-name version.

IS THE FDA
DOING ENOUGH?

Drug companies must apply to the FDA to sell generic versions of drugs. To gain FDA approval, a generic drug must contain the same active ingredients as brand-name medications and meet the same criteria for such factors as quality, strength and purity. *Possible problems with generic drugs...*

•**Periodic checks for impurities.** The FDA monitors generic drugs, testing for such things as proper dosing and active ingredients. But the agency only checks about 300 "dosage forms," such as tablets and capsules, among brand-name and generic products a year—out of a total of more than three billion prescriptions.

•**Infrequent inspections.** The FDA is supposed to inspect each US drug manufacturing plant every two years—but lacks the resources to meet that requirement.

•**Overseas manufacturing.** An enormous percentage of drug ingredients and raw materials for drugs (primarily generic and over-the-counter) come from India, China and other countries where quality assurance is not as rigorous as in the US—and where drug counterfeiting has been a problem.

Trap: Overseas plants are inspected much less frequently than those in the US. Without testing, there's no way to tell whether drugs and drug ingredients derived from these plants have impurities—or come in "subtherapeutic" dosages (for example, a drug labeled 10 milligrams [mg] may be only 6 mg).

STAYING SAFE

Most of the evidence for problems with generic drugs is based on anecdotal reports. However, research published in *Neurology* in 2004 reported that people with epilepsy who switched from the brand-name form of the antiseizure medicine *phenytoin* (Dilantin) to the generic form of the drug began to have higher-than-expected rates of seizures. Investigators found that in many patients, blood levels of the active ingredient had dropped by 30%.

Even so, patients should not give up on generic drugs. Your cost savings can be considerable...and there is no evidence thus far that the majority of generic drugs will cause problems in most patients. *Patients using generic medicines should simply take extra precautions...*

•**Stick with one manufacturer.** This is particularly important if you're taking a drug with a narrow therapeutic index (NTI), such as the anticoagulant *warfarin*, the antipsychotic *lithium* or the anticonvulsant *carbamazepine*. NTI drugs, which typically require periodic blood tests to measure blood levels of the medications, have a very thin margin between an effective dose and a toxic dose. If you're taking a generic form, ask your pharmacist for the name of the manufacturer—and request that the pharmacy stick with that company, if possible, to avoid variations between products.

•**Monitor your numbers.** Many conditions, such as hypertension or high cholesterol, don't cause obvious symptoms. The best way to tell whether a drug is working is to monitor your numbers—by taking daily blood pressure readings, monitoring blood-sugar levels and keeping track of cholesterol levels with frequent blood tests at your doctor's office.

Important: Ask your doctor to give you copies of your test results. Check them periodically to make sure that you're maintaining adequate control—particularly if you've recently switched from a brand name medication to a generic, or the reverse.

• **Trust your instincts.** Some medications affect the body in subtle ways. A patient taking a thyroid drug, for example, might feel slightly run-down if it isn't working exactly the way it should, even if test results appear to be normal. Pay attention. If you have switched to a generic and notice a difference—either in effectiveness or side effects—tell your doctor.

• **Do a "challenge, rechallenge" test.** If you suspect that a generic drug isn't working the way it should, write down changes in how long the drug works and side effects. Then, ask your doctor to switch you to the brand-name equivalent, and see if there's improvement—in most cases, it will be apparent in about two weeks. Under the close supervision of your doctor, repeat the test, going back and forth until you have a clear idea which drug is more effective for you.

• **Report problems to the FDA.*** The FDA can analyze generic drugs to determine if they contain the stated amount of active ingredient. When reporting any drug to the FDA, ask your pharmacist to provide the name of the manufacturer, the lot number and exactly when the drug was dispensed to you.

If you'd also like to report problems with generic drugs to us, go to The People's Pharmacy Web site, *www.peoplespharmacy.org*.

*Go to the FDA Web site, *www.fda.gov/medwatch*, or call 888-463-6332.

Boost Your Medication's Healing Powers

Leo Galland, MD, an internist in private practice and the founder and director of the Foundation for Integrated Medicine, both in New York City, *www.mdheal.org*. He is also the creator of the *Drug-Nutrient Workshop*, a software tool for analyzing interactions among medicine, foods and supplements, *www.nutritionworkshop.com*, and the author of *The Fat Resistance Diet* (Broadway) and *Power Healing* (Random House).

If you're part of the millions of Americans taking medication for pain, asthma or allergies, hypertension, high cholesterol or depression, research shows that you may be able to maximize all the benefits...curb the side effects...and maybe even lower the dosages of your drugs by combining them with the right supplements.

Important: Consult your doctor before adding a supplement to your drug regimen. Some supplements can interact adversely with medications—for example, some research indicates that fish oil can decrease the time it takes for blood to clot and should be used with caution by anyone who uses a blood thinner, such as *warfarin* (Coumadin).

Supplements (available at health-food stores) to consider using if you are taking any of the following...

ANTIDEPRESSANT

Supplement with: 1,000 milligrams (mg) to 2,000 mg daily of *eicosapentaenoic acid* (EPA), an omega-3 fatty acid found in fish oil. (Ask your doctor which dosage is right for you.)

What it does: Omega-3s are believed to enhance the ability of the brain chemical serotonin to act on the nervous system. In a recent British study, when depressed patients who were taking a prescription antidepressant, such as *fluoxetine* (Prozac) or *sertraline* (Zoloft), added 1,000 mg of EPA to their daily regimen for 12 weeks, they reported significantly less depression, anxiety and suicidal thoughts, as well as improved sleep, libido and energy.

Most standard fish oil supplements contain only 200 mg to 300 mg of EPA, so you'd need up to 10 capsules daily to get the recommended 1,000 mg to 2,000 mg of EPA. If you don't want to take that many capsules, take liquid fish oil—

in an amount equal to 1,000 mg to 2,000 mg daily of EPA.

Helpful: To avoid "fishy-tasting" burping (the most frequent complaint), try taking the capsules on an empty stomach with a large glass of water. Some people also find that this unpleasant aftertaste is less likely to occur with liquid fish oil.

Also try: 500 micrograms (mcg) daily of folic acid, which promotes proper functioning of the nervous system. Low levels of folic acid have been linked to depression.

Researchers at Harvard Medical School report that depressed patients who had achieved remission with fluoxetine were 13 times more likely to relapse during a six-month period if they had low blood levels of folic acid.

Caution: Supplemental folic acid may mask a vitamin B-12 deficiency, which could lead to nerve damage. Take a 500-mcg to 1,000-mcg B-12 supplement daily to prevent worsening of a B-12 deficiency.

NONSTEROIDAL ANTI-INFLAMMATORY DRUG

Supplement with: 350 mg of deglycyrrhizinated licorice (DGL), three times daily.

What it does: Studies show that DGL may decrease or prevent the gastrointestinal (GI) inflammation, bleeding and ulcerations caused by aspirin and other nonsteroidal anti-inflammatory drugs (NSAIDs)—both prescription and over-the-counter.

Caution: Whole licorice extract also protects the stomach, but it contains *glycyrrhetinic acid*, which even in small doses may raise blood pressure. Stick with DGL.

Also try: 1,000 mg to 2,000 mg daily of vitamin C (in two divided doses) and 7 grams (g) of powdered *glutamine* (one heaping teaspoon dissolved in water, three times per day). Studies suggest that taking 1,000 mg of vitamin C twice daily may help prevent aspirin-induced inflammation of the small intestine.

Meanwhile, the amino acid glutamine, long used to help heal ulcers, may decrease the intestinal toxicity of NSAIDs.

ASTHMA OR ALLERGY DRUG

Supplement with: 1,000 mg daily of gamma-linolenic acid (GLA) and 500 mg daily of EPA.

What it does: GLA, an omega-6 fatty acid derived from evening primrose oil or borage oil, may inhibit production of *leukotrienes*, molecules that trigger inflammation and constriction of the bronchial airways. The asthma drug *montelukast* (Singulair) also works by inhibiting leukotrienes.

Important: Most omega-6 fatty acids (including those found in many processed foods) increase inflammation, unless they're balanced by sufficient amounts of anti-inflammatory omega-3s. GLA, however, is an anti-inflammatory, but at high doses—and in the absence of omega-3s—it could become inflammatory. The recommended 500 mg of EPA daily creates an optimal balance of omega-6s and omega-3s.

Also try: *Quercetin*, a bioflavonoid derived from red onions, apples and other foods. In laboratory studies, quercetin has demonstrated both antihistamine and antiallergenic properties. Clinical trials are needed, but given its safety, I often recommend quercetin to my asthma and allergy patients. Try using 500 mg to 600 mg, twice daily, of quercetin—taken on an empty stomach for maximum benefit—as an adjunct to your antihistamine and/or GLA.

BLOOD PRESSURE DRUG

Supplement with: 1,000 mg of *arginine* two times daily.

What it does: Arginine (also called L-arginine) is an amino acid used by the body to produce nitric oxide (NO), the molecule that helps keep blood vessels flexible and able to dilate—both of which stabilize blood pressure. Legumes (such as lentils, black beans and kidney beans) and whole grains (such as brown rice) contain some arginine, but you'll need a supplement to get the 2,000 mg daily that is recommended for blood vessel health.

Caution: Because some research has shown that arginine can be dangerous for people who have suffered a heart attack, it should not be used by these individuals. If you have the herpes simplex virus and want to take arginine, you may need to add 1,500 mg daily of lysine, another amino acid. The virus grows in the presence of arginine but is inhibited by lysine.

Also try: 100 mg daily of *Pycnogenol*. This plant extract appears to enhance NO synthesis in blood vessels. In a recent placebo-controlled trial, Chinese researchers found that hypertensive patients who took 100 mg of Pycnogenol daily over 12 weeks were able to significantly lower their dose of a calcium channel blocker, a popular hypertension drug.

STATIN

Supplement with: 100 mg daily of coenzyme Q10 (CoQ10).

What it does: Cholesterol-lowering statins deplete the naturally produced molecule coenzyme Q10—this depletion may lead to muscle damage.

Research done at Stony Brook University in Stony Brook, New York, found that patients taking statins who added 100 mg of CoQ10 daily for one month reported a 40% reduction in severity of muscle pain, a common side effect of statins.

CoQ10 also may prevent oxidation of LDL "bad" cholesterol—an unfortunate side effect of statins that occurs to LDL cholesterol particles not eliminated by the drug.

Also try: Fish oil that contains 1,500 mg of EPA and 1,300 mg of *docosahexaenoic acid* (DHA) daily. Studies show that these essential fatty acids raise HDL "good" cholesterol and lower dangerous blood fats known as triglycerides—making EPA and DHA a valuable adjunct to statins, which mainly target elevated LDL cholesterol.

●**Ask your doctor the exact name of the drug and its dosage.** Check the name and dosage on the label when you receive it.

●**Ask your doctor to write the purpose of the drug on the prescription form—**the pharmacist will be alerted if the purpose doesn't fit the name of the drug.

●**If your doctor sends a prescription to a pharmacy electronically,** be sure to get a copy for yourself.

●**If a drug bottle arrives in a box or other packaging,** check to be sure the label on the bottle matches that on the packaging.

●**Take your prescription to the pharmacist during his or her off-peak hours.** Then talk to the pharmacist about it to verify it and ask any questions you have.

Key: During off-peak hours, the pharmacist is more free to talk—and less likely to be rushed in a way that could cause a mistake.

●**Learn about drugs that are prescribed to you from on-line sources.**

Good sites: Drugs.com (*www.drugs.com*)... RxList (*www.rxlist.com*).

For other on-line sources of information regarding a particular drug, enter its name in the Web search engine of your choice.

Protect Yourself from Pharmacy Drug Errors

David Wood, freelance consumer advocate and writer on senior scams and fraud, Washington, DC.

At least 1.5 million patients annually in the US are harmed or killed by prescription drug errors.

Major causes: Doctors' messy handwriting that is misread by pharmacists...distractions that cause doctors and pharmacists, as well as nurses and other caregivers—including those working in hospitals—to make mistakes.

Self-defense: Know your prescription and its purpose...

Hospital Medical Errors Are Painful, Costly and Deadly: How to Protect Yourself

Charles B. Inlander, a consumer advocate and healthcare consultant located in Fogelsville, Pennsylvania. He was the founding president of the nonprofit People's Medical Society, the consumer advocacy organization credited with key improvement in the quality of US health care in the 1980s and 1990s, and is the author of 20 books, including *Take This Book to the Hospital with You: A Consumer Guide to Surviving Your Hospital Stay* (St. Martin's).

Medicare has announced that it will no longer pay hospitals for the extra costs of treating patients with complications due to medical mistakes—infections, hospital-acquired bedsores, etc.

Medical mistakes are the eighth leading cause of hospital deaths among Americans. The National Academy of Sciences indicates that more people die from hospital errors than from auto accidents, breast cancer or AIDS.

Examples: Mistakes in drug use, such as giving the wrong dose or even the wrong drug, account for tens of thousands of deaths annually in hospitals and outpatient facilities. Hospital-acquired infections result in 80,000 to 100,000 deaths. But, the vast majority of these deaths are preventable.

Most hospital mistakes are relatively minor. A patient might be given an unnecessary test, or a drug that's not optimal for his/her condition. But some mistakes are life threatening—and, in most cases, completely avoidable.

MEDICATION MISTAKES

It's estimated that hospitals in the US make more than 1.5 million drug-related mistakes annually, causing the deaths of 40,000 to 80,000 patients. Name confusion is the most common cause of medication errors.

Example: A patient who's supposed to get Celebrex for arthritis might be given Cerebyx (used for seizures) or Celexa (an antidepressant) instead of the correct drug.

Handwritten prescriptions should not be allowed in hospitals. It's common for pharmacists to accidentally substitute medicines with similar-sounding names…give the wrong dose (by confusing the numbers "3" and "8," for example)…or miss a decimal point (confusing 10.00 mg with 100.00 mg). *To prevent a medication mistake in the hospital…*

●**If possible, choose a hospital with a bar-coding system** that automatically matches drug prescriptions/labels with coding on patient bracelets. Only 7% to 8% of hospitals now use this technology. All prescriptions are entered directly into computers—and the computers are programmed to recognize potential errors.

●**Question any drug that looks different from what you've been getting.** If you have been taking blue pills for two days, and then are given a green pill, ask what it is…what it's for…why you're being given something different from before…and who ordered it.

●**Notice changes in side effects and report them to your doctor or nurse.** You may have been given a wrong drug and/or dose.

INFECTIONS

The Centers for Disease Control and Prevention estimates that an average of 4% to 6% of hospital patients develop hospital-acquired infections annually. In some hospitals, the percentage is much higher. With the emergence of antibiotic-resistant organisms, such as the potentially deadly *methicillin-resistant Staphylococcus aureus* (or MRSA), some of these infections are threatening to life. *Ways to prevent unnecessary infections…*

●**Not washing hands accounts for half of all hospital-acquired infections.** Don't let health-care workers touch you—or equipment that's attached to you, such as intravenous (IV) lines—unless they wash their hands while you watch. They should wash even if they're putting on gloves before doing a procedure, because the outside of the gloves could get contaminated from germs on the hands.

●**Bladder or blood-vessel catheters are open doors to infection.** Every time a nurse comes into the room to monitor your catheters, ask him to check them for cleanliness, and to make sure that the entry site is clean and sterilized each time. It is also important to sterilize the connections every time the catheter bag is changed.

●**Food-service workers who come into your room should touch only the trays they bring** and retrieve and the food on the trays. If they touch anything else—such as by propping up a patient in the bed next to you—ask them to change their gloves before giving you your tray.

Key protection: If you have the time, get a pneumonia vaccination from your doctor as far in advance as possible before entering the hospital. Hospital patients often have weakened immune systems—and pneumonia is among the leading causes of death in hospitals. In patients who develop pneumonia while hospitalized for another condition, the mortality rate can be as high as 70%. The pneumonia vaccine protects against 23 strains of the most common bacterial pneumonia.

BEDSORES

Also known as pressure ulcers, bedsores occur when circulation to the skin and underlying tissues is blocked in immobile patients. This usually occurs on the elbows, hips, buttocks and/or heels. Older patients, and those with diabetes or other diseases that cause circulatory problems, have an especially high risk for bedsores.

Warning: Bedsores are often painless until the damage has become extensive. Patients and health-care workers have to watch out for them. *Self-defense...*

•**Move your arms and legs as often as you comfortably can.**

•**Change your position** or ask friends/family members to help you change position about every hour or two.

Also important: Ask them (or nurses) to inspect areas that you can't see to make sure sores aren't developing.

FALLS

Falls are the second leading cause of accidental deaths in hospitals, and they're a main cause of broken hips. They often occur when patients need to use the bathroom but do not get a response after pressing the call button—and attempt to climb out of bed without waiting for assistance.

Other causes: Unsteadiness due to sedation from medications...tripping over an IV line and other obstacles...and slipping on wet floors. *To ward off falls...*

•**If a nurse doesn't respond when you press the bedside call button, use the phone** (assuming you are able) to call the main switchboard. Ask for the nursing station on your floor. Someone will always answer.

•**Have a friend/family member bring you a pair of slippers with nonskid soles.**

Important: For safety's sake, do not get up without assistance, even if you believe you are strong enough to do so. Some hospitals have bed alarms that alert the nurses if you try to get up on your own—but many don't.

SURGICAL SAFETY

Under the new rules, Medicare will not pay hospitals for treating complications from serious preventable errors, such as recovering a sponge or other object that was left inside a patient after surgery.

Patients have little control over surgical outcomes, but they can pick a surgeon who has a lot of experience doing a particular procedure. Statistically, the error rate is significantly lower when surgeons perform a surgical procedure at least 100 times a year.

Also important: Before surgery, use a marker to write an "X" on the body part—knee, hip, elbow, etc.—that's supposed to be operated on. Some hospitals already take this precaution, but some do not.

There aren't reliable statistics on the frequency of "wrong-site" surgeries, but it occurs frequently enough that the Joint Commission on Accreditation of Healthcare Organizations, a not-for-profit organization that evaluates and accredits healthcare organizations, issued an emergency alert in 2001 about the rise in frequency. It now advises marking the surgical site ahead of time.

Charles Inlander on risky surgeries...

Beware of Surgeries In Doctors' Offices

Do you need a colonoscopy? What about a hernia repair or arthroscopic knee surgery? Are you thinking about having your cataract removed or maybe undergoing breast augmentation? These and hundreds of other procedures, once performed only in the hospital operating room, are now routinely being done in doctors' offices. Even though this arrangement is usually convenient, and oftentimes less costly than going to a hospital, doctors report—and research confirms—that office-based procedures can be risky.

How risky are they? A 2004 Florida study of office-based surgeries performed over a two-year period found that the risk for complications or death was 10 times greater than in hospital or hospital-affiliated settings, such as surgical facilities. Other states indicate similar findings. With more than 25 million office-based surgeries performed each year in the US, you would expect states to be closely monitoring this practice. But that's not the case. Unlike hospitals, which are highly regulated and inspected, only 12 states have rules or regulations that govern office-based surgery. And even in those states, the oversight is minimal. But you can lower your risk for a botched office procedure. *Questions to ask...*

• **Is the doctor qualified to do the procedure?** Make sure the doctor is board certified in the specialty that covers the procedure he/she is performing. For example, a doctor who is performing a colonoscopy should be board certified in gastroenterology. To check on a doctor's certification, consult the American Board of Medical Specialties (ABMS) at 866-275-2267 or *www.abms.org.*

• **Have complaints been filed?** Check with your state medical licensing board to see if there have been any serious complaints or actions taken against the doctor. (To get the board's telephone number, check your state's official Web site or call your state legislator.)

• **How are emergencies handled?** Ask the doctor whether he has an agreement with a local ambulance service and a nearby hospital to move you in case of an emergency, such as a heart attack or failure to regain consciousness. Then confirm it with the ambulance company and the hospital administrator's office.

• **What is the projected recovery time?** The office should have a recovery area that has the same type of equipment a hospital would use for patients undergoing a similar procedure. Call the medical director's office at a local hospital and ask what the standard equipment and practices are when the procedure is done there. A registered nurse or physician should be available until you are completely recovered from the anesthesia.

• **Does the doctor possess malpractice insurance?** It may surprise you, but a number of physicians performing office-based surgeries do not have malpractice insurance. While it might save the doctor some money, it can be costly for you if things go wrong. So ask the doctor what company provides his insurance, and get his approval to check it out with the carrier.

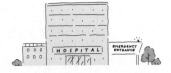

Surviving the Intensive Care Unit

Richard P. Shannon, MD, chair of the department of medicine at Allegheny General Hospital in Pittsburgh, PA, where he pioneered the highly effective model program for reducing catheter-associated bacterial infections. Dr. Shannon also is chair of the department of medicine at the University of Pennsylvania School of Medicine and the Hospital of the University of Pennsylvania, both in Philadelphia. His efforts to improve patient safety were highlighted in the PBS television series *Remaking American Medicine.*

Having a loved one in the intensive care unit (ICU) is unavoidably stressful. Patients placed in this part of the hospital are seriously injured or sick enough to require the most sophisticated around-the-clock medical care.

Frightening: About 12% of the estimated 5 million Americans admitted annually to ICUs die before leaving intensive care. While the seriousness and uncertainty of your loved one's condition may leave you feeling powerless, there are ways you can help.

AVOIDING INFECTIONS

Almost 2 million infections are acquired in hospitals each year—about 260,000 of them fatal. ICU patients are most vulnerable—their immune systems are already greatly challenged because of their illnesses or injuries, and they frequently require invasive procedures that can inadvertently introduce harmful bacteria into the body.

What you can do...

Be aware of the two steps for hand hygiene. Although you may not always be able to stay in the patient's room, when you are present, remind health-care staff and visitors to wash their hands with soap *and* water and use an alcohol hand-sanitizing gel upon entering the room.

An alcohol hand-sanitizing gel is highly effective against bacteria, but plain soap and water is necessary to eliminate hardy, infection-causing spores, such as those formed by the bacterium *Clostridium difficile,* a primary cause of severe diarrhea in hospitalized patients who are taking antibiotics.

BREATHING TUBES

Here is what to do to help protect a patient who has trouble breathing...

If a breathing tube is recommended for your loved one, ask the doctor if it is absolutely necessary. Patients who are unable to breathe on their own due to heart failure or severe pneumonia are usually "intubated" (a plastic tube is passed through the nose or mouth into the trachea to force air from a mechanical ventilator into the lungs). Because intubation is an invasive procedure that greatly increases the risk for infection, it is often safer to first try a noninvasive bilevel positive airway pressure (BiPAP) mask. The BiPAP mask, which fits snugly over the nose and mouth to open the airways, delivers oxygen to the lungs and assists exhalation. This device is an appropriate first step in cases of mild respiratory failure.

Ask the doctor daily, "Is this breathing tube still necessary?" The longer any patient remains on mechanical ventilation, the greater the threat for an often-fatal complication known as ventilator-associated pneumonia (VAP). Patients on mechanical ventilators are routinely sedated to reduce anxiety and discomfort. But some studies suggest that lightening the sedation for a brief and carefully monitored period daily, to assess the patient's readiness to breathe independently, may reduce time on the ventilator by an average of two-and-a-half days.

Make sure the head of the patient's bed is always elevated at least 30 degrees if mechanical ventilation is necessary. Studies suggest that elevating the head significantly reduces the risk for VAP, probably by preventing mucus from pooling in the back of the throat and becoming a reservoir of bacteria that can be inhaled into the airways. A semi-upright position also may minimize reflux (backup of stomach acid), reducing the chances that gastrointestinal bacteria will be inhaled into the lungs. If the bed doesn't have an elevation indicator, the desired elevation can be measured and marked on the wall.

Confirm that your loved one's mouth is being thoroughly cleaned and swabbed twice each day with *chlorhexidine*, an antiseptic that prevents the growth of oral bacteria. A recent study at the University at Buffalo School of Dental Medicine found that patients' own dental plaque is often the source of VAP-causing bacteria.

CARING FOR CATHETERS

Central venous catheters—which often are inserted through the patient's jugular (neck) vein to allow for the delivery of medication and ready access for blood withdrawal—give bacteria direct access to the bloodstream, greatly increasing a patient's risk for a bloodstream infection (BSI). Such infections cause more than 26,000 deaths in US hospitals each year.

*A **new lifesaving approach:*** At Allegheny General Hospital in Pittsburgh, we developed a program to prevent BSIs after one of our heart-transplant candidates died because of a catheter-associated infection. The program (consisting of basic measures, such as always cleansing the insertion site with a topical antiseptic) decreased catheter-associated BSIs by 87%.

Unfortunately, not all hospitals are equally vigilant—this means that you need to be. *What you can do...*

• **Ask daily, "How many catheters are being used?"** Many ICU patients require several catheters to deliver medications and nutrients and eliminate wastes. Make a daily note of the number and location of the patient's catheters. Ask each day whether any of the catheters can be removed.

• **Watch to ensure that the catheters are being properly maintained.** Nurses should check the condition of all catheters and dressings each time they see the patient.

• **Ask daily, "Are any of the catheters at risk of causing an infection?"** Speak up if you notice red skin and/or oozing of a watery substance around an insertion site.

OTHER WAYS TO HELP

Researchers have identified other ways that family members or friends can help protect an ICU patient. *My advice...*

• **Inquire about early physical therapy.** A recent two-year study found that patients on mechanical ventilation who received early physical therapy (PT)—within 48 hours of intubation—cut their ICU stays by more than a day and their overall hospital stays by about three days, on average, compared with completely immobilized patients. A nursing assistant or physical therapist, for example, can flex a mechanically ventilated patient's arm and leg joints three times daily, until he/she recovers sufficiently to participate in more active therapy.

• **Request a weekday transfer prior to 7 pm.** The ICU is fully operational 24 hours daily, but the same is typically not true of less intensive hospital units, where ICU patients are transferred before going home. That's why I am generally reluctant to transfer patients out of the ICU after 7 pm. A recent Canadian study involving almost 79,000 ICU patients at 31 hospitals found that those transferred at night had about a 22% higher risk for death following the transfer, compared with those transferred during the day. While you won't always be able to choose when your loved one leaves the ICU—it will depend largely on the demand for ICU beds—it's worth lobbying for a weekday, daytime transfer.

• **Communicate with the ICU team.** Within two hours of your loved one's admission to the ICU, try to arrange an initial meeting between family members and your ICU physicians and nurses to discuss your loved one's status and a treatment strategy. Find out who will be leading the care (in the ICU, this is typically a specialist called an intensivist) and ask when he makes daily rounds.

Arriving at the hospital and asking, "Is the doctor here?" Is an inefficient and often frustrating way to try to stay updated on your loved one's progress.

Better: Call ahead to the ICU nurses' station and ask, "When will the doctor be there?"—and time your hospital visits accordingly. Jot down any questions ahead of time—that way, you'll remember to ask them when seeing the physician. Communicating regularly with the doctor may ease your own anxiety while helping to ensure that your loved one receives optimal care.

Curb Surgery Side Effects

In a recent study of 200 women scheduled for breast cancer surgery, a psychologist treated one group with 15 minutes of hypnosis (including suggestions on how to reduce pain) within one hour prior to surgery, while the other group simply spoke with a psychologist about whatever they wished.

Result: The hypnosis group needed less anesthesia and reported less pain than the other group.

Theory: Hypnosis induces relaxation, which helps reduce pain.

To find a hypnotist: Contact the American Society of Clinical Hypnosis, 630-980-4740, *www.asch.net.*

Guy Montgomery, PhD, associate professor, Mount Sinai School of Medicine, New York City.

Medical Miracles Really Do Happen

Larry Dossey, MD, executive editor of *Explore: The Journal of Science and Healing* and the former executive editor of the journal *Alternative Therapies in Health and Medicine.* He is the author of 10 books, including *Healing Words* and *Prayer Is Good Medicine* (both Harper One) and *The Extraordinary Healing Power of Ordinary Things* (Harmony/Random House).

Most of us have read about people who recover from diseases that were considered not curable. This phenomenon, referred to in medical literature as a spontaneous remission, occurs when a serious, often deadly illness such as cancer quickly and inexplicably—and some would even claim miraculously—disappears.

No one knows exactly how often such cases occur. Approximately 3,500 medically documented cases of seeming miracles—based on reports from doctors in America and around the world dating from 1967—have appeared in 800 peer-reviewed medical journals and cover all major illnesses, including cancer, heart disease, diabetes and arthritis.*

Here, Larry Dossey, MD, answers questions on medically documented "miracles"—and what

*These cases are reviewed in *Spontaneous Remission* (The Institute of Noetic Sciences). An on-line version of the bibliography is available at *www.noetic.org.*

they might mean for improving everyday health and healing...

• **What is a "medically documented miracle"?** The word miracle is from the Latin *mirari*, meaning to look at in awe. For me, a medical miracle is an awe-inspiring healing event, a disease that just goes away suddenly, unexpectedly and completely.

Attempts have been made to define and medically document miracle-type cures. For example, in 1954, the Catholic Church established the International Medical Committee of Lourdes, a panel that includes dozens of experts from the European medical community. These physicians decide whether the cure reported by a person who has visited the healing shrine at Lourdes in southwestern France is an "authentic" miracle, utilizing scrupulous criteria, including a permanent remission of the disease. As of 2006, the committee had documented 67 cases.

• **Have any of your patients ever experienced this type of healing?** Early in my career, I had an elderly patient with cancer in both lungs that had spread throughout his body. We had no medical therapies for this type of cancer, but during visiting hours, people from his church stood near his bed, praying and singing gospel music. I expected him to die within days, and when he asked to go home, I respected his wishes and discharged him.

About one year later, this patient was back in the hospital—this time with a bad case of the flu. I went to the radiology department to look at his current chest X-ray, and it was completely normal. I thought that in the past year he must have had a dramatic response to additional therapy of some kind, but he hadn't undergone any therapy. To me, this was a true miracle cure.

• **Are religious and supernatural influences believed to play a role in most medical miracles?** Many medical miracles occur in a religious, spiritual or supernatural context—people pray to God, or to saints, or rely on what they believe to be the healing energies of the universe. Maybe some unrecognized mind-body process is triggered from belief. But even this is pure speculation—because atheists and agnostics also experience what appear to be miracle cures.

Not really knowing why something works is not necessarily a problem. Throughout the history of medicine, we often have known that a treatment works before we understand how it works. Aspirin and penicillin are two examples. We can add miracle-type cures to that list. Perhaps science will someday explain these occurrences. For now, they remain inexplicable.

• **How do people who experience these cures explain their recoveries?** In interviews conducted for a book that is titled *Remarkable Recovery* (Riverhead), individuals whose illnesses were reversed pointed to a variety of factors they thought played an important role in their healing.

Paradoxically, the two most commonly cited factors seem like opposites—75% attributed the recovery to the "belief in a positive outcome," while 71% said it was based on "acceptance of the disease." This shows that there is no single "personality type" that experiences miracle-type healings.

Sixty-eight percent believed that prayer was responsible, followed up by meditation and faith. Self-help regimens, including exercise, music and singing, were also cited.

• **Some doctors believe that telling patients about miracle-type cures instills "false hope." What do you think?** Yes, some doctors may believe that speaking about medically documented miracles promotes "false hope" in seriously ill patients. But I would say that not informing and educating your patients about this possibility promotes "false pessimism"—a negative viewpoint that is not justified by the facts. Documented miracle cures are a fact of medical history. For someone who is ill, that knowledge can provide comfort and consolation.

3

Common Health Problems

The Wilen Sisters' Home Remedies That Work Better Than Drugs

The Wilen sisters have been using home remedies all of their lives, and for the last quarter of a century, they've been researching and writing about them as well.

Below, the Wilens share the remedies they use most often for a variety of health challenges. The sisters may not always be able to explain why the remedies work—but they work. All use ingredients readily available in most kitchens, supermarkets or health-food stores. Of course, always check with your doctor before taking any dietary supplement or herb.

SORE THROAT

At the first sign of a sore or scratchy throat, mix two teaspoons of apple cider vinegar in six-to-eight ounces of warm water. Take a mouthful, gargle with it and spit it out—then swallow a mouthful. Repeat the gargle/swallow pattern until there is nothing left in the glass. Do this every hour until your throat is better. We usually feel better within two or three hours.

COLDS

We eat chicken soup when we feel a cold coming on. Aside from being a comfort food, it helps prevent a cold from becoming full-blown and/or it shortens the duration of one. We either prepare the soup from scratch, adding lots of veggies (carrots, onions, parsnip, celery, string beans), or we do the next best thing—buy packaged soup found in the supermarket's frozen food section, then add vegetables. In either case, we add the most potent and health-restoring ingredient—garlic. To derive the full healing powers of garlic, add one or two finely minced raw cloves after the warmed soup is in the bowl.

Lydia Wilen and Joan Wilen, folk-remedy experts based in New York City. The sisters are coauthors of many books, including Bottom Line's Healing Remedies: Over 1,000 Astounding Ways to Heal Arthritis, Asthma, High Blood Pressure, Varicose Veins, Warts and More! *(Bottom Line Books, 800-678-5838, www.BottomLineSecrets.com/store).*

49

STOP BLEEDING

A simple first-aid procedure to stop a minor cut or gash from bleeding is to cover the cut with cayenne pepper from your spice cabinet. Gently pour on the pepper. Yes, it will sting a bit. And yes, the bleeding will stop quickly.

DIARRHEA

If you must be away from a restroom, prepare slippery elm tea (we use the inner bark powder available at health-food stores). Pour eight ounces of just-boiled water over a heaping teaspoon of the powder. Let it steep for about eight minutes, then strain the liquid into a mug and drink it. It works quickly. For severe cases, do not strain it—just drink this soothing, gloppy tea.

HEARTBURN

We use our mother's remedy. As soon as the burning starts, eat a palmful of almonds—that's about one ounce—and the heartburn stops immediately. Our mom used dry-roasted almonds. We buy raw almond slivers.

STY

A sty is an inflamed swelling on the eyelid. This classic folk remedy sounds ridiculous but has worked for us many times. The minute you feel as though you're getting a sty, take a 14-carat gold ring (wash it first) and rub it several times across your eyelid every 15 minutes or so, until that "sty-ish" feeling disappears...along with the sty. In our experience, it works right away.

BURNED FINGERTIPS

Ever reach for a pot handle that's surprisingly hot? How about grabbing the wrong side of a plugged-in iron? We have a unique way of treating these minor first-degree burns, where the skin is painful and red but unbroken. It's a form of acupressure. Place your thumb on the back side of your earlobe, and the burned fingertips on the front side of the same earlobe. Press firmly. After a minute, the pain is gone.

INSOMNIA

Our new best friends are nuts—in this case, walnuts. They are rich in serotonin, the brain chemical that calms anxiety and allows us to turn off the pressures of the day to get a good night's sleep. Eat a palmful (one ounce) of raw walnuts before going to bed. It's important to chew each mouthful thoroughly, until the nut pieces are ground down.

The Healing Power of Aromatherapy

Mindy Green, a practicing aromatherapist for more than 25 years. The Minneapolis-based coauthor of *Aromatherapy: A Complete Guide to the Healing Art* (Ten Speed) is a founding member of the American Herbalists' Guild.

A scented spray or candle may smell good, but true "aromatherapy" does so much more. This ancient healing practice involves the therapeutic use of aromatic substances known as essential oils (highly concentrated extracts distilled from plants).

Some people scoff at the idea of using aromatherapy, but ongoing research has shown that essential oils are effective in treating a variety of common health problems, including muscle cramps, cough, fatigue and insomnia.

How does it work? Smelling an essential oil releases neurotransmitters and other chemicals that affect the brain. When used topically, chemical constituents in essential oils are absorbed through the skin and enter the bloodstream, where they affect overall physiology, including hormones and enzymes.

Best way to use topical therapy: Add five to 10 drops of essential oil to one ounce of a "carrier" oil, such as almond oil, which is odorless, and apply this to the affected part of your body. For a bath, add five to eight drops of essential oil mixed with a teaspoon of a carrier oil to a tub full of warm bathwater.

Best way to use inhalation therapy: Add three to six drops of essential oil to a basin of hot water (boil then cool slightly). Bend your head over the bowl and cover your head with a towel, creating a tent to trap the scented steam. Staying at least 12 inches away from the water source, inhale deeply for three to five minutes.

My favorite essential oils and their uses...

MARJORAM FOR MUSCLE CRAMPS

Add a mixture of marjoram and a carrier oil to your bath and soak for 20 minutes. Or massage marjoram oil and a carrier oil into the painful area as needed.

EUCALYPTUS FOR COUGH AND CONGESTION

Rub a mixture of eucalyptus and a carrier oil onto your chest and back. The oils work via skin absorption and inhalation to ease coughs and congestion. For congestion, do an inhalation therapy three times daily for five minutes each session.

Caution: Do not try this therapy during an asthma attack—it can exacerbate symptoms. If you don't get relief within a few days, see your doctor.

ROSEMARY FOR FATIGUE

Add rosemary and a carrier oil to a warm bath and soak for 10 to 15 minutes as needed.

LAVENDER FOR INSOMNIA

Add lavender and a carrier oil to warm bathwater and soak for 20 minutes before going to bed.

GINGER AND PEPPERMINT FOR NAUSEA

Mix two drops of ginger oil with one drop of peppermint oil and one tablespoon of a carrier oil. While lying on your back, gently massage the mixture onto the abdomen. When rubbing, follow the natural flow of intestinal movement—move your hand up the right side of your stomach, across the middle and down the left side. This is the way food normally moves through the large intestine. For even greater relief, also drink one cup of ginger or peppermint tea after the massage.

ESSENTIAL OIL BASICS

Essential oils are available at most health-food stores and on-line.

Typical cost: $5 to $15 for a small bottle.*

High-quality oils can now be purchased from Aura Cacia, 800-437-3301, *www.auracacia.com*… The Essential Oil Company, 800-729-5912, *www.essentialoil.com*…or Oshadhi, 888-674-2344, *www.oshadhiusa.com*.

*Prices subject to change.

Eat Just One a Day... And Fight Colds, Flu and More

Carol Johnston, PhD, RD, professor and chair, department of nutrition, Arizona State University in Mesa, Arizona. She has published more than 75 research papers and book chapters on nutrition subjects and received the 2004 Grace A. Goldsmith Award from the American College of Nutrition in recognition of her research.

Wouldn't it be great if you could add one simple item to your diet each day to help your body fight colds, flu, fatigue and other ailments related to a weakened immune system?

You can, according to some recent research conducted at the University of California at Los Angeles. The six-year study of 17,688 men and women, published in the *Journal of the American Dietetic Association*, found that people who eat at least a one-cup portion of salad, including raw vegetables and salad dressing, every day have high blood levels of vitamins C and E as well as folic acid, all of which help promote a healthy immune system.

But some salads provide more disease-fighting nutrients than others. *Here's how to make sure your salad is as healthful as possible…*

• **Use salad dressing.** In an effort to reduce fat and calories, many people sprinkle greens with just a little lemon juice or vinegar. That's a mistake.

A small amount of fat actually helps promote the absorption of fat-soluble vitamins, such as vitamins A, E, D and K. In addition to the health benefits these vitamins themselves provide, they also aid in the absorption of certain other nutrients—for example, vitamin D helps facilitate the absorption of calcium. Aim to include about two tablespoons daily of olive oil or another healthy oil, such as canola, in your salad dressing.

Smart idea: To ensure that your salad dressing is healthful, make your own.

An easy recipe: Combine one-half cup of balsamic vinegar, one-quarter cup of olive oil, two tablespoons each of finely grated Parmesan cheese and sugar, one teaspoon of oregano and one-half teaspoon of garlic salt.

Breakdown: About 80 calories per two-tablespoon serving...60 milligrams (mg) of sodium...7.5 grams (g) of fat.

If you want the convenience of a bottled salad dressing, shop carefully. Many brands contain as much as 700 mg of sodium per serving (the recommended daily allowance is 1,500 mg for people age 50 and older) as well as partially hydrogenated or hydrogenated oils—code words for trans fat, which has been shown to increase risk of blood cholesterol and heart disease—and 100 calories per tablespoon. If your salad contains healthful fat from avocado or nuts, consider using a low-fat dressing.

(For recommendations on nutritious bottled salad dressing see page 69 in Chapter 4.)

• **Don't overdo the fatty ingredients.** Even though a certain amount of healthful fat is good for you, people who try to make a meal of their salad often end up adding too much fat by piling on processed meats, fried chicken, creamy salad mixtures, such as egg salad, tuna salad or macaroni salad, and high-fat cheeses.

Smart idea: Add in low- or nonfat cheeses, cubed tofu, poultry (except fried or breaded versions) or fish (salmon and tuna are good choices because of their omega-3 fats).

• **Choose lettuce that is dark green or reddish.** The majority of Americans make their salads with iceberg lettuce. However, this is the least nutritious type of lettuce because it contains mostly water.

Smart idea: Select romaine lettuce for your salad, then for variety, add any combination of dandelion greens, arugula, endive, chicory, butterhead lettuce or spinach, all of which are rich in folic acid, a vitamin that is important to cardiovascular health.

In general, the darker the color of the lettuce leaf, the more vitamins and minerals the lettuce contains.

• **Choose a variety of richly colored vegetables.** Americans tend to pile their salads with celery and cucumbers. Even though these vegetables make good snacks—they are very low in calories—they are also relatively low in nutrients, compared with some other vegetables.

Smart idea: Add tomatoes, broccoli, snow peas and bell peppers to your salad. They are all excellent sources of vitamin C and other key nutrients.

Rule of thumb: The brighter the vegetable's color is the more vitamins and minerals it will contain.

• **Get your phytochemicals.** These chemicals are antioxidants or enzyme inhibitors that protect us from disease-causing free radicals and help slow down the aging process.

Smart idea: Add white, yellow or red onions, garlic (crushed or chopped up) and mushrooms (such as shiitake and maitake)—all are loaded with healthful phytochemicals.

• **Add nuts.** Many people like to top their salads with croutons or bacon bits to add flavor, but croutons often are high in calories and most bacon-bit products contain nitrates—which have been linked to cancers of the digestive tract and the pancreas—as well as bad fats and sodium.

Smart idea: Add a tablespoon or two of unsalted nuts, such as almonds, pistachios, cashews, walnuts, hazelnuts or peanuts. All these nuts contain the healthful fats and are excellent sources of vitamin E. As an alternative, add unsalted sunflower seeds, which are high in fiber, potassium, phosphorus and other nutrients.

Cold Remedy Update— How Good Are Vitamin C, Echinacea and Zinc?

William Schaffner, MD, an infectious disease specialist and vice president of the National Foundation for Infectious Diseases, Bethesda, Maryland. He is chair of the department of preventive medicine at Vanderbilt University Medical Center, Nashville.

P harmacies provide hundreds of cold and cough remedies, including natural treatments and preventives, such as zinc and vitamin C. But which ones really work?

One proven way to prevent colds is to wash your hands frequently. You do not have to be around people who are coughing or sneezing to get sick—a person can be ill with a cold for 24 hours before symptoms start.

Best: Assume that you've been exposed—and wash your hands before viruses have a chance to enter the mucous membranes in your nose, eyes or mouth. If you are unable to wash your hands, use waterless hand sanitizers containing alcohol instead.

Unfortunately, not all the cold preventives and remedies are so effective. *Here is the real story about common cold remedies...*

ECHINACEA

A study published in the July 2007 issue of *The Lancet* analyzed the findings of 14 previous studies and reported that the herb echinacea reduced the risk of catching a cold by 58%, and it also shortened the duration of a cold. Yet previous research, including a large study published in *The New England Journal of Medicine*, found that echinacea doesn't make a significant difference in cold prevention.

A number of factors might explain the conflicting results. It is possible that some, but not all of these cold viruses are susceptible to echinacea. Also, because the US Food and Drug Administration does not regulate any herbal products, the doses and quality of echinacea—and even the species—could vary from study to study, affecting the results.

My conclusion: Echinacea might have a minor effect on cold treatment and prevention, but the evidence is too weak to recommend it. It is one of the safer herbs, though, so apart from the modest expense, there's no downside to trying it.

VITAMIN C

More than 35 years ago, Nobel prizewinner Linus Pauling suggested that large doses of vitamin C—1,000 milligrams (mg) or more daily—could prevent a cold. Research since then has been inconsistent. Some studies indicate that vitamin C can reduce the duration and severity of cold symptoms and possibly aid in prevention. Other studies find no benefits.

Latest finding: Researchers looked at 30 previous clinical studies, which included a total of 11,350 participants. They concluded that vitamin C does not prevent colds. However, they also noted that patients with colds who took at least 200 mg of vitamin C daily did experience a slight reduction in symptoms and duration of the cold.

My conclusion: Vitamin C appears to reduce cold symptoms, but the improvement is so modest that many people won't notice the difference. Higher doses do not appear to help...and taking more than 200 mg per day increases the risk of kidney stones and diarrhea.

Important: Drink two extra glasses of water daily when taking vitamin C. It helps to prevent kidney stones and moistens mucous membranes, which is helpful for reducing cold symptoms.

ZINC LOZENGES

Despite their unpleasant taste, zinc lozenges were popular during the 1990s. Early studies indicated that they could significantly shorten the duration of colds. The latest evidence, however, has shown that they probably are not effective. Other forms of zinc, including zinc-treated nasal swabs, are still being investigated.

My conclusion: Zinc lozenges are not effective for cold treatment or prevention.

DECONGESTANTS

Oral, long-lasting decongestants (which contain *pseudoephedrine*), such as Sudafed, and the short-acting nasal sprays (which contain *oxymetazoline*), such as Afrin, work in a similar fashion. By shrinking blood vessels in the nose and sinuses, they decrease congestion, but they can cause side effects, including insomnia and the "jitters," in some people. They also can occasionally cause an increase in blood pressure. Using them for more than a few days often results in rebound congestion—inflammation of the mucous membranes that increases stuffiness.

My conclusion: Decongestants don't shorten the duration of colds, but they are very effective at reducing stuffiness—the sprays work almost instantly. To limit side effects, use them for no more than 72 hours at a stretch.

COUGH SUPPRESSANTS

Most over-the-counter (OTC) cough suppressants contain *dextromethorphan*, a chemical that is supposed to suppress the cough reflex but it doesn't work all that well. The suppressants that contain codeine are far more effective, but they are available only with a prescription. Physicians prescribe cough suppressants for a dry, nagging cough, particularly if it's keeping you up at night. You do not want to suppress a productive cough, which can help remove mucus from the airways.

My conclusion: OTC cough suppressants give only modest relief. Stronger drugs, available by prescription, are a better choice for people with serious, persistent coughs.

ANTIHISTAMINES

They are a common ingredient in combination cough and cold remedies. Antihistamines dry mucous membranes and provide some relief from sneezing and/or a runny nose. However, their main effect is to block the effects of histamine, a chemical that's produced by allergies, not colds.

My conclusion: Don't take antihistamines for colds. They don't work. In fact, they can thicken cold secretions and make symptoms worse.

Surprising Causes Of Sinus Infections

Ralph B. Metson, MD, a clinical professor of otology (diseases of the ear) and laryngology (diseases of the nose and throat) at Harvard Medical School and director of the rhinology fellowship program at the Massachusetts Eye and Ear Infirmary, both in Boston. He is also author of *The Harvard Medical School Guide to Healing Your Sinuses* (McGraw-Hill).

It is bad enough when a cold or an allergic reaction to dust or pet dander leads to the pain and congestion of acute sinusitis (infection of the sinuses that lasts no more than four weeks). But for an estimated 35 million Americans, sinusitis is a chronic problem that takes a surprisingly serious toll on energy levels and quality of life.

The sad thing is that much of this suffering is not necessary. With a proper understanding of what causes sinusitis and appropriate preventive steps, you can get the upper hand against this all-too-common medical problem.

THE INSIDE STORY

The nasal cavity and sinuses are lined with membranes containing cells that produce mucus (up to eight ounces daily). Airborne irritants, such as dust, pollen and pet dander, are trapped by the mucus and moved out of the sinuses and into the nose through tiny openings called ostia,

so that the mucus (and irritants) can then be swallowed or expelled by blowing the nose.

Trouble starts when the area inside the nose where the ostia drain becomes blocked as a result of a cold, allergy or some other condition. Mucus then becomes trapped in the sinuses—creating a perfect environment for bacteria to flourish and infection to develop.

Pressure in the sinuses builds, making it hard to breathe, and infected mucus turns a thick, cloudy green or yellow. If a culture determines that the infection is bacterial, an antibiotic will probably be prescribed to quell the infection. Viral infections usually improve on their own. For people with chronic sinusitis, such episodes recur four or more times a year, often requiring prolonged, repeated antibiotic therapy—or even surgery to open the blocked sinus drainage passages.

OVERLOOKED TRIGGERS

Next to the common cold, allergies are the second most common cause of sinusitis, playing a role in about one-third of chronic sinusitis cases. With this type of sinusitis, the inflammatory response triggered by the allergen blocks the flow of mucus from the sinuses and sets the stage for infection. Skin testing by an allergist can often identify the allergens involved, and dust control, allergy shots and antihistamine drugs, such as *loratadine* (Claritin) and *fexofenadine* (Allegra), can help alleviate the sinus problem.

However, few doctors recognize that allergic-type reactions to foods also could be involved. Most often, this is triggered by certain alcoholic beverages, such as red wine, whiskey and some beers. The alcohol itself is not the problem, but rather the constituents of alcoholic drinks called congeners—these substances provide taste and aroma to alcohol, but they can inflame sensitive mucous membranes.

My advice: If your sinus symptoms worsen the day after consuming certain alcoholic beverages, such as merlot or pinot noir, try switching to white wine, clear spirits (vodka or gin, for example) or lighter beers.

For some sinusitis sufferers, symptoms are aggravated by foods containing milk. To find out if you are milk sensitive, eliminate all dairy products from your diet for three weeks. If milk and other dairy products are the trigger, your symptoms will noticeably improve.

KEEP YOUR NOSE CLEAN

Simply keeping the nose clear of mucus that contains bacteria and allergen particles is one of the most effective ways to prevent and relieve sinusitis. Nasal irrigation—a safe and simple practice you can do at home—is more efficient than nose blowing for clearing mucus.

Caution: Vigorous nose blowing can force bacteria-filled mucus back into the sinuses.

Nasal irrigation requires only a rubber bulb syringe (the kind used to clean an infant's nose and widely available at drugstores for about $5*).

What to do: Mix about a teaspoon of salt with eight ounces of warm water. Fill the syringe with the salt water, gently squeeze it into one nostril, and let it run out that nostril. Repeat the process, first in one nostril and then the other until all the water is gone, twice daily. If the mixture stings or burns, try more or less salt, to match the salinity of the mucus. Adding in one-half teaspoon of baking soda can make the solution more soothing—it helps adjust the irrigant to the pH (level of acidity and alkalinity) of mucus.

Other options: A plastic squeeze bottle specifically designed to fit in the nose (available at drugstores for about $5 to $10) or a neti pot (a cup-sized container with a spout at one end, a style that has been used in India for centuries to open up nasal passages). Squeeze bottles come prefilled with saline (a salt and water solution) or with premeasured packets that you mix with tap water. Neti pots are available at some drugstores and most health-food stores for about $15. The neti pot is gentler than the bulb syringe or squeeze bottle, but may not be forceful enough if mucus is thick.

Important: If you've never done nasal irrigation before, it may seem unsettling the first few times—it might remind you of getting water up your nose when swimming. But most people get used to it quickly and find it worth the brief initial discomfort.

My advice: Irrigate twice daily around the same time you brush your teeth. Be sure to rinse the irrigation tool between uses.

Some people find saline nasal sprays, such as Simply Saline or Xlear nasal wash (available at drugstores for about $4 to $13), to be easier to

*Prices subject to change.

use than nasal irrigation methods. Nasal sprays can relieve nasal dryness and may loosen mucus, but a recent study at the University of Michigan found them to be significantly less effective than irrigation in reducing sinusitis symptoms.

BREATHE EASIER

Some people with sinus problems also develop crusty deposits (composed of dried mucus) inside the nose, particularly in winter when nasal membranes are dried out by indoor heating. Crusts can further obstruct breathing already reduced by sinusitis congestion.

My advice: To fight multiplying bacteria that can develop on nasal crusts, apply an over-the-counter antibiotic ointment, such as Bacitracin or Neosporin, two times daily on the inside of the nose. Use of a humidifier, especially during the winter, also can help reduce indoor dryness.

For some sinusitis sufferers, an obstruction is worsened by a narrowing of the nasal valve—an area of soft tissue in the middle of the nose that tends to collapse when you inhale. Nasal tapes, such as Breathe Right nasal strips, which fit across the top of the nose and lift the sides, can keep the valve from closing, allowing you to breathe more freely. These products are available at most drugstores for about $13.

IMPROVED TREATMENTS

Sinus surgery becomes an option when infections are frequent despite medical treatment, including antibiotics and the allergy medications. Surgery aims to correct anatomical obstructions in the nose and sinuses. For example, a narrow sinus opening may be enlarged or an obstruction, such as a polyp (a usually benign growth), may be removed.

Endoscopic surgery, using a thin tube to insert miniaturized instruments into the sinus passages via the nostrils, has improved the outcome of sinus operations.

The latest innovation, image-guided surgery, adds to the precision—it is similar to global positioning technology (the guidance systems drivers use) and helps locate the exact site that needs repair. This technology enables the surgeon to monitor the location of instruments during the procedure—and is helpful in difficult cases, such as those involving patients who have extensive disease or who have undergone previous sinus surgery.

Are Saunas Good for Your Health?

Saunas promote relaxation and alleviate nasal congestion. They also may ease soreness and fatigue after exertion by increasing blood flow to muscles...and help the body sweat out toxins, such as mercury and *polychlorinated biphenyls* (PCBs).

Caution: Saunas dilate blood vessels, affecting blood flow—so if you have high blood pressure or take drugs that affect the heart (such as beta-blockers), use a sauna only under a doctor's guidance.

Leo Galland, MD, director of the Foundation for Integrated Medicine in New York City, and author of *Power Healing* (Random House). His Web site is *www.mdheal. org.*

Hot Help for Allergies

Washing clothes in 140°F water kills all dust mites versus just 6.5% of those in clothes washed at 104°F. Hot water is also more effective at removing pet dander and pollen.

American Thoracic Society, New York City, on the Web at *www.thoracic.org.*

Faster Allergy Relief

A burst of carbon dioxide into the nose relieves congestion and other nasal symptoms within 10 minutes, and keeps working for 24 hours. The treatment—not yet FDA-approved—may be an effective alternative to steroid sprays.

Creighton University, Omaha, Nebraska, on the Web at *www.creighton.org.*

OTC vs. Prescription For Allergies

Over-the-counter (OTC) allergy therapy beats prescription drugs for some allergies.

Recent study: Of 58 people with ragweed allergies, 30 took 10 milligrams (mg) daily of the prescription drug *montelukast* (Singulair), and 28 took 240 mg daily of OTC *pseudoephedrine* (Sudafed) for two weeks.

Result: Both the drugs were equally effective at easing runny nose, sneezing and itchy eyes, while pseudoephedrine was slightly more effective at clearing nasal congestion.

If you suffer from seasonal allergies: Ask your doctor if OTC pseudoephedrine is appropriate for you.

Caution: Don't use pseudoephedrine if you have high blood pressure, a history of stroke or diabetes.

Fuad Baroody, MD, associate professor of otolaryngology, University of Chicago.

Skip the Salt If You Have Asthma

Improve asthma symptoms by decreasing your salt intake.

Recent finding: A review of 26 published studies found that lowering salt intake to 1,500 milligrams (mg) of sodium per day can reduce asthma severity and improve breathing in two to five weeks.

Theory: High-sodium foods may play a role in bronchial inflammation, which can worsen asthma.

If you have asthma: Limit sodium intake to 1,500 mg daily and eat a diet rich in fresh foods.

T. D. Mickleborough, PhD, associate professor, department of kinesiology, Indiana University, Bloomington.

Antibiotics Help Treat Difficult Asthma Cases

In a recent study, patients whose asthma was poorly controlled through traditional medications, such as inhaled steroids, were given the antibiotic *clarithromycin* twice daily for eight weeks.

Result: Airway inflammation was significantly reduced. One marker of inflammation—the *sputum IL-8* (or interleukin-8) concentration—dropped by 48%.

Patients whose asthma is not under control should consult their physicians.

Peter Gibson, MBBS, a professor of respiratory medicine, Hunter Medical Research Institute, Newcastle, New South Wales, Australia, and senior author of a study published in American Journal of Respiratory and Critical Care Medicine.

Asthma Linked to Spray Cleaners

In a nine-year study of 3,500 adults, researchers found that the study subjects who used cleaning sprays (such as the glass and furniture cleaners) at least once weekly had a 30% to 50% higher risk, on average, for asthma than people who used such sprays less often.

Theory: The chemicals in these products irritate the airways.

Self-defense: Try to use nonspray cleaning products.

Jan-Paul Zock, PhD, senior research fellow, Municipal Institute of Medical Research, Barcelona, Spain.

A Breathing Technique That Eases Asthma

The Papworth method, created in the 1960s at Papworth Hospital in Cambridgeshire, England, can help individuals who start breathing rapidly and shallowly because of anxiety. It had not been studied in asthma sufferers until just recently. It has now been shown to cut asthma symptoms by one-third, but it does not improve lung function or replace medications.

This type of physical therapy integrates both breathing and relaxation exercises to discourage shallow breaths while focusing on slow nasal expiration using the abdomen and diaphragm. It teaches patients to recognize stress and use breathing to physically manage that stress. Ask your doctor for a referral to a respiratory therapist who teaches the technique.

Martha V. White, MD, director of research, Institute for Asthma and Allergy, Wheaton, Maryland.

Which Painkiller Works Best for a Tension Headache?

Tension-type headaches most often respond to anti-inflammatory drugs, such as aspirin or *ibuprofen* (Motrin). If you have high blood pressure or a digestive disorder, it's safer to use *acetaminophen*, either alone (Tylenol)…or combined with caffeine (Excedrin Tension). Some people get longer-lasting relief from *naproxen* (Aleve).

Caution: To avoid rebound headaches and other side effects, restrict painkiller use to two days per week.

Alan M. Rapoport, MD, clinical professor of neurology at the David Geffen School of Medicine, University of California, Los Angeles. He is also founder of the New England Center for Headache, Stamford, Connecticut.

More from Dr. Alan Rapoport…

New Treatment for Cluster Headaches

In one recent finding, 63% of cluster headache episodes in patients who were given 10 milligrams (mg) of the migraine nasal spray *zolmitriptan* (Zomig) were significantly relieved in as little as 30 minutes. Some patients had relief within 10 minutes. Just 5 mg eased pain in half of participants. Cluster headaches are among the most painful form of headaches, and there are few FDA-approved treatments available. Zolmitriptan's side effects include drowsiness, tingling and chest discomfort. Zolmitriptan is a triptan, a type of drug that should not be given to patients who have heart disease, high blood pressure or blood vessel problems.

Also from Dr. Alan Rapoport...

Botox for Migraine

When other treatments fail, some doctors offer injections of prescription *botulinum toxin* (Botox). This use of Botox is "off label"— meaning it is legal but the drug has not been FDA-approved for this purpose. Since the therapy is considered experimental, insurance generally does not cover it. If a clinical trial, now in its final stage, shows Botox to be effective against migraine, it may receive FDA approval within a few years.

Some evidence suggests that multiple Botox injections in the head and/or neck can reduce the severity and frequency of migraine attacks for three to four months by decreasing the release of certain chemicals from nerve endings. Cost varies widely, from $700 to $2,000 or more.*

*Prices subject to change.

New Migraine Treatment

Injections of local anesthetic can reduce both the number and severity of migraine attacks. Many migraine sufferers have trigger points in the neck that, when stimulated, elicit the same pain as their migraine attacks. In a recent study, anesthetic was injected into participants' trigger points four times over a two-month period.

Result: The number of attacks decreased by 46%, and the intensity decreased by 17%.

Maria Adele Giamberardino, MD, an associate professor of internal medicine and director of the centers for headache and fibromyalgia, "G. d'Annunzio" University of Chieti, Chieti, Italy.

A Lightbulb Warning

Energy-saving lightbulbs might bring on migraines or epileptic seizures. The fluorescent low-energy lightbulbs have a high rate of "flicker" that normally isn't noticeable. But the British Migraine Action Association says that the flicker may trigger migraine headaches, and the organization Epilepsy Action indicates that the bulbs apparently have caused seizures in a small number of epilepsy sufferers.

If you or a family member suffers from either of these conditions, consult your doctor before installing such bulbs.

Karen Manning, spokesperson, Migraine Action Association, Great Oakley, Northamptonshire, England, *www.migraine.org.uk.*

Better Low Back Treatment

Researchers analyzed 22 studies that involved more than 1,700 adults who had chronic low back pain.

Result: Psychological treatments, such as behavioral techniques, hypnosis, biofeedback and counseling, were more effective than standard treatments, such as surgery, narcotic drugs and implantable drug delivery systems.

Theory: Psychological treatments reduce patients' experience of pain.

If you suffer from chronic lower back pain: Ask your doctor whether psychological treatments are an alternative for you. To locate a psychologist near you, call 202-783-7663 or go to *www.findapsychologist.org.*

Robert D. Kerns, PhD, professor of psychiatry, neurology and psychology at Yale University in New Haven, Connecticut.

Why Sitting Up Straight Is Bad for Your Back

Despite the age-old advice that "sitting up straight" is good for your back, research indicates that in reality it increases pressure on the disks in your back. Hunching forward is bad for your back, too.

Recent study: The best sitting position for one's back is a 135-degree thigh-to-trunk angle with feet planted on the floor. This minimizes the strain on disks.

The best way to achieve the 135-degree angle is by sitting on a wedge-shaped cushion with the thicker end under your tailbone to raise it slightly. But any position in which you open up the angle between thighs and back to reduce back strain and prevent back pain—such as by leaning backward—is better for you than sitting with your legs and back at right angles.

Waseem Amir Bashir, MBCbB, MRCP, radiologist, University of Alberta Hospital, Edmonton, Canada.

Plantar Fasciitis Relief

Plantar fasciitis is an inflammation of the ligament along the bottom of the foot that connects the heel bone and the toes. It can cause stabbing or burning pain, especially after periods of inactivity.

To relieve pain, hold an ice pack on the area for 15 to 20 minutes several times a day or after exercise and/or take ibuprofen or another anti-inflammatory as directed by your doctor. To treat the condition and lessen the chance of recurrence, stretch the Achilles tendon—stand on the edge of a step and lower heels together or one at a time…hold the stretch for one minute…repeat as many times as it feels comfortable to you.

Insoles also might be prescribed if the pain continues…or the doctor may inject the area with corticosteroids. If symptoms persist, surgery may release the ligament.

Neil Campbell, DPM, spokesperson for the American College of Foot and Ankle Surgeons, Chicago, and a podiatrist in Yoakum, Texas.

Help for Ropy Veins On Hands

Hands have thin, delicate skin and little subcutaneous fat. That's why cosmetic procedures, such as chemical peels and injections that minimize the appearance of veins elsewhere on the body, don't work for hands.

Better: A prescription *tretinoin* cream, such as Renova, that stimulates collagen production, making the skin plumper and smoother…or try nonprescription Olay Regenerist Targeted Tone Enhancer.

Marianne O'Donoghue, MD, an associate professor of dermatology at Rush University Medical Center in Chicago and a past president of the Women's Dermatologic Society.

 # Licorice Licks Canker Pain

A dissolving oral patch shrinks painful canker sores by 90%, while untreated sores often get bigger. The patch, CankerMelts, releases licorice root extract for two to six hours—and eases pain in about 10 minutes.

Ivanhoe Newswire, *www.ivanhoe.com.*

Hydration Help

What is a good rule of thumb for figuring out how much water to drink each day? Drink at least one-half ounce of fluid per pound of body weight.

Example: If you weigh 130 pounds, drink 65 ounces of fluids daily—at least five to six cups of which should be water.

When you exercise, add another two cups. And then add another two cups per day if you are traveling, pregnant, nursing, dieting or ill. Finally add two cups more (for a total of up to six additional cups) when you are at a high altitude or in a warm climate.

Helpful: Check your urine. It should be relatively odorless and have a color no darker than straw. Odor and/or a dark yellow color suggest dehydration.

Exception: Urine sometimes looks darker after taking a vitamin supplement, but it should lighten after you've urinated once or twice.

Susan M. Kleiner, PhD, RD, owner and president of nutritional sciences, High Performance Nutrition, a consulting firm in Mercer Island, Washington, and author of *The Good Mood Diet: Feel Great While You Lose Weight* (Little, Brown).

Beautiful Skin the Natural Way

Jamison Starbuck, ND, a naturopathic physician in family practice and lecturer at the University of Montana, both in Missoula. She is past president of the American Association of Naturopathic Physicians and a contributing editor to *The Alternative Advisor: The Complete Guide to Natural Therapies and Alternative Treatments* (Time Life).

Americans spend up to $5 billion a year on skin-care products, but, in my opinion, many of these lotions, balms and gels are not necessary. *Here's my natural approach that not only helps keep your skin supple and vibrant, but also improves your overall health…*

•**Hydrate.** For skin to function properly as a protective layer and a vehicle for eliminating toxins, the body needs to be hydrated. With dehydration, the skin loses all its "turgor," or fullness, and it begins to sag. For good skin health, consume one-half ounce of water for each pound of body weight daily. (Some of this can come from herbal tea.) You will need more water if the temperature is above 90°F or if you are perspiring a lot.

•**Use a dry brush.** Using a natural bristle brush or loofah (the dried interior of fruit from the loofah plant)—both are available at most drugstores—brush your skin with small, circular motions for two minutes before getting into the shower or bath several times a week. Dry brushing improves circulation to your skin and removes old, dead skin cells.

•**Take cod-liver oil.** My favorite omega-3 fish oil choice for people who have skin conditions is cod-liver oil. It not only contains essential fatty acids necessary for healthy skin, but also vitamins A and D, which are both fundamental to good health.

Daily dose: 1,500 milligrams (mg) in capsule or liquid form, taken with a meal. Make sure the label says the oil has been purified—and consult your doctor before exceeding 10,000 international units (IU) of vitamin A daily from all supplement sources.* If you have skin problems and already take fish oil, check the label to determine the fish source. If it's not cod, consider switching.

•**Reduce your toxic load.** The skin is an organ that, like the liver, kidneys and lungs, helps excrete toxins. The health of your skin declines in proportion to the amount of toxic substances you ingest through medication and food and/or are exposed to via pollution, herbicides and household chemicals. Do not smoke, and don't allow others to smoke in your home. Use naturally based cleaning products, including baking soda and vinegar. Consider obtaining a high efficiency particulate air (HEPA) filter, available at most of the big home stores, for your home and/or office.

•**Eat turmeric.** Curry, the traditional Indian dish, is often made using turmeric, which contains curcumin, a substance that has antioxidant, anti-inflammatory and anticancer properties. Curcumin may help prevent acne and damage from the sun.

Caution: If you have a stomach ulcer, avoid curry.

•**Choose the right sunscreen.** Use a sunscreen that contains zinc oxide as its main sun-blocking agent, as well as vitamins E and C and the mineral selenium, and has a sun protection factor (SPF) of 15 or higher. Researchers have found that sunscreens containing these antioxidants are more likely to prevent skin damage than sunscreens that don't have these protective compounds.

*Pregnant or lactating women should check with their doctors before using cod-liver oil.

Natural Cures for Constipation

Mark Stengler, ND, a naturopathic physician, director of the La Jolla Whole Health Clinic in La Jolla, California, and adjunct associate clinical professor, National College of Natural Medicine, Portland, Oregon. He is also author of the newsletter *Bottom Line Natural Healing*, available at *www.DrStengler.com*.

Twice as many women as men suffer from constipation and all of its side effects—abdominal pain, bloating, hard stool and hemorrhoids. Long-term laxative use only worsens the problem by stopping digestive contractions. *Prevention...*

• **First thing every morning, drink eight ounces of warm water** with two teaspoons of lemon juice to improve flow of bile, a laxative digestive fluid.

• **Sit on the toilet for two minutes at the same time each morning,** even if you can't move your bowels, to help train your nervous system to go on schedule.

• **Avoid cow's milk, bananas and fried foods...** eat high-fiber whole grains, fruits and vegetables.

• **Ask your doctor about nonconstipating alternatives** if you use an antacid, iron supplement, antidepressant or blood pressure drug.

• **When you are constipated, try the remedies below,** one at a time, in the order listed. If one does not help within a week, switch to the next. All are sold in health-food stores (see labels for dosages).

• Flaxseed oil, which lubricates stool.

• Triphala tablets, an herbal formula that helps stimulate digestive contractions.

• Dandelion root capsules to promote the flow of bile.

• Probiotics (beneficial bacteria)—supplements that restore the digestive tract's normal balance of flora.

Constipation can signal an underlying medical problem, such as a thyroid disorder, uterine prolapse (uterus drops down into the vagina) or colon cancer. If natural remedies don't help, see your doctor.

Botox for Constipation

Botox shots may relieve constipation if your condition is caused by inappropriate contraction or inability to relax pelvic-floor muscles. Ask your doctor about local injections of Botox if traditional approaches, such as eating a lot of fiber and taking laxatives, are not effective.

Guiseppe Brisinda, MD, senior investigator, University Hospital Agostino Gemelli, Rome, Italy, and leader of a study of Botox use in people with constipation, published in *The American Journal of Gastroenterology*.

Sleep Better— Without Drugs

Ara DerMarderosian, PhD, professor of pharmacognosy (the study of natural products used in medicine) and Roth chair of natural products at the University of the Sciences in Philadelphia.

It's no secret that prescription sleeping pills are hugely popular in the US. But it is less well-known that these drugs are not always effective, and that side effects, like headache and dizziness, can be troublesome for many.

Some people are now turning to *melatonin,* a "sleep hormone" already made by our bodies, which can be boosted by taking it as a dietary supplement. Melatonin (0.3 milligrams [mg] to 5 mg) is typically taken 30 minutes to four hours before bedtime. It is generally safe but may increase blood pressure and should not be taken by pregnant or lactating women. Melatonin does not work for everyone, though.

Another option is the herb *valerian.** In one double-blind study, valerian extract was as effective as the prescription tranquilizer *oxazepam* (Serax). Valerian can cause mild side effects, including stomach upset and morning sleepiness, but these are rare. Valerian should not be used by anyone taking a *benzodiazepine* tranquilizer, such as *diazepam* (Valium).

If you would like to try valerian, take the capsule form 30 minutes before bedtime. (Choose a product standardized to 0.5% to 1.0% valerenic

*Pregnant or lactating women should consult a doctor before taking herbs.

acids and follow label instructions.) Tea drinkers can try steeping 2 grams (g) to 3 g of the dried root (or the equivalent in a standardized extract) or adding one tea bag to six ounces of boiling water. Drink 30 minutes before bedtime. If you're like most people, you should start sleeping better the same night you try this remedy.

When It's Good To Eat Carbs

Eating starchy carbohydrates before bed may help you fall asleep faster.

Possible reason: Carbohydrates loaded with simple sugar and little fiber, such as the jasmine rice used in this study, increase levels of *tryptophan* and *serotonin*, brain chemicals involved in sleep.

Chin Moi Chow, PhD, University of Sydney, Australia, and lead author of a study published in *The American Journal of Clinical Nutrition*.

The Best Position for Sleeping

When sleeping, avoid lying on your stomach, which arches and strains the lower back and stretches the neck asymmetrically.

Better: Sleep on your side or back, using a contoured pillow (sold at bedding stores) that is thicker along one or two edges than in the center—it supports your neck while keeping the head and spine aligned.

Side sleepers: Place a pillow between your knees so your pelvis doesn't twist.

Back sleepers: Place a bolster under your knees to relax leg and hip muscles.

Karen Erickson, DC, chiropractor in private practice in New York City, and spokesperson for the American Chiropractic Association.

The Right Pillow For You

Your pillow should support your head in a way that lets your neck muscles relax. *Consider your primary sleeping position...*

•**Back sleepers usually prefer medium- to low-density pillows** (typically labeled as "medium" and "soft") because they provide the appropriate level of neck support.

•**Belly sleepers are usually more comfortable with low-density pillows**—they allow you to easily turn your head to one side to breathe.

•**Side sleepers often prefer a medium- to full-density ("firm") pillow,** depending on the distance from the head to the mattress (a person with broader shoulders, for example, would require a more supportive or a thicker pillow). A contour pillow (with a recess for the head and support for the neck) may be a good choice if you sleep on your back and/or side.

Roger Herr, PT, a Seattle-based physical therapist, past president of the American Physical Therapy Association's Home Health section and member of the Physical Therapy Association of Washington.

Sing a Song

Group singing—in a community chorus or another group—lowers stress and boosts mood and the immune system. Because singing requires deep, controlled breathing and focuses the singer's attention on the lungs, diaphragm and abdominal muscles, it offers the same stress-relieving benefits as deep breathing exercises. Also, studies indicate that people with speech problems, particularly if caused by damage to the left sides of their brains, can sometimes sing words they have trouble speaking.

Harvard Health Letter, 10 Shattuck St., Boston 02115, *www.health.harvard.edu/newsletters*.

4

Bodyworks

The Diet That Really Works and Why Most Others Don't

ant to lose pounds? Most nutritionists suggest eating less while exercising a lot more. But, award-winning science journalist Gary Taubes disagrees with this conventional wisdom. After more than five years of poring over medical and dietary research, he has come to the conclusion that what most of us believe about weight loss is wrong. *Here, he answers questions about his controversial findings and shares with readers what he really believes does work well…*

•It seems like common sense that eating less leads to weight loss. Why doesn't this work? Yes, if we eat less, fewer calories will enter our bodies, which sounds as if it should equal weight loss. But the actual evidence indicates this doesn't work.

When people force themselves to eat less, they not only get hungry—they also expend less energy. This is the way our bodies work—they try to match intake to expenditure. So even with willpower, calorie-restricted diets eventually will fail.

An eight-year study conducted by the Women's Health Initiative in the 1990s reported that women on diets that cut daily consumption by 360 calories lost an average of only two pounds during those eight years and saw their waist size expand. In 2001, the US Department of Agriculture examined the results of 28 diet studies and discovered no evidence that significant weight loss could be achieved through low-fat or low-calorie diets.

•Why doesn't exercise work? If we exercise more, we'll burn more calories, which also

---

Gary Taubes, New York City–based correspondent for *Science* magazine. He is the only print journalist to have won three Science-in-Society Journalism awards from the National Association of Science Writers. Taubes is the author of *Good Calories, Bad Calories: Challenging the Conventional Wisdom on Diet, Weight Control, and Disease* (Knopf).

seems like it should lead to weight loss. But this ignores the fact that exercise makes us hungry and so we eat more afterward. Think of it this way—we perspire when we exercise, but that does not mean we can survive on less water. It just means that we drink more to replace the water we have sweat out. Our bodies seek to replace the calories we burn off during exercise the same way.

Lab rats do not weigh significantly less if you force them to exercise, unless you force them to exercise for so many hours each day that they lack the energy to eat when they are done. The most comprehensive analysis of the scientific evidence—a 2000 study by Finnish scientists—concluded that the link between physical activity and weight loss was at best unproven and might not exist at all.

• **If trying to eat less and exercise more does not work, how can we lose weight?** We need to consider what regulates fat accumulation in our bodies. The science here has never been controversial. It's just been considered irrelevant to the question of why we gain weight. Our fat tissue is regulated by our hormones, the hormone insulin in particular. The higher your insulin level, the more calories your body will store as fat…and the more difficult it will become for your body to rid itself of this fat.

• **What causes high insulin levels?** Carbohydrates. The more carbohydrates in your diet, the more insulin your body will secrete. Genetics is a factor as well. Some people seem to be able to consume all the carbohydrates they want without significantly increased insulin production, while others will experience dramatic insulin level variations depending on their carbohydrate consumption.

So the big secret to weight loss is not simply to eat less or to exercise more—it is to consume fewer carbohydrates.

• **The low-carb Atkins program has been around now for more than 35 years. If this works, why does it remain so controversial?** The idea that carbohydrates are responsible for obesity was not at all controversial prior to the 1960s. Few questioned that pasta, bread, beer, pastries, sweets and bagels were the sorts of foods that made people fat.

Best-selling diet books, such as Dr. Herman Taller's 1961 *Calories Don't Count* and Dr. Robert Atkins' top seller *Dr. Atkins' Diet Revolution,* picked up on the idea and began popularizing low-carb diets. But low-carb diets are by definition high-fat diets. The medical establishment—including the American Medical Association and the American Heart Association—believed that high-fat, high-cholesterol diets were responsible for heart disease and obesity, so they branded these authors quacks, despite evidence that low-carb diets work.

At the time, a half-dozen university professors took almost total control over America's obesity research. These men wrote all the textbooks, hosted the conferences and decided which studies received funding. The beliefs propagated by these men and, later, their students, continue to be defended with near-religious fervor—specifically, the position that fat and calories, not carbohydrates, are to blame for obesity and heart disease—even though there is no compelling evidence to defend this.

America's obesity epidemic began by the early 1980s, exactly when Americans increasingly were following these men's advice to eat low-fat, high-carb diets. Government surveys conducted in the 1960s and 1970s found that between 12% and 14% of Americans were obese. That figure topped 20% by the end of the 1980s and approached 30% by the end of the 1990s.

• **Your position is that high-fat diets are not to blame for heart disease either?** Despite all we're told, there is little evidence that high-fat diets cause heart disease. The evidence is far more compelling that high-carb diets are to blame. In fact, when you actually look at the studies evoked to support the benefits of low-fat or low-saturated-fat diets, which no one bothers to do anymore, you find just as much evidence that these diets cause heart disease as that they prevent it.

• **Do we have to eliminate carbs entirely to lose weight?** Most people can lose excess pounds simply by cutting back on carbs, but some will have to remove all carbs from their diets. It depends on how your body tolerates carbohydrates.

People who are significantly overweight might want to do something that Dr. Atkins originally suggested—eliminate all carbohydrates from their diets until they get down to their target weight. Once they reach their target weight, they might try adding small amounts of one or two carbohydrate-containing foods back into their diets. For example, they might allow themselves a morning glass of fresh orange juice. If they remain close to their target weight, fine. If they start to pack the pounds back on, they might need to avoid carbs completely to keep the weight down. The good news is that once the carbs are removed, these people will be able to eat as much meat, cheese, eggs and other carb-free food as they like.

•**What are the worst of high-carb foods?** The worst are probably all sugars, including refined sugar and high-fructose corn syrup. There is reason to believe that most people could shed their excess weight simply by eliminating sugary foods and beverages from their diet.

It also is good to avoid anything containing white flour, white potatoes and white rice. Fruits, beans and vegetables also contain carbohydrates to varying degrees. Leafy green vegetables, such as broccoli, kale and spinach, are the vegetables with the least carbs.

•**Which of the low-carb diets do you recommend in particular?** The diet that will best help you lose the weight is the diet that does the best job of eliminating carbohydrates. When my friends ask me to recommend a particular diet book, I tell them to try the original 1972 edition of *Dr. Atkins' Diet Revolution*. Atkins made adjustments to the diet in later editions that made it slightly less helpful in avoiding carbohydrates. Used copies of the original book often are available on Amazon.com, and sometimes for less than $1.*

*Price subject to change.

What's Really Making So Many of Us Fat?

JoAnn E. Manson, MD, DrPH, a professor of medicine and women's health at Harvard Medical School and chief of the division of preventive medicine at Brigham and Women's Hospital, both in Boston. She is also one of the lead investigators for two highly influential studies on women's health—the Harvard Nurses' Health Study and the Women's Health Initiative. Dr. Manson is the author, with Shari Bassuk, ScD, of *Hot Flashes, Hormones & Your Health* (McGraw-Hill).

The statistics are scary—62% of American women are overweight today, and more than half of these women are obese. Everyone knows that too much food and too little exercise lead to weight gain. *But to reach and maintain a healthy weight, it's important to recognize lesser-known culprits...*

•**Stress.** Whenever we're stressed, our adrenal glands release the hormone *cortisol,* which boosts activity of the enzyme *lipoprotein lipase,* causing the body to store extra fat.

Smart: Make exercising a priority—it triggers the release of soothing brain chemicals called *endorphins.* Speak to your doctor if you suffer from depression or an anxiety disorder, as these also are linked to elevated levels of cortisol.

•**Sleep deprivation.** The average American sleeps fewer than seven hours per weeknight—and many of us log six hours or less. In surveys, overweight people generally report sleeping less than slim people do.

Theories: Sleep deprivation may slow carbohydrate metabolism...increase levels of cortisol ...lower the hunger-suppressing hormone *leptin* ...and increase the appetite-stimulating hormone *ghrelin.*

Solutions: Avoid late-evening meals and caffeine...turn off all phones (including cell phones) at night...take the computer and TV out of the bedroom...and keep to a consistent bedtime that allows for eight hours of rest.

•**Stillness.** Obese people tend to sit still (literally), spending, on average, 2.5 fewer hours per day pacing and fidgeting than lean people do.

Surprising: All these seemingly insignificant movements burn about 350 calories per day—preventing a gain of about 36 pounds per year.

A tendency toward stillness may be genetically determined, but long hours at a desk or in a car exacerbate the situation.

Good habit: Don't sit when you can stand or ride when you can walk.

• **Fat friends and family.** Our chances of becoming obese may rise by 57% if a close friend becomes obese…40% if a sibling becomes obese …and 37% if a spouse becomes obese.

One reason: When judgments are based on comparison with others, a loved one's obesity may shift our perception of an acceptable weight.

Best: Ask loved ones to begin a weight-loss program with you, and avoid picking up their bad habits.

• **Diet composition.** The high-glycemic foods rapidly increase blood sugar levels, triggering a surge of the hormone *insulin*. These foods may be more likely to cause weight gain, independent of their calorie content, because insulin increases fat storage and prevents fat breakdown in the body.

Slenderizing: Limit the high-glycemic foods, such as white bread, pasta, sugary cereals, baked goods and soda. Eat more low-glycemic foods —fruits, vegetables, legumes and whole grains— which stabilize blood sugar.

The New Rules for Body Weight

Barbara Rolls, PhD, the endowed Guthrie Chair in Nutritional Sciences at Pennsylvania State University in University Park. She is the author of more than 200 studies on weight management and related topics and four books, including *The Volumetrics Eating Plan* (HarperCollins), which *Consumer Reports* has named a top diet plan.

Until recently, being overweight was regarded primarily as a matter of physical appearance—and as a stepping-stone toward developing diabetes and heart disease.

Now: Extensive research shows that excess pounds are associated with a variety of serious health problems, including asthma, high blood pressure, stroke, dementia, sleep apnea (a sleep disorder that interrupts breathing during sleep) and certain types of cancer.

But the bathroom scale might not give you all the information you need about your body weight. For decades, physicians have used the body mass index (BMI), a measure of weight relative to height.*

However, the BMI has limitations. For example, someone who is very muscular may end up with a high weight-to-height ratio even though he/she is extremely fit. Older and/or frail adults may have a normal BMI when their nutritional intake is insufficient for good health.

It's also possible to have a normal BMI with a level of body fat that increases health risks. People who diet but do not exercise regularly, for example, may keep their weight under control, but they may have dangerous fat deposits around the abdomen, heart and other internal organs.

Recent studies confirm that weighing yourself on a scale or measuring your BMI may not be enough to determine whether you're at risk for health problems.

Other options to consider…

BEYOND THE SCALE AND THE BMI

There are a variety of ways to tell whether you may need to slim down. *Best methods…*

• **Waist circumference.** Visceral fat, which is located primarily in the abdomen and around the organs, is especially harmful because of its tendency to promote fatty buildup (plaque) in the arteries as well as dangerous increases in cholesterol and triglycerides (blood fats). A computed tomography (CT) or magnetic resonance imaging (MRI) scan is required to identify visceral fat, but waist measurement is a reasonable substitute.

Recent research: Waist measurement may be more reliable than body weight in identifying increased risk for certain health problems, such as heart disease, diabetes and cancer. Risk for heart disease and diabetes has been shown to increase if waist circumference exceeds 35 inches for women and 40 inches for men. For cancer, women with the most fat in the abdominal area (more than a 36-inch waistline) have a 34% greater risk of developing breast cancer, for

*To determine your BMI, log on to the National Heart, Lung and Blood Institute at *www.nhlbisupport.com/bmi*. A BMI of 19 to 24 is normal…25 to 29 is overweight… and 30 and above is obese.

example, than women with the least abdominal fat (less than a 28-inch waistline).

What to watch out for: It is easy to make a mistake if you're measuring your own waist. To get the most accurate measurement, stand up and place a tape measure around your bare waist at or just below your navel…make sure that the tape measure is straight and parallel to the floor…exhale and measure.

• **Body fat.** Body weight is the total of lean weight (muscles, bones, tendons, ligaments and water) and fat weight (fat stored in cells and organs of the body). The normal range for body fat percentages in men is 10% to 20%…in women, it's 15% to 25%.

Measuring body fat is useful because it gives you a better idea of your body composition and whether any fat needs to be lost.

A dual-energy X-ray absorptiometry (DEXA) scan, which is widely utilized to measure bone density, can determine body fat percentages because it measures muscle and fat composition. Weighing a person underwater also measures body fat. However, both approaches are expensive and not readily available.

A more convenient way to determine body fat is to use a pincerlike device (calipers) to externally measure skinfolds at specific parts of the body, such as the waist. This type of body fat measurement is available at most health clubs.

One other option is bioelectrical impedance analysis, a method that is used in a body fat monitor. This device looks like a bathroom scale and delivers a painless and harmless low-level electrical signal throughout the body to calculate the percentage of body fat. Monitors are available at many drugstores and on-line.

Typical cost: $50 to $100.*

What to watch out for: Skinfold measurements are often not accurate unless the person administering the test is well trained. Body fat monitors are not always accurate, particularly for people who are extremely obese or who are in the process of losing weight.

IF YOU NEED TO LOSE WEIGHT

There are dozens of fad diets that promise new, more effective ways to lose weight. The truth is, however, that most people can lose one

*Prices subject to change.

pound per week by simply taking in 500 fewer calories each day while increasing their physical activity. As a first step, aim to reduce your body weight by 5% to 10%. Depending on the individual, additional weight loss may be necessary after that initial goal is met.

No diets or pills will target visceral fat alone. Sit-ups and crunches strengthen the abdominal muscles, but they do not reduce belly fat more than other fat deposits. Building muscle is critical, however, because muscle burns more calories than fat—even when you are resting—which revs up your metabolism to help you maintain a healthy weight.

In general, a good exercise regimen consists of at least 30 minutes of moderate-intensity exercise, such as brisk walking, daily.

This diet-and-exercise approach typically ensures a steady weight loss of one to two pounds a week—a rate that is considered healthful and sustainable.

Caution: If you've been sedentary, start out slowly—maybe by walking 10 minutes daily.

Helpful: Keep a daily food-and-exercise log. Write down what you eat, how much and when, as well as the type and amount of exercise that you do. Then, at the close of each day, use the diary to calculate calories consumed and calories burned. For information on the calories in foods, log on to the US Department of Agriculture Web site at *www.nal.usda.gov/fnic/foodcomp/search*. To determine the number of calories burned by various activities, go to the Shape Up America! Web site (*www.shapeup.org/fitness/assess/level1. php*).

"Diet" Mixer Warning

Alcoholic beverages that are made with artificial sweeteners enter the bloodstream more quickly than a regular, sugar-sweetened drink. Just one "diet" mixed drink can put you over the legal blood alcohol limit.

American Journal of Preventive Medicine, La Jolla, California, *www.ajpm-online.net*.

Are You Drinking Too Many Calories?

Barry Popkin, PhD, a researcher specializing in obesity. He is also the Carla Smith Chamblee Distinguished Professor of Global Nutrition at the University of North Carolina and director of the university's Interdisciplinary Center for Obesity, both in Chapel Hill. He led a panel of scholars that developed a Beverage Guidance System for American consumers.

Most Americans obtain more than 20% of their total daily calories from beverages —twice as many as they did 30 years ago. In fact, the alarming increase in obesity rates in the US—two-thirds of Americans are considered overweight or obese—seems to be directly related to our consumption of caloric beverages.

The dramatic increase in the typical beverage serving size is part of the problem. Bottle sizes for soda are up 65% from a century ago—and in just the 12 years from 1990 to 2002 (the last year for which statistics are available), the number of ounces in the typical soda bottle increased by 25%. Drinking just one 16-ounce cola a day can increase body weight by nearly 21 pounds, on average, over the course of a year.

The growing popularity of sports drinks and other high-calorie beverages, including coffee drinks, "energy" drinks and sweetened iced-tea beverages, plays a role as well. And even though most people are drinking more of these beverages than in the past, they are not eating any less.

Why not? Our brains do not register that we feel full when we drink calorie-rich beverages. That is because humans have historically satisfied their thirst by consuming water—a beverage with no calories. If we felt hungry but filled up on water and did not eat as a result, our health would be severely compromised. Therefore, our brains still recognize hunger and thirst as needs that can only be satiated separately.

WHAT TO DRINK

To stay healthy, you do not have to limit your beverage consumption to water alone. Instead, you should begin by becoming aware of what you are drinking. On average, American adults consume 101.5 ounces of beverages daily.

The Beverage Guidance System, recently developed by a panel of leading nutrition experts, recommends maximum intakes for each of the following beverages...

• **Water.** Seventy-two to 104 ounces of water daily (tap or bottled).

• **Black, unsweetened coffee or tea.** Up to 32 ounces of coffee or 64 ounces of tea daily. (Adding up to one teaspoon of sugar to each eight ounces of coffee or tea is acceptable.)

• **Diet soda or other zero-calorie sweetened beverages.** Up to 32 ounces per day.

• **Skim or low-fat milk.** Up to 16 ounces daily.

• **100% fruit juices, whole milk, sports drinks, soft drinks and other sweetened beverages.** Up to eight ounces per day.

• **Alcohol.** Up to one drink a day for women and up to two drinks daily for men. One drink equals 12 ounces of beer, 5 ounces of wine or 1.5 ounces of distilled spirits.

WHAT NOT TO DRINK

New vitamin-fortified beverages have been introduced, including Diet Coke Plus (fortified with niacin, vitamins B-6 and B-12, zinc and magnesium) and PepsiCo's Tava (fortified with vitamins B-3, B-6 and E and chromium). Vitamin-fortified water has been available for the past decade.

Virtually all research indicating that fortified beverages are beneficial to your health—by increasing energy, for example—is funded by the beverage companies.

Many medical experts are concerned that these beverages can be dangerous if consumed in excess—vitamin deficiencies are rare in the US, so drinking too many fortified beverages could result in a toxic buildup of some nutrients.

For example, too much beta-carotene, a nutrient found in some mixed vegetable/fruit drinks, can raise heart disease risk, while high amounts of caffeine can cause spikes in blood pressure.

Better way to get your essential nutrients: Eat a well-balanced diet and take a daily multivitamin.

Beware of Trans Fat Replacement

So-called interesterified fat (formed by chemically incorporating a saturated fatty acid into a vegetable oil to harden it) is now being used in some foods to replace trans fat.

New study: When 30 healthy volunteers ate a diet containing 30% of calories from interesterified fat for four weeks, their HDL "good" cholesterol declined while their blood sugar rose by 20%.

Self-defense: Avoid foods that list "interesterified" fat as an ingredient.

K.C. Hayes, DVM, PhD, professor of biology, Brandeis University, Waltham, Massachusetts.

Most Healthful Store-Bought Salad Dressings

That nutritious salad you carefully create using dark-colored lettuce and brightly colored vegetables can easily turn into a high-fat nutritional nightmare if you choose the wrong salad dressing. *Here are three nutritious options...*

• **Annie's Naturals Tuscany Italian**

Nutritional breakdown per serving (2 tablespoons): 80 calories...7 grams (g) fat...0.5 g saturated fat...0 g trans fat...240 milligrams (mg) sodium.

• **Ken's Lite Country French**

Nutritional breakdown per serving (2 tablespoons): 100 calories...6 g fat...1 g saturated fat...0 g trans fat...230 mg sodium.

• **Wish-Bone Salad Spritzer Asian Silk Sesame Ginger Vinaigrette**

Nutritional breakdown per serving (10 sprays, equal to about one tablespoon): 10 calories...0.5 g fat...0 g saturated fat...0 g trans fat ...100 mg sodium.

Lisa R. Young, PhD, RD, an adjunct professor of nutrition at New York University and a nutritionist in private practice, both in New York City. She is the author of *The Portion Teller Plan: The No-Diet Reality Guide to Eating, Cheating and Losing Weight* (Morgan Road).

Checkout-Counter Caution

Checkout-counter impulse buying can pack on pounds. Items women typically buy at checkout add up to about 14,300 calories each year, enough for a four-pound weight gain. The items men buy average 11,000 calories per year, a three-pound gain.

Greg Buzek, founder and president, IHL Consulting Group, Franklin, Tennessee, which polled 1,000 shoppers for its 2007 North American Self-Checkout Systems market study.

The Best Breakfast for Weight Loss

People who eat oatmeal, other hot breakfast cereals or cold ready-to-eat cereals tend to weigh less than those who have other typical breakfast foods for their morning meal. Those who skip breakfast entirely weigh more, and those who eat eggs with bacon and potatoes are the heaviest.

Theory: Skipping breakfast may lead to eating more later in the day.

Gladys Block, PhD, director, public health nutrition program, School of Public Health, University of California in Berkeley.

 # Eggs for Weight Loss?

In one study, women who ate eggs for breakfast consumed about 418 fewer calories throughout the day than women who ate a bagel containing the same number of calories.

Reason: Eggs are a good source of protein and nutrients, inducing greater satiety and reducing overall daily caloric intake.

Among individuals who are healthy, daily egg consumption has not been shown to negatively impact cholesterol levels.

J.S. Vander Wal, PhD, assistant professor, department of psychology, Saint Louis University, and the leader of a study of 30 women, published in *Journal of the American College of Nutrition.*

Smarter Nighttime Noshing

Stephen P. Gullo, PhD, president of the Center for Healthful Living at the Institute for Health and Weight Sciences in New York City. Dr. Gullo is a member of the *Bottom Line/Women's Health* advisory board and author of *The Thin Commandments Diet* (Rodale).

Many people enjoy an evening snack, and that's fine—as long as you stick mostly to healthful foods and reasonable portions. Yet it is all too simple to overindulge if your willpower weakens as the evening wears on or if you are too distracted to notice how much you're nibbling.

This is known as "night eating syndrome." As I have learned in treating nearly 15,000 patients, it's quite common, especially among people who stay up late (past 10 pm). Fortunately, changing this pattern does not require depriving yourself of an evening snack. *Here's how...*

• **Don't mistake sleepiness for hunger.** A few hours after dinner, hormonal shifts indicate that there is no more need for food as you prepare for sleep. If instead of going to bed, you stay up to read or to pay bills, you may feel an increased urge to eat. This is not true hunger, because you've probably already eaten enough food for the day—but nonetheless it can trigger a snack attack.

• **Identify snacking patterns.** Evening activities lend themselves to mindless or mood-triggered eating. You may munch as you watch TV or balance your checkbook, scarcely noticing as the food disappears. Or perhaps you are bored or anxious about the day's events, so you eat to fill the void or forget your troubles.

Reality check: For one week, keep a journal of what and how much you eat at night...and what you're doing and how you're feeling as you snack. Thereafter, to overcome bad habits, plan your snack schedule in advance, listing healthful foods and what time you will eat them.

• **Make a "no-shopping" list.** Do you go out at night to buy the foods you crave? Probably not. Most people keep the kitchen stocked with favorite snacks, yet this creates a constant temptation. It's easier to resist just once—when you're at the grocery store.

How: On your shopping list, include a separate section for foods you won't buy.

• **Eat dinner—again.** Sometimes one small treat stimulates rather than satisfies the appetite, so a morsel only leads to frustration. Instead of a calorie-dense smidgen of fudge or a sliver of cheese, have a satisfying mini-meal.

Consider: An egg-white omelet with fat-free cheese (try Borden Fat-Free American Singles, 30 calories)...two low-fat hot dogs (such as Hebrew National 97% Fat Free Beef Franks, 45 calories each) on a bed of sauerkraut (skip the buns)...or shrimp cocktail with a green salad.

• **Indulge yourself—100 calories' worth.** Go ahead and have a sweet nighttime treat or a favorite salty snack—but control the portion. Products that come in 100-calorie single-serving sizes include pudding (Jell-O Fat-Free Chocolate Vanilla Swirl), frozen treats (Breyers Pure Fruit strawberry bar), popcorn (Pop Secret and Orville Redenbacher) and crackers (Goldfish and Wheat Thins). Sure, you get more food for your buck when you buy in bulk, but if the single-serving packages help you to slim down and safeguard your health, the extra money is well spent.

More from Dr. Stephen Gullo...

Tricks for Resisting Sweet Cravings

To curb cravings for sweets, keep your mouth busy with a sugarless gum. Also try sipping artificially sweetened iced tea through a straw to prolong the sweet taste. A clean taste curbs cravings, so brush teeth or pop a breath-freshening strip. Salty or spicy foods may quell a yen for sugar as well—try pickles or V8 juice.

New: Sugar Blocker Gum (*www.eatingman agement.com*) contains herbs that bind with receptor sites on your palate, temporarily blocking the ability to taste sugar—so sweets lose their power to tempt.

Foods That Seem Healthy...but Really Are Not

David Grotto, RD, president and founder of Nutrition Housecall, LLC, a consulting firm specializing in family nutrition programs, Chicago. He serves on the scientific advisory board of *Men's Health* magazine and is author of *101 Foods That Could Save Your Life* (Bantam). He is past spokesman for the American Dietetic Association.

Nearly everyone wants to eat healthier. The food industry, which keeps a close eye on America's changing tastes, has introduced thousands of foods that purport to be healthy—but are they really?

Too many people assume that anything that comes from a health-food store is good for you or that quantities don't matter when you're eating a "good" food.

Personal story: One of my first clients was a strict vegetarian, but this woman was 5' 2" and weighed 250 pounds. Something was obviously amiss. She told me that she used nearly a pint of olive oil in recipes because it's a "healthy" fat.

Some foods, such as vegetables, whole grains, legumes, etc., are almost always good for you. But many of the foods that are promoted with healthy-sounding terms, such as "natural" or "vitamin-packed," actually are loaded with sugar and/or fat and are unacceptably high in calories.

Some common offenders—and healthier alternatives you might want to try...

SMOOTHIES

Some smoothies can have more calories than sodas do, making them an unhealthy choice to have regularly. My daughter once bought a peanut butter smoothie. I did the calculations and found that it had about 1,000 calories.

Healthier: Make your own smoothie using just fresh fruit and adding skim milk if you want. Or mix four ounces of fruit juice with four ounces of sparkling water. It tastes delicious, is relatively low in calories and has the same nutrients as a serving of whole fruit (though less fiber).

PROTEIN BARS

Millions of Americans substitute one or more meals daily with bars—granola bars, high-protein bars, meal-replacement bars, etc. Many of these are high in sugar and/or fat and deliver 300 calories or more. It's fine to occasionally use one of these bars as a meal replacement, but they're too high in calories to have in addition to meals.

Healthier: Make up your own healthy snacks, using a mixture of nuts, seeds and dried fruit. One-half ounce of almonds (about 12) and one tablespoon of dried fruit totals about 140 calories. When you do crave a bar, have one that has at least three grams of fiber, with no more than 150 calories. Try Luna small-size organic bars.

FROZEN YOGURT

Healthier than ice cream? Not necessarily. Yogurt is one of the healthiest foods you can eat, but most frozen brands have more in common with desserts than with health foods.

Check the label: Some frozen yogurts have the same number of calories as ice cream. They may even have similar amounts of sugar and fat. Also, it's rare to find live and active cultures—the probiotic organisms that make natural yogurt so healthy—in frozen products.

Healthier: One of the newer versions of frozen yogurt. For example, Berry Chill, a yogurt chain based in Chicago, is producing products that are relatively low in fat and sugar and contain live and active cultures. Other manufacturers are following suit, such as New England–based Brigham's with its premium frozen yogurt, élan. Look for the LAC seal on frozen yogurt containers —it means that the product has at least 10 million live and active cultures.

PRETZELS

They are often touted as a healthier alternative to potato chips because they have less fat. A one-ounce pretzel serving usually has about one gram of fat, compared to up to 10 grams (g) in a one-ounce serving of some potato chips. However, most pretzels are high in salt. They also have a high glycemic index because they consist mostly of refined wheat flour and cornstarch —they are quickly transformed to sugar during digestion, which can increase blood glucose levels and lead to weight gain.

Be wary of pretzels with added wheat or oat bran—these often are just "window dressing" and not a significant source of whole grains.

Healthier: Satisfy your "crunch craving" with a mix of nuts, seeds and dried fruit (see Protein Bars on the previous page).

FAKE WHOLE-WHEAT BREAD

Real whole-wheat bread is among the healthiest of foods you can eat. Some brands, however, only look like whole wheat—manufacturers often add a brown color to make them look more wholesome.

Another trick: Manufacturers super-size the slices so that they can make higher fiber claims on the label.

Healthier: A bread with normal-size slices that contains at least three grams of fiber per serving. Read the ingredient label. The word "whole"—whole wheat, whole grain, etc.—should be first in the list.

MUFFINS

Today's big muffins often seem like they are loaded with nutritious ingredients, such as fruit or bran, but many muffins that are sold in supermarkets or coffee shops, such as Starbucks, are loaded with fat and sugar and range from 400 to 500 calories each.

Healthier: A smaller one-and-a-half ounce muffin that's made with bran or a whole grain. A muffin this size that's not loaded with sugar and/or fat usually contains about 100 calories.

RICE MIXES

Brown rice has more fiber and disease-fighting phytochemicals than white rice, but people don't always want to take the time to cook brown rice. Instead, they buy the packaged rice pilaf, both for convenience and extra flavor. Most of these products are very high in sodium, as well as fat.

Healthier: Uncle Ben's microwavable brown rice. It's ready in just a few minutes, and you can season it to your own taste—without adding salt or oil.

Eat More Slowly to Cut Calories

In a recent finding, women ingested 67 fewer calories and felt more satisfied after taking 29 minutes to eat a meal than when they took nine minutes to consume the same meal.

Best: Savor meals by taking smaller bites… chewing thoroughly…pausing between bites… and consuming calorie-free beverages, such as water or unsweetened tea, with the meal.

Kathleen J. Melanson, PhD, RD, associate professor, nutrition and food sciences department at the University of Rhode Island, Kingston, and leader of a study of 30 women, presented at the annual meeting of the Obesity Society.

A Quick Calorie Count

Get a quick calorie count before ordering at a restaurant by using your personal digital assistant (PDA) or cell phone to send an e-mail to *calories@dietdetective.com*. Specify the name of the food, such as corn muffin or pork chop, and you will get a free response within minutes, giving you a calorie count and information on carbs and grams of fat.

If You Spend A Lot of Time Sitting…

Exercise is not enough to take off the pounds if you spend a lot of time sitting. When people sit for long periods—doing desk jobs, using computers, playing video games, watching television or for other reasons—the enzymes that are responsible for burning fat shut down.

Result: People who sit too much have significantly greater risk for premature heart attack, diabetes and death.

Self-defense: In addition to exercising, it is important to stand up and move around as much as possible throughout your day—walk around the office, go up and down stairs, take a break from the computer and go outdoors, or do something else to get out of a seated position.

Marc Hamilton, PhD, associate professor of biomedical sciences, University of Missouri-Columbia, and leader of research on the physiological effects of sitting, published in *Diabetes*.

10 Easy Ways to Sneak Exercise Into Your Day

Carol Krucoff, a registered yoga therapist at Duke Integrative Medicine in Durham, North Carolina, where she creates individualized yoga programs for those who have health challenges. She is a coauthor with her husband, Mitchell Krucoff, MD, of *Healing Moves: How to Cure, Relieve, and Prevent Common Ailments with Exercise* (Writer's Collective).

Getting the recommended 30 minutes of exercise a day can be challenging during the cold, dark days of winter. But the good news is that you do not have to work out for a half-hour straight to boost your health. Guidelines from the American Heart Association and the American College of Sports Medicine indicate that three 10-minute periods of moderate-intensity physical activity (such as a brisk walk) can be just as effective as exercising for 30 minutes straight. While other evidence suggests that even shorter periods of an activity—in fact, every step you take—adds up to better health. *Try these simple strategies to slip exercise into your day...*

1. Break the elevator/escalator habit. Climbing stairs is a great way to strengthen your heart, muscles and bones. The Harvard Alumni Health Study, which followed 11,130 men (mean age 58 at the beginning of the study) for about 20 years, found that those who climbed 20 to 34 floors per week had about a 30% lower risk of stroke. Take the stairs at every opportunity and even look for ways to add extra flights, such as using the bathroom on a different floor. If you must take an elevator up a tall building, get off a few flights early and walk.

2. Use muscle, avoid machines. In our push-button world, we expend about 300 to 700 fewer calories per day than did our grandparents, who had to do things like chop wood and fetch water. Drop the "labor saving" mentality, and embrace opportunities to activate your life. Use a rake instead of a leaf blower...wash your car by hand...get up and change the TV channel.

3. Walk over to a coworker's office instead of sending an e-mail. William Haskell, PhD, calculated, in *The Journal of the American Medical Association,* that the energy expenditure lost by writing e-mails for two minutes every hour for eight hours per day, five days a week—instead of two minutes of slow walking around the office to deliver messages—adds up to the equivalent of 1.1 pounds of fat in one year and 11 pounds of fat in 10 years.

4. Take exercise breaks. Energize your body with movement instead of caffeine by turning your coffee break into a "walk break." Every hour or two, get up and walk around or stretch.

5. Wait actively. If you are forced to wait for an airplane, hairdresser, dentist, doctor, restaurant table, etc., take a walk. To boost the calorie burn of your walk, move purposefully—as if you're late for a meeting—rather than just strolling along.

6. Do the housework boogie. Play lively music when you are doing household chores, and dance off extra calories by moving to the beat.

7. Try aerobic shopping. Take one lap or two around the mall or grocery store before you go into a store or put anything in your cart.

8. Socialize actively. Instead of sitting around talking (or eating) with friends and/or family, do something active, such as bowling, playing Ping-Pong, shooting baskets or dancing.

9. Install a chin-up bar in a convenient doorway. Whenever you walk through, do a pull-up or simply "hang out" and stretch. Chin-up bars are available at sporting-goods stores and online for less than $20.*

10. Practice "phone fitness." Stretch, walk or climb stairs while you are talking on your cell phone or cordless phone.

*Price subject to change.

Walk and Work

A workstation incorporating a treadmill with a computer could enable obese workers to lose up to 66 pounds a year. People burn about 72 calories per hour while doing work at a desk, compared with 191 at the vertical workstation.

British Medical Journal, London, *www.bmj.com.*

The Ultimate Stay-Young Workout

Joel Harper, a New York City–based certified personal trainer who designs equipment-free workouts for Olympic athletes and business executives. His exercise DVDs are *YOU: Staying Young Workout, YOU: On a Diet Workout, FitPack Workout, FitPack Chair Workout* and *Dorm Room Diet*. The exercises described in this article are adapted from the program he created for *YOU: Staying Young* by Dr. Mehmet Oz and Dr. Michael Roizen (Free Press).

If you would love to have strong, limber muscles but hate the idea of trudging off to the gym to lift weights or use exercise machines, there's a new no-equipment workout that uses your body to create strength-building resistance.

Muscle strength is key to remaining robust as you age. Research shows that building up strong muscles can keep you out of a nursing home.

The following exercise plan should be performed three times a week, with at least one day of rest between workouts. The exercises, which take about 10 minutes to complete, are generally appropriate for people of any age or fitness level. Just be sure to check with your doctor before starting this program—particularly if you have a chronic health problem. If the basic exercises seem too easy, try the advanced versions.

Important: If you observe yourself holding your breath during the workout, immediately begin counting your repetitions out loud. This is a simple way to force yourself to breathe properly. Always count backward rather than forward—it tricks your mind into thinking that you're headed toward a finish line.

My stay-young workout...

TITANIC

Purpose: Stretches your chest, shoulders and arms.

Helps with: Maintaining correct posture—especially for people who work at computers.

What to do: While standing with your feet slightly apart, hold your arms out to your sides, palms facing forward, two inches below your shoulders. Keeping your torso upright, stretch your hands back as far

Workout illustrations by Shawn Banner.

as you can reach. Hold it for 20 seconds, while breathing deeply into your chest. This will expand your diaphragm, the large muscle that separates the chest and abdominal cavities.

Advanced version: Bend your wrists back and reach the backs of your hands toward each other.

DREAM OF JEANNIE

Purpose: Strengthens your quadricep muscles (in the fronts of the thighs), abdominals and shoulders.

Helps with: Walking up stairs.

What to do: While kneeling, cross your arms and hold them in front of your body like a genie, maintaining a straight line from the top of your head to your knees. Keeping this straight line, lean back very slightly, pulling your middle in and squeezing the buttocks together. Hold for 30 seconds, while breathing deeply. If necessary, cushion your knees with a folded towel.

Advanced version: Lean back as far as possible while continuing to maintain the straight line from your head to your knees.

SUPERMAN TOE TAPS

Purpose: Strengthens your lower back and buttocks.

Helps with: Gardening, making the bed or carrying luggage.

What to do: Lie on your stomach with your head turned to the side and resting on your interlaced fingers. Keeping your legs straight, lift them up off the ground and raise up your knees as high  as you can. Tap your toes together 40 times.

Advanced version: Reach your arms (palm side down) as far as you can in front of you. While looking down, lift up your elbows as far above the ground as possible, then press your thumbs together and apart 40 times, while tapping your toes together.

HAMMOCK STRETCH

Purpose: Stretches your hips and hamstring muscles (in the backs of the thighs).

Helps with: Easing low-back tension—especially when caused by sitting for long periods, such as during an airplane flight.

What to do: Sit on the floor with your hands behind you and your palms on the floor. Keep your fingers pointing backward and your elbows just a little bent. Bend your knees and draw in your heels until they're just two feet from your tailbone. Keeping the sole of your left foot flat on the ground, place your right ankle on top of your left knee and sit up as straight as possible. Focus on pressing your lower back forward toward your right calf. Resist raising your shoulders toward your ears. Hold for 15 seconds, then switch legs and repeat.

Advanced version: To get a deeper stretch, gently press the knee of your crossed leg away from you while doing this exercise.

ABDOMINAL BUTTERFLY

Purpose: Strengthens your abdominals.

Helps with: Building strength in the core muscles of the trunk, which, in turn, supports the back.

What to do: Lie on your back and bring your legs into the "butterfly position"—knees pointing out to the sides and the soles of your feet touching. Relax your legs and lace your hands in back of your head, resting your thumbs on your neck to be sure that it remains relaxed. Using only your abdominals, lift your upper body two inches off the ground then lower it back down, pressing your belly button toward your lower back. Repeat 25 times. Next, hold your upper body off the ground and lift your legs two inches, then tap the sides of your feet on the ground 25 times.

Advanced version: Lift your legs as high as you can off the ground and simultaneously raise your upper body into a "crunch" 25 times, while tapping the sides of your feet on the ground after each crunch.

CROSS-LEGGED TWIST

Purpose: Stretches out the back, abdominals and hips.

Helps with: Releasing low-back tension and opening up the hips—good for those who sit at a desk all day and for activities such as tennis and skiing.

What to do: Sit on the floor with your legs crossed. Keeping your torso upright and the top of your head directly above your tailbone, place your left hand on the right knee and your right hand on the ground just behind you. Slowly twist to the right. Take two deep breaths while holding the stretch. Switch sides and repeat, then do once more on each side.

Advanced version: Do this in the lotus position (legs crossed with ankles on top of your crossed legs).

To Strengthen Muscles...

A recent finding showed that people over age 65 who engage in weight-bearing exercise for one hour twice a week for six months may increase muscle strength by 50%.

A bonus: Participants went from being 59% weaker than their younger counterparts to being only 38% weaker.

Simon Melov, PhD, associate professor and director of genomics, Buck Institute for Age Research, Novato, California, and coauthor of a study of 25 people, published in the on-line journal *PLoS One.*

Magnesium—the Strength Builder

In a study of 1,138 men and women, participants with the highest blood levels of magnesium were stronger (based on tests for handgrip strength and power in leg muscles) than those with the lowest levels.

Theory: Magnesium is essential to the body's cellular energy production, thereby promoting optimal muscle performance.

Suggested: To get the recommended intake of magnesium (420 milligrams [mg] daily for men age 31 or older...320 mg daily for women age 31 or older), eat such foods as dark green, leafy vegetables, navy beans and pumpkin seeds.

Ligia J. Dominguez, MD, researcher, geriatric unit, University of Palermo, Palermo, Italy.

Fitness Beats Thinness

Fitness beats thinness for promoting longevity. A recent study compared the effects of fitness and obesity on longevity by tracking 2,600 people over age 60 for 12 years.

Findings: People who were overweight or obese but judged physically fit by performance on a treadmill test had a lower death rate than those who had normal body weight but were not fit.

Importance: It's best to be fit and not overweight. But even if you are seriously overweight, just moderate exercise can greatly improve your health. Increasing fitness from the level of the "bottom fifth" to only the next-lowest fifth reduced mortality risk by 50%.

Steven Blair, PED, fitness expert, department of exercise science, Arnold School of Public Health, University of South Carolina, Columbia.

If You Have Tennis Elbow...

Steroid injections for tennis elbow are not as effective over the long term as other treatments.

Injecting a steroid into a tendon in the elbow may ease pain and discomfort for the short term, but there is a high risk of recurrence.

Recent finding: One year after receiving corticosteroid injections for tennis elbow pain, only 68% of patients said their symptoms were significantly improved, versus 90% of patients who were told to take analgesic drugs, such as aspirin or ibuprofen, and avoid activities that aggravated their pain...and 94% of those who received physical therapy.

Bill Vicenzino, PhD, professor of sports physiotherapy and head of physiotherapy, School of Health and Rehabilitation Sciences, University of Queensland in St. Lucia, Australia, and chief investigator of a study of 198 people, published in *British Medical Journal*.

 # New Exercise Guidelines

The latest exercise guidelines from the American Heart Association and the American College of Sports Medicine call for moderate aerobic exercise 30 minutes per day, five days a week, or vigorous aerobic exercise 20 minutes every day, three days a week...and strength-training twice a week.

People age 65 and older also should do exercises to improve or maintain balance three times a week to minimize their risk for falling.

Steven Blair, PED, fitness expert, department of exercise science, Arnold School of Public Health, University of South Carolina, Columbia, and contributor to new recommendations for exercise by the American Heart Association and the American College of Sports Medicine.

5

Natural Health

Dr. Oz's Simple Ways to Add Years to Your Life

Today life expectancy is 75 years for men and 80 years for women. That is better than it was in 1970—when life expectancy was 69 for men and 74 for women—but people still could be living much longer. Many of us can increase life expectancy and have an excellent chance of reaching 100. *Here's how...*

FIGHT FREE RADICALS

All our cells have hundreds of *mitochondria*, which convert nutrients into energy. But during this conversion process, the mitochondria create waste—particularly *free radicals*, molecules that cause inflammation and cell damage. The mitochondria in someone over age 60 are 40% less efficient than the mitochondria in someone age 40.

Result: More inflammation...more damaged cells...and more age-related diseases.

Solution 1: Eat colorful produce. Fruits and vegetables with bright colors—red grapes, blueberries, tomatoes, etc.—are high in flavonoids and carotenoids, antioxidants that inhibit free radicals and reduce inflammation.

Solution 2: Take coenzyme Q10 (CoQ10). If you don't eat lots of produce—and most people don't—consider this supplement, which can improve the efficiency of mitochondria. It also is a potent antioxidant that helps to neutralize free radicals. I usually recommend that people start taking CoQ10 after age 35.

Dose: 200 milligrams (mg) daily (100 mg in the morning and 100 mg in the afternoon). The gel-cap form is easier for the body to absorb than the tablets.

Mehmet C. Oz, MD, professor of surgery at Columbia University in New York City. He is medical director of the integrative medicine program and director of the Cardiovascular Institute at New York–Presbyterian Hospital/Columbia University Medical Center. Dr. Oz is coauthor, with Michael F. Roizen, MD, of many books, including *YOU... Staying Young: The Owner's Manual for Extending Your Warranty* (Free Press). He also is the health expert for *The Oprah Winfrey Show.*

EAT FISH INSTEAD OF MEAT

Americans eat a lot of red meat, one of the main sources of saturated fat. Saturated fat increases LDL "bad" cholesterol, one of the main risk factors for heart disease, and stimulates the body's production of inflammatory proteins, believed to be an underlying cause of most age-related diseases, including cancer.

Solution 1: Eat fish three times a week. The omega-3 fatty acids in fish decrease inflammation…increase lubrication of joints…decrease risk for atherosclerosis (or hardening of the arteries) and arterial clotting…improve immunity…reduce menopausal discomfort…and improve memory and other cognitive functions.

Solution 2: Take DHA if you don't eat fish on a regular basis. Fish oil supplements contain the omega-3s *docosahexaenoic acid* (DHA) and *eicosapentaenoic acid* (EPA)—but humans need only the DHA.

Daily dose: 400 mg of DHA for women, and 600 mg for men. Buy the algae form. It doesn't have the fishy taste—or the undesirable additives that prolong shelf life—found in many fish oil supplements.

TAKE ASPIRIN

It's estimated that about 50 million Americans should be taking an aspirin daily, but only about 20 million are doing so.

Reasons: Some people don't know that they should be taking an aspirin. Others experience stomach upset when using it. And some tend to think that a drug that is so cheap and readily available isn't likely to be effective.

Fact: In studies, taking 162 mg of aspirin daily reduces the risk for a heart attack by about 36% and the risk for colon, esophageal, throat and stomach cancers by about 45%.

Solution: Take one-half of a regular aspirin or two 81-mg (baby) aspirins daily (162 mg total)—but check with your doctor first. Buy the cheapest tablets. These usually come unbuffered and dissolve more quickly in the stomach.

Also helpful: Drink one-half glass of warm water before and after taking aspirin. It causes the aspirin to dissolve more rapidly, so it doesn't stick to the stomach wall—the main cause of discomfort.

BOOST NITRIC OXIDE

Nitric oxide is a naturally occurring, short-lived gas that is produced mainly in the lining of blood vessels. It plays a critical role in *vasodilation*—the expansion of blood vessels that allows blood to circulate with less force. Nitric oxide is thought to lower blood pressure, decrease the buildup of plaque in atherosclerosis and foster enhanced lung function. The traditional American diet, which promotes the accumulation of fat-laden deposits on artery walls, lowers nitric oxide in the blood.

Solution: Eat less saturated fat. Limit foods that are high in saturated fat, including meats, butter and whole-milk dairy products. Studies indicate that the body's production of nitric oxide declines immediately after people eat a meal that is high in saturated fat—and nitric oxide levels stay depressed for about four hours after such a meal.

REDUCE STRESS

Researchers have observed that chronic stress prematurely shortens *telomeres*, the tips of chromosomes that control the ability of cells to divide and repair damaged tissues. Impaired cell division is among the main causes of age-related diseases. Research has shown that people who achieve control over daily stress have lower levels of harmful stress hormones, reduced blood pressure and better immunity.

Solution: Meditate for five minutes daily. Sit silently, and try to clear your mind of thoughts. To help do this, pick a word (it does not matter what it is), then repeat it to yourself over and over. Focusing on the one word helps prevent other thoughts from entering your mind. Yet another stress reducer is exercise, such as yoga or walking.

LIMIT SUGAR

Sugar consumption in the US has increased almost every year since the early 1980s. The average American now has 20 teaspoons of added sugar each day—from sweets, soft drinks, table sugar, etc.

Because sugary foods often do replace more healthful foods in the diet, they are a primary cause of heart disease, cancer and osteoporosis. Of course, a high-sugar diet contributes to obesity, a primary cause of diabetes. Excessive sugar (glucose) in the blood can result in nerve damage, kidney failure, memory problems, eye disease and arthritis.

Solution: Avoid sugar. Also avoid other white carbohydrates, such as white rice, white potatoes and white flour. These "simple sugars" have few nutrients and cause blood sugar to spike.

Diabetes indicator: If you have to urinate more than 12 times a day, or more than three times in a three-hour period, ask your doctor to test your urine for sugar, an early indicator of diabetes.

STRENGTHEN BONES

Falls, and resulting broken bones and complications, are among the top five causes of death.

Solution: Regular exercise—and particularly all of the weight-bearing exercises, including lifting weights and using exercise bands—increases muscle strength and bone density. Taking a daily walk strengthens leg bones, but you also need exercises that target the upper body.

Self-test: Stand on one foot with your arms out to the sides. Close your eyes, and count the seconds until you fall off balance. If you can't stay balanced for 15 seconds at age 40 or seven seconds at age 60 or older, your balance and/or strength aren't optimal. Ask your doctor about balancing exercises, etc.

The Health Secret Most Doctors Don't Know About: The Healing Benefits of Yoga

Timothy McCall, MD, a board-certified internist and medical editor of *Yoga Journal*. Dr. McCall's articles have appeared in dozens of publications, including *The New England Journal of Medicine* and *The Journal of the American Medical Association*. He was the *Bottom Line/ Health* columnist from 1995 to 2003 and is the author of *Yoga as Medicine: The Yogic Prescription for Health and Healing* (Bantam). His Web site is *www.DrMcCall.com*.

Yoga is one of the most underutilized and underrated medical therapies in the US. It is extremely rare for American medical doctors to prescribe yoga—most are just not knowledgeable about its wide array of health benefits.

What you may not know: More than 100 scientific studies show that yoga can improve health problems ranging from heart disease to insomnia…diabetes to arthritis…and cancer to multiple sclerosis.

As a medical doctor who has practiced yoga for 12 years, I firmly believe that it is the most powerful system of overall health and well-being that I have ever seen. By promoting overall health, yoga increases the benefits you may derive from conventional and/or other alternative/complementary therapies—and may even eliminate your need for medication.

WHAT IS YOGA?

Yoga is a holistic system of exercise and controlled breathing aimed at optimizing physical and mental well-being. Developed in ancient India, yoga stretches all muscle groups while gently squeezing the internal organs, a practice that lowers blood pressure and respiratory rate and increases cardiac efficiency.

HOW YOGA HELPS

Studies show that virtually all health problems respond positively to yoga.

Landmark research: When 2,700 people suffering from a wide variety of ailments practiced yoga (for at least two hours a week for one year or longer), it helped 96% of those with back disorders…94% of those with heart disease…90% of those with cancer…90% of those with arthritis…88% of those with bronchitis or asthma…and 86% of those with diabetes.

What is responsible for all of these beneficial effects? Yoga, which is practiced by children as well as adults well into their 80s and 90s, helps with such a wide range of medical conditions because of its many different mechanisms of action. *Yoga can…*

• **Increase flexibility,** strengthen muscle and improve posture and balance.

• **Boost immunity** by reducing levels of the stress hormone cortisol and increasing the circulation of lymph (a fluid rich in lymphocytes and other immune cells).

• **Enhance lung function** by using slower and deeper breathing which promotes oxygenation of tissues.

• **Strengthen bones and joints** and nourish the cartilage in spinal discs by improving range of motion and by using a variety of movements that help deliver nutrients to the cartilage.

• **Condition your heart and circulatory system** by lowering elevated blood sugars and artery-damaging high blood pressure...and improving levels of both cholesterol and triglycerides (blood fats).

• **Relieve pain** due to conditions such as arthritis, back problems, fibromyalgia and carpal tunnel syndrome, by reducing muscle spasms, improving the alignment of bones in joints and teaching people to separate their pain from an emotional response to the pain.

• **Improve brain function** by increasing levels of certain neurotransmitters (brain chemicals) and activating an area of the brain (the left prefrontal cortex) that is associated with lower levels of stress and anger.

GETTING THE BENEFITS

There are a variety of ways to maximize the effectiveness and safety of yoga therapy. *Some advice...*

• **Talk to your doctor.** Certain yoga practices are not recommended for people who suffer from specific medical conditions.

Example: People who have diabetic retinopathy (damage to the retina as a result of diabetes) should avoid upside-down poses, such as shoulder stands and headstands, because these poses can increase pressure on the blood vessels in the eyes.

Helpful: When you visit your doctor, bring a book with photos of yoga poses that reflect the yoga style that you are considering. Since your physician may not be aware of all possible contraindications, be sure to also discuss your concerns with your yoga teacher.

• **Choose the right type of instruction.** Yoga therapy ideally is tailored to the individual based on the evaluation of an experienced yoga teacher. While large group yoga classes can be great preventive medicine for people who are relatively fit and flexible, those who have chronic medical conditions are usually better off working with a teacher privately or in a small group (two to four students). The cost of private lessons ranges from about $40 to $100 or more an hour.* Large group classes range from about $10 to $20 a session.

Helpful: If you're not sure whether a class is right for you, phone or e-mail the teacher before you attend and explain your situation. If the class doesn't fit your needs, ask for a recommendation for another class or teacher.

• **Find an experienced teacher.** Some styles of yoga require teachers to undergo 200 to 500 hours of training to be certified. However, there is no universal accrediting organization.**

Warning: Some yoga teachers might have completed only a weekend training course to become "certified." Before attending a yoga class, ask the instructor how long he/she trained. (At least 200 hours is standard.)

• **Pay attention to your body.** If you experience sharp pain when you do a yoga posture, stop. If you perform a breathing exercise and feel short of breath, stop. In either case, tell the teacher as soon as possible—during or after the class.

• **Practice regularly.** The key to success with yoga is steady practice—once each day is ideal, even if it is only for a few minutes. Yoga works well as part of an overall fitness program that includes aerobic exercise and strength training.

Helpful: Set your goal for daily practice and make an appointment with yourself, just as you would make plans to meet a friend for lunch.

• **Be patient.** Most drugs work fast, but the longer you take them, the less effective they tend to become. Yoga is not a quick fix. But the longer you practice it, the more effective it tends to become. Yoga is slow—but strong—medicine.

That does not mean you will not have immediate results. It is a well-known fact among yoga teachers that people starting yoga make quicker progress with health problems than people who have been practicing for a long time. Just a little bit of added flexibility, strength and balance can make a huge difference in how you function day to day—by reducing back pain, for example, or helping you climb stairs more easily.

*Prices subject to change.

**To find a yoga therapist near you, go to the Web site of the International Association of Yoga Therapists, *www.iayt.org.*

And some yoga techniques can help you instantly in stress-provoking situations, such as getting stuck in traffic.

Example: Counting to yourself, inhale for three seconds and exhale for six seconds, for a single breath. Take a few normal breaths, then repeat the first sequence, breathing smoothly. In a few breaths, you should start to feel calmer.

The Miraculous Power of Nuts

Joy Bauer, MS, RD, CDN, nutrition expert for the *Today* show and nutritionist for the New York City Ballet as well as several Olympic athletes, New York City, *www.joy bauernutrition.com.* She is coauthor, with Carol Svec, of *Joy Bauer's Food Cures* (Rodale).

Nuts are among the most healthful foods you can eat. Rich in nutrients, they can help prevent some of the most common —and most serious—diseases.

Example: In a long-running health study conducted by researchers at Loma Linda University, participants were asked what foods they ate most often. Those who ate nuts five or more times a week were about 50% less likely to have a heart attack than those who ate them less than once a week.

FORGET THE FAT

Many Americans don't eat nuts because they want to cut back on fat and calories. It's true that a single serving of nuts can have 20 grams (g) or more of fat and 180 to 200 calories, but most of the fats are healthful fats, such as omega-3 fatty acids and monounsaturated fat. Americans need to get more, not less, of these fats. As long as you limit yourself to a small handful of nuts daily—the recommended amount, unless otherwise noted—you don't need to worry about the "extra" calories.

Each type of nut contains a different mix of nutrients, fats and protective antioxidants, which can "neutralize" the cell-damaging free radicals. People who have a variety of nuts will get the widest range of benefits. Raw, toasted or roasted nuts are fine as long as they are unsalted.

Here's what nuts can do…

NUTS FOR THE HEART

All nuts are good for the heart, but the following nuts are especially beneficial…

• **Macadamia nuts.** Of the 21 g of total fat in a serving of macadamias, 17 g are monounsaturated—the kind of fat that lowers a person's levels of harmful LDL cholesterol without lowering levels of beneficial HDL cholesterol. Both the antioxidants and the monounsaturated fat in macadamias provide anti-inflammatory effects— important for curtailing arterial damage that can lead to heart disease.

• **Peanuts.** Actually a type of legume, not a true nut, peanuts contain 34 micrograms (mcg) of folate per one-ounce serving, a little less than 10% of the recommended daily amount. Folate is a B vitamin that lowers levels of *homocysteine,* the amino acid that damages arteries and also increases the risk of heart disease.

Peanuts also are high in *L-arginine,* an amino acid that is converted by cells in blood vessels into *nitric oxide.* Nitric oxide improves circulation and may inhibit fatty buildups in the arteries.

• **Pistachios.** One 2007 study conducted by Penn State University found that pistachios lower blood pressure. Men who added 1.5 ounces of shelled pistachios to their daily diets had drops in systolic pressure (the top number in a blood pressure reading) of 4.8 points. The antioxidants and healthy fats in pistachios relax blood vessels and allow blood to circulate with less force.

ALMONDS FOR BONES

Just about everyone needs more calcium, the mineral that strengthens bones and reduces the risk of osteoporosis. Almonds provide more calcium than other nuts, with about 80 milligrams (mg) in 20 to 25 nuts. For people with lactose intolerance, who have trouble digesting dairy, one daily dose of almonds helps increase calcium to bone-protecting levels.

Blood pressure bonus: A single serving of almonds provides 98 mg of magnesium, about one-fourth of the recommended daily amount. Magnesium, along with potassium and calcium, controls the relaxation and contraction of blood vessels and can help control blood pressure.

BRAZIL NUTS FOR PROSTATE

Brazil nuts are a superb source of selenium, with about 155 mcg in just two nuts. The recommended daily amount is 55 mcg. They are also very high in vitamin E. One study, the Selenium and Vitamin E Cancer Prevention Trial, found that men getting selenium and vitamin E, alone or in combination, reduced their risk of prostate cancer by up to 60%. Selenium can improve the ability of the immune system to recognize and destroy cancer cells in the prostate. Vitamin E is an antioxidant that also has been linked to reduced cancer risk.

Caution: People who get too much selenium may have decreased immunity. Because Brazil nuts are so high in selenium and calories (50 calories in two nuts), don't have more than two nuts daily. If you take a multivitamin that has more than 50% of the daily value of selenium, opt for one nut.

PECANS FOR THE EYES

The most serious eye diseases, including cataracts and macular degeneration, are caused, in part, by free radicals. The antioxidants in nuts and other plant foods fight free radicals to keep the eyes healthy.

A study conducted by the US Department of Agriculture (USDA) found that pecans are particularly rich in antioxidants. And, the National Eye Institute's Age-Related Eye Diseases Study reported that participants with macular degeneration who had adequate intakes of antioxidants were 29% less likely to experience disease progression than those who got lower levels.

Bonus for heart health: The vitamin E in pecans reduces the tendency of LDL cholesterol to oxidize and stick to artery walls. Pecans also are high in *phytosterols*—plant compounds that are similar to active ingredients in cholesterol-lowering margarines, such as Benecol.

WALNUTS FOR MOOD

Apart from fish and flaxseed, walnuts are one of the best sources of omega-3 fatty acids. They're the only nut that contains *alpha linolenic acid* (ALA), a polyunsaturated fat that is converted to omega-3s in the body.

The omega-3s appear to help maintain healthy brain levels of serotonin, the neurochemical involved in mood. People who eat walnuts and/or two to three fish meals a week may experience a reduction in symptoms of depression.

Bonus for heart health: Omega-3s lower LDL cholesterol and triglycerides, another type of blood fat...increase HDL "good" cholesterol... inhibit blood clots in the arteries...and reduce arterial inflammation.

Coffee: The "New" Miracle Health Drink

Peter Martin, MD, professor of psychiatry and pharmacology, Vanderbilt University, Nashville.

Accourding to the latest research, coffee is an extremely healthful beverage. *Recent studies have found that coffee...*

• **Decreases the risk for cardiovascular disease.**

• **Helps the liver**—reducing risk for liver cancer (by up to 50%, in one study) and protecting against chronic liver diseases, such as alcohol-related cirrhosis.

• **Reduces risk for Parkinson's disease** by as much as half.

• **Is the number-one source of antioxidants** in the American diet. It's ahead of fruits, vegetables, tea, wine and chocolate.

• **Contains a high level of soluble dietary fiber,** reducing risk for gallstones (by up to 25% in one study).

• **Contains elements that are known to help prevent colon cancer.**

• **Reduces soreness in the muscles** after exercising.

• **Improves mental ability among seniors.** In one study, people over age 65 who drank coffee 30 minutes before a memory test scored higher than those who did not.

How much to drink: Experts suggest two to four cups per day, but many say there is no need to worry about an upper limit. In general, if you can sleep at night, you are not drinking too much. If you enjoy coffee, drink it.

You Don't Need Drugs to Control Your Cholesterol

Allan Magaziner, DO, a clinical instructor in the department of family practice at the Robert Wood Johnson University of Medicine and Dentistry in New Brunswick, New Jersey, and the medical director of the Magaziner Center for Wellness and Anti-Aging Medicine in Cherry Hill, New Jersey, *www.drmagaziner.com*. A prior president of the American College for Advancement in Medicine, he's also the author of *The All-Natural Cardio Cure* (Avery).

It's widely known that low cholesterol levels help prevent heart attack and stroke. But that's only part of the story. Levels of HDL "good" cholesterol must be high enough to carry harmful forms of cholesterol to the liver to be excreted.

New finding: Research has shown that decreasing LDL "bad" cholesterol by 40% and increasing HDL by 30% lowers the risk for heart attack or stroke by 70%—a much greater reduction of risk than occurs from lowering either total cholesterol or LDL levels.

The pharmaceutical industry has worked feverishly to introduce a prescription medication that significantly increases HDL levels, to be used as a complement to cholesterol-lowering statins that focus primarily on lowering LDL levels.

Latest development: The new drug *torcetrapib* was pegged as a blockbuster that increases HDL levels by 60%—that is until some late-stage clinical trials showed that torcetrapib actually increased heart problems and death rates.

What you may not know: Therapeutic doses of niacin (vitamin B-3) effectively boost HDL levels—and lower LDL and total cholesterol.

THE "CHOLESTEROL VITAMIN"

Fifty years ago, Canadian researchers discovered that high doses of *nicotinic acid*—a form of niacin—could lower total cholesterol. And in a 1975 study of men with heart disease, niacin was shown to decrease the rate of second heart attacks. Later, niacin was found to boost heart-protective HDL levels.

Although niacin alone cannot help everyone with abnormal cholesterol levels—often it is best used in combination with a statin—the vitamin is one of the most effective nondrug therapies available.

Ask your doctor about taking niacin if after trying cholesterol-lowering medication you have suffered side effects or if your cholesterol levels have not improved within three months. Or consider trying niacin with the nondrug treatments described below.

How to use: Start with 100 milligrams (mg) of niacin daily and build up over one week to 500 mg a day. Every week, increase the dose by 500 mg until you achieve 2,000 mg a day, taken in three divided doses, with meals. Be certain to use *nicotinic acid*, not *niacinamide*, a form of B vitamin that does not improve cholesterol levels. Consult your doctor before taking niacin.

The most common side effect of using niacin is flushing—a warm, itchy, rash-like reddening of the face, neck and chest, which lasts about 10 minutes. Flushing is caused by niacin's ability to trigger vasodilation (widening of blood vessels).

To lessen this side effect, choose a form of niacin known as *inositol hexanicotinate*. It helps to prevent the flush without decreasing niacin's effectiveness.

Caution: Niacin should be avoided by people with a history of liver problems or stomach ulcers and used with caution by all patients with diabetes and/or gallbladder disease. In addition, high-doses of niacin (2,000 mg or more) may interact with certain medications, including alpha-blockers, such as *doxazosin* (Cardura), and the diabetes drug *metformin* (Glucophage).

OTHER NONDRUG THERAPIES

A diet that keeps sugar and processed food to an absolute minimum and emphasizes fruits and vegetables...whole grains...beans...fish...leaner meats...and nuts and seeds can help lower LDL cholesterol and raise HDL levels. So can regular exercise, such as brisk walking, and losing excess weight.

Other nondrug approaches can lower total and LDL cholesterol and boost HDL. *Combine the following nondrug therapies with niacin for maximum effectiveness...*

• **Red yeast rice.** This Chinese medicine—a yeast that is grown on white rice, then fermented—contains *monacolins*, substances that act as naturally occurring statins. Research in China shows that red yeast rice can lower total cholesterol by 11% to 30%.

Typical use: Take 1,200 to 2,400 mg a day of red yeast rice, in two to four doses, with meals.

Not recommended: *Policosanol*—a supplement derived from cane sugar that also contains all-natural statins—has been widely promoted as effective for lowering cholesterol. However, several recent studies show that policosanol has *no* significant effect on cholesterol.

• **Fish oil and flaxseed.** Fish oil and flaxseed supply omega-3 fatty acids, which decrease total cholesterol and LDL levels and raise HDL levels.

Typical dose: For fish oil, take supplements containing a total of 3 grams (g) daily of *eicosapentaenoic acid* (EPA) and *docosahexaenoic acid* (DHA). But, if you take a blood-thinning drug, such as aspirin or *warfarin* (Coumadin), check with your doctor before taking this dose of fish oil. Or have one to three teaspoons of ground flaxseed a day, sprinkled on food or mixed with water or juice. Flaxseed also can help stop constipation and ease arthritis pain.

• **Soy.** Many studies show that soy can help lower total and LDL cholesterol.

Typical use: Try to get 20 g of soy protein a day—the equivalent of eight ounces of tofu...or one cup of edamame (soy) beans.

Important: Soy ice cream and the other processed soy foods do not deliver enough soy to help reduce cholesterol.

Caution: If you have been diagnosed with any hormone-dependent cancer, such as some breast malignancies, or you are at risk for such a condition, check with your doctor before adding soy to your diet.

• **Plant sterols.** These all-natural substances, which block the absorption of cholesterol in the intestines, are found in fruits, vegetables, beans, grains and other plants. Regular intake can reduce total cholesterol by 10% and LDL by 14%. Products with plant sterols (or the similar form, plant stanols) include spreads, salad dressings, snack bars and dietary supplements.

Typical use: Aim for 1 g to 2 g daily of plant sterols.

• **Walnuts.** One recent study published in the medical journal *Angiology* showed that people who ate one handful of walnuts daily for eight weeks had a 9% increase in HDL. Walnuts contain *polyphenol* antioxidants, which also inhibit oxidation of LDL cholesterol.

Recommended intake: One ounce of raw walnuts three times daily.

The Food That Lowers Cholesterol 24%...in Just Five Weeks

Andrea Chernus, RD, a registered dietitian, certified diabetes educator and exercise physiologist who maintains a private practice in New York City. She counsels her patients on high cholesterol, diabetes, weight management and sports nutrition. She was formerly the clinical nutritionist for Columbia University, New York City. Her Web site is *www.nutritionhandouts.com.*

I f you are one of the millions of Americans with high cholesterol, chances are your doctor has told you what not to have—high-fat meats and dairy, for example. But certain foods actually can lower your cholesterol and, in some cases, eliminate the need for cholesterol-lowering drugs. Regularly including these foods can have a particularly powerful effect on reducing LDL—the "bad" cholesterol that damages arteries and other blood vessels. High LDL levels are associated with an increased risk for heart attack and stroke.

OAT BRAN, BARLEY AND MORE

Soluble fiber is present in plant-based foods in the form of gums and pectins. The National Cholesterol Education Program Adult Treatment Panel states that five to 10 grams (g) of soluble fiber daily can help to lower LDL by 5%.

A specific type of soluble fiber—*beta-glucan* (found in oat bran and barley)—offers an even more potent cholesterol-lowering effect...

• **In a 2004 study,** men eating 6 g of soluble fiber from barley per day lowered their LDL cholesterol by an average of 24% in five weeks.

•**In another study,** men given 6 g of beta-glucan in a fortified bread—who also were following a low-fat diet and walking 60 minutes per day—experienced an average reduction in LDL cholesterol of 28%.

How it works: In the intestines, soluble fiber attaches itself to cholesterol and bile acids. Bile acids help with fat digestion. They are made from cholesterol, thus when the body needs to make more bile acids, it pulls cholesterol from the bloodstream. The process of binding soluble fiber to bile acids forces the body to make more bile and use up cholesterol from the body's supply. Because fiber is not digested, it carries the cholesterol and bile acids out of the body, lowering the body's cholesterol.

Best sources of soluble fiber: Oat bran, oatmeal, barley, apples, citrus fruits, pears, kidney and lima beans, carrots, broccoli and brussels sprouts. Psyllium seed husks also are a good resource and are found in some cereals, such as Kellogg's All-Bran Buds cereal.

Hot cereal made of 100% oat bran has about 3 g of soluble fiber per serving...plain oatmeal has about 2 g. Most cold oat-based cereals have one gram. Fruits and vegetables have 0.5 g to 1 g of soluble fiber per serving.

Be aware: Commercially prepared muffins, pretzels and breads made with oat bran may not contain much soluble fiber. Also, some may be high in saturated or trans fats, sugars and sodium. As a general guide, check the label to make sure oat bran is one of the first ingredients listed on the food label. (Soluble fiber does not have to be listed separately from total fiber.)

PLANT STEROLS AND STANOLS

Plant sterols (*phytosterols*) and plant stanols (*phytostanols*) are substances that block absorption of cholesterol. They are particularly high in vegetable oils and, to a lesser degree, in fruits, vegetables, nuts and seeds. More than 25 studies have proved their effectiveness in cholesterol reduction. *Examples...*

•**In a 2001 study,** 155 adults with high cholesterol took in 1.5 g per day of plant sterols from margarine. After six months, they had an average reduction in LDL cholesterol of 11% (and 9% reduction in total cholesterol).

•**In another study,** 72 adults with high cholesterol took in 2 g per day of plant sterols from a phytosterol-fortified orange juice. Eight weeks later their average reduction in LDL cholesterol was 12% (7% reduction in total cholesterol).

How they work: Plant sterols and stanols help block the absorption of dietary cholesterol and the reabsorption of cholesterol back into our intestinal tract. They compete with cholesterol for incorporation into mixed *micelles*, which are composite molecules that contain both water- and fat-soluble substances. In the body, micelles are used to carry fats through the bloodstream. When cholesterol is prevented from being absorbed and incorporated into these molecules, it is excreted from the body.

Best sources: To get a cholesterol-lowering dose from ordinary food, you would have to eat hundreds of calories worth of oils each day or bushels of fruits and vegetables. But researchers have isolated plant sterols and stanols, and food companies have incorporated them into "functional foods."

Until fairly recently, only certain margarines contained these cholesterol-lowering ingredients, but food companies now have added them into lower-fat foods, including yogurts, juices, breads and more. A dose of 2 g to 3 g of plant sterols and stanols per day has the greatest impact on lowering LDL cholesterol, reducing it by 6% to 15%. Higher doses of sterols and stanols are not more effective.

Those foods containing effective amounts of plant sterols and stanols include Promise, Benecol and Take Control margarines...Minute Maid Heartwise Orange Juice...Nature Valley Healthy Heart Granola Bars...Hain Celestial Rice Dream drink...Lifetime low-fat cheese...Orowheat whole-grain bread...and VitaMuffins.

The FDA now allows foods containing sterols and stanols, that meet certain criteria, to put a health claim on the label that they can help reduce the risk of coronary heart disease.

Beware: Margarines and juices are dense in calories. Check food labels to see how much you need to eat to obtain 2 g to 3 g of sterols and stanols.

If you're worried about calories, you can take the sterol/stanol supplements. Generally, they are called beta-sitosterol or sitostanol. It is safe to use these supplements along with statin drugs for an additional cholesterol-lowering effect.

NUTS

People who are trying to decrease cholesterol levels often eliminate nuts from their diets because nuts are high in fat and calories. But nuts contain primarily monounsaturated fats, which, when substituted for the saturated fats found in high-fat meats and dairy, not only can lower LDL levels but also boost HDL "good" cholesterol levels.

Studies have shown the greatest effect when nuts comprise 20% of one's total calories, which typically amounts to 1.5 to 3.5 ounces of nuts a day (about one-quarter to one-half cup).

On average, LDL cholesterol levels fall 8% to 12% when walnuts or almonds are substituted for saturated fats. HDL levels may increase by 9% to 20%. Other nuts, such as peanuts (technically a legume), pistachios and pecans, have been shown to decrease cholesterol, but fewer studies are available on these varieties.

How they work: The exact mechanism of nuts' healthful effects has not been discovered yet, but nuts contain a combination of plant sterols, fiber and healthy fats.

Beware: Because nuts are high in calories, the trick is to substitute nuts for less healthful, high-fat foods, including cheese and meat.

Stress Raises Cholesterol

In a recent study, when 199 healthy, middle-aged men and women performed moderately stressful tasks—such as quickly identifying the mislabeled colors on a computer monitor—their cholesterol rose. And three years later, the study participants who had reacted most strongly to the tasks (with stress and cholesterol spikes) had the largest cholesterol increases.

Theory: Fatty acids and glucose are released during stressful situations. This can cause the liver to produce more LDL "bad" cholesterol, which can have long-term health consequences.

If you lead a stressful life: Explore stress-relieving activities, such as aerobic exercise and/or meditation.

Andrew Steptoe, DSc, professor of psychology, University College, London.

Lower Blood Pressure Through Diet

In a recent study, postmenopausal women with high blood pressure who replaced 25 grams (g) of protein in their daily diets with one-half cup of unsalted soy nuts (roasted whole soybeans) for eight weeks decreased their blood pressure by an average of 9.9% systolic (top number) and 6.8% diastolic. Postmenopausal women who had normal blood pressure also had a healthy decrease in blood pressure.

A caution: Women with thyroid problems, pregnant women and nursing mothers should all avoid soy.

Francine K. Welty, MD, PhD, associate professor, department of medicine at Beth Israel Deaconess Medical Center, Boston, and leader of a study of 60 women, published in *Archives of Internal Medicine*.

Better Chocolate Choice

In a recent analysis of five studies involving 173 people, those who ate dark chocolate or other cocoa-rich products daily for two weeks had an average 4.7-point lower systolic (the top number) blood pressure compared with those who ate white chocolate or other products without cocoa.

Theory: Cocoa is high in procyanidins, antioxidants that boost the body's production of nitric oxide, a chemical that relaxes blood vessels.

For healthier blood pressure: Substitute one-half ounce daily of dark chocolate for other high-calorie or high-fat desserts.

Dirk Taubert, MD, PhD, senior lecturer, University Hospital, Cologne, Germany.

Sleep More to Lower Blood Pressure

People who got five hours or less of sleep a night were more than two times as likely to develop high blood pressure as the people who slept seven to eight hours, according to a recent study.

Theory: Blood pressure drops by 10% to 20% during sleep, so a sleep deficit increases average 24-hour blood pressure and increases the workload on the cardiovascular system. Lack of sleep also boosts stress, which increases appetite for salt and decreases salt excretion—further raising hypertension risk in some people.

James E. Gangwisch, PhD, an assistant professor, department of psychiatry, Columbia University, New York City, and leader of a study of 4,810 people, published in *Hypertension*.

Make New Friends

Loneliness is harder on older adults than it is on younger people.

Recent findings: Lonely middle-aged and older people have higher blood pressure and higher levels of the stress hormone *epinephrine* than people of the same age who are not lonely. And, this increases their risk for cardiovascular problems.

Self-defense: Maintain or expand your range of social acquaintances as you age.

John Cacioppo, PhD, a professor and director of the Center for Cognitive and Social Neuroscience at the University of Chicago, and coauthor of a study published in *Current Directions in Psychological Science*.

Anger Can Be Deadly

Angry outbursts can increase your heart disease risk.

Recent finding: In a nine-year study of 185 people (age 50 or older), imaging tests showed

that participants who expressed anger outwardly, such as by yelling, were more likely to have calcium deposits in their coronary arteries (one risk factor for cardiovascular disease) than were people who suppressed anger or infrequently experienced it.

Theory: Outwardly expressed anger causes a temporary surge in blood pressure and heart rate that may damage blood vessel walls.

If you are prone to angry outbursts: Talk to your doctor about healthier ways of managing anger, including relaxation and problem-solving techniques.

Bruce Wright, MD, medical director, Washington State University Health and Wellness Services, located in Pullman, Washington.

Nap Your Way to Better Health

In a six-year study of 23,681 people (average age 53), those who napped at midday for 30 minutes or more at least three times per week were 37% less likely to die of heart disease than those who never napped.

Theory: Midday naps help protect the heart from stress-related problems, such as high blood pressure.

Self-defense: If you have risk factors for heart disease, such as high blood pressure, ask your doctor about napping for at least 30 minutes every day, if your schedule allows.

Androniki Naska, PhD, lecturer, University of Athens School of Medicine, Athens, Greece.

Citrus Protection

Grapefruit and oranges have been proven to protect the heart.

Recent finding: In a 16-year study of nearly 35,000 women ages 55 to 69, researchers found that women who consumed the most flavanones, a flavonoid antioxidant found primarily in citrus fruits (such as oranges, grapefruits and lemons) had a 22% lower risk for death from heart disease than those who consumed the least.

Theory: Flavonoids help prevent blood clots and promote blood vessel health.

If you take medication, ask your physician if citrus affects the drug's effectiveness.

Pamela Mink, PhD, MPH, senior managing scientist, Health Sciences, Exponent Inc., Washington, DC.

Whole Grain for The Heart

Whole-grain cereal reduces heart failure risk by 28% and helps to lower blood pressure and risk for diabetes.

Best: Eat one-half to one cup of whole-grain cereal every day. Look for a cereal that provides at least four grams of fiber per serving.

Luc Djoussé, MD, MPH, DSc, associate epidemiologist at Brigham and Women's Hospital, and assistant professor of medicine at Harvard Medical School, both in Boston. He was leader of a study of the breakfast habits of more than 21,000 people, published in Archives of Internal Medicine.

Best Wines for Health

Roger Corder, PhD, professor of experimental therapeutics at the William Harvey Research Institute, Queen Mary's School of Medicine and Dentistry in London. The author or coauthor of more than 100 scientific studies, his primary research interests are the relationship between diabetes and heart disease, and the health benefits of red wine. He is the author of The Red Wine Diet (Avery).

For many years, researchers theorized that the "French Paradox"—the phenomenon of relatively lower rates of heart disease among the French, who are renowned for their rich, fatty foods—may be due, in part, to their daily consumption of red wine.

Now: The cumulative body of scientific evidence shows that moderate consumption of red wine not only reduces the risk for heart disease, but also for stroke and metabolic syndrome (a constellation of health problems that can lead to heart disease and diabetes). Wine also helps people live longer and avoid dementia. Only recently, however, have scientists begun to identify the specific compounds in red wine that confer health benefits.

Trap: Mass-produced, sweet red wines with high alcohol content (above 14%) do *not* offer high levels of health-promoting chemicals.

What you need to know to choose the most healthful wines—as well as the best alternatives for nondrinkers…

WINE'S PROTECTIVE EFFECTS

Recent research shows that white wine may provide some of the same health benefits of red wine, such as protection from heart disease, but the bulk of scientific evidence focuses in on red wine.

Latest developments: Animal experiments show that *polyphenols*—chemicals found abundantly in dark and/or colorful foods, including red and purple grapes, cocoa and pomegranates—can stop atherosclerosis (fatty buildup in the arteries). That's because polyphenols affect the *endothelium* (cells lining the arteries), causing blood vessels to widen (vasodilate), increasing blood flow.

Breakthrough: In November 2006, English scientists published a paper in *Nature*—the renowned scientific journal—showing that…

• **The most potent of polyphenols in red wines are *procyanidins*,** healthful plant substances that over time become condensed *tannins*, compounds that give the astringent taste to wine. The more procyanidins consumed, the greater degree of vasodilation that occurs.

• **Regions in Europe having the highest rates of proven longevity** produce wines with two to four times more procyanidins than the other regions.

Examples: Many varieties of the Bordeaux wines from France and Chianti wines from Italy.

What you may not know: Resveratrol is often mentioned as the key heart-protecting component of red wine. But to get enough resveratrol to benefit the heart, you would need to drink 1,000 quarts of wine a day. Resveratrol supplements haven't been proven safe or effective.

HEART-FRIENDLY WINES

Many factors influence the level of procyanidins in red wine.

Certain varieties of grapes, including cabernet sauvignon and malbec, are higher in procyanidins than other red and white grapes. Other positive factors include the altitude of the vineyard (the higher, the better)…a slower ripening process…a lower yield (the amount of grapes produced per vine)…and older vines.

Useful: Wines described as having "firm" tannins are more likely to have high levels of procyanidins than wines with "soft" or "ripe" tannins. Check for this description in wine reviews and at the Web sites of wine retailers, such as K&L Wine Merchants (*www.klwines.com*) and Wine. com, Inc. (*www.wine.com*).

DRINK WITH MEALS

The most healthful way to drink red wine is in the classic French style—one or two smallish glasses with lunch and/or with dinner, as food slows alcohol absorption. Most research shows that women should not exceed five ounces of wine per day, and men should limit their daily consumption to 10 ounces.

When red wine is consumed in excess, the health benefits are outweighed by the risks associated with alcohol abuse, including increased risks for many types of cancer, as well as heart disease, obesity and diabetes.

Caution: Drinking wine quickly or with an empty stomach speeds alcohol absorption, increasing the risk for high blood pressure.

NONALCOHOLIC PROCYANIDINS

If you prefer not to drink red wine, consider these procyanidin-rich foods…

• **Dark chocolate.** Look for a bittersweet or extra-dark chocolate that is 70% to 85% cacao. One ounce of dark chocolate delivers the amount of procyanidins in four ounces of red wine.

Caution: To restrict your calories, do not eat more than one ounce to one-and-a-half ounces of dark chocolate daily.

• **Apples.** Red Delicious and Granny Smith have high levels of procyanidins. One medium-sized apple is equivalent to four ounces of red wine.

• **Cranberry juice.** An eight-ounce serving of juice containing 25% cranberry is roughly equivalent to a four-ounce glass of red wine. Choose low-sugar versions with at least 25% cranberry content.

Other sources for heart-healthy procyanidins: Raspberries, blackberries and strawberries, Concord grape juice, pomegranates, walnuts, pinto beans and cinnamon.

Wine with Your Meal

Drinking white wine with a high-carbohydrate meal decreases the postmeal spike in blood sugar levels. Although only white wine was studied, the effect is expected to be similar for red wine. Wine lowers the meal's glycemic index by 37%, probably because its high acidity helps slow digestion—so sugar does not enter the bloodstream as quickly. Keeping blood sugar under control can help prevent diabetes and heart disease.

Jennie Brand-Miller, PhD, professor of human nutrition, University of Sydney, Australia, and the leader of a study of alcohol consumption with meals, published in *The American Journal of Clinical Nutrition.*

Deep Sleep May Protect Against Diabetes

Nine 20- to 31-year-old participants whose deep sleep was limited for only three days became less sensitive to insulin—but their bodies did not produce more of it. The change was comparable to the impact of gaining 20 to 30 pounds.

Self-defense: If you sleep about six to eight hours a night but still feel tired or have trouble concentrating, you may not be getting enough deep sleep. Check with your doctor about what to do.

Esra Tasali, MD, assistant professor of medicine, division of biological sciences, The University of Chicago.

Folic Acid Helps Prevent Strokes

In one recent finding, taking folic acid supplements daily for more than three years reduced risk of stroke by 29%. Most Americans should be able to get sufficient amounts (400 micrograms [mcg] per day) of this B vitamin from spinach, dried beans, fortified cereals and other foods. Ask your physician whether you would benefit from extra folic acid.

Xiaobin Wang, MD, MPH, ScD, professor of pediatrics at Northwestern University and director of the Smith Child Health Research Program at Children's Memorial Medical Center, both in Chicago. She led an analysis of eight clinical trials of folic acid involving a total of 16,841 adults, published in *The Lancet*.

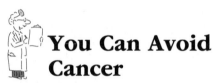 # You Can Avoid Cancer

More than 50% of cancer deaths are avoidable. In fact, only about 5% of all cancers are strongly hereditary.

Good news: Simple lifestyle changes—such as eliminating all tobacco use…eating healthy foods…exercising to maintain a healthful body weight…and getting regular cancer screenings—can decrease your risk for dying from cancer.

Ahmedin Jemal, PhD, program director for cancer surveillance, American Cancer Society, Atlanta.

Onions and Garlic Curb Cancer Risk

In a 13-year study of the diets of about 25,000 people, participants who ate the most onions and/or garlic were 10% to 88% less likely to develop several types of cancer—including colorectal, esophageal, oral and ovarian—than those who ate the least.

Theory: Onions and garlic contain antioxidants, including *allicin* and *quercetin*, that prevent cell damage that can lead to cancer.

Self-defense: Aim to eat one-half cup of onions (any type) and/or one to two cloves of garlic (chopped or crushed) several times weekly.

Carlotta Galeone, PhD, researcher, Mario Negri Institute of Pharmacological Research, Milan, Italy.

More Nutritious Broccoli

Broccoli provides *glucosinolates*, a group of compounds that's thought to detoxify carcinogens (cancer-causing substances) and increase human resistance to cancer. In a 2007 study, we found that the levels of glucosinolates in broccoli fell by up to 77% after the vegetable was boiled for 30 minutes. Most of broccoli's biologically active compounds are water-soluble and leak into the cooking water during heating, which reduces their nutritional benefits, since the water is typically not consumed.

If you want to get the most benefit from your cruciferous vegetables, including broccoli, do not boil them. Instead, steam, microwave or stir-fry (cook rapidly with a little oil) vegetables—cooking styles that showed no significant loss of glucosinolates in our study.

Paul J. Thornalley, PhD, professor of systems biology, University of Warwick Medical School, University Hospital, Coventry, England.

C "Suffocates" Cancer

Researchers once thought that vitamin C and other antioxidants helped prevent cancer by neutralizing free radicals.

Recent finding: Vitamin C appears to block a protein that allows cancers to survive in a low-oxygen environment.

Johns Hopkins Medical Institutions, Baltimore, Maryland, *www.hopkinsmedicine.org*.

A Double Whammy for Skin Cancer

Exercise and coffee may help to fight off skin cancer. Skin cancer develops in cells whose DNA has been damaged by UV radiation—but damaged cells do often die before they become malignant. The death rate of precancerous skin cells in mice that received exercise and oral caffeine was nearly 400% greater than in mice that had neither exercise nor caffeine.

Allan Conney, PhD, director of the Susan Lehman Cullman Laboratory for Cancer Research, Rutgers, The State University of New Jersey, Piscataway, and coauthor of a study published in *Proceedings of the National Academy of Sciences.*

Green Tea Combats Skin Cancer

Polyphenols, a type of antioxidant found in green tea, protect skin from the sun's damaging ultraviolet radiation and help prevent the formation of skin tumors.

Best: Drink five to six cups of green tea a day—the fresher, the better.

Fresh green tea leaves have a light yellow or green color. A brownish color indicates that the tea has undergone oxidation, which destroys antioxidants. Tea bags and loose leaves are better than instant and bottled teas.

Santosh Katiyar, PhD, associate professor of dermatology, University of Alabama, Birmingham, and leader of a study of green tea and skin tumor development in mice, published in *The Journal of Nutritional Biochemistry.*

Pancreatic Cancer Prevention

Antioxidants may help to decrease pancreatic cancer risk.

A recent finding: In the analysis of dietary data for 183,518 men and women, those who had the highest overall intake of *flavonols* (antioxidant compounds)—found in such foods as black tea, onions and apples—had a 23% lower risk for pancreatic cancer than those who had the lowest intake.

Theory: Flavonols help eliminate unhealthy cells that may develop into pancreatic cancer.

Self-defense: Aim to eat several weekly servings of flavonol-rich foods.

Ute Nöthlings, PhD, researcher, German Institute of Human Nutrition, Potsdam-Rehbruecke, Nuthetal, Germany.

Soda Warning

Reduce risk for pancreatic cancer by cutting back on soda and other sugary beverages. People who drink regular soda at least twice a day have a 90% greater risk of developing pancreatic cancer than people who don't drink soda at all.

Self-defense: Drink no more than one serving of soda a day, and limit refined sugars.

Research from the Karolinska Institutet in Sweden, reported in *Health,* 2100 Lakeshore Dr., Birmingham, Alabama 35209, *www.health.com.*

Cut Back on Bacon

The more bacon you eat, the higher your risk for stomach cancer. Bacon and other processed meats, such as sausage, hot dogs, salami, ham and smoked or cured meat, contain excessive amounts of salt, which can damage the gastric mucosa and may increase susceptibility to carcinogenic substances. Most varieties also contain nitrates and/or nitrites, which can be converted to carcinogenic nitrosamines in the stomach.

Susanna Larsson, MSc, nutrition epidemiology division, Karolinska Institutet, Stockholm, Sweden, and leader of a review of 15 studies on stomach cancer, published in *Journal of the National Cancer Institute.*

Beware the Beef...and Poultry and Pork

Timothy C. Birdsall, ND, vice president of integrative medicine for the Cancer Treatment Centers of America, a national network of cancer care facilities, *www.cancercenter.com*. Based in Zion, Illinois, he is the coauthor of *How to Prevent and Treat Cancer with Natural Medicine* (Riverhead).

A diet high in meat and poultry increases cancer risk. *Here is why and what you can do to protect yourself...*

•**Sedentary farm animals tend to have more body fat than wild or free-range animals.** High-fat meat and poultry contain more *arachidonic acid,* a fatty acid that promotes cell-damaging inflammation.

•**Cattle often are fed hormones to make them bigger.** When we eat their meat, we ingest residual hormones that may stimulate cancer growth.

•**Preserved, cured and smoked meats—** such as hot dogs, ham, bacon, salami and turkey that's smoked—contain preservatives called nitrites, which the body can convert into carcinogenic nitrosamines.

•**Grilling meat or poultry allows fat to drip onto coals,** forming carcinogenic *polycyclic aromatic hydrocarbons* (PAHs)—which smoke then deposits onto the food.

TO DECREASE
YOUR RISK OF CANCER

•**Choose meats and poultry labeled "free-range,"** which generally contain less fat.

•**To avoid hormones, opt for poultry or pork** (the USDA prohibits hormone use in these animals)...or buy beef labeled "hormone-free."

•**Select nitrite-free brands of deli meats,** hot dogs and bacon.

•**When grilling, stick to vegetables,** which do not form PAHs. If you do grill meat, cut off charred bits.

•**Limit serving sizes of meat and poultry to three or four ounces—**about the size of a woman's palm.

Playing the Harmonica Promotes Lung Health

Blowing in and out of the harmonica lowers air pressure in the airways and expands the air sacs in the lungs, reducing the risk that they will constrict or collapse, as occurs in patients with asthma or emphysema. It also forces you to frequently change the pace and depth of your breath, which strengthens the diaphragm (a muscle separating the lungs from the abdomen).

If you have asthma, chronic bronchitis or emphysema: Consider learning to play the harmonica.

Dan Hamner, MD, a physiatrist and sports medicine physician, New York City.

Fish Oil for MS

Fish oil may benefit multiple sclerosis (MS) patients. MS is a neurological disorder. Symptoms include weakness, pain and vision loss.

Recent finding: MS patients who took just over two teaspoons daily of fish oil containing omega-3 fatty acids had lower levels of an inflammatory blood protein that is often higher in MS patients.

Lynne Shinto, ND, MPH, assistant professor, department of neurology, Oregon Health & Science University, Portland, and principal investigator of a study presented at a meeting of the American Association of Naturopathic Physicians.

Coffee for Gout

Coffee has been shown to reduce risk of gout in men.

Recent study: Men who drank four to five cups of coffee a day had a 40% lower risk of gout than men who drank none. Men who drank six or more cups daily had a 59% decreased risk.

Reason: Gout—a painful inflammatory disease that's characterized by attacks of arthritis—is caused by excessive buildup of uric acid. Coffee tends to lower uric acid levels.

Hyon K. Choi, MD, DrPH, associate professor, department of rheumatology, University of British Columbia, Vancouver, Canada, and the leader of a study of 45,869 men, published in *Arthritis & Rheumatism*.

The Arthritis Fix Few People Use

Kate Lorig, RN, DrPH, director of the Patient Education Research Center at the Stanford University School of Medicine, and coauthor of *The Arthritis Helpbook* (Da Capo) and *Living a Healthy Life with Chronic Conditions* (Bull).

A ll too often, people with arthritis give up activities that they enjoy because of their pain and stiffness. That is unfortunate—and usually unnecessary.

WHAT YOU CAN DO

Most doctors remind arthritis sufferers that exercise is necessary to decrease the discomfort associated with the condition. Still, many people who suffer from arthritis "overprotect" affected joints. This is a truly dangerous approach because their joints don't get the circulation and nutrients they require, and their muscles atrophy. Without strong muscles to stabilize the body and act as shock absorbers, the joints are more vulnerable to damage.

Helpful: Start with whatever amount of physical activity, such as walking or bicycling, you can do now, even if that means only one minute every hour or five minutes twice a day. Perform the activity four or five times weekly, increasing your time by about 10% every couple of weeks. If at any point you feel worse after you exercise than you did before, cut back and wait a week before increasing your time again.

Maintaining a healthy weight also is crucial to managing arthritis pain. If you are overweight, losing just five to 15 pounds can significantly reduce knee osteoarthritis pain as well as improve overall flexibility and mobility.

Helpful: If you need to lose weight, try the "200-a-day" plan. By eliminating just 200 calories daily through diet and/or exercise, the average person will lose about 20 pounds in a year. To reduce your daily intake by 200 calories, skip one slice of bread and take a 20-minute walk, for example...or eat two fewer cookies.

THE TOOL THAT TOO FEW PEOPLE USE

There is one other approach that many arthritis sufferers overlook. At the Patient Education Research Center at Stanford University School of Medicine, we've now helped thousands of arthritis sufferers achieve increased mobility and less physical discomfort with our six-week "self-management" program that teaches problem-solving strategies that can be used in a variety of situations. In addition to self-management techniques, the program includes exercise and diet strategies as well as the use of arthritis medications.*

Several randomized studies have shown that people who follow our program for at least four months experience less pain and disability, have fewer visits to doctors and enjoy greater quality of life than arthritis patients who have not participated in the program.

What's the secret? People who become good "self-managers" of arthritis problems learn how to work around all the physical limitations that prevent them from activities they enjoy. Whether you want to walk the beach, climb up the stairs to your friend's front door or visit your sister in Chicago, following a self-management program will help you. *Here's how...*

• **Set a specific goal.** Is there something specific you would like to do, but are avoiding because of your arthritis?

Example: I would love to go to the movies, but I worry about sitting for two hours.

• **Pinpoint the obstacles.** What, precisely, is the problem with prolonged sitting? Do you get stiff? Do your knees hurt?

• **Brainstorm possible solutions.** Would it help to sit in an aisle seat, so you can stretch your legs during the movie? Could doing warm-up exercises beforehand and/or bending and stretching your knees during the movie make

*Exercise guides and DVDs, as well as self-help information, are available from the Arthritis Foundation (800-568-4045, *www.arthritis.org*).

a difference? How about changing the angle of your knees by sitting on your jacket...or timing your medication so its effect peaks during the movie? Would you do better at a matinee or early-evening show, when the theater is less crowded?

•**Devise a short-term action strategy.** Find something specific that you can do now to move closer to your goal.

Example: I will practice sitting for 30 minutes, four times this week, at different times of the day to see when I'm most comfortable.

Write down your action plan and post it on your bathroom mirror or any other place where you will see it often. Keep a notebook to record all setbacks and successes. Review your progress and update your action plan weekly. If you are able to sit comfortably for 30 minutes in the afternoon, see if you can extend that time by doing knee exercises before or during sitting.

•**Test different approaches.** In many cases, a combination of solutions will be most effective. While simply choosing a matinee, for example, may not be enough to get you comfortably through a two-hour movie, you may find that you are able to enjoy the cinema if you attend an early-afternoon show, take your medication an hour beforehand, use a warm pack on your knees and sit in an aisle seat so you can periodically stroll to the back of the theater.

OTHER WAYS TO BEAT ARTHRITIS

Arthritis pain and stiffness often interfere not only with the things you would like to do, but also the things you have to do. With a little ingenuity, however, you can reduce your discomfort.

Example: Bulky handles (about one inch in diameter) are much easier to grasp than narrow handles when using tableware, pens, pencils, kitchen utensils and tools. Less tension is required to maintain your grasp on a bulky handle, so it's easier to hold if your hands are weak or your fingers won't close all the way.

Helpful: To modify all your existing utensil handles, wrap them with foam pipe-insulation tubing (available at most hardware stores). Tubing with a three-eighths inch to three-quarter inch diameter opening usually provides a good fit. It's inexpensive and can be cut to size with a knife or scissors.

Other approaches...

•**To save your hands from painful wringing of a dishcloth, use a sponge instead—** the water can be easily squeezed out by putting the sponge in the sink and pressing on it with your palm.

•**To avoid the sometimes painful movements needed to towel dry, put on a terrycloth robe** after showering to absorb much of the water.

•**Put small laundry items (socks, underwear) in mesh bags** (available at home-goods stores) for easier retrieval from the washer.

•**To avoid morning stiffness, keep joints warm at night** with a lightweight electric blanket. Or sleep inside a sleeping bag—it will turn with you, preventing cold air pockets, and keep you warmer than a blanket.

•**Use a large spatula to tuck in sheets when making the bed.**

Say No to Joint Surgery

Rebecca Shannonhouse, editor of *Bottom Line/Health*, Boardroom Inc., 281 Tresser Blvd., Stamford, Connecticut 06901.

With the demand for knee and hip replacements increasing so rapidly, by 2030 there might not be enough surgeons to perform these operations, researchers have recently reported.

Why are so many Americans receiving joint replacements now? Some of the explanation is the rampant use of *naproxen* (Aleve) and other anti-inflammatory medicine, according to Joseph Weisberg, PhD, a physical therapist and dean of Touro College's School of Health in Bay Shore, New York. These drugs temporarily relieve joint pain, but they mask—rather than eliminate—the underlying dysfunction that irritates the tissues of the joint.

Inflammation is a healthy response to trauma affecting the joint, explains Dr. Weisberg. It enables cells that repair damaged cartilage and other tissues to accumulate at the site and heal the tissues. Stopping inflammation with drugs prevents normal healing—and permits chronic irritation that eventually can destroy the joints.

Better approach: For immediate relief, apply a cold pack to the affected area (from 15 to 20 minutes twice daily). For the long-term effect of accelerating joint repair, perform stretching exercises to enable the joint to operate through the full range of motion without further injury. A typical stretch (held for 30 seconds and performed two to six times daily)…

For knee pain (front of knee): Lie on your stomach…reach back and grip your ankle…pull your heel as close to the buttocks as possible without causing pain.

As soon as you have joint pain, consult your doctor or a physical therapist about stretching exercises. This approach could allow your joints to last a lifetime.

More from Rebecca Shannonhouse…

Foods That Aren't So Nutritious After All

If a food label touts its product as "100% natural" or "100% whole grain," you might assume that all the ingredients are nutritious. But that's not always the case.

For instance, it's no surprise to find the sweetener high-fructose corn syrup (HFCS) in supersweet sodas, but many people are shocked to learn that it is also found in many food products that are promoted as healthful.

Examples: Some whole-grain breads and cereals, granola bars, yogurts, "low-fat, low-cholesterol" cookies and many brands of fruit juice. Manufacturers often use HFCS because it is usually much cheaper than sugar.

Some scientists have speculated that HFCS (derived from corn) might provide different biological effects than regular sugar (derived from sugarcane or sugar beets), making it more likely to trigger diabetes, obesity and other health problems.

While there are clear concerns about HFCS, there's no conclusive evidence at this point that it is worse than table sugar (sucrose), says Peter J.

Havel, PhD, a nutrition researcher at the University of California at Davis. "Both table sugar and HFCS contain similar amounts of fructose, the component that is considered to have potentially adverse effects," explains Dr. Havel. "Results from studies comparing both types of sugar suggest that overconsumption of either could lead to higher levels of fats in the blood, known as triglycerides, and possibly weight gain."

Americans consume an average of about 85 pounds of sweeteners—both HFCS and white sugar—a year. We would all do better if we limited our consumption of foods made with any added sugar.

Whole Grains Help Inflammatory Disorders

When researchers analyzed eating habits of 27,312 women over a 17-year period, they found that those who ate 19 or more servings weekly of whole grains, including oatmeal and brown rice, were 34% less likely to have an inflammatory condition, such as rheumatoid arthritis or heart disease, when they died than those who rarely or never ate whole-grain foods.

Theory: Phytochemicals in whole-grain foods neutralize free radicals (molecules that can lead to disease-causing inflammation).

Self-defense: Eat at least three servings daily of whole-grain foods.

David R. Jacobs, Jr., PhD, professor, division of epidemiology and community health, University of Minnesota, Minneapolis.

Vitamin C for the Knee

Vitamin C may help to stem arthritis of the knee.

Recent finding: In a study of 293 healthy men and women, those who had higher levels of dietary vitamin C and ate the most fruit (any type) had fewer bone marrow lesions (a marker for osteoarthritis) than those who consumed the least amount. Researchers think antioxidants may boost bone mineral density.

To reduce your risk for osteoarthritis of the knee: Eat five to nine half-cup servings daily of fruits and vegetables.

Yuanyuan Wang, PhD, research fellow, department of epidemiology and preventive medicine, Monash University, Melbourne, Australia.

Tea Builds Bones

In one study of 1,500 healthy women (ages 70 to 85), hip-bone density was 2.8% higher in women who drank caffeinated or caffeine-free black tea, compared with people who did not drink tea. Tea drinkers consumed an average of three cups daily.

Theory: Flavonoid antioxidants in black tea may stimulate production of new cells that build bone.

Self-defense: Drinking black tea daily may help protect your bones as you age.

If your doctor has advised you not to drink caffeine, opt for caffeine-free black tea.

Amanda Devine, PhD, senior lecturer, nutrition program, Edith Cowan University, Joondalup, Australia.

What Your Fingernails Tell About Your Health

Jamison Starbuck, ND, a naturopathic physician in family practice and lecturer at the University of Montana, both in Missoula. She is past president of the American Association of Naturopathic Physicians and a contributing editor to *The Alternative Advisor: The Complete Guide to Natural Therapies and Alternative Treatments* (Time Life).

Since the time of Hippocrates, most doctors have examined a patient's fingernails during routine physical exams. That's because the fingernail is an important window through which an astute physician can see signs of some diseases and even clues about a person's nutritional status, lifestyle and emotional health.

Fingernails should be strong, with a light pink color to the nail bed (the skin on which the nail rests). A few white spots and/or lines are usually due to injury to the nail bed and are harmless. However, if you have any of the conditions described below, see your physician for an evaluation and treatment, such as the use of medication and/or supplements. *What to look for...*

• **Brittle, dry, splitting nails,** with deep longitudinal (from the cuticle up to the fingernail tip) ridges, can indicate hypothyroidism (an underactive thyroid). It also can be a sign of a mineral deficiency, particularly calcium or zinc.

• **Nails loosening or separating from the nail bed** can indicate hyperthyroidism (an overactive thyroid). This condition also can be a sign of psoriasis (a chronic skin disease) or a reaction to synthetic nails or a nail injury.

• **Nail pitting (or deep depressions)** could indicate psoriasis, psoriatic arthritis (a condition with symptoms of both arthritis and psoriasis) or chronic dermatitis (skin rash). Nail pitting also can be seen in people with *alopecia areata,* an autoimmune disease that causes sudden patchy hair loss, usually in the scalp or beard.

• **Nails curved around enlarged fingertips (known as clubbing)** can be a harmless condition that runs in families, or it can be a sign of low oxygen in the blood, a common marker for chronic lung disease.

• **Hollowed or dipped nails (known as spoon nails)** are often associated with an iron deficiency. A three-year-old boy I recently saw had 10 tiny scooped-out fingernails that could have each contained a drop of water.

• **Opaque (white) nails with a dark band at the fingertip (known as Terry's nails)** can be a harmless sign of aging, or it can indicate cardiac disease, particularly congestive heart failure.

• **Yellow nails** can be due to nicotine stains, bacterial infection, fungus in the nail and nail bed, chronic bronchitis or lymphedema (swelling and congestion of the lymph system).

• **Bitten nails** can indicate anxiety, severe stress or compulsive behavior.

The best way to keep your nails healthy is to keep them clean, trim and warm. Don't pick at hangnails. Clip them. Limit nail polish remover use to twice a month (it dries nails and makes them more brittle). Protect your nails from harsh chemicals by wearing gloves and avoiding synthetic nails. With normal growth, an injured nail will be replaced in about four to six months.

Hidden Risk for Eye Disease

In an eight-year study of 3,977 people, those who ate the most carbohydrates with a high glycemic index (a measurement of how quickly a food boosts blood sugar levels)—such as cake, cookies or white bread—had a 40% higher risk for macular degeneration (a retinal disease that destroys vision) than those who ate the least.

Theory: Such foods cause cellular damage to the retina (the light-sensitive membrane in the back of the eye).

Allen Taylor, PhD, director, laboratory for nutrition and vision research, Tufts University, Boston.

A Chocolate Smile

A recent study has shown that a cocoa extract found naturally in chocolate hardens tooth enamel and may prevent decay. A cocoa-spiked toothpaste may be available within four years.

Tulane University, New Orleans, *tulane.edu.*

Now, Hear This!

A combination of nutrients (vitamins A, C, E and magnesium) may protect the ears. After laboratory animals were exposed to five hours of loud noise, those given the nutrients for five days showed the least amount of hearing loss.

Free Radical Biology & Medicine, Indianapolis, Indiana, *www.sfrbm.org.*

Depression Linked to Low Folate Levels

In a recent study, people with low levels of the nutrient folate (folic acid) had as much as a 55% higher risk of depression.

Self-defense: Individuals who have a personal or family history of depression should have their blood tested for folate.

If levels are low: Have folate-rich foods—breakfast cereals, leafy green vegetables, lentils, dried beans, liver and wheat germ—and take a daily multivitamin with 400 micrograms (mcg) of folic acid.

Mark Stengler, ND, a naturopathic physician and director of La Jolla Whole Health Clinic, La Jolla, California. He is also author of the newsletter *Bottom Line Natural Healing*, available at *www.DrStengler.com.*

Depression and Diet

In a recent study, researchers took blood samples from 43 subjects and learned that those who had significantly higher levels of omega-6s (found in refined vegetable oils, such as corn oil) compared with omega-3s (found in cold-water fish, such as salmon or trout...walnuts...and flaxseeds) reported more symptoms of depression than those who had lower levels.

Theory: Omega-6s can cause chronic inflammation, which has been linked to depression, while omega-3s have anti-inflammatory effects.

Self-defense: Have at least two three-ounce servings weekly of cold-water fish or take a supplement containing omega-3s.

Jan Kiecolt-Glaser, PhD, professor and director, division of health psychology, Ohio State University College of Medicine, Columbus.

Get Dirty, Be Happy!

A bacterium that lives in soil might increase brain levels of *serotonin* and improve people's mood. Rodents that were treated with the *Mycobacterium vaccae* had behavioral changes that resembled those caused by antidepressant drugs.

University of Bristol, England, *www.bristol.ac.uk.*

Dirty Medicine?

A French clay has recently been found to kill off disease-causing bacteria, including the dangerous *methicillin-resistant Staphylococcus aureus* (MRSA).

Geological Society of America in Boulder, Colorado, *www.geosociety.org.*

Better Pneumonia Protection

When 617 nursing home residents were given daily supplements containing 50% of the recommended dietary allowance (RDA) of essential vitamins and minerals (including zinc), patients with low blood levels of zinc at the end of the one-year study had a higher incidence of pneumonia than the patients with normal zinc levels.

Theory: Zinc is essential to the function of cells in the immune system, which helps to fight infection.

If you are age 65 or older: Ask your doctor if you should take a multivitamin containing the RDA of zinc (11 milligrams [mg] for men and 8 mg for women).

Simin Nikbin Meydani, DVM, PhD, associate director, Jean Mayer USDA Human Nutrition Research Center on Aging, Tufts University, Boston.

How to Eat Fruits and Vegetables Safely

Marion Nestle, PhD, the Paulette Goddard professor of nutrition, food studies and public health at New York University in New York City. She is the author or editor of five books, including *What to Eat* (North Point).

In the wake of a *Salmonella* or *E. coli* outbreak from contaminated fruits or vegetables, many Americans just stop eating the offending fruit or vegetable or become more rigorous in washing it. However, there are probably few people who adopt long-term strategies to protect themselves against dangerous contaminants that could be found in any fruits or vegetables.

WHY OUR FOOD IS AT RISK

Concern about safety should not prevent you from eating fruits and vegetables—as the health benefits of produce far outweigh the risks. Nevertheless, health officials estimate that each year, foodborne bacteria, parasites and viruses sicken 76 million Americans, resulting in 325,000 hospitalizations and 5,000 deaths.

Contaminated fresh produce is the number-one cause of individual cases of foodborne illnesses, according to the Washington, DC–based consumer-advocacy group Center for Science in the Public Interest.

In the US, the safety of fruits and vegetables falls under the jurisdiction of the Food and Drug Administration (FDA). However, in general, less than 2% of imported food products is inspected by the FDA, and domestic produce is rarely inspected at all.

The FDA and US Department of Agriculture (USDA) guidelines for the safe handling of produce—known as "Good Agricultural Practices"—suggest methods to help prevent contamination with dangerous microorganisms from manure, water, soil or unhygienic food handlers.

However, these guidelines are voluntary—the fruit and vegetable companies do not have to follow them. What's more, the reality is that the FDA does not possess the financial resources or personnel to effectively monitor industry practices or the safety of the 741 pounds of produce that are consumed, on average, by every person in the US each year.

Fruits and vegetables are grown in what the FDA typically calls "nonsterile environments"—that is, they grow in dirt. If they come in contact with feces of grazing cattle, wild animals or birds, farm workers or any other source, they can become contaminated with potentially harmful microorganisms. This is clearly unappetizing, and fecal contamination can cause health problems if the microorganisms are dangerous types.

BEST SELF-DEFENSE STRATEGIES

Most produce is safe to eat, but regardless of where you shop, there's no way to be 100% certain that the fruits and vegetables you're buying are free of contamination from dangerous bacteria and microbes.

To do the best you can to protect yourself and your family from unsafe produce, *follow all these simple steps...*

• **Be sure to remove the outer leaves of leafy greens.** That's the area that is most likely to come in contact with manure or other sources of dangerous contamination while leafy vegetables are growing in the soil or processed after harvesting.

A caution: The FDA has not required food safety procedures to be followed for most produce, and this includes the leafy greens, such as spinach and lettuce, as well as carrots.

But, sprouts are an exception. They must be grown under strict safety rules, and problems with them have decreased since those precautions went into effect.

• **Store produce in the refrigerator, and wash it before eating.** Harmful microorganisms can multiply on fresh fruits and vegetables, especially when they are transported great distances, sit in supermarket produce bins for extended periods and are not kept cold enough.

Best way to wash produce: Thoroughly rinse produce under running cool tap water. In addition, carefully scrub firm-skinned fruits and vegetables, such as apples and cucumbers, with a clean vegetable brush. Make sure to clean the vegetable brush, utensils and other kitchen tools in hot water (or the dishwasher) after each time you use them.

Caution: It is a good idea to wash bagged lettuce, spinach and all other vegetables—even

if the bag says the contents have been "triple washed." If the bags were not kept cold enough, bacteria could have quickly multiplied inside of the package.

To be extra safe, rinse off the inedible rinds of fruits, including cantaloupe and avocados. If microbes are on the rind, the fruit inside can become contaminated when the rind is pierced by a knife.

Helpful: Don't splurge on expensive fruit and vegetable washes sold in supermarket produce departments. There is zero evidence that these special washes are any more effective than chlorinated tap water.

Important: Although washing helps protect against foodborne illnesses from produce, the only way to guarantee that fruits and vegetables do not contain harmful microbes is to boil, bake or peel them.

• **Buy certified organic.** Studies show that certified organic produce, which is grown with composted manure instead of chemical fertilizers, is no more likely to be contaminated with microbes than conventionally cultivated produce. That is because, to receive organic certification, farmers must adhere to strict rules to ensure that harmful microbes in manure are destroyed (typically through a high-heat decontamination process). Growers of conventional produce are not required to follow such rules.

Organic produce also is a good option if you want to avoid the synthetic pesticides and other chemicals that are typically used to kill insects in conventionally grown crops. These chemicals do not reduce your risk for contamination with bacteria and other microbes.

In addition, some research shows that organic produce may be superior to the conventionally grown produce in its nutritional value.

Important: When buying organic produce, be sure that it is labeled with a "USDA organic" seal. This means that the producers follow organic growing rules established by the USDA Organic Standards Board and they have been inspected by agencies licensed by the USDA to make sure the rules are followed.

Because organic produce is usually more expensive than nonorganic varieties, most people don't buy organic all of the time. The Environmental Working Group (or EWG), a Washington, DC–based, nonprofit environmental research organization, recommends buying organic varieties of produce whose nonorganic counterparts are typically highest in pesticides.

Best to buy organic: Peaches, apples, sweet bell peppers, celery, nectarines, strawberries, cherries, pears, imported grapes, spinach, lettuce and potatoes. For a list of other fruits and vegetables evaluated by the EWG, go to the group's Web site, *www.foodnews.org.*

• **Buy from local farmers.** When produce is shipped from far away and/or it stays in the supermarket for long periods prior to being sold and eaten, there is more time for microbes to multiply.

Example: If you live on the East Coast, some of the produce in your supermarket sits on a truck for 10 days to two weeks after being harvested in California.

Locally grown foods are fresher and do taste better, but there are no guarantees that they are safe. Like any produce, they can come in contact with harmful microbes in the field or during handling, so washing is still essential. And as always, the only way to ensure complete safety is to cook the foods before eating them.

Important: If you grow your own produce, use a fence to prevent pets and wild animals from defecating in your garden, and be sure to wash everything that you've grown.

If you go to pick-your-own farms for apples, berries, pumpkins or other seasonal produce, be sure to wash these foods, too.

Canned vs. Fresh

Canned vegetables can be just as nutritious as their fresher counterparts. Vegetables are canned during the harvest, when nutrients are at their peak, so some canned varieties may have even more nutrients.

Best: To get a mix of the essential nutrients, purchase canned, fresh and frozen vegetables.

Opt for low-sodium versions, or rinse canned produce to reduce sodium.

Christine Bruhn, PhD, specialist in the cooperative extension, food science and technology at the University of California, Davis, and leader of a study of canned vegetables, published in Journal of the Science of Food and Agriculture.

Buy the Right Olive Oil

The brand of olive oil you buy is far less important than making sure that you choose only *extra-virgin* olive oil. Because it is extracted from olives without the use of chemicals, extra-virgin olive oil is the least processed. For this reason, it contains the highest levels of disease-combatting antioxidants. Whenever possible, it's also smart to buy *organic* extra-virgin olive oil. This ensures that you are not consuming toxic pesticides. And, do choose an olive oil in a dark glass bottle, which helps prevent the oil from generating toxic free radicals and fats as a result of light exposure.

Mark Hyman, MD, a board-certified family medicine physician in private practice, Lenox, Massachusetts, and the author of Ultrametabolism *(Scribner).*

Spinach Is Not a Good Source of Iron

Spinach contains about as much iron as any green vegetable, but it contains *oxalic acid,* which prevents about 90% of the iron from being absorbed. Spinach is high in vitamins A and E, as well as many antioxidants, including beta-carotene. Good sources of iron are clams, liver and fortified cereals. Also, consuming vitamin C at the same time as iron-rich foods can help increase iron absorption.

Reza Hakkak, PhD, chairman, department of dietetics and nutrition, University of Arkansas for Medical Sciences, Little Rock.

6

Very Personal

Reclaiming Desire: Good Sex at Any Age

Even though we live in a culture that sometimes seems to be obsessed with sex, we are not always very knowledgeable about sexuality. And one of the worst myths in our society is the idea that sexual desire—or libido—always fades with age.

Our sexuality does change as we grow older, but the reality is that we can stay as tuned in to our senses and remain as sensual as we want to be. For both men and women, sexuality and libido can stay an important and enjoyable part of life.

UNDERSTANDING LIBIDO

Sexual desire differs between men and women. That seems obvious, but it's actually a major source of misunderstanding in our culture. For a woman, a healthy libido tends to be experienced as being receptive. She responds to her partner, but her libido is less assertive. Over time in long-term relationships, women tend to become less spontaneous in their desire and less interested in initiating sexual activity.

Men, on the other hand, do generally remain more willing to initiate sex throughout a long-term relationship. That's a very basic difference between men and women, and it's important to understand—because a woman might misinterpret her response and think that she has low libido, when in fact she's perfectly normal and is responding as a healthy woman would.

Similarly, as a man ages, his ability to have sex (though not his desire) changes. The quality of his erections may diminish, and he may not be able to have an erection as frequently as when he was younger. These changes are normal, but they can cause a lot of distress.

Important: There's a big difference between low desire and genuine dysfunction. Psychologists do recognize a disorder called hypoactive

Marianne Brandon, PhD, codirector, The Sexual Wellness Center, Annapolis, Maryland. She is coauthor, with Andrew Goldstein, MD, of *Reclaiming Desire: 4 Keys to Finding Your Lost Libido* (Rodale). Her Web site is *www.wellminds.com*.

101

sexual desire disorder. In both men and women, it's characterized by a lack of interest in sex and a lack of sexual fantasy. The disorder must cause marked distress to be considered diagnosable. And even then, this is a controversial diagnosis. Some professionals believe it's motivated by drug companies that want to have a disorder that can be diagnosed and treated with prescription drugs, such as supplemental testosterone. Many feel that there have not yet been enough high-quality scientific studies to confirm that the disorder affects as many people as some of the researchers claim.

THE PHYSICAL PIECE
OF THE PUZZLE

The physiological aspects of sex and desire are just one small piece of what makes up our experience of our sexuality. Our society is very focused on all the physical aspects of sex, but if you're in a loving relationship and you want to expand intimacy, having a high libido isn't the primary requirement.

When two individuals share intimacy—their hearts and bodies—they will create something beautiful. That intimacy doesn't have to rely on intercourse and orgasm. When the sexual patterns that used to work for you start to change, as they naturally do as we age, it's time to look into other aspects of how to give and receive love well with your body.

But if your body isn't healthy, it's hard to enjoy any kind of sex life. *Many things can interfere with your libido…*

•**Sleep deprivation.** Someone who is tired from lack of sleep, too much travel, chronic illness or some other reason, is far less likely to be interested in sex.

•**Poor diet.** Not eating right can cause fatigue, digestive upsets and other problems that interfere with your sex drive. Being obese can also cause sexual difficulties.

•**Medications.** Some common prescription medications, including the antidepressants and blood pressure drugs, can interfere with sexual pleasure by altering blood flow to the genital area. Antidepressant medicines, such as *fluoxetine* (Prozac), *citalopram* (Celexa) and *sertraline* (Zoloft), can also hurt the libido. Sometimes just reducing the dosage or changing to a different medication helps. Don't hesitate to have a frank discussion with your doctor if you think that a drug you take is impacting your sex life.

•**Chronic conditions, including diabetes, arthritis and high blood pressure,** can affect your libido by interfering with blood flow or making sex uncomfortable. There are ways to work around these medical challenges.

Unfortunately, many doctors don't know much about this. Also, you and your doctor may be too embarrassed to discuss the topic. But don't give up on sex! Consider consulting a sex therapist instead.

•**Menopause.** The hormonal changes during menopause can make intercourse physically uncomfortable for women. This problem can easily be solved with lubricants, such as K-Y jelly and Vagisil, and, when appropriate, the use of hormones to relieve vaginal dryness. Discuss this issue with your doctor.

EMOTIONAL ASPECTS

When a man or woman is feeling depressed, anxious or stressed, he/she is unlikely to be interested in sex or to feel a desire to be close. In fact, a reduced libido is one diagnostic indicator of depression.

When serious depression is ruled out, however, we can still have anxiety and negative feelings about our bodies. Our culture tells us that to be "sexy," bodies should look a certain way, but very few of us actually ever looked like that, and we certainly don't look that way when we get older.

Being comfortable with our bodies and avoiding unrealistic expectations helps avoid a lot of emotional anguish.

Understanding what arouses your desire—and what doesn't—is an important part of improving your libido. This means exploring your own sexuality and sharing that knowledge frankly with your partner.

By learning what you enjoy most and communicating it in an emotionally open way, you increase your own enjoyment of sex. And when you start to enjoy something more, you become more interested in participating in it and initiating it.

Our culture tells us that as people age, they lose all their sensuality and sexuality, but that's simply not true. We don't lose the need for intimate contact, we don't lose the need for touch and we don't have to lose our sexual desire. Research shows us that people can be sexually active for as long as they want to be.

As we get older and our bodies change, making love can be a fabulous way to feel pleasure in our bodies and have a sense of growing and expanding.

SPIRITUAL FULFILLMENT

Spiritual contentment is what turns sex into making love. I'm referring to the experience of a deeper and more profound sense of life and also of a deeper and more profound connection to yourself and your partner. That is achieved through an open heart—by living more fully in a loving way.

Spiritual contentment in a relationship can be nurtured in part simply by slowing down and taking more time for each other. Spending quality time together outside of sex, for instance, will help partners share life goals and get to know each other at a deeper level.

Older adults often have more time to experiment with this way of thinking because they're at a point in life where they're less focused on schedules and the rat race. They can relax more into the experience of being loving outside of sex as well as during sex, and they can more fully experience giving and receiving.

Sex Really Is Good for Your Heart

A recent finding showed that having sex two to three times per week can reduce risk of heart disease and stroke by up to 50% and increase life expectancy by three years. Sex burns calories, lowers blood pressure, boosts immunity and releases heart-protective hormones.

Health, 2100 Lakeshore Dr., Birmingham, Alabama 35209, *www.health.com*.

Sex Can Ease Migraine Pain

Women who have sex when they feel a migraine coming on experience less head and neck pain, fatigue and moodiness. In one finding, almost one-third of women who had sex at the start of a migraine reported reduced symptoms...and for 12%, sex stopped the migraine completely.

Possible reason: Sex and orgasm boost levels of the pleasure hormone serotonin—which is known to be low in migraine sufferers.

James Couch, MD, PhD, professor and chair of neurology, University of Oklahoma Health Sciences Center, Oklahoma City, and leader of a study of 82 women with migraines, published in *Headache: The Journal of Head and Face Pain*.

Iron Boosts Fertility

Iron increases a woman's chance of becoming pregnant.

Recent finding: Women who took daily iron supplements had, on average, a 40% lower risk of infertility caused by ovulation problems than those who did not take iron supplements. The higher the dosage of iron, the lower the risk for infertility. Women who took the highest doses —41 milligrams (mg) a day—reduced their risk of infertility by 62%.

Caution: Take iron supplements only under a doctor's supervision. Iron overload can cause damage to internal organs.

Jorge E. Chavarro, MD, ScD, research fellow, department of nutrition, Harvard School of Public Health, Boston, and the lead author of an eight-year study of women ages 24 to 42, published in *Obstetrics & Gynecology*.

More from Dr. Jorge Chavarro...

If You Are Trying To Conceive...

Trans fats may increase the risk for infertility among women.

Recent finding: Women who obtained as little as 2% of total calories from trans fats instead of monounsaturated fats were twice as likely to have ovulation-related fertility problems. Every 2% increase in trans fat consumption increased ovulation-related infertility by 73%.

Trans fats are found mainly in commercially baked and fried products.

Self-defense: Be extra vigilant about avoiding trans fats if you are of childbearing age and are planning to have children.

Heavy Period Help

The best treatment for heavy periods is usually a hormone-releasing intrauterine device (IUD). Other treatments include endometrial ablation (the removal of the lining of the uterus) or hysterectomy, but studies show that women who choose the IUD are as satisfied as women who opt for a surgical technique.

Also: The IUD has no long-term effects on conception. Pregnancy is not safe after ablation and not possible after having a hysterectomy.

Jonathan Scher, MD, obstetrician/gynecologist in private practice, New York City.

Hearing Loss and HRT

Women on hormone replacement therapy (HRT) may suffer hearing loss.

Recent finding: Women who took progestin —the most common form of HRT—had a 10% to 30% higher risk of hearing loss than women taking estrogen alone or not using HRT at all.

If you are taking progestin: Have your hearing checked every six months.

Robert D. Frisina, PhD, University of Rochester Medical Center, Rochester, New York, and senior author of a study of 124 women, published in *The Proceedings of the National Academy of Sciences.*

Flaxseed for Hot Flashes

Flaxseed may help to reduce hot flashes in menopausal women.

Recent study: 29 menopausal women cut the frequency of hot flashes in half by eating 20 grams (g) (two tablespoons) of ground flaxseed twice daily for six weeks.

Theory: *Lignans,* estrogen-emulating antioxidants found in flaxseed, may relieve hot flashes.

If you have hot flashes: Add two tablespoons of ground flaxseed to your yogurt or cereal once daily for two weeks, then increase to twice daily.

Sandhya Pruthi, MD, breast health specialist at Mayo Clinic, Rochester, Minnesota.

Help for Excess Body Hair

High levels of free testosterone in women can result in hirsutism, characterized by hair growth on the face, breasts and stomach. In a study, participants drank two cups of spearmint tea daily for five days.

Finding: Spearmint tea may lower levels of free-circulating testosterone.

Caution: People who have gastroesophageal reflux disease (GERD), which is a severe form of heartburn, or who are prone to acute gallstone attacks should not ingest spearmint.

M. Numan Tamer, MD, professor, department of internal medicine, Suleymann Demirel University, Turkey, and leader of a study of 21 hirsute women, published in *Phytotherapy Research.*

Better Overactive Bladder Therapy

In a new study, women with overactive bladder received either acupuncture using acupuncture points targeted for bladder control or general, nontargeted acupuncture once weekly for four weeks.

Result: Women who received bladder-specific acupuncture had improved bladder capacity, while the other group showed no change in symptoms.

Theory: Targeted acupuncture decreases the excess nerve stimulation that causes the bladder to feel full even when it is not.

Sandra L. Emmons, MD, associate professor of obstetrics and gynecology, Oregon Health and Sciences University, Portland.

Red Meat Linked to Breast Cancer Risk

Researchers analyzed dietary intake data for 90,659 women over a 12-year period.

Result: Women who ate more than one-and-one-half daily servings of red meat had nearly twice the risk of developing hormone receptor–positive breast cancer (a type of breast cancer fueled by estrogen and progesterone), compared with those who ate three or fewer servings weekly.

Theory: Red meat (including beef, lamb and pork) may contain cancer-causing residues of hormones given to animals raised for meat.

Eunyoung Cho, ScD, assistant professor of medicine, Harvard Medical School, Boston.

Beware of This Common Breakfast Food

In one recent study, postmenopausal women who ate a quarter grapefruit daily increased their risk for breast cancer by as much as 30%. Grapefruit is thought to boost levels of estrogen, a hormone associated with higher risk. This is the first study to link a commonly eaten food to increased breast cancer risk in older women.

Kristine R. Monroe, researcher, department of preventive medicine at Keck School of Medicine, University of Southern California, Los Angeles.

Wide Hips Linked to Breast Cancer

Women are more likely to get breast cancer if their mothers had wide, round hips. This body shape, which indicates high levels of the hormone estrogen, can more than double a daughter's cancer risk in some cases.

Oregon Health & Science University, Portland, *www. ohsu.edu.*

Better Breast Cancer Detection

In a recent study, 969 women who had recently been diagnosed with cancer in one breast but had no abnormalities in the opposite breast (based on mammography and clinical examination) received a magnetic resonance imaging (MRI) scan. In 30 women, these scans revealed opposite-breast malignancies that were missed by the standard testing methods.

Theory: MRI scans evaluate the subtle differences in blood flow of cancerous tissue versus normal tissue.

If you have breast cancer or are at high risk (due to family history): Ask your doctor about receiving an MRI scan in addition to your mammogram. The American Cancer Society is recommending that all high-risk women receive scans and mammograms once a year starting at age 30.

Connie Lehman, MD, PhD, director of radiology, Seattle Cancer Care Alliance.

Better Mammograms

Comparing a new mammogram with previous ones improves accuracy of diagnosis.

Recent finding: When radiologists followed this protocol, the number of false-positive diagnoses declined by 44%.

Self-defense: Provide a radiologist with prior mammogram films whenever possible.

Nico Karssemeijer, PhD, associate professor, department of radiology, Radboud University Nijmegen Medical Center, the Netherlands, and coauthor of a study published in *Radiology*.

More Mammogram Advice

Researchers evaluated the performance of 123 radiologists who interpreted nearly 36,000 mammograms at 72 US medical facilities.

Result: The radiologists who were based at academic medical centers or those who spent at least 20% of their time in breast imaging interpretation were more likely to accurately detect cancers and not as likely to have false-positive findings (incorrectly identifying a mammogram finding as a potential malignancy).

When scheduling a mammogram to evaluate a breast concern (such as a lump): Ask if a breast imaging specialist will be interpreting the results of your mammogram.

Diana Miglioretti, PhD, associate investigator and biostatistician at the Group Health Center for Health Studies, Seattle.

This Breast Cancer Treatment Increases Survival

Women with early-stage breast cancer who took *tamoxifen* over two to three years, then an aromatase inhibitor (AI), such as *anastrazole* (Arimidex) or *letrozole* (Femara), were less likely to have a recurrence than those who kept taking tamoxifen, one study has shown.

Caution: Women taking AIs should be monitored for high cholesterol, musculoskeletal disorders and heart disease.

R. Charles Coombes, MD, PhD, professor, medical oncology, Imperial College, London, and leader of a study of 4,724 women, published in *The Lancet*.

Breast Cancer Surgery Breakthrough

Laura A. Klein, MD, director of breast surgical oncology at St. Barnabus Hospital and an instructor in clinical surgery at Columbia University College of Physicians and Surgeons, both in New York City. Dr. Klein is one of the few surgeons trained in oncoplastic surgery and is an innovator in its continued development.

Traditionally, women whose breast cancers have been treated with lumpectomies (a surgical removal of the tumor that leaves the rest of the breast intact) often had to either live with a breast marred by the procedure…or plan to have reconstructive breast surgery in the future.

Good news: An innovative new approach enables women undergoing lumpectomy to receive cosmetic repair at the same time. The result is a more attractive and natural-looking breast—right away. Called oncoplastic surgery, this technique combines oncology surgery (treatment of cancer) and plastic surgery (reconstruction of the breast).

How it's done: Using a technique called the "advancement flap," the surgeon moves or rotates replacement tissue from the same breast, without detaching it from the original blood supply. While the result is a somewhat smaller breast, the doctor can immediately reshape the other to match so there's no need for further surgery. Usually the patient ends up with a breast lift—a silver lining of sorts. This technique eliminates the need to use implants or relocate tissue from another part of the body.

Who it's for: Oncoplastic surgery is an alternative for many breast cancer patients, even smaller-breasted women who might otherwise have required mastectomy. Also, this approach is particularly advantageous when treating the noninvasive cancer called *ductal carcinoma in situ* (DCIS). This refers to cancer that does not migrate outside the ducts and into the breast tissue, and comprises about 20% of diagnosed breast cancers today. DCIS will radiate from the nipple and may be distributed throughout the ductal system, and can necessitate removal of a substantial amount of breast tissue.

Important: This is a new and emerging technique, and only a limited number of surgeons in this country have experience with it. To learn more or locate a physician who performs this breakthrough surgery, consult with a fellowship-trained breast surgeon or someone whose practice is 100% breast surgery, since he/she is apt to be most current in breast surgery advances.

New Breast Cancer Treatment

A new breast cancer treatment eliminates the need for later radiation. With intraoperative radiation therapy, during surgery to remove the cancerous tissue, a one-time dosage of radiation is given. The procedure adds about one hour to the surgery.

Best for: Women over age 55 with early-stage breast cancer that has not spread.

David McCready, MD, head of Princess Margaret Hospital Breast Cancer Program, Toronto.

Ginkgo Biloba May Cut Ovarian Cancer Risk

In a study of 668 women with ovarian cancer and 721 healthy women, those who took the herbal supplement ginkgo biloba for at least six months (for any reason) were 60% less likely to develop ovarian cancer.

Theory: Ginkgo inhibits *platelet activating factor,* which can stimulate cancer cell growth.

Self-defense: Women with an elevated risk for ovarian cancer (due to a family history, for example) may want to ask their doctors about taking ginkgo biloba.

Caution: Do not use ginkgo if you take a blood thinner.

Daniel W. Cramer, MD, ScD, professor of obstetrics, gynecology and reproductive biology at Brigham and Women's Hospital in Boston.

Pay Attention to These Symptoms!

Ovarian cancer does cause symptoms in early stages. Cancer experts recently agreed on some early common symptoms of the disease, long believed to give no warning until it is far advanced. Ovarian cancer has a 90% cure rate when detected early.

Symptoms to watch out for: Bloating…pelvic or abdominal pain…difficulty eating or feeling full quickly…and feeling a frequent or urgent need to urinate.

A woman who has had any of these symptoms nearly every day for more than two weeks should see her gynecologist.

Barbara Goff, MD, a gynecologic oncologist and researcher at the University of Washington School of Medicine in Seattle, and a member of the Gynecologic Cancer Foundation.

What Doctors Don't Know About Men's Health

Marianne J. Legato, MD, founder of the Partnership for Gender-Specific Medicine at Columbia University and professor of clinical medicine at Columbia's College of Physicians and Surgeons, both in New York City, and adjunct professor of medicine at Johns Hopkins University School of Medicine in Baltimore. The author of *Eve's Rib: The New Science of Gender-Specific Medicine and How It Can Save Your Life* (Harmony), she is a member of the *Bottom Line/Health* Board of Advisers.

Many men joke about the fact that their life expectancy is shorter than a woman's. In the US, the average man dies by age 75 versus 80 for a woman. But it is no laughing matter.

For years, the medical community has been puzzled by the disparity, but researchers are now discovering some viable explanations—and important steps that men can take to protect their health.

GENDER-BASED MEDICINE

It's true that scientific research has historically focused on men—two-thirds of all diseases that affect both men and women have been studied exclusively in men. But as increased resources are now being allocated to studying women's health problems, there are still a number of special risks that affect men. *Some of the most important are...*

DEPRESSION

Only half as many men as women are diagnosed with depression. And, at one time, it was believed that men were less vulnerable to depression because their brain levels of serotonin (a neurotransmitter that influences mood) are 52% higher, on average, than in women.

New thinking: Men probably get depressed as often as women, but they express it differently. For example, men are taught not to cry...not to show emotion...and to be self-reliant. They're less likely than women to admit to depression.

What to do: Men who exhibit "male signs" of depression—becoming less social and more solitary...more prone to excessive drinking or other addictive behaviors...and more irritable or violent—should speak to their doctors about possible treatment.

LOW TESTOSTERONE

In men, levels of testosterone drop by about 1% a year after age 30. Men with lower-than-average testosterone (hypogonadism) experience declines in muscle mass and bone density. They also have less energy, lower libido, greater abdominal obesity and a higher risk for heart disease, diabetes and cognitive decline.

A recent study in *Archives of Internal Medicine* found that men with low testosterone had a mortality rate of 35%, compared with 20% in those with normal testosterone.

What to do: Men with the symptoms described above should get their testosterone checked—if the level is low, a doctor should be consulted about the pros and cons of testosterone replacement (in the form of patches, gels, etc.).

HEART DISEASE

Cardiovascular disease is one of the primary reasons that men die earlier than women. Men usually develop coronary artery disease 10 to 15 years earlier than women do, and they are more likely to die from it before age 65. *Main reasons...*

• **Abdominal obesity.** Women tend to accumulate excess weight in the buttocks and hips... men tend to get a "beer belly." Abdominal obesity indicates high levels of visceral fat, which is stored around the abdominal organs, and is one of the main risk factors for cardiovascular disease.

What to do: Men should measure their waist-to-hip ratio (waist circumference divided by hip circumference) at least once a year. A ratio higher than 0.9 for men is a risk factor for cardiovascular disease.

• **Low HDL cholesterol.** Inadequate HDL "good" cholesterol may predict heart disease or a heart attack better than elevated levels of total or LDL "bad" cholesterol.

What to do: In addition to tracking blood pressure (anything that's 120/80 or above needs medical attention), men should be aware of their cholesterol readings, keeping HDL levels high and LDL levels low. If a man's HDL is below 35 milligrams per deciliter (mg/dL), he should ask his doctor about taking niacin to elevate HDL levels (40 mg/dL and above is desirable).

Important: Men with erectile dysfunction (or ED) should be screened for cardiovascular disease. New research indicates that men with ED are nearly 50% more likely to suffer from diabetes or metabolic syndrome (a constellation of symptoms including high blood pressure and obesity)—conditions that greatly increase risk for cardiovascular disease.

OSTEOPOROSIS

Men account for 20% of all osteoporosis cases diagnosed in the US. Because osteoporosis is often considered a "women's disease," many men who are at increased risk—due to smoking, a sedentary lifestyle, excessive intake of alcohol and/or prolonged use of steroid medication—go undiagnosed.

What to do: Men who have osteoporosis risk factors should ask their doctors about receiving a bone density test. Therapy may include calcium (1,200 milligrams [mg] daily for men over age 50…1,000 mg for those under age 50), weight-bearing exercises and osteoporosis drugs.

SKIN CANCER

After age 50, men begin to have higher rates than women of melanoma, the deadliest form of skin cancer. Skin cancers affect women most often on the legs and upper chest…in men, these malignancies are most common on the upper back and neck. Men's greater susceptibility to skin cancer is believed to be because they tend to spend more time outdoors and are less inclined to wear sunscreen.

What to do: Perform monthly skin checks. In addition, all men over age 40 should have annual total-body skin exams. They also should use sunscreen with a sun-protection factor (SPF) of at least 15—and/or cover up with a hat and clothing.

SEEING THE DOCTOR

Men are only about half as likely as women to go to a doctor regularly. As a result, when a man is finally diagnosed with a chronic health problem, such as diabetes or heart disease, the condition tends to be more advanced and harder to treat.

Only about two-thirds of men have a personal physician. After age 18, every man should see a board-certified internist—and get a physical exam every two years until age 30, then annually thereafter.

Veggies Protect the Prostate

During a 14-year study of the diets of 32,000 men, researchers found that men who ate the most vegetables—six one-half cup servings daily—had an 11% lower risk for benign prostatic hyperplasia (BPH), or enlarged prostate, than men who consumed the least—an average of 1.5 servings daily.

Theory: Antioxidants in vegetables may reduce the negative effect of free radicals on prostate cells.

Sabine Rohrmann, PhD, MPH, researcher, German Cancer Research Center, Heidelberg, Germany.

Omega-3 Help

Omega-3 fatty acids may cut prostate cancer risk in males with a family history of this disease. Omega-3s (contained in fish-oil capsules and certain fish) slowed disease progression in mice genetically engineered to develop prostate cancer.

Yong Q. Chen, PhD, researcher, Wake Forest University School of Medicine, Winston-Salem, North Carolina, and leader of a study published in *The Journal of Clinical Investigation*.

A Powerful Juice

In one recent study, drinking eight ounces of pomegranate juice per day increased the doubling time of prostate specific antigen (PSA) by more than 300% (more research is needed to determine why). The longer the doubling time, the slower the prostate tumor growth.

Extra benefit: Pomegranate juice may slow the progression of breast, testicular and lung cancers, as well as help reduce blood pressure and protect against heart disease.

Kelly Morrow, RD, assistant professor of nutrition at Bastyr University, Kenmore, Washington.

 # Multivitamin Warning

Taking lots of multivitamins may increase the risk for fatal prostate cancer, according to a recent finding. There was no link with early or localized prostate cancer, but the risk for fatal cancer was almost doubled in men who took multivitamins more than once per day. The correlation was strongest for men with a family history of the disease and who also took selenium, beta-carotene or zinc supplements.

Suggestion: Eat a healthy diet rich in fiber, vegetables and fruit to reduce your risk for cancer (and the need for additional multivitamins).

Karla Lawson, PhD, epidemiologist, National Institutes of Health, National Cancer Institute, Bethesda, Maryland, *www.cancer.gov.*

A More Accurate Prostate Cancer Test

The current test for prostate cancer, which measures blood levels of prostate-specific antigen (PSA), can identify 85% of prostate cancer cases, but it gives a "false positive" (a test result that wrongly indicates the presence of disease) in 80% of cases.

New study: Researchers tested 330 men for elevated levels of early prostate cancer antigen-2 (EPCA-2).

Result: EPCA-2 detected 94% of prostate cancer cases with only a 3% false-positive rate.

EPCA-2 testing could be available to the public within a year or two.

Robert H. Getzenberg, PhD, director of urology research at Johns Hopkins University School of Medicine, Baltimore.

Flaxseed Oil Caution

Most experts suggest avoiding flaxseed oil if you have prostate cancer or have risk factors, such as family history or elevated prostate-specific antigen (PSA) levels. Though flaxseed and flaxseed oil are good sources of healthful omega-3 fatty acids, several recent studies have raised serious concerns that flaxseed oil actually

may stimulate prostate cancer cells to grow. This effect is linked to the high amount of alpha-linolenic acid (ALA) in flaxseed oil. But, it appears to not be an issue with ground flaxseed, which contains lower levels of ALA as well as healthful lignans, a type of fiber.

However, until we obtain more research, the best way to increase your essential omega-3 fatty acids is to eat a diet high in fatty fish, such as salmon, and to supplement your diet with fish oil every day.

Sheldon H.F. Marks, MD, adjunct assistant professor of urology, University of Arizona College of Medicine in Tucson.

When to Stop Aspirin Therapy

Aspirin makes prostate cancer treatment less effective. Men who are taking a daily low-dose aspirin to head off a heart attack should stop taking it before starting hormone therapy for prostate cancer and then resume taking it after the treatment ends. For men who already have had a heart attack or other "cardiovascular event" and who are taking aspirin to prevent another one, it might be necessary to continue taking aspirin and forgo part of the hormone therapy.

Anthony V. D'Amico, MD, PhD, professor of radiation oncology, Harvard Medical School, and chair of gastrourinary radiation oncology, Dana-Farber Cancer Institute, both in Boston.

ED Drug Danger

Some patients taking the erectile dysfunction (ED) drugs *sildenafil* (Viagra), *tadalafil* (Cialis) and *vardenafil* (Levitra) have reported sudden hearing loss (temporary or permanent), sometimes with dizziness and ringing in the ears.

Development: The FDA has asked manufacturers of these drugs to more prominently display warnings about this potential side effect.

If you have sudden hearing loss while taking an ED drug: Immediately stop using it, and seek medical attention.

Janet Woodcock, MD, chief medical officer, acting director, FDA's Center for Drug Evaluation and Research, Washington, DC.

conditions, such as cardiovascular disease and age-related memory loss.

Edward L. Giovannucci, MD, ScD, professor of nutrition and epidemiology, Harvard School of Public Health, Boston.

Better Baldness Treatment

The foam form of Rogaine may be safer and easier to use than the liquid. The foam does not contain *propylene glycol,* which can cause irritation or contact dermatitis in some users. And it does not drip. Male subjects in a recent study funded by Rogaine's manufacturer, Pfizer, said they found the foam easier to apply, quicker to dry and simpler to fit into their daily routines. The retail price for the foam is the same as for the solution—$25 for a two-ounce bottle.*

Elise A. Olsen, MD, professor of medicine, divisions of dermatology and oncology, Duke University Medical Center, Durham, North Carolina, and leader of a Rogaine study published in *Journal of the American Academy of Dermatology.*

*Price subject to change.

Fight Colon Cancer With Fruit

An analysis of data on 34,467 women who had received screening tests for colon cancer showed that those who ate five or more daily servings of fruit over a 14-year period had a 40% lower risk of developing intestinal polyps (precancerous growths) than women who ate one or fewer servings daily. Those who ate five or more daily servings of vegetables had only a slightly lower risk.

Theory: Fruit may be a better source of specific nutrients that fight colon cancer.

Self-defense: Eat at least five servings of fruit daily. Vegetables may help prevent other

Natural IBS Help

In a recent study, fifty-nine people diagnosed with irritable bowel syndrome (IBS), a condition characterized by abdominal pain, bloating, diarrhea and/or constipation, received either 10 sessions of a behavioral therapy program in a clinic…four sessions administered at home…or no treatment.

Result: After 10 weeks, about 70% of the behaviorally treated patients indicated significant improvement in IBS problems. The home-based program was just as effective as the clinic-based program. Untreated patients reported that their symptoms did not significantly improve.

Theory: Behavioral therapy can relieve physical tension as well as excessive worrying, both of which can aggravate IBS symptoms.

Self-defense: If you have IBS, ask your doctor about behavioral therapy.

For further information, contact the Behavioral Medicine Clinic at the University of Buffalo Medical School, 716-898-6251 or *www.wings.buffalo. edu/research/ibs/.*

Jeffrey M. Lackner, PsyD, assistant professor of medicine, University of Buffalo Medical School, State University of New York, Buffalo, New York.

New Finding on Diverticular Disease

Researchers analyzed 18 years of dietary data for about 47,000 men, checking for the development of complications from diverticulosis (pouches, or diverticulum in the colon wall), including diverticulitis (infection of a diverticulum). Consumption of nuts and popcorn—previously thought to aggravate the condition—did not lead to an increase in diverticular complications.

Theory: The anti-inflammatory properties of these foods may explain this effect.

If you suffer from diverticulitis: Discuss your diet with your doctor.

Lisa L. Strate, MD, MPH, assistant professor of medicine, division of gastroenterology, University of Washington, Seattle.

A New Treatment for Hemorrhoids

If the standard treatments—warm baths, stool softeners, increased fiber intake and over-the-counter or prescription hemorrhoid creams and suppositories—do not work, an infrared coagulator can decrease hemorrhoids. The treatment works 75% of the time, takes just five minutes, does not require anesthesia and has little recovery time—but it is not yet widely available.

For more information: Contact the manufacturer—Redfield Corporation, 800-678-4472 or *www.redfieldcorp.com.*

Benjamin Krevsky, MD, MPH, director of gastrointestinal endoscopy at Temple University Hospital, located in Philadelphia.

When Sweating Means Medical Trouble

Bouts of secondary hyperhidrosis (excessive sweating) that begin suddenly in adulthood may be caused by an underlying disease, such as overactive thyroid disorder or an infection. An irregular sweat pattern—for instance, if one hand is wet while the other is completely dry—may indicate a neurological problem. Abnormal sweating at the site of an old but still painful arm or leg injury is a sign of complex regional pain syndrome (CRPS), a form of nerve damage. Sweating excessively during sleep could be a sign of Hodgkin's disease or HIV, or it could be a side effect of taking niacin or using antidepressants.

If you have unusual or excessive sweating, talk to your doctor.

John H. Eisenach, MD, exercise-and-sweat expert at Mayo Clinic College of Medicine, Rochester, Minnesota.

Don't Sweat It

If you sweat a lot, try topical treatments for sweat absorption, such as antiperspirants containing aluminum compounds. Some are available over the counter, such as New Secret Clinical Strength. Stronger products require a prescription.

If topical treatment does not work, a dermatologist could utilize Botox to shut down sweat glands or liposuction to remove them. You also can try *iontophoresis,* in which you use an electrical device—available over-the-counter or by prescription—to temporarily block sweat ducts. If all else fails, a dermatologic surgeon can destroy the nerves that cause excessive sweating in an area—but this can lead to increased sweating elsewhere. To find a surgeon, go to the site of the American Society for Dermatologic Surgery, *www.asds.net.*

Harold J. Brody, MD, clinical professor of dermatology, Emory University Medical School, and a dermatologist in private practice, both in Atlanta.

For Problem Drinkers...

The drug *varenicline* (Chantix), which helps smokers kick their habit, could help heavy drinkers quit their addiction, too, according to a recent study. Nicotine and alcohol act on the same locations in the brain. Varenicline blocks the release of dopamine in the brain's pleasure centers. Down the road, the drug might be prescribed for addictions to everything from gambling to painkillers.

Be sure to discuss side effect concerns with your doctor.

Selena E. Bartlett, BPharm, PhD, director, preclinical development group, Gallo Research Center, University of California at San Francisco.

7

Money Coach

How to Avoid Very Sneaky Bank Fees

I
ncreasingly, the banks are finding ways to impose bigger and trickier fees on account holders. *Some of the sneakiest fees right now and how to avoid them...*

ATM FEES

•**ATMs allowing customers to overdraw their accounts.** Request cash from your bank's ATM, and you will almost certainly receive it—even when there is not enough money in your account to cover the withdrawal. Banks could easily program their ATMs to decline such transactions or to warn you that such a transaction will trigger a hefty overdraft fee, but that would mean a loss of extra fees for the banks.

Self-defense: Check your balance before making the withdrawal if you are not certain there is enough money in your account.

•**Double ATM fees.** Bank of America has increased its ATM fee for nonaccount holders

from $2 to $3,* and other banks are likely to follow suit. ATMs warn customers of this type of charge, but many ATM users do not realize that their own banks often charge an additional fee of between $1 and $2.50 for using an ATM that belongs to another bank chain. That means the total fee for an out-of-network ATM transaction can top $5.

Self-defense: Use only your bank's ATMs.

CHECK FEES

•**Clearing the biggest checks first to maximize overdraft penalties.** Most banks charge a fee of $30 to $40 each time an account holder bounces a check. (Any merchant who received your bad check might charge you a penalty as well.) In addition, many banks now follow a

*Rates and fees subject to change.

Ed Mierzwinski, federal consumer program director with the US Public Interest Research Group (PIRG), Washington, DC, and Emily Rusch, a consumer advocate with the California PIRG in San Francisco. PIRG is a nonprofit, nonpartisan consumer, governmental and environmental watchdog group, *www.uspirg.org.*

practice that often automatically increases the number of checks that their customers bounce. They do this by first deducting from your account the largest check amounts when processing a batch of your checks.

The banks claim they do this because large checks tend to be the most important, but consumer advocates contend that it is just a way to maximize their fees. Bank of America, Citibank, HSBC, Wells Fargo and many other banks engage in the practice.

Example: Five checks you wrote arrive at your bank on a given day—four checks for small items followed by a $1,600 mortgage payment. If there is only $1,500 in your account, only the final check—the big mortgage payment—should bounce. Instead, your bank processes the large mortgage payment first, which means that five checks will bounce. Rather than one $30 or $40 overdraft fee and one upset check recipient, you now face $150 to $200 in overdraft fees and five perturbed check recipients.

Self-defense: Avoid writing many checks or making several debit card purchases in a short period if you are not 100% certain that there will be enough money in your account to cover all of them.

• **Fees for someone else's bounced check.** A charge when you bounce *your* check is one thing—but many banks now charge a fee of $5 to $10 to the *recipient* of a bad check as well.

Self-defense: Do not accept checks as payment unless you are confident that you can trust the payer.

ACCOUNT FEES

• **Dormancy fees.** Some banks charge a fee of several dollars per month to keep an "inactive" or "dormant" account open. Banks have different criteria for what they consider a dormant account, so be sure to ask your bank about its rules.

Self-defense: Close any unnecessary accounts.

• **Account closing charges.** Your bank might charge you a fee of $5 or more if you close an account within six to 12 months of opening it. These fees are particularly common at the bank branches located in college towns, because the banks know that students often close accounts at the end of each semester or school year.

Example: KeyBank charges an early closure fee of $25 whenever "Express Checking" accounts are closed within 180 days of being opened.

Self-defense: Ask about account closing fees before you open the account. Don't open an account at a bank that charges such a fee if you expect to leave the region or close the account for another reason anytime soon.

• **Gift card fees.** Banks sell gift cards similar to those offered by retailers. They can be used just as you would use your bank-issued debit or a credit card. Unlike retailer gift cards, however, bank gift cards often carry account fees of as much as $2 or $3 every month. If the recipient does not spend the money quickly, a significant portion of it might gradually disappear.

Self-defense: Give cash or a check—or a retailer gift card—rather than a bank gift card.

TRANSACTION FEES

• **Teller and phone fees.** Some banks now charge $1 to $5 or more every time an account holder interacts with a teller or customer service representative in person or on the phone (or every time the account holder exceeds the preset monthly teller transaction limit). At some banks, this charge applies even when customers call the bank but interact only with the automated system. Customers are not told that they are being charged a fee at the time of the transaction, and they often are unaware of the rules.

Some banks will even charge fees for certain ATM services, such as requesting a "mini-statement" that summarizes recent transactions.

Self-defense: Ask your bank if your account has a limit on the number of free teller visits or calls. If it does, do as much banking as possible through ATMs or on-line.

Ask to have any teller or phone fee waived when your call or visit is about a bank mistake, involves opening an account or is because the bank's ATM is out of service. You also may avoid these fees if you maintain a certain balance in some accounts.

• **PIN fees.** Some banks now charge a fee of 25 cents to $1.50 each time a customer uses a personal identification number (PIN) for a debit card transaction at a retailer. Debit card users typically can choose to either sign for purchases or type in their PINs.

Banks impose PIN fees to encourage customers to sign for all purchases, because banks can charge retailers higher fees when they do. Trouble is, many cardholders don't even know that PIN fees exist.

Self-defense: Try to use credit cards rather than a debit card. If you do use a debit card, check whether your bank imposes a fee when you enter a PIN. Consider switching banks if it does.

HOW TO AVOID FEES

Many bank customers find out that fees exist only when the charges appear on their account statements—if they bother to review their statements at all. Banks are required to give all new customers a "Truth in Savings Disclosure" statement detailing all of their fees and to notify customers in writing when policies change, but few customers read the fine print of bank literature. All bank customers should request a copy of the fee-disclosure statement for their accounts.

Banks once waived charges upon request for good customers, but this is less common now. At many banks, low-level employees no longer even have the right to waive fees, and the managers who do are increasingly unwilling to be lenient—though it is still worth asking to have questionable fees waived when they appear on your statement.

Credit unions tend to impose the fewest and lowest fees, followed by local community banks. Large bank chains usually have the greatest number of big fees—though they also have extensive ATM networks, which can at least help customers avoid paying out-of-network ATM fees.

...when overcharges happen, you might be less likely to catch them, because payments are automatic and you do not have to review every month's bill before paying it...it can be hard to stop making payments when you decide you no longer want either a product or service...canceling multiple payments at the same time—for instance, if you were robbed and need to protect against identity theft—can be difficult and time-consuming.

Rick Miller, CEO of Sensible Financial Planning and Management in Cambridge, Massachusetts, *www.sensible financial.com.*

For Higher Yields...

You may be able to negotiate higher yields at your local bank—if you are depositing enough money. Branch managers do have some discretion on interest rates. If you decide to take out a CD in a smaller city or an area where big deposits are rare, the manager may be willing to increase the interest rate by about one-quarter of a point if you invest as little as $25,000. In larger cities, you may be able to negotiate with $200,000 or more.

The best rates nationwide are easy to find—go to *www.bankrate.com.* Obtaining those rates may require using an Internet-only bank or one far from your home. If that makes you uncomfortable, you can try to negotiate locally.

Alan Lavine and Gail Liberman, personal finance columnists, Palm Beach Gardens, Florida, and authors of *Quick Steps to Financial Stability* (Pearson Education).

Automatic Bill Payment Risk

An increasing number of people have bill payments taken directly out of their bank accounts.

Risks: You may incur late charges because of computer errors that can take months to correct

CD Smarts

When cashing in your certificate of deposit (CD) during the grace period, send your request by certified mail. CD holders get a grace period in which to decide whether to renew a CD. Many depositors wait for the grace period—usually 10 days after the CD matures—to see what the latest rates would be, but if the bank loses a cash-in request or does not receive it in time, you automatically will be rolled over to a CD at the new rates and may forfeit six months of interest if you withdraw the money before the new CD matures. Sending a request by certified mail provides proof of the date on which you submitted it and is cheaper than registered mail.

Note: If your CD is at a local bank, it may be faster to go there in person.

Greg McBride, CFA, senior financial analyst, Bankrate. com, North Palm Beach, Florida.

Debit Cards Are Dangerous: How to Avoid Very Tricky Traps

Frederick Lowe, editor of *ATM & Debit News,* a weekly electronic newsletter in Chicago that tracks news and trends shaping the ATM, debit card and electronic-funds transfer markets, *www.cardforum.com.*

The use of debit cards has grown so much that it rivals the use of credit cards in the US, especially for purchases costing less than $25. And with the help of heavy marketing muscle, debit card issuers are finding more ways to entice cardholders to use them—including rewards programs and "contactless" cards, which don't require swiping at a store.

However, the drawbacks of using debit cards often outweigh their convenience as substitutes for cash, checks and credit cards. *Few consumers fully understand the pros and cons of using a debit card or even exactly how they work...*

DEBIT CARD FEATURES

Though they look just like credit cards, debit cards don't accumulate balances. Instead, debit cards, which often double as ATM bank cards, automatically draw money from your checking or brokerage account to pay for purchases. *Debit cards are best for...*

• **People who have trouble limiting spending** or paying off credit balances.

• **People who have weak credit ratings,** because debit cards are easier to obtain than credit cards.

There are two ways that debit card transactions are processed, and the choice of method can affect the rewards you receive and the liability you face.

For many purchases, you can choose to press the "credit" button and sign for the purchase, which means the transaction will be processed by the Visa or MasterCard network.

Alternatively, you can press a "debit" button and punch in a personal identification number (PIN), which means the transaction will be handled by a regional processing network, such as NYCE or Pulse.

For the merchant, a signature-based transaction generally is more costly since it requires a payment of perhaps 2% to the bank because of Visa and MasterCard requirements. A PIN-based transaction may cost the merchant only 10 to 40 cents. Some merchants, including Walmart, will request PINs for all debit card purchases, even though banks try to encourage signatures.

Bottom line for consumers: Generally, if you choose to use a debit card, sign for a purchase when you want to maximize your rewards or when your checking account balance is running low and you want to avoid having an extra amount frozen (see below). Use a PIN when you want cash back.

THE BIGGEST TRAPS

Trap: Frozen funds. To make sure that you can cover your bill, many hotels automatically freeze money in your account when you use a debit card to check in. Hotels also may freeze extra amounts when you check out to handle any additional charges that arise later, such as a missing robe or items used from the minibar. The holds are later released automatically—minus any extra charges—but that can take up to three full days, reducing the amount of cash that you have available and possibly causing you to bounce a check.

Gas stations also tend to impose these holds, typically for $50 or more, when you swipe a debit card at the pump, because the gas station is not sure how much gas you will end up purchasing. If you sign for the purchase instead of using a PIN, however, a hold is not imposed.

Self-defense: Avoid using debit cards at hotels and gas stations. Do not use up anywhere near your total checking account balance when paying with a debit card.

Trap: Overdraft fees. Many banks automatically enroll debit card customers in "courtesy" overdraft protection programs. Then if you do overdraw your account, the bank will honor the payment up to a predetermined amount, but it will charge you a fee—typically, $30 for the first overdraft and more for the next one. This service is lucrative for financial institutions, as they collect $17.5 billion annually from overdraft fees. Debit card transactions have become the main cause of overdrafts, according to the Center for Responsible Lending.

Self-defense: Opt instead for less costly protection, such as linking your checking account to your savings account...or signing up for a less onerous type of overdraft line of credit. Then if you overdraw your account, you typically incur a $3 to $5 transfer fee and an annual interest rate of about 19% to 21% on the borrowed money (about $1.50 per month for a $100 overdraft) until you pay it back, which you should try to do immediately.

Trap: Fraud liability. Under federal regulations, a consumer is liable for up to $50 in unauthorized purchases if his or her debit card is reported lost or stolen within two days of discovery...$500 if reported within 60 days...and unlimited amounts if reported after 60 days.

Some banks are more forgiving. If the unauthorized debit card purchase is processed by either Visa or MasterCard, which is the case when a signature is used, they require banks to follow a "zero liability" policy on unauthorized transactions—meaning that you are not charged. Some but not all banks apply zero-liability policies even if a PIN is used. Credit card users usually face no liability for unauthorized purchases that are reported—no matter how late they are reported.

Federal regulations allow banks up to 10 business days to restore money from an unauthorized debit card transaction to your account, which increases the risk that you bounce a check during that period. However, some banks try to restore the money within two days. For credit cards, unauthorized charges often are immediately taken off the monthly bill when reported, pending an investigation.

Self-defense: Report unauthorized debit card purchases quickly. Check your debit card issuer's liability policy, and switch to a different bank if yours does not offer enough protection.

Trap: Less protection in a dispute. Your ability to challenge a transaction with a merchant—for instance, if an item you receive is defective or you never ordered it—is decreased once the money is paid out, as can happen quickly with a debit card purchase.

Self-defense: Use credit cards for purchases of high-priced items, especially those prone to big problems, such as major appliances and electronics.

Trap: Less attractive rewards. Debit card rewards programs tend to be less generous and more restrictive than credit card rewards.

For instance, some debit cards give only one frequent-flier mile for every $2 you spend, compared with one mile for every $1 you spend with most frequent-flier credit cards. The cash rebates from debit cards often are less generous than the 1% or more that many credit cards offer.

Self-defense: If rewards are really important to you, use a credit card.

Credit Card Traps— Even Savvy Consumers Fall For

Scott Bilker, author of three books about credit cards, including *Talk Your Way Out of Credit Card Debt!* (Press One), which includes 52 transcripts of telephone calls to banks that saved more than $43,000 in interest and fees. Bilker lives in Barnegat, New Jersey, and now holds 80 credit cards with more than $300,000 in available credit and $10,000 in credit card debt that he manages at 0% interest. His Web site features articles on credit cards and other financial topics, *www.debtsmart.com.*

D on't get caught in a credit card trap. You may think you know your way through the credit card jungle—but credit card issuers have laid new traps at every turn for unwary consumers.

Some relief may be on the way. Congress recently held hearings to review fees, interest rates, grace periods and other provisions in credit card agreements. In the face of such pressure, a few banks have recently eased up on some of their most onerous terms.

Even so, you can't let down your guard. *Here are six ways to avoid the traps...*

DON'T PAY YOUR FIRST LATE FEE

Credit card fees have been rising rapidly in recent years. Expect to be charged as much as $39 if you are even one day late with the minimum payment due on a credit card, especially if you have a large overdue balance.

Example: American Express started charging a $38 late fee* on Delta SkyMiles accounts that have balances of $400 or above. Accounts with balances less than $400 are charged a $19 fee.

Virtually all card issuers will waive the first late fee on an account if the cardholder calls and asks them to do this. (Fees for subsequent late payments are difficult to avoid.)

Strategy: Tell the customer service representative that this is your first late payment and that you want the charge to be waived. Be persistent if the phone rep resists. Threaten to take your credit card business elsewhere. If that does not work, ask to speak with a supervisor and repeat your request. If necessary, call back a few days later and try again with a different phone rep.

KEEP SOME OLD CARDS

You shouldn't necessarily close an old, rarely used credit card account. The companies that compute credit card ratings consider long-term accounts a factor in your favor. Canceling older cards can lower your credit score, which makes it harder and more costly to obtain loans in the future.

Retaining a few no-longer-used, zero-balance credit card accounts also helps keep your options open in case a card that you do use suddenly alters its terms in a way you don't like. If that happens, you could phone the customer service departments for the cards you have not used for a while and ask what incentives they can offer for you to transfer your balance, then start using their cards again. The issuers of those cards will likely offer you low interest rates to entice you back.

*Fees and offers subject to change.

118

BEWARE OF REWARDS PROGRAMS

In addition to frequent-flier miles, credit card rewards programs provide gifts, discounts, cash and other perks. These programs are most appropriate for those cardholders who don't carry balances, because rewards cards rarely offer the lowest interest rates. Unfortunately, the rewards programs that look the most appealing on paper often come with the most traps, as well as steep annual membership fees.

Examples: Airline-branded cards provide frequent-flier miles, but because of increasingly overcrowded flights, these miles are very difficult to cash in. Automaker-branded cards promise rebates on new vehicles, but the dealership might play hardball when you try to purchase the car you want. Your rebate is restricted to a particular make of car, such as General Motors—so the salesperson knows your options are limited.

Some cards offer more flexibility, but there still are catches.

Example: Capital One has a "No Hassle Miles" rewards card with no blackout dates, no annual fee, no limit and no expiration date for frequent-flier miles earned, as long as your account remains open. These miles can be used to pay for tickets on any airline, but they cannot be combined with those of any other airline frequent-flier program. Also, the required number of miles rises as the price of a ticket does. A ticket costing from $150.01 to $350 requires 35,000 miles, more than the usual 25,000 for US flights in standard frequent-flier programs...and tickets costing $350.01 to $600 require 60,000 miles.

Strategy: I prefer the simplicity of the cash-back cards. These include Discover cards and Blue Cash from American Express, which rebate between 0.5% and 5% of purchase prices, depending on how much you spend in a year and where you spend it.

AVOID THE SPLIT-RATE TRAP

Credit card companies occasionally offer their cardholders interest-free, no-fee loans. The offer sounds like a great deal, but if you already carry an old balance on the card, there's a catch. You still have to pay interest at the old rate on the money you already owe, and all new payments go toward the 0% interest cash advance until it is paid off.

Example: Say you have a $10,000 spending limit and a $6,000 balance on a card charging 15% annual interest. The issuer offers you a 0% interest, no-fee cash advance. You take this offer and spend another $4,000. The issuer will apply 100% of your future monthly payments toward your new $4,000 cash advance until that has been paid in full. Meanwhile, your original $6,000 balance will continue to rack up interest charges at the original 15% rate, costing you hundreds of dollars per year.

Strategy: To eliminate monthly charges at the 15% rate, first transfer your $6,000 outstanding balance to another credit card, then get a cash advance for at least $6,000 at the 0% rate on the first card. Next, use that $6,000 to pay off the balance on the second card. That leaves you with a 0% rate on the first card's full balance.

Other rate traps: Some card issuers calculate interest using your average daily outstanding balance over two months, rather than one. Even if you pay off nearly all of the balance at the end of the first month, the interest charged the next month will be based on the average over the entire two-month period. Chase Bank recently dropped this practice, but other banks have not.

Also, issuers often increase rates or fees without waiting for your old credit card and agreement to expire.

DON'T EXCEED YOUR CREDIT LIMIT

You can face lofty fees for going even $1 over your limit. It also can hurt your credit score.

Strategies: Ask your card issuer to raise your limit...don't spend anywhere near your limit in case you lose track...or switch to another card that grants you higher limits.

TRIGGERING "UNIVERSAL DEFAULT"

If you are late with a payment to any lender, all of your credit cards might try to jack up your interest rate—perhaps to 30% or more—even if your payments to most of these cards have always been on time. This universal default rate increase is disguised in the fine print of many credit card agreements. Citi dropped the provision, but many banks have not.

Strategy: One solution is to always pay at least the minimum amount due on time. Also, review the fine print of credit card applications closely, and favor those that do not include a universal default provision. If you are hit with a universal default rate increase, call customer service and threaten to switch your balance to another card.

Don't Pay Bills By Phone

Paying credit card bills by phone can trigger fees—as high as $15—at many major banks. These fees have been rising for several years. Thirteen of 20 big banks in one recent survey charge fees, from $3* at Amalgamated Bank of Chicago to $15 at HSBC. Citibank and Washington Mutual charge $14.95.

Self-defense: If you think your credit card payment could be late if you mail it, pay with an on-line transfer from a checking or savings account before the due date—this does not trigger a fee.

Linda Sherry, director of national priorities at Consumer Action, a nonprofit consumer education and advocacy organization in Washington, DC, *www.consumer-action.org*.

*Fees subject to change.

Store Credit Card Trap

Store credit cards can cause problems after you enjoy your initial 10% to 15% discount typically offered for signing up. Store cards generally have higher interest rates on outstanding balances than general-purpose cards. Store cards also are not subject to the same regulations as bank-issued credit cards, and stores can be difficult to deal with in case of disputes. Also, if you have a large number of store cards plus several major credit cards, your credit score may suffer because you have too many open accounts.

Robert McKinley, founder/CEO of CardTrak.com, Port Charlotte, Florida.

Why You May Not Have to Pay Old Debts

Don't believe debt collectors who start pestering you about nonpayment of credit card debt from long ago. There are statutes of limitations in each state, after which a debt may no longer be collected. Find out your state's rules at *www.fair-debt-collection.com/SOL-by-State.html*. Even if the debt collector offers you a discount for prompt payment, do not agree to pay.

Insist that the debt collector give you, in writing, the name and address of the original debt holder, the account number, the date of the last transaction and the amount of original debt. You have a right to this information—and cannot be required to pay what you no longer owe.

Barbara Weltman, Esq., an attorney based in Millwood, New York, and publisher of the free on-line newsletter, Big Ideas for Small Business, www.barbaraweltman.com.

Free Credit Reports For You

Don't pay for your credit report. Some Web sites offer "free" credit reports when you subscribe to a "credit monitoring" service that alerts you each time a lender checks your credit history. The cost of the subscription is $12 to $15 per month.*

But: Annualcreditreport.com provides truly free annual credit reports without subscribing to any service.

Also: Each of the three major credit bureaus—TransUnion, Experian and Equifax—must provide you one free report every 12 months on request. You can request all three reports simultaneously or you can spread your requests throughout the year.

USA Today, McClean, Virginia, www.usatoday.com.
*Prices subject to change.

Credit Score Smarts

Adding a relative or friend to your credit card no longer helps raise his/her credit score.

In the past, FICO scores—a credit score used by banks and businesses—counted "authorized user" accounts (cardholders would get a card on their account for someone else, without him/her filling out an application). This could boost the score of someone with little or no credit. Now these people must establish their own credit references, which can take at least six months.

Alternatives: If a spouse or an adult child has no credit history, have him apply for a secured credit card, which requires a cash deposit and lets him transfer to a regular card after he proves creditworthy. If a child is at college, he can get his own card—issuers are likely to approve cards for college students.

Gerri Detweiler, credit adviser, Credit.com, San Francisco, as well as author of The Ultimate Credit Handbook (Plume).

More from Gerri Detweiler...

Bankruptcy Can Boost Credit Score

After filing for bankruptcy, the credit score is determined by comparing the filer's performance with that of other people who have filed. If you file for bankruptcy and then manage your credit carefully, you can have a higher score than before bankruptcy. However, credit scores are only one element to consider when deciding whether or not to file. The real issue is your ability to get back on your feet if you are deeply in debt.

If possible, avoid filing for bankruptcy—you can be forced to sell assets, perhaps even your home and car, if you do file.

Also from Gerri Detweiler...

Mortgage Know-How

When getting a mortgage, beware of yield spread premiums (YSPs). YSPs are broker commissions added on to the par rate, which is the rate that lenders are charging brokers. YSPs add $800 to $3,000 to the cost of obtaining a mortgage, as well as higher interest costs for the life of the loan.

Self-defense: When getting a mortgage, ask the broker to tell you the par rate, which is like the "dealer invoice" on a car. Compare rates at *www.bsh.com* or go to *www.freeratesearch.com,* which breaks out par rates.

Similar to a consumer who knows the dealer invoice when shopping for a car, a home buyer who knows the best available par rate when shopping for a mortgage is in a much better position to negotiate the best loan terms.

What's Ahead for Real Estate: From the Man Who Predicted the Housing Crisis

Robert Wiedemer, president of Business Valuation Center in Reston, Virginia, a primary business-valuation adviser for the Small Business Administration. He is a coauthor of *America's Bubble Economy: Profit When It Pops* (Wiley). His Web site is *www.americasbubbleeconomy.com.*

I n early 2007, many analysts were predicting that real estate prices would soon rebound from a mild slump. But economic forecaster Robert Wiedemer knew better. He warned that home prices were only at the beginning of an extended decline. *Here, Wiedemer gives an update and his latest forecast...*

MORE DECLINES AHEAD

The US is in the early stages of this correction. Nationwide, real estate prices have declined just a few percent, on average, even though it's been much worse in some areas of the US. Easy financing has largely disappeared, a key element pushing down prices now. Banks are demanding that borrowers have much better credit and larger down payments than before. This trend will accelerate as prices fall further.

During the next three to five years, real estate prices could fall to as low as their 2001 levels. That means declines in some regions of 20% or even 35%, and potentially more. Goldman Sachs has said that home prices in California are overvalued by 35% to 40%, for example.

Subprime mortgages, which allowed borrowers with weak credit to buy houses, were merely the first shoe to drop. Once home prices in any region fall by more than 20%, even many borrowers with solid credit and mainstream mortgages will face serious problems. A home owner whose equity has disappeared because of falling prices might have to cough up $50,000 or more just to escape his/her mortgage if he is forced to sell his home because of a relocation or divorce. And refinancing has become more difficult.

BUYERS ABANDON MARKET

When a slump in housing drags on, potential home buyers choose to stay on the sidelines and wait for a rebound. Few people are anxious to make the biggest investment of their lives while prices are still falling. Potential buyers will abandon the housing market in ever greater numbers as prices begin to fall more rapidly—and prices will start to fall even more sharply as these additional buyers leave the market.

Consumer spending will slow significantly as falling home values undercut consumer confidence and make it more difficult to tap home equity for spending money. Declining consumer confidence and spending will undercut the retail sector...the hospitality and leisure sector...and automakers. During 2009, the economic downturn will broaden, and many Americans will lose their jobs, leading to more foreclosures.

Even traditionally secure jobs in government might not be safe during this economic downturn. Plummeting home values mean billions in lost property-tax revenue for local governments, causing budget shortfalls and layoffs.

WHEN TO BUY

When the worst of the problems start to recede years from now, home prices will go back to increasing by 2% to 3% per year, as they used to do before the recent bubble. If you are waiting to buy a home, do not try to identify the exact moment when the real estate rebound begins. Real estate prices rebound slowly, not all at once as the stock market has been known to do.

Rule of thumb: During a real estate correction, it is better to wait a little too long to buy a home than it is to buy too early.

Houses Are Not High-Return Investments

One dollar invested in residential real estate in 1963 has, on average, barely outperformed the 4% average annual return of short-term Treasury bills in the more than four decades since then—even including the big run-up in home prices during the last housing boom.

Statistics from a report by Fidelity Research Institute, Boston, www.fidelityresearchinstitute.com.

Buying or Selling a Home? The Internet Can Help You Get a Better Deal

Blanche Evans, editor of *Realty Times,* the Internet's most visited independent real estate news service, Dallas, *www.realtytimes.com.* She is author of *Bubbles, Booms, and Busts: Make Money in Any Real Estate Market* (McGraw-Hill). In 2006, she was named one of the "25 Most Influential People in Real Estate" by *Realtor Magazine.*

Over the past decade, real estate tools on the Internet have morphed from novelty to near necessity. Eight out of every 10 buyers launch their home hunts on the Web today. In a California survey, buyers who used the Internet spent an average of only 2.2 weeks looking with a real estate agent before buying a home—less than one-third the amount of time spent by non-Internet users.

The Web can simplify your search for home-related information, including listings of newly built homes and older ones. It can provide mortgage rates...estimated home values and selling prices...local demographics, crime statistics and cost-of-living data...school ratings...descriptions of activities and amenities, such as restaurants... and detailed interactive maps, satellite images and "virtual tours" of homes—all without leaving your desk. Most sites are free.

For sellers, there are sites where you can list your home yourself, thereby reducing or eliminating real estate agent commissions.

Strategies for using the Web to help you buy or sell a home...

BUYING A HOME

•**Determine your price range.** There are millions of homes listed on the Web. Instead of wasting time wading through listings for homes you cannot afford, go to *www.bankrate.com* or *www.mortgagecalc.com* for calculators that help you figure out what you can afford.

•**Sort through listings.** Until several years ago, only real estate agents had access to lists of homes from the massive information-sharing Multiple Listing Service (MLS). Now you can access many of those listings yourself, although some details, such as the original listing price and commission rates, may be available only to real estate agents.

Start with *www.realtor.com,* which has three million listings, along with prices—much more than any other site. This site also enables you to screen for homes by style, number of bedrooms and bathrooms, waterfront or mountain views and dozens of other factors. For many areas, the site also includes comments about local market conditions from real estate professionals. A 360-degree virtual tour of some homes lets you use your mouse to navigate through several rooms as if you were there.

Next, move on to the local real estate agent Web sites. You often can find these through Realtor.com, which provides e-mail addresses and links to Web sites for listing agents of particular homes. Local sites often have more accurate and up-to-date information about homes than national sites.

•**Compare prices.** Get the tax records, sales histories and prices of "comparables"—homes in the area that are similar to the home you are interested in—at *www.zillow.com.* The site has more than 60 million estimated home valuations across the US. It offers maps showing prices in neighborhoods, plus loads of historical charts and graphs displaying how a particular home's value has risen or fallen in the past 30 days or since its last sale.

Another site, *www.homegain.com,* combines several services—letting you estimate home values, get prequalified for a mortgage, view listings, compare real estate agents and commission rates, and even find a moving company.

Caution: Estimated home values do vary on different sites and are not based on appraisals. Property details can be inaccurate, and offering prices can be out-of-date. Double-check details with agents and home owners. Also, go to the house and talk to neighbors.

• **Compare features.** Using satellite imagery, *www.trulia.com* has now teamed with Google Earth to let you "fly" down to treetop level to look at available properties in near 3-D. Yahoo's real estate site—*realestate.yahoo.com*—and *www.bestplaces.net* let you research a neighborhood for schools, recreational facilities, crime statistics …even Starbucks coffee shops.

If you are willing to pay a fee to get more detailed information than is available on free sites, check out *www.neighborhoodscout.com,* which provides nearly 200 types of statistics and characteristics, including school district ratings and crime rates, as well as how much median home values have changed. Subscription plans range from seven days ($19.95) to one year ($99.95).*

• **Consider a newly built home.** Amid the plunge in new-home sales, builders are slashing prices by as much as 20% and offering other incentives. Homes available from three of the largest US home builders are now provided at *www.beazerhomes.com…www.kbhome.com…*and *www.tollbrothers.com.*

Aggregator sites: Newly constructed homes in the US are listed at *www.americanhomeguides.com…www.inest.com…*and *www.newhomeguide.com.* Homes are listed by type, location, price, size and other factors. Inest.com offers rebates of 1% of the purchase price for homes bought based on their listings.

• **Compare the mortgage rates from more than 70 mortgage lenders at *www.e-loan.com.*** You also can call an associate on a toll-free number (888-533-5333) for help. At *www.priceline.com,* indicate the mortgage terms you want, then see whether such a loan is available.

*Prices subject to change.

At *www.bsh.com,* compare mortgage rates and find names of lenders by state. Also visit *www.mortgage.com…www.quickenmortgage.com…* and *www.bankrate.com* for similar information.

• **Get preapproved for a loan.** Buyers with strong credit can get loan preapproval from an on-line lender, print out the preapproval notice and carry it with them while looking at houses.

SELLING A HOME

• **List your home.** If you're willing to list and show your home yourself, you can save thousands of dollars in real estate agent commissions with the Internet.

At *www.owners.com,* you can choose from a variety of listing packages. The basic one is free and allows you to write a description of unlimited length and run it on the site with a photo for as long as it takes to sell your house. For $377, Owners.com will list your home on your local MLS for six months. If a broker brings you a home buyer in response to your listings, you can negotiate the commission rate—which usually is up to 3%—but you won't have to pay a seller's agent, saving you up to 3%. (In a typical non-Internet real estate agent agreement, commission charges often are negotiated down. The combined rate these days is typically 5% or less.) If a home buyer responds to your Web listing directly, there is no commission.

• **Set your dream price.** Even if you do not necessarily expect to sell your home, on *www.zillow.com* you could post a "Make Me Move" price that is so high it might convince you to change your mind if someone offers that price.

Caution: Even though the Internet can be a powerful selling device, a real estate agent may bring more potential buyers to the house…help you avoid mistakes, such as overpricing…stage a successful open house…help you negotiate a better price…and even help coordinate your work with a real estate attorney.

Investing in Foreclosures

Michael Perl, owner of Equity Res-Q in West Palm Beach, Florida, *www.equityresq.com.* The company has bought and sold more than 400 foreclosures and preforeclosures in the past six years.

Rising interest rates and the proliferation of high-risk variable-rate mortgages have pushed foreclosures to record levels.

Opportunity: Agile investors can buy foreclosed homes for as little as 80% or even 70% of fair market value (the price the home might normally sell for) from home owners seeking to avoid a public auction...from lenders wanting to get foreclosed properties off their books fast...or at a public auction.

A careful study of the foreclosure process can lead to great bargains, whether you are seeking a home to live in...to rent out...or to sell quickly for a profit.

Danger: Foreclosed homes are not always a good deal. A buyer who moves too fast can end up with a money pit.

Among the questions to consider...

• **How much will it cost to fix up and maintain the home,** including insurance and taxes?

• **How long will it take to locate a new buyer** if you think of this home as a short-term investment?

If you still want to buy a foreclosure once you have considered the challenges, here's how to get the best deal...

UNDERSTAND THE FORECLOSURE PROCESS

It is important to know the steps leading to foreclosure...

• **The home owner "defaults" on mortgage payments,** typically after falling 90 days behind.

• **The lender serves the home owner with a summons,** and the property enters the state of "preforeclosure."

• **Attorneys for the lender detail the debt owed in court.**

• **A "final judgment" hearing is held,** and an auction date is set.

The owner can sell the property at any point before it is sold at auction. Or the lender could assume ownership, either through an agreement with the owner during preforeclosure or by winning the auction. The property is then known as an REO property (real estate owned by the lender).

GETTING STARTED

• **Consult with your bank or a mortgage broker to determine how much of a loan you could comfortably handle,** and look for properties in that price range. If the home is an investment that you intend to sell, the most profitable neighborhoods often are up-and-coming locations, where about 80% of the residents are renters.

• **Check foreclosure filings.** Check for the most recent foreclosure filings at your county courthouse. In many counties, there will be dozens or even hundreds of listings every week or two. You also could use a foreclosure tracking service, such as First American Core Logic (800-345-7334, *www.facorelogic.com*).

Typical cost: $40 per month per county.*

After spotting a potential bargain, review recent sale prices of homes in the same neighborhood, making sure that the houses are comparable based on such factors as size and condition. The free Web site *www.zillow.com* is a useful resource.

BEST TIME IS BEFORE AUCTION

Some of the better foreclosure bargains are found before the auction removes the sales decision from the home owner. Contact home owners of prospective properties as soon as a notice of foreclosure appears. You might send a letter to introduce yourself and express interest, but don't expect the average home owner in foreclosure to respond to your letter until about a month before a public auction would take place. By then, the owner might welcome an offer to buy the property quickly for a price that allows him/her to pay off the mortgage and perhaps end up with a little extra cash. That might mean 75% of the property's fair market value.

If the home owner doesn't agree to sell until less than a month remains before the auction, you might not have time to arrange a mortgage.

*Prices subject to change.

In such a case, both you and the home owner should file a motion with the court for an emergency hearing (possible court fee is about $50) and a delay of the auction so you can secure financing.

Even if you cannot work out a deal with the home owner, approaching him prior to the auction might give you an opportunity to inspect the house—which could no longer be possible once a lender takes possession.

If you decide to take this route…

• **Be ultrasensitive to the home owner's situation.** Don't use the word "foreclosure." Say you are interested in buying if the owner "decides" to sell.

• **Ask if the owner has looked into "forbearance" from the mortgage lender.** Home owners sometimes can bring their loans up-to-date by making one relatively small forbearance payment to the lender. You will lose out on the house if the home owner does get forbearance, but your helpful suggestion should build some goodwill and raise your chances of a purchase if forbearance is not granted, as is usually the case.

Many home owners in foreclosure these days owe the lender more money on properties than the properties would be worth if sold. To get a great deal, you could arrange something called a "short sale"—the bank agrees to take less for the property than is owed. In the current real estate market, banks often are willing to accept as little as 60% to 75% of the amount owed, particularly in states such as Florida, where home values have fallen substantially.

AUCTIONS ARE TRICKY

It is not easy for a buyer to get a great deal at a foreclosure auction. There are experienced real estate investors at most auctions, ready to snatch up any bargains. At most auctions, the lender will bid the amount owed on the property to keep the sale price from going too low. If no one bids more, the lender—which does not yet own the property—will end up buying it at auction.

Auction winners generally must pay with cash or by certified check before the close of the business day—leaving no time to arrange financing. There may not be much time before an auction to research the title and arrange a professional inspection, and auctioned homes are sold "as is," so once you buy the property, you get it in whatever condition it is in. It's a good idea to attend a few auctions, just as an observer. I would not recommend auction bidding for the novice foreclosure buyer.

BUYING FROM THE BANK

If the bank ends up owning the home, it will try to sell it as quickly as possible, particularly in today's depressed real estate market. A bank will not give you a great deal, but it might give you a very good deal, perhaps as little as 80% to 85% of fair market value. The bank typically will make sure the title is clear of liens (which use the property as collateral) and other barriers to transfer and do some basic repairs to make the property more appealing to prospective buyers.

To find the REO properties in your area, call the real estate agencies and ask if any of their agents specialize in REO homes. The bank will pay the agent's commission if you do eventually buy a property through him. Or call area banks and say you're interested in seeing their lists of foreclosed properties.

GREATEST DANGERS

• **Liens, that include property taxes and mortgages.** The buyer of foreclosed property may not know that it carries one or more liens. Some liens, such as those filed by tradespeople, are wiped away by the foreclosure process, but when it's a government agency, such as the IRS, or a home owner's association that is owed money, the debt typically passes to the new owner. A title search performed after the foreclosure or an attorney with experience in this field can tell you what liens remain.

Cost: A title company might charge $100 to $150 to search a title for liens…a real estate attorney costs a bit more.

• **Condition.** The property you buy might be in worse shape than you realized.

Example: The previous occupants trashed the inside of the home to get back at the bank for the eviction. Try to inspect before you buy.

• **Some foreclosed properties are occupied** by a home owner who refuses to leave.

Use Your Cell Phone to Buy a Home

Get prices of homes from your cell phone. Just send in the address as a text message to 46873 (HOUSE) on your cell phone or go to Housefront.com and type in the address on the Web form. You will get information on asking price, size and number of bedrooms and bathrooms, and other data. The service is free,* but your mobile phone carrier might charge for the text messages.

The Wall Street Journal, 200 Liberty St., New York City 10281, *online.wsj.com.*

*Subject to change.

Real Estate Rebates

Ask for rebates from real estate brokers now that the housing market is cooling off. Some firms offer as much as 75% off of their commissions for potential buyers. Others try to sweeten the pot by giving large-denomination gift cards or airline mileage awards.

The Wall Street Journal, 200 Liberty St., New York City 10281, *online.wsj.com.*

Up-Front Mortgage Brokers

To find a truthful mortgage broker, visit *www.mtgprofessor.com.* Developed by retired business school professor and mortgage expert Jack Guttentag, it provides a list of "Upfront Mortgage Brokers," who will find good mortgage rates for you without imposing hidden charges. It is up to you to negotiate a reasonable markup, but you can make sure that you are getting a good rate by comparing on-line.

Newsweek, 251 W. 57 St., New York City 10019, *www.newsweek.com.*

Get Money Back When You Pay Your Mortgage

American Express cardholders with mortgages from IndyMac Bank can charge monthly mortgage payments and earn cash back or reward points (800-528-4800).* American Express charges a one-time fee of $395, but if you charge enough, the rewards outweigh the fee.

Other cards linked to mortgages: With a Wells Fargo Home Rebate card, even though you cannot charge mortgage payments, you can get a $25 rebate applied to your principal for every $2,500 that you charge on a Platinum Visa Card (800-869-3557). Countrywide, the nation's largest mortgage lender, decreases principal by $25 for every $2,500 charged on its Platinum Visa Card (888-200-6071).

Curtis Arnold, founder of US Citizens for Fair Credit Terms, Inc., North Little Rock, Arkansas, a consumer advocacy organization that educates consumers on credit cards, *www.cardratings.com.*

*Offers subject to change.

 # Open Houses Don't Help Sell Houses

Open houses benefit the real estate agents—who meet individuals in the market to buy homes—but they are of almost no value to the seller. Fewer than 1% of homes sell because of an open house.

Colleen Pearsall, owner of 4% Properties, Fort Myers, Florida.

When Remodeling Is *Not* a Good Idea

Don't remodel to increase a home's value if you plan to sell soon. You would be lucky to recover even a portion of your investment if you sell before the depressed housing market recovers. Also, affordability is moving up in importance to home buyers, given the tight credit conditions. "Sprucing up" your home still is always worthwhile.

Examples: Painting walls, trimming bushes and straightening up your garage.

Kermit Baker, PhD, chief economist for the American Institute of Architects (AIA), Washington, DC, *www.aia. org*, and senior research fellow, Joint Center for Housing Studies, Harvard University, Cambridge, Massachusetts.

For Sale By Owner...

Nancy Dunnan, a New York City–based financial and travel adviser and author or coauthor of 25 books. Her latest book is the ninth edition of her best seller *How to Invest $50–$5,000* (HarperCollins).

Some suggestions to keep in mind if you are looking to sell your home without a real estate agent...

•**Don't overprice.** Doing so means that the property could wind up being on the market for a long time and thus appear to have something wrong with it. So, find out what other similar properties are listing for. Check your local newspapers and various Web sites, including Realtor. com, HouseValues.com or ForSaleByOwner.com. And attend open houses in your area to compare prices of like properties.

•**Make the house look appealing.** It should be clean, freshly painted (indoors and out) and not cluttered. Put fresh flowers about. Keep pets out of the way. Turn on lights. Ask a friend to do a walk-through and point out things that he/she might not like as a buyer. An impartial view can be extremely helpful. After all, you are accustomed to the house's flaws.

•**Actively market the house.** In addition to posting it on the Internet sites, such as ForSale ByOwner.com or on Owners.com, purchase ads in area newspapers, including their on-line versions. Many people find listing on Craigslist.org helpful. ForSaleByOwner.com has various pricing packages with listings starting at $89.95 per month.* An old-fashioned lawn sign should also be part of the plan (check your area's law about signs first) as well as posting the information on community bulletin boards and at work.

*Price subject to change.

•**Work only with buyers who are pre-approved for mortgages**—ask for documentation. You don't want to arrive at your closing only to find out that the person cannot afford the house and you must start all over again.

Note: You still need an attorney, but for additional information, read Piper Nichole's book, *The For Sale By Owner Handbook* (Career Press).

More from Nancy Dunnan...

Money-Saving Lessons for Grown Kids

Basic savings techniques are essential to creating a sound financial life, one that doesn't bounce from emergency to emergency. *Saving suggestions for children or grandchildren...*

•**Pay yourself first.** *When you are paying your monthly bills...*

•Deposit a check into your money market or savings account (or make the transfer on-line).

•Save 1% of your take-home pay in the first month, then increase the amount by one percentage point each month. In one year, you will be socking away 12% of your pay.

•**Use automatic savings plans.** If you don't see it, you will not spend it. Arrange with your employer for a certain amount, perhaps it's $50 or $100, to be taken out of your paycheck and transferred into your savings or money market fund. If you can, do this in addition to "paying yourself first," as described above. In the same vein, be sure to participate in a company 401(k) plan, if offered.

•**Limit walking-around money.** Decide how much you need each week for bus or taxi fare, gas, lunch and newspapers. Make every effort to stick to it.

•**Keep making payments.** When you have paid off a mortgage, car loan or college debt, continue to write a check every month for that same amount (or at least half the amount) and put it into savings. You've been living without it, so you won't miss it.

•**Save your change at the end of the day.** This forces you to focus, every day, on the concept of saving. So, drop your coins—or, even better, dollar bills—in a jar every evening, then deposit all the money when the jar fills up.

• **Save your raise.** If you can't save all of a pay increase, save at least half of it and put it into a relatively safe investment, such as a successful mutual fund.

• **Compare interest rates.** Go to Bankrate. com *(www.bankrate.com)* for the interest rates being paid on money market funds, bank CDs and savings and checking accounts.

Free College

Some universities provide cooperative under-graduate and graduate educations, in which the students switch back and forth between the classroom and the workplace while earning college credit. They are either in school or at work all year—no summers off—and are paid for their work.

Result: Some students graduate with no debt …60% are hired by their co-op employers…95% find jobs immediately upon graduation.

Co-op education started at University of Cincinnati in 1906—now it is available at 500 colleges in the US, and it is becoming increasingly available internationally. Some schools offer this only for specific majors, such as accounting, architecture, engineering and urban planning. Others require it for all students.

More information: National Commission for Cooperative Education (617-373-3770, *www. co-op.edu*). Also, try Directory of College Cooperative Education Programs (Greenwood, *www. greenwood.com,* $68.95*).

M.B. Reilly, public information officer at the University of Cincinnati, and author of *The Ivory Tower and the Smokestack: 100 Years of Cooperative Education at the University of Cincinnati* (Emmis).

*Price subject to change.

Graduate School Aid

Graduate school aid—which comes directly from the school—is based more on merit than on need. These awards need not be paid back. But, students should meet the application deadlines for these awards, which often are earlier than regular admissions deadlines. Students studying physical sciences, engineering, religion and theology have access to the most aid and fellowships. Doctoral candidates generally have a better chance of receiving such aid than students seeking master's degrees.

Kalman A. Chany, president, Campus Consultants, Inc., New York City, and author of *Paying for College Without Going Broke* (Random House).

Smarter Charitable Donations

To get the most funds to a charity, eliminate the middleman. Charities employ for-profit fundraisers who keep up to 90% of the contributions they collect in a charity's name through mailings and telephone solicitations, something they don't tell you.

Shrewd: To get the most funds to a charity, do not use the envelope you receive in a mailing or send your check to the address you are given in a phone solicitation. Instead, look up the charity's address in the phone book or on its Web site, and send your check to it directly, so it will receive 100% of what you send.

Sandra Miniutti, vice president, Charity Navigator, a nonprofit independent charity evaluator, Mahwah, New Jersey, *www.charitynavigator.org.*

How to Protect Your Assets from Creditors And Lawsuits

Robert S. Keebler, CPA, MST, partner, Virchow, Krause & Co., LLP, a CPA and consulting firm, 1400 Lombardi Ave., Green Bay, Wisconsin 54304. Keebler is the author of *A CPA's Guide to Making the Most of the New IRAs* (American Institute of Certified Public Accountants).

Your personal assets are vulnerable to the claims of creditors, the government, an individual who might want to sue, and, perhaps, an ex-spouse. *What can you do to protect them? Here are sound ways to use the tax law and other means to protect your assets...*

COMPREHENSIVE APPROACH

There is no single action to bulletproof your assets from claims. You need to look at all aspects of your personal and business activities. *Areas for review...*

• **Insurance coverage.** The liability limits on most homeowner's and auto insurance policies are too low in light of the size of many of today's personal injury awards.

Solution: Add on umbrella coverage, which picks up where those other policies leave off. For example, a $5 million liability policy will cost about $1,200 a year. *Other insurance to assess...*

• If you are a professional (such as a doctor, attorney or accountant), carry appropriate professional liability coverage, also known as malpractice insurance, that provides unlimited duration. Continue coverage, even after you've retired from practice, usually with a onetime premium (that protects you against future claims arising from actions taken before you retired).

• If you serve on a board of directors, including one for a nonprofit organization, make sure that the organization carries directors' and officers' coverage to protect you from claims arising from actions you took (or did not take) in your capacity as board member.

• **Prenuptial agreements.** Those concerned with protecting property acquired prior to a marriage, or ensuring the rights of children from a former marriage, should use a prenuptial agreement. This kind of contract spells out property rights, among other things, and can protect your assets from your spouse's claims should your marriage fail.

If using a prenuptial agreement to protect retirement plan assets, be sure to have your new spouse sign a waiver of his or her rights to those assets. The waiver must be signed after you get married. A prenuptial agreement does not work to protect retirement plan assets in the absence of such a waiver.

If you are already married but do not have a prenuptial agreement, consider a postnuptial agreement to accomplish the same goals.

• **Business organization.** Anyone owning a business should consider using a type of organization that provides personal liability protection—a corporation or limited liability company can do this. However, all owners should understand the limits of these legal protections. For example, a corporate shareholder who personally guarantees a third-party loan to his corporation is personally liable for all of the debt if the corporation fails to pay—incorporation does not give any protection in this situation.

• **State of residence.** Some states offer special protection for certain assets. For example, Florida allows residents unlimited protection for personal residences. And, Texas and Wisconsin exempt all IRAs from creditor claims.

RETIREMENT AND EDUCATION SAVINGS PLANS

• **Retirement plans and IRAs.** Investments held in qualified retirement plans, such as 401(k) accounts, enjoy federal asset protection (meaning they are protected against all creditors) because of the *Employee Retirement Security Act of 1974* (ERISA) and the *Bankruptcy Abuse Prevention and Consumer Protection Act of 2005*.

Limitation: Although funds in rollover IRAs are fully protected, there is a $1 million limit on protection for assets in a contributory IRA (as opposed to a rollover).

Rollover strategy: When rolling over funds from a qualified plan to an IRA, use an account that is separate from your contributory IRA to obtain unlimited protection for the rolled over amount. Do not make any additional contribution to the rollover account—continue to keep it separate from any contributory IRAs.

Option: When leaving a job or retiring, for even stronger asset protection consider keeping funds within a qualified plan rather than rolling them over to an IRA. ERISA protection for assets held in any qualified retirement plan is "impenetrable," meaning that creditors cannot get the funds under any circumstances. IRA funds enjoy only bankruptcy protection, so unless you go bankrupt, your funds are vulnerable.

• **Education savings plans.** Funds held in 529 plans maintained by a state or eligible institution are exempt from creditors' claims in case of bankruptcy.

Requirement: The account beneficiary must be the debtor's child, grandchild, stepchild, or stepgrandchild.

Limitation: Funds contributed within one year of filing for bankruptcy are not immune from creditors' claims. Contributions made more than one year but less than two years before filing are protected only up to $5,000—full exemption applies after two years.

Note: Your state may offer greater protection for 529 plan assets than allowed under the federal bankruptcy law, and you can choose this state protection over federal protection.

TRUSTS

Assets held in a trust for a beneficiary generally are protected from creditors' claims—if the right type of trust is used. *Options...*

• **Spendthrift trust.** This is a trust that includes a clause preventing undistributed income and principal from being utilized to satisfy the claims of a beneficiary's creditor. For example, the beneficiary cannot assign his interest in the trust to a creditor to satisfy a debt. Usually, this type of trust is used only for a beneficiary other than the person who sets up the trust, such as that person's spouse, child or grandchild.

Caution: Asset transfers to a trust may be subject to gift tax (depending on the size of the gifts and who the beneficiary is).

• **Domestic asset protection trust.** This is a trust that's designed to protect the assets of the trust's creator from claims of his own creditors. Only certain states permit them—Alaska, Delaware, Nevada, Rhode Island and Utah. Whether a resident of another state can protect assets by setting up a trust in one of these states has yet to be tested in court, so, for now, asset protection trusts probably work best for residents.

• **Foreign trust.** Set up in jurisdictions that do not enforce judgments of US courts, these trusts are not necessarily unreachable. So, before using them, discuss asset protection with an attorney who specializes in the subject.

LONG-TERM CARE

Needing long-term care because of accident-related injuries or chronic illness can be financially devastating. AARP estimates that 60% of those over age 65 will need some type of long-

term care during their lives. Many people don't realize that standard medical policies and Medicare do not cover this type of care, which can quickly wipe out a lifetime of personal savings.

Solution 1: Those with a sizable chunk of assets to protect (generally, $500,000 or more) should consider buying a long-term-care insurance policy. For federal income tax purposes, part of the premium is a tax-deductible medical expense (the portion depends on current age). State law may provide additional tax breaks (for example, in New York, there's a 20% tax credit for all such premiums).

Solution 2: Those with more modest assets, who can't afford the long-term-care premiums, should consider transferring almost all their assets (other than assets exempt under Medicaid) to family members in order to qualify for Medicaid, which does pay for long-term care.

Plan ahead: Transfers that are made within 60 months of a Medicaid application are taken into account in determining eligibility and may prevent this government assistance.

Those with family histories of chronic diseases that typically require long-term personal care not covered by regular medical insurance policies, such as Alzheimer's disease, should discuss long-term planning with a knowledgeable elder law attorney. (Locate one near you through the National Academy of Elder Law Attorneys Web site, *www.naela.org.*)

Is Your Lawyer Overcharging You? Watch for Warning Signs

Daniel L. Abrams, JD, partner, Daniel L. Abrams, PLLC, New York City, specializing in legal malpractice cases, legal fee disputes and commercial litigation, *lawyerquality. com.*

Even if you never break the law, at some point in your life you will need a lawyer to buy a home...write a will...or administer an estate. Unfortunately, you might not get what you pay for.

The 2007 survey of 251 attorneys by William Ross, a professor of law at Samford University's Cumberland School of Law, found that a staggering two-thirds of attorneys either admitted to padding client bills or said they know an attorney who regularly pads bills.

Even many lawyers who do not intentionally cheat clients may push the ethical envelope to bill them in a manner that maximizes revenue. Either way, the result is legal bills that are hundreds or thousands of dollars higher than they should be. *How to make sure your lawyer's fees are reasonable...*

NEGOTIATE THE FEE

Discuss money matters with the attorney before hiring him/her.

A simple flat fee (plus expenses), agreed to up front, is usually best for the client—because it ensures that the cost won't go over a certain amount. And lawyers often accept a flat fee for simple matters, such as uncomplicated wills or real estate closings. However, many lawyers will not agree to a flat fee if there is a risk that the legal matter could become more complex and time-consuming than anticipated.

Instead, lawyers frequently demand an hourly fee.

Exception: Some matters, such as personal injury lawsuits, commonly involve contingency fees—meaning that the attorney agrees to take a predetermined percentage of any settlement or court award.

Some lawyers claim terms are not at all negotiable, but there usually is some room for flexibility or even creative compromise, assuming that the lawyer wants your business.

Example: Offer to pay a certain amount that you both consider reasonable as a guaranteed minimum flat fee for the expected amount of work. In addition, agree to pay an hourly fee at a lower-than-usual rate if the matter becomes more complicated than expected—for instance, if you are an executor and a beneficiary contests your execution of the will.

Other terms to negotiate in advance if you are paying an hourly fee...

•**Billing increments.** Most law firms bill in six-minute increments. Protest if any firm wants to bill in 15-minute increments even when, say, only one minute is spent on your case.

•**Photocopying rates.** Some law firms will charge as much as 20 or 25 cents for one copy, which can really add up if there are thousands of copies. You should push for as little as 10 or 12 cents.

•**Travel time.** Most attorneys bill their full hourly rate for time spent in transit for a case. Savvy clients ask that travel time be billed at half the attorney's usual rate...or that the attorney be required to use travel time for which he bills you to work only on your case.

RED FLAGS

An attorney who is hired for an hourly fee occasionally may slip questionable charges onto a client's bills. *Watch for these common warning signs...*

•**Poorly itemized bills.** Your bill should explain what your attorney was doing during each time segment billed.

What to do: Insist on a detailed bill. Vague terminology, including "research" and "preparation" should be explained.

•**Complex bills.** Bills written in impenetrable legalese might hide overcharges.

Example: Latin terminology used without explanation.

What to do: Insist on a bill that a layman can understand.

•**Too many junior lawyers.** When business is slow, law firms often assign extra junior lawyers to cases where they are not needed.

What to do: If more than two attorneys are listed on your bill, call and ask why such a large team was necessary...and what special talents each attorney brought to the table.

•**Attorneys doing nonlegal duties.** Your lawyer should not bill you for time that he spent filing, scanning, assembling documents or doing other clerical work.

What to do: Tell your attorney that he should have handed off these clerical tasks to a legal secretary. Legal secretaries' salaries are part of law firms' overhead and should not appear on your bill. (Do expect to be billed for paralegals' time, however, at lower rates than for lawyers.)

•**Staff changes.** You should not be responsible for the added time it takes a new attorney to get up to speed on your case if the law firm assigns you a different attorney midstream and you did not ask for the change.

Best: Watch for inflated hours on your monthly bill following an attorney change.

•**Billing for billing.** You shouldn't ever be charged for the time spent compiling your bill or answering questions regarding the bill.

Best: Scan your itemized bill for entries related to billing. Try to keep conversations about billing separate from other conversations, and track them in a diary.

RESOLVING A BILLING DISPUTE

If you are not satisfied with your bill and can't get the lawyer to alter it, contact your state's bar association to find out how legal fee disputes are resolved in your state. Most states offer some form of arbitration. State bar associations can be found at the American Bar Association Web site (*www.abanet.org/barserv/stlobar.html*).

How Much a Lawyer Costs

Robert L. Heston, Jr., attorney and president and CEO of LegalPlans USA, LLC, Houston, Texas. LegalPlans USA provides legal services at no additional charge to its 13.3 million members. More than 4,600 employers offer Legal-Plans services as a benefit to their employees. Log on to *www.combinedlegalplans.com* for more information.

How much should you have to pay for a lawyer? Charges vary significantly by region...your attorney's experience...legal specialty...the firm's reputation...and the complexity of your situation. *All that said, a typical person in need of basic legal services might reasonably spend roughly the following...*

•**Bankruptcy.** $1,500 to $2,500.*

*Fees subject to change.

•**Consumer dispute resolution.** $150 to $750.

•**Divorce.** $750 to $2,500, but it can be much more in some cases.

•**Misdemeanor defense.** $2,000. Common misdemeanors include public intoxication and petty theft.

•**Preparation of living trusts, wills or other estate-planning documents.** $75 to $2,500 per document, depending on complexity.

•**Preparation of other legal documents, including deeds, leases or affidavits.** $75 to $400 apiece.

•**Real estate closing.** $300 to $700 or more in some areas.

•**Suspended driver's license.** $500 to $1,000 to oppose the suspension.

•**Tax audit.** $2,000.

Portable Password Manager

RoboForm2Go software remembers all your passwords and logs you into Web sites automatically. Plus, it can store your contact information and automatically fill in address forms with a click. You can install it on a USB drive that you own or buy it preinstalled on a USB drive. Just plug the USB into a computer you're using—the software stays on the drive so that no personal data is left on the computer when you're done.

Cost: $39.95 for the software...$49.90 for the software installed on a USB drive.*

More information: Siber Systems at *www. roboform.com/pass2go.html*.

David Boyer, a research editor and resident computer guru, *Bottom Line/Personal,* Boardroom Inc., 281 Tresser Blvd., Stamford, Connecticut 06901.

*Prices subject to change.

8

Insurance Solutions

Are You Saving Enough For Your Health Care?

ar too many people assume that health-care costs will no longer be a worry once they reach age 65 and become eligible to receive Medicare coverage. That's a mistake.

According to the nonprofit Employee Benefit Research Institute, a 65-year-old couple who retire in 2008 and live into their mid-80s will need $164,000 to $324,000 (in today's dollars) to cover out-of-pocket medical costs for insurance premiums (including Medicare), insurance-related copayments and deductibles, and prescription drugs. That doesn't include the cost of over-the-counter medications, long-term care (if you opt for it) and most dental expenses.

But the situation is not necessarily as grim as it sounds. Whether you are planning for retirement—or are already there—you can significantly lower your out-of-pocket health-care costs. *Here's how...*

• **Look for the best price.** Even some people who would never make a purchase at the grocery store without comparing prices believe that health-care costs are final. But, that is not always the case.

Drug prices, even for generic drugs, vary significantly among local pharmacies, chain drugstores, large retailers and mail-order companies. Before you fill a prescription, check at least three stores in your area (including pharmacies in the same chain, where prices often vary). Mail-order drug programs, such as those offered by AARP or drugstore chains, are often cheaper than local stores. If you use the same drug continuously, ask your doctor to write a 90-day (rather than a 30-day) prescription—this can save you up to 20% (via mail order or at a drugstore).

Charles B. Inlander, a consumer advocate and health-care consultant, located in Fogelsville, Pennsylvania. He was the founding president of the nonprofit People's Medical Society, the consumer advocacy organization credited with key improvements in the quality of US health care in the 1980s and 1990s, and is the author of 20 books, including Take This Book to the Hospital with You: A Consumer Guide to Surviving Your Hospital Stay *(St. Martin's).*

When you purchase Medicare supplemental insurance, make sure that you carefully check the same policy from at least five different companies. The federal government controls what the various policies cover, but not their prices. You can get a list of all approved insurers from your state's insurance department (it's usually listed in the phone book). You will find that the cost of the same policy may vary by as much as 40% among companies. Do the same when looking at Medicare prescription drug plans. Each state has at least three dozen plans available in many price ranges. Buy what you need and can afford. Also, don't use a specialist, such as a cardiologist, for a general problem like a sinus infection. Use a family physician or internist. His/her rates will be lower, and he will have more experience in treating general health problems. Your out-of-pocket expenses also will be lower.

•**Start building a health reserve.** If you are younger than age 65 and planning for retirement, put aside some money each month for postretirement out-of-pocket health costs. If you have just received a tax refund, put all or part of it into an account earmarked for postretirement health expenses.

•**Plan ahead.** If you have more than $150,000 in stocks, bonds and similar investments, consider buying long-term-care insurance. This will cover such expenses as nursing-home care. The younger you are when you purchase such coverage, the less expensive it is. Even for a 65-year-old, the cost is about 40% less than it is if you wait until age 70. Again, shop around for the policy that provides the best coverage for the money.

More from Charles Inlander...

Insider Tips on Getting Health Insurance

Despite all the recent talk about future reforms in health insurance, the fact remains that this year, an estimated 82 million Americans will be looking for health insurance. These people are not employed by a business that offers health benefits or they are not eligible for a government-sponsored health-care program, such as Medicare or Medicaid—and they cannot

afford an individual policy themselves or are too unhealthy to be eligible for one. If our next president champions health insurance reforms, any measures that make it through Congress won't be in place until at least 2011. Fortunately, there are many more options available now. *But you must know where to look...*

•**Know all the benefits of COBRA.** COBRA—the acronym for the *Consolidated Omnibus Budget Reconciliation Act of 1986*—is a sweeping law that requires employers (with 20 or more employees) to give departing employees the option to purchase the same group health insurance policy for up to 18 months. But many people don't know how to take full advantage of COBRA. You have 60 days after leaving your job to exercise your option, and it doesn't matter why you left your job. You simply tell your former employer that you want COBRA, and you cannot be turned down for medical reasons.

My special advice: COBRA usually covers all members of your family. So if you get another job with health benefits—but they don't cover your spouse or children—you still can use COBRA, through your former employer, to cover your family for up to 18 months.

•**Investigate group plans.** Many unions, alumni associations, fraternal and business organizations, including chambers of commerce, and large national groups, such as AARP, offer their members a selection of health insurance plans. Be aware, however, that simply joining one of these groups does not necessarily mean you will qualify for health coverage. Some exclude preexisting conditions, while others base their premiums on your age and medical history. Check your eligibility for the group's health plan before joining.

My special advice: If you can afford to pay a deductible of $1,000 to $3,000 per year for your health care before your policy starts to kick in, your monthly premiums can drop by half.

•**Consider using a broker.** Prices for individual health policies vary by as much as 50%, depending on your medical history and the type of policy you buy. You can search on-line under "individual health insurance" for policies sold by private insurance companies in your state, but I would recommend that you contact your local insurance broker for help (check the phone book and on-line directories). Insurance brokers often represent many companies and can help determine what you qualify for and what you can afford.

My special advice: Before you sign up for a policy, check with your state's insurance department to be sure that the insurer you want to use is licensed to sell in your state and does not have a history of multiple consumer complaints.

Rewards for Healthful Living

Some health insurance plans now provide rewards to encourage healthful living. United Healthcare, the country's largest insurer, is offering employers a health plan that enables employees to earn up to $2,000 in deductible credits when they reach health benchmarks for vital measures, such as blood pressure and cholesterol.* Virgin Life Care, as part of an employer's benefits package, rewards employees with HealthMiles as they reach their fitness goals, which can be exchanged for gift cards to retailers, such as Bloomingdale's and Blockbuster. Check with your provider to see if it is offering similar rewards programs for employees with healthy lifestyles.

Kevin Flynn, president of HealthCare Advocates, Inc., Philadelphia.

*Offers subject to change.

Get Paid

Track all health insurance claims to be sure you receive payment. If you phone about a problem, get the name and extension of anyone you talk to. If someone asks you to resend a claim, ask him/her to hold on while you fax it. And, be sure that he acknowledges receipt. If you file a claim and hear nothing for 60 days,

call and ask for the supervisor. Continue doing this until you reach someone who helps you.

Money, Time-Life Bldg., Rockefeller Center, New York City 10020, *money.cnn.com*.

Medicare Reminder

If you are a US citizen, or have a resident visa and have lived in the US for five consecutive years, you are eligible to get Medicare at age 65. This is unlike Social Security eligibility, where the normal retirement age is gradually being increased. But don't let your ineligibility for Social Security cause you to miss your enrollment period for Medicare, which starts three months before the month you turn 65 and ends at the end of the third month after it.

Danger: If you miss your Medicare enrollment period, you will have to wait until the next year's enrollment period. You will forfeit Part B coverage (outpatient care) in the meantime. You may also incur lifetime penalties for late enrollment in Part D (prescription drugs). So, be sure you enroll on time.

Deane Beebe, public affairs director, Medicare Rights Center, New York City, *www.medicarerights.org*.

What You Must Know Now About Long-Term Care

Joseph L. Matthews, JD, a San Francisco–located attorney specializing in issues relating to seniors. He is the author of numerous books, including *Long-Term Care: How to Plan & Pay for It* (Nolo). For a free on-line guide to long-term-care insurance, go to Caring.com and put "long-term care" in the search window.

The average cost of a private room in a nursing home today has reached $78,000 per year, according to the 2007 MetLife Market Survey of Nursing Home & Home Care Costs. Top facilities can cost well into six figures a year. Recently revised government rules make it more difficult than ever to obtain Medicaid assistance to pay these bills.

Most people never require an extended nursing home stay, but for those who do, the result can be financial devastation. By understanding the ways you can finance long-term care, you can reduce the chances that it will have such a devastating impact on your finances.

How to decide which of the options are best for you…

LONG-TERM-CARE INSURANCE

Insurance that pays for long-term-care bills sounds like a "no brainer" idea—until you take a closer look at the details. These policies cost thousands of dollars a year. You may pay premiums for decades before coverage is needed, if it is ever even needed at all…and the premiums can increase significantly over the years, even with the so-called "fixed-rate" policy. For these reasons, long-term-care insurance generally isn't a very effective investment. Also, collecting on the policies is often difficult. Between 2003 and 2006, complaints to state regulators over denied claims soared 74%.

So why even consider this form of insurance? If you would sleep better at night knowing that a lengthy stay in a long-term-care facility would not deplete your assets, consider purchasing a policy.

However, as a rule of thumb, if coverage costs in excess of 5% of the combined total of your pension, Social Security, retirement plan distributions and any other income, it is too expensive, because you would be sacrificing too much elsewhere in your retirement budget. Speak with a financial planner to determine your projected monthly budget in retirement.

Despite all of the drawbacks, the popularity of these long-term-care policies has increased. Total premiums collected have jumped 21%, from $8.2 billion in 2004 to $10 billion in 2007.

The best time to consider long-term-care insurance is when you are between the ages of 50 and 65 and still healthy—any sooner and you would have to pay out premiums for too many years…but any later and the annual premiums would become so expensive that you probably would be better off paying for long-term care out of pocket. (Most insurance companies charge

sharply higher premiums for people over age 60 or 65.)

For information on how to choose a policy, see page 137.

MEDICAID

Half of all nursing home residents depend on Medicaid, the government health insurance program for the poor, to pay for their stays. (Some states have different names for Medicaid, such as Medi-Cal in California, and Medicaid laws vary from state to state.) Unfortunately, Medicaid will not pick up your nursing home bills until you have depleted virtually all of your assets. In the past, many people who thought that they were likely to require a nursing home stay in coming years gave their assets to their children, making themselves poor enough to qualify for Medicaid.

New, stricter rules make this much more difficult. Any assets given away or sold for less than their true value within five years of applying for Medicaid are included in calculations of your wealth, and that could delay the date on which you qualify for Medicaid.

Medicaid recipients are allowed to own a car, a burial plot, a limited amount of life insurance, a wedding ring and a few other possessions. A recipient can keep his/her home if his spouse is living in it.

Many nursing homes will not be available to you if you use Medicaid to pay for long-term care. Those with the strongest of reputations and the highest demand for beds often do not accept Medicaid as payment…or have space for only a few Medicaid patients.

On the bright side, once you are in a nursing home, you cannot legally be forced to leave just because you have run out of money. Even facilities that do not accept Medicaid patients still must let you pay with Medicaid once you have been accepted, should you outlive your assets or a long-term-care insurance policy. (You might, however, be demoted to smaller or less appealing accommodations after Medicaid starts paying your bill.)

VA FACILITIES

The Veterans Administration (or VA) operates a large number of surprisingly well-funded and well-run long-term-care facilities. They are free for most former military personnel—but because millions of former service people are in need of nursing home care, demand far exceeds supply.

The VA has a complex formula for determining which applicants are accepted into its facilities. First priority is given to veterans suffering service-related disabilities...those in extreme financial need...and retired career service people. Veterans should contact the VA (877-222-8387 or *www.va.gov/directory*) as soon as it becomes apparent that a stay in a long-term-care facility is likely in the future.

OTHER TYPES OF CARE

Twenty years ago, nursing homes were virtually the only option. But, today there is a range of long-term-care facilities. *Most of them are less expensive than nursing homes, and they may be covered by long-term-care insurance...*

• **Independent-living residences** are small apartments that provide limited assistance as is needed and cost less than assisted-living facilities. Twenty-four-hour security and emergency-response systems are usually provided.

• **Assisted-living facilities** will cost perhaps one-third to one-half less than nursing homes. They do not provide 24-hour care, but their services, including assistance with transportation and shopping, bathing and eating, are sufficient for many seniors.

• **Continuing-care retirement communities.** Some senior-care facilities have different types of accommodations ranging from senior residences to nursing home care on one site. Residents move from one level of care to the next as their needs dictate.

PAYING OUT OF POCKET

If you choose not to buy long-term-care insurance...have too much money to qualify for Medicaid...and are not eligible for VA care, you likely will have to pay for long-term care out of your own pocket. To stretch your money, depend on in-home care from family members for as long as possible before resorting to professional care. Some seniors postpone their nursing home stays by months or years with the assistance of spouses or adult children. Discuss this with your family before your health deteriorates.

If you must move to a long-term-care facility, do not pay for more assistance than you actually need. Consider independent living and assisted living first.

If you have only enough assets to pay for three to six months of long-term care, consider moving into a nursing home even if an assisted-living facility or an independent-living residence would be sufficient for your needs, particularly if you have a degenerative condition. Once you are in a nursing home, you cannot legally be kicked out for lack of funds.

More from Joseph Matthews, JD...

Selecting a Long-Term-Care Policy

If you do decide to purchase long-term-care insurance, be sure to buy it from an established insurance company. Certainly a familiar company name is a good sign, but also check out the company's financial strength. The best insurance companies earn grades of AAA or AA from Standard & Poor's.

Long-term-care coverage should include...

• **Long exclusion period.** To reduce the cost of coverage, select a policy with a 90-day to six-month "exclusion period." This means that if you ever need care, you would have to pay out of pocket for this period before the benefits begin. Your premiums would be as much as one-third lower than with a 30-day exclusion period, the most common exclusion option.

• **Inflation protection.** This protection is best when it is linked to increases in the actual cost of living, and not to an arbitrary preset inflation rate.

• **Premium protection.** Select a policy that does not allow your insurance company to raise your premium unless it also raises the premium for everyone holding the same policy. Insurance companies must apply to the state regulators for this type of premium raise, making excessive increases less likely (though still possible).

• **Payout flexibility.** Your policy should pay for home care, assisted-living care and nursing home care.

• **Minimal impairment to trigger coverage.** A good policy will offer benefits when you cannot perform two or three daily living tasks, while a poor one might require four or five.

• **At least three years of coverage.** An extended stay in a facility is unlikely, but the purpose of insurance is to protect against unlikely but financially crippling scenarios.

A Smart Way To Cut Your Long-Term-Care Insurance Costs

John Ryan, CFP, principal, Ryan Insurance Strategy Consultants, Greenwood Village, Colorado, *www.ryan-insurance.net*.

Nursing-home care, assisted living or home health care can be very expensive, so many people buy long-term-care insurance policies with lifetime benefits to protect family wealth against the risk of ever having to pay for it. But these high-cost insurance policies usually provide much more coverage than you'll ever need.

Study: Among 70-year-old claimants under these insurance policies, only 8% needed coverage exceeding five years.

A better strategy: Most insurers now offer shared-benefit policies for married couples and domestic partners, which provide all the benefits they are likely to need at lower cost.

Example: A couple could purchase one 10-year shared-benefit policy. If one spouse receives benefits for four years, the other will be eligible for benefits for six.

A 10-year shared benefit protects against the small risk that one spouse will need benefits for more than five years. And because it is unlikely that both spouses will need more than five years of benefits, it is likely that the policy will also meet their combined needs. The cost is less than that of buying a separate 10-year policy for each spouse, and much less than buying lifetime benefits for each.

Shared benefits can be purchased for longer and shorter terms, so consult an expert about your family needs.

Life Insurance Loopholes

Edward Mendlowitz, CPA, partner in the CPA firm of WithumSmith+Brown at One Spring St., New Brunswick, New Jersey 08901. He's also author of *The Adviser's Guide to Family Business Succession Planning* (American Institute of Certified Public Accountants).

You can maximize the profitability of an insurance policy by buying and holding it in tax-smart ways. *Consider the loopholes below...*

Loophole: **Nearly all life insurance proceeds paid upon death are never subject to income taxes.** This also applies to "viatical settlements," which are payments made to someone who is terminally ill (defined as having a life expectancy of less than 24 months).

Caution: If the policy is improperly titled—for example, if it is in the name of the insured, payable to the insured's estate, or the insured retained "incidents of ownership," such as the ability to change a beneficiary—life insurance proceeds could be subject to estate tax.

Loophole: **The policyholders who borrow against a policy's cash surrender value do not recognize taxable income.** Money that is borrowed can be used for purposes unrelated to the insurance, such as home remodeling.

Note: Interest paid on loans used to pay policy premiums is not deductible. Interest on loans used for other purposes is subject to "interest tracking" rules that determine whether interest is deductible depending on how the money is used.

Example: Interest on loans used to finance vacations is not deductible. Interest on loans for a business purpose is deductible.

Loophole: **Policyholders who surrender an insurance policy owe no tax on the policy proceeds, up to the total amount paid for premiums.** However, proceeds in excess of the premiums are taxed as ordinary income. Death benefits that include the policy's cash value are not taxed.

Loophole: **The proceeds from the sales of whole life and term life insurance policies**

in excess of these policies' cash values are taxed as long-term capital gains. However, proceeds up to the cash value exceeding total premiums paid are taxed as ordinary income.

Caution: This is a new and unsettled area of the law. If you are considering selling your policy, discuss the consequences with a tax expert.

Loophole: **Policyholders could exchange their policies for similar policies tax free.** However, no cash or other property can be received in the transaction. These exchange rules also apply to endowment policies and annuity contracts.

Examples: A life insurance policy with a high cash value and high premium can be exchanged for a policy that has a smaller premium and higher death benefit. While exchanges of "second to die" policies for "single life" policies generally do not qualify for tax-free status, they do qualify after the death of one of the original beneficiaries of the "second to die" policy. Policies with outstanding loans can be exchanged tax free if the level of indebtedness is unchanged in the swap. A life insurance policy can be exchanged for an annuity with a cash flow.

Loophole: **Avoid the "transfer for value" trap when you buy a life insurance policy.** "Transfer for value" rules apply when an owner sells a policy to someone other than the insured, a partner of the insured, a partnership in which the insured is a partner, or a corporation in which the insured is an officer or shareholder. When a policy is sold this way to the "wrong" person, the sum of the excess of the proceeds over the cost to acquire the policy and any premiums paid going forward is taxed as ordinary income when the insured dies.

Loophole: **A tax-effective way to make charitable donations of a life insurance policy is to sell the policy and then donate the proceeds to charity.**

Reason: While you can transfer a life insurance policy to a charity, the tax law is unclear how the tax deduction is calculated. Generally, it is a complex calculation based on the donor's original cost, the ordinary income portion of the policy, and its untaxed capital gain. Therefore, it makes more sense to simply sell the policy and donate the cash.

Loophole: **Earn tax-free income by keeping an unneeded insurance policy instead of letting it lapse or cashing it in.**

How it works: The insurance premium rates are set to account for policies that lapse or are terminated before death—for which insurance companies never pay out benefits. Many policies held until death are not profitable for insurance companies.

Recently, the hedge funds and other investors have been buying policies whose owners would have let them lapse, then holding them until the death benefits are paid. They will typically earn 20% to 30% on their investment. If an owner instead retains such a policy, the death benefit may eventually represent significant tax-free income to the family.

Life Insurance Smarts

Pay your life insurance premiums annually if you can. Insurers usually offer multiple payment options—annual, semiannual, quarterly or monthly. But, there's a charge for paying more often than once a year, and insurers often don't disclose the effective annual rate of interest. To calculate the annual percentage rate (APR) for a given payment option on any policy, use the APR calculator offered at *www.accuquote.com/modal.cfm*.

Byron Udell, founder and CEO of Accuquote.com, a life insurance quoting and brokerage firm in Wheeling, Illinois.

Cost of Auto Insurance Drops

The average price of auto insurance has decreased for the first time since 1999. That means more opportunities to pay much lower premiums.

Reasons: Safer cars, fewer accidents and insurance companies' focusing more on credit histories to determine pricing.

Strategy: Strive to improve your credit record and correct any errors. Compare auto insurance prices at *www.insurance.com*.

Linda Sherry, director of national priorities at Consumer Action, a nonprofit consumer education and advocacy organization in Washington, DC, *www.consumer-action.org.*

Home and Auto Insurance Traps Can Cost You Big: Make Sure You're Covered

J.D. Howard, executive director of Insurance Consumer Advocate Network, a not-for-profit insurance consumer advocacy organization in Branson West, Missouri, *www. ican2000.com*. He has worked in the insurance industry since 1965, mainly as an insurance adjuster.

Insurance is supposed to protect us from financial disasters—but both homeowner's and automotive insurance policies do not cover some potentially expensive problems and situations. *The most common coverage gaps and how to protect yourself...*

HOMEOWNER'S POLICIES

You may already know that damage caused by an earthquake, flood or war is not covered by typical homeowner's insurance policies and that generally there are special limits on coverage for jewelry, furs, cash, collectibles and other pricey items. *Additional coverage gaps...*

• **Limits on inflation protection.** Replacement-cost coverage that has an "inflation guard" feature is supposed to pay the true cost of repairs (minus your deductible) when something goes wrong. Unfortunately, the insurance companies quietly have begun setting a percentage limit—generally 6% to 10% each year—on the inflation protection. If home construction costs rise so rapidly that your coverage falls below 80% of the true cost of rebuilding or repairing the damaged portions of your home, your insurance company might have the right to void your replacement-cost coverage. In such a case,

the company would instead calculate the depreciated value of the damaged portions. Then it could further reduce that amount to reflect how far short of the 80% figure your coverage falls.

Example: The cost to rebuild your home has grown to $160,000, but your initial $100,000 coverage has increased to only $119,100 over the past three years. That means you have only 74.4% of the coverage you require. Your replacement-cost coverage is voided because of the shortfall. When your 10-year-old roof is demolished in a storm, the company pegs the depreciated value at $5,000 (half the original cost), then multiplies that by 74.4%, subtracts the $500 deductible and ends up paying you only $3,220—a small fraction of the actual replacement cost.

Self-defense: Call your insurance agent every two to three years to make sure that your coverage has kept pace with the full replacement value of your home. If he/she says it has, get it in writing. If the agent tells you that your coverage has not kept pace, consider increasing your coverage. If you follow your agent's advice and your coverage still falls short, the carrier usually will cover the difference.

• **Leaks and mold.** Water damage caused by slow leaks from pipes, plumbing fixtures or heating/ventilation/air-conditioning (HVAC) components is not generally covered by homeowner's insurance—although damage from a burst pipe is. The removal of mold, mold spores or mildew from a home also typically is not covered unless it's the result of a covered event, such as a burst pipe or water sprayed onto the house to extinguish a fire. It could cost you tens of thousands of dollars to correct problems caused by slow water leaks.

Self-defense: Be alert for any signs of hidden moisture, such as peeling paint...discolored ceilings or floors...or musty odors. And if you find them, call a contractor to identify the cause and scope of the damage. If it is in its early stages, a simple bleach solution and proper ventilation should solve it.

• **Sewer backups and/or septic problems.** Standard homeowner's policies do not pay for repairs to broken or clogged sewer lines or septic systems...or for cleaning sewage from your home and replacing damaged carpets and furniture if these systems back up.

Self-defense: Ask an agent what sewer/septic coverage will cost. It is not always available. Call a plumber or septic system specialist at the first sign of sluggishness in your sewer line or septic tank. If a landscaping company, contractor or municipal worker is to blame for the problem, you can try to recover your expenses through the responsible party's insurance or in court.

- **Home offices.** The equipment and furniture used for business purposes are not covered by standard homeowner's insurance policies. Likewise, the liability portion of your homeowner's insurance will not protect you if someone gets injured on your property while visiting for business reasons.

Self-defense: Add a "business pursuits" endorsement to your homeowner's coverage if you do business from home. Expect this to increase your premiums by approximately 5%.

- **College students.** Your child's possessions are not covered by your homeowner's policy if he/she lives in off-campus housing while attending college. However, a college student's possessions typically are covered by your policy if he lives in a college dorm, usually up to 10% of the policy limits.

Self-defense: Purchase renter's insurance for college-age kids who live in noncollege housing. It typically costs a few hundred dollars a year.

AUTO POLICIES

You might already know that most US auto insurance, especially for liability coverage, does not apply south of the Mexican border, which means you have to arrange for temporary "tourist" vehicle coverage from a Mexican insurance company. *Two other potential problem areas...*

- **Deer and other road obstacles.** If you have an accident with something that's moving (other than a vehicle)—such as a deer running across the road...or a rock rolling down from a hillside—your losses will not be covered by collision insurance. Your losses will be covered only if you have comprehensive insurance, which is often dropped by owners of older vehicles.

On the other hand, if you have an accident with something that's standing still—such as a deer that is frozen in your headlights in the mid-

dle of the road...or a rock that has rolled down a hillside and come to rest in your lane—you are covered by collision insurance.

Self-defense: If you don't have comprehensive insurance, make sure your insurance agent understands that the deer or rock you hit was standing perfectly still, assuming that was the case. If you have both collision and comprehensive coverage but your comprehensive deductible is lower, make sure your insurance agent understands that the deer or rock was moving.

- **Lending a car to a friend or relative.** Some auto insurance policies are "family style," meaning that they cover anyone who drives the vehicle with the owner's permission. Others are "named-insured only," meaning that they cover only drivers specifically named on the policy. If a car owner with a named-insured-only policy lends the vehicle to a friend or relative who then causes an accident, the car owner could be personally liable for all damages. If serious injuries are involved, the car owner might lose everything he owns in a lawsuit.

Self-defense: Do not lend out your vehicle unless you are certain that your insurance covers all drivers. Call your insurance company to check if the contract isn't clear. You also are on relatively safe ground if the person you lend your car to has auto insurance that covers him when he is driving someone else's vehicle.

Reduce Homeowner's Insurance Premiums

In addition to raising your deductible and using the same insurer for car and homeowner's policies, ask about discounts if you are over age 55—some insurers now cut rates by as much as 10% to 15%. Also, ask for loyalty rewards based on the number of years you have been a policyholder in good standing—5% discounts are common after three to five years and 10% discounts after six years.

Consumer Reports, 101 Truman Ave., Yonkers, New York 10703, www.consumerreports.org.

Home Insurance Know-How

Home insurers might raise your rates or even refuse to renew your policy if you have filed three or more small insurance claims in a single year.

Self-defense: Do not file a claim for only a few hundred dollars more than your deductible. Also, increase your deductible—a $1,000 deductible can lower your premium by 25%, compared with a typical $500 deductible, and will discourage you from filing small claims.

Carolyn Gorman, vice president, Insurance Information Institute at 110 William St., Washington, DC 10023, *www.iii.org.*

Homeowner's Insurance Danger

Since Hurricane Katrina, clauses that exclude damage from wind, water and mold are being inserted into homeowner's insurance policies across the Gulf coast, as well as in other parts of the US.

Self-defense: Review renewal contracts carefully to make sure these clauses have not been added. If they have, ask the insurer to remove them or consider switching insurers. For new policies, seek complete coverage.

Amy Bach, executive director of United Policyholders, a nonprofit insurance consumer-rights organization in San Francisco, *www.unitedpolicyholders.org.*

Take Inventory

Free home-inventory software helps you create a computer listing of everything you own. The Insurance Information Institute offers *Know Your Stuff* for PCs and Macs, free at *www.know yourstuff.org.* You can print out a paper copy and store a backup on a key chain–sized "Flash" drive to keep in a safe location outside the home, such as a safe-deposit box. Once completed, the inventory list is easy to update. A complete inventory, with details including serial numbers, photos and receipts, will make the insurance claims process much easier if you ever have a significant loss.

Should You Get Wedding Insurance?

Wedding insurance can be a good buy now that the average cost of a wedding is close to $30,000. Different insurance policies cover different contingencies.

Examples: Cancellation because of a death in the family...a natural disaster...the deployment of one member of the couple on military assignment.

Cost ranges from less than $200 to $1,000 or more.* Available at WedSafe.com (877-723-3933) and BridalAssociationofAmerica.com (866-699-3334).

Christa Vagnozzi, senior weddings editor, TheKnot.com, New York City.

*Prices subject to change.

9

Tax Time

Top Tax Planning Strategies for Now... And Beyond

Consider using these powerful strategies to reduce your next tax bill, from the savvy coauthor of *101 Tax Saving Ideas...*

INVESTMENTS

To get the most tax-free income from your investment portfolio...

•**Use the 0% federal tax bracket.** People in the 10% and 15% regular income tax brackets can receive long-term capital gains and qualified dividends free from federal tax in 2008.

These brackets cover taxable income up to $65,100 on a joint return and $32,550 on a single return. "Taxable income" is computed after subtracting all personal exemptions and deductions from your total income, so taxpayers with total income significantly over these amounts could qualify for the 0% tax rate. You must include the capital gain amount when determining if your taxable income falls within the 0% capital gains tax bracket.

If you can't use the 0% tax bracket because your income is too high, consider shifting investments to other family members who can use it—such as retired parents—to lower the family tax bill.

If you make a gift of...

•Stock that pays qualified dividends, the 0% tax bracket gift recipient can receive the dividends tax free.

•Capital gain property that you've held for more than one year, the 0% tax bracket recipient can sell the property using the long-term holding period carried over from you while paying tax at his/her own 0% rate.

Julie Welch, CPA, CFP, director, tax department, Meara Welch Browne, PC at 800 W. 47 St., Kansas City, Missouri 64112, *www.meara.com*. The coauthor of *101 Tax Saving Ideas* (Wealth Builders), she serves as a discussion leader for the American Institute of Certified Public Accountants' National Tax Education Program and is a past chairperson of the Taxation Committee of the Missouri Society of Certified Public Accountants.

143

• **Match up gains and losses.** First, check to see if you have a capital loss carryforward into 2008 of losses incurred in 2007 or prior years. Then tally up your realized gains and losses to date this year, plus unrealized gains and losses in your portfolio that you could take.

Goal: Match gains and losses so that gains are taken tax free. If you have net losses to date, take gains that offset them. If you have net gains to date, take losses that will offset them.

Extra benefit: Regularly taking losses to offset gains also gets you into the habit of continually reviewing your investments to prune out all the disappointments in a timely manner—and so may increase your investment returns.

GIFTS

Gifts of valuable assets made to other family members can save taxes two ways, by…

• **Shifting income-producing assets over to those in lower tax brackets.** Beware of the new "kiddie tax" rules in 2008. See IRS Publication 553, *Highlights of 2007 Tax Changes*.

• **Reducing the size of your estate to reduce your future estate tax bill.**

Making such gifts as early in the year as possible will maximize these tax benefits by shifting more income and, potentially, more appreciation than if the gifts are made later.

Rules: Gifts as much as $12,000 per recipient annually are exempt from gift tax. This limit is $24,000 when the gift is made jointly by a consenting married couple.

In addition, every person can make up to $1 million of lifetime gifts (over the $12,000 annual exempt amount) free of gift tax. These lifetime gifts decrease the amount of an estate that will be exempt from estate tax (currently $2 million). However, if your estate will be too small to owe estate tax, the gift costs nothing.

Even if you will owe estate taxes, these gifts can save tax by removing appreciation on assets from your estate as well as by reducing current income tax.

RETIREMENT ACCOUNTS

The sooner you place funds in a tax-favored retirement account, the more tax-favored investment returns it may receive during the year. So don't wait until the last minute to make an IRA contribution.

Safety: If you contribute more to an IRA than you are eligible to—say, due to an unexpected change in your circumstances that occurs later in the year (such as an increase in your income level or a change in your employment status)—you can withdraw the excess amount by April 15 of the following year without penalty.

If you participate in any other kind of retirement plan to which you can make contributions early in the year, such as a Keogh plan for the self-employed, do so as well. Check your plan's rules.

CHARITABLE GIFTS

Many people make charitable gifts with cash when they possess appreciated stock or mutual fund shares upon which they will, someday, incur taxable gain.

Better: Rather than cash, donate long-term-gain securities to a charity. You get a deduction for their full market value while avoiding ever paying capital gains tax on them.

EDUCATION

Congress has created a host of tax breaks to help pay for education—including adult education.

Examples: A business expense deduction for work-related education…student loan interest deduction…Hope credit…Lifetime Learning tax credit…Section 529 tax-favored college savings…Coverdell Education Savings Accounts…tax-free interest from Series EE and Series I savings bonds when the interest is used for tuition and fees at a higher education institution for yourself, your spouse or a dependent.

Snags: Each benefit has its own rules, including differing income limits for those eligible to use them…and using one may preclude using another.

Best: Examine all the options available to you and select the best for your situation. Find them all explained in IRS Publication 970, *Tax Benefits for Education*.

STATE TAXES

Most people focus on managing federal taxes, but state taxes can be costly as well—even more costly than federal taxes for many. State taxes include not only income taxes but also property taxes, sales taxes, inheritance taxes and others.

Don't overlook opportunities to cut these taxes. *Examples…*

• **If your home or other real estate you own has recently declined in value,** you may be able to have the property tax assessment on it reduced. Check the assessment appeal rules in your locality.

• **State tax rules create many specific local tax breaks**—such as income tax and property tax exemptions for seniors, tax deductions for medical costs, sales tax exemptions for specific items and others. There's no way to learn of these except by checking local rules, so do so with an expert.

Moving opportunity: Before moving from one state to another, check the tax effects. For instance, you might want to take capital gains on securities before or after the move, so you're living in the state that imposes the least tax.

RECORD KEEPING

It's very basic but important—the better your record keeping, the easier it will be to find tax-saving strategies…prepare your tax return…and defend all your deductions and other tax-saving strategies on it in an IRS audit.

Improve your record keeping by using one of the leading financial computer programs, such as Intuit's Quicken or Microsoft Money Plus, to record all of your investment activities and expenditures that may affect taxes.

Important: Whenever you sell an item, you'll need to know its "tax basis"—its cost to you for tax purposes—from which gain or loss will be determined.

Trap: People often lack basis records for items received as gifts or by inheritance or that have been held many years. But without a record of basis, the IRS may treat all of the proceeds from a sale as taxable gain.

This may occur with items ranging from an interest in the family business to a long-owned family vacation retreat to antiques and old family heirlooms.

If you received an item for a gift, you may need to learn the gift-maker's basis in it so that you can calculate your own. If you received an item by bequest, you might need information from the executor of the estate that left it to you. Collect such records now while you have time

and while the people who can give them to you are still available.

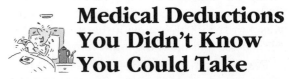

Medical Deductions You Didn't Know You Could Take

Benjamin Bohlmann, CPA, shareholder, Mallah, Furman at Brickell Bay Office Tower, 1001 Brickell Bay Dr., Miami, Florida 33131. The past chair of the South Florida–located US Taxation of Multinationals Discussion Group, Bohlmann's also a past president of the Greater Miami Tax Institute.

You may think that there is little or zero chance you can deduct medical expenses. After all, only unreimbursed outlays are deductible, and only to the extent that they exceed 7.5% of your adjusted gross income (or AGI). Even worse, if you are subject to the alternative minimum tax (AMT), only those medical costs over 10% of your AGI are deductible.

Harsh reality: As medical costs keep rising, many taxpayers' shares of medical bills will start to creep over the threshold. That may already be true for you if you are paying higher health insurance premiums with after-tax dollars and have high deductibles, copays and coinsurance (in which you pay a specific percentage of the total bill).

Silver lining: Some little-known Tax Code wrinkles may help you add to your list of tax-deductible medical expenses.

HOUSE CALLS

In some cases, capital improvements to your home qualify as deductible medical expenses.

Required: The capital improvement must be incurred primarily to alleviate a specific health condition.

Examples: A doctor tells you to install central air-conditioning to help you cope with asthma, allergies or other respiratory conditions. Alternatively, a daily swim is prescribed for your arthritis, so you install a pool. In yet another scenario, an elevator is said to be necessary because someone in your house has a heart condition.

What to do: Get before-and-after appraisals of your home. The amount you spend, minus the increase in your home's value, will be your medical deduction.

Say that you spend $25,000 installing central air-conditioning. A local real estate agent provides a written appraisal saying that your house, which was worth $300,000 previously, is now worth $315,000 as a result of the improvement.

Result: You spent $25,000 and your house appreciated by $15,000. The difference ($25,000 - $15,000 = $10,000) can be used as an itemized medical deduction.

In addition, ongoing operation and maintenance costs of the air-conditioning (or the pool or the elevator) may qualify as medical expenses. To calculate your deduction for air-conditioning, for example, you might figure the difference between your electricity expenses before central air-conditioning and your electricity costs after central air-conditioning, and include other costs, such as service contract, repairs, filters, etc.

Strategy: Before starting in on the home improvement, get a written recommendation from the physician who treats the individual with the health condition. Ask him or her to spell out the reasons the home improvement is necessary to treat that condition.

The physician's note, along with your before-and-after real estate appraisals, can support your medical deduction.

Note: The full cost of installing ramps or other improvements to accommodate a disability is a deductible medical expense.

ALL IN THE FAMILY

You probably know that money you spend on health care for yourself, your spouse and dependent children can be included when you're tallying medical bills.

Loophole: You also may be able to add money you spend for a parent's medical expenses. In fact, health-care costs that you pay for other relatives, such as siblings, grandchildren and in-laws, may be eligible for write-off, too.

Strategy: For these expenses to qualify, you must pay the provider of the health-care service or product directly. Don't give money to someone else so that he can pay.

Required: The person whose bills you pay needs to be a US citizen or a resident of North America (US, Canada, Mexico). In addition, you must provide more than half of what it costs for that person to live—all costs, not just medical expenses—during the year.

Loophole: You do not have to claim a relative as a dependent in order to take deductions for medical bills you pay for him. That relative needn't live with you, either.

Nonrelatives: You also can take deductions for medical bills paid for someone who isn't a relative, such as a domestic partner. That person must meet the qualifications mentioned above (a US citizen or a resident of the US, Canada or Mexico, for whom you provide more than half of living costs).

However, the nonrelative must live in your principal place of residence for the entire year.

OVERLOOKED DEDUCTIONS

Even if you are not improving your home for health reasons or you are supporting a nondependent, you may be able to boost your medical deductions. *Many taxpayers neglect to write off expenses for...*

• **Travel for medical care.** If you go by car, you can use the standard rate for medical travel. That's 19 cents a mile for the first six months of 2008, and 27 cents a mile for the last six months. You can add in money you spend for tolls and parking. If you don't use a car, then train fares, taxi fares, etc., can be included.

• **Weight-loss programs.** They're deductible if the weight loss is a treatment for a specific disease (such as obesity, hypertension or heart disease) diagnosed by a physician. You can write off fees you pay for membership in a weight reduction group and the cost of attending meetings.

• **Cosmetic surgery.** Although surgery solely to improve your appearance is not deductible, cosmetic surgery could be written off if it promotes the proper function of the body (for example, reconstructive dental work after an auto accident) or prevents or treats illness or disease (such as removing a precancerous mole).

Also, cosmetic surgery could be tax deductible if it's done to ameliorate a deformity caused by trauma, injury or disease. Repairing a nose ruined in a vehicle accident probably would qualify.

• **Dental treatment.** The costs are generally deductible, except for purely cosmetic processes, such as teeth whitening. If there's a question, get a statement from your dentist saying that the work was done for a specific health reason rather than for cosmetic purposes.

• **Vision care.** The costs of prescription eyeglasses, contact lenses and laser eye surgery may be included in deductible medical expenses.

• **Self-initiated diagnostic tests.** Amounts paid by a healthy individual for a full body scan or a home pregnancy test are deductible.

• **Smoking-cessation programs.** The costs of prescription drugs to help you deal with nicotine withdrawal are deductible, but not outlays for nonprescription nicotine gum and patches.

• **Long-term-care (LTC) insurance.** The premiums you pay for yourself, your spouse and someone else (dependents and nondependents, as explained on the previous page) are deductible, subject to age-based limits.

In 2008, those age 40 or younger can deduct up to $310 paid for LTC insurance. That scales up as you grow older and peaks for those over 70, who can deduct as much as $3,850 in LTC premiums in 2008. To find LTC deductible amounts, see page 14 of *IRS Revenue Procedure 2007-66* (*www.irs.gov/pub/irs-drop/rp-07-66.pdf*).

• **Other long-term-care services.** If you are paying for the long-term care of someone who cannot care for himself, those expenses—such as hiring a caregiver to assist a chronically sick individual with activities of daily living—may be deductible. The person you are caring for must meet the eligibility tests for deducting medical expenses described above.

have passed muster with the IRS (*www.irs.gov*) and/or the United States Tax Court (*www.ustaxcourt.gov*). Even if they do not apply directly to you, they may spark some ideas on how to be creative at tax time.

• **Pets as property.** The cost of moving the family pet is tax deductible when relocating for a job (the pet is treated as a personal household effect). If you own business property, such as a used car lot, and place food out to attract feral cats that also eat mice and snakes, thus making the property safer for customers, the cost of the pet food is deductible.

• **Enrollment in a boarding school.** Travel, room and board expenses—but not the tuition—were deductible as medical expenses for a child's enrollment in a boarding school in Arizona to help with his/her respiratory problems.

• **African safari.** The owners of a dairy business that used wild animals in its marketing were allowed to deduct the cost of a trip to Africa as an ordinary and necessary business expense. If you take a trip that benefits your business or job, you also might be able to deduct all or a portion of the expenses.

• **Clarinet lessons.** These were allowed as a deductible medical expense when recommended by a dentist to improve a child's overbite.

• **Lead paint removal.** When a home owner's child got sick from eating lead paint, the cost of paint removal was a deductible medical expense—but not the cost of repainting the home with nonlead paint.

• **Organic foods.** An allergy sufferer who is advised by a doctor to eat chemical-free foods could deduct the extra cost of buying organic foods—the cost in excess of buying conventional food.

Unusual Tax Deductions

Barbara Weltman, Esq., an attorney located in Millwood, New York, and author of *J.K. Lasser's 1001 Deductions & Tax Breaks* (Wiley). She is publisher of the free monthly on-line newsletter *Big Ideas for Small Business*, *www.barbaraweltman.com*.

When it comes to tax deductions, thinking outside the box can be productive. The following unusual tax deductions

Special School Expenses Now Deductible

The cost of sending a child to a special school to remedy a learning disability is deductible

147

as a medical expense, the IRS says in a new ruling.

Saver: The full cost of the school effectively becomes deductible if you pay for it through an employer's medical flexible spending account, into which you contribute part of pay on a tax-free basis to pay medical costs. Otherwise, the school costs are subject to the normal rule that limits the medical deduction to the amount by which it exceeds 7.5% of adjusted gross income.

Key: For the cost of the special school to be deductible, it must be recommended by a physician to help remedy a diagnosed disability (*Letter Ruling* 200704001).

Peter Weitsen, CPA/PFS, partner, WithumSmith+Brown, CPAs, One Spring St., New Brunswick, New Jersey 08901.

More from Peter Weitsen, CPA/PFS...

Are Cash Rewards Taxable?

Cash rewards received for using a credit card are tax free to the card owner who receives them. The IRS considers such cash rewards to be price discounts—and a promotional or volume discount off of the price of a product or a service is tax free.

How to Get Uncle Sam to Help Pay For Your Continuing Education

Sandy Soltis, CPA, tax partner, Blackman Kallick, 10 S. Riverside Plaza, Chicago 60606. Soltis provides tax-consulting services to middle-market businesses and their owners.

The Tax Code treats education kindly. Section 529 college saving plans, for example, have become familiar to parents and grandparents of college-bound youngsters.

Inside of 529 accounts, investment earnings aren't taxed. And there may be no tax on withdrawals if at least the same amount is spent on the beneficiary's higher education in the same year.

Beyond 529 plans: Tax benefits for education don't stop there by a long shot. Even when you are out of school, the IRS may give you a hand paying for ongoing learning.

WRITE-OFFS WHILE YOU WORK

If your employer requires you to take a course and you're not reimbursed, you can deduct your expenses. (Outlays will not be deductible if the course is taken to meet the minimum education requirements of your employer.)

Option plays: Even if you sign up for a class that is not required by your employer, unreimbursed outlays may be deductible.

Required: Such a course must help you to stay current or to advance in your present career.

Example: If you're an executive, the money you pay to take a management or a computer science course at the local college probably will be deductible, because these courses are likely to help in your career.

Trap: A course you take that prepares you for a new career will not generate tax-deductible expenses.

The IRS's position: If you are an employee, a change of duties that involves the same general kind of work is not a new trade or business. See Publication 970, *Tax Benefits for Education*, at *www.irs.gov.*

Example: You're an executive who goes to law school at night. Law school prepares you for a new career—as a lawyer—so the money you pay won't be deductible.

That will be true even if you do not intend to practice law but are taking the course to learn some legal fine points which will help you do your current job better. What counts to the IRS is whether you could use the course as preparation for a new career.

Allowed: Suppose you are taking a course that improves your current job skills but does not prepare you for a new career. You can deduct the costs of tuition and fees.

When a course is deductible as a career booster, you also can write off outlays for books and supplies. If you travel to the course from your work, you can deduct the corresponding travel expenses.

Current rate: The IRS standard rate for business-related auto use is 50.5 cents a mile for the first six months of 2008 and 58.5 cents for the last six months. This is the rate you can use for taking your car from work to a job-related course.

What if you pay your way to attend an out-of-town seminar? The costs are deductible if the trip was primarily for education, as long as the classes will help you in your current career.

TROUBLE ON YOUR TAX RETURN

Even though the education-related costs mentioned above are tax deductible, you might have difficulty actually getting any tax savings.

Reason: If you're an employee, such outlays are considered unreimbursed employee business expenses. Those expenses, in turn, fall into the category of miscellaneous itemized deductions on Schedule A of your tax return.

Hurdle: The miscellaneous deductions are deductible only to the extent that they exceed 2% of your adjusted gross income (AGI).

Example: Your AGI this year is $100,000, and all of your miscellaneous deductions total $3,200.

The first $2,000 of your miscellaneous itemized deductions is not deductible, so you can deduct only $1,200. If your miscellaneous deductions total, say, $1,900, no deduction will be allowed.

Trap: Miscellaneous itemized deductions are not allowed at all when calculating your alternative minimum tax (AMT) obligation. Under the AMT, you will not be able to write off any education expenses you incur as an employee, no matter how the total compares with your AGI.

SOLE SATISFACTION

There are some strategies that might help you take education-related deductions.

Example: You are an employee and you are not subject to the AMT. To take deductions for qualifying tuition, fees, books, supplies and travel, try to bunch your education outlays with prepayments of deductible items or delayed payments, where possible.

Bunching these payments into every other year might help you build up sufficient miscellaneous deductions to go beyond the 2%-of-AGI obstacle every other year. Instead of itemizing

education costs, check eligibility for the tuition and fees above-the-line deduction.

The self-employed solution: If you're self-employed, you can deduct qualified education outlays on Schedule C of your tax return. Even if you are only incidentally or casually self-employed, those expenditures may be deductible if you file a Schedule C to report some of your self-employment income.

Example: You have a full-time job, but you also earn $10,000 a year as a consultant. You pay $3,000 for a computer course that will enhance your skills when you consult for clients.

That $3,000 can be taken as a deduction on the Schedule C you file to report your consulting income.

Loophole: Taking education deductions on a Schedule C permits tax saving without having to contend with the 2%-of-AGI issue.

Big bonus: You can decrease your business income with these deductions even if you are subject to the AMT.

WHEN CREDIT IS DUE

Another possibility for education-related tax relief is to take a Lifetime Learning credit.

Required: You need to pay for a post–high school course given at an accredited institution. The course must be either part of a degree program or taken to acquire or improve job skills related to your current career.

Note: The IRS does not further narrow down eligible types of study. See IRS Publication 970, *Tax Benefits for Education.*

If the education qualifies, you may get a 20% credit on the money you spend for outlays up to $10,000 per year (maximum tax saving of $2,000 each year).

Income limits: For the maximum tax credit in 2008, your AGI (with minor modifications) must be less than $48,000 ($96,000 on a joint return). With up to $58,000 in AGI ($116,000 on a joint return), you can get a partial tax credit.

Assessing the AMT: Those otherwise eligible for the Lifetime Learning credit were able to use it in 2007 even if they were subject to the AMT that year, but that tax break has expired. Unless this provision is renewed for subsequent years, you won't be able to take the credit if you pay AMT.

Note: You cannot use the Lifetime Learning credit to offset expenses you are claiming as a deduction.

---

529 Plans Are Great, But Not for Everyone

Martin Shenkman, CPA and attorney who specializes in trusts and estates in New York City and Teaneck, New Jersey. He is also the author of many books, including *The Complete Book of Trusts* (Wiley). His Web site, *www.law easy.com*, provides sample forms and documents.

S ection 529 college saving plans do provide income tax, gift tax, estate tax and asset protection benefits. But, in spite of all the hype and publicity (which they deserve), 529s aren't for everyone.

If you are on either end of the wealth spectrum, there might be better options, which are often lost in the marketing barrage for 529 plans. *While 529s may be great for most people saving for a child's or grandchild's college, it depends on your specific situation...*

• **You are on the low end of the income/ wealth spectrum.** You may be better off with keeping the finances in your name. You might need the money for yourself. From an emotional perspective, you may not want to have your child see 529 money that he/she will assume is for college only to see you pull it out to meet a family emergency.

Also: Your tax bracket may not be so high that the tax advantages of a 529 account are that significant.

• **You're on the high end of the income/ wealth spectrum.** You might benefit your family more if, as part of an overall financial, asset protection and estate planning strategy, you establish trusts for all your children and grandchildren to which you can gift interests in a family business or investments at a discount, fractionalize ownership of family entities by these gifts, remove future appreciation from your estate and achieve other goals. You can, at these levels, al-

ways pay for tuition costs directly gift-tax free over and above the annual gifts you can make to the trusts (currently $12,000/year).

Lesson: 529 plans, like other estate and financial techniques, are a wise choice for some people, but not for everyone. Use discretion to be sure you're taking all the steps that are right for you.

 # Save Money (Even Make Money) on Housing for Your College Student

Greg Weyandt, CPA, MPA, director of operations for Welch Group, 3940 Montclair Rd., Birmingham, Alabama 35213. A partner in a wealth-management firm, Weyandt profited from an investment in housing when two of his children went to Auburn University.

I f you're sending a child to college away from home, be prepared to pay up big, and not just for tuition. For the 2007–2008 academic year, the average expense for room and board at public universities was more than $7,400, the College Board reports, up 5.3% from a year earlier. For private colleges, the average cost was around $8,600, up 5% from the previous year. Those are averages, so some schools were charging even more.

The bottom line: You can expect to spend $30,000 or more for room and board for each child who goes away to college for four years.

Strategy: Buy your child a place to live near the campus. In today's buyer's market for housing, you might find a very good deal.

If you sell the property a few years from now, you may get a better price. Even if you just break even on the real estate, you'll save by not paying for college housing.

What's more, tax breaks can increase your chances of coming out ahead.

REAL TAX BREAKS

In a simple example, you might buy an apartment where your daughter can live while she goes to school.

Tax benefits: If you itemize, and as long as you are not subject to the alternative minimum tax (AMT), you'll be able to deduct the property taxes you pay. If you use a mortgage to help finance the purchase, the interest you pay will be tax deductible as well. In essence, this apartment would be taxed as if you were using it as a second home.

Final accounting: When you sell the apartment, assuming that you've owned it for more than a year, any gain will be taxed at only 15%, as a long-term capital gain.

Trap: A loss on your sale won't be treated as a capital loss because you can't take a capital loss on the sale of a residence, so you would get no tax benefit.

Strategy: Rather than take a loss, you might prefer to rent out your apartment, perhaps to a different student, after your daughter moves on. You can receive rental income while you wait for your apartment's value to recover.

ALL IN THE FAMILY

A more ambitious venture is to buy a larger apartment than your child requires or a house near the campus.

Next step: Have your own child live in this residence and rent space in it to one or more other students. Because they'll pay rent to you, the residence will become an income-producing property.

Tax treatment: Operating costs will become tax deductible. That could include everything from utility bills to insurance.

You also will be able to take depreciation deductions for the real estate, furnishings, fixtures, etc.

Management fees: Name your child as the property manager. Your child's responsibilities can include screening tenants, getting leases signed, collecting rents, arranging for property maintenance and so on.

For those services, you could pay your child a management fee. Approximately 10% to 12% of the rental income received from tenants might be reasonable, depending on property management fees in the area.

Loophole: Such management fees will be deductible for you, the property owner. They can reduce taxable income from rents or contribute to a loss for tax purposes.

At the same time, all income from these management fees probably will be tax free to your child. In 2008, because of the standard deduction, single taxpayers may have up to $5,450 in earned income and owe no tax.

Therefore, this arrangement can be a tax-efficient way to give your collegian some spending money.

Travel smart: What's more, your trips to visit the college town may be deductible if your primary purpose is to check up on your investment property.

Note: Be sure to document that you checked on the house's condition, spoke with the property manager (your child) about maintenance, met with student-tenants to see if they have concerns, researched nearby rents, etc.

LOSS LEADER

Deductions for management fees, depreciation, travel and other expenses may generate a taxable loss from the property each year. This might be the case even if you have positive cash flow from rental income.

Tax treatment: Such a loss would be considered a passive loss. As long as your adjusted gross income (AGI) is less than $100,000, up to $25,000 worth of passive losses can be deducted each year.

As your AGI goes from $100,000 to $150,000, your maximum passive loss phases out, from $25,000 to zero.

Situation: Say your AGI in 2008 is $145,000. You are 90% through the phaseout range, so you are entitled to deduct only 10% of the maximum —you can deduct up to $2,500 worth of passive losses.

Say your college housing investment shows a $4,000 loss this year. You could deduct $2,500 in 2008.

The $1,500 that was not deducted can be carried forward into future years. If you have taxable passive income, such as from other rental properties, that $1,500 passive loss can serve as an offset.

End of the deal: When you ultimately sell the property, you can use any passive losses not previously deducted. Those losses can decrease a taxable gain or increase a capital loss from rental property.

PROCEED WITH CAUTION

Tax benefits will help a near-campus investment, but there is risk with any real estate venture. Some basic precautions can increase your chance of success.

Location: This is always crucial for real estate investing. Look for a place not far from the school in a neighborhood that's safe and doesn't seem intimidating in any way. A good location will help make student-tenants and their parents feel comfortable. Moreover, it will make it easier to eventually sell the property.

Tenant tactics: Be cautious about selecting tenants. Get references from employers to see if these students have been reliable. Have the students' parents sign 12-month leases and provide guarantees that they will be responsible for the rent. You might have to give those parents permission to sublet over the summer months.

Bonus: If you get your child involved in tenant screening and other aspects of managing the property, he/she could have some valuable insights to offer…and will probably pick up some valuable life lessons on what it takes to make a profit from a business venture.

How the IRS Will Help You Support Your Retired Parents

Sidney Kess, attorney and CPA at 10 Rockefeller Plaza, New York City 10020, coauthor/consulting editor of *Financial and Estate Planning* and coauthor of *1040 Preparation and Planning Guide 2008* (CCH). Over the years, he has taught tax law to more than 700,000 tax professionals.

I f your parents are retired and require some financial help, the IRS may help out by subsidizing the assistance you to give to them. *Tax-advantaged ways to get money to them…*

PRIVATE REVERSE MORTGAGE

Many retirees own valuable paid-off homes, but lack cash to spend.

A reverse mortgage provides funds to a home owner at least 62 years old with the owner's equity in the home securing the loan. Funds can be received through periodic payments (such as monthly) or a lump sum, and are tax free.

The home owner can continue to live in the home for life. The loan doesn't have to be repaid until the owner dies or sells the home, and is then paid off from the home-sale proceeds or from heirs refinancing the home. *But commercial reverse mortgages have two drawbacks that make many seniors reluctant to use them…*

• **Equity in the home is transferred outside the family.**

• **Fees and expenses tend to be high compared with those of other loans.** And maximum dollars paid out are restricted to a certain percentage that is based on the home owner's age. For more information, visit the reverse mortgage page of the AARP Web site, *www.aarp.org/money/revmort.*

STRATEGY

Make a private reverse mortgage loan to your parents. This keeps ownership of the home in the family with no expensive bank charges. *The tax effects…*

• **You can provide a large sum to your parents** without any gift tax problems.

• **Future estate taxes your parents could owe on the home are cut** by transferring their equity in it to you.

• **Fees and expenses incurred in making the loan are deductible** by the lender as an expense of earning interest income.

• **When the loan is repaid, your parents (or their estate) get a deduction** for the accumulated interest, which is paid to you.

Stepped-up basis still applies to a home you inherit when you provided a reverse mortgage on it—so all taxable gain on it until the date you inherit it is eliminated.

The interest you earn from making a reverse mortgage is taxable to you when you receive it at the time the loan is paid back—though the deduction available to your parents or their estate may offset it for overall family tax savings.

Caution: Private reverse mortgages must be legally enforceable and carry a market interest rate, so consult a lawyer as well as a tax adviser when making one.

GROUP LOANS

If you can't afford to fund a reverse mortgage by yourself, a group of individuals (family members and friends) can do so with you.

The on-line site for Virgin Money US (*www. virginmoneyus.com*) facilitates such group loans by providing its group members with electronic fund transfers, escrow and tax payment administration, title searches, record keeping and related services. Loan terms can be customized.

LONG-TERM-GAIN ASSETS

You can make gifts of long-term-gain assets and/or dividend-generating assets to parents in the 15% or lower tax bracket. They can then sell the capital gain assets and/or receive dividends tax free.

In 2008, the tax rate on long-term capital gains and qualified dividends is 0% for persons in the regular 10% or 15% tax bracket. This may include married couples with approximately $80,000 of income or less, and singles with about $40,000.

Calculated: During 2008, the 15% tax bracket covers taxable income up to $65,100 for joint filers, who also receive a standard deduction of $10,900, with a spouse receiving a personal exemption of $3,500, and, if age 65 or above, another $1,050 added to the standard deduction. For a couple who are both age 65, this totals to gross income of $85,100, leaving them still in the 15% tax bracket. Single filers get about half these amounts. These numbers are adjusted annually for inflation.

The annual gift tax exclusion means gifts of up to $12,000 per recipient are free of gift tax ($24,000 to two spouses, or $48,000 from a couple to two spouses).

HIRE PARENTS

Though often recommended for children, hiring parents in a family business can have big advantages, too…

• **Salaries are deductible at your (or your business's) high tax rate** and taxed at your parent's lower rate.

• **Retirement benefits for your parents may be increased.** They could qualify, along with other employees, for 401(k) and other tax-favored benefits, including a health plan. And if younger than age 70½, parents may be able to contribute to a deductible IRA to increase their retirement finances while you effectively deduct the cost.

MEDICAL EXPENSES

If you pay more than half a parent's support, you may be able to deduct on your return medical expenses you pay on your parent's behalf—even if the parent does not live with you and does not qualify as your dependent.

Long-term-care insurance could be especially valuable as such an item—to protect your parents' home and other wealth (and your inheritance) from costly nursing-home care that may be needed in the future. If your parents can't afford to buy insurance, or are in too low a tax bracket to get a significant deduction for it, you may be able to buy it for them and then deduct it yourself.

For people ages 61 to 70, $3,080 of the premium cost is deductible in 2008. For people older than age 70, $3,850 is deductible.

Planning: You do not have to provide most of a parent's income to provide most of his/her support. "Support" consists of expenditures on living expenses. So, if your parent saves pension income in a savings account while you pay his medical and other living costs, you may provide most of your parent's support while providing less than half his income.

Other medical costs you might deduct if you pay them for a parent include the cost of a caregiver, prescription medications, medical equipment, medical care at a nursing home, etc.

CLAIM AS A DEPENDENT

If you provide more than 50% of a parent's support and the parent has less than $3,500 of taxable income during 2008, you may be able to claim the parent as a dependent and take an exemption of $3,500 against your income.

Example: Your parent's income consists of $2,500 of taxable interest on savings and $12,000 of Social Security benefits, which are tax free. The parent meets the income test to be claimed as a dependent.

If multiple family members combine to support a parent but no one person provides more than 50% of the parent's support, they can file IRS Form 2120, *Multiple Support Declaration*, to

153

obtain a dependency exemption for one among them.

PROVIDE A HOUSEHOLD

If your tax filing status is single, but a parent comes to reside in a home (including a nursing home) for which you provide more than half of the household cost, you could qualify for head of household tax status, which provides lower tax rates.

Helpful: For more details on the rules defining support, qualifying a parent as a dependent and qualifying to deduct a parent's medical expenses, check IRS Publication 501, *Exemptions, Standard Deduction, and Filing Information,* and Publication 502, *Medical and Dental Expenses.*

Surefire Ways to Fight a Property Tax Assessment

Nicholas A. Nesi, JD, CPA, multistate tax partner, BDO Seidman, LLP, 330 Madison Ave., New York City 10017. Nesi specializes in state and local tax audits.

When the property tax bill on your home arrives, don't assume it's correct—especially if your home's assessed value has changed sharply during the recent up-and-down swing in the real estate market.

Checking the correctness of your assessment could be easier than you think—and save you hundreds or even thousands of dollars in property taxes annually. *What to know...*

FINDING ERRORS

Errors in local property tax assessments are common. It's easy to see why—local tax assessors almost never have the time and resources to examine all their local properties individually in detail.

Instead, they assess numbers of properties by general descriptive factors, like type of building, location, date of construction, initial price and similar factors. But this process can omit specific traits of individual properties that have a significant effect on their value.

Moreover, as the real estate prices move up or down generally over time, assessors adjust assessed values for groups of properties in a manner similar to applying an inflation factor.

But the average change in value of a group of properties as a whole can be very different from the change in value of one particular property within the group—yet another source of assessment error.

The big swing in real estate prices in recent years—first up, then down in many areas—increases the risk that the valuation adjustments applied generally by the assessor's office will produce a result that differs from a property's real market value.

When you receive your property tax bill, take a good look at all the information on it (which will vary by locality). A bill should provide the assessed value of your home, give the deadline by which the assessment must be challenged to reduce tax for the current year, and give contact information for the local assessor's office.

CHECK YOUR ASSESSMENT

Examine the tax assessor's description of your home in detail. This won't be found on the assessment notice mailed to you—you will have to visit the assessor's office and look at the information on file there describing your home. This information is freely available to you (and to anyone). *Look for...*

● **Errors in the factual description.** For instance, your home might be described as containing more square footage, more rooms, more bedrooms or bathrooms, or even more stories than it actually does. Or it might be described as being newer than it really is.

● **Omissions of unique factors that might decrease value.** Your home might be located on a lot with a drainage problem, or be situated next to railroad tracks...its foundation might be cracking due to faulty construction...recent renovations, such as updated bathrooms, might have been overvalued...the land it is on might be subject to a restrictive legal easement that reduces its value.

Pointing out such factual errors and omissions in your file to the assessor's office may obtain you a reduced assessment right there. And you can do this all by yourself just by checking the records.

Also, verify the market value of your home against the assessor's estimate. If your home's actual market value is less than the value that's assigned by the assessor, you should be entitled to a reduction in assessed value.

You may suspect that this is the case if homes similar to yours in your neighborhood have recently sold for less than the assessor's valuation of your home…or if you bought your home at the "market high," its assessed value is the price you paid for it, and prices have since fallen in your area.

However, to convincingly document market value of your home, you'll need a professional appraisal from a real estate appraiser.

Cost: Around $400.

Saver: If you recently refinanced your home, the appraisal of it obtained for the bank may serve your purpose. (By the same token, whenever you refinance your property, check the appraisal obtained for the bank to see if it suggests that you should challenge your current property tax valuation.)

Important: Do not confuse the "tax value" or "assessed value" of your home, to which the property tax rate is applied when computing tax owed, with its market value.

Many localities tax only a portion of a property's market value—as little as 10% in Louisiana. That may make it look like your property is undertaxed, when in fact it is overtaxed.

Example: Your home has a market value of $400,000. The property tax bill you receive shows tax applying only to a value of $250,000, so you think you are getting a bargain. But by law, your locality taxes just 50% of a property's market value. So, in reality, the assessor has assigned your home a market value of $500,000—two times the $250,000 assessment and $100,000 more than the actual market value—and you are being overtaxed.

CHECK "COMPARABLES"

The property taxes you pay for your home should be about the same as that paid by others who own homes similar to yours. Property taxes are a matter of public record, so you can check this out. *How…*

• **Ask the assessor's office what homes it uses as being comparable with yours,** and check their descriptions.

• **Ask a real estate agent who uses a multiple listing service for a listing of homes comparable with yours.** Then check the list to see the taxes paid on these homes.

If you pay more tax on your home than others pay on comparable homes, document this for the assessor.

APPEALS

Fixing errors in your property tax assessment can be easier than you would expect—with no lawyer necessary in the typical home owner's case.

Key: The assessor's job is to get assessments right. So correcting an assessment is not an adversarial proceeding like a court trial or a dispute with the IRS over a contested tax deduction.

The tax assessment review proceedings, also known as "certiorari," vary by locality, but generally there are three steps to contesting a tax assessment…

• **Talk to the assessor.** This is an informal, person-to-person conversation during which you simply explain your case. If you show the assessor that a factual error has been made with your property, you are likely to get a correction—and a tax reduction—right there.

The property tax bill you receive should tell how to contact the assessor, or you can inquire with your local governmental offices.

If meeting with the assessor does not produce the desired result …

• **Meet with the local property tax appeal panel or a board of review.** With factual errors corrected at the assessor's office, an appeal is most likely to deal with an "arguable" issue, such as a valuation based on comparable properties. The appeal board will specify filings you must provide to document your case (such as an appraisal or list of comparable properties).

Again, no lawyer is necessary in the typical home-owner case, and the process is relatively informal compared with other legal proceedings, with negotiation possible to reach a compromise result.

• **File with a higher appeal board,** or go to court, if the appeal result is not satisfactory. This will likely involve obtaining professional representation because the issues involved are complicated, and you'll have to weigh the expense against the tax involved. But most home-owner cases are settled before reaching this level.

Important: Before you decide to question an assessment, learn about the appeal procedures in your state from the assessor's office. States set the procedures, and local jurisdictions set their own tax rates. Some states set very quick deadlines for questioning a tax assessment—and you don't want to fail to get a tax reduction just because you didn't ask for it on time.

Useful: The property tax authorities in many states and localities now have Web sites. If yours does, scour it early in the process to learn what you can.

Mortgage Interest Deduction Loopholes

Edward Mendlowitz, CPA, partner in the CPA firm of WithumSmith+Brown at One Spring St., New Brunswick, New Jersey 08901. He's also author of *The Adviser's Guide to Family Business Succession Planning* (American Institute of Certified Public Accountants).

Certain interest paid on mortgages, home-equity loans and investments can be deducted on Schedule A, Form 1040. *How to maximize your home-ownership-related interest deductions...*

Loophole: **Interest on home-equity loans up to $100,000 can be deducted no matter how the funds are used.** If a home-equity loan is secured by a mortgage on property, you can use the proceeds to pay off credit card debt, for car purchases and for other items for which interest ordinarily would not be deductible. When a home mortgage is refinanced and the money is used for personal purposes, the interest is not deductible.

Caution: Interest on the maximum amount of home-equity debt can be deducted only if the taxpayer has net equity in the residence of at least $100,000 after subtracting the value of any other mortgages.

Loophole: **Interest on home mortgages of up to $1 million is deductible if the money is used to construct, acquire or improve a residence (known as "acquisition indebtedness").** Interest is also deductible on multiple mortgages on the same primary residential property and/or a second personal residence, as long as the total debt on both houses doesn't exceed $1 million.

Strategy 1: Taxpayers with multiple "second" residences or vacation homes can designate annually which property will generate the mortgage interest deduction for the year.

Note: Real estate taxes are deducted for all multiple residential properties.

Strategy 2: Time interest payments on outstanding loans, if possible, depending on your need for annual tax deductions. If no deduction is needed in one year, for instance, because you will be using the standard deduction, allow the interest charges to accumulate until a year when the payment would create a tax savings.

Note: Interest paid in advance (except for the points paid on a mortgage—see below) isn't tax deductible.

Caution: Interest that accrues on mortgages (including reverse mortgages) is not deductible until it is paid. Interest is not deemed paid if a promissory note is issued for the interest owed.

Loophole: **Borrowers of a qualified mortgage (one used to construct, acquire or improve a residence) greater than $1 million up to and including $1.1 million can allocate the mortgage between acquisition indebtedness and home-equity indebtedness.** This allows them to deduct interest on the extra $100,000.

Loophole: **Points paid to a lender by an individual taxpayer (who does not use accrual-basis accounting) on a qualified home mortgage are deductible in the year paid.** Points paid when a mortgage is refinanced are deducted over the life of the mortgage. Any remaining points on mortgages repaid before the mortgage falls due are deductible in the year of the repayment.

If refinancing proceeds are used to improve a residence, the points are deductible in full when paid.

Loophole: **Get a long-term mortgage from a family member with interest at the applicable federal rate.** This is the minimum rate required by the IRS on intrafamily loans. Rates are published by the IRS monthly (at *www.irs.gov*, just type "applicable federal rates" into the search box). The loan could carry a fixed long-term rate for 20 or 30 years, or a short-term rate that is reset every three years.

Reasons: When a family member holding a long-term mortgage dies, you can discount the mortgage for estate tax purposes, reducing the amount that would be subject to estate taxes, if the current mortgage market interest rate exceeds the family mortgage's rate. Or with a reset provision, the mortgage value can be discounted even more if short-term interest rates are lower than the long-term rates at the time of death.

Caution: File the mortgage with the county clerk to secure your tax deduction. If interest is not paid on family mortgages, then it is imputed, triggering interest income and a taxable gift by the mortgagor.

Loophole: **The interest on mortgages and home-equity loans in excess of $1.1 million can be deducted if the proceeds are used for investment or for business reasons and the proceeds are specifically traced to a deductible business/investment expense.**

How to do it: Document the flow of the funds into the business or investment. If the funds are segregated into a separate account before they are disbursed, any disbursement within 30 days (before or after) of receiving the loan can be attributed to the deductible activity.

You must maintain records tracing the flow of funds. These tracing rules apply to all loans not directly used to acquire investment or business property. It also applies to partnerships and closely held C corporations that borrow money that is distributed to owners or stockholders.

Example: You write a check for more than $100,000 from your home-equity line of credit and deposit it into your sole proprietorship account—then use all of that money to pay for the purchase of business equipment within 30 days of the initial deposit. To deduct interest on the portion of the home mortgage loan related to the business purchase, you must document the purchase and allocate the correct amount of home-equity interest. Had you instead purchased the equipment directly, using the home-equity line of credit, tracing would not be necessary.

Avoid the Big Tax Hit

Looking to sell your home even though you have lived in it for less than two years? Normally, selling any home for a profit within two years of purchasing it triggers a tax hit.

But: If you need to sell the house because of certain unforeseen circumstances—being the victim of a crime…a change in place of employment…or health reasons—you may qualify for special tax relief that reduces or eliminates the tax penalty.

Best: Talk to a knowledgeable tax expert.

Gail Levin Richmond, JD, associate dean of academic affairs at Nova Southeastern University Law Center, Fort Lauderdale, Florida.

The Tax Rules For eBay Sellers

Barbara Weltman, Esq., an attorney based in Millwood, New York, and coauthor of *The Complete Idiot's Guide to Starting an eBay Business* (Alpha). She is publisher of the free monthly on-line newsletter *Big Ideas for Small Business, www.barbaraweltman.com.*

With more than 233 million registered users, eBay is the world's largest marketplace. Millions take advantage of this on-line venue to sell anything and everything—from junk that is around the house to diamond rings, cars and forklifts.

Just because sales activities are on-line, doesn't mean they are invisible. You still need to know the tax rules to follow in reporting your eBay sales.

When you sell items on eBay, the tax law may view you as belonging to one of three categories—casual seller, hobbyist or business owner.

Where you report income and whether you can deduct expenses depends on your category. There's no bright line based on revenue or number of sales dividing these categories—a lot of factors come into play. *Here is what you need to know...*

FOR CASUAL SELLERS

If you sell an item or two from time to time, such as unused sports equipment sitting in your garage, you are a casual seller. (There is no formal designation in the tax law of "casual seller." It's a descriptive term.)

Most sales like this will result in a loss—the price you receive on eBay will be less than what you paid for the item. You are not required to report the loss on your tax return—you cannot deduct it, because it is viewed as a personal loss, and personal losses are not deductible.

On the other hand, if you sell something at a profit—say, the antique porcelain vase you inherited from your aunt or the collectible child's game you purchased at a garage sale—you must report the gain on your tax return. (Of course, to determine your gain, you'll have to know your basis in an item—generally, either the amount you paid for it...or, if it was given to you, the donor's basis...or, if you inherited it, its value at death of the decedent.) If you don't know what your basis is, then all of the proceeds are considered profit (gain).

Note: You can minimize taxable gain by adding your selling expenses to your basis. Selling expenses include eBay listing fees (the "insertion fees" paid to eBay to post items for sale) and "final value fees" (a percentage of the item's final selling price that is also paid to eBay). The fees are paid by the seller.

There is no threshold amount of gain or number of sales before you are required to report eBay transactions. All gain must be reported on Schedule D. (You cannot take capital losses because these are personal items.)

Gains on the sale of items are capital gains—long-term if the items have been held for more than a year, or short-term if they are held for a year or less.

However, unlike most long-term capital gains that are taxed at no more than 15%, gains on the sales of collectibles are taxed at 28% for those in income tax brackets of 28% and above.

Collectibles for this purpose are defined in the instructions for Schedule D as works of art, rugs, antiques, precious metals (such as gold, silver and platinum bullion), gems, stamps, coins and certain other tangible property.

FOR HOBBYISTS

If you sell items on eBay more frequently but your sales aren't profitable (your expenses exceed your revenue), you may be looked upon by the IRS as merely having a hobby, rather than a business. Unless you can prove that you have a profit motive, then income is ordinary income reported as "Other income" on Form 1040, but deductions can only be claimed to the extent of this income. If you make $1,000, your deductions cannot exceed $1,000.

These limited deductions from a hobby are treated as miscellaneous itemized expenses deductible to the extent that they exceed 2% of adjusted gross income (AGI).

Trap: Individuals subject to the alternative minimum tax (AMT) lose any benefit from hobby write-offs because miscellaneous itemized expenses are not deductible for AMT purposes.

eBAY BUSINESS OWNERS

To move out of the hobby classification, you need to have a profit motive. This elevates your hobby to a business and lets you deduct business expenses—and losses. *Profit motive is demonstrated by...*

- **Running your activity in a businesslike way** (have a business plan, keep good books and records and maintain a separate business bank account and credit card).

- **Devoting considerable time to your activities on eBay.**

- **Consulting with business experts,** such as accountants and successful eBay sellers, on how to improve profitability.

TAX RESPONSIBILITIES

More than 1.3 million people have full-time or part-time businesses on eBay. *If you are one of these people, be sure to observe the following tax responsibilities...*

- **Report income and expenses.** Like any other sole proprietor, you must file Schedule C to report your income and expenses for the year. (If you form a legal entity for your business, such as a corporation, you must file appropriate tax returns for the business.)

The difference between your gross receipts for the items you sell and your cost of inventory, called the "cost of goods sold," less any returns, is your income from eBay activities.

Being in business also means that you can write off eBay-related expenses. *Examples...*

• Car expenses. You can deduct business use of your personal car for travel to garage sales, flea markets, and other locations where you buy your items or otherwise conduct business, as well as trips to the post office or other shipping companies to mail your items to buyers. Write off your actual costs of business use of your car or take the IRS's standard mileage rate of 50.5¢ per mile for the first six months of 2008 and 58.5¢ for the second six months, plus any parking fees and tolls.

• Fees paid to eBay and PayPal (an on-line payment company).

• Home-office costs, provided you use your space, such as a spare room, regularly and exclusively for your eBay business.

• Internet access fees if personal use is kept to a minimum.

• Tools for sales and management. Typically, these devices, which help you automate listing and tracking eBay sales, involve deductible monthly or annual subscription fees. Software costs may be expensed (deducted) or depreciated.

• **Pay self-employment tax.** If your eBay activities are profitable, you owe self-employment tax, which covers Social Security and Medicare taxes.

Break: If eBay is a sideline business for you (you are an employee at another company), the Social Security portion of this tax may be covered at your place of work through FICA withholding. The wage base for 2008 is at $103,000, so anyone with wages at or above this amount from which FICA has been withheld won't owe the Social Security portion of self-employment tax. However, there is no wage base restriction for the Medicare portion of the tax, so profitable eBay businesses will always owe some self-employment tax. See instructions to IRS Schedule SE (which is part of Form 1040) for details.

• **Collect sales tax.** Just because a business is conducted on the Web doesn't automatically exempt transactions from state and local sales tax rules. With more than 8,000 sales tax jurisdictions nationwide, sales tax is complicated. In general terms, a seller needs to collect sales tax on items sold to buyers within his/her state, so check with your state revenue department for information about your collection and reporting responsibilities.

Break: eBay business owners should obtain a state sales tax number (also known as resale number) under which to report sales tax collections. You can get the number from your state revenue department. Sellers can then use this number to avoid paying sales tax on items purchased for resale (i.e., their inventory).

Very-Last-Minute Year-End Tax Savers

Laurence I. Foster, CPA/PFS, tax consultant based in New York City and former partner at Eisner LLP. Foster was chairman of the Personal Financial Specialist Credential Committee at the American Institute of Certified Public Accountants (AICPA).

You can use these ideas right through December 31 to cut your 2008 tax bill.* *But if you wait until after that date, it will be too late...*

PERSONAL COSTS

• **Deductible expenses.** Be sure to pay by year-end all of the year's expenses for which tax deductions are permitted on a personal return, and if you don't have the cash, charge them (see "Personal Write-Offs" at the end of this article).

Examples: Medical expenditures—to the extent that they exceed 7.5% of adjusted gross income (AGI)—mortgage interest, alimony, investment fees, legal expenses, subscriptions to financial publications and tax advisory fees.

• **Dependency exemptions.** Protect dependency exemptions (for other than qualified children) by being sure that you pay more than half the support of any person you intend to claim as a dependent. A year-end support payment may

---

*Eligibility for these strategies varies, and some of the rules are complex—so consult your tax consultant as to which, if any, of these moves applies to your situation.

be needed to get you over the limit. Also, remember to get Social Security numbers for your children.

• **College savings.** Some states permit state income tax deductions for contributions to Section 529 college savings plans. If your state does, and you're planning to send a child to college, consider making one.

• **Adoptions.** An adoption tax credit of up to $11,650 is allowed for expenses of adopting a child. The credit reduces your 2008 tax bill dollar for dollar. So, if you're adopting a child, make sure qualifying expenses are paid by year-end to get the credit. Rules are complicated—check with your tax adviser.

PREPAID EXPENSES

• **Tuition and education expenses incurred for higher education** for an academic period starting in the first quarter of 2009 can qualify to give you a tuition deduction, Hope credit or Lifetime Learning credit on the 2008 tax return, if paid by year-end.

• **Mortgage interest** owed in January 2009 is deductible this year if paid in December.

• **State and local income tax and property tax payments** due in 2009 (such as an estimated payment due on January 15) are deductible on the federal 2008 return if prepaid in 2008, and if state law allows you to prepay such taxes.

Note: Don't prepay if you're subject to the alternative minimum tax.

CHARITY

• **Last-minute donations are deductible as long as they are made by year-end.** Be sure to have proper documentation of any donation. Rules vary by size and type of donation. Check IRS Publication 526, *Charitable Contributions*, for details.

• **Direct gifts from your IRA to charity.** If you are age 70½ or older, you can transfer up to $100,000 directly from your IRA to a qualified charity tax free. The transfer will count toward your minimum required annual distribution that otherwise would be taxable. This break expired December 31, 2007, but Congress may extend it.

RETIREMENT PLANS

• **401(k) accounts.** Although you contribute during the year to your 401(k), some plans allow

extra year-end contributions if you haven't contributed the maximum permitted. Consult your plan administrator.

• **Annual minimum distributions.** Take any annual minimum distribution that you are required to receive from your IRA, Keogh or other retirement savings plan. If you are age 70½ or older, you are subject to such distributions—and failure to take them by year-end results in a 50% penalty.

• **IRAs.** Convert a traditional IRA to a Roth IRA to obtain future tax-free investment returns from a Roth IRA while escaping the minimum annual distribution requirements. (You could reconsider and reverse an IRA conversion—for example, if you find later that your modified AGI exceeded eligibility limits or that you can make the IRA conversion at lower tax cost later if the value of your account has dropped—as late as October 15, 2009. You may reverse a conversion only once in a single year.)

INVESTMENTS

• **Capital losses.** Take capital losses to wind up with a $3,000 net loss for the year. A loss of up to that much is deductible against ordinary income.

• **Bond swaps.** Make bond swaps to generate tax losses without significantly changing your investment position. This strategy is for individual bonds—not shares in a bond fund.

How: Sell a bond that has declined in value, and use these proceeds to buy another similar but not identical one (to avoid violating the IRS wash-sale rule that would disallow the loss)—such as a bond with the same credit rating, paying the same interest rate, issued by a different firm in the same industry. The capital loss on the sale is deductible, but your bond holdings stay almost exactly the same.

• **Worthless securities.** Sell near-worthless securities and investments by year-end to get a capital loss in 2008 for their loss in value.

• **Early withdrawals.** Penalties incurred on early withdrawals of savings (such as time deposits and CDs) are tax deductible—so if you're planning to make such a withdrawal soon, doing so before year-end will accelerate the penalty deduction into 2008.

SMALL BUSINESS

• **Expensing.** The cost of equipment up to $250,000 is deductible if the equipment is put into service, not just purchased, by the end of 2008.

• **Business cars.** Depreciation deductions are sharply limited on autos, so business autos usually have a depreciated basis (purchase cost minus depreciation deductions) that's higher than their market value. When such an auto is sold for market value, this difference is a deductible loss. Do not trade such a vehicle in toward the cost of a new one, or no loss deduction will be currently allowed—it will be deferred until the replacement auto is sold.

• **Deductible expenses.** Run up discretionary deductible expenses.

How: Buy supplies, pay for nonemergency repairs, buy advertising and incur other business costs over which you control the timing.

• **Bills.** Pay all outstanding bills if the business uses cash-basis accounting to nail down deductions for this year.

• **Depreciation.** Abandon all excess inventories and unneeded equipment that is not fully depreciated to deduct your firm's cost basis in them. Don't merely write these items off on the books—they must be physically disposed of (or donated to a qualifying charity) by year-end.

• **Holiday helpers.** Hire children and family members to work for the business during the holidays. Their salaries will be deducted at the business's higher rate and taxed at their lower rates—and could be used by them to fund tax-favored IRAs.

• **Holiday business gifts.** Gifts are generally deductible up to $25 per recipient when used to generate "goodwill" among current and potential business customers and associates.

PERSONAL WRITE-OFFS

• **Marital status.** Get married or divorced, or delay doing so. Year-end marital status can have a big effect on your tax bill. Ask your adviser whether it is better for you to "hurry it up" or to wait awhile.

• **Gifts.** Make gifts to younger family members using the $12,000 per recipient annual gift tax exclusion. While a gift on December 31 won't save income tax in 2008, it can save it from the very start of 2009 if it shifts income earned on the gift amount into a lower tax bracket. The gift may also reduce future estate tax. But, if it's not made by year-end, 2008's tax-free gift amount will be lost.

• **Gambling.** Winnings are taxable, but losses are deductible against them on an itemized return. So, if you have net winnings to date, a last-minute gambling trip will either produce more winnings or produce deductible losses that save tax on your winnings to date.

• **Credit cards.** Remember, use credit cards to make last-minute deductible expenditures if you lack cash to pay them. Charges made on a general-use card (not a store card) are deductible when made, even if paid off in a later year.

• **Tax withholding.** Adjust tax withholding from your last paychecks.

How: Estimate whether your final tax bill for the year will be more or less than what you've paid through estimated taxes and withholding. If more, reduce withholding from your last paychecks to get an "advance tax refund." If less, increase withholding from your last paychecks to eliminate or reduce an underpayment penalty.

More from Laurence Foster, CPA/PFS...

When Is Your Return Safe from Audit?

The IRS generally has three years to audit a tax return starting from the later of its original due date or the date on which it was actually filed. So, if you file your return before April 15, the three-year period starts on April 15, while if you file later, it starts on your return's actual filing date.

Caution: The limitation period is six years if your return understates income by more than 25%, and there is no limitation period if you commit fraud on your return or don't file at all.

Common Filing Errors

Martin S. Kaplan, CPA, 11 Penn Plaza, New York City 10001, *www.irsmaven.com*. He is a frequent guest speaker at insurance, banking and financial planning seminars and is author of *What the IRS Doesn't Want You to Know* (Villard).

Be on the lookout for these common filing mistakes the next time you prepare your tax return...

•**Not filing because you can't pay what you owe.** The penalty for late paying is only 0.5% per month, but for late filing it is 5% per month. So, file on time no matter what, and pay later if you have to.

•**Attaching receipts or other papers to a return.** At most, write a short explanation on the return next to unusual items—such as "heart surgery" next to very large medical expenses.

•**Delaying filing because information returns are missing.** If Forms W-2, 1099 or K-1 are late or missing, estimate the income they'll report and then include it on the return. File an amended return later.

•**Form 1099 mismatches.** If 1099 income does not match with the corresponding amount reported on a return, IRS computers will notice the mismatch and send an audit notice. If you think a 1099 is erroneous, write the amount that is incorrect on your return with an adjustment showing the correct amount and a brief note of explanation.

•**Social Security number mistakes.** When "married filing separately," make sure that you include your spouse's Social Security number. The IRS will want to check for inconsistencies in both spouses' returns.

•**Leaving out an employer identification number** if you employ child-care providers.

•**Schedule C expense misallocations.** The costs of tax planning, legal expenses, business publications, etc., are fully deductible as business expenses by a proprietor on Schedule C. Be able to justify your allocations—if you put 100% of them on Schedule C, an auditor may question whether some weren't really personal costs.

•**Basis miscalculations on capital gains.** Calculate basis very carefully.

More from Martin Kaplan, CPA...

Home-Office Audit Danger?

The home-office deduction is much less of an audit red flag today than it was a generation ago. It is far more common, and Congress and the IRS have regularized rules that once led to tax disputes. Today, it doesn't particularly create more audit risk than any other common business deduction unless it is unusual in size or in some other way—which is true of all deductions.

If you file an honest return and are legitimately entitled to any deduction, you should take it and not fear an IRS auditor. There's no point in paying more than you owe to the IRS.

Safety: Check all the rules in IRS Publication 587, *Business Use of Your Home*, and take photos of your office to document how you use it in case the IRS asks.

The Check Sent with Your Return May Be Paying a Different Tax

Fred A. Windover, TC Summary Opinion 2007-50.

When you send a check to the IRS, always write on it specifically what tax it is to be applied against, for example, "2008 Form 1040." If you don't do this, the IRS can apply the check as it chooses—to your surprise and cost.

New case: Even a check attached to a tax return may be applied to a different tax bill.

Facts: Fred Windover filed his 1999 tax return and included a check for $13,178, the exact amount shown as due on the return. But the IRS applied more than $12,000 of the check to other tax bills that it said Windover owed. Windover didn't realize this until he received a later IRS tax bill for 1999 that had grown to more than $17,000 with interest and additions to tax. Soon after, the IRS threatened to levy to collect the tax, and Windover protested by going to court.

Tax Court: According to the IRS's published procedures, if no particular written instructions designating how to apply a tax payment are accompanying it, "the Service will apply the payment to periods in the order of priority that the Service determines will serve its best interest." Windover didn't provide any written instructions on or with his check as to what tax it was to be applied against. Moreover, the "common sense" belief that a check sent with a tax return will be applied to the tax reported on the return does not constitute written instruction indicating how the check is to be applied.

So, the IRS was free to apply the check sent with the return as it wished, and it can proceed with the levy.

Money-Saving Steps When You Get a Tax Bill

E. Martin Davidoff, CPA, Esq., president and founder, E. Martin Davidoff & Associates, 353 Georges Rd., Dayton, New Jersey 08810, *www.taxattorneycpa.com*. He was selected by *Accounting Today* magazine for inclusion in their "100 Most Influential People in Accounting" list for three consecutive years (2004–2006). He is also founder and national chairperson of the IRS Tax Liaison Committee of the American Association of Attorney-Certified Public Accountants.

Here is what to do when you think you might owe some of the tax the IRS is trying to collect, but you want more time to pay what you owe, minimize interest and penalties and prevent the IRS from taking improper collection actions. *Four savers...*

•**Verify the IRS's tax computation.** People facing tax bills often fail to take the basic step of checking the IRS's numbers to see if they make sense—surprisingly often, they don't.

What to do: Request a free IRS Record of Accounts by calling 800-829-1040 or by mailing Form 4506-T to the IRS—the record will show the amounts that the IRS has credited and debited to the tax period. Go through their record item by item to see if all the numbers add up as they should.

Possible mistakes: Tax payments you made may be omitted from your account, or applied to a different period or type of tax than you intended. Or tax charges may be wrong.

Example: When one client received a surprising tax bill, I found that the IRS had erroneously assessed an additional $9,000 of payroll taxes.

Bottom line: Reviewing the IRS's numbers can eliminate or decrease a tax liability quickly, before you incur any cost from fighting it—and save you from paying a tax you don't owe.

•**Make a "deposit in the nature of a cash bond."** This can help to minimize penalties and interest if you receive a large tax bill from the IRS and think that you'll wind up owing some, but not all, of it.

Situation: You claimed a large amount for an arguable "gray area" deduction. An IRS auditor now is trying to disallow most of it. You're pretty sure that in the end, you'll get more of the deduction than the auditor wants to allow but less than you claimed—so you'll owe some tax.

Problem: The audit dispute may take a long time, possibly years including appeals, so you may incur a big bill for interest and possibly penalties on any tax you finally owe.

Strategy: Advance an amount to the IRS at the beginning of the audit to cover some or all of the disputed tax, not as a "payment" but as a "deposit in the nature of a cash bond." This preserves your right to fight the tax through the entire audit and appeals process, and stops interest and penalties from running on the portion of the tax that you paid.

It also entitles you to collect interest on any amount of the deposit ultimately returned to you by the IRS if you're found not to owe some of the tax. The rules for tax deposits were amended by the 2004 tax law changes to become more "taxpayer friendly." For the full rules, see Section 6603 of the Tax Code and IRS Revenue Procedure 2005-18, available on the IRS Web site at *www.irs.gov*.

•**Use fast track settlement (FTS) if available.** Fast track mediation (FTM) is the alternative dispute resolution process used by the IRS to greatly speed the voluntary disposition of tax disputes.

163

Fast track settlement is an improvement on this, now being tested by the IRS. As with FTM, an IRS appeals officer who has no prior contact with the case, and who is trained in mediation techniques, acts as a neutral party who tries to bring the taxpayer and the IRS's auditing agent to a voluntary agreement.

What's better about FTS is that the appeals officer can propose a specific settlement, and do so considering the "hazards of litigation" to the IRS (such as the risk of losing on appeal or in court). This proposal is likely to be better than any an auditor will make, even in FTM, because auditors are barred from considering hazards of litigation.

Moreover, an appeals officer's proposal, while voluntary for the taxpayer and also the auditor, is likely to be persuasive as it represents an independent view of the issues in dispute.

FTS can be used at any time in an audit, and the IRS seeks to resolve all FTS cases in 60 days. The speeded-up resolution saves not only professional fees for audit representation but also interest and penalties on any taxes you may finally owe.

FTS is available in Chicago, Houston and St. Paul. If successful in these cities, it will be expanded nationwide. If you live in one of these three cities, you can request FTS from your auditor. If not, you may be able to use it in the near future. For details on FTS, enter "alternative dispute resolution" in the search box at the IRS Web site.

• **Stretch out your payment.** If you finally do owe a tax, you may be able to delay paying the IRS, and do so on terms that you request or negotiate with the IRS.

Deferred payment of tax incurs interest and penalties. The rate of interest varies quarterly, is compounded daily, and is not deductible. The current rate of interest is 8%. The penalty for late payment varies from as little as 0.25% per month to 1% per month.

The IRS will generally allow you 120 days to pay the tax balance in full before starting collection procedures. Often this request is granted in a telephone conversation.

If the amount of taxes, interest and penalties "assessed" against you with respect to your Form 1040 taxes is $25,000 or less, you qualify

to enter into the streamlined installment agreement. Under these installment agreements, the IRS does not require the disclosure of financial information if the entire tax can be paid within three years. Streamlined agreements can be secured over the telephone, in person at a walk-in center, or on-line at *www.irs.gov* by clicking on "Individuals" and then "Online Payment Agreement (OPA) Application." Generally, such agreements are automatically approved for those who are current on their other US tax liabilities.

In all other cases, you can enter into a standard installment agreement to fully pay the tax liability. The amount of the monthly installments and the period of time can be negotiated with the IRS. Generally, the IRS will require financial disclosure through the use of Forms 433-A, 433-B, and/or 433-F. In setting the amount of your monthly installments, the IRS must allow you to meet your basic living needs as set forth in the Internal Revenue Manual (IRM), available for free on the IRS Web site. The IRM does provide for the exercise of judgment by the IRS to take into consideration any special circumstances.

Strategy: Never consent to any installment agreement that you cannot afford. If you cannot come to an agreement with the IRS employee, you could always get help from the employee's manager, the Taxpayer Advocate or IRS Office of Appeals.

Learn the general payment terms that may be acceptable to the IRS by looking at the "Collection Financial Standards" and reviewing chapter five in the IRM.

If you cannot pay: Other alternatives, such as offers in compromise, partial pay installment agreements, bankruptcy and uncollectible status are available for those who cannot pay, even after making all reasonable efforts to do so. These options will be the subject of a future article.

Note: For information on how to fight the IRS when it initiates aggressive collection activity, see "The Best Ways to Fight an IRS Tax Bill." Go to *www.bottomlinesecrets.com/delights/taxhotline.html* and click on the article.

Random Tax Audits Are Back! What to Do If You Get Scary Mail from the IRS

Scott Estill, JD, former senior trial attorney with the IRS who now is a partner in the business and tax law firm Estill and Long, LLC, Littleton, Colorado. He is author of *Tax This! An Insider's Guide to Standing Up to the IRS* (Self-Counsel).

T ax audits are on the rise now. Starting in October 2007, the IRS revived a practice of doing random audits—targeting about 13,000 individual 2006 income tax returns for no particular reason.

Fortunately, the vast majority of the more than 100 million IRS notices sent out every year do not signal full-blown audits. Most concern minor issues that can be handled quickly without the assistance of an accountant or tax attorney. But if you do not respond in the correct way, some issues that start out small could easily grow into big problems.

Here's what to do, and how much to worry, if you get a letter from the IRS...

CLARIFICATION NOTICE

These letters request additional forms or figures, or they indicate errors the IRS believes it has found on your tax return. *Common triggers include...*

•**Apparent errors in math** or in transcribing numbers.

•**Missing documents or forms** you should have sent with your return.

•**Numbers that don't agree with ones reported to the IRS** by other sources.

Appropriate concern level: Very low. The IRS is just trying to clear up several details on your return. There is no reason to believe that you have been selected for a full audit. The fact that your return has attracted an agent's attention, however, does slightly increase the odds that you will be audited later.

What to do: If the request is for a specific form or piece of information, mail it along with a copy of the notice and a brief letter explaining that you are responding to the IRS request. Your letter should contain your Social Security number and contact information, including a daytime phone number.

If the clarification notice reports a mistake in your return, the IRS might recalculate the taxes you owe and ask you to pay the difference. If you agree, send this payment as directed—but do not just assume that the changes are correct without double-checking their figures. The IRS makes millions of mistakes each year. You can contest the change in writing if you don't agree, but if the amount involved is just a few dollars, it might not be worth the time.

It usually is not worth consulting a tax attorney or an accountant regarding a clarification notice unless you believe that the IRS is mistaken and the amount involves thousands of dollars. Attorney or CPA fees are likely to top $500. (If a mistake by your accountant triggered the IRS notice, the accountant should not charge to advise you on the matter.)

PENALTY NOTICE

These notices will include a phrase along the lines of "You are being penalized because...," followed up with the explanation. The IRS believes that you underpaid taxes owed due to dishonesty or negligence. You now face a fine in addition to the money the IRS believes you originally owed.

You can be charged a penalty even for honest mistakes. *Situations that often trigger penalties include...*

•**Late tax payments after receiving an extension.** Many taxpayers do not realize that they must pay taxes owed by the April deadline even if they are granted an extension to file the tax return.

•**Failing to make quarterly tax payments.** Taxpayers generally are required to pay tax in installments throughout the year if their withholding is less than 90% of their tax liability. To figure out what you owe, go to *www.irs.gov* and search for "Estimated Taxes."

Penalties can typically range from 5% to 25% of the amount the IRS believes was underpaid. Penalties as high as 75% could be levied if the IRS believes there was fraud rather than simple negligence.

Appropriate concern level: Mild to moderate, depending on the penalty.

What to do: Consider hiring a tax attorney or a CPA to contest the penalty if thousands of dollars are on the line and you do not believe that you have done something wrong. Penalties often can be decreased or waived. When a penalty amounts to hundreds of dollars, it usually is cheaper to pay it than to hire a pro to fight it. You can contest IRS penalties on your own by filing Form 843, *Claim for Refund and Request for Abatement* (800-TAX-FORM or *www.irs.gov*), though taxpayers typically have less luck overturning penalties than pros do.

CORRESPONDENCE
AUDIT NOTICE

These IRS letters say that your tax return has been "selected for examination." You are asked to mail copies of supporting documents or other materials related to selected entries to a specified IRS agent. The bad news is that you are being audited, but the good news is that it is by mail or phone—not a full-blown in-person audit. This audit likely will be narrowly focused, usually on four or fewer figures. Correspondence audits are on the rise because they are quick, easy and inexpensive for the IRS.

Appropriate concern level: Moderate. Correspondence audits are nowhere near as painful as full audits, but they are likely to result in some amount of mental stress, wasted time and added taxes. Your correspondence audit could be expanded into a larger audit if the IRS agent discovers significant problems during the initial investigation.

What to do: Send in the specific information the IRS requested to the address it provided. It generally is not necessary to hire a tax attorney or CPA for the correspondence audit unless the figures involved are very large.

OFFICE OR FIELD
AUDIT NOTICE

These letters say that your return has been "selected for examination" and that an appointment has been scheduled for a certain date and time. If this is an "office audit," you will be asked to visit a local IRS office. If it is a "field audit," the agent will seek to visit your home or place of business.

Returns involving family limited partnerships, S corporations and large charitable noncash gifts are now being audited with particular zeal.

Appropriate level of concern: Significant. These are the full-blown audits that every taxpayer dreads. Field audits are the IRS's most exacting of examinations, and they are performed by the IRS's most experienced agents. It is very likely that the field audit will cost you significant amounts of time and money.

What to do: In the event of an office audit, call and ask the auditor assigned to your case whether it would be possible to handle the audit by mail instead. If the agent agrees, this will essentially become a correspondence audit, the less demanding procedure previously discussed. If he/she doesn't agree, bring all the documents requested (but nothing extra that could provide more ammunition to the IRS) to your meeting.

In the event of a field audit, phone the IRS auditor to confirm or to reschedule your appointment. If the field audit notice does not specify which elements of your return the agent wishes to discuss, say, "By the way, I noticed that you didn't mention the scope of the audit in the notice. I would like to know what in particular you want to cover so I can be prepared." The agent likely will mention only a relatively small number of topics. Have the documentation regarding only these topics at hand during the meeting, to reduce the odds that the audit will expand.

Ask the agent if you could meet in his office. (Agents pick up clues about your income based on your home and belongings.) If he insists on a field audit, you have the right to hold the meeting in an attorney's or a CPA's office.

Answer the agent's questions during the meeting but otherwise say little.

In either case, consider hiring a tax attorney or CPA, which is likely to cost $2,500 to $5,000 or even more.

FOR ANY NOTICE

•**If you cannot figure out what the IRS wants, write to the address provided** and explain that you wish to comply but don't understand the request and need clarification. Include a copy of the notice with your letter. If you do not hear back within 30 days, call the IRS taxpayer advocate in your region for assistance (*www.irs. gov/advocate*).

• **Send all correspondence to the IRS via certified mail** with return receipt requested.

Inside the IRS

In the following articles, Ms. X, Esq., a former IRS agent who is well connected reveals insider secrets from the IRS...

BE PREPARED TO DOCUMENT YOUR DEDUCTIONS

The IRS is now requiring tax return preparers to adopt a standard of "more likely than not" before they claim a tax deduction or take a particular tax position on a client's income tax return—meaning it is more likely than not that the return would be upheld (ultimately by a court). The tax return preparer is now liable for a penalty of up to the greater of $5,000 or 50% of the income he or she earned from preparing the tax return.

IRS CAN REQUEST YOUR CREDIT REPORT

The IRS can access your credit report and find out about financial transactions you might not otherwise want to share with it. Suppose, for example, that your credit report indicates that you borrowed money to purchase an expensive car or boat, and suppose the IRS finds this out. Its next step could easily be to contact your bank and obtain a copy of your credit application. If it does that, you have a problem—if the credit application reflects assets or sources of income that you are trying to hide from the IRS, it just found them. And what if you overstated your assets on the credit application? While this is not a tax crime, it is a crime under federal law.

MORE ON CREDIT REPORTS AND THE IRS

It is permissible under the federal *Fair Credit Reporting Act* for the IRS to request your credit report if you owe back taxes. The collection division of the IRS routinely orders credit reports to determine what assets a delinquent taxpayer owns, or to confirm the financial information provided by a taxpayer who requests an installment agreement or an offer in compromise.

Caution: Not paying tax because you don't have money generally is not a crime. But submitting false financial information to the IRS is a crime.

REQUESTING INFO FROM THE IRS

The *Freedom of Information Act* permits you to ask the IRS for copies of all documents in its possession relating to your audit examination or collection proceeding. The request is made by addressing a letter to the local disclosure officer of the IRS and identifying the documents you want. A request should be made for all documents in your possession relating to a specific matter.

Problems: Sometimes, disclosure office caseworkers will tell you that the documents you've requested are not available although they really are available.

Best approach: Speak to a manager and ask him/her to review the case because it appears that information you have requested has been omitted.

IRS AUDIT TRAP

Suppose that in the course of your audit an agent asks you a question and you don't understand why it is being asked.

What to do: Ask the agent why he/she wants to know. Don't answer any such question until you receive an understandable, and acceptable, answer from the agent.

Example: The agent asks where you went on your vacation last year. Why would he want to know such a thing? He is probably trying to ascertain your standard of living and how the amount of income you reported on your tax return jibes with your confessed lifestyle.

Be careful about offering an answer that may be incriminating—consult with your lawyer.

GETTING AUDITED BY MAIL

In recent years, the IRS has increased its audit coverage of individual taxpayers by conducting "correspondence" audits. Correspondence audits topped one million in 2007. What if, say, you are selected for a correspondence audit...you know that your return includes some "gray areas" having to do with income...but the IRS says that it only wants to examine your medical expenses?

Strategy: Consider not responding at all, in which case the IRS might simply disallow the medical expenses, leaving your income alone.

Caution: You should not begin any correspondence that could lead to a question about whether all of your income was reported. Speak with a qualified tax adviser.

FILING YOUR TAX RETURN WHILE UNDER AUDIT

It is generally not advisable to file an income tax return while you are in the midst of an IRS audit. The reason is simple—the revenue agent can decide to extend the scope of the audit to include the most recent year filed and raise the issue of additional adjustments.

What to do: File an extension and hope that the examination is finished before the extended due date of the return.

If you run out of time: Make sure that the tax return you file is absolutely correct and does not contain only aggressive deductions. A plain vanilla tax return is unlikely to be examined. If you want to take an aggressive position, you can always consider filing an amended tax return after the examination is closed—you have three years to amend your tax return.

USING AN OFFSHORE BANK

Individuals who want to maintain an offshore bank account (the existence of which must generally be disclosed to the IRS annually) should keep in mind that the IRS could summons the bank to obtain copies of account holders' statements reflecting deposits and withdrawals.

Exception: If the offshore bank doesn't have an office in the US, a motion to quash the summons should be successful. The IRS can enforce a summons in a US district court only if it can show that the summonsed person (or entity) resides, or is found in, the court's geographical jurisdiction.

Best bet: Choose an offshore bank with no branch office or business connection, such as an investment banking operation, in the US.

MAKE SURE IT'S IN WRITING WHEN DEALING WITH THE IRS

Creating a written record is very important if you later need to prove either that you took a specific action or that someone at the IRS was supposed to remedy a problem.

Situation: You filed an amended return reflecting a refund but did not receive a check within 90 days.

What to do: Send the IRS a letter setting forth the date that you filed the amended return and requesting that it process the return and send you a check. Also in your letter, ask the IRS to confirm that it received the amended return.

Failure to create such a written record, especially if you did not send the return by certified or registered mail, can make it difficult, even impossible, to prove that you filed the return should the deadline for filing pass without your refund showing up.

USE THE RIGHT SITE

The Treasury Inspector General for Tax Administration (TIGTA) has the authority to maintain the integrity of tax administration. In that capacity, TIGTA is working to free the Internet of sites that may sound like that of the IRS, but are not. The correct Web address for the IRS is "*www.irs.gov.*" However, the taxpayers who use *www.irs.com*, *www.irs.net* and a host of other private, commercial sites may pay for services or products that they can get for free on the *www.irs.gov* site. Check resources on the official IRS site before paying for tax-related information!

10

Investment Adviser

The Truth About Money: Don't Fall for These Lies That Financial Advisers Tell

Financial consultant Ric Edelman believes that the world of investment advice is filled with lies that place your financial security in jeopardy. They include lies that stockbrokers and mutual fund executives tell you—and, worst of all, the lies that you tell yourself. But there also is good news—you can discover the truth and achieve your investment goals.

Ric Edelman should know. *Barron's* has five times (2004–2008) ranked him among the top 100 independent financial advisers in America. His 20-year-old firm has the most clients—more than 7,500—of any independent financial adviser. And his best-selling books have one million copies in print.

Below, Edelman tells how to spot the biggest financial lies and how to keep them from ruining your investment portfolio...

Lie: You should rebalance your portfolio once a year.

Truth: Once each year probably isn't often enough. Rebalancing involves bulking up asset groups that have underperformed and paring down ones that have overperformed. By doing this, you can take advantage of the inevitable shifts in whichever categories are strongest. Because markets move like roller coasters, if you rebalance just once, you might choose the wrong time of year to do it or you might be waiting too long to react to significant shifts.

Strategy: Rebalance as soon as any category of investments you hold shifts by a predetermined amount. For instance, say you decide that

Ric Edelman, chairman of Edelman Financial Services, Fairfax, Virginia, which manages $3.5 billion in assets for clients nationwide. He writes a syndicated newspaper advice column, hosts a nationwide call-in show on the ABC Radio network and is the author of *The Lies About Money* (Free Press).

small-cap value stocks should total 10% of the stock portion of your portfolio. If that allocation appreciates to 12% or shrinks to 8%, rebalance by selling or buying enough to get it back to 10%.

Important: Rebalancing can result in extra taxes and commissions, so this strategy works best in a retirement account.

Lie: You should shift all your accounts—including 401(k)s and IRAs—to more conservative investments the closer you get to your retirement date. That's because you want to lower your risk of running short of spendable money during a market downturn.

Truth: Few retirees I have worked with draw heavily from their tax-sheltered retirement accounts as soon as they stop working. It's often many years before they even touch that money, because of Social Security, investment income from taxable assets and other sources.

Strategy: Focus on when you will start drawing on a particular account, rather than when you will retire. Maintain relatively aggressive investments in that account as long as you're several years away from drawing on it.

My rule of thumb: As long as you maintain the planned level of diversification in your overall portfolio and you are more than seven years from using the money in your 401(k) and/or IRA, place all newer contributions to these accounts in diversified stock mutual funds. If you are between seven and three years from withdrawals, shift the mix of your retirement account assets to an increasingly conservative stance that you will maintain from then on.

Lie: The stock market will crash between 2017 and 2024. That's when huge waves of aging baby boomers are expected to sell their stock holdings on a massive scale, so you should cash out before then.

Truth: Retiring baby boomers won't all liquidate their investments in one short time span. They will do what retirees have always done—sell and spend assets slowly and judiciously over the rest of their lives.

Strategy: Maintain a diversified portfolio. I advise clients to have at least 17 different asset classes. That mutes volatility.

Lie: Retirees who depend on investment income should focus primarily on interest-yielding bonds and bank certificates of deposit (CDs).

Truth: A portfolio of bonds and CDs causes your available income to fluctuate too much. Every time a bond or CD matures, you are forced to roll it into a new one. If interest rates have fallen, you end up with less cash each month. Trying to protect yourself with a "ladder"—a series of bonds and CDs having a variety of rates that mature on various dates—leaves you vulnerable to inflation because your principal remains the same year after year.

Strategy: In addition to bonds and CDs, include a substantial investment in the dividend-paying stocks in your retirement portfolio. If the resulting income is not enough to pay for living expenses, close up the gap by selling off shares of assets that have become overvalued. That way, your income does not fluctuate.

Example: One client in his 60s needed to draw 5% a year from his investments to pay his expenses. I created a portfolio designed to grow by 8% a year but throw off only 3% in dividends and interest, after taxes. We made up the two-percentage-point gap by selling shares of outperforming stocks and funds.

Lie: If your child or grandchild will be entering college in, for instance, 10 years, try to have enough saved up by then to pay for four years of college based on what college costs are expected to be 10 years from now.

Truth: Inflation will most likely continue to drive up college costs by 7% every year the child remains in school, as it has done, on average, for the past several decades. If tuition is $30,000 a year when your child enters college, you will need $133,198 over four years, not $120,000—although a combination of loans, scholarships, grants and a student's employment income can cover a portion of the expenses.

Strategy: When you start saving for a child's education, calculate what inflation rates will do to college expenses through graduation. Once a child starts college, you can't keep this money in anything riskier than CDs.

Important Investment Advice From a Legend

John C. Bogle, founder, previous chief executive and former chairman of The Vanguard Group, Inc., one of the largest mutual fund groups in the world. He helped to create the first index mutual fund in 1975. He is president of Bogle Financial Markets Research Center in Malvern, Pennsylvania. In 2004, *Time* named Bogle one of the 100 "Most Influential People in the World," and in 1999, *Fortune* named him one of four "investment giants" of the 20th century.

For four decades, Vanguard founder John C. Bogle has been a hero to small investors. He also has been a gadfly to the mutual fund industry, which, he claims, too often charges fees that are too high while delivering lackluster performance.

Bogle, 77, has remained active on mutual fund issues since he retired from Vanguard in 1999. He lobbied in Washington, DC, for tighter regulation of mutual fund advertising and authored his sixth book, *The Little Book of Common Sense Investing* (Wiley).

Below, Bogle answers questions on how investors can prepare for a future that includes a downturn in the US economy and low investment returns...

• **How do you expect stocks to perform in the next several years?** I predict annualized returns of 7% to 8% for the Standard & Poor's 500 stock index over the next decade. I know that's not what investors want to hear, and it's certainly not what stockbrokers will tell them. But I base my predictions on the numbers, which I call the "relentless rule of humble arithmetic."

Stock market returns are created by the growth of actual businesses. In the past century, those businesses have paid dividends averaging 4.5% of stock prices, and their earnings have grown an average of 5%—a total of 9.5% per year. However, since 1980, the S&P 500—my proxy for the market—has provided total returns of 12.5% per year. Those extra three percentage points each year reflect the premium in the price investors were willing to pay for each dollar of earnings. That increase has kept the returns artificially inflated for a long, long time. In effect, investors were convinced each year that the US economy would continue to do better and better.

• **Why can't returns remain high for many years to come?** There are two basic reasons. First, even if companies continue to grow their earnings at the long-term average of 5% per year, their dividend yields—which are part of total returns—are nowhere near 4.5% now. In fact, they average less than 2.2%.*

And second, the current price-to-earnings ratio (P/E) is about 15.81. To continue to have annualized returns of 12.5% a year from stocks, the market's P/E would need to rise to 25. That's just not sustainable. It wasn't sustainable back in the giddy days of 1999, and it will not be sustainable over the next decade.

• **How can fund investors prepare for years of lower returns?** For starters, they should control what they have control over when choosing mutual fund investments—costs, expense ratios and tax efficiency.

Next, consider having a large chunk of foreign equity in the portfolio. I'm well-known for ignoring overseas investments—I thought they were much too expensive and full of speculative accounting practices. However, I'm worried about the US economy now—our excessive borrowing for costly wars, an underfinanced pension system and the dollar's weakness. In the next few years, I'm planning to put as much as 20% of my equity holdings into foreign stocks. That includes 10% in developed countries and 10% in emerging markets.

Third, don't equate simplicity with stupidity. Warren Buffett likes to say that for investors as a whole, returns decrease as motion increases. In other words, more trades will not necessarily boost returns. In fact, the less trading investors do, the better off they tend to be.

• **How do you pick investments?** I allocate my assets in such a manner that I have to peek at how they are doing only once a year, and I probably won't change that formula for the rest of my life. It provides decent returns in both good and bad market years.

My portfolio now includes 60% equities and 40% bonds. In the equity portion, I have 80% in the Vanguard Total Stock Market Index Fund (VTSMX) and 20% in other types of Vanguard

*Figures as of July 9, 2008.

funds that include Explorer (small-cap growth stocks, VEXPX)…PRIMECAP (a large-cap blend of growth and value stocks, VPMCX)…Wellesley Income (high-yielding stocks as well as bonds, VWINX)…Wellington (various stocks and bonds, VWELX)…and Windsor (large-cap value stocks, VWNDX). In the bond portion, I have 50% in Vanguard Total Bond Market Index Fund (VBM-FX) and 50% in the Vanguard Intermediate-Term Tax-Exempt Fund (VWITX).

• **You favor index funds, but indexing peaked at about 10% of all mutual fund assets in 2000. Why hasn't its popularity grown?** Broad stock market returns have not been great, so people are not content to simply match broad indices by investing in traditional index funds. There are newer index funds that give more weight to the small-cap and value stocks, which have had a stellar run for the past seven years—but they don't have enough of a track record to attract many investors.

I don't think traditional index funds need to be fixed—they're not broken. Not only do they work beautifully in bull markets, but they also hold up well in periods of modest returns, when investment management fees, transaction costs and taxes take a disproportionate bite out of most funds. These costs don't take as much out of index funds, because they trade less frequently.

Even though S&P 500 index funds have returned only 8.3% per year this decade, on average, they have beaten 69% of all large-cap funds. And as foreign stocks beat domestic stocks over the past five years, the Vanguard Total International Stock Index Fund (VGTSX) beat 90% of the funds in its category.

• **But there are still plenty of actively managed funds doing much better than index funds.** Agreed, but will the managers responsible for superior returns stick around for the next 10 years? Will the funds become so popular that they get bloated and their returns revert to the mean?

I tell investors who are sick of hearing me tout the benefits of index funds that they must, at least, be disciplined. Keep 95% of your portfolio in index funds, and use the rest to pick stocks or actively managed funds. Choose the managers who invest in their own funds and who follow

distinctive, long-term philosophies without hugging the benchmarks.

Here are some of my favorite mutual fund families now, Dodge & Cox (800-621-3979 or *www.dodgeandcox.com*)…Oakmark (800-625-6275 or *www.oakmark.com*)…Royce Funds (800-221-4268 or *www.roycefunds.com*)…Torray (800-443-3036 or *www.torray.com*)…Tweedy, Browne Co. (800-432-4789 or *www.tweedy.com*)…and Weitz (800-304-9745 or *www.weitzfunds.com*).

Make a 10-year commitment, and do not bail out if your managed fund underperforms the benchmark index in any given year.

How to Predict the Stock Market

Jeffrey A. Hirsch, editor of the *Almanac Investor* newsletter in Nyack, New York. He also is the editor-in-chief of *Stock Trader's Almanac 2008* (Wiley), the latest edition of the book that was developed by his father, Yale Hirsch. It has been published annually since 1967, with more than one million copies sold. Both publications can be found at *www.stocktradersalmanac.com*.

Many investors spend countless hours analyzing historical stock market patterns for clues to what may happen in the future. *Here, market historian Jeffrey Hirsch helps separate the clues that could lead you to wealth from those that could mislead you…*

THE JANUARY EFFECT

Small-cap stock prices tend to surge in early January, outpacing large-cap stocks. This happened 93% of the time from 1953 to 1995.

Reason: Investors often sell off stocks in December for various purposes, including to lock in profits or harvest losses to lower capital gains taxes. This drives down the prices of small-cap stocks, in particular, because they swing more sharply in reaction to waves of selling or buying. Then, in January, these stocks rebound as the selling pressure evaporates. The effect is greatest among the 10% of the stock market's smallest companies.

THE JANUARY BAROMETER

The January performance of the Standard & Poor's 500 stock index usually foreshadows how the stock market will perform for the year overall. This has been true for about three-quarters of the time since 1950.

Reason: Many political policies, corporate priorities and investment strategies set in January influence events for the next 11 months.

PRESIDENTIAL ELECTION YEAR

The stock market tends to rise in the third and fourth years of a presidential term.

Reason: The incumbent administration often boosts spending and/or cuts taxes to give the economy a lift so that voters will keep its party in power. Then, once the election is over, markets tend to pull back markedly in the first and second years of a presidency. Most bear markets and recessions have begun in the two calendar years following a presidential election. That's because presidents prefer to take any unpopular actions, such as increasing taxes or cutting back funding for popular programs, early in their administrations. That's when their approval ratings tend to be highest and long before they will run for reelection.

Since 1941, the Dow Jones Industrial Average has posted an average annual return of 3.7% in the first year of presidential terms…5.6% in year two…17.2% in year three…and 7.1% in year four.

SELL IN MAY AND GO AWAY

Typically, stocks start the year very strong… grow sluggish during the summer…bottom out in September, which is often the worst month of the year…then rally again near year-end. As a result, staying invested in the stock market for only six of every 12 months, from November 1 to April 30, has proved to be one of the most profitable strategies an investor can follow.

If you had invested $10,000 in the Dow starting in November 1950, kept it invested for only those six months of each year—and reinvested all capital gains—then your money would have compounded through 2006 to $588,413 (taxes, dividends and commissions not factored in). If, instead, you had been Dow invested only from May through October, which is more likely to be a down or weak period, the total would be $10,341. Even if you do not want to follow this strategy fully, it is a good guide to when it might be best to increase, decrease or delay increasing your investments.

THE THANKSGIVING MARKET

Over more than a half-century, the Dow has risen in 82% of the years, by an average of 1%, for the two sessions on the day before and the day after Thanksgiving. It's hard to say why this occurs, other than holiday euphoria.

SANTA CLAUS RALLY

Santa Claus usually visits Wall Street with a short rally in the last five trading days of December and the first two in January. This has held true 78% of the time since 1952, with gains averaging 1.4%.

Reason: Investors gear up for the new year, invest a portion of their year-end bonuses and add to their IRA contributions.

Reverse indicator: If the Santa Claus rally does not appear, it has tended to be bad news historically, a harbinger of lower prices. For instance, the S&P 500 plunged 4% over this time period in 1999, followed by a 49% drop in the S&P 500 from March 2000 to October 2002.

Stocks That Get a Boost When the Dollar Goes Down

John P. Dessauer, president of John Dessauer Investments in Naples, Florida, which manages $80 million for private clients. He is also editor of *John Dessauer's Investor's World, www.dessauerinvestorsworld.com.*

Although the weakness of the US dollar in relation to many foreign currencies continues to pummel Americans who travel overseas, it also helps boost revenue and profits for US companies that do a lot of business in other countries.

The dollar's fluctuation will depend mostly on the state of the US economy. I do expect the dollar to strengthen slightly against the euro once it becomes clear that the Federal Reserve's interest rate cuts are reviving the US economy. But the dollar will remain relatively weak for the foreseeable future because oil producers and US trading partners around the world continue to diversify their cash holdings among other currencies, such as the euro.

How to take advantage…

• **Buy shares of big US-based multinational companies.** If they do business as local companies overseas, their profits are boosted when the foreign currencies are translated to US dollars. If they export goods from the US, the prices of those goods translate as bargains for customers abroad, which can greatly increase sales.

Some of my favorite stocks…

• AFLAC (AFL), the health and life insurer, derives about 70% of its sales from abroad. The firm's prospects are brightest in Japan, where an aging population has growing insurance needs and government deregulation has opened up banks as a sales channel for insurance products. *Recent share price:* $62.80.*

• Cisco Systems, Inc. (CSCO). Sales in Europe for this technology giant are accelerating. In Asia, Cisco can depend on a 35%–45% annual increase in revenue for at least several years. Cisco's stock price could double within five years. *Recent share price:* $22.88.

• Colgate-Palmolive Co. (CL) is a good choice for more conservative investors. It is a steady and relatively low-risk stock with a growth rate that is likely to surprise Wall Street, thanks to its gains in emerging markets. *Recent share price:* $69.88.

• Pfizer Inc. (PFE) has seen its stock beaten down to a point far below fair value. The global pharmaceutical firm suffered from the loss of patent protection of its best-selling drug, Zoloft, and competition from generic pharmaceutical manufacturers. But Wall Street doesn't see the positives, which include a nearly $8 billion annual research budget and new drugs with blockbuster potential, such as the oncology drug Sutent, that target aging populations overseas. *Recent share price:* $18.19.

• **Invest in companies that benefit from tourism.** Cheap greenbacks mean an increase in the number of foreign tourists who now can afford to spend lavishly in the US. *My pick now…*

• Carnival Cruise Lines (CCL), North America's largest cruise provider and one of the world's largest vacation companies. Not only is the company attracting Asians, Europeans and Canadians who have rising disposable income, but more Americans are opting for cruises, which let them travel abroad and still pay in US dollars. *Recent share price:* $34.26.

*Prices as of July 9, 2008.

Smart Stock-Picking Strategy

Purchasing stocks during their 52-week highs has been a smart strategy historically. These stocks often have momentum which can move them still higher, according to a study published in *The Journal of Finance*. In a separate study, the *Chicago Tribune* reported that of 256 firms whose shares saw 52-week highs on the New York Stock Exchange in mid-January, more than half outperformed the S&P 500 through the end of the first quarter—and one-tenth rose by more than 15%. But choosing the correct stock is crucial, as some stocks at their highs are poised to fall, while ones with rising earnings that exceed analysts' forecasts and strong cash flow could go still higher.

Self-defense: Look for stocks with price-to-earnings ratios (P/Es) under 15, which indicate a bargain.

Chicago Tribune, www.chicagotribune.com.

What Makes a Good Stock Buy

Beating earnings expectations is not enough to make a stock a good buy. Nearly 70% of the S&P 500 companies have beaten consensus estimates in recent quarters. To evaluate stocks' performance, find ones that rally on strong earnings reports…see whether sales, as well as earnings, beat expectations—if they do, it is a good sign…find out if the company has revised earnings expectations upward for future quarters—a signal that business is really improving.

Various earnings-surprise stocks to consider: Cleveland-Cliffs Inc. (CLF), Hurco Companies, Inc. (HURC) and WellCare Health Plans, Inc. (WCG).

Richard J. Moroney, CFA, portfolio manager of Horizon Investment Services, Hammond, Indiana, and editor of *Dow Theory Forecasts, www.dowtheory.com.*

What's in a Name?

Acompany's good name can work against it in the stock market. Stocks of less admired firms significantly outperformed the stocks of more admired firms in the 23 years from 1983 to 2006.

Possible reason: The admiration that investors feel for a company may make them willing to pay a higher price for its stock than the underlying fundamentals of the company justify over the long term.

Self-defense: Analyze any company's performance objectively, no matter what its reputation.

Meir Statman, PhD, a professor of finance and chair, finance department, Leavey School of Business at Santa Clara University, California, and coauthor of a study of the relative performance of more admired and less admired companies.

Buybacks Often Backfire

Company stock buybacks often backfire, especially amid problems such as the current credit crunch and slowing economy. According to new research, stock prices for firms that have bought back shares tend to underperform the overall market. Investors typically applaud buybacks, which raise earnings per share by reducing the number of outstanding shares. But often the firms would be better off using the cash for other purposes.

Self-defense: Consider a stock buyback program to be a neutral factor, at best, when making investment decisions.

Todd Rosenbluth, an analyst for Standard & Poor's Equity Research Services, New York City.

 **Put Some Feeling Into It**

Emotional investors tend to make better decisions than unemotional ones. The higher the average intensity of the investor's feelings, the better his/her returns tend to be.

Reason: Investors who experience emotions more intensely are more actively attuned to investing and more engaged in the process—and those investors who have a clearer understanding of their emotions (rather than ignoring them) are better able to regulate them and thus achieve better returns.

Smart: Don't ignore your emotional reactions when making investment decisions.

Myeong-Gu Seo, PhD, assistant professor of management and organization, University of Maryland, Robert H. Smith School of Business, College Park, and coauthor of a study of 101 stock investors in a simulated four-week trading exercise, published in the *Academy of Management Journal.*

For Older Investors...

Impulsiveness may hurt portfolio performance among older investors.

Reason: They are easily swayed by appeals to positive emotions by brokers and scammers.

Self-defense: Install caller ID on an elderly person's phone and a spam filter on e-mail to keep scammers away. Form a relationship with a trusted financial adviser, and have him/her review any interesting opportunities.

Jason Zweig, financial columnist and author of *Your Money and Your Brain* (Simon & Schuster).

A Low-Cost Way to Invest in Undervalued Sectors

Sonya Morris, CPA, editor, *Morningstar ETFInvestor,* a publication offered by Morningstar, Inc., that helps readers find ETF opportunities.

One way to make money in the market is to invest in "undervalued" stocks—stocks whose market prices appear to be below their fair value (what the stock would be selling for today if its value were accurately perceived). The idea is that these stocks will ultimately rise to their fair value.

The risk, of course, is that an "undervalued" stock could have fundamental problems, and never appreciate to levels that investors expected.

What follows is a simple trading strategy to allow you to minimize the hazards of owning individual undervalued stocks and to do so at a low cost.

MAKING MONEY WITH SECTOR ETFs

By investing in an entire undervalued industry sector, you eliminate the risk of picking only a single stock. If the outlook improves for the entire sector, many, if not most, of the stocks in it should advance in price. One way to capture a complete sector is by investing in an industry-focused stock mutual fund. Nearly every industry, from utilities to telecommunications, is represented by one or more mutual funds.

But another way to invest in sectors is with exchange-traded funds (ETFs)—baskets of securities that are traded on an exchange. Their annual expense ratios are usually much lower than mutual funds with similar portfolios, and they are also more "tax efficient"—investors can time their gains and losses, and thereby control their tax liabilities, better than with mutual funds. (Remember that besides the expenses charged by the ETFs, there are also broker commissions for trading them.) To keep expenses down, adopt a buy-and-hold strategy.

There are more than 500 ETFs listed on US exchanges, more than 150 of which are sector funds.

PICKING UNDERVALUED SECTORS

Morningstar looks for sector ETFs that own a slew of cheap stocks and that hold down trading costs by keeping them for at least three to five years.

In picking undervalued sectors, we use what we term a price/fair value ratio. This can tell us whether an ETF portfolio is cheap or expensive by showing whether its holdings, on average, are trading above or below our estimate of their fair value, the potential market price of the stock.

To get the price/fair value ratio of an ETF, we calculate the average market value (current prices) of all of its holdings for which we've made fair value estimates. Then, we use the fair value estimates of those stocks to calculate what we believe is the fair value of the portfolio.

Finally, we compare these two numbers and calculate the percentage premium or discount of the market price relative to the fair value estimate. This will allow us to see whether the ETF portfolio is undervalued or overvalued.

As with all ETFs, sector ETFs not only have market risk—as the market, including the sector, could go down—but can be volatile in any kind of market, since sectors tend to swing in and out of favor. To decrease risk, invest only a portion, say 10%, of your portfolio in sector ETFs. *Some undervalued sectors…*

HOME BUILDERS

As measured by the price/fair value ratio, the home-building sector is one of the cheapest corners of the market. Home-building stocks have been severely punished by investors' reactions to a weakening housing market triggered by turmoil in the subprime mortgage business. Meanwhile, many potential home buyers are delaying their purchases, looking for definite signs that home prices have bottomed.

Home-builder ETFs are trading at significant discounts to our estimates of their fair values. Although they are not for investors who are risk averse, it is an intriguing area for bolder bargain-hunters with the patience and risk tolerance for a more aggressive play.

FINANCIALS

The stream of bad news from the subprime lending industry has adversely affected this sector, too. But many of the financially sturdy blue chips have minimal exposure to subprime mortgages, yet they have been punished along with the sector's raciest names.

TECHNOLOGY

Many investors have been gun-shy about this sector since the technology stock crash of 2000, and tech stocks have lagged all the other industry sectors for the past five years. With the rapid growth in the use of the Internet and with the continuing stream of better technology devices, such as the iPhone, and new software, such as Microsoft's Vista operating system, many companies in this sector could start to report strong earnings increases.

Note: When you invest in an "equal-weight" sector ETF, you are investing evenly in all stocks in one sector—not just the biggest of the big. In nonequal-weighted sector ETFs (most ETFs), a "cap-weighted" approach is used—most of your money will go into a handful of large companies with large market capitalizations and less into that sector's smaller companies. If you believe that large-cap stocks will do better, then own nonequal-weighted sector ETFs. If you believe small- and mid-caps will do best, then own equal-weighted sector ETFs.

MEGACAPS

ETFs that focus on the market's biggest companies look inexpensive right now compared to those that emphasize small- and mid-cap stocks. After trailing their smaller cousins for years, megacaps have become more attractive.

Megacaps are not screaming bargains, but they are the best buys on average. If your portfolio's allocation to smaller stocks has grown beyond your targeted weighting, now's a good time to rebalance in favor of large companies.

Best Investment Newsletters

Mark Hulbert, editor of *The Hulbert Financial Digest*, Annandale, Virginia, which provides performance data on the investment strategies recommended by financial newsletters, *www.marketwatch.com/Hulbert*.

There are many different roads to good returns. *Three top newsletters pursue widely divergent investment approaches…*

• *The Buyback Letter Standard Edition* focuses on companies that are buying back their stocks.

Information: 12 issues. $195/yr.* 888-289-2225, *www.buybackletter.com*.

• *Investment Quality Trends* analyzes blue-chip stocks. They provide a relatively conservative approach that reduces volatility.

*Prices subject to change.

Information: 24 issues. $310/yr. for printed copy…$265/yr. for on-line access. 866-927-5250, *www.iqtrends.com*.

• *NoLoad Fund*X* explores top-performing mutual funds.

Information: 12 issues. $179/yr. for printed copy and on-line access…$149/yr. for on-line access only. 800-763-8639, *www.fundx.com*.

Despite their different investment approaches, these newsletters share a disciplined approach to following a single system of investing. That means adherence even during downturns, when the newsletter's favored system is out of favor. That's crucial because every system will be out of sync with the markets at some points.

In choosing the best investment newsletters, long-term performance—and the longer, the better—is key. If you evaluate them for less than 10 years, a few lucky stock picks or a style choice that's temporarily in favor may provide an outsized boost to returns that doesn't last.

Also, instead of measuring simple total return, it's best to gauge risk-adjusted return. Otherwise, a newsletter with volatile picks may impress you with an outstanding performance, but you might not have the stomach for the large up-and-down swings that accompany it.

Of course, when picking a newsletter to follow, it's wise to consider your individual goals and tolerance for ups and downs in the value of your portfolio.

Don't Buy These Mutual Funds

Mutual funds run by insurance companies lag behind noninsurance company funds, on average. A new study shows that insurance company funds suffer from a "flow performance" problem. When a noninsurance company fund performs poorly, investors often take out their money. But the investors in insurance company funds who buy them in conjunction with other insurance products often cannot remove their investments from the company without triggering a premium increase or having their policy canceled. You may be able to shift to a better fund within the company.

Tong Yu, PhD, associate finance professor, College of Business Administration, University of Rhode Island in Kingston.

Top Mutual Fund Web Sites

If you are looking for information on mutual funds, the Web is a good place to begin. *See the sites below…*

•**Beginners** who want to know how funds work can try *www.investopedia.com*, which offers free articles, and *www.troweprice.com*, whose guide makes it easy to choose the right fund.

•**Moderately experienced investors** can log on to *www.morningstar.com* for articles and fund ratings…*www.bigcharts.com* for interactive charts and investment research…or *www.mfea. com*, the Mutual Fund Investor's Center, for helpful portfolio-tracking tools.

•**Experienced investors** can try *www.fund alarm.com*, which compares performance and suggests which funds to consider selling.

AARP, 601 E St. NW, Washington, DC 20049, *www. aarp.org*.

Gold Prices Keep On Rising

As the economy slows and the interest rates decline, gold prices should continue to rise even if other commodity prices don't.

Reasons: Despite rising demand, gold production has been stagnant for 10 years, output from older mines is dwindling and newer mines are not replacing old production levels. Also, the current volatility of world currencies will likely increase the demand for gold as a monetary reserve. Moreover, countries that hold huge dollar

reserves, like China, may begin to diversify into other currencies and gold.

One solid gold mining stock: Barrick Gold (ABX).

Leo Larkin, equity metals and mining analyst, *Standard & Poor's*, 55 Water St., New York City 10041.

Newest Way to Invest in Gold

Prices for gold have nearly doubled in three years and could hit $1,000 an ounce before long, compared with about $860 an ounce* recently. Exchange-traded funds (ETFs), including streetTRACKS Gold Shares (GLD), is a new way to invest in gold that is less cumbersome than the bars or coins. Because gold is a very volatile investment, make it no more than 5% to 10% of your portfolio. Also, realize that capital gains on gold ETFs held more than 12 months are taxed at a 28% rate, rather than the standard 15%, because the IRS considers gold to be a collectible —even in an ETF.

Robert T. Lutts, president and chief investment officer of Cabot Money Management, Inc., Salem, Massachusetts.

*Price subject to change.

Don't Be Fooled by an "Alternative Investment"

Some brokers and consultants are marketing currencies, commodities, options, real estate deals and other risky investments, implying that they are now acceptable alternatives to traditional stocks and bonds.

Reality: There is nothing new about these investments. Many are higher-risk and generate significant commissions, fees and profits for the people who are selling them, but not necessarily for investors.

Bottom line: Make an investment only if you fully understand it.

Paul B. Farrell, JD, PhD, investment columnist, *Dow Jones MarketWatch*, Arroyo Grande, California, and author of *The Millionaire Meditation* (a free download on *www.paulbfarrell.com*).

Tax-Wise Investment Planning

Janice M. Johnson, CPA, JD, A.B. Watley Group at 50 Broad St., New York City 10004, *www.abwatley.com*. She has more than 25 years of experience in advising high-net-worth investors, hedge funds and broker-dealers on the tax consequences of investing.

G et the most after-tax returns from investments with smart tax planning. *Moves to consider right now...*

RECORD KEEPING

Too many investors pull together their records only at year-end—or even after year-end, when preparing their tax returns.

It's much better to keep records on a current basis throughout the year. The information in them can let you make tax-management moves as the year progresses.

Records to keep: Cost basis of investments... the holding period of investments...all reinvested amounts (including dividends) added to basis... the dividend dates of qualified dividends...interest expense...brokerage expenses...other investment-related expenses, such as subscription costs and investment management and legal fees.

If you always know where you stand, you can make opportunistic tax moves during the year.

SPECIFIC SHARE IDENTIFICATION

Normally, when you sell shares of a stock or mutual fund, the first shares bought are deemed the first sold when determining gain or loss. But when you've bought shares at different prices, it can be better tax-wise to identify specific shares for sale.

Example: You own shares of XYZ stock purchased at prices of $20, $40 and $50, in consecutive purchases, and the stock currently is worth $45. If you sell some of the shares today, under the first-bought, first-sold rule, the taxable gain will be $25 per share on the shares sold.

However, if you identify specific shares for sale, you can choose to have a gain of $25 or $10, or a loss of $5 on shares you sell for $45—whichever is best for your tax position.

Requirements: To use this "specific identification" method, you must have price records for individual shares. You also must inform your broker of the specific shares to be sold and get broker confirmation that they were sold.

Problems: There are generally no exact procedures for taxpayers to follow when using the specific identification method and when trading through on-line brokers.

Helpful: An IRS private ruling has held that a letter from a client to a broker giving "standing instructions" to always sell highest-cost shares first (to minimize gain), followed by a post-sale confirmation from the broker stating that instructions have been followed, is sufficient to satisfy the rules. See *Letter Ruling* 9728021.

What to do: Consult with your broker about how you can meet the IRS requirements for specific identification sales using the broker's system. If he/she doesn't have a way to do so, move to another broker.

DIVIDENDS

In today's stock market, a growing number of large-company stocks have very attractive dividend yields, because share prices have declined significantly in the recent market tumult. When share prices go down, the dividend's percentage return increases.

Example: A financially troubled company is paying a 6.7% dividend, but this substantial yield should be weighed against the possibility that the company will cut its dividend because of its financial problems.

The top tax charge on "qualified" dividends (where you hold the shares for more than 60 days during the 120-day period surrounding the declaration of the dividend, and the company has earnings and profits to support the dividend) is now only 15% (and is zero for some, see below), so such high yields can very attractively provide a high rate of tax-favored income—while you also have the chance to gain further from the stock's appreciation in value.

Caution: Stocks also can fall in value, and, if a business is troubled, its dividend may be cut.

In 2008, for the first time, the tax rate on long-term capital gains and qualified dividends is 0% for those in the 15%-or-lower tax brackets. This covers people with taxable income up to $65,100 on a joint return or $32,550 on a single return.

If your income is too high to use the 0% rate on your own return, you can still benefit from it by making gifts of investments that qualify for long-term-gain treatment, and of dividend-paying stocks, to family members who are in the 15%-or-lower tax bracket—such as retired parents you help support. They can then sell the stock and/or take the dividends and pay tax at their own lower rate.

HARVEST GAINS AND LOSSES

Throughout the year, using the improved records, review your portfolio monthly (or continuously) to take gains and losses advantageously and avoid making costly mistakes. *Examples…*

• **If you receive a qualified dividend, preserve its tax-favored status** by holding the shares that pay it for at least 61 days including the dividend date.

• **Sell loss investments before holding one year** to get a short-term capital loss deductible against highly taxed short-term-gain income, and sell gain investments after holding them a year to get tax-favored long-term treatment.

• **Realize losses as the year progresses to offset tax on gains.**

BOND SWAPS

Interest rates for bonds have been at long-term lows recently. If rates rise, the prices of outstanding bonds will fall.

Opportunity: If a bond's price falls, sell it and simultaneously buy another higher-quality bond. Not much has to differ from the old bond for you to avoid the wash-sale rule (see the next page). Simply get a higher interest rate or a longer maturity or more protection from the bond being called than your old bond provided, and you're safe from the wash-sale rule. This is true even when both bonds have the same issuer.

Result: You'll get a tax-saving capital loss on the sale without fundamentally changing your investment position.

TAXABLE AND TAX-DEFERRED ALLOCATIONS

A tax drawback of 401(k) accounts and traditional IRAs is that all distributions from them are taxed at high ordinary income rates.

A strategy: If your portfolio includes both assets producing ordinary taxable income (such as taxable bonds or CDs) and investments held for long-term gains, consider keeping the latter in taxable accounts so they benefit from the tax-favored capital-gains tax rates, and keeping the income-generating assets in tax-deferred retirement accounts so interest benefits from pretax compounding.

Also: If you're an active stock trader, consider doing this through a tax-favored retirement account. The normally high-tax short-term gains you earn will be tax deferred, and you will avoid the need to keep records regarding the holding periods and cost basis of these investments.

KIDDIE TAX

In years past, the "kiddie tax," which taxes the investment income of children at their parents' tax rate, applied only to children under age 14—so many children under 14 had investments placed in their names with the expectation that the children would soon be able to pay tax on them at their own low rates.

But in 2008, the kiddie tax applies to children under age 19 and to dependent children under age 24 who are full-time students.

What to do: Have children subject to the kiddie tax invest in appreciating assets (Series EE or I savings bonds, growth stocks) and tax-favored assets (municipal bonds) until they can pay tax at their own rate.

AMT

Long-term capital gains remain tax-favored under the alternative minimum tax (AMT), but taking them can nonetheless increase the amount of AMT you owe or make you subject to the AMT when you otherwise wouldn't be.

This is because capital gains are included in your income for AMT purposes, and, therefore, use up all of your AMT exempt amount. This can cause other income that otherwise would escape all AMT through the exempt amount to become subject to the AMT.

State and local taxes owed on investment income can create AMT liability as well.

Also: Interest paid on certain kinds of tax-exempt bonds is subject to AMT. Check on the AMT status of a bond (or a bond fund) before buying it.

More from Janice Johnson, CPA, JD...

How Traders Can Get Better Deductions

If you frequently trade stocks or other investments (such as options and commodities) for short-term gain, consider electing "trader" status and making a "mark-to-market" election under Section 475(f) of the Tax Code. This means that your position will be valued at year-end, with any increase over cost taxed at ordinary rates and any decrease being fully deductible against ordinary income. All your gains and losses (realized and unrealized) will be deemed short term. But if you trade for short-term gains anyhow, this makes no difference. *Advantages...*

• **Investing expenses will be deductible on Schedule C of your tax return,** as opposed to counting them among your miscellaneous expenses, which are deductible only to the extent that they exceed 2% of adjusted gross income.

Schedule C deductions could include a home office and related expenses, such as computing equipment, if this is your principal place of business for your trading activities.

• **All net investing losses will be deductible against ordinary income**—instead of only $3,000 of your net capital losses being deductible annually.

• **You'll no longer need to keep records of holding periods** or to be concerned about the wash-sale rule (which otherwise applies when the same security is sold and repurchased within 30 days).

For flexibility: Conduct your trading through a pass-through entity, such as a family partnership or a one-person limited liability company, and you can still invest separately for long-term gains in your personal portfolio.

Trader status for 2009 with the mark-to-market election must be elected by April 15, 2009—

attach your statement to the 2008 return or to your extension request. Consult your tax adviser for details.

Cash In Your Losses To Save on Taxes

Jason Hsu, PhD, principal and director of research and investment management, Research Affiliates, 155 N. Lake Ave., Pasadena, California 91101. A visiting professor at the Paul Merage School of Business at the University of California, Irvine, he is a coauthor of *The Fundamental Index: A Better Way to Invest* (Wiley).

Stocks are down sharply since reaching record highs in 2007. You might now hold stocks and stock funds that are trading at less than the price for which you bought them.

Strategy: Harvest capital losses in your taxable investment accounts. You'll lock in immediate tax savings and position yourself for greater long-term after-tax returns.

Ground rules: Net capital losses of up to $3,000 may be deducted against your ordinary income each year. Losses that can't be deducted may be carried forward indefinitely to help offset gains in future years.

HOW MOST PEOPLE DO IT

Most people think of tax-loss harvesting as something you do at the end of the year.

Situation: Tom Williams tallies all his 2008 stock trades for year-to-date in early December. He realizes that he has net long-term gains of $10,000 for the year.

If he takes no additional action, Williams will owe $1,500 on these transactions, at a 15% rate for long-term capital gains (as high as 35% for short-term gains), when he files his tax return next year.

Instead, Williams sells off enough shares of his bank stock to realize a $13,000 capital loss. He immediately reinvests the proceeds in another bank stock, which he expects will perform about the same as the stock he sold. It is important that he does not repurchase the same stock—otherwise, the wash-sale rule would be triggered and disallow the recognition of the $13,000 capital loss.

Result: Williams's $10,000 net realized gain has been converted to a $3,000 net capital loss for calendar year 2008, with no major change to his overall investment posture.

Instead of owing $1,500 to the IRS, he'll have a $3,000 tax deduction (against his ordinary income), worth $1,050 in the top 35% federal income tax bracket.

Therefore, Williams will be ahead by $2,550 (minus transaction costs) as a result of these out and in trades to harvest losses, which may be invested in additional stocks or stock funds.

State and even local income tax savings might increase the dollar savings resulting from the loss harvesting strategy.

YEAR-ROUND STRATEGY

Rather than wait until December, the better strategy is to harvest your losses continually.

Why this makes sense: Cutting your losses at, say, 10% enables you to avoid larger losses, which can be a good stop-loss discipline. In addition, there is no guarantee that you will have unrealized losses that you can take late in the year to achieve the desired $3,000 net capital loss for the year.

By harvesting losses more steadily, you can build up a bank of losses. Then you will be able to offset capital gains and take a $3,000 deduction on each tax return without any last-minute maneuvering.

How to do it: Track your taxable accounts carefully and sell whenever an issue is trading significantly below its purchase price.

General guideline: If you have a 10% unrealized loss, sell the stock or stock fund and invest the proceeds in another similar investment.

Flex plan: Harvesting losses gives investors a great deal of flexibility.

Situation: Suppose that Williams harvests sufficient losses during 2008 to build up a "bank" of $35,000 in net capital losses. But meanwhile, one stock that he holds has shot up sharply in price and future gains are uncertain. Selling that stock would trigger a $30,000 taxable gain.

Without loss harvesting, Williams might be reluctant to sell the stock and realize a taxable gain. (This would be particularly true if the gain were short term.) With the banked losses, in this example, he can sell the stock without incurring

tax obligations and reinvest the full amount in an issue he finds more promising now. The losses previously taken will offset the taxable gain.

Diversification: Some investors have highly concentrated portfolios—a great deal of their net worth is tied up in just one stock, which makes them vulnerable to a drop in that issue.

If you are in this situation, a sale and reinvestment is the prudent move. You sell some of the shares of stock that make up most of your net worth, then reinvest the sales proceeds in something else to diversify your holdings. However, a sale might trigger sizable capital gains.

Taking losses on other positions may permit you to sell some of the appreciated assets and reinvest elsewhere to diversify and reduce overall risk without owing tax on the realized gains.

Beyond the stock market: Many individuals hold investments other than stocks.

Example: In a given year, you might have taxable gains from hedge fund shares, commodities, collectibles, investment property, the sale of a closely held company, sale of your vacation home, etc.

Net losses that have been harvested from a stock market portfolio can balance all of these types of gains. Thus, taking such losses can reduce your overall tax bill in many situations for years to come.

REINVEST AND REAP

To harvest higher long-term returns, when you sell to take a loss, reinvest the sales proceeds immediately in a new investment.

Benefit: With this discipline, you'll be fully invested and, if you're a skilled stock picker, you'll be continually investing in timely prospects.

You probably will hold several different stocks or funds. Some may go up while others will go down. By constantly harvesting losses and reinvesting in more promising picks, you will reduce the tendency of selling winners too soon and holding on to losers for too long—a behavioral bias that has been documented to hurt investment performance for individual investors.

Your disciplined tax loss harvesting program will delay taxable capital gains for a very long time. The improvement in after-tax return, compounded over decades, can mean a later portfolio value that is many times the value of the portfolio with no tax loss harvesting strategy.

DEALING WITH THE DOWNSIDE

Drawbacks to tax-loss harvesting…

•**Transaction costs.** Frequently selling and buying stocks and/or funds can boost your investment expenses.

Strategies: If you prefer to invest in mutual funds, stick with no-load funds, which have no sales charges, and funds without redemption fees.

For stocks, use a discount broker. Fees may be negligible, especially if you do your trading on-line.

If you prefer to work with a full-service broker or an investment adviser, request a fee-based account. The amount you pay will be based on the size of your portfolio—generally, from 1% to 2% a year—often without any extra charges for trades. Portfolio minimums for these fee-based accounts, which most brokers offer, have come down to as low as $25,000.

•**Wash sales.** According to the wash-sale rule, if you sell any stock but also buy it back within 30 days before or after the date of the sale, your loss on the sale won't be a capital loss, for tax purposes. So, be careful not to do this if you are trying to take a capital loss.

After realizing a loss, be sure to reinvest in a different stock or fund.

Mutual Fund Alert: A Big Tax Hit Is Coming

Christopher Davis, mutual fund analyst, Morningstar, Inc., Chicago, which provides data on more than 250,000 investment offerings and has operations in 16 countries. He writes on tax topics for Morningstar's Web site, *www. morningstar.com.*

During the bear market early this decade, many mutual funds suffered big losses. But there was one hidden gift amid the bad news for shareholders—a gift that has kept on giving for years. Those losses translated into smaller annual capital gains tax bites for many fund investors, not just during the market's down years but also as the stock market rose strongly.

Under the US Tax Code, net losses can be used to offset future gains not only in the same year but also for years to come.

However, most of all those leftover tax breaks have been used up. That means many fund investors are facing much more in potential capital gains taxes this year, especially as funds sell off stocks after years of big price increases.

STRATEGIES

•**Don't buy fund shares late in the year.** Funds tend to register capital gains around December, so if you buy shares just before your gains are registered, you end up paying the tax even though you may not have benefited from most of the fund's gains for that year. (Eventually, however, when you sell the shares, this will reduce the size of the capital gain on which you must pay taxes.)

•**Limit fund sales.** Once you buy the fund, stick with it unless its long-term prospects sour or its strategy changes in a way that you don't like. Each time you sell fund shares, you may trigger capital gains taxes based on your profits—as opposed to the fund portfolio's internal profits. At the very least, try to hold fund shares for more than one year before selling. This way, you pay tax at the long-term capital gains rate—a maximum of 15%—instead of at the ordinary tax rate, which is as high as 35% for the top tax bracket.

•**Sell for capital losses.** If your fund shares have dropped in value substantially since you bought them, consider selling them and realizing a capital loss which can be utilized to offset capital gains. You then can buy a similar fund or buy back the same fund later.

Caution: After you sell a fund, wait more than 30 days to buy it back or it will be counted as a "wash sale," preventing you from claiming the capital loss.

•**Check the fund's potential capital gains exposure.** This is based on the size of the profits that a mutual fund has accumulated without distributing them as capital gains. The larger the percentage of assets this represents, the more potential exposure to big tax liabilities the shareholders could be facing when the fund sells its holdings. To determine potential exposure, go to my company's Web site, *www.morningstar.com*, and click the tax analysis tab for each fund.

The funds with the greatest profits in recent years may have accumulated the biggest potential capital gains. These include funds focused in on foreign stocks, as well as value and small-cap stocks and certain sectors, such as natural resources and precious metals.

•**Use retirement shelters.** Generally, keep funds that are the least "tax efficient" of all your investment picks in your 401(k), IRA and other retirement accounts. In a deductible IRA, for example, the assets won't be taxed until you remove them from the sheltered account.

Examples of tax-inefficient funds: Bond funds that pay out taxable dividends...and stock funds sitting on substantial capital gains which may trigger significant taxes for shareholders in taxable accounts.

TAX-EFFICIENT FUNDS

The most tax-efficient stock funds tend to be those that actively seek to restrict taxable gains, follow specific indexes and/or keep their holdings for many years, rather than buying and selling them often.

•**Tax-managed funds.** Funds that have the term "tax managed" in their names seek to limit taxable gains by keeping their turnover of stocks relatively low and by offsetting realized gains with sales of investments that have lost value. *Top choices include...*

•The Vanguard Tax-Managed Growth and Income Fund (VTGIX). It roughly tracks Standard & Poor's 500 stock index but decreases the tax bite more than the Vanguard 500 Index Fund by selling some falling stocks to offset capital gains. It's never had a capital gains distribution. 800-523-7731, *www.vanguard.com. Performance:* 6.69%.*

*Performance figures represent annualized returns for the five years ending June 30, 2008.

•The Vanguard Tax-Managed Capital Appreciation (VMCAX). This fund roughly tracks the Russell 1000. It's comprised of relatively large-company stocks—but it avoids all the higher-yielding dividend stocks in the index. It has never issued a capital gains distribution, and its fees are lower than those of 95% of rival exchange-traded funds (ETFs). 800-523-7731, *www.vanguard.com. Performance:* 7.59%.

•**Index funds.** Many index funds are naturally tax-efficient because they seldom trade. A typical index fund buys a basket of shares and sells only when a company is dropped from the index. *One of the best...*

•Fidelity Spartan Total Market Index Fund (FSTMX). This tracks the Dow Jones Wilshire 5000 Total Market Index, which includes nearly every US stock. 800-343-3548, *www.fidelity.com. Performance:* 7.62%.

•**Low-turnover funds.** Even though they do not have "tax managed" in their names, some actively managed funds are tax-efficient because they hold on to stocks for many years. *Some top funds with low turnover...*

•Fairholme Fund (FAIRX). This fund buys the stocks of stronger companies with solid business markets. 866-202-2263, *www.fairholmefunds.com. Performance:* 15.05%.

•Selected American Fund (SLASX). This fund has produced steady results from buying strong companies at bargain prices. 800-243-1575, *www.selectedfunds.com. Performance:* 8.23%.

•Third Avenue Value Fund (TAVFX). Its fund manager looks for "safe" stocks, including beaten-down ones, whether the companies are based in the US or are overseas. 800-443-1021, *www.thirdavenuefunds.com. Performance:* 11.27%.

11

Smart Consumer

14 Ways to Save Money With Your Home Computer

**Y**our computer and its Internet connection don't have to cost you a cent—in fact, they can save money and even make money for you. *Here are practical ways to do it...*

1. Find the best gasoline prices in your area. Go to GasPriceWatch.com (*www.gaspricewatch. com*) and GasBuddy.com (*www.gasbuddy.com*).

2. Slash your phone bill. Get unlimited long-distance phone calls, paying only one flat rate of around $25 per month for all your calls,* by using a Voice over Internet Protocol (VoIP) service. These services usually include extras, such as caller-ID and voice-mail messages that can be forwarded as e-mail. You need a high-speed Internet connection. Standard phone equipment can be used—the VoIP provider will give you

*Offers and prices subject to change.

an adapter to hook up with the service free or for a small charge. Calls are made just as you would with a standard land line, and the person you are calling does not need to have VoIP.

VoIP is available through specialty providers, such as Vonage (*www.vonage.com*)...from major phone companies, such as AT&T (*www.usa.att. com*)...and from cable providers, such as Road Runner (*www.roadrunner.com*).

More information: The Federal Communications Commission (*www.fcc.gov/voip*).

3. Get bargain airline fares. The airlines' best bargain prices often are available only on their own Web sites. Many airlines like to send e-mail "alerts" or newsletters to people who subscribe for free through the airlines' Web site. Check the Web site of any airline that you are considering flying on.

4. Save on mortgage expenses. If you are considering taking out a primary mortgage, second

Patricia Robison, president, Computing Independence, Box 2031, New York City 10011. She is a technology security specialist and gives seminars on using computers and technology safely and efficiently.

mortgage or home-equity loan, locate the best deals at HSH Associates (*www.hsh.com*) and at Bankrate.com (*www.bankrate.com*).

5. Earn more interest on savings. The Internet banks pay higher rates on savings because they don't have to cover the cost of paying for prime "bricks and mortar" banking locations.

Top Internet banks include VirtualBank (*www. virtualbank.com*) as well as Juniper Bank (*www. juniper.com*). To find even more Internet banks, go to Google (*www.google.com*) or Yahoo (*www. yahoo.com*) and enter "Internet banks" in their search box.

More information: Federal Deposit Insurance Corporation (*www.fdic.gov/bank/individual/ online/safe.html*).

6. Stay in touch with family and friends free. Start a private blog at *www.blogger.com*. This is a personal Web page on which you (and people you select) can post messages, pictures and even voice recordings for free. You save postage on letters and also the cost of printing and shipping photographs, etc., as well as keep everyone in touch no matter how far apart they may be.

7. Have a yard sale on-line. You will probably reap better prices through an on-line auction at eBay than through a yard sale.

Why: Instead of getting bids only from the few people who pass your yard in a few hours, you'll be able to hold items up for sale for days before a market of millions of people nationwide.

More information: To learn how to be an eBay seller, go to *www.ebay.com* and click on "Getting Started" under "Sell."

8. Get books cheap—or free. *Opportunities…*

• Get new books at prices lower than in retail stores at *www.amazon.com, www.barnesandnoble. com*, eBay or the Web site of the publisher.

• Used books, many in nearly new condition, are available at up to 70% or more off of list price at Amazon.com. Click on the "used and new" option when making your purchase.

• Classic books that are in the public domain because a copyright has expired or has not been enforced are downloadable to print—and can be viewed on-line—for free. Bartleby.com (*www.bartle by.com*) has thousands of texts dating from ancient Greece up until today, plus many leading reference works, on-line free.

Also, if you're looking for a particular "classic" book or play, enter its name in the Google search box, and you may find it downloadable free on a university Web site.

9. Read newspapers for free. Most of the newspapers now offer on-line editions—and most of these are free (though you may need to register by providing an e-mail address, etc.). You'll save the cost of your daily newspaper, and also be able to read newspapers from around the world. If you are planning a trip to a distant city or foreign country, reading its newspapers can be the best way to learn about it in advance.

Newspapers.com (*www.newspapers.com*) has a searchable directory of more than 10,000 newspapers worldwide.

10. Download music. Music can be cheaper than paying $16 for a CD when you download single songs for only $1 or so, and you can play them through your computer, a portable digital music device or on your home stereo (using the appropriate audio cables purchased from an electronics store).

Resources: Apple's iTunes store (*www.apple. com/itunes*) is most well-known, but there are many other sources, including the Smithsonian's Global Sound collection of music from around the world (*www.smithsonianglobalsound.org*). To find other sources, enter "music downloads" in your search engine.

11. Get digital radio free. While satellite radio stations charge a monthly subscription service fee, there are thousands of radio stations around the world that "Webcast" their programming so it can be heard on any computer for free, and many more new stations are "on Internet only." Radio-Locator.com (*www.radio-locator.com*) is a searchable directory of thousands of Webcasting radio stations worldwide.

Example: You can even hear music from Antarctica on Anetstation.com (*www.anetstation. com*).

12. Get free maps and trip planning. Before you take a road trip, get all the maps you need for free from Mapquest (*www.mapquest.com*) or at Google Maps (*www.google.com/maps*). These sites also give detailed directions to your destination, so you'll get there as quickly, and use as little gas, as possible.

13. Find local help, goods and services. Craigslist (*www.craigslist.org*) offers classified listings for many local areas. If you require household help, you can find it here. Or if you want to buy (or sell) an item locally, this is a fine site to help you do it.

Example: I recently needed a replacement power adapter for a laptop computer. The lowest price I could locate from the manufacturer or in an electronics store was $85. But through Craigslist, I was able to pick one up locally for $22 from an individual seller.

14. Continue your education. More and more colleges and universities are putting their courses on-line for easy access.

To obtain college credits, there's usually a fee, usually much less than the cost of going back on campus to get credits in person.

On-line learning, whether for credit or not, can boost your career, help you move to a second career and enrich your life.

More information: Visit Degreetutor.com at *www.degreetutor.com*, which provides a directory of colleges and universities that offer degree and nondegree programs, and the Web sites of colleges and community colleges of interest to you.

Nine Sneaky Fees And How *Not* to Pay Them

Joe Ridout, spokesperson for Consumer Action, a non-profit consumer education and advocacy organization located in San Francisco. Consumer Action features a "fee of the week" on its Web site, *www.consumer-action.org/feeoftheweek*.

You shopped around and found a great deal on a hotel room…a checking account…or a rental vehicle—or so you believed. Then lots of fees popped up, inflating the bill way beyond your expectations.

It may be perfectly reasonable for companies to charge additional fees when customers request special services or break established rules. But some companies push fees too far, tacking on hefty charges without warning or legitimate cause.

Several industries are especially notorious for charging unwarranted fees. *Here are some of the worst…*

HOTELS

1. Smoke-odor charges. Hotel chains impose stiff penalties when they think that guests have smoked in nonsmoking rooms.

Example: At many of the Marriott hotels, a smoke-odor cleanup fee is $250.* A charge has been imposed even when the only evidence of smoking is a report from a hotel housekeeper who smelled tobacco.

You might be charged a smoke-odor fee if the person who had your room before you smoked and the smell wasn't immediately noticed…or if your clothes picked up a tobacco odor after an evening in a smoky place.

What to do: If the hotel management won't remove the fee, call your credit card provider to protest this portion of your bill and request a "chargeback." The card provider will contact the merchant, which, in many cases, will then reverse the charge.

2. "Resort fees." An increasing number of hotels add "resort fees" of $5 to $30 each day to guest bills to cover the cost of maintaining the gym and pool—expenses that most travelers assume are included in the room rate. This fee applies even if you don't use these facilities. Occasionally it is tacked on at hotels that don't even have a gym or pool.

What to do: If a resort fee is unexpectedly added to your hotel bill, ask to have it removed, especially if you did not use the gym or pool. Point out that it was not mentioned when you confirmed your price.

AIRLINES

3. Frequent-flier-mile reactivation charges. US Airways has begun to erase frequent-flier miles for holders who haven't added any miles or redeemed them for 18 months, down from the old time limit of 36 months. The only way to get the expired miles back from US Airways is to pay a reactivation fee of $50 plus one cent per mile. Other airlines may follow.

*Fees, rates and offers subject to change.

What to do: Watch out for rule-tightening by airlines. Always use frequent-flier miles as soon as possible. Keep your US Airways mileage account active by making small transactions before 18 months go by. For example, you can extend your miles by occasionally buying one iTunes song for $1 on the airline's shopping site.

4. Bike transport fees. Most airlines charge a fee for checking a bicycle as luggage—even if the bike is disassembled and packed in a box that meets all luggage size and weight requirements. The bike fee is usually between $50 and $110 per round-trip, depending on the airline.

What to do: Mail your bike to your destination, or rent one when you get there. If you must bring your bike on a plane, pack it in a box with the pedals and handlebars disassembled, and tell the baggage-check employee that it is "exercise equipment." This isn't a lie—and shouldn't trigger a fee, assuming that the box meets luggage size and weight requirements and that the airline employee doesn't open it and discover the bike.

CAR RENTAL FIRMS

5. Airport rental charges. Rental firms impose hefty surcharges on car rentals at many airports. This can add $10 or more per day to the cost of a rental.

What to do: Ask the car rental agency to confirm your total price before you reserve a vehicle. If the airport fees are significant, check prices at car rental facilities located a few miles from the airport, where these fees might not apply. Off-site car rental companies sometimes even run airport shuttle buses to save customers cab fare.

BANKS AND CREDIT CARDS

6. "Free checking" fee. So-called free checking isn't always as free as it first appears, and sometimes it doesn't remain free.

Example: One bank recently switched its customers who had signed up for free checking accounts to new accounts that carry a $5.95 monthly fee unless these customers authorized automatic paycheck direct deposits or made bill payments on-line through the bank.

What to do: Consider closing any accounts that impose unexpected fees, and find a bank that truly provides free checking without strings at *www.bankrate.com*. Or you can open a credit

union account instead. Credit unions typically charge fewer and lower fees than banks charge. The Credit Union National Association (800-356-9655, *www.cuna.org*) can help you to locate a credit union in your area.

7. Double ATM charges. When you withdraw cash from an ATM at a bank other than your own, you might expect to pay that bank a fee of $1.50 to $2. In addition, however, your own bank may impose a fee of $1 to $2 for using another bank's ATM. All told, you could be charged $4 or more to withdraw as little as $20.

What to do: If it isn't convenient to use one of your own bank's ATMs, ask for cash back when you make a purchase using your bank debit card—that automatically removes funds from your bank account, and most retailers don't charge a fee for this service.

8. Gift card dormancy fees. Gift cards with a Visa, MasterCard, Discover or American Express logo often assess an "inactivity fee" of about $2.50 per month if a balance remains on the gift card after six months.

Gift cards issued by specific retailers are less likely to charge this fee, though Amazon, Blockbuster and American Eagle impose dormancy fees where they are permitted by state law.

What to do: Use gift cards quickly to avoid fees. If you don't have a use for a gift card, sell it to a friend or on eBay.

VIDEO RENTALS

9. "No late fee" video rental fees. Video rental giant Blockbuster has heavily promoted its "no late fee" program, but the late fee is not really gone—it is just hidden. If a movie is seven days late, Blockbuster converts the rental into a sale and charges your credit card the full price of the movie—in some cases, $40 or $50. Blockbuster will let you return the movie for a refund after this charge is imposed, but you will have to pay a "restocking fee" of $1.25. After a month, if the video is not returned, the sale becomes final.

Adding to the confusion is that some Blockbuster franchises are not participating in the "no late fee" program and charge traditional late fees.

What to do: Make sure you understand your video store's late-fee policy, including the fine print—even if the store claims not to charge late fees.

Best Time to Buy...

Shopping for a gym membership or new car? *Check out the best time to buy below...*

New suit: January or July. Winter collections can be marked down by about 30% in January, when spring collections are released. The summer collections are marked down in July.

Caribbean vacation: March and April. It still is cold in most parts of the US, but you'll save 25% by avoiding the December–February peak travel season.

Gym membership: July and August. Gyms are quiet during hot-weather months.

Car: November and December—that's when dealers are concerned about clearing out inventory before year-end, and winter is typically the slowest car-selling season.

House: October to December. The supply exceeds demand after the school year starts.

Airline tickets: 1 am on Wednesdays—airlines reset their fares every Wednesday just after midnight.

Men's Health, 33 E. Minor St., Emmaus, Pennsylvania 18098, *www.menshealth.com.*

The Underground Shopper's Secrets to Getting the Absolutely Lowest Prices This Holiday Season

Sue Goldstein, founder of The Underground Shopper, a 36-year-old organization focused on bargain-shopping tips. Goldstein has written more than 75 guidebooks on the topic. She hosts a morning call-in radio show at radio station KVCE-AM in Dallas. Her Web site is *www.under groundshopper.com.*

I find some of the best shopping discounts of the entire year the day after Thanksgiving and the day after Christmas. On these two dates—Black Friday (traditionally when retailers get out of the "red" for the year and start making a profit) and December 26—the stores routinely mark down items by 50% to 90%. To gain an edge over the crowds of shoppers on these days, I have learned to follow a few key strategies. *My secrets...*

PREPARE IN ADVANCE

Read sale ads before they are officially released. Check Web sites that manage to obtain major retailer sale ads a week or two before they are published. That way, you can delay buying items that you know will be on sale.

Best sites: *www.bfads.net...www.blackfriday ads.com...www.theblackfriday.com...www. dealtaker.com...www.fatwallet.com...www. savingsvine.com.*

Helpful: Know the sales abbreviations that are used often on the Web sites and in newspaper ads...

• **AR is after rebate.**

• **B&M is bricks and mortar,** which means deals are available only in stores, not on-line.

• **CPN is coupon.**

• **MIR is mail-in rebate.**

• **RP is return policy.**

• **S&H is shipping and handling.**

Take advantage of a store's policy on "price adjustments" for items that go on sale after you buy them. If, for instance, a store adjusts prices up to 14 days after you have purchased an item, buy it two weeks early if you expect it to go on sale the day after Thanksgiving. If the item goes on sale, go into the store with your receipt and ask that customer service refund the difference between what you paid and the sale price. If the item doesn't go on sale, you can return it.

Helpful: Check whether your credit card issuer provides a "lowest-price guarantee," which will usually give you up to 30 or 60 days after you make a purchase to find the same product at a lower advertised price and get a refund for the difference. For example, the Citi Diamond Preferred Rewards American Express Card will refund up to $250 if you locate the item at a lower price within 60 days.*

Check whether a store "price matches" during holiday sales. Many stores will match a competitor's advertised prices on the same items—an advantage if the price-matching store is more conveniently located.

*Offers subject to change.

Beat all the early birds without leaving home. Plenty of stores open at the crack of dawn for post-holiday sales—and lots of shoppers show up hours beforehand to get in line.

To avoid this madness: With some popular chains, you can start ordering on the retailer's Web site at midnight—at the sale prices—even if the stores don't open until 6 am. Often, you can avoid shipping costs by arranging to pick up the item on the day of the sale at your local store.

Important: Check with the particular retail stores in your area because their policies can vary from year to year and in different regions.

Alert your credit card issuer ahead of time. If you plan to make a lot of purchases or atypical purchases, call the credit card's customer service phone number. Otherwise, you may waste valuable time at the store dealing with card transactions that are questioned or rejected because your purchases don't fit in with your usual pattern and the issuer becomes suspicious that the card may have been stolen.

AT THE STORES

Bring magazine or newspaper ad clippings of what you want to buy. It will save time when you are asking clerks about what you are looking for.

Shop for the most heavily promoted items last if you have a long shopping list and fear that items will sell out. Unless they say "supplies are limited," stores usually carry large inventories of their most prominently advertised specials but only limited supplies of other advertised items.

Check out an electronics chain's Web site on a store computer while you are in the store. At retailers, including Best Buy and Circuit City, the chain's Web prices are sometimes lower than its in-store prices. If a salesperson doesn't agree to match the Web price, talk to the manager. If that doesn't work, call customer service executives at the chain's corporate headquarters.

Request a rain check. If a sale item is out of stock, many stores will agree to sell it to you at the same price weeks later when their inventories are replenished and/or customers start to make returns.

THE MONDAY AFTER

Get a second chance on "CyberMonday." This is the first day of the workweek following the extended Thanksgiving weekend, when many people check the retail Web sites on their office computers. This is when retailers unveil special holiday promotions on-line, as well as free shipping offers.

Resource: *www.cybermonday.com.* It links to various retailers' on-line deals.

Amazon's Biggest Discounts

The Web site called JungleCrazy.com features Amazon.com products currently discounted by 70% or more.* Search for a specific product, or browse dozens of categories.

Real Simple, 1271 Avenue of the Americas, New York City 10020, *www.realsimple.com.*

*Rate subject to change.

Jeans That Fit

You can "try on" jeans on-line at *www.zafu. com.* Answer a few questions about how you would like jeans to fit, then the free Web site Zafu lists the brands that will fit you the best.

How to Spot a Designer Knockoff

Luxury goods are made with care, so sloppy stitching in less visible areas, such as inside pockets, is a sign of a counterfeit. Also, on the real thing, the logo usually appears on all of the metal pieces, including zippers and snaps. And, make sure that a logo is spelled and capitalized correctly. Finally, the packaging should be made of quality material—if an item is covered in plastic wrap, it's probably a fake.

FakesAreNeverInFashion.com.

Don't Buy Flowers Here

Don't buy cut flowers from the supermarket. Grocery stores tend to keep flowers in the open, instead of in the refrigerator (cold keeps flowers alive longer).

Also, flowers in the grocery store often are close to the fruit, which gives off *ethylene* that makes flowers wilt faster.

Money, Time-Life Building, Rockefeller Center, New York City 10020, *money.cnn.com*.

Save on Pet Medicines By Buying On-Line

Filling prescriptions at a veterinary clinic is expensive—many clinics have not joined with others to negotiate discounts on drugs. Getting the prescription from your vet and filling it at a Web site, such as *www.1800petmeds.com*, can save 50% or more.*

Also: Ask your vet if a less expensive generic version of a medicine is available...and find out if your pet can take the human form of a medicine, many drugs prescribed for people also are used for animals and may cost less at a traditional pharmacy.

Kiplinger's Personal Finance, 1729 H St., NW, Washington, DC 20006, *www.kiplinger.com*.

*Rate subject to change.

Patience Pays

To buy trendy electronics for less, simply be patient. Apple quickly cut the price of the

recently released iPhone by $200...the first iPod had 10 gigabytes of memory and cost $500, but the price fell to $300 when a 20-gigabyte model was introduced. Sony has reduced its PlayStation 3 price, and Microsoft has cut the price of its Xbox 360.

Bottom line: Let other people wait in long lines to be the first with a new product—you can hold off and get the identical product, or a better one, for less money.

Steve Kruschen, an independent consumer electronics reviewer known as Mr. Gadget, Los Angeles, *www.mrgadget.com*.

Beware Interest-Free Loans

Interest-free loans for major purchases, such as furniture, may not be good deals.

Example: You buy a piece of furniture that costs $5,000. The store interest rate is 20%, but you do not have to pay interest for three years. At the end of three years, you are able to pay off all but the last $1,000. Most people think they will owe only $200 in interest (20% of $1,000). In reality, interest is calculated on the original purchase price so that you owe $1,000 in interest (20% of $5,000).

Self-defense: Pay off the purchase price before the interest-free period ends.

Danny Kofke, special education teacher based in Hoschton, Georgia, and author of *How to Survive (and Perhaps Thrive) on a Teacher's Salary* (Tate).

Cut Down on Catalogs

Sign up for a free account at Catalog Choice (*www.catalogchoice.org*)...type in your name and mailing address...and state which catalogs you would like to stop receiving. Catalog Choice will then work on your behalf to remove your name from the company's mailing lists.

Secrets of the eBay Millionaire's Club: Easy Ways For Sellers to Boost Profits

Amy Joyner, the author of several books about eBay, including *The eBay Billionaires' Club: Exclusive Secrets for Building an Even Bigger and More Profitable Online Business* (Wiley). She has conducted nearly 1,000 transactions and has a 100% positive eBay feedback rating. Her Web site is *www.theonlinemillionaire.com*.

The Professional eBay Seller's Alliance is an organization of more than 700 eBay "power-er sellers" who together generate nearly a half billion dollars in annual sales. *eBay enthusiast Amy Joyner interviewed more than 30 of these on-line auction stars to learn their strategies...*

PRICING AND SELLING

• **Start the bidding at 99 cents.** Experienced eBay sellers know that more bidders are drawn to listings when the bidding starts very low, even when selling merchandise worth hundreds of dollars. Lots of bidders tend to mean a higher final price, because some bidders are likely to get carried away by the auction excitement and bid more than they originally intended. Setting your opening bid at 99 cents instead of $1 or more also qualifies you for the lowest eBay starting (insertion) fee of 20 cents. ("Final value" fees based on the auction's closing price also apply.)

Exception: Do not set an ultralow opening price when there are numerous items similar to yours already for sale and they are not attracting multiple bidders. When sellers outnumber buyers, buyers sometimes win with their opening bids. This is particularly common with books and DVDs.

• **Skip the reserve.** In a "reserve auction," the item is not sold if bidding does not reach a seller-selected reserve (minimum) price. Cautious sellers will use reserve auctions to protect themselves from selling items at much less than they are worth. However, top eBay sellers tend to agree that setting a reserve is a very bad idea.

Most eBay bidders are bargain hunters. When they read the message "reserve price not met," they conclude that the seller will not part with this item at a bargain price and they move on to other auctions. Setting a reserve price also adds to your eBay insertion fees.

Helpful: If you simply cannot live with the risk that your item will sell for a very low price, increase the opening bid instead of adding a reserve. High opening bids are the lesser of two evils.

• **Don't gouge buyers on shipping.** Some eBay sellers inflate shipping charges to increase their profits. Top sellers rarely do this. They have learned that many potential buyers consider excessive shipping costs a sign of an untrustworthy seller. The proper amount to charge for shipping is slightly more than your actual cost of postage and packing materials.

Helpful: If you have an eBay store (a personalized Web page on eBay, where you can sell merchandise at a fixed price), encourage more sales by offering shipping discounts when buyers purchase more than one item.

• **Pay for the gallery photo but not the bold print.** When listing your items for auction on eBay, you are offered numerous "listing upgrades" that are meant to help your auction catch shoppers' attention. Top sellers all agree that the "gallery photo"—the small picture that appears next to the title when listings are displayed—is money well spent. Buyers tend to scroll past all listings that lack these.

Cost: 35 cents.*

Do not opt for bold print titles. They do not draw enough extra attention to justify the extra $1 fee.

• **Offer second-chance auctions when you sell multiple quantities.** If you have more than one of the same item to sell, don't list each in a separate auction. Auction one of the items, then send an e-mail through eBay to the bidder who made the second-highest bid, offering him/her the chance to purchase an identical product for the amount of his final bid.

Second-chance auctions save you money because you will be charged an eBay insertion fee only on the first item (final value fees do apply

*Prices subject to change.

to each item sold)…they provide you a guaranteed selling price on the second item, assuming that the bidder accepts the offer…and they let you choose a bidder you trust, based on positive feedback scores. If the second-place bidder has negative feedback, make your offer to the third- or fourth-place bidder instead.

BUSINESS STRATEGIES

Would you like to turn selling on eBay into a business? *To make it work…*

• **Stay in touch with customers.** Inexperienced eBay sellers often fail to take full advantage of their satisfied customers. Ask buyers for permission to add their names to your e-mail list so that you can update them about auctions.

• **Include a free gift with purchases to foster goodwill.**

Example: A successful camera seller adds free lens cloths to shipments.

• **Do not waste time at the post office.** Long post office lines can be major time drains for people who sell on eBay regularly. Instead, schedule free post office package pickups from your home/store through the post office's Web site (*www.usps.gov*). The site also lets you print shipping labels and pay for shipping costs with your credit card. You can even order free priority mail shipping boxes.

Important: You will need an accurate scale to weigh your shipments.

• **Protect your feedback score at all costs.** Top eBay sellers know that a high eBay feedback score is a necessity to get high bids. Adopt a policy of "the buyer is always right"—even when he is not. Even if just a few buyers leave you negative feedback, potential bidders in future auctions might not trust you.

• Offer money-back refunds to unsatisfied customers whenever possible.

• Do not type resentful responses when you receive undeserved negative feedback. If you explain poor feedback in a calm, reasonable manner, future bidders are more likely to assume that the buyer was to blame for the problem.

• Be responsive to bidder questions. Try to be at your computer as your auctions draw to a close so that you can answer any last-minute questions.

• Do not list negative-sounding policies on your auction pages. State your sales policies in a positive way. *Example:* Write "I accept only Pay-Pal," rather than "Under no circumstances will I take a check or money order."

• **Select appropriate auction management software.** These programs can take the grunt work out of posting multiple items for auction by offering tools to quickly create, edit and format multiple listings. Turbo Lister from eBay is appropriate for most sellers (free at *pages.ebay. com/turbo_lister*).

People who sell hundreds of items or more a month might choose to get a more sophisticated program, such as ChannelAdvisor Pro ($29.95/ month, 866-264-8594, *pro.channeladvisor.com*) or eBay's Blackthorne Basic ($9.99/month, *pages. ebay.com/blackthorne*).

• **Become a consignment seller.** Let friends know that you can handle their eBay sales for them, and ask them to recommend you to their friends.

Consignment sellers typically charge between 35% and 50% of the net sale price, after eBay fees. The item's owner should pay the auction fees if the product doesn't sell.

Helpful: Check completed auctions of similar items before posting a consigned item for sale. If you can let the item's owner know what price the product is likely to fetch, you will reduce the risk of disappointment.

Cash for Your Books

W̲ant to get rid of some gently used books? Just go to *www.cash4books.net* and enter the ISBN (10- or 13-digit identification number found on the copyright page) of a book to find out how much this site will pay for it. If you agree, set up an account and print out a packing list and shipping label. When your books are received, you will get either a check or a deposit to a PayPal account.

Cash In on Old Gadgets

If you have an older cell phone, music player, camera, etc., that you no longer use, you can sell it to SecondRotation.com. Just answer a few questions about the condition of your device, and the site will estimate its value. Next, print out a postage-paid mailing label, and send the device on to SecondRotation. After they receive your gadget, they will make a final condition valuation and notify you by e-mail. If you accept the offer, they will send you a check. If you decline the offer, the item will be returned to you within five to 10 business days at no charge.

End It Early

When your provider alters cell phone service in a "materially adverse" way (such as a fee increase), you can cancel your contract without paying the early termination fee. This escape period typically lasts 14 to 60 days after notification of the plan change.

Self-defense: Read all contract changes when they arrive. Be ready to explain why the change in service affects you adversely.

Linda Sherry, director of national priorities at Consumer Action, a nonprofit consumer education and advocacy organization in Washington, DC, *www.consumer-action.org.*

Cell Phone Smarts

To avoid a bad cell phone deal, request a trial period. Most carriers allow new customers to try out a plan for up to four weeks. Sign up for the shortest contract possible—even if you have to pay for the phone. Early-termination fees range from $150 to $200.* Also, pay attention to the fine print. If you don't understand something in the contract, ask for an explanation. If a policy

*Fees subject to change.

concerns you and the carrier won't negotiate, consider another carrier.

Buyer beware: Buying a service plan from a company that represents multiple carriers can result in double penalties should you need to cancel your contract.

Consumer Reports, 101 Truman Ave., Yonkers, New York 10703, *www.consumerreports.org.*

Escape Your Cell Phone Plan

The CellSwapper Web site (*www.cellswapper. com*) acts as a sort of eBay for cell phone plans.

How: To dispose of a contract, you post its details and, if you wish, offer an incentive for someone to take it over—such as a small money payment or the phone carrying case. Your offer remains posted until someone is lured by the shortened contract (since you have already used part of it) and lack of activation fee to pick it up.

Charge: $18.95 for a successful transfer.*

Flip side: You can also use the site to obtain a bargain phone plan, plus maybe a sweetener from its seller.

*Prices subject to change.

Four Ways to Cut Your Phone Bill

Looking for some smart ways to slash your phone bill? *Check out the list below…*

•**Switch to Internet calling using Voice over Internet Protocol** (VoIP) if you have a broadband connection. You can save $400 per year* on long distance—but you will need a basic land line as backup in case electricity goes out.

VoIP providers: Packet8, *www.packet8.com* …Vonage, *www.vonage.com.*

*Rates subject to change.

• **Consider dropping your land line** and using your cell phone for all calls, saving the cost of your current local and long-distance service.

• **Buy a local-and-long-distance bundle** for $35 to $55 a month, if you already spend that much on long distance alone. You will essentially be getting local service free.

• **Make long-distance calls with a prepaid card.** Cost can be less than four cents a minute —but you have to punch extra numbers every time you make a call.

Consumer Reports, 101 Truman Ave., Yonkers, New York 10703, *www.consumerreports.org.*

Cheaper Long Distance

Cut long-distance phone bills by using your computer to make calls. Yahoo Messenger with Voice and Google Talk are free for use between computers.* You need to download the messaging service software and purchase a microphone and a headset for each computer.

David Boyer, a research editor and resident computer guru, *Bottom Line/Personal,* Boardroom Inc., 281 Tresser Blvd., Stamford, Connecticut 06901.

*Offer subject to change.

Free 411 Information Calls

Telephone directory assistance calls today often cost from $1.50 to as much as $3.50,* whether made by cell phone or land line.

Several smart options: Google Voice Local Search (800-466-4411) will give the phone listing of any business in the US for free. You can search by a specific name or business category. Or phone 800-FREE-411 to access the same full database used by the phone companies that includes personal, business and government numbers. There is no fee, but the service does play one short advertisement before it provides your

*Rates and offer subject to change.

number (and it cannot connect you directly to your requested number).

David Wood, freelance consumer advocate and writer on senior scams and fraud, Washington, DC.

✂ Cut Your Heating Bills By 20%...and Trim Cooling Costs, Too

Richard Trethewey, master heating, ventilation and air-conditioning technician for the PBS TV shows *This Old House* and *Ask This Old House.* He is also a coauthor of *This Old House Heating, Ventilation and Air Conditioning* (Little, Brown).

A programmable thermostat—one that lets you automatically adjust the temperature in your home for different times of the day and week—can cut your heating and cooling costs by as much as 20%. *My easy plan for programming your thermostat...*

HOW TO SELECT TEMPERATURES

• **Chart your daily habits for a few weeks.** If you have two or more heating/cooling zones, with two separate thermostats, track how much time you spend in each area and when you shift from one to the other. If you are comfortable with less heat or cooling while you sleep, program the thermostat to different temperatures for those hours. Do the same if everyone is going to be out of the house for at least six hours during the day—or if you will spend little time in one area for that long. It does not save energy to cut back heating or cooling for less than six hours at a time, because to restore the more comfortable temperatures afterward, you would use up as much energy as you saved. Over a period of eight hours, you will save 1% in energy costs for each degree you cut back on heating or cooling.

For optimal efficiency: Winter, 65°F to 70°F when you're at home and awake...60°F to 65°F while you're asleep or not home. Summer, 70°F to 75°F when you're home and awake...75°F to 80°F while asleep or not home.

• **Avoid trying to heat or cool your home quickly.** Cranking the heat up to 90°F or the air conditioner down to 50°F will not help you reach your desired temperature faster.

Reason: Central heating and cooling systems produce the same amount of heat or chilled air in a given period of time regardless of how high or low the thermostat is set. What varies is the amount of time they remain on to reach the designated temperature.

If your thermostat does not have the "smart recovery" feature that gradually shifts it to the desired temperature, track how long it takes to reach that temperature and set the unit to start shifting that far in advance.

PICKING A NEW THERMOSTAT

•**Choose an Energy Star–compliant thermostat,** including from two to four automated temperature settings a day, depending on your needs…an override switch that lets you temporarily change settings without reprogramming… and smart recovery, which gradually shifts the temperature to the desired level.

•**Make sure that the thermostat is user-friendly.** It should have digital backlit displays… bold letters or lights to tell you the override is on …and backup batteries so that you don't have to reprogram the unit if a blackout interrupts the electricity that powers it.

•**Choose one that is easy to install.** Home owners can install most units in about a half-hour. To get a free instructional video on how to install a thermostat, go to *www.thisoldhouse.com* and search for "Install Thermostat." If you are uncomfortable dealing with electrical wires, have an electrician or plumber do the job.

BEST THERMOSTATS

Both of the units below include the features cited above.

•**Lux Smart Temp Touch Screen** TX9000TS ($80*) lets you set a different program for every day of the week. 856-234-8803 or *www.luxproducts.com.*

•**Honeywell Focus Pro 6000** ($87) and Lux Smart Temp TX1500 ($37). Both allow one program for weekdays and two for weekends. The Honeywell unit has a flip-out door that allows for simple battery replacement. 800-328-5111 or *www.honeywell.com.*

*Prices subject to change.

Clean Refrigerator Coils To Save Money

Lucie B. Amundsen, contributing editor to *The Family Handyman,* 2915 Commers Dr., Eagan, Minnesota 55121, *www.familyhandyman.com.*

Refrigerator cooling coils can become covered with a lot of dust, dirt and especially pet hair.

This buildup makes your refrigerator run less efficiently, increases your energy bill and could cause the refrigerator's compressor to overheat, triggering an overload switch—stopping the refrigerator from running.

Service professionals claim that fully half of all refrigerator service calls are caused by dirty cooling coils. But cleaning the coils yourself is easy and much less expensive than paying for a service call—or buying a brand-new refrigerator because the old one stopped running and you mistakenly thought it was broken.

How to do it: Coils are usually located on the back of the refrigerator, where they can simply be brushed off. Or, if located at the bottom in a compartment behind a grille, remove the grille and use a coil-cleaning brush (available at home stores for about $10*). Simply insert the brush, pull it back and vacuum it.

If your refrigerator stopped running due to dirty coils, after they are cleaned and its compressor cools down, it will start running again on its own.

Payoff: Cleaning dirty cooling coils can save as much as $10 per month in electricity bills—well over $100 a year.

*Prices subject to change.

Energy Drain

Various electronics and appliances, including those that come with remote controls or digital clocks, never do power down completely unless they are unplugged. This drains as much as 65 billion kilowatt-hours per year and costs US consumers $5.8 billion.

Best: Unplug devices you don't use regularly …be sure that your computer screen turns off when the computer does…and only buy Energy Star appliances, which use less standby power. Also unplug chargers for phones, cameras, etc., when not needed—if a charger is warm to the touch, power is being used.

Jeff Deyette, an energy analyst, Union of Concerned Scientists, Cambridge, Massachusetts, *www.ucsusa.org*.

Beware of Medical Discount Plans

Charles B. Inlander, a consumer advocate and health-care consultant located in Fogelsville, Pennsylvania. He was the founding president of the nonprofit People's Medical Society, the consumer advocacy organization credited with key improvements in the quality of US health care in the 1980s and 1990s, and is the author of 20 books, including *Take This Book to the Hospital with You: A Consumer Guide to Surviving Your Hospital Stay* (St. Martin's).

Forty-seven million Americans do not have health insurance, but there are also now 50 million Americans—including 30% of adults over the age of 65—who are said to be "underinsured." This means that their insurance does not sufficiently cover some key aspect of medical care, such as physical therapy, psychological counseling or prescription medication. If you don't have health insurance—or it's inadequate—it can be tempting to respond to those ubiquitous advertisements for "discount" medical cards. With come-ons like "Discounts of up to 60%" and "No deductibles or co-pays," these services sound like the answer to your prayers. But are they? *What you should know…*

• **Medical discount cards are not health insurance.** Medical discount providers make arrangements with physicians, dentists, pharmacies, hospitals, chiropractors and other providers to offer a discount off their normal retail prices for services. But you still must pay the bill out of your own pocket. In addition, most medical discount cards charge a monthly fee ($9.99 to more than $50,* on average) for the use of their services.

*Prices and rates subject to change.

• **Discounts may not be worth it.** Over the years, several states, including New York and Florida, have investigated some of the companies providing medical discount cards and found that many offer only small—or no—savings.

Example: If the doctor you go to offers a 10% discount, and his or her fee is $100 per visit, you save $10 each visit. But if the card fee is $10 per month, you won't save anything unless you see the doctor more than 12 times per year!

The discounts also can vary widely from provider to provider, making it difficult for you to get the best use out of the service unless you invest considerable time in finding the best discounts.

Eyeglasses, medical equipment and foot care are among the few instances in which a valid discount card may be worthwhile.

• **Provider lists are often out-of-date.** Medical discount plans give clients a list of participating providers. But quite often, those lists are outdated, or the providers will accept only a limited number of customers from one card sponsor. If you are considering signing up for a card, be sure that the providers or pharmacies that you want to use participate in the discount plan. Call each provider and ask if he accepts this card, what the discounts will be and the retail prices for the medical services that you are most likely to need.

• **You can negotiate discounts yourself.** Most people don't realize this, but many doctors, dentists and other providers will offer a discount if you ask them, particularly if you're a longtime patient. For example, a doctor may charge a discounted fee for a physical exam, while a dentist might discount fees for fillings and crowns. AARP and other organizations, including the drug companies, have discount programs for medications that are worth checking into. Many pharmacies also have their own discount plans, with discounts ranging from 10% to 70%, depending on the drug and whether it is a brand-name or a generic.

By negotiating your own discounts with your health-care providers, you can cut out a middleman fee, which means you'll receive the greatest possible savings.

Eat Right, Spend Less

A new finding shows that Americans who eat six to 10 daily servings of fruits and vegetables spend about $2,000 less on health-care expenses annually than those who eat less of these foods...and if everyone ate six to 10 servings daily, cases of heart disease could drop by about 30%.

Journal of the American Dietetic Association, Chicago, Illinois, *www.eatright.org*.

Better Than Bottled Water

Tamara Eberlein, editor, *Bottom Line/Women's Health*, Boardroom Inc., 281 Tresser Blvd., Stamford, Connecticut 06901.

A ttracted by images of pristine springs and wary of dehydration, I guzzle bottled water, as many health-conscious Americans do. But is bottled water more healthful than tap —or am I needlessly squeamish about drinking from the same household water source I use to flush my toilets? *What I've learned...*

• **The emissions from manufacturing and shipping plastic bottles add to global warming.** An estimated 86% of water bottles wind up in landfills instead of recycling centers, and they will take centuries to biodegrade.

• **Repeatedly reusing bottles meant for one-time use cuts down on pollution**—but it can promote bacterial growth as the plastic degrades.

• **Government standards for bottled water purity often are less strict than for tap water.** Bottled water packaged and sold within the same state is exempt from FDA oversight.

My plan for switching to tap...

• **Install a faucet-mounted or carafe-style carbon filter ($20 to $60 at drugstores*) to remove lead,** chlorine and other contaminants from tap water...or install a reverse-osmosis filter

*Prices subject to change.

($300 to $800) on the main water line to your house.

• **Carry water in a stainless steel or enamel-lined thermos.** Avoid reusable bottles made with #7 polycarbonate plastic—potentially carcinogenic and/or hormone-disrupting chemicals may leach from the plastic into the water, especially when exposed to heat or sunlight.

Bottled water can cost up to 10,000 times more than tap. The money that I save can pay my gym fees.

Dangers from China

William Hubbard, a former associate commissioner for policy and planning at the US Food and Drug Administration (FDA). He is an adviser to the nonprofit Coalition for a Stronger FDA in Washington, DC, *www.fdacoalition.org*, and Donald L. Mays, senior director of product safety planning and technical administration at Consumers Union, publisher of *Consumer Reports*, Yonkers, New York, *www.consumerreports.org*. Mays is on the boards of directors of the American National Standards Institute and International Consumer Products Health and Safety Organization.

R ecent recalls of imports from China have mounted to encompass millions of defective or tainted items, including seafood, toothpaste, pet food, tires and toys. The recalls have focused attention on just how dependent the US is on China for an array of goods—about 80% of all toys we buy and nearly 22% of all seafood—as well as on how risky those goods can be.

Recalls also have highlighted the inadequacy of our inspection system. The US Food & Drug Administration (FDA) has only 450 inspectors to inspect the nearly 20 million shipments of food that enter the country every year, which means each consumer has to be extra vigilant.

Below, two leading consumer advocates, who have testified at congressional hearings, share insights into how to protect against dangerous items from China...

FOOD AND DRUGS
William Hubbard

Federal rules requiring retailers to label country of origin for a wide range of foods were supposed to take effect in 2004 but were postponed for most types of food until September 30, 2008. Those rules are in effect for seafood but are widely ignored. Also, if you buy a prepared seafood product, such as shrimp scampi in a package, as long as the processing occurred here, it is labeled "Made in USA" no matter where the seafood and other ingredients originated.

SEAFOOD

Problem: Toxic contaminants.

Recall: In July 2007, the FDA declared an import alert for five types of seafood from China—catfish, shrimp, eel, dace (a carplike fish) and basa (similar to catfish). Contaminants—including residues of *nitrofuran*, the antibiotic that is used to keep fish free from certain bacteria…the toxic chemicals *malachite green* and *gentian violet*…and the *fluoroquinolone* antibiotics—were found in more than 15% of the tested fish. The first three substances are carcinogens, and the fourth may increase resistance to important antibiotics, such as Cipro.

Under the alert, seafood shipments are held at the US border until importers conduct independent testing to show that the seafood is safe. Despite the alert on imports, at least one million pounds of suspect Chinese seafood has slipped past the inspectors.

Self-defense: Don't eat seafood from China. Whenever it's possible, buy local freshwater fish, such as rainbow trout. Buy prepared products only at stores and from companies that you trust and that assure you that they do not buy seafood from China.

Check on seafood recalls with your state agricultural department. State agencies often do more extensive testing on food than the federal government does. To find the Web site of your state agricultural department, go to *www.statelocalgov. net* and click on "Agriculture."

TOOTHPASTE

Problem: Contains *diethylene glycol* (DEG), a chemical used in antifreeze and as an industrial solvent. It can damage the kidneys as well as the central nervous system. DEG tastes sweet and is used as a cheaper substitute for pharmaceutical-grade glycerin, a sweetening thickener.

Recalls: In June 2007, the FDA warned consumers to discard all toothpaste that was labeled as made in China after DEG was discovered in

some tubes. In August 2007, the manufacturer Gilchrest & Soames recalled complimentary tubes distributed to hotels in many countries. To date, there have been no reports of poisoning.

Self-defense: Buy major brands at local drugstores and supermarkets. Do not buy toothpaste at flea markets or at 99-cent stores, where most of these questionable products were distributed. Counterfeit toothpastes may have a foreign language instead of English on the packaging.

PHARMACEUTICALS

Problem: DEG contamination. Cough syrups and an acetaminophen syrup from China that contained DEG have caused a number of deaths among children in Panama and Haiti. In addition, in early 2008 there was the problem of tainted heparin from a Chinese plant.

Self-defense: Make sure that any medicine you use is a known and trusted brand name and that it has an English-language label.

PET FOOD

Problem: Contains *melamine*, a chemical that is used to make plastics and fertilizer. Pet food contaminated with melamine resulted in the illness or death of at least 4,000 cats and dogs.

Recall: More than 150 varieties of pet food tainted with melamine were recalled in 2007.

Self-defense: Check for sources of protein, such as chicken, chicken meal, beef and lamb meal—rather than cheap fillers, including cornmeal, wheat, oatmeal or millet—as the main ingredient in the pet food you buy. Visit *www.fda. gov/oc/opacom/hottopics/petfood.html* to get the latest information on pet food recalls.

RECALL UPDATES

Stay alert to future dangers by monitoring recalls listed on the FDA Web site, *www.recalls. gov.*

CONSUMER PRODUCTS
Donald L. Mays

In 2006, three out of every four US recalls of imported products involved imports from China. The Consumer Products Safety Commission (CPSC), which handles all product safety inspections, has suffered severe staff and budget cuts. Also, it is not legally allowed to alert the public to a hazard until the case against the manufacturer is resolved.

TIRES

Problem: A missing safety feature called a "gum strip" that binds belts of a tire together so the tread does not separate from the tire…or gum strips that were not large enough. Tread separation can cause loss of vehicle control.

Recall: The National Highway Traffic Safety Administration (NHTSA) ordered the distributor Foreign Tire Sales Inc. to recall its defective tires intended for pickups, sport-utility vehicles and light trucks. The distributor has recalled 255,000 tires, with the brand names Westlake, Compass and YKS.

Self-defense: US Customs requires country-of-origin labels on all tires made outside the US. Avoid tires from China.

CHILDREN'S TOYS

Problem: Lead.

Recalls: In the summer of 2007, Mattel announced worldwide recalls of 2.7 million toys with paint that had high levels of lead. Since 2003, the CPSC has announced recalls of more than 165 million pieces of children's jewelry containing high levels of lead, many of them sold in vending machines.

Self-defense: Only buy toys labeled "Made in USA" or those made by European companies with good reputations for safety, such as LEGO of Denmark and Haba of Germany. Avoid cheap children's jewelry found in vending machines and discount stores and all children's metal jewelry. Favor brand-name retailers.

Example: Toys "R" Us has now increased third-party testing for lead in toys it sells and increased its quality-assurance budget by 25%.

RECALL UPDATES

Sign up for the CPSC alerts at *www.cpsc.gov/cpsclist.aspx* so that when a product is recalled, you will get an e-mail.

Lead in Lipstick

In a study of lipsticks, of 33 tested, 20 had measurable lead levels. Lead is a neurotoxin that builds up in the body over time. It can cause memory and concentration problems, miscarriage in pregnant women and lowered IQ and behavioral problems in children.

Stacy Malkan, cofounder, Campaign for Safe Cosmetics, *www.safecosmetics.org*, a national coalition of health and environmental groups working to eliminate all toxic chemicals in personal-care products, San Francisco, and author of *Not Just a Pretty Face* (New Society).

Auction Site Warning

Health and beauty products sold at auction sites may have been stolen and, if stored improperly, could have spoiled or become less effective. Criminals steal items, including toothpaste, painkillers and razors, from retail chains and resell them on-line.

Caution: There is no way to know whether the items have been stored safely or were damaged or contaminated.

Bottom line: Buy health and beauty items on-line only at retail Web sites, not at auction sites.

USA Today, McClean, Virginia, *www.usatoday.com*.

 # Don't Pay to Learn About Free Federal Grants

TV infomercials promise information about federal grants that offer free money to individuals—if you pay for it. But the federal grant programs are listed for free on the Catalog of Federal Domestic Assistance (CFDA) Web site at *www.cfda.gov*. Most federal grant programs provide funds through state or local governments, or nonprofit organizations through which you must apply. The CFDA site lists all such grants, lets you search for those you might qualify for and tells where and how to apply.

Mary Hunt, editor, *Debt-Proof Living*, Box 2135, Paramount, California 90723, *www.debtproofliving.com*.

12

Retirement Update

How to Cut the Risk of Ever Running Out of Money...the 4% Solution

For the last 80 years, the average annual total return of large-capitalization US stocks has been more than 10% per year, while long-term corporate bonds have returned nearly 6% a year.

Assuming that the next 20 to 40 years will generate similar returns, a portfolio that is balanced equally between stocks and bonds may deliver 8% annualized returns throughout your retirement.

Given all these assumptions, you could draw down 8% of your portfolio a year to use for retirement spending. That would be $40,000 on a $500,000 portfolio. With such a plan, you could live off your investment earnings. You would still have $500,000 of principal for emergencies that come up or long-term-care needs or to leave as an inheritance.

Trap: Such a strategy has serious flaws. In reality, you probably would not enjoy the type of retirement that you assumed you would.

Better: Withdraw 4%—half the amount—to begin your retirement. Then set your withdrawals for automatic (regardless of market performance) by increasing the dollar amount of your withdrawal each year by the inflation rate to maintain your spending power.

WILD RIDE

This seemingly logical "8% solution" creates such problems because the 10% stock returns and 6% bond returns mentioned above are long-term averages.

Stocks and bonds do not produce such regular returns, year after year. The returns of bonds and especially stocks will fluctuate, sometimes dramatically.

Michael Kitces, CFP, CLU, ChFC, MSFS, MTAX, director of financial planning, Pinnacle Advisory Group, Inc., Columbia, Maryland, *www.pinnacleadvisory.com.* President of the Financial Planning Association of Maryland, he is also coauthor of *The Annuity Advisor* (National Underwriter).

As recently as 2000, 2001 and 2002, the S&P 500 stock index, which is a common benchmark for the US stock market, lost 9%, 12% and 22%, respectively. Such drops could create a disaster for a withdraw-8%-each-year strategy.

Situation: You have a $500,000 portfolio and in year one withdraw 8% ($40,000). The same year, stocks slide sharply, so your total portfolio loses 10% ($50,000). Now, you have $410,000 left.

Withdrawing 8% in year two gives you only $32,800 to spend that year. That could mean a severe cutback in your lifestyle from one year to the next.

Result: This simple 8% withdrawal strategy means that your retirement income will vary—perhaps enormously—from year to year, and you will probably deplete all of your investments before long.

Numbers crunch: A 10% loss in year one means you would need a 31.7% return in year two, if you want to spend $40,000 again and see your portfolio get back to the original $500,000.

WHY 4% IS THE MAGIC NUMBER

If a steady 8% won't work, why should you choose 4%—rather than something in between —as the ideal way to tap a retirement portfolio? Studies have shown that a 4% initial withdrawal, increased annually to keep pace with inflation, has a high probability of keeping you from running your portfolio down to zero over a 30-year retirement.

These studies generally assume that around half of your portfolio remains in the stock market and that investment returns and inflation will stay within the ranges they've displayed over the past 80 years.

Situation: From a $500,000 portfolio, you withdraw $20,000 (4% of $500,000) in 2008.

Suppose that the inflation rate in 2008 is 3%. You would boost your withdrawals by 3%, from $20,000 to $20,600, in 2009.

Suppose that inflation kicks up to 4% in 2009. For 2010, you would increase your withdrawal by 4%, from $20,600 to around $21,400.

And so on. Over time, your portfolio withdrawals will reach $25,000, $30,000 and more.

Payoff: You won't run out of money within 30 years. In most scenarios founded on historic

results from stocks and bonds, you'll still have a substantial sum in your portfolio. You'll also most likely be able to increase spending above the inflation rate in future years.

DEVILISH DETAILS

In addition to how much to tap your portfolio, you need a plan for which assets to withdraw.

Strategy: Tap only your taxable accounts before age 70½. Once you go past that point, you will probably be required to withdraw specified minimum amounts from your IRA or other retirement accounts. Waiting to tap them provides extended tax deferral, which is the prime reason to save money in an IRA, 401(k), etc., in the first place.

Tactic: Elect to have your interest and dividends paid to you, rather than reinvested. Those payments can make up a portion of your portfolio withdrawals, decreasing the amount of selling you have to do to raise spending money.

Situation: As above, you expect to draw $20,000 (4%) from your $500,000 portfolio during 2008, and that $500,000 is evenly divided between your IRA and your taxable accounts.

With this example, your $250,000 in taxable accounts includes both stocks and bonds. Dividends and interest payments from those securities are, say, $7,500. If you take out $20,000 from taxable accounts in 2008, and $7,500 of that is paid in dividends or in interest, another $12,500 must come from selling securities.

One approach is to sell whichever securities have appreciated the most. This "sell-high" strategy lets you "lock in" profits and gives your lagging investments time to catch up.

Another technique is to sell off assets that will deliver the greatest tax savings. You might sell securities that have lost value—so there is no capital gains tax due on them—and sell profitable securities with the smallest possible taxable gains.

Bottom line: Selling high probably will yield better investment results, long term. Selling for tax savings is best if you want certain, near-term tax savings.

Going forward: Say you want to withdraw $20,600 in 2009 but only receive $7,100 in dividends or interest income. You would need to sell $13,500 of securities. And so on, each year.

Alternative: Take some or all of the money from your IRA, if this can be done in a low tax bracket.

MINIMUM WITHDRAWALS

The situation changes when you exceed age 70½. For most tax-deferred accounts, there are required minimum distribution (RMD) rules you must follow.

Therefore, you'll probably have to withdraw money out of your IRA. According to IRS tables, your first-year RMD generally is around 3.7% of your IRA balance. Each year, as your official life expectancy decreases, this percentage increases slightly. It will reach about 5% at age 78, about 6% at 83, etc.

Situation: As above, you started out with a $250,000 IRA. If you tapped all your taxable accounts first, your IRA might have increased to $350,000 by the time RMDs must begin. During the same time, the amount you plan to withdraw from your portfolio may have moved up from $20,000 to $25,000, due to inflation.

Result: If you must take 3.7% of a $350,000 IRA, that's $12,950. You can spend that amount, plus another $12,050 from your taxable accounts, bringing the total withdrawal to $25,000 for the year.

Again, the $12,050 you take from your taxable accounts can be your interest and dividend income, plus whatever is needed from sales of securities. If you sell off those investments that have appreciated the most, you could rebalance your portfolio and bring your allocation of assets into line, rejiggering your assets among stocks, bonds, a real estate fund and other asset classes to meet a target allocation for each class.

RETIRING IN THE REAL WORLD

As a practical matter, you won't pull exactly $20,600 from your portfolio in a given year, selling exactly $13,500 worth of securities to match $7,100 in interest and dividends. The "4% solution" is merely a guideline.

However, if you start out with a withdrawal of around 4% of your portfolio and increase the amount of money withdrawn by a few percent every year, you likely will avoid running short of spending money as you grow older, even in volatile markets.

When Can You Afford to Retire? Top Adviser Tells How to Ensure Your Financial Security

Jonathan D. Pond, president, Financial Planning Information, Inc. in Newton, Massachusetts. He has hosted 16 prime-time TV specials for PBS, winning several awards, including one Emmy. He is author of *You Can Do It! The Boomer's Guide to a Great Retirement* and *Grow Your Money! 101 Easy Tips to Plan, Save, and Invest* (both from Collins). His Web site is *www.jonathanpond.com*.

Even though many Americans are working past the age of 65 to bolster their savings and investments or just to remain active, others are retiring early—either by choice or circumstance. The number of retirees is expected to mount now that baby boomers have started turning 62. But many are not prepared for the many challenges or realistic about the financial considerations and assumptions that will determine how comfortable their retirement will be.

Critical factors you must consider to prepare for your retirement...

•**Life expectancy and portfolio performance.** Many retirees underestimate how long they will live and overestimate how much their investments will return annually. A Fidelity Research Institute study found that a 65-year-old man has as much chance of living to age 95 as dying before age 70.

What to do: To be financially safe, I tell my clients to expect to live to the age of 95—and to expect a 6% annualized return on investments, based on a mix of 60% stocks and 40% bonds and other interest-earning securities.

•**Inflation.** Based on the historical inflation trends, people who retire at age 60 are likely to experience an 80% rise in living expenses by age 80. Those who retire at 65 will probably experience a 60% increase.

What to do: To calculate your income needs, figure inflation could average 3% annually. Then withdraw an annual amount in the early years of retirement—say, 4% of savings—that is enough to meet your income needs but is below the assumed growth rate of investments. That way you won't drain your assets too quickly.

• **Taxes.** Don't expect your tax bite to decline sharply in retirement—it probably won't. Keep in mind that you will pay income tax on withdrawals from traditional 401(k) accounts and IRAs.

What to do: Expect your taxes to drop by no more than 10%—and realize that they even may increase.

• **Expenses.** My retired clients find that each year, they spend 75% as much as they did in their final working years. Will your investments generate enough income to fund that spending?

What to do: Assume that you will spend at least that much, and develop a financial strategy that provides enough income to support all that spending.

Important: Do not leave out big-ticket expenses that still will pop up, including replacing your vehicle, large-scale repairs to the home and dental work.

• **Health insurance.** Unless you get an early retirement package that extends your company's health insurance coverage until you become eligible for Medicare, you will need to factor in the premiums for an individually purchased policy if you retire before age 65.

What to do: Consider obtaining temporary insurance through the stopgap federal program COBRA…check with state programs…or search for private individual coverage with high deductibles to lower premiums.

• **Part-time work.** Finding satisfying work to supplement your income can be challenging, when you fall out of the loop of your lifelong profession. And if you do find work, this extra income may mean reduced benefits from Social Security and/or higher income taxes.

What to do: I tell my clients who are considering retirement to assume that they won't find part-time work to bolster their income and to map a financial plan that doesn't count on extra income.

• **Retirement savings.** The longer you put off drawing on investment accounts—assuming that they gain value—the more income you will eventually be able to draw each year. And because of compounding, the longer you wait, the more this effect accelerates.

Examples: Assuming an annual rate of return of 6%, if you work an extra two years before starting withdrawals, you can increase the amount of income you draw annually by 10%… if you wait an extra three years, by 25%…and if you wait an extra five years, by 40%. This assumes that you would use up all of your money by age 92.

What to do: Put off retirement until your accounts are big enough to support your spending needs.

• **Social Security.** The earlier you start taking Social Security payments before you qualify for the full monthly base amount—which could be as late as age 67, depending on when you were born—the lower your monthly checks will be. They could be as much as 30% lower. Any future cost-of-living increases to Social Security checks also will be lower, because they will be calculated from a lower initial benefit amount.

What to do: Unless you really need the money or are in poor health, it's often better to delay starting benefits until you reach full retirement age.

• **Early retirement incentive package.** Your pension usually is based on the average of what you earned in the last few years of your employment. Even if your employer's early retirement incentive plan adds bonus years of employment and bonus years of age to your pension formula, it usually won't make up the difference between your average salary for your last five years and the presumably higher average salary you would have earned for your last five years if you had continued working.

What to do: Be careful not to overestimate the value of an early retirement package. You may want to consult a financial adviser for help analyzing the package.

RETIREMENT CALCULATOR

My favorite Web-based retirement calculator is free at *www.analyzenow.com*.

What you will find: Free on-line information that helps you to determine when to begin taking Social Security payments, how much to allocate to different investment categories, how much you need to save for retirement and how withdrawals from your retirement accounts will affect your taxes. It was created and is run by

Henry K. Hebeler, a former chief economic forecaster for Boeing Company.

Beware of Early Retirement Pitches

Misleading early retirement pitches are being marketed by some brokers. These brokers claim to be able to manage baby boomers' funds so successfully that the boomers can stop working now and still be secure throughout retirement. Many of these claims cross over a line. The Financial Industry Regulatory Authority (a nongovernmental regulating body) recently ordered two firms to pay $30 million in fines and restitution for allegedly letting their brokers pitch early retirement by overstating likely investment returns.

Self-defense: It is generally better to use a fee-only adviser than one who profits from trading securities. Get a second opinion from an independent financial adviser or accountant to be sure that you have enough saved for retirement, based on your lifestyle and a reasonable rate of return on investments.

David Wray, president, Profit Sharing/401(k) Council of America, Chicago.

Guaranteed Retirement Income: Myths and Reality

Mark Cortazzo, CFP, senior partner, Macro Consulting Group, 1639 Rte. 10 E., Parsippany, New Jersey 07054. A member of the Financial Planning Association and the Estate Planning Council of Northern New Jersey, he has been named one of the best financial advisers in the US by *Worth, Registered Rep* and *Research* magazines.

Many people want an income stream in retirement that will last as long as they do—guaranteed. *That's possible, just as long as you can separate fact from fiction about guaranteed retirement income...*

SOCIAL SECURITY

Myth: Social Security will not be around for much longer.

Reality: Social Security is immune from being annulled.

But: The taxes on earned income could be increased to keep this system together...taxes on benefits may be increased...and cost-of-living adjustments could be curtailed. Any or all of these might occur, but you'll receive at least some lifetime income from Social Security.

Myth: Social Security will provide income sufficient to maintain a lifestyle similar to the one you now enjoy.

Reality: The average Social Security check is about $1,000 per month...the average retired couple receives around $1,700.

Even for someone who paid the maximum amount of Social Security taxes over the years, the current maximum benefit at normal retirement age (around age 66) is just over $2,100 a month, about $26,000 a year. That will be much less than such a person would be used to taking home.

Myth: Social Security benefits are so small as to be inconsequential.

Reality: Receiving $25,000 a year from Social Security is equivalent to getting a 5% yield from $500,000 worth of bonds. That's not bad at all.

By considering these benefits a bond equivalent, you can hold more stocks in your portfolio, which likely will help long-term investment returns.

Another positive: Benefits rise with inflation.

PENSIONS/ANNUITIES

Myth: Pensions hardly exist any more.

Reality: Lifelong pensions are still offered to government workers, many union members and to some employees of large organizations, provided that they worked the required number of years.

Many other workers have accumulated substantial amounts in employer-sponsored retirement plans.

Often, retiring employees are given the choice of receiving their retirement funds in the form of an annuity. Such an annuity can provide income for a retiree or for a retiree and spouse as long as either is alive.

Myth: Taking the annuity offered by an employer is a good way to lock in a guaranteed retirement income.

Reality: There could be times when this is a good choice. At some companies, there is a "sweet spot" in which particular annuities are very attractive.

>**Example:** The company might subsidize annuities that pay a 50% benefit to an employee's surviving spouse, making it more attractive than similar annuities sold directly to investors by insurers.

In other cases, though, the payout offered by an employer might be on the low side compared with what you could get commercially. And a company-provided annuity might be inflexible, lacking newer features, such as access to money and investments that provide growth potential.

Myth: If you don't take the annuity offered by your employer, you won't get guaranteed retirement income to supplement Social Security.

Reality: You can buy an annuity.

One option: Roll money that is in your employer-sponsored retirement plan into an IRA, which will maintain the tax deferral of the assets. Then purchase an annuity with some or all of that money. Alternatively, you can use non-IRA funds to buy an annuity.

Myth: No matter where you get your annuity, the rates will be about the same.

Reality: The annuity payment rates can vary greatly.

Myth: When you buy an annuity, you lose access to your money, you lock yourself in to a given payment amount and the issuer will reap a windfall if you die soon.

Reality: Immediate annuities, also known as "payout" or "income" annuities, have added features in recent years...

>•Some do allow access to the principal. This flexibility, however, comes at the price of lower payouts.

>•Some are variable rather than fixed, so your payments could rise or fall, depending on investment account performance.

>•Some offer payments for at least a certain number of years to a beneficiary, if necessary.

Myth: An immediate fixed annuity is always the best way to lock in a guaranteed retirement income.

Reality: Some immediate variable annuities have minimum ("floor") payout rates that are as high or higher than immediate fixed annuity rates, in today's low-yield environment. You can get guaranteed minimum income from the floor plus potentially higher returns, if your investments do well.

Myth: You must purchase an immediate annuity to get guaranteed retirement income that does not come from a pension or from Social Security.

Reality: Deferred annuities also may provide guaranteed lifelong income. In a deferred annuity, investment income is untaxed until the investor takes out money. There is usually a 10% penalty, in addition to the income tax, for withdrawals before age 59½. These annuities come in two varieties—fixed and variable. Fixed annuities pay a specific return for a specific time period. Variable annuities have varied returns, depending on the performance of your chosen investment accounts.

Deferred variable annuities, in particular, usually offer some form of guaranteed income.

Myth: You have to "annuitize" any deferred variable annuity—meaning convert the account value into a payment stream—to get guaranteed income.

Reality: From one deferred variable annuity to another, guarantees contain different terms. *They generally fall into one of two categories...*

>•Guaranteed income benefits. You are promised an income based on whichever is higher—a minimum guaranteed return or the actual performance of your investment accounts.

>•Guaranteed withdrawal benefits. You are permitted to withdraw a certain percentage of your investment for a fixed number of years or for your lifetime.

Either way, you can invest in stock funds, for upside potential, while being protected against loss.

Myth: Variable annuities are always an overpriced rip-off.

Reality: Variable annuities available now differ tremendously.

Some are very expensive with limited benefits and virtually no access to your money for years without significant penalties.

Others are issued by reputable firms. The fees are comparable to what you would pay for other financial products and the guarantees may provide peace of mind.

These products aren't for everyone. However, if you want guaranteed retirement income, they are worth considering.

Strategy: Ask your financial adviser if you need to invest in a type of account that generates guaranteed retirement income. Before you buy, request a full explanation of the costs. Also determine whether your adviser offers a widespread array of products from which to choose. Ask to see a spreadsheet showing how several of these offerings compare. That way, you will have a greater chance of getting generous retirement income and a short surrender period (the time during which you'll pay a penalty for taking money from an annuity), for more access to your money.

Saving for Retirement

Saving just 10% of your salary is not enough to guarantee financial stability in retirement. The often suggested 10% figure works only if you start saving no later than age 35 and save 10% every year. If you start later, the amount required grows significantly.

Example: A 50-year-old with no retirement savings and making $80,000 a year must save 30% a year until retirement to maintain the same standard of living. If he/she is making $120,000 a year, the savings amount must be 35%.

Discuss your specific situation with a financial adviser.

Roger G. Ibbotson, PhD, professor in practice at Yale University School of Management, New Haven, Connecticut, and founder of Ibbotson Associates, Chicago, *www.ibbotson.com.* He was leader of a study on national savings rate guidelines, reported in *The Journal of Financial Planning.*

Don't Use Your Home for Retirement Income

The traditional ways of tapping your home's value—such as home-equity loans and lines of credit—are poor ideas for retirees, because these loans must be repaid. That can be difficult for people on a fixed income.

Troubling: 70% of 60-year-olds do consider their home part of their retirement plan. Of that group, 24% say their homes' equity represents half or more of their total savings.

Diahann Lassus, CFA, CFP, president of Lassus Wherley & Associates, a wealth management firm, New Providence, New Jersey.

Thinking of Retiring Abroad?

Some costs of retiring outside the US may not be apparent before people move.

Example: US federal income taxes still are due to the IRS if you move outside the country —Social Security benefits and distributions from pensions, 401(k) accounts and traditional IRAs still are taxable.

US citizens are taxed on their worldwide income, including income earned abroad. Treaty provisions and the foreign earned-income exclusion may decrease or eliminate the tax. Consult your tax adviser. Of course, local cost of living and the value of the dollar are factors.

Also: Health care may be a significant issue— Medicare does not cover treatment outside the US. Some countries have good medical facilities, but before moving, be sure to find out how foreign residents are treated.

Helpful: Go to *www.irs.gov,* and download IRS Publication 54—*Tax Guide for US Citizens and Resident Aliens Abroad.*

Ingrid P. John, CPA, director of Capital Management Group, LLC, Washington, DC 20036.

How to Beat One of The Toughest Penalties In the Tax Code... And Preserve Your Retirement Funds

Mary Kay Foss, CPA, partner at Marzluft Tulis & Foss CPAs, 185 Front St., Danville, California 94526. Foss has chaired the California Society of CPAs Committee on Taxation as well as its Estate Planning Committee.

From 401(k) plans to IRAs to a host of other plans, deferring tax in a retirement account often makes sense. The tax benefits will not go on forever, though. At some point, you'll have to withdraw funds and pay tax.

Your own accounts: Required minimum distributions (RMDs) generally need to begin by April 1 of the year after the year you reach age 70½.

Inherited accounts: Beneficiaries also must take RMDs and pay tax. Often, the schedule is based on the beneficiary's life expectancy and requires minimum distributions beginning in the year after the account owner's death.

If you do not withdraw at least the amount of your RMD, you'll be slapped with one of the highest penalties in the Tax Code—50% of the shortfall. *Ways to avoid it...*

FLEX PLAN

RMDs must be made from traditional IRAs (not Roth IRAs) and from employer-sponsored retirement plans. For employer plans, RMDs can be deferred as long as you keep working, if you own less than 5% of the company—as long as the plan allows it.

Trap: RMDs apply to all of your retirement accounts, which may be scattered.

Situation: You have a $400,000 IRA with a mutual fund company plus three other IRAs, that come to $50,000, with three different banks. Your RMD for the year is based on $450,000. If you take an RMD based only on $400,000, you'll owe a 50% penalty on the RMD based on the difference.

Flex plan: Say your RMD for the year is $18,000. That $18,000 may come from just one

of your IRAs or from more than one account—as long as you withdraw the right amount, the government doesn't care which of your accounts (subject to the RMD) you tap.

Note: This only applies to IRAs. RMDs from qualified plans must be figured separately for each plan.

SHIFTING INTO AUTOMATIC

One way you can avoid RMD penalties is to make advance arrangements with all of the financial firms holding your retirement accounts to automatically distribute RMDs.

What to arrange: Every month or every quarter, money can be transferred from each of your IRAs directly into your bank account or a money market fund.

Over the limit: These transfers can be designed to meet the RMD rules, which determine minimum withdrawals. You can take out larger amounts if you need the cash and are willing to pay the required tax.

MEETING THE DEADLINES

Regardless of whether you have arranged for automatic RMDs, be vigilant about taking necessary withdrawals.

Due date: Except for the initial April 1 deadline, all RMDs must be made by December 31 each year.

Go to IRA expert Ed Slott's Web site at *www.irahelp.com* to see the IRS tables you can use to calculate RMDs, or visit the IRS site at *www.irs.gov*.

SPOTTING A SHORTFALL

A part of your year-end tax planning can be checking to see that you comply with the RMD rules by December 31.

After the fact: You can double-check on your RMDs during the beginning of each year, when you prepare your income tax return for the preceding year.

What to look for: Forms 1099-R, which you receive at the start of the year, where distributions from IRAs and other retirement vehicles throughout the previous year are reported by the firms holding the assets. Compare those reported distributions with your RMD.

Strategy: If you see that you have not complied with the RMD rules, act immediately to make the required withdrawal.

Example: Carol Smith's RMD for 2008 is $50,000. In early 2009, she sees that only $10,000 has been reported on Forms 1099-R.

Carol could immediately withdraw $40,000 from her IRA, which she will report as income for 2009. She should also make sure to take the required RMD for 2009 by December 31 of that year.

But now Carol faces the 50% penalty on inadequate RMDs. However, the process that's described below can help avoid the fine, even if the deadline is missed.

AVOIDING FINES

Merely taking a required minimum distribution in 2009 that should have been taken in 2008 will not spare you automatically from the 50% penalty. Another action is required.

After taking such a "make-up" RMD, attach IRS Form 5329, *Additional Taxes on Qualified Plans (Including IRAs) and Other Tax-Favored Accounts,* to your income tax return. With this form, request a waiver of the 50% penalty. You do not have to pay the penalty up front (enter "RC" and the amount you want waived on the form).

Include your own explanation of why you neglected to take the RMD and attach it to Form 5329. You might say that family health problems diverted your attention from your financial obligations. If Form 1040 is not required, Form 5329 can be filed separately.

Likely outcome: The IRS has been willing to waive this penalty for most taxpayers. Be sure to withdraw any shortfall from your IRA before filing Form 5329. The IRS cannot waive the penalty unless you have already done so. Then write a reasonable explanation on Form 5329.

Note: Things are more difficult if you lag by multiple years—and much more difficult if the IRS discovers a shortfall before you ask for a waiver.

What you can expect: The IRS probably will not tell you that your request has been accepted, even if it has been. If it is refused, the IRS will simply send you a bill for the penalty. However, before you pay this, write to confirm that your

waiver request was actually received. If it wasn't, send them a copy of what you filed.

Assuming that you don't get billed after filing for a waiver, once three years from the due date of the tax return on which you were supposed to report the withdrawal have passed, you will be beyond the statute of limitations. Therefore, you won't owe the 50% penalty. (If Form 5329 is not filed, the statute of limitations doesn't run.)

Strategy: Withdraw your required amounts and file Form 5329, as a stand-alone form, for each year there has been a shortfall. Again, the IRS might not impose the penalty if you have a reasonable explanation.

It is important to act very quickly. File your appeal before the shortfall has been discovered, say, during an audit, and a penalty has been assessed. Once the IRS has served notice that you owe a 50% penalty, getting relief becomes much more difficult.

Penalty-Free Ways To Take Early IRA Distributions

William J. Stecker, CPA, president, The Marble Group, Ltd., 28 E. Jackson Bldg., Chicago 60604, which specializes in retirement distribution planning. He is author of the e-book, *A Practical Guide to Substantially Equal Periodic Payments and Internal Revenue Code §72(t)* (The Marble Group, *www.72t.net*).

At age 62, you can begin to collect Social Security checks. However, many early retirees, among other people, need money sooner—perhaps much sooner. They therefore need to tap their IRAs for living expenses because after they stop working, they have less income than they did during the years they were earning paychecks.

Upside: Because of their lower income, early retirees may be in a lower tax bracket than before. This will reduce the income tax they'll owe on IRA withdrawals.

Trap: Before age 59½, IRA withdrawals generally are subject to a 10% surtax.

Situation: James Green, age 50, retires and finds that he is in the 25% federal income tax bracket this year. He takes a $25,000 distribution from his IRA for living expenses.

On that withdrawal, he owes $6,250 in federal income tax (25% of $25,000). But he also owes a $2,500 surtax (10% of $25,000).

The extra tax effectively pushes this moderate-income retiree into the top 35% federal income tax bracket.

ESCAPE FROM PENALTY

Section 72(t) of the Tax Code includes several exceptions to the 10% surtax.

Examples: After an IRA owner's death, a younger beneficiary may take distributions from the decedent's account without owing the surtax. Similarly, if you are disabled and cannot be expected to earn income for many years, the surtax won't apply.

As you can see, these exceptions might not help many early retirees.

What you can use: Most early retirees wishing to tap an IRA focus on one of the other exceptions listed in Section 72(t)—the option to take "substantially equal periodic payments" (SEPPs) from their IRAs. Such payments can provide a stream of IRA withdrawals, penalty free. What's more, you have a great deal of flexibility in structuring these payments to meet your needs.

SEPPs BY THE NUMBERS

SEPPs must be calculated in accordance with your life expectancy, from an IRS table. To find the Single Life Expectancy Table for Inherited IRAs, go to *www.irahelp.com,* then click on "Consumers" and "Single Life Table for Beneficiaries."

Situation: James Green is 50, as mentioned. His life expectancy is 34.2 years. Thus, he can use the 34.2-year schedule for tapping his IRA, penalty free.

Loophole: James does not have to maintain SEPPs for 34.2 years in order to avoid the 10% surtax.

Required: Taxpayers must maintain SEPPs for at least five years. If SEPPs are started before age 54½, they must be continued for more than five years—at least until age 59½.

Trap: If you fail to complete the required SEPP schedule, you'll owe the 10% surtax on all

the withdrawals you've taken, plus interest. This is true if you deviate from the schedule by any amount.

Important: You'll also owe the surtax if you make more contributions to this IRA while taking the scheduled SEPPs. (Reinvestment of earnings within the IRA is allowed.) You are allowed to make contributions to another IRA.

MULTIPLE METHODS

The Tax Code specifies three methods of taking SEPPs…

• **Minimum distribution.** Official life expectancies usually go down by 0.9 every year, therefore, James can take $\frac{1}{34.2}$ of his IRA balance in year one, $\frac{1}{33.3}$ of the balance in year two, etc.

This method might make sense if you need to withdraw a relatively small amount from your IRA. If you are married, you can use a joint life expectancy with your spouse and thus withdraw even smaller amounts each year.

• **Amortization and annuitization methods.** With both of these methods, you assume that your IRA will grow during your lifetime at a rate that you specify. (IRS regulations cap the amount you can assume.) This assumed growth allows you to take out more from your IRA each year, penalty free, than you can take out if you use the minimum distribution method. (You use these methods for five years or until age 59½, whichever comes later.)

Amortization: Most people who use SEPPs choose this method. Payments under the amortization method are fixed, based on the amount determined when the SEPP is first calculated. A calculation under this method requires that the account balance be amortized (paid in installments) over the individual's single, joint or uniform life expectancy. (Uniform life expectancy is used whenever you name a beneficiary who is 10 or more years younger than you are.) The amount is calculated utilizing the earnings rate chosen by the individual. This typically permits slightly higher penalty-free withdrawals than the annuitization method (see next page) and much higher withdrawals than the minimum distribution method.

Example: Using the current interest rates, 50-year-old James would be able to withdraw $14,620 this year, penalty free, from a $500,000

IRA, by using the minimum distribution method. But, with the amortization method, James could withdraw approximately $30,800 (depending on interest rates used) each year, penalty free, until age 59½.

Annuitization: Your annual payment for each year is determined by dividing the account balance by a factor based on the age of the individual, and continuing for the life of the taxpayer (or the joint lives of the individual and beneficiary). The annuity factor is derived using the mortality table labeled "Appendix B" in *Revenue Ruling* 2002-62, along with the interest rate chosen by the taxpayer.

The annuitization method would allow James to withdraw $30,400 per year over five or more years penalty free.

These calculations are complex, so it is best to work with a tax CPA, enrolled actuary, or tax attorney to come up with the permitted amount. Keep good records to demonstrate compliance in case your tax return is examined.

SPLIT DECISIONS

If James wants to withdraw $30,800 from his IRA each year, he can simply apply the amortization method to his $500,000 IRA. Real life is seldom this simple, though.

Situation: James had $520,000 in his IRA as of December 31, 2007. In 2008 and succeeding years, he would like to withdraw only $25,000 per year from his IRA.

James determines that using the amortization method and current interest rates, he can withdraw $25,000 a year from a $406,000 IRA.

How this is possible: James divides up his $520,000 IRA into one $406,000 IRA and one $114,000 IRA. Then, he takes SEPPs of $25,000 a year from the $406,000 IRA.

The $114,000 IRA is not affected by his scheduled withdrawals. If James decides to make an IRA contribution during the SEPP period, that contribution can go into the $114,000 IRA.

FUTURE FLEXIBILITY

Many things can happen during the period when you are taking SEPPs...

• **You need more money.** You may discover that your $25,000 annual SEPP withdrawals are inadequate. However, if you take larger withdrawals from the IRA connected to your SEPPs,

you will owe a 10% surtax, plus interest, on all previous IRA withdrawals.

Instead, you can tap another IRA for the extra cash. If you're under age 59½, you'll owe a 10% penalty on these withdrawals—but to avoid that, you can begin a new series of SEPPs from this other IRA.

• **You need less money.** You may go back to work or come into an inheritance. Then you won't need the $25,000 IRA withdrawals.

However, if you stop taking the SEPPs prematurely, you'll owe penalties and interest.

Strategy: In *Revenue Ruling* 2002-62, the IRS announced that taxpayers in the midst of SEPPs can make a onetime switch from the amortization method or the annuitization method to the minimum-distribution method.

This would allow you to take out much smaller amounts each year, thus leaving more money in your IRA for ongoing tax deferral. No penalties would be due.

Working After Retirement Has a Big Impact on Benefits and Taxes

Joan Moffitt, CPA, a senior tax manager with the accounting firm Weiser LLP, 399 Thornall St., Edison, New Jersey 08837. She specializes in tax planning and compliance for professional corporations, high-net-worth individuals and estates and trusts.

Today, retirement from a job for many people is only a transition into a new phase of work. More and more seniors are starting up businesses or beginning new careers, and some of those never plan to fully retire. Often, they do this for the money as well as to stay active and challenged.

What impact does continuing to work have on retirement benefits, such as Social Security, Medicare and the funds in qualified retirement plans and IRAs? To maximize after-retirement income and wealth, it is important to know all of the rules.

SOCIAL SECURITY BENEFITS

Working into one's "retirement" years affects Social Security retirement benefits. The impact depends on when you start taking your benefits. *Three choices...*

• **Start taking benefits as early as age 62.** This is the minimum age to start taking benefits. But there are two drawbacks to this option. First, benefits will be permanently reduced because you're taking them prior to attaining your full federal retirement age (e.g., 66 for those born in 1943). Second, those who earn over a threshold amount ($13,560 in 2008) will see benefits reduced by one dollar for each two dollars they earn over this amount until they reach full retirement age.

• **Start at full retirement age.** This age depends on your year of birth. For those born in 1943 through 1954, the full retirement age is 66. Once this age is achieved, there is no reduction in benefits if you continue to earn income, regardless of the amount earned.

A break: The Social Security Administration will continue to adjust your benefits annually to take into account any higher-earning years. So, working after you retire from one job, regardless of your age (up to age 70), could increase your monthly retirement benefits—even after you've started taking benefits.

Reason: Benefits are based on a look-back period of your best 35 years of work history.

• **Put off benefits until age 70.** For every year that you wait to start collecting benefits, the amount you collect increases—up until age 70. Those born in 1943 and later will earn an 8% increase in benefits for each year they wait to collect after their full retirement age and until age 70—there is no reward for waiting any longer.

You can use the on-line calculator from the Social Security Administration to see the impact of age on your benefits (*www.ssa.gov/planners/calculators.htm*).

Tax impact: Working while collecting Social Security benefits has two important tax results that need to be factored into your decision of when to commence benefits...

• Taxes on Social Security benefits. Any benefits received will be included in income at the rate of 50%, 85% or 0%, depending on your other income. Those who work likely will trigger the 85% inclusion amount (85% of their benefits will be subject to tax).

• Continued payment of Social Security tax. Whether or not you are collecting benefits and regardless of your age, as long as you continue to receive income, through a job or self-employment, you continue to pay Social Security (and Medicare) taxes on that income.

MEDICARE

Regardless of whether you are collecting Social Security benefits or are applying for them, be sure to apply for Medicare coverage at age 65. Contact the Social Security Administration several months before this birthday to enroll. If you still possess "creditable" health coverage through an employer or union, apply only for Medicare Part A—it does not cost you anything and will provide secondary coverage, paying some things that your commercially provided coverage does not. ("Creditable" means at least as good coverage as Medicare provides. Ask your employer for a letter confirming that your coverage meets the standard.)

Once you no longer have employer coverage, you should enroll in Medicare Parts B (primarily for doctors' fees) and D (for prescription drugs). The fact that you delayed this coverage past age 65 won't result in a penalty as long as you sign up no later than eight months after your employer coverage terminates for Part B. For Part D, you need to sign up no later than 63 calendar days after employer coverage ceases, and you must show Medicare a letter from the employer stating that you had creditable coverage through a certain date.

For details, including penalty information, go to *www.medicare.gov.*

RETIREMENT PLANS

For those who continue to work after retiring from a job, the maze of rules for putting money in and taking money out of qualified retirement plans and IRAs is complex. *Some considerations to be aware of...*

• **Qualified retirement plans.** A workplace plan must include these older workers and cannot exclude them because of age. For example, if you work past retirement age for any company that contributes to a plan, you are eligible to receive contributions (assuming you meet other eligibility requirements). But, you usually must at the same time commence receipt of benefits from qualified retirement plans—such as 401(k), profit-sharing, and defined-benefit plans—at age 70½ in order to avoid a 50% penalty on insufficient withdrawals.

Caution: While distributions from a qualified retirement plan can be postponed past this age if you continue working for the company that maintains the plan, and the plan allows it, this break doesn't apply after you leave the company and work elsewhere.

•**IRAs.** As long as you continue to work, deductible IRA contributions are permitted—until age 70½, assuming adjusted gross income (AGI) is below set limits for those who are active participants in company retirement plans. *To contribute past this age…*

•Contribute on the behalf of a younger non-working spouse. As long as the spouse is under age 70½, you can fund his/her IRA based on your earnings.

•Contribute to a Roth IRA. There is no age limit on making contributions. Also, there are no mandatory lifetime distributions. However, there are still AGI limits on eligibility to put money into a Roth IRA, so too much income can prevent these contributions.

RELOCATING

If you relocate after you leave your job, factor in the state tax rules for the treatment of various types of retirement income, even if you continue to work. Consider the impact on all your new earnings as well as on your previously accumulated retirement benefits. Some states do provide generous exemptions for Social Security and/or distributions of qualified retirement benefits and IRAs. View the treatment of retirement income in the different states at the Retirement Living site (*www.retirementliving.com/RLtaxes.html*).

Note: Your old state cannot tax the benefits you collect from qualified plans and IRAs in your new state, even though you earned those benefits in the old state.

Moving costs: You can deduct the cost of moving as long as you continue to work for a set time in your new location. For instance, if you relocate from Connecticut to Arizona when you retire, you can deduct the cost of moving your household items if you work full time for at least 39 weeks within a 12-month period in your new location (78 weeks within a 24-month period if you start your own business in the new location).

More information: Review IRS Publication 521, *Moving Expenses.*

Don't Miss the Saver's Tax Credit

The saver's tax credit can offset part of the cost of the initial $2,000 that an individual contributes to an IRA, 401(k) or other retirement plan—but it is one of the most commonly overlooked of credits.

For 2008, the credit is available to people filing joint returns with adjusted gross income of up to $53,000, or up to $26,500 for single filers. The maximum credit is $1,000 ($2,000 if filing jointly), with the exact amount determined by a formula on Form 8880, *Credit for Qualified Retirement Savings Contributions*, which you file to claim the credit.

Note: Those eligible who have missed out on the credit can file amended tax returns to claim it up to three years back and get a tax refund.

Barbara Weltman, Esq., an attorney based in Millwood, New York, and publisher of the free on-line newsletter, *Big Ideas for Small Business, www.barbaraweltman.com.*

Help Your Kids Set Up an IRA

If children have money from summer or vacation jobs, help them set up their own Roth IRAs. One $5,000 contribution for a 15-year-old, earning an 8% annual return, will increase to $235,000 by the time he/she is 65. Roth IRA contributions can be withdrawn anytime, tax free, to pay for college, a home or other needs. Parents could encourage saving by matching funds that children contribute as long as the amount of the contribution is no more than the earned income. Among the companies that permit minors to open IRAs are T. Rowe Price, Vanguard, Charles Schwab and E*Trade.

Ed Slott, CPA, editor, *Ed Slott's IRA Advisor,* 100 Merrick Rd., Rockville Centre, New York 11570, *www.irahelp. com.* He is a nationally recognized IRA distributions expert and author of *Your Complete Retirement Planning Road Map* (Ballantine).

IRA Alert

Do not have a family member manage your IRA and get paid a fee for doing so. If you do, the entire IRA could become taxable. The Tax Code says that you cannot have your IRA "directly or indirectly pay any compensation" to a family member or to yourself. That includes siblings, spouses and children who are financial professionals. The law may change, and the IRS is unlikely to seek out violators, but meanwhile, you may not want to take a chance on jeopardizing the IRA's tax-sheltered status.

Seymour Goldberg, Esq., CPA, Goldberg & Goldberg, PC, 100 Jericho Quadrangle, Jericho, New York 11753, *www.goldbergira.com.*

Increase Benefits and Get a Deduction

Bob Carlson, editor, *Bob Carlson's Retirement Watch,* Box 970, Oxon Hill, Maryland 20750.

If you chose to begin receiving your Social Security benefits early, at age 62, you may regret it when your normal retirement age arrives and your monthly benefit is lower by 20% or more from what it would have been had you waited to receive it.

But, even in this case, it is not too late to obtain the larger benefit. By filing a "withdrawal of claim" with the Social Security Administration (SSA), you can give up the smaller benefit you

claimed at the earlier age. You can then take the larger benefit you are entitled to at the later age. Of course, you will have to repay to the SSA the earlier benefits you received. In the year that you do so, the SSA will issue you a Form 1099 reporting your benefit for the year as a negative number—equal to the amount it paid you for the year minus the amount of benefits you repaid to it for the prior years.

Tax saver: This negative number is deductible on your tax return—giving you a deduction for your repayment.

Alternative: You can look at your previous years' tax returns, figure out how much tax you actually paid on the Social Security benefits you repaid, and claim a tax credit for that amount. You can claim either the deduction or the credit, whichever has the greater cash value.

For details about the deduction and credit, see IRS Publication 915, *Social Security and Equivalent Railroad Retirement Benefits.* For more information about filing a "withdrawal of claim" with the SSA to increase your benefits, consult an expert Social Security adviser.

10 Fun Ways to Make an Extra Buck

Abigail R. Gehring, author of *Odd Jobs–101 Ways to Make an Extra Buck* (Skyhorse). She lives in Edgewater, New Jersey, and has held 24 of the jobs included in the book.

In today's world, making extra money is often a necessity. But even when it isn't, taking on an odd job can be challenging and fun. Working—even occasionally—can bring excitement in doing something totally different and in meeting new people. *Ideas to consider...*

1. A male dance host on cruise ships. Dance with partygoers who don't have partners. You must be a competent ballroom dancer, dress appropriately and have charm and confidence.

Downside: You won't always want to dance with everyone who wants to dance with you. Also, you're on call for all social activities on the entire trip.

What you'll earn: $25 to $100 an hour plus the cost of the cruise.*

More information: Dancing List (800-815-9158, *www.dancinglist.com/hosts/host1.htm*).

2. Mystery shopper. This work requires you to visit a bank, shop, car dealership or restaurant posing as a customer and to evaluate your experience—for example, you'll report back on the service, product quality and how items are displayed. Sometimes you may be given a small amount of money to make a purchase. Other times, such as at a car dealership, you only pretend to be interested in buying.

A caution: Beware of help-wanted ads for mystery shoppers. Most of these are scams requiring money up front.

Downside: Sporadic assignments.

What you'll earn: About $100 a month in cash, food and/or merchandise if you work two to four hours.

Note: You are hired by the mystery shopping company. They pay you and bill the company you visit.

More information: Idea Lady (*www.mystery shoppersmanual.com*).

3. Movie or TV extra. You do not need to belong to a performer's union to work as a movie or TV extra (since you have no spoken lines). Sign up with a local talent agency or watch for newspaper ads to learn about work opportunities. To do this work, you must have the particular look that the production company requires—such as a certain age, ethnicity, hair color, etc.

Downside: Twelve-hour days—including sitting around for hours doing nothing—are not unusual.

What you'll earn: About $100 to $200 a day if you are not a member of the Screen Actors Guild. Agencies take a 20% commission.

More information: Entertainment Careers (*www.entertainmentcareers.net*).

4. A resort receptionist. During busy holiday periods, the resorts are always short-staffed, and they are very happy to have extra help checking people in and out of their rooms, answering the phone and accommodating guest requests. Generally, you get to stay at the resort for free.

*Rates and fees subject to change.

To do this work, you'll need customer service skills and good command of English (fluency in other languages is a plus).

Downside: You're expected to present a positive image by always being particularly polite and helpful around hotel guests, even when not working.

What you'll earn: About $10 an hour (varies with location and type of resort).

More information: Resort Jobs (*www.resort jobs.com*).

5. Focus group participant. Meet with a group led by a moderator to give your opinion on an idea, evaluate a service or test a product. A session can be one to two hours. Requirements for participation vary according to the needs of the client paying for the session. You'll need to supply information about yourself—education and income levels, profession, marital status.

Downside: Sporadic work—since many companies only allow you to participate once every six months.

What you'll earn: About $40 to $100 per hour.

More information: Try FocusRoom (212-935-6820, *www.focusroom.com*) for New York City groups. Focus Pointe Global (*www.focusgroup. com*) for groups in other locations. Or, type "focus group" into a Web search engine, such as Google.

6. Home-based sales representative. You can sell a product (maybe cosmetics or vitamin supplements) for a company through "parties" or personal contacts. Some companies require you to buy a certain amount of product at a wholesale price (for example, the cosmetics company Mary Kay requires you to buy a minimum starting inventory). Others require you to pay to become a member of their sales force (for example, the natural health supplement organization Shaklee charges $19.95 for membership). And you'll need a knack for selling.

Downside: The pay depends entirely on the amount you sell.

More information: Avon (800-367-2866 or *www.avon.com*)…Shaklee (800-742-5533 or *www. shaklee.com*)…Mary Kay (800-627-9529 or *www. marykay.com*).

7. School crossing guard. Most guards work two to four hours a day. Qualifications do vary by state—you may need a driver's license, high school diploma and first-aid certification. Depending on the school district, you may be given some minimal training. Good eyesight and hearing are a must. This is an ideal job for early risers, and those who want the satisfaction of providing safety for school children.

Downside: This can be stressful work—for example, drivers may not stop even though you are standing in the middle of the road, but instead zoom around you. You may have to work in inclement weather.

What you'll earn: An average of $7 to $10 an hour.

More information: National Center for Safe Routes to Schools (866-610-7787, *www.saferoutes info.org/guide/crossing_guard/index.cfm*).

8. House sitter. Just stay in a home while the residents are away—all you need for this work is to be responsible and have common sense.

Downside: If something goes wrong (fire, flood, robbery or the dog dies), there is a good chance you will get blamed. Protect yourself by asking your lawyer to write up a liability contract (or fill out an "Employment Contract" form at *www.lawdepot.com*) with the home owner that spells out what happens if you need to leave for a personal emergency and you can't fulfill your obligation.

What you'll earn: Free rent is the biggest payment, plus you can house-sit anywhere in the world. If you have additional responsibilities, such as caring for a pet or doing yard work, you could make up to $300 a week.

More information: HouseSitters 4u (*www. housesitters4u.com*).

9. Gift wrapper. Have presents brought to your home—or pick them up from customers—and wrap them in style. Or ask a local store owner if you can wrap gifts during busy periods. The cost of getting started is modest—$40 to $100 for supplies (wrapping paper, tissue paper, tape, gift bags). You need creativity and efficiency. Put an ad in your local paper to get customers. Also, add a rider to your homeowner's insurance to cover loss or damage to items that you're wrapping.

Downside: Paper cuts.

What you will earn: $3 to $10 a package.

More information: Mommys Place (*www. mommysplace.net/gift_wrapping_business.html*).

10. Complete surveys. Sign up on the Web to complete surveys on anything from coffee preferences to toothbrush usage. All you need is a computer, Internet access and patience. Surveys generally take five to 25 minutes.

Downside: You can waste time starting a survey only to be told after several pages of questions that you're not eligible because you don't fit the desired profile of the survey group.

What you'll earn: About $3 to $5 per survey.

More information: Survey Savvy (*www.sur veysavvy.com*).

Seniors Lose Buying Power

Seniors have lost 40% of their buying power since the beginning of the decade.

New study: Cost-of-living adjustments have increased average Social Security benefits only 22% since 2000, while typical senior expenses, such as food, heating oil, drugs and transportation, have risen by 71%.

Problem: A majority of seniors on Social Security depend on it for at least 50% of their total income.

Shannon Benton, research director, The Senior Citizens League, nonpartisan seniors group, Alexandria, Virginia, *www.seniorsleague.org*.

Just for Seniors

There's a new Web site for seniors from the National Institutes of Health. The NIHSenior-Health (*www.nihseniorhealth.gov*) site contains medical information on 34 health topics of high interest to seniors, including arthritis, cataracts, exercise, blood pressure, sleep, medicines and more.

The Three Secrets To a Happier Life in Retirement

Richard N. Bolles and John E. Nelson, the coauthors of *What Color Is Your Parachute? For Retirement: Planning Now for the Life You Want* (Ten Speed). Located in the San Francisco Bay Area, Bolles has been a leader in the field of career development for more than 30 years. He is author of *What Color Is Your Parachute?* (Ten Speed), which has sold more than nine million copies. His Web site is at *www.jobhuntersbible.com*. Wisconsin-based Nelson is a renowned retirement-planning researcher, speaker and writer, *www.retirementwellbeing.com*.

Working people often think of retirement as a time for perpetual leisure. They expect to play golf, read books, travel and do all the other pleasurable things that they never found enough time for during their careers. But when these people actually retire, many are surprised by how bored and unfulfilled those leisurely retirements leave them.

The idea that leisure activities alone can produce an enjoyable retirement is out-of-date. In the early 20th century, most retirees had only a few years of declining health remaining after lifetimes of hard labor. For them, relaxation and leisure were just what the doctor ordered. But today's retirees often enjoy decades of healthy years remaining. Leisure alone isn't enough to get them through it. Even the word "retirement" is out-of-date, as it implies disengagement and evokes images of being put out to pasture.

Here are the three elements of a satisfying "retirement"…

PLEASURE

Leisure activities alone might not be enough for a fulfilling retirement, but they certainly have their place. If you always have dreamed of fishing seven days a week…having season tickets to the symphony or for the ballpark…or traveling extensively, then by all means do so. But do not be surprised if these leisure activities are not as enjoyable as they were when you were working. *If you start to get bored, consider the possibilities below…*

• **You enjoyed these things mainly because their relaxing nature served as a counterbalance** to the stresses of the workplace. Now that you are not working, they don't serve this purpose.

• **You find these places and activities fun only in smaller doses.** The quaint little town that was the perfect spot for weeklong vacations might not provide enough variety to keep you entertained as a full-time resident.

• **It may not be the leisure activity itself that you enjoyed but some aspect related to it that's now missing.** Maybe you enjoyed renting a boat on summer weekends, not because you loved boating but because your grandkids came along on your trips. Buy a boat, and your grandkids might not be able to join you as often as you had hoped.

What to do: Ask yourself what, in particular, makes your favorite leisure activities fun for you. Is it what you are doing? Where you are doing it? With whom you are doing it?

Avoid making a large financial commitment to any leisure activity until you have confirmed and reconfirmed that your interest won't wane when you devote lots of time to it in retirement. Rent big-ticket items, such as boats, RVs and vacation homes, for several extended periods (just a week or two is not long enough) before purchasing them.

A wide variety of companies market leisure products to retirees—but whether they are marketing backyard pools or recreational vehicles, their advertisements inevitably focus less on the products being offered than on how the products will allow buyers to share happy times with their friends and family members. What these marketers do not admit is that you might enjoy spending time with these people just as much without their products.

ENGAGEMENT

When retirees feel there's "something missing" in their lives, that something often is engagement. Being engaged means being actively involved in something, not just watching things happen. The difference between pleasure and engagement is the difference between attending a soccer game and joining a sports team…or between listening to a symphony and learning to play an instrument. It's investing ourselves in life and getting back more than we put in. Engagement supplies an element of challenge without which life becomes boring.

During our working lives, we're most likely to experience engagement in the workplace. Even if we didn't love a job, it probably provided interesting challenges and opportunities for growth.

Postcareer engagement can be found in gardening…woodworking…photography…a part-time job…or thousands of other hobbies and activities.

What to do: To find the most rewarding challenges for your retirement, think about the occasions when you have been most engaged in the past…

•**When did time seem to fly by?** When did you get so caught up in a certain activity that you didn't notice the passing hours? When time seems to have flown, you've been engaged.

•**What are your greatest qualities and strengths?** We tend to feel most engaged when we put our skills and strengths to use. The Web site *www.viastrengths.org* can help you identify strengths that you didn't even realize you had. (The site is free, but registration is required.)

•**Which aspects of your career gave you the greatest sense of accomplishment?** Perhaps you can replicate some of these activities in retirement.

Example: One retired supervisor felt most engaged when he was providing honest and accurate performance reviews that helped younger workers to discover their ideal career paths. To recapture that engagement in retirement, he volunteered as a guidance counselor at a local business school.

MEANING

As people age, they are increasingly likely to question whether their lives have had meaning. When the answer is no, the result often is despair. Retirement can be a major blow for such people. If they never achieved meaning in their careers, they may now fear that it is too late to ever do so.

Retirement also can be a blow to those who feel their lives did have meaning. They might have found meaning in their ability to support their family…or in a career that made the world a better place. But because their sense of meaning was tied closely to their careers or paychecks, retirement robs them of purpose.

What to do: Fortunately, retirees still have plenty of time to discover a sense of meaning, whether or not they believe they had one before. We often find meaning when we serve causes greater than ourselves. Help your neighbors or local community groups…enter politics…mentor a young person…take a more active role in your church…volunteer with a charity…or start a business to bring jobs or necessary services to your area.

The only firm rule is that the cause must be meaningful to you. It can take years to discover the cause that's right for you, so don't get discouraged. Ask yourself what causes you care about and how you can help. Experiment until you find your answer.

Resilience: The Key To a Stress-Free Retirement

Robert Brooks, PhD, a psychologist on the faculty of Harvard Medical School and in private practice in Needham, Massachusetts, *www.drrobertbrooks.com*. He is author or coauthor of many books, including *The Power of Resilience: Achieving Balance, Confidence and Personal Strength in Your Life* (McGraw-Hill).

By age 50 or 60, most of us have learned that life offers many hard knocks. The key to handling these jabs is resilience.

Resilience serves as a reservoir of emotional strength that can be drawn on for everyday challenges, such as interactions with others, as well as life-altering events, such as a loved one's death or a financial setback. I see resilience as the ability to respond to difficult situations with inner strength. *Steps toward developing that ability…*

LETTING GO

Substantial research indicates that those who concentrate on what they have control over are more hopeful, more optimistic and more likely to enjoy life and withstand its hardships than those who focus on forces and issues beyond their control. *Examples…*

•**Sports.** Friends of mine who love participating in sports obsess about their deteriorating skills. When aging or injury wrecks their performance, they quit.

Solution: Recognize that few of us are as athletically fit at age 60 as we were at 40. I'm still jogging in my 60s. So what if I'm slower than I used to be? I'm not entering the Olympics.

•**Relationships.** If a relationship isn't working well, avoid blaming others—you can't control them. Ask yourself, What can I do to fix this?

My private psychology practice includes marital counseling. Some couples complain that their lengthy marriages are turning stale because they don't feel the excitement or interest in each other that they used to. I always suggest that instead of waiting for their spouses to change, disgruntled partners should ask themselves, How can I explain why I'm unhappy about what's going on in our relationship in a manner that demonstrates my love and concern, but avoids finger-pointing? and Do I discuss our relationship only when I'm complaining about it, or do I make an effort to mention the good things, too?

Negativity, a relentless drain, improves nothing, whereas bringing a positive attitude to all daily communications can create an optimistic environment that feels open to change and embraces it.

Exception: For a person who is truly miserable in a marriage, ending it is often best.

Examples: Several months after one close family friend in her early 60s left her husband of many years, my wife noted, "I've never seen her so happy." My older brother, married for nearly 48 years, left his wife when he was almost 70. For him, it was the right decision.

One form of personal resilience is to cease enduring the unacceptable situations that you can change.

REMAIN CONNECTED

According to extensive studies, the more connected people feel to something that's outside of themselves—a group, a cause, a religious belief—the longer they live. Feeling part of something larger than oneself supports a resilient mind-set.

As we age, especially in retirement, establishing new forms of connectedness is essential. What counts is the quality, not the quantity, of your relationships. Do you make an effort to be part of a social group? If you love backgammon, horseshoes or checkers, do you find a partner and play? If you are religious, do you regularly attend services or a discussion group?

Those relocating for retirement need to put "Make new friends" near the tops of their to-do lists. This is hard if you aren't used to befriending strangers, but as you seek out people with similar interests, friendships will begin naturally. Friends provide social support, which helps build resilience.

HELP OTHERS

Older people who help others do tend to live longer, studies show. Contributing your time and talents states, "Because I'm on Earth, Earth is a better place."

I believe strongly that retirees should volunteer for a personally meaningful cause.

Example: Furthering a political or environmental cause that you're passionate about.

Bonus: Contributing to society adds purpose to life, and strengthens meaningful ties to others, another key to building resilience.

STAY FIT

Our mental and physical lives are intertwined. To stay resilient physiologically and psychologically, eat a healthy diet and exercise. Any level is fine. When my legs give out and I can't jog, I'll walk or swim.

An Australian doctor who works with retirees has written that many feel like victims. As a result, they become victims. They say, "I can't lose weight because being overweight runs in my family." Or, "I cannot exercise because my joints hurt." Although genes play a role in our ability to stay fit, you may have more control over your fitness level than you think.

Nothing curtails an exercise regimen more swiftly than unrealistic goals.

Example: Mr. Whitaker had trapped himself into believing that unless he could institute a major change quickly, he was a failure. I helped him to develop an appropriate exercise-and-diet program that has specific, achievable, short-term goals. He began with a one-mile walk—not the five miles he had envisioned—and met with a good nutritionist whose simple recommendations worked better than the starvation diets he had previously tried. You can begin with a half-mile walk—or even less, and build up. You can start by cutting just 100 calories from your daily diet. The important thing—start somewhere.

BE GRATEFUL—IN WRITING

It is easy to lose sight of the gratifying aspects of life. To retain perspective, every day or two write down things for which you feel grateful. Feel free to repeat yourself.

My own list includes: "Four lovely grand-children…my wonderful marriage…being able to follow my passion in my work."

The idea is not to deny or minimize the serious or sad things in life, but to remember the good parts. Once you have reminded yourself, reinforce what makes you happy. For me, that means visiting my grandchildren, being a good husband and working creatively to help others.

FOLLOW YOUR PASSIONS

Many new retirees find that for the first time they can follow their interests and passions.

Examples: My father-in-law took up golf after he retired from the police force…a friend who had always wanted to play the piano began lessons…my close friend Mickey started taking pictures of town events and quickly became a sought-after photographer.

Start something new or expend more effort on an activity you already perform. Loving what you do gives you a wealth of happiness, which, in turn, boosts your resilience.

Home Sharing Helps Seniors

Home sharing may allow seniors to stay in their homes. Some seniors offer their extra room rent-free to a younger person in exchange for cooking and light housecleaning. Others do charge rent and expect no services but feel more comfortable knowing that a younger person is nearby in case of an emergency. Younger people benefit because these arrangements tend to cost less than living in a rented apartment.

Janet Witkin, executive director of Alternative Living for the Aging in West Hollywood, California, which has matched more than 7,800 seniors with roommates, *www.alternativeliving.org*.

Social Networking At the Computer

Facebook, at *www.facebook.com*, is becoming popular with adults as well as teenagers—as a place to meet, chat and exchange information. And several free networking sites have now been set up *specifically* for older adults. Among them, I like BoomerTowne.com at *www.boomertowne.com*, which focuses on finance, health, lifestyle and legal subjects…BOOMj at *www.boomj.com*, which covers these same topics and also shopping and politics…Eons at *www.eons.com*, which includes groups interested in careers, games, romance and mind and spirit…and TeeBeeDee at *www.teebeedee.com*, which provides discussion groups on music, travel, money and more.

Caution: Avoid giving financial or other personal information on a public Web site.

Speaking Your Mind More?

As we get older, the frontal cortex—the part of the brain that censors thoughts—begins to shrink. This could explain why many elderly people seem to say just what they mean.

But: The decline is not inevitable. Aerobic exercise enhances functioning among older adults.

William von Hippel, PhD, professor, School of Psychology, University of Queensland, Australia, and author of a study published in *Current Directions in Psychological Science*.

13

Estate Planning Now

Does Your Will Contain These Terrible Errors? What to Do If It Does

ake one seemingly minor misstep when you draft up your will, and your assets might be divided in a very different manner from what you had intended.

The biggest mistake of all is dying without a will, so don't let fear of making a mistake prevent you from drafting one—either with the assistance of an attorney or on your own with the help of a guidebook or a will-creation software program. *Just be sure that you—and your attorney—avoid these common errors…*

●**Overdoing equal apportionments.** Parents will often try to divide every asset exactly equally among their children in wills. This can cause problems when it means that a large, difficult-to-divide asset, such as a vacation home or a valuable vase, is left to more than one person.

Example: You leave to each of your four children a share of your vacation home. Two of your kids love the home and want to keep it in the family, but the other two are not doing as well financially and would rather sell it. Despite your good intentions, your gift sparks a family fight that could last for years.

Better: Find out in advance how each of your children feels about your most valuable possessions. If some of them are especially partial to particular items, consider leaving these assets exclusively to them. Give other children the larger share of other assets to balance things out. Explain your decision in a letter kept with your will so that everyone understands your reasoning.

●**Including unexplained "surprise" heirs.** Surprises are dangerous in wills. They can lead to hurt feelings, confusion and even legal battles. Family members often become suspicious and

---

Mary Randolph, JD, senior vice president of legal publisher Nolo Press, *www.nolo.com,* and author of four books on estate matters and avoiding probate. She is coauthor of the book and software package *Quicken WillMaker Plus 2008* (Nolo). She is based in Berkeley, California.

resentful when someone they do not know very well receives a significant portion of an estate.

Better: To minimize problems, include a letter with your will explaining who this "surprise" heir is and why he/she is receiving the bequest. An explanation should minimize any concerns among—and potential legal claims from—family members that this person exerted undue influence on you when you wrote the will.

Example: "I'm leaving this money to my neighbor to thank him for the many hours he spent taking care of me and my home during these past few years, when I no longer could get around well myself."

● **Setting conditions.** Some wills say that the kids or grandkids must graduate from college, get married or reach some other goal to receive their inheritances. Unfortunately, these attempts to influence heirs from beyond the grave usually result only in headaches for the executors, because heirs often find ways to subvert the intent of the contingencies.

Examples: A potential heir might "graduate" from a Caribbean diploma mill to satisfy a college requirement…or marry and then quickly divorce to satisfy a marriage requirement.

Better: If you trust your heirs, give them their bequests outright (or outright upon reaching a certain age). If you do not, do not leave them much money under any circumstances.

● **Trying to cut your spouse out of a will.** In most states, spouses are legally entitled to no less than one-quarter to one-half of the estate. (The exact minimum depends on the state.) In community property states—Arizona, California, Idaho, Louisiana, Nevada, New Mexico, Texas, Washington and Wisconsin—spouses do legally own half of anything acquired or earned during the marriage (exceptions include items received as gifts or inheritances), so up to half of "your" property may not really be yours to give away. If you leave a surviving spouse out of the will despite these restrictions, he can claim the share allowed by state law. This means that other beneficiaries would have their shares reduced.

Better: If you want your spouse to receive less than the amount legally mandated and the spouse agrees, he can waive the right to claim the share provided by state law.

● **Leaving everything to a spouse.** Married people often simply leave all of their assets to a surviving spouse. If your spouse later remarries and then dies before his new partner does, the partner might wind up with all of your money, leaving your children and/or any other intended heirs with nothing.

Better: If you want to be sure your assets stay in your family, an attorney can help you set up a trust that passes your assets from you to your spouse, then on to your children after your spouse's death.

● **Disinheriting any children (or grandchildren) by omitting them from the will.** You are not legally required to leave money to all (or any) of your children or grandchildren. If you do choose to disinherit a descendant, however, it still is smart to mention this person in your will. If you fail to do this, depending on circumstances, the descendant might be able to contest the will on the grounds that you simply forgot to include his name. Some people try to solve this problem by giving the disinherited descendant a token bequest of $1…or by writing straight out that this particular descendant receives nothing. These strategies are unnecessary.

Better: Include a list of all of your descendants in the will—including the disinherited person—to show you have not forgotten anyone and then state who gets what.

● **Assuming a will takes precedence over other financial documents.** The beneficiary designations on all your retirement accounts, life insurance policies and living trusts do supersede your will. People often neglect to update beneficiaries for these accounts on the assumption that the instructions in their wills dictate the distribution of these funds after death.

Examples: If you fail to change the beneficiaries on your retirement accounts when you divorce, an ex-spouse could wind up with your IRA, even if your will indicates that your assets —including specifically this IRA—should go to someone else.

Better: Update of all your beneficiary designations whenever there is a major event in your life that would warrant such a change, such as a birth, death, divorce or marriage.

•**Being extra specific.** Some people try to spell out in a will who should get every last teacup. Extreme specificity in wills is more likely to cause problems than solve them. You are bound to accidentally leave something off the list, and your inventory of possessions is likely to change many times between the time your will is written and your death, forcing frequent updates.

Better: Provide specific instructions for the distribution of possessions of particular financial or sentimental value, then let your heirs divide up the rest, perhaps by stipulating that they select items in turn.

•**Not signing the will legally.** People sometimes fail to realize the importance of signing the will in the presence of witnesses. Wills have been invalidated because people stepped into the next room to find a flat surface to sign on while a witness remained behind.

Better: Sign your will in the presence of at least two adult witnesses.

Property Inheritance Smarts

If you own property as "tenants in common," each of you will have his/her separate interest in the house. When one of you dies, that person's interest will pass to an heir or heirs per the terms of that person's will. The interest will pass to the other owner only if that's what the will calls for.

If you own the property as "joint tenants with right of survivorship," when one of you dies, the survivor becomes the owner of the entire house. To make this happen, your deed must specify that you hold the property as joint tenants.

Example: "John Doe and Mary Smith, as joint tenants with the right of survivorship and not as tenants in common."

Consult an attorney familiar with your state and local laws.

Nancy Dunnan, a New York City–based financial and travel adviser and author or coauthor of 25 books. Her latest book is the ninth edition of her best seller, *How to Invest $50–$5,000* (HarperCollins).

How to Record Your Last Wishes

Sanford J. Schlesinger, Esq., a founding partner and head of wills and estates, Schlesinger Gannon & Lazetera LLP, 499 Park Ave., New York City 10022.

By preparing a document listing your last wishes, you can help lessen your loved ones' problems during the time of your death—they'll have a record of what you would like them to know and do.

Some of your wishes may seem inconsequential—no flowers at your funeral, for example. But such issues can cause family discord at this highly emotional time.

MORE THAN JUST A WILL

Everyone needs to have legal documents. *In addition to a will, be sure to have…*

•**Advanced health-care directive (e.g., living will)**—covers specific directives as to the course of your medical treatment should you be unable to give informed consent.

•**Power of attorney**—gives an agent the power to handle your financial affairs during your lifetime in case you are not able to.

•**Organ donation card**—you can also indicate that you are a donor on your driver's license. Visit *www.organdonor.gov.*

•**Other legally binding directives**—trusts you've set up for your heirs, transfers on death, bank books for accounts in trust, etc.

But these legal documents will not adequately address some of the issues sure to come up when you die.

What to do: Prepare a document of instructions for your family. Keep it in a place where it will be found immediately after your demise. It certainly won't do you, or your family, much good if one of your last wishes is to be cremated and the document that says this is found two weeks after you have been buried! Make copies and give them to those you have designated to carry out your instructions, such as a spouse, relative or trusted friend.

Include in this document the actions that you would like to see your family take within a few days of your demise.

KEY LISTS

Think about what your relatives or friends would need to know to settle your estate, then include this information in your document. *Lists to include...*

•**Advisers.** Provide a complete listing of all your professional consultants—such as your accountant, attorney, life insurance agent and financial planner—along with their phone numbers and/or e-mail addresses. Also organize a listing of your doctors and dentists, so that family members can trace medical histories (which may be helpful in the case of genetic diseases).

•**Location of assets and information**—account numbers, PINs, passwords, etc. Prepare a list of places, in addition to accounts with financial institutions, where you keep your money, papers and other valuables—a safe-deposit box (and location of the key), a closet or a desk (perhaps a secret drawer).

Identify items found in these places, such as appraisals, birth certificates, cemetery deeds, divorce decrees and insurance policies. Prepare a detailed list within every category showing the identification numbers of insurance policies, brokerage accounts and annuities and estimated values, if at all possible. *Examples...*

•For all insurance policies, provide the name of the owner, insured, beneficiary, policy number, company, type of coverage, amount of coverage, agent's name, agent's address and agent's phone number.

•For all brokerage accounts, provide account number, firm, address, phone number and name of sales representative, if any.

•For retirement plans or annuities, which may provide significant death benefits to named beneficiaries, list the companies with which they can be found (e.g., former employer, insurance company).

Also create a list of your credit card numbers (along with the toll-free phone numbers) so they can be canceled immediately after your death. This will avoid any unauthorized use. Include any passwords or PINs required for immediate access. For instance, if you maintain a comprehensive list of assets on your computer, but your computer can be accessed only by entering the password, your list won't easily be found unless someone knows the password.

•**Dogs, cats and other pets are considered part of the family to most people.** Because they require immediate care, simply including information in a will about who should inherit them is not sufficient. Specify who should take immediate possession of your pet, what type of special care the pet may require (or you might want it to have) and contact information for the pet's veterinarian.*

•**Those who have served in the military may be entitled to special benefits** (including burial in a military cemetery). Indicate your service number, branch, rank and the discharge date so that heirs can easily obtain information about possible benefits.

WHERE TO TURN FOR HELP

You can create your own document of last wishes.

Helpful: The Illinois CPA Society offers a free form that you can download and fill in (*www. icpas.org/uploadedfiles/consumer/last-wishes. pdf*).

It is important to understand that the information you put in your last wishes document is not legally binding. For instance, if your will leaves your diamond engagement ring to your oldest daughter, you can't change that in the last wishes document. You would need to have your will updated.

If you want professional help in creating a last wishes document, discuss the matter with your attorney. There are also companies that will create a document for you (at *www.privatematters. com*, you can have such a document created for a $69.99 charge with annual renewal for $12**).

*For a copy of "Setting Up a Pet Trust," log on to *www. bottomlinesecrets.com.*

**Prices subject to change.

More from Sanford Schlesinger, Esq....

Instructions for Last Wishes

Questions you might want to address in instructions you leave for loved ones...

• **What are your last wishes about your funeral?** Cover topics like music, flowers, eulogizer and type of casket.

• **Do you want to be buried, placed in a mausoleum or cremated?**

• **If cremated, what do you want done with your ashes?**

• **Where do you want your funeral service to take place?**

• **Do you want a wake, immediate burial, private service?**

• **What type of monument do you want? Epitaph?**

Also from Sanford Schlesinger, Esq....

Estate Tax Planning for Uncertain Law

The future of the estate tax has never been more uncertain. *Under current tax law, the amount of an estate that is exempt from tax...*

• **In 2008 is $2 million.**

• **In 2009 will be $3.5 million.**

• **In 2010 will be unlimited,** with the estate tax repealed.

• **In 2011 will be $1 million,** with the top estate tax rate increased to 55% from the current rate of 45%.

Nobody believes that this bizarre, currently legislated course will be followed over the next four years—but nobody knows what will take its place.

Most likely: The elimination of the estate tax in year 2010 will not take place and the tax will be made permanent again, but with an exempt amount higher and tax rate lower than that provided in the currently legislated 2011 "restoration." *Planning now...*

• **Don't assume that the estate tax will ever be repealed.** If you've made this assumption, review your estate plan with an estate tax adviser and begin using such tax-cutting strategies as gifts.

• **Be sure that any provisions in your will tied to the amount of an estate that is exempt from tax** do not contain the wrong number, as that amount will change almost every year in coming years.

• **Keep informed about all new developments in the law** and consult with your estate planning advisers about their importance to you as they occur.

Smartest Ways to Make Tax-Free Gifts

Gloria S. Neuwirth, Esq., partner in the law firm Davidson, Dawson & Clark LLP at 60 E. 42 St., New York City 10165. The firm concentrates on tax, trust and estate law, as well as not-for-profit organizations. Neuwirth lectures and writes on estate planning and trust and tax issues.

The annual gift tax exclusion is a prime tax-planning tool, and rightly so. This exclusion may permit you to remove assets from your taxable estate tax free.

Don't stop there: You also can make "taxable gifts," those that are not covered by the annual gift tax exclusion. Don't let the name fool you—such gifts might not cause you to pay any tax.

When used wisely, such taxable gifts can reduce the estate tax bill that your heirs eventually will have to face.

EMPLOYING THE EXEMPTION

As mentioned, your first priority in trimming your taxable estate via gifts is to use the annual gift tax exclusion.

Current limit: $12,000 worth of assets per giver, per recipient, per year, to any number of recipients.

This ceiling will gradually rise up to $13,000, $14,000, etc., in the future, to keep pace with inflation.

Example: Bill Jones has three children. In 2008, he can give each of them up to $12,000 worth of assets. He doesn't even have to file a gift tax return.

Bill's wife, Mary, also can give $12,000 to each of their children. Thus, the couple can shed as much as $72,000 worth of assets this year, tax free, and pass those assets to the next generation. (The gifts are not taxable income to the recipients.) Similar gifts can be made every year.

OVER THE LIMIT

Suppose, in the above example, Mary Jones gives each of their three children $12,000 this year. Bill Jones, gives them $20,000 each.

Result: These gifts are over the limit by $8,000 per child, or $24,000 altogether. Bill must report all these gifts on IRS Form 709, *United States Gift (and Generation-Skipping Transfer) Tax Return.*

Loophole: Assuming that no other excessive gifts have been made in this year or prior years, no tax need be paid. Instead, Bill can use his lifetime exemption from the gift tax.

Current limit: $1 million. At present, there are no plans to raise this exemption amount, but future increases are possible.

That limit is $1 million per giver. Thus, a married couple can give away a total of $2 million, without owing gift tax, in addition to amounts that are covered by the annual gift tax exclusion.

How it works: Suppose that Bill Jones, who had not made any taxable gifts previously, gives $60,000 equally to his three children this year. The first $36,000 is covered by three $12,000 exclusions, but the excess $24,000 is reported on a gift tax return.

Result: Bill's lifetime gift tax exemption is reduced from $1 million to $976,000. If he reports another $24,000 of excess gifts next year, his exemption will be down to $952,000. And so on.

Final accounting: Suppose that Bill makes a total of $200,000 in excess gifts before death. Assume he dies in a future year when the estate tax exemption is set at $2 million.

Instead of a $2 million exemption, Bill has a $1.8 million estate tax exemption. His $200,000 in reportable gifts, on which he has paid no tax, effectively reduces his estate's tax shelter.

Vital: Married couples may elect to split all their gifts 50-50 in a given year for tax-reporting purposes. Such gift splitting, elected on a gift tax return, effectively allows the spouse who owns the property being gifted to use the other's annual gift tax exclusion and lifetime exemption amounts.

Gift splitting may make sense when most or all of the gifts actually come from the assets of only one spouse.

SOONER THE BETTER

Why would you make these reportable gifts now, even though they'll reduce your estate tax shelter later?

• **Generosity.** You might want to give someone a gift that is larger than $12,000, or larger than the $24,000 a married couple can give. Such large gifts can help your children buy homes.

• **Reduction of estate tax.** By transferring assets that are likely to gain value, you'll remove that potential appreciation from your estate.

Example: You own investment real estate now worth $600,000. You think that if you hold on to it until your death, it may be worth $2 million or more. Thus, you give the real estate to your three children. The first $36,000 in its value will be covered by the annual gift tax exclusion (three times $12,000), while the excess $564,000 is reported on a gift tax return.

Therefore, you have reduced your estate tax shelter by $564,000, but you have effectively removed a $2 million-plus asset from your estate.

Tax concerns: Gift recipients assume the giver's basis on property received. On a sale, they might owe capital gains tax if the sales price exceeds the giver's basis.

However, it might make sense to have your children pay capital gains tax, at a low federal rate of 15%, instead of estate taxes, where federal tax rates now are up to 45%.

Depend on discounts: Some creative planning may help you get extra tax shelter when making large gifts. You might not have to pay tax on the full value of the asset given away.

Example: When you give a $600,000 investment real estate property to your three children, as described above, you first form a limited partnership or a limited liability company (LLC) to own it. You can retain a small controlling interest and give your children an interest representing most of the ownership of the property.

The interest given to the children often will have no management rights. If so, a qualified, unrelated appraiser might say that the children's interest is worth less than the nominal value of their stake in the property because they lack control and liquidity.

Result: Although the IRS is likely to look hard at any valuation discount, with a well-reasoned appraisal, you may sustain a reported gift that is less than the face value of the transferred asset.

Going forward, unless there are issues of your having kept control, future appreciation will be largely out of your estate because the children own most of the investment real estate as limited partners or LLC members.

PAYING TAX CAN PAY OFF

In some cases, it might even make sense to go over the $1 million lifetime gift tax exemption.

Example: You give your children a 30% interest in your wholly owned company, which is valued at $7 million. Instead of $2.1 million (30% of $7 million), their minority interest might be valued at a lower amount, perhaps $1.4 million.

Tax brackets: For gifts from $1 million to $1.25 million, gift tax must be paid at a 41% rate. From $1.25 million to $1.5 million, the rate is 43%. And under current law, all reportable lifetime gifts of more than $1.5 million are taxed at a 45% rate.

Strategy: Paying such a gift tax now may be wise if you can move appreciating assets out of your estate and spare your heirs from having to pay larger amounts later.

And paying gift tax actually moves more assets (the cash you use to pay the tax) out of your estate, too. Thus, it pays to plan—and act—soon. Last-minute gifts won't save estate tax.

The Right Way To Use the Most Popular Trusts...and Traps to Avoid

Martin Shenkman, CPA and attorney who specializes in trusts and estates in New York City and Teaneck, New Jersey. He is also the author of many books, including *The Complete Book of Trusts* (Wiley). His Web site, *www.law easy.com*, provides sample forms and documents.

Trusts can serve as very valuable and effective tools for protecting and managing family wealth, and minimizing family taxes. But trust abuse is one of the IRS's "dirty dozen" most common tax scams.

Reason: Any number of unscrupulous operators are in the business of making false tax-

saving claims so that they can sell bogus trusts to unsuspecting taxpayers.

Here are the key kinds of legitimate trusts every family should know about—and the warning signs that may signal trust abuse. *Top four legitimate trusts to use...*

REVOCABLE LIVING TRUSTS

Revocable living trusts (RLTs) are often promoted as a means to avoid probate, since probate fees in some states can be high and probate proceedings can be time consuming, not to mention public (wills are public documents).

But an RLT may provide you even more valuable benefits as a tool that ensures the secure management of your assets—according to your wishes—should you become unable to manage them yourself due to unexpected disability, or in old age.

How it works: You create the trust and...

• **Transfer to it legal ownership of assets you choose,** such as your home and key investments.

• **Name a trustee to manage the assets.** The trustee can be you, but then you must also name the successor trustee to take your place should you die, become disabled or resign from managing the trust.

• **Direct in the trust's documents how its assets are to be managed while you live,** and how they are to be distributed or managed upon disability and death.

Key: You can revoke the trust completely or change its provisions at any time, which means that the trust has no practical effect until you become disabled, or you decide to resign from actively managing your affairs (as in old age), or die. *Advantages...*

• You ensure continuing management of your assets as you desire if you become disabled, while retaining full control over them while you remain well.

• When you die, your trust assets are distributed outside of probate. This means that your heirs may receive them faster, because the trust has control of them already and there is no delaying court involvement. (Usually estate tax must also be paid before distributions can be made.) Also, the entire process takes place in privacy—unless there is a contest (i.e., lawsuit).

Tax planning: An RLT has no effect on income taxes. Because you retain full control over the trust assets, the IRS ignores the trust for income tax purposes. Also, the assets in an RLT remain part of your taxable estate, so the RLT does not by itself affect estate tax liability.

However, you can accomplish with your RLT anything that you can with a will—make deductible charitable bequests, create additional family trusts (such as for children and grandchildren), direct how assets in such trusts are to be invested (such as in tax-exempt bonds), and so on.

Thus, an RLT can be designed to play an important role in any larger estate plan that minimizes taxes for the family.

IRREVOCABLE LIFE INSURANCE TRUST

If you die owning a life insurance policy on your own life, the policy proceeds will be part of your taxable estate even if you named another individual as the beneficiary of the policy. *Dangers...*

• **The policy proceeds could be lost** in large part to the IRS and state taxing authorities through estate tax instead of going to your intended beneficiaries (except a spouse).

• **If you named your estate as beneficiary of the policy, the proceeds will be part of your probate estate**—meaning that they will pass through your will subject to legal expenses, claims and delays.

• **Policy proceeds may pass outright in a lump sum to a beneficiary** who does not have the discipline or financial skills to manage the amount or who may divorce—leading to a squandering of your legacy.

An irrevocable life insurance trust can enable you to avoid these problems to get the most benefit from every insurance premium dollar.

How it works: You create a trust to buy and be the legal owner of an insurance policy on your life, with all policy proceeds to be paid to the trust. When the trust receives the proceeds upon your death, the trustee will manage and distribute them as you direct—providing professional management of funds to beneficiaries who might need it, paying them out over time as you direct.

A tax benefit: The policy proceeds escape both estate tax (since the policy isn't owned by you) and income tax (as life insurance proceeds do generally), so they are totally tax free.

The proceeds also avoid your probate estate and can be managed by the trust in the way you direct for many years after your death.

APPLICABLE EXCLUSION TRUST

Also known as a credit shelter or bypass trust, an applicable exclusion trust (or AET) enables a married couple to use two full estate tax exempt amounts to pass wealth to heirs.

Danger: The tax law lets one spouse bequeath any amount to the other free of estate tax. But then the couple's total assets may "pile up" in the surviving spouse's estate with only one exempt amount available to protect them from tax.

Example: The current federal estate tax exempt amount is $2 million. If a couple owns assets worth $3.8 million and they end up owned by the longest-lived spouse, when that spouse dies, estate tax will be due on $1.8 million.

To prevent this tax, both spouses should make bequests to people other than each other of up to $2 million. In this way, the two spouses together can leave up to $4 million free of tax ($2 million each)—avoiding tax on $1.8 million.

The AET is set up to receive such a bequest from the first spouse to die. The trust can then, if its creator desires, pay its income to the surviving spouse for life, and then distribute its assets to other beneficiaries (such as children) on the death of the second spouse. Alternatively, the trust can benefit both the spouse and beneficiaries other than a spouse from its creation—still using the creator's full estate tax exempt amount.

CHILDREN'S TRUST

When you give or bequeath significant assets to a son or daughter, it can be a good idea to do so through a trust even if you believe that the child is fully capable of managing the assets responsibly.

If a child is a minor, it is legally required to place ownership of the assets described above in a trust benefiting the child (a minor cannot legally own anything). And if you fear that an adult child is too inexperienced or irresponsible to manage valuable assets, it is wise to do so.

But even a fully mature and responsible adult child can lose valuable family assets in a divorce, or through a liability lawsuit (such as malpractice suits that doctors and lawyers risk). Placing ownership of the assets in a trust that benefits the child can secure the assets for the family in spite of claims brought forth by a hostile divorcing spouse or creditors.

TRUST SAFETY

Many variations of the above trusts are possible, as well as other trust options.

Important: Trusts are legal documents that should be custom-designed to your personal situation. So any trust that you consider should be reviewed by a lawyer hired by you—not by any person, such as a trust salesperson or a lawyer suggested by him, advising you to use the trust.

Also, be wary of doing business with someone who tries to sell you any trademarked trust (a particular trust for which the name has been trademarked). The label means nothing. Anyone who has patented or trademarked the name of the trust he is offering is likely to be more interested in marketing than in providing you with good legal service.

Finally, check the IRS Web site's "Abusive Trust Tax Evasion Schemes" warning page at *www.irs. gov.* Enter "abusive trusts" in the search box.

Avoid the Double-Tax on Retirement Accounts

Christopher R. Hoyt, Esq., professor of law, University of Missouri–Kansas City School of Law, Kansas City, Missouri. He was cochair of the American Bar Association's Committee on Lifetime and Testamentary Charitable Gift Planning.

The money that's in your retirement plan accounts could very well be most of your life savings.

Trap: It may be taxed at rates of 64% or even more when you die, due to the double-tax effect of combined income and estate taxes. *How to leave less of these savings to the IRS and more to your heirs...*

THE DANGER

Funds held in a qualified retirement plan account—such as a 401(k) or a company pension account—or an IRA are subject to estate taxes when you die, just like all other assets you own. The same funds are subject to income tax when distributed from a retirement plan account or traditional IRA to an account beneficiary.

Federal estate tax currently applies at a 45% rate to portions of estates larger than $2 million ...and income tax applies to retirement plan distributions at ordinary rates of up to 35%. When estate and income tax rates are combined on a retirement plan account, the combined federal rate can reach 64%.

Calculation: A retirement plan account has a balance of $100,000, is included in a taxable estate, and will distribute its balance in the year of the owner's death to a beneficiary in the 35% income tax bracket. *Result...*

• **The estate will owe $45,000 of estate tax on the account.**

• **The beneficiary will have $100,000 of taxable income from the distribution.** But the beneficiary will also be entitled to a $45,000 income tax deduction for the estate tax paid on the account—a deduction for "income in respect of a decedent" (IRD). Therefore, the beneficiary has net taxable income of $55,000, which, when subject to a 35% tax rate, results in income tax of $19,250.

• **The combination of $45,000 of estate tax plus $19,250 of income tax comes to $64,250**—a tax rate of more than 64%—and leaves only $35,750 to the heir, after taxes, from the $100,000.

EVEN WORSE

In reality, the total tax bill may be even larger. *Why...*

• **State taxes are extra.** The above calculation covers only federal taxes. The cost of state taxes is extra and in high-tax states may be large.

Example: In New York State, income tax reaches 6.85% (10.5% in New York City). Estate tax rates range from 6.4% to 16%, with only $1 million of an estate exempt from tax (only half the amount that's exempt from federal estate tax).

Such state taxes can push the combined federal and state tax rate to more than 80%.

•The deduction for IRD is difficult to claim. The deduction for IRD gives the heir to a retirement account an income tax deduction for estate taxes paid on it that can be claimed against taxable income received from the account. This somewhat reduces the cost of the estate tax (as seen in the calculation on page 229).

Snag: In practice, the deduction for IRD can be difficult to take, and much or all of its value often is lost.

Why: Rules are very complex and not understood by most people who prepare their own returns and even many tax professionals. Many overlook the deduction entirely.

Also, the deduction is available only if you itemize deductions—so persons who don't itemize can't take it at all.

And, finally, the deduction can be taken only as income from a retirement account is received, which may be over a period of many years. Thus, much of it may be deferred for many years.

Result: The deduction for IRD may be much less valuable than it appears—making estate tax even more costly.

WHAT TO DO

There are several things you can do to avoid the double taxation of retirement savings that you leave to your heirs…

•Make charitable gifts and bequests. If your estate is large enough to owe estate taxes, and you intend to make charitable gifts or bequests, make them using the funds in retirement accounts instead of other assets.

Benefit: When received by a charity, these funds will escape income tax and estate tax. The taxes saved on such a bequest can let you leave more to heirs after tax.

Example: You have $100,000 in an IRA and another $100,000 in mutual fund shares in a taxable account, and wish to leave $100,000 each to a child and a favorite charity. If you leave the taxable fund shares to charity and the IRA to your child, the child will owe income tax on the IRA proceeds at up to a 35% rate—costing up to $35,000 of tax if the IRA funds are withdrawn immediately.

But if you leave the IRA to charity and the mutual fund shares to your child, nobody will owe income tax—the charity is tax exempt, and

the mutual fund shares will be received by the child with "stepped-up basis" (market value at the date of death), eliminating all taxable gain on them to date.

So, up to $35,000 of tax is saved to increase what you leave to heirs.

Planning options…

•Name a charity as beneficiary of your qualified retirement plan or IRA.

•In 2007, the law permitted you to directly transfer (before death) up to $100,000 from an IRA to charity on a tax-free basis if you were at least 70½ years old. This break may be extended for 2008.

•A charitable planning expert can offer you other possible tax-saving options, such as the creation and use of a private foundation.

•Avoid saving too much in retirement accounts. Once you have sufficient funds in retirement accounts to meet retirement needs, put additional savings in other investments.

Example: Life insurance proceeds are free of income tax, and can be estate tax free, too, if the policy's ownership is properly arranged. So, your insurance premiums can provide a bequest to heirs that is double tax free instead of double taxed.

•Withdraw excess funds from retirement accounts. Take distributions from retirement accounts and use them to buy investments such as life insurance or appreciating capital gain assets that will be income tax free to heirs. Similarly, convert a traditional IRA to a Roth IRA (starting in 2010, there is no income limit on eligibility to convert). Income taxes will be due currently on the value of the distributed funds or converted IRA. But future appreciation in the value of these funds will be income tax free to your heirs—and thus avoid double tax.

•Minimize your estate. Reduce the size of your taxable estate by measures such as making maximum use of the $12,000 per recipient annual gift tax exclusion, to move assets from your estate to heirs free of gift and estate tax while you still live.

This will reduce any estate tax you owe, and may reduce your tax bracket rate if the estate tax "comes back" at higher rates after 2010 (under current law, the estate tax will be repealed in 2010, but will be reinstated in 2011).

14

Travel Guide

A Travel Pro's Money-Saving Secrets

The travel industry does not make it easy for a consumer to save money. Airfares, hotel prices and auto rental charges fluctuate daily...hidden fees unexpectedly increase bills...and historically high gas prices and a weak US dollar have made it even harder to plan inexpensive vacations. *Still, there are ways for savvy travelers to save money...*

•**Skip the hotel room.** With hotel rates at all-time highs, lodging alone can burn through most of your vacation budget. *Rather than overpay, consider these money-saving alternatives...*

•Time-share rentals. Time-share owners sometimes rent out their places when they cannot use them themselves. They often ask a fraction of what a hotel would charge for comparable lodgings. To locate a time-share available for rent, check time-share rental and exchange Web sites, such as Red Week.com and TradingPlaces.com. Also, search the

Craigslist.org site for the region you plan to visit under the "Housing" section.

•Home exchanges. Home-exchange organizations, such as HomeExchange.com and Homelink. org, help members swap homes for one week or two. These programs work best for people who live near popular tourist destinations.

Membership in a home-exchange organization typically costs around $100 per year,* but the savings on the accommodations more than pay for the membership prices if you take even one trip each year.

•Campgrounds. Many people do imagine dirt flooring and outhouses when they hear "campground," but some facilities provide clean, up-to-date cabins or rooms for rent so that guests sleep indoors, often for considerably less than a hotel would charge. Some of the rooms and cabins even include private bathrooms and wireless Internet

*Price subject to change.

Christopher Elliott, host of the television series *What You Get for the Money: Vacations on the Fine Living Network.* Based in Winter Springs, Florida, he writes a travel column for MSNBC.com and serves as ombudsman for *National Geographic Traveler.* His Web site is *www.elliott.org.*

231

access. Local visitors' bureaus can help you find campgrounds in the region.

•**Shop on-line for package deals.** You may have wondered if the package deals offered by on-line travel sites really do save you money. Often, they do. Expedia.com, Travelocity.com and Orbitz.com purchase airline tickets, hotel rooms and rental car reservations in bulk at low rates—and pass some of their bulk-buy savings along to customers who buy these services together.

The package deals can often be considerably cheaper than anything you could find by purchasing airline tickets, hotel rooms and rental cars separately. Occasionally a hotel-and-airfare package actually is cheaper than airfare alone.

These sites' package deals tend to be most attractive for travel to common vacation destinations, such as Hawaii, New York City, Orlando and Las Vegas.

•**Make a low bid for a rental vehicle on Priceline.com prior to reserving a car.** The Web site Priceline.com lets users bid for rental cars and other travel services. The site either accepts these bids or rejects them—you have nothing to lose by bidding, because there's no charge to do this. Priceline.com is particularly likely to provide great rental car rates.

The difficult part is deciding how little you should bid. Rental car prices vary greatly from city to city and even day to day, making it hard to determine a fair price.

I begin by finding the best rental rate I can through major rental car company Web sites and 800 numbers. (Rental car companies often offer better deals over the phone than they do on their Web sites.)

Next, I search for rental car deals on Hotwire. com, a Web site that often has very attractive prices. Then, I take the best price I have found and bid 30% less on Priceline.com. Often, my bid is accepted. If not, I accept the best deal I have found elsewhere.

Also: Consider reserving an economy car, even if you would prefer something larger. Rental agencies often run out of economy cars and provide free upgrades to customers. This is not worth trying if you absolutely must have a larger vehicle.

•**Upgrade your airline legroom for free.** You might not have to ante up big bucks (or frequent-flier miles) for an upgrade to first-class

legroom. Just reserve a coach seat that's in an emergency exit row. This row typically has several more inches of legroom than other coach rows—sometimes even as much as first class—to make it easier for passengers to exit in the event of an emergency. A few airlines do charge extra for exit-row seats, but most don't.

When I am not able to reserve a seat in the emergency exit row, I ask the gate agent to place me on the waiting list for this row as soon as I check in for my flight. You must be able-bodied to sit in the emergency exit row and physically able to open the emergency door.

Bulkhead seats—those seats at the front of a seating section—typically also provide extra legroom. However, bulkhead seating often is reserved for people with disabilities, families with young children and frequent-fliers.

Helpful: Buy airline tickets as early as possible this year. Many of the major American airlines are considering mergers. Airline mergers tend to reduce competition and increase prices, at least for a while. It is better to lock in today's fares.

•**Eat lunch out but dinner in.** Many restaurants charge about twice as much for dinner as they do for lunch—even though the food is the same and the portions comparable.

Trim vacation costs by eating lunch in the fancy restaurants you want to visit but dinner in less expensive restaurants or even back in your room if you have a kitchen or can bring in takeout.

•**Look out for hidden fees.** Virtually every company in the travel industry these days seems to be tacking on "hidden" fees. Cruise lines impose "fuel surcharges"…car rental agencies have become stricter about fuel "top off" fees…hotels add "concierge charges" or "resort fees."

Scan the fine print of rental contracts and other travel documents for fee disclosures before signing. If you feel that a fee is not justified, say so—you may be able to get it waived.

If fees are not stated in your documents, explain that you were not told about these fees and request that they be waived. If this request is denied, dispute the fee charge through your credit card company after your trip.

•**Consider using a travel agent for complex itineraries or a cruise.** In this era of book-your-own-ticket Internet sites, most consumers consider travel agents unnecessary. But an experienced travel agent can save you money on complicated international trips with numerous stops.

When consumers book complex trips on their own, they often suffer missed air connections or other unforeseen complications—these problems can be very expensive to resolve. Working with an experienced travel agent makes problems less likely and gives you an emergency on-call problem solver if something does go wrong.

Also, travel agents who are associated with large consortiums often have access to special rates for cruises and hotels that you couldn't find on your own.

Last-Minute Package Deals

Last-minute package travel bargains can cost less than airfare alone. When checking prices on-line, go to *www.lastminute.com*, one service that specializes in last-minute travel. Search for flight-and-rental-car packages, as well as flights alone.

Recent example: Flight-plus-rental-car from New York City to Savannah, Georgia, was listed at $248...compared with $424 for just the flight.*

George Hobica, publisher of Airfarewatchdog.com, a site that searches and lists unusually low fares, New York City.

*Rates subject to change.

Amazing Travel Bargains for Seniors

Joan Rattner Heilman, an award-winning travel writer based in New York. She is author of *Unbelievably Good Deals and Great Adventures That You Absolutely Can't Get Unless You're Over 50* (McGraw-Hill).

Only 49? Forget it! But if you've turned 50—or better yet, 60, 62 or 65—you can make your age pay off. These days,

all kinds of companies are offering special privileges and discounts that can save you a lot of money. *Here are my favorites...*

BARGAIN HOTEL ROOMS

Age 50 is the threshold for many hotel and motel discounts, some as generous as half off. Virtually all lodging chains and most individual establishments will give you a break on room rates. Most take only 10% off your bill—better than nothing—but some do much better, especially if you're at least 60. *Examples...*

• **Starwood Hotels** (Westin, Sheraton, W, Luxury Collections and Four Points) provides up to 50% off, depending on the location and season, when you're age 50 or older and an AARP member.* You must arrive on a Thursday, Friday or Saturday and make a reservation at least 21 days in advance. If you do not, you get 15% to 25% off, also depending on location and season (877-778-2277, *www.starwood.com/aarp*).

• **Choice Hotels.** The Sixty-Plus Rate from Choice Hotels (Comfort Inn, Quality Inn, Clarion, Econo Lodge, MainStay Suites, Sleep Inn, Rodeway Inns, Cambria Suites) gives you a discount, based on availability, of 20% to 30% at age 60 and older when you call ahead to make reservations. At age 50, you're entitled to 15% for AARP members, 10% for nonmembers (800-424-6423, *www.choicehotels.com*).

FRUGAL FLIGHTS

If you're age 65 or older, get Southwest Airlines' Senior Fare tickets at much less than full fare.

Senior tickets are available on all routes and all flights, and they have no advance-purchase requirements or fees for changing or canceling your flights. Seats are limited, however, so make your plans early and be flexible.

Saver: Southwest runs many seat sales for people of any age that cut prices even further, so check them out before you book a senior fare. For a route map and other information, visit *www.southwest.com* (click on "Travel Tools," then on "Southwest Policies," then on "Seniors").

OVERSEAS OFFERS

If heading overseas, you'll find senior bargains mainly on transportation, such as train and bus

*Offers, rates and prices subject to change.

travel. And, of course, at museums, historic sites, movies, etc., just as in the US.

Many foreign airlines take 10% off most non-promotional fares on flights to and from the US for travelers 60 or 62 and older (and sometimes for a younger companion, too).

Among them: Austrian Airlines, El Al Israel Airlines, Lufthansa German Airlines and Mexicana Airlines.

In most cases, you must request the discount by telephone.

A LIFETIME PARK PASS

Obtain an America the Beautiful—Senior Pass (formerly known as the Golden Age Passport) for $10 at age 62 or older, and for the rest of your life you will be admitted free of charge to all national parks, forests, refuges, monuments and recreation areas and get half off the federal user fees for certain facilities and services such as camping, swimming and parking.

The free admission deal applies not only to you but also to up to three additional adults in your vehicle. (All children under age 16 are free.) You can get your lifetime pass at a park entrance or on-line at *www.nps.gov/fees_passes.htm*. If you are younger than 62, you'll need the America the Beautiful—Annual Pass that costs $80 a year and offers the same privileges.

BREAKS ON CAR INSURANCE

At age 50 or 55 you may become eligible for a discount of up to 10% on your auto policy because insurance companies consider you a more cautious driver than you were in your youth. (After 70 or 75, however, the rates start going back up again.) Check out several insurers and choose the one that gives you the best deal, then be sure to take a defensive-driving course that entitles you to even more off the bill. At the same time, find out if you can get a similar discount on your homeowner's policy.

HOP A TRAIN, BUS OR SUBWAY

Just about all commuter railroad and metropolitan transit systems in the country charge you less once you're eligible for Medicare (age 65 in most cases). Usually they take half off the regular fare, although sometimes it's only in off-peak periods.

Examples: For travel by bus, subway or train in New York, Chicago, Washington, DC,

Honolulu and other big cities, you pay half the usual adult fare. Things are even better in the entire state of Pennsylvania, where taking a bus, trolley or subway is free, and only $1 on the regional rail lines. (Regular fares apply during rush hour—7 am to 8 am and 4:30 pm to 5:30 pm.) In most cases, all you need to qualify is proof of age.

SLEEP CHEAP

Join a bed-and-breakfast club and pay only a pittance for a bed in the US or Canada. The Evergreen B&B Club (800-962-2392, *www.ever greenclub.com*), limited to people over age 50, charges annual dues of $60 for a single and $75 for two for the privilege of staying at the homes of other members here and abroad for $10 single or $15 double per night.

When you sign up for the Affordable Travel Club (253-858-2172, *www.affordabletravelclub. net*) at age 40 or older, you pay dues of $75 a year and nominal charges of $15 (single) or $20 (double) directly to your hospitable fellow members for every night you sleep in their homes. Count on them not only to offer you a full or continental breakfast but to show you around the neighborhood, too.

Europe Too Expensive? Insider Secrets

Pauline Frommer, creator of *Pauline Frommer Guidebooks*, guides designed to help vacationers save money on trips in the US and to Europe and other destinations, *www.frommers.com/pauline*. She is the daughter of the legendary travel expert Arthur Frommer.

D on't give up plans for a European vacation just because the dollar has gone down so much in value. Yes, in the last few years, the dollar has lost value compared with other currencies—prices are up by more than 50%, in dollar terms, for Americans in many parts of Europe. *But there are still great places you can visit without spending a fortune…*

KRAKOW, POLAND

Located on the beautiful Vistula River, Krakow is a city rich with history. The capital of Poland for more than 400 years (until 1596), Krakow is home to centuries-old churches and synagogues. Another gem is the Wawel Royal Castle, a 16th-century structure that reflects architectural styles from many parts of Europe. Or if you want to shop for bargain jewelry, clothing or food, stroll through Rynek Glówny, an 800-year-old market square.

A half hour from Krakow is Auschwitz. After seeing the former death camp, few people ever look at history in the same way.

Small hotels and bed-and-breakfasts in Krakow cost as little as $70 to $80 a night for two,* and you can figure on about $20 to $30 per person more for food and sightseeing expenses. For a money-saving alternative to hotels, try short-term apartment rentals in Krakow and other cities. See the rental Web sites listed on page 236.

BOHEMIA, THE CZECH REPUBLIC

The capital of the Czech Republic, Prague has become just as expensive as Rome, Madrid and other popular European cities, but the close by countryside of Bohemia is a bargain. Top-rated hotels in numerous charming Bohemian villages charge less than $75 a night for a room for two, and meals and sightseeing typically run about $20 to $25 a day per person.

Bohemia is known for its nature trails, music festivals, historic castles and spas. Český Krumlov, for instance, is a UNESCO World Heritage site on the banks of the Vitava River. (The designation is given to only 851 sites that are judged to be among the most historically important in the world.)

Visitors can go boating, walk through castles and stop by the town's many cultural attractions, including the Egon Schiele Art Centrum, devoted to works of influential classical and contemporary art. Or tour all the breweries in the town of Česke Budějovice, whose name became Budweiser in the US.

In addition to various Web sites mentioned on page 236, Czech Republic Bookings (*http://hotels. czech-republic-bookings.com*) provides bargain accommodations throughout Bohemia.

LISBON

The capital of Portugal, Lisbon is 20% to 25% less expensive than most other European capitals.

*Prices, rates and offers subject to change.

The city is also one of the most beautiful, with great boulevards, magnificent parks and vestiges of its Roman and Moorish history. The Alfama neighborhood, for instance, dates from the Moorish occupation of the eighth century.

Or visit Saint George's Castle, situated on a hill that overlooks the city. It was built in the sixth century and recaptured from the Moors 600 years later. If it's nightlife you're after, spend the evening in the Bairro Alto, home to dozens of friendly restaurants and clubs.

Spring is a great time to go to Lisbon. While it is still chilly and damp in northern Europe, Lisbon—on the southwestern tip of the continent—usually sees lots of sunny days with temperatures in the 60s and 70s.

It's easy to save money in this city by renting an apartment for as short a time as a day or two. The agency Travelling to Lisbon at 351-21-888-6072, *www.travelingtolisbon.com*, links up apartment owners with vacationers and often offers lodgings for as little as $75 a night per family.

LONDON

Though it's one of the most expensive cities in Europe, you can save substantially by going off season, booking a package deal (check page 236) and/or staying in one of a number of low-cost hotels or in a private house.

Airlines, hotels and even many restaurants do lower their prices from October through April. Overall, a week in London is often 50% cheaper during this time, than it would be in July or August, the peak season.

Off season is high season for theater. You can see new shows long before they come to the US. So, bundle up and have a ball!

No matter when you go, to save on food, eat in pubs. They tend to be much less expensive than touristy restaurants.

To save on accommodations, consider easyHotel (44-20-7216-1717, *www.easyhotel.com*), the new chain of inexpensive hotels. I would especially recommend their hotel in Kensington, a quiet area of London that is a short subway ride from the theater district and many other attractions. Rates start at about $90 per night, double occupancy.

Typical rates in a private house are about $150 per couple per night. Home owners who rent apartments and rooms to tourists can be located through At Home In London (44-20-8748-1943 *www.athomeinlondon.co.uk*) and the Bulldog Club (44-870-803-4414, *www.bulldogclub.com*).

PARIS

While top hotels often charge more than $700 a night, Paris still has dozens of excellent hotels where two people can sleep for less than $150 a night. The Web site Paris.org (*www.paris.org/Hotels*) is useful in finding them.

You can often save even more by staying in an apartment instead of in a hotel. The agency Parisian Home (*www.parisianhome.com*) links up apartment owners with travelers. Some well-located studio apartments listed on the site recently rented for about $550 a week.

For the most authentic and affordable meals, ask a local for advice (and avoid restaurants that have English language menus posted outside).

Examples: A helpful Parisian might send you to Le Pré Verre (8 rue Thénard), where a high-quality three-course, prix-fixe meal would be about $53...or to Café Constant (139 rue St. Dominique), where you can feast for about $40.

Most museums in Paris offer free admission at least one day a month.

Example: The Musée du Louvre is free on the first Sunday of the month. Check the Web sites of other museums for their free days.

More from Pauline Frommer...

Favorite Money-Saving Travel Tips

Planning a vacation? *Check out these smart money savers...*

•**Buy package deals that combine airfare with a hotel stay.**

Two of the best resources: Go-today.com (*www.go-today.com*) and Gate 1 Travel (*www.gate 1travel.com*). Go-today.com recently offered airfare to London and six nights in a good hotel for $859, per person, double occupancy.*

Also: Paul Laifer Tours (*www.paullaifertours. com*) and Virgin Vacations (*www.virgin-vacations. com*).

•**Stay in an apartment.** Apartments, owned either by companies in the lodging business or

*Prices subject to change.

by individuals, often save you 50% to 60% over hotels of comparable quality.

Web sites that offer vacation rentals include Sublet.com (*www.sublet.com*)...Vacation Rentals (*www.vacationrentals.com*)...ESLWorldwide (*www.eslworldwide.com*)...The Right Vacation Rental (*www.therightvacationrental.com*)...Interhome (*www.interhome.com*)...Vacation Rental by Owner (*www.vrbo.com*)...At Home Abroad (*www.athome abroadinc.com*).

Planning a Trip To Europe?

Bob Bestor, publisher, *Gemütlichkeit: The Travel Letter for Germany, Austria & Switzerland*, 288 Ridge Rd., Ashland, Oregon 97520, *www.gemut.com*.

Whether you are booking a trip to Europe yourself or buying through your agent, you will save money by making sure prices are guaranteed in US dollars not in euros.

How it works: Rates for vehicle rentals, rail passes, some river cruises and a few luxury hotels can be paid for prior to US departure and thus guaranteed in US dollars rather than in euros. If the dollar continues to drop against the euro—which many experts say is likely—euro-guaranteed bookings will cost more when converted to dollars by your credit card company after payment is made in Europe. By paying in dollars, you'll also avoid the 2% to 3% foreign transaction fee which is charged by most credit card companies.

However: When you get to Europe, pay all transactions in local currency.

Hotel, restaurant and other bills presented in US dollars include a hidden 3% to 5% currency exchange fee known as Dynamic Currency Conversion (DCC). Do try to use your credit card whenever possible—you'll still have to pay the foreign transaction fee, but it is usually a better rate than the DCC.

Cheaper Calls When You Travel

Voice over Internet Protocol (VoIP) lets you use the Internet instead of a regular phone line to place and receive calls. Plug your US telephone into an analog telephone adapter (ATA), and connect it to a high-speed wired Internet connection. If you're staying at a hotel, you may need to use a laptop to turn on the Internet connection in your room before the VoIP will work.

For more information: *www.fcc.gov/voip.*

The Wall Street Journal, 200 Liberty St., New York City, *online.wsj.com.*

Ship It Home

Ship souvenirs home when traveling abroad instead of carrying them back on your return flight. US Customs allows American travelers to ship up to $200 worth of goods per day to themselves at a US address, as well as gifts totaling up to $100 per recipient per day to friends and family members.*

Arthur Frommer's Budget Travel, 530 Seventh Ave., New York City 10018, *www.frommers.com.*

*Subject to change.

Cruise Smarts

Rowdy passengers on cruise ships can pose a problem anytime—but particularly during colleges' spring breaks. Cruise ships have lowered some prices to attract younger passengers, who sometimes act up, drink too much or cause problems for others on board.

Self-defense: Find out the cruise line's booking restrictions—some require anyone under 21 to share a room with a parent or guardian age 25 or older. Consider booking at times of less interest to students—that is, avoid March and April cruises.

ConsumerAffairs.com, a free consumer news publication, Washington, DC.

Travel Detective's Secrets to Avoiding Airline Nightmares

Peter Greenberg, known as the "Travel Detective," is the travel editor for NBC's *Today* show and editor of the travel Web site *www.petergreenberg.com.* His latest book is *The Complete Travel Detective Bible* (Rodale).

Airline trip hassles are common. Delayed or canceled flights, missed connections, lost luggage and getting bumped are just a few problems travelers experience too often.

The good news: You can avoid or minimize many of these problems.

CALL AHEAD

Many travelers phone the airline before they leave for the airport and ask if their flight is on time—but they usually get misleading information. The airline agents often tell you whether the flight is "scheduled" to leave on time. This is useless.

Instead, when calling the airline, ask for the "ship" number (or tail number) of the aircraft assigned to your flight. If the reservations agent doesn't know, ask him/her to call the operations office to get the number. Then ask for the status of the ship number. If the plane is running late, you can hang out at home a while longer or try to rebook your flight. (The Web sites that keep up on airline delays include *www.bts.gov, www. flightstats.com* and *www.avoiddelays.com.*)

TRY ALTERNATE AIRPORTS

Big city airports often are near smaller airports. Those airports offer fewer flights, but that means less congestion and fewer delays. *Try...*

- **Oakland, instead of San Francisco.**
- **Providence, instead of Boston.**
- **Burbank, instead of Los Angeles.**
- **Milwaukee, instead of Chicago.**
- **Islip or White Plains, instead of New York City.**
- **Fort Lauderdale, instead of Miami.**

INVOKE RULE 240

Rule 240 states that if your domestic flight is delayed for any reason other than weather or factors outside an airline's control, such as a riot or work stoppage, the airline must transfer you to another carrier if the second airline has available seats and can get you to your destination more quickly. If your flight is canceled or delayed, say to the ticket agent, "I'd like to invoke rule 240."

This rule does not apply to airlines that don't have existing interline agreements with other carriers (such as Southwest and JetBlue), but it does apply to most US airlines, including Continental, American, Delta, Northwest, United and USAir.

GET A SEAT ASSIGNMENT

In 2006, nearly 56,000 people who had tickets for a flight on a US airline did not get on because of overbooking. Atlantic Southeast Airlines (ASA) bumped the most people, followed by Delta. JetBlue bumped the fewest.

The key to avoiding getting bumped is to have an assigned seat and a boarding pass. Whenever possible, get a seat assignment when you make your reservation. Many airlines let you use the Internet to check in for a flight within 24 hours of flight time. Smart travelers log in from home, work or a hotel to print out their own boarding passes in advance.

Barring that, always try to book the first flight of the day. If you get bumped, you stand a better chance of getting out on the next flight.

SEND LUGGAGE AHEAD

If you want to avoid losing your luggage, do not check bags, especially on flights that connect through hubs with tight connection times. You can avoid checking bags by taking only one carry-on bag. (See the following article for tips on packing one bag.)

Or ship your bags ahead of you. FedEx, UPS, DHL and other companies provide baggage service, where bags are picked up at your home and delivered to your hotel. A suitcase weighing between 40 and 50 pounds costs between $100 and $200 for overnight delivery.* Discounts are offered for sending your bags a day or two ahead. By shipping your bags, you'll save an average of two hours every time you fly—you won't be standing in lines to check luggage and won't be waiting around baggage carousels after you land.

Also, by not having checked bags, you will have no problems switching flights if yours is delayed.

*Rates subject to change.

238

IDENTIFY YOUR BAGS

If you have to check bags...

• **Make your bag stand out.** Tie a brightly colored ribbon around the handle, or attach a sticker or decal.

• **Put your name and cell phone number on a luggage tag on the outside of your bag.** Don't put your address on the outside—it's an advertisement to burglars that you're not home.

Put contact information, including your address, home and cell phone numbers and e-mail address, inside each bag so it's visible as soon as the bag is opened. Conveyor belts may destroy outside tags. If your bag is lost with no ID inside, it could be lost forever.

• **Take a photo of your bag, and carry it with you when you travel.** This way, if your bag is lost, you can give the photo to the baggage claims representative.

• **When getting your checked bag at your destination, don't just grab it and leave** the terminal. Open it and inspect the contents before you leave the carousel area. It's always better to report the crime at the scene. If your bag does go missing, keep in mind that the airline liability limit for domestic flights is $3,000 per incident, not per bag, and is based on the actual value of your belongings, not the replacement value. For international flights, the limit is $9.07 per pound for checked baggage.

Pack for a 10-Day Trip In One Carry-On Bag

Joanne Lichten, PhD, a professional speaker and media spokesperson based in Marietta, Georgia, who travels about 100 days a year. She is author of *Dr. Jo's How to Stay Healthy & Fit on the Road* (Nutrifit). Her Web site is *www.drjo.com*.

You can pack everything needed for a 10-day vacation into a single 22"-x-9"-x-14" bag that complies with today's strict airline carry-on rules. Of course, you won't be able to wear a different outfit every day or get really dressed up for dinner, but frequent travelers find the convenience worth it. *What to pack...*

TWO-OUTFIT STRATEGY

In addition to the clothes you wear, you need pack only a core wardrobe of two outfits if you do the following...

• **Pick one color scheme.** Choose a neutral color—black, navy, brown or olive—and pack only clothing in this color or that goes well with this color. This makes it easy to create new outfits by mixing and matching pants, skirts, shirts, etc. Avoid lighter neutrals, such as tan and white, which are more likely to show dirt.

• **Buy wrinkle-resistant clothes.** Garments made from high-tech fabrics that resist wrinkles can be worn several times during a trip without looking messy. A wrinkle-resistant T-shirt is particularly versatile for men and women—it looks great with jeans or under a sport coat.

Good sources of travel clothing include Magellan's (800-962-4943, *www.magellans.com*)...TravelSmith (800-950-1600, *www.travelsmith.com*)...L.L. Bean (800-441-5713, *www.llbean.com*).

• **You may want to bring a microfiber T-shirt and one pair of shorts for workout clothes.** Microfiber is breathable and fast-drying. You can wash it and wear it again the next day. A large microfiber T-shirt works as a nightshirt and a bathing suit cover-up. You also may want to bring microfiber socks and underwear (enough for each day of the trip).

• **If you must bring a coat, make it a compact, wrinkle-resistant, all-weather raincoat.** With a sweater underneath, it's good even in 20-degree weather if you're not outside too long.

Examples: TravelSmith's Men's Packable Classic Raincoat ($169 to $179*) or the Women's Packable Microfiber Classic Raincoat ($149) provides lightweight wrinkle-resistant warmth.

• **If you need a suit or sport coat, check for wrinkle resistance.** Roll or knot the suit sleeve. If it still looks good when it is straightened out, it should work well during your trip.

• **Wear either sneakers or walking shoes,** and pack one pair of dressier, but still comfortable, shoes in your carry-on bag.

Examples: SoftWalk shoes for women (888-218-7275, *www.softwalkshoes.com*)...Johnston & Murphy "Signature Comfort System" dress shoes

*Prices subject to change.

for men (800-424-2854, *www.johnstonmurphy. com*).

OTHER ITEMS

• **Buy travel-sized bottles for toiletries,** if you're not staying in a hotel that supplies them. The Container Store sells plastic bottles perfect for small supplies of shampoo, conditioner, body lotion and aftershave.

Cost: 79 cents and up, depending on the size (888-266-8246, *www.containerstore.com*). Small bottles comply with the new US air travel rules, which ban bottles that hold more than three ounces of fluid from carry-on luggage.

Helpful: Magellan's offers compact brushes, curling irons, toothbrushes, etc., that save additional room.

• **Bring paperbacks or magazines**—reading material that you can throw away when you are done.

• **Wear a watch with an alarm if you don't want to rely on a hotel alarm clock.** Or use a cell phone alarm.

How Thieves Steal Carry-On Bags

Don't let crooks grab your carry-on. *Check out their tricks below...*

• **They stage a scene to distract people's attention away from their belongings.**

• **They work in pairs**—one asks for help or offers to help while the other steals a bag or wallet.

• **They sometimes spill something on a passenger** so that they can get close and offer to help with cleanup—and then make the theft.

Self-defense: Keep your carry-on bag completely zipped or fastened closed and in front of you, not at the side or on your back, and not on a cart. If you think that you are being targeted, and there are no security officers nearby, draw attention to yourself so people around you will see what is going on.

C.J. Tolson, editor in chief, *MotorWatch*, Box 123, Butler, Maryland 21023, *www.motorwatch.com*.

Avoid Flight Delays

When traveling to the East Coast, most flight delays are caused by afternoon thunderstorms, so take flights that land by lunchtime. When traveling to the West Coast, the opposite is true—most flight delays are caused by morning fog along the coast, so schedule flights that land in the afternoon or later.

MotorWatch, Box 123, Butler, Maryland 21023, *www. motorwatch.com.*

Tricks for Turning Frequent-Flier Miles into Tickets

Randy Petersen, editor and publisher for *InsideFlyer* in Colorado Springs, *www.insideflyer.com.* He has earned more than 10 million frequent-flier miles and points.

Frequent-flier miles are supposed to earn free tickets for air travelers—but more often, the miles just get them hours on hold waiting for customer service representatives to tell them that no award seats remain on the flights they want. Various obstacles, many of which are set up purposely by the airlines, make converting hard-earned miles into tickets an increasingly frustrating chore.

The airlines finally have begun to respond to the mounting frustration with flashy new on-line tools and updated policies that make miles a little easier to redeem—but only for travelers who are savvy enough to understand their options. *The best strategies to help you turn award miles into flights...*

CHECK WEB SITES

All of the major airlines now offer Web sites that let frequent fliers secure award tickets without waiting on hold for a phone rep. If the date you initially select is sold out, color-coded calendars make it easy to identify alternative dates when tickets are available. (See contact information for individual airlines on the next page.)

Unfortunately, these Web sites do have some limitations...

- **They are not very good at finding alternate itineraries.** If no ticket is available for, say, Los Angeles to Denver on the day you want to fly, the site may not automatically check flights out of other LA area airports, such as Burbank or Ontario (California) International, or flights into Colorado Springs. You would have to try all of the possible combinations yourself.

- **They do not always check for indirect flights,** which would require stops and possibly transfers to different planes along the way, particularly for shorter trips that normally would be direct flights.

- **They will not find available award tickets on all partner airlines.** All of the major airlines have partners, including many foreign partners, but the Web sites won't show you all of their flights even if your frequent-flier miles make you eligible for them.

Examples: Delta, Continental, Northwest or Alaska Airlines miles can be cashed in for tickets on any of those four air carriers—but not through their Web sites.

Solution: A good airline phone rep knows how to handle all of these problems, so it is worth calling if you cannot find the flight you want on-line.

IMPROVING YOUR ODDS

- **Reserve six months in advance.** The best time to try to reserve your frequent-flier ticket is about six months before your travel date, not 331 days (about 11 months) before, as is widely believed. Although you are allowed to book up to 331 days in advance, airlines generally don't load all of the frequent-flier seats into the system that soon. If the award tickets you want are not available when you first call or check on-line, try again every week or two. Approximately one in five frequent fliers alters travel plans after making the initial reservations, putting the seats that were initially reserved back on the market.

- **Call after midnight.** Consider checking on availability when it is shortly after midnight in the time zone from which the flight would be departing. Midnight local time is when tickets that were put on "hold" tend to return to circulation if the transactions are not finalized.

- **Try to fly on Tuesday, Wednesday or Thursday.** That's when your odds of finding a seat improve by 20% to 30%. When your travel schedule is flexible, consider finding frequent-flier award seats before you pick a vacation week.

•**Consider connecting through an alternative airport.** If your travel dates are inflexible and the award tickets you need are not available for departure from any nearby airport, consider expanding your ticket search to include departure from an airport you could fly to for a small amount of cash before you start the award portion of your trip.

Example: You cannot find a frequent-flier ticket for San Francisco to Burlington, Vermont, but one is available from Los Angeles to Burlington. Round-trip flights from San Francisco to Los Angeles are available for less than $100—about $400 less than you would have to pay for the San Francisco to Burlington flight.*

•**Don't bother with a waiting list.** They often don't exist. They're just something customer service reps offer to get unhappy customers off the phone. And while you're waiting for the airline to contact you, you could be missing out on newly available seats.

•**Check out first class.** When tickets are not available for the standard number of frequent-flier miles, do not automatically resort to paying double the number of miles, which airlines often suggest you do because more seats are available at that award level. First check whether a first-class award ticket is available. First-class round-trip award tickets for domestic flights typically cost 40,000 miles—10,000 less than double-miles coach tickets.

•**Split the difference.** "Split-award" redemption is an option on US Airways, Delta and Alaska Airlines. If you can find the frequent-flier seat you need for the standard number of award miles in one direction of your round-trip but not the other, you can opt to spend double miles for half the trip. For a domestic trip, that would mean 12,500 miles one way and 25,000 the other.

MAJOR AIRLINE PROGRAMS

•**American Airlines AAdvantage.** 800-421-0600, *www.aa.com.*

•**Continental Airlines OnePass.** 713-952-1630, *www.continental.com.*

*Prices subject to change.

•**Delta SkyMiles.** 800-323-2323, *www.delta.com.*

•**Northwest Airlines WorldPerks.** 800-447-3757, *www.nwa.com/worldperks.*

•**United Airlines Mileage Plus.** 800-421-4655, *www.united.com.*

•**US Airways.** 800-428-4322, *www.usairways.com.*

SMALLER AIRLINES

These three airlines make lots of seats available to frequent fliers...

•**Alaska Airlines.** 800-252-7522, *www.alaskaair.com/mileageplan.*

•**Frontier Airlines.** 866-263-2759, *www.frontierairlines.com.*

•**Southwest Airlines.** 800-248-4377, *www.southwest.com/rapid_rewards.*

A different type of program...

•**JetBlue TrueBlue.** Instead of award miles, you earn points that range from two points for short flights to six for cross-country flights. For every 100 points, you get a free round-trip domestic flight. 800-JETBLUE, *www.jetblue.com/trueblue.*

Best Way to Use Miles

Airlines are making miles easier to earn—and harder to redeem for tickets. The best way to use frequent-flier miles is to upgrade to first class. In addition to upgrades, miles can be used for hotels or rental cars but can't be easily redeemed for merchandise—several airlines restrict using them for that purpose.

Tim Winship, Los Angeles–based editor-at-large for SmarterTravel.com, and coauthor of *Mileage Pro: The Insider's Guide to Frequent Flyer Programs* (OAG).

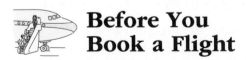 # Before You Book a Flight

Learn whether airfares are likely to go up or down before you book a flight. Farecast.com uses historic pricing data to determine whether an airfare is likely to fluctuate during the coming week, helping you book a flight at a lower fare. The Farecast.com site covers travel to most major US cities.

Another option: If the price of your airline ticket drops, you can obtain a refund or a travel voucher for tickets purchased on-line at the airline's own Web site with the help of Yapta at *www.yapta.com*. Simply type the confirmation number into their free downloadable program and the program will track the fare for you. Or simply forward your e-ticket confirmation e-mail to *flights@yapta.com*. If the price drops, you will get an e-mail with instructions on how to claim a refund from the airline.

How to Get Bumped

If you *want* to get bumped from a flight so you can receive free tickets, cash, upgrades or other incentives, research which airlines seem to bump more often at *airconsumer.ost.dot.gov* (click on "Air Travel Consumer Report"). Arrive early and ask the gate attendant if the flight is overbooked—if it is, put your name on the bump list. Do not check bags—airlines may refuse to bump passengers whose luggage is already on the plane.

Also, try booking the flight for the day before you actually need to get somewhere—then if you are bumped and delayed by a day, you still will arrive on time.

Catch: If your strategy gets you to your destination a day early, be prepared to pay for an extra day's hotel stay.

Nancy Dunnan, editor of *TravelSmart,* Dobbs Ferry, New York 10522, *www.travelsmartnewsletter.com.*

More from Nancy Dunnan...

Air Travel with a Cat or Dog

For better air travel with a cat or dog, put instructions for food and medicine inside the carrier, in case it is misplaced...carry a current photograph of your pet, in case he/she gets lost ...clip the pet's nails, and check that your pet's collar cannot get caught on the carrier...exercise

your pet before leaving for the airport, and do not give food for four to six hours before the flight—except for a small drink of water before flight time...travel on off-peak days, during off-peak hours...and try to take only direct flights—no stops or layovers.

Get the Best Price On a Rental Car

Rental car prices change as often as 20 times a day, with swings as great as 28%. Thanks to the Internet, rental firms repeatedly compare prices charged by competitors and adjust their own prices quickly.

Strategy: Compare prices on Web sites such as Orbitz and Expedia, then check if the rental firm's own site charges less...lock in low rates by making a reservation, then keep checking and rebook if the price goes even lower.

Michael J. Kane, president of the auto-rental consulting company Vehicle Replacement Consulting Group, Inc., in Southfield, Michigan, *www.vrcg.com.* Kane has more than 20 years of experience in the auto-rental and leasing business.

Rental Car Strategy

Don't pay for a car rental upgrade that you can get free. When an auto rental location runs out of vehicles like the one you have reserved, it will usually upgrade your rental to a higher-quality vehicle for free.

Trap: Before doing so, the rental agent may try to talk you into voluntarily paying more for the "better" vehicle without revealing that the one you reserved isn't available—getting you to pay for what you would otherwise get for free.

What to do: When the rental agent offers to rent you a better car than the one you reserved, simply say no. You are likely to get the better car anyway.

Internet ScamBusters, Boone, North Carolina, *www.scambusters.org.*

How to Stay Well On Vacation

Charles B. Inlander, a consumer advocate and health-care consultant located in Fogelsville, Pennsylvania. He was the founding president of the nonprofit People's Medical Society, the consumer advocacy organization credited with key improvements in the quality of US health care in the 1980s and 1990s, and is the author of 20 books, including *Take This Book to the Hospital with You: A Consumer Guide to Surviving Your Hospital Stay* (St. Martin's).

I'm always so amazed when people devote hours and hours to planning their itineraries for vacations, while virtually ignoring any special measures for ensuring their health while they are away. Whether you are traveling to an exotic foreign destination, taking a family cruise or simply spending a few weeks at the seashore, *here's what you need to know to protect yourself —and your family...*

•**Plan for your health before you go.** Pre-trip planning—as far ahead as possible—is crucial. If you are going overseas, for example, you may need vaccinations and preventive medications. To find out what shots and medicines are recommended, check the Web site of the Centers for Disease Control and Prevention (CDC) at *www.cdc.gov/travel/*. Regardless of where you are traveling—even if it's in Canada or Europe—check this Web site.

Important: Don't wait until the last minute. Antimalarial drugs, if needed, should be started three to four weeks before your trip, and some shots, such as those for hepatitis B, should be started about six months in advance.

•**Pack up your medications.** The Transportation Security Administration now recommends that all prescription and over-the-counter (OTC) medications be kept in their original dispensers to help with the airport screening process. Also, pack everyday OTC health products that you may take for granted at home but that may not be easy to find if you get sick while abroad or even in a remote rural area of the US. This includes medications like Pepto Bismol or Imodium AD for diarrhea, contact lens supplies and any other medicines your doctor might recommend.

•**Use precautions on the way.** Airplanes, which are often packed with runny-nosed kids and coughing adults, are prime areas for contracting an illness. But don't blame the airplane air. Studies have shown that the filters airlines use are terrific at weeding out viruses and other germs in the air. The problem is what you touch! Passing a cup, reaching for the handle in the airplane bathroom or touching the traytop at your seat can expose you to a multitude of germs. Wash your hands often, carry antibacterial wipes when you don't have access to soap, and keep your hands away from your mouth, nose and eyes. By taking these steps, you will dramatically lower your chances of getting sick. Follow these same strategies on cruise ships.

•**Staying healthy when you are there.** Jet lag is the number-one complaint among international (and even long-haul domestic) travelers. Take it easy for the first few days at your destination. Your body is still operating on its normal schedule. Also, watch what you eat when traveling, even here in the US, because sometimes food you're not accustomed to can cause gastrointestinal upset. And pack light. One of the most common travel injuries is "traveler's back," a painful condition caused from hauling heavy suitcases and other travel bags. Finally, bring a list of your medical conditions and medications in case you need medical attention while you are away. Major hotel chains and travel agencies usually can provide a list of qualified physicians and hospitals available in the local area.

Help for Motion Sickness

To prevent motion sickness, take 1,000 milligrams (mg) of powdered gingerroot 30 to 60 minutes before your trip. If you still feel sick, pop another 500 mg every two to four hours.

Caution: Don't use gingerroot if you are taking a blood thinner, such as warfarin.

Also: Sit in the front seat of a vehicle, open the window to get fresh air and don't read while riding in a vehicle.

If you start to feel nauseated: Apply pressure to your wrist, just three finger-widths above your inner wrist, between the two tendons…or wear a wristband designed to put pressure on that spot. Queaz-Away or Sea-Band wristbands are available at drugstores and cost $10.* Or take an over-the-counter remedy, such as Dramamine II, Bonine or Marezine—these are the ones least likely to make you drowsy.

Health, 2100 Lakeshore Dr., Birmingham, Alabama 35209, *www.health.com*.

*Price subject to change.

Beach Alert

Bacteria levels at some beaches exceed EPA standards as much as 30% of the time.

Among them: Avalon Beach, Catalina Island, CA…Cook's Brook, Eastham, MA.

Self-defense: Most polluted beaches are near clean ones.

Examples: Pebbly Beach instead of Avalon…and Coast Guard Beach instead of Cook's Brook.

Go to *www.epa.gov/beaches* for information on your favorite beach.

The Wall Street Journal, 200 Liberty St., New York City 10281, *online.wsj.com*.

How to Handle A Rip Current

If you are caught up in a rip current—a fast-moving channel of water flowing away from shore—don't swim against the current. Instead, swim parallel to the shoreline to escape the current. If that doesn't work, tread water until the current weakens, then swim back to shore. Rip currents are responsible for more than 80% of lifeguard rescues at beaches. Signs of a rip current include a change in water color…a channel

of churning, choppy water…a line of foam, seaweed or debris moving seaward…or a break in the incoming wave pattern.

US Lifesaving Association, *www.usla.org*.

Rules of the Road Outside the US

Traffic accidents are the largest cause of non-natural death among US citizens abroad.

Important tips: Do not hesitate to use the horn—it can sound a warning and prevent an accident…many countries do not permit a right turn on red lights…traffic circles are common outside the US—be sure you know how to enter and leave them.

Helpful: The US Department of State's "Road Safety Overseas" Web page (*http://travel.state.gov/travel/tips/safety/safety_1179.html*) features links to information on specific countries, an explanation of how to obtain an international driver's license, insurance coverage information, etc.

Betsy L. Anderson, senior consular official, US Department of State, Washington, DC.

Live Like the Locals

Get the real flavor of places you visit through VIAmigo.com. This site connects travelers with personal tour guides—some professional, some amateur—who have knowledge that goes beyond typical tourist spots and can help travelers experience an area as local residents do. The site provides ways to contact guides and includes ratings by other travelers who have gone on adventures with them. There are numerous categories, from wine and walking tours to history, bird-watching and safaris. The site is free for travelers.

15

Just for Fun

How to Throw a Wonderful Party

Big celebrations can be very expensive today. The average wedding in America can come to about $28,700 now, according to wedding trend tracker The Wedding Report Inc. But cheer up. Costs can be trimmed by thousands of dollars without drastically compromising the quality of any big celebration.

INVITATIONS

• **Skip the colored paper.** Dark-hued invitations must be engraved, but ivory or cream-colored paper can be printed using much less expensive processes, such as thermography. The paler versions can save you about $2 per invitation.* If you want to add some color, tie a piece of ribbon on each invitation.

• **Avoid overweight and oversized invitations.** They cost more to buy and to mail, add-

*Prices subject to change.

ing another dollar or more per invitation. For well-made yet reasonably priced stationery, try the brands William Arthur (800-985-6581, *www.williamarthur.com*) or Crane & Co. (800-268-2281, *www.crane.com*).

FLOWERS

• **Stay in season.** Flower expenses are highest when people choose flowers that aren't in bloom on the date of their event, meaning that the flowers must be grown in greenhouses or flown in from overseas. A local florist or garden shop can point you to appropriate flowers for the region. This should save you 10% or more on the cost of your floral arrangements—which could mean a savings of $20 or more per centerpiece or bouquet.

Consider renting potted plants from a local nursery rather than buying flowers. Some nurseries rent out trees, shrubs and other plants for as little as 25% of their retail price, though there

Christa Vagnozzi, senior weddings editor of TheKnot.com, New York City, which offers a magazine called *The Knot* and a Web site that provides advice and lists of local resources to help plan weddings.

245

might be an additional hourly labor charge if delivery and setup are required. Or order flowers wholesale from a local garden center or on-line merchant, and ask a friend who is good at decorating to arrange them.

GrowersBox.com offers packages for as little as $155. The $155 package includes 100 roses, baby's breath, tree fern and lily grass.

Most of the plants and flowers might already be in place if you hold a wedding ceremony in a garden or a church around Christmas. Do not schedule a wedding for the week of Valentine's Day or Mother's Day, when flower prices peak. (If this can't be avoided, at least skip the roses, which get jacked way up in price.)

Helpful: Ask the bridesmaids to arrange their bouquets on the cake table after the ceremony to take full advantage of these flowers.

RECEPTION SITE

• **In many locales, you can get a discounted rate by scheduling for any time other than Saturday...**or for any month other than June, July, August, September or October. That could save you between $1,000 and $5,000.

• **If you're a member of a country club or alumni club, you might qualify for an attractive rate** on a meeting hall that could serve as a reception room. Also, investigate city- and state-run rentals. There might be a beautiful historic building that can be rented for a low price.

• **In many cities and towns, marriages can be held in public parks for free,** but try to make sure a noisy sporting event or concert isn't scheduled nearby for the same day by avoiding Saturday and Sunday afternoons and holidays.

MUSIC

A DJ can cost $500 to $5,000...a band, $2,000 to $10,000. Today, many people program their own iPods and hook them up to the reception hall's speaker system. They get the songs they want and don't pay an extra charge.

Important: Make sure that your iPod can be connected to your speaker system and that it sounds good. Or rent a speaker system that does connect or bring your stereo from home. Enlist a tech-savvy friend to take charge of the iPod at the event so that you don't have to worry about music matters.

246

FOOD AND DRINK

• **Save by providing pasta or chicken dishes rather than lobster, salmon, shrimp or filet mignon.** A sit-down dinner with a chicken entrée (plus the service charge, tax and gratuity) could run $150 per person. The more expensive dishes can run as high as $200 to $300 per person. Or skip a sit-down meal entirely in favor of simple hors d'oeuvres—spring rolls, stuffed pastries, etc.—and you could keep your food costs to less than $100 per guest, as long as the reception lasts no longer than four hours.

Exception: The savings opportunity might not apply if your reception hall includes the cost of a sit-down meal in the basic price.

• **Offer wine, draft beer and pitchers of a single favorite cocktail** instead of a full bar to save $10 to $20 per guest.

• **Save on wedding cake.** Even if your guest list is long, you don't need a huge wedding cake, which could cost thousands of dollars. Order a modest wedding cake that will look magnificent on display—and a large sheet cake or two with similar icing, cake and filling.

Wedding cakes are most often priced according to the number of servings and depend on the design and options you choose. On average, the wedding cake costs $2 to $3 per serving, though more elaborate cakes could cost as much as $30 per serving. A half sheet cake, on the other hand, costs around $95 and serves approximately 70 people. Your caterer can slice up the sheet cake in the kitchen and distribute the pieces mixed in with pieces of your fancy cake. Your guests may never know that most of them are eating sheet cake, and you will save about 20%—potentially $200 to $1,400.

PHOTOGRAPHER

• **Hire a photographer for only part of the day,** and you will save a few hundred dollars. Six hours should be enough to get pictures of a wedding ceremony and the beginning of the reception. You don't really need pictures of anything that happens after that.

Example: Nationwide wedding photography company Bella Pictures (888-556-7590 or *www. bellapictures.com*) charges as little as $1,950 plus tax for half-day wedding packages that include six hours of a photographer's time, a wedding album and the rights to reproduce your photos. The comparable eight-hour package costs $2,200 and includes unlimited pictures. All packages include digital negatives, on-line image editing and a personal photography consultant.

• **Keep the prints simple.** Sepia tones, multiple exposures and split frames drive up cost.

LIMOUSINE

• **If you want a limousine, hire one for a single trip,** perhaps the ride to the wedding ceremony or from the ceremony to the reception. That way, your driver won't spend hours in a parking lot, getting paid to do nothing. Limo company full-day wedding packages can cost thousands, but you often can hire a limo for one quick trip for $200 or less.

Party Entertainment On a Budget

For less expensive party entertainment, phone music schools for the names of students and ensembles available for parties. Many offer almost professional-level playing for a fraction of the cost of full-time musicians. Review a performance tape, and get references before agreeing to hire anyone.

Money, Time-Life Bldg., Rockefeller Center, New York City 10020, *money.cnn.com.*

Shy at Parties? Strategies That Let You Join In

Susan RoAne, best-selling author of *How to Work a Room: Your Essential Guide to Savvy Socializing* (Collins). She is a keynote speaker and communications coach in the San Francisco Bay Area, *www.susanroane.com.*

Shyness can interfere with our enjoyment of life and also limit our advancement in the workplace. This is an astonishingly common problem—93% of Americans identify themselves as shy in some or all situations. *Here's how to get past shyness at parties, business gatherings and other social events...*

• **Research the guest list.** Prior to a business event, ask the host who else will be attending. If the names are unfamiliar to you, research them on-line through a Google search or their companies' Web sites. The more you know about all your fellow guests, the less they will seem like strangers and the easier it will be to strike up a conversation.

• **Collect three offbeat news stories before any social gathering.** Scan past big headlines to compelling smaller stories that other people might have missed. These make great conversation fodder when you don't know what to say.

• **Recognize your social strengths.** Shy individuals tend to assume that no one wants to speak with them. The reality is that shy people make great conversation partners in social settings. Unlike "life of the party" types, shy people actually listen during conversations, and they do not scan the room while talking to a conversation partner.

• **Dress appropriately.** Shy people generally become even less comfortable when their clothing does not match that of others present. If you are not sure what to wear to a gathering, phone the host and ask...or wear an outfit that can be adjusted for the occasion, perhaps by removing a tie or jacket or adding a necklace or scarf.

• **Arrive on time.** When you arrive late to social gatherings, everyone else already is in a group, making it more difficult to join in. It is easier to arrive on time and position yourself near the door or bar, where you can easily start up conversations with other early arrivers before groups form.

• **Learn how to identify other shy people.** When shy people enter crowded rooms and no one invites them over, they tend to assume that everyone else is aloof and uninterested in conversing with them.

In truth, people who appear aloof usually are shy themselves. These people would probably love it if you walked up to them and started a conversation.

• **Point yourself toward the most animated group.** It is difficult to simply walk up to a group of people you do not know and join in their conversation. To minimize the chance of awkwardness, select the group that is doing the most talking and laughing. People tend to be at their most open and inviting when they are enjoying themselves.

Stand on the periphery of this group, and when there is a break in the conversation, ask, "Mind if I join you?" You will never be turned down. If you feel you must explain your presence, add, "This group looks like it's having the most fun."

Helpful: In general, it is not advisable to attempt to join groups of two. You might be butting in on a private conversation.

Important: For extreme shyness—that is, if your pulse races and you become drenched in sweat at the very thought of attending any party...or if social fear causes you to avoid virtually all interaction with strangers—seek professional counseling.

How to Rent the Good Life

Clayton Clavette, owner of Lavish Living LLC, an online listing service that brings together owners of more than 1,000 luxury assets—such as mansions, yachts, aircraft and automobiles—with people looking to rent them. He resides in Miami Beach, Florida. His Web site is *www.lavishliving.com*.

If you want to get a taste of the trendy, lavish or exotic without busting your budget, you can rent ritzy items for a day or a month at a time.

AUTOMOBILES

People rent luxury cars for anniversaries and birthdays...special trips...and business events.

Example: Gotham Dream Cars, which operates in the Northeast and in southern Florida, offers daily and weekly rates.

Details: An Aston Martin Vanquish Phantom, which sells for $230,000, rents for $1,450 a day during weekdays*...a Porsche 911 GT3, priced at $116,000, rents for $895. Delivery and pickup are available to and from your door or any area

*Prices subject to change.

airport. 877-2-GOTHAM, *www.gothamdreamcars.com*.

For a directory of exotic and sports car rental companies across the US, go to *www.exoticcarrental.com* or *www.bnm.com*.

HANDBAGS

For a special event, you might want to rent a high-end handbag, such as the latest one from Louis Vuitton, Prada, Fendi or Jimmy Choo. Bag Borrow Or Steal lets you keep the rental for one week to one year with an option to buy.

Details: Weekly rental charges for members range from $15 to $150. Membership fees start at $9.95 per month, or $59.95 per year. Round-trip shipping charges start at $9.95. 866-922-2267, *www.bagborroworsteal.com*.

JEWELRY

Why buy expensive jewels to wear them only on special occasions? Borrowed Bling rents out all kinds of jeweled accessories that would typically cost from $100 to several thousand dollars.

Details: For a membership fee of $29.95 per month (three-month minimum), you could pick out and hold on to two items at a time from a restricted selection for up to four months. For $49.95 or $99.95 a month, you can choose from a wider selection. You pay a round-trip shipping fee of $9.99 each time items are sent. 877-672-7978, *www.borrowedbling.com*.

ART

You can rent artwork by famous or up-and-coming artists from museums and galleries.

Example: Los Angeles County Museum of Art provides paintings, prints and photographs from southern California–based artists for three months, after which the rental can be renewed.

Details: $17 to $149 a month. You must be a member of the museum to rent. 323-857-6500, *www.lacma.org/info/arsg.aspx*.

Other examples of museums and galleries providing rental programs include Agora Gallery in New York City (212-226-4151, *agora-gallery.com*) ...Larsen Gallery in Scottsdale, Arizona (480-941-0900, *www.larsengallery.com*)...Portland Museum of Art in Portland, Oregon (503-226-2811, *www.portlandartmuseum.org*)...and the San Francisco Museum of Modern Art (415-357-4000, *www.sfmoma.org*).

Additional resources: Check your phone book or on-line for galleries and museums in your area.

INSURANCE NOTE

In some cases, your homeowner's or auto insurance policy will cover a luxury item rental, at least in part. If not, ask about adding a rider to your existing policy. You also can get insurance from most of the rental companies, typically for less than 5% of the rental fee.

Buying Tickets to Sold-Out Events... And Selling Tickets You Don't Need

Alfred Branch, Jr., news editor of TicketNews.com, a ticket industry news resource, Vernon, Connecticut.

S old-out programs have become increasingly common in recent times, triggering frustration for those seeking tickets to concerts, shows or sporting events.

Fortunately, the secondary market for tickets is safer than in the past. Traditional back-alley scalpers have been largely replaced by Internet-based ticket-resale organizations and Web sites where you can resell tickets.

Expect tickets for the hottest shows and events to trade for several times their face value, while less popular events might trade at a more modest premium or no premium at all.

Caution: Scalping laws have been relaxed in recent years as state governments bow to the reality that they have little power to prevent Internet transactions. Still, it remains illegal in most states to resell tickets near the venue where the event will take place, particularly for more than face value, and some states even restrict how a ticket can be resold over the Internet. To learn more about ticket-resale laws in your state, consult your state attorney general's office...or click on your state's name on eBay's ticket sales rules page at *http://pages.ebay.com/buyselltickets/rules. html.*

BUYING TICKETS

The largest of Internet ticket resellers include StubHub.com (it's now owned by eBay, 866-788-2482)...TicketsPlus.com (800-444-7464)...Tickets Now.com (800-927-2770)...Ticket Exchange (part of TicketMaster, phone number varies by state, *www.ticketmaster.com/ticketexchangehome*)... and RazorGator.com (800-542-4466).

Prices on comparable tickets can vary significantly among all these resale sites, so comparison-shop all five. There are other, smaller ticket brokers as well, but make sure that any site you use is a member of the National Association of Ticket Brokers (*www.NATB.org*). NATB members offer customers a money-back guarantee should something go wrong.

For sporting events, check the team's Web site. Some teams have set up exchanges where season-ticket holders can sell tickets they are not using.

Tickets often are sold through eBay.com and Craigslist.org as well. It sometimes is possible to locate attractive ticket prices on these sites, but you'll likely be buying from an individual. That means counterfeit tickets and other scams are a bit more likely.

On rare occasions, a very small number of last-minute tickets might be available to sold-out events at the arena or stadium ticket window on the day of the event. This is most likely to work if you require only a single seat, not two seats together.

SELLING YOUR TICKETS

Sell unneeded tickets on any of the major Internet ticket reseller sites listed above. You can also try to sell them on eBay.com or Craigslist. org. Look up how much the major ticket broker Web sites are charging for similar seats, then set your eBay "Buy It Now" price or Craigslist asking price at least 10% lower.

Make sure your auction ends a week or more before the event date so that you have time to mail the tickets to the winning bidder.

If you have no buyers after several days, recheck the prices on ticket broker sites. If ticket prices have decreased, you might need to lower your price.

Some sports teams indicate additional restrictions that govern how ticket holders can resell their seats. Season-ticket holders caught breaking these rules might lose their chance to buy tickets in future years. Check a team's Web site for rules.

The Best Casinos You Never Heard Of

Steve Bourie, a Florida-based gambling expert who has studied American casinos for more than 20 years. His latest book is *American Casino Guide: 2008 Edition* (Casino Vacations).

When you go to a casino, there's more than one way to win. Of course, it is great to get four of a kind in a poker game or hit the jackpot at the slots. But you can also win by just having a great time—eating good food, relaxing in the spa or catching a show by a performer you've always wanted to see.

It's unfortunate, but people are usually disappointed by a casino for one reason—their expectations aren't met. They want to gamble, but choose a casino where the odds are poor. Or they want to play golf while their spouse plays the slots...only to go to a casino without a good golf course.

Solution: Don't go to a casino without finding out what it has to offer. Speak with people who have recently been there. Visit the casino's Web site, and read publications with information about what casinos offer. One of the best is Casino Player (800-969-0711, *www.casinoplayer. com*, 12 issues, $27.95/yr.*). Their free directory of casinos is available on-line.

My Web site, *www.americancasinoguide.com*, can also be helpful. It invites people to report on what they like and dislike about casinos and lets Web browsers view these comments (at no charge).

The best casinos have...

● **Games with odds that give players a comparatively good chance of winning.**

Example: Slot machines that pay back an average of 94 cents for every dollar you play, compared with some casinos' machines that pay back only 89 cents.

*Prices and rates subject to change.

● **Attractions,** such as gourmet dining, spas, first-class entertainment, golf courses and interesting boutiques and other worthwhile shopping opportunities. Also important are high-quality hotel rooms and service.

Best of all: Casinos that have combinations of these attributes.

THE BEST ODDS

If you like to gamble, be aware that the slot machines and blackjack are two popular games where your chances of winning can vary substantially from casino to casino. Slot machines with the best odds are usually found in Las Vegas, but a few blocks from the famous Strip.

Example: Casinos on the Strip pay back an average of 93.3 cents for every dollar you put in a slot machine. Not far away, the casinos on Boulder Highway pay back an average of 94.87 cents.

The disparity does not seem large, but even a small advantage gives you a chance at more wins, which will make a casino weekend much more fun.

Your chances of winning at blackjack can depend heavily on the number of decks that the dealer uses. In Reno, Nevada, for instance, some casinos still have single-deck blackjack. Given identical rules and payoffs, single-deck blackjack always has a lower casino advantage than a multiple-deck game. In Atlantic City, eight-deck blackjack is the norm.

THE TOP SEVEN

The casinos listed here all provide excellent room accommodations, service, amenities, dining and entertainment...

● **Barona Valley Ranch and Casino,** Lakeside, California (619-443-2300 or 888-722-7662, *www.barona.com*). Located just outside of San Diego and owned by the Barona Band of Mission Indians, the casino is great for anyone who enjoys blackjack.

Reason: At the Barona, you'll win $7.50 for each $5 you bet in single-deck blackjack, compared with only $6 for every $5 at many other casinos.

The casino also offers offtrack betting. The entertainment typically consists of blues, salsa or soft rock. At the hotel, rooms are luxurious.

Rates: Moderate.

•**Borgata Hotel Casino and Spa,** Atlantic City (609-317-1000 or *www.theborgata.com*). The four-year-old Borgata is very luxurious and large. It offers about 2,000 hotel rooms, 4,100 slot machines, 200 table games, an 85-table poker room and a 54,000-square-foot spa. Among the 13 restaurants is the Wolfgang Puck American Grille that features a large lounge and bar as well as a dining room and its legendary California chef.

The casino is the only one in Atlantic City that uses six-deck blackjack exclusively, giving players an advantage they wouldn't have at other casinos in the city, where eight decks are the norm.

Rates: Expensive.

•**Boulder Station Hotel & Casino,** Las Vegas (702-432-7777, 800-683-7777, *www.boulderstation. com*). Slot machines along the Boulder Highway, including Boulder Station, boast the highest average payback in Las Vegas at 94.87%. The casino has an 11-screen movie theater, five restaurants and hotel rooms for the physically impaired. Entertainers often include groups that play rock and other music from the 1960s and 1970s.

Rates: Budget.

•**Casino Queen,** East St. Louis, Illinois (800-777-0777, *www.casinoqueen.com*). Just across the Mississippi River from the famous St. Louis Gateway Arch, Casino Queen is a new facility, replacing the popular but smaller riverboat version.

Casino Queen's blackjack games give players advantages they don't have at most other Midwest casinos because the dealer stands on "soft 17" (ace-six)—meaning that the dealer does not draw another card if his or her hand includes an ace and it can be counted as 7 or 17.

The casino is also one of the few with an RV park.

Rates: Budget.

•**Foxwoods Resort Casino,** Mashantucket, Connecticut (800-369-7777, 800-369-9663, *www. foxwoods.com*). Owned by the Mashantucket Pequot Tribal Nation, Foxwoods is now the world's largest casino and has so many attractions that even if you do not like gambling, there's plenty of places to have fun. You can play golf, shop for designer-label clothing or spend some time at the spa.

Foxwoods offers a huge range of games, including blackjack, craps, roulette, baccarat, bingo,

keno and several varieties of poker. And if you can't get enough action at the tables, Foxwoods also lets you bet on horses, greyhounds and jai-alai.

Rates: Moderate.

•**Silver Legacy Resort Casino,** Reno (800-687-8733, *www.silverlegacyreno.com*). The resort offers games with especially attractive odds.

Example: If you get four of a kind at the casino's "full-pay, deuces-wild" video poker, you will win five coins for each coin that you bet, compared with four coins for each coin at most other casinos.

Restaurants offer a wide variety of food, including a buffet with Chinese, Mexican and Italian dishes.

Rates: Budget.

•**Trump Plaza,** Atlantic City (609-441-6000, *www.trumpplaza.com*). The world-famous casino offers a large variety of games, including some that other casinos do not offer, such as Pai Gow Poker (a variation on a Chinese domino game) and All American Video Poker. This game, found mainly in the Midwest, has a theoretical return of more than 100%. That means if you play perfectly—which very, very few people ever do—you have a chance of beating the house.

Trump Plaza has luxurious beach facilities, including a swimming pool, spa and bar. Inside are cocktail lounges and three high-quality dining rooms. One of them, Roberto's, is an Italian restaurant that overlooks the ocean.

Rates: Expensive.

Tricks to Winning Sweepstakes

Jay Sokolow, MD, who practices diagnostic radiology in New Haven, Connecticut. He has entered more than a half-million contests and sweepstakes since he was a teenager and has won about 2,000 prizes. The items he doesn't keep, he gives away to family members, friends and charities.

The Internet has revolutionized the sweepstakes world, allowing people to share tips, enter more contests and win prizes more frequently. Radiologist Jay Sokolow, MD, has taken full advantage of this great Internet windfall. In his spare time, Dr. Sokolow, enters thousands of Internet contests a month. He gets great satisfaction from beating the odds, as evidenced by the constant stream of prizes delivered to his home.

Over the years, he has won Super Bowl tickets, iPods, Dell computers, Nokia cell phones, Caribbean vacations, a golf holiday in Scotland and a white-water rafting vacation. He won one daily contest so many times that the sponsors decided to institute a once-a-month win restriction that they now frequently refer to as the "Jay Sokolow Law."

Here, Dr. Sokolow reveals the secrets to his sweepstakes success...

CONTESTS TO ENTER

To boost my chances of winning, I make a point to enter contests that...

● **Offer many consolation prizes in addition to a grand prize.**

Example: Procter & Gamble, through one of its Web sites offered one grand prize, worth $145,600, that included first-class travel for the winner and three friends to the Super Bowl. The odds of winning that were slim, but there were five first prizes (attending a single NFL home game of your choice with one guest, worth $3,900) and 24 second prizes (a $100 gift certificate to *www.nflshop.com*).

● **Have short entry periods of no longer than a few weeks.**

Reason: The longer a sweepstake is available, the more people find and enter it.

● **Are restricted in some way,** such as to a certain state or even a specific store.

Example: Sweepstakes sponsored by wineries or breweries often avoid states with strict restrictions regarding liquor-related contests, such as California and Tennessee. That will eliminate a lot of potential contestants.

● **I've already won.** When I win a contest, that often means the Web site isn't getting much traffic, which improves my chances of winning again.

Example: I've won the football trivia contest at *www.nflplayers.com/games/main.aspx* numerous times.

CONTESTS TO AVOID

I don't bother with contests that...

● **Have so many contestants that the odds of winning are astronomical.**

Example: I ignore the Publishers Clearing House Sweepstakes and the contests that credit card companies promote around holidays.

● **Require a lot of work,** such as filling out a survey or clipping UPC codes off boxes. I like to enter sweepstakes when I am talking on the phone or watching sports on TV, so they can't be too labor-intensive.

● **Are heavily advertised.** If I keep seeing a contest in newspapers and hearing about it on TV and radio, I know that the number of entries will be staggering.

WINNING STRATEGIES

Once you have selected the sweepstakes to enter, here is how to improve your chances of winning...

● **Submit multiple entry forms.** Most sweepstakes allow different people from the same address to enter.

Example: I quadrupled my chances of winning the huge sweepstakes at *www.nationalgeographic.com/conquer* by entering my name, my wife's and my two children's. (My kids are 16 and 18 years old—always check contest rules on age restrictions.) First prize was a trip for two with a National Geographic expert to either Alaska, Belize or the Galapagos islands ($17,500). There were also 85 secondary prizes, including books and snorkel sets.

● **Automate the process.** Most sites require you to provide basic information, such as your e-mail address, birthday, phone numbers and home address. But typing this into entry forms again and again is very time-consuming, so I use the function on the Web browser Safari (for Macintosh) that automatically fills out standard entry forms with one simple click of my mouse. This allows me to enter as many as 100 on-line sweepstakes in an hour.

252

Google includes a similar program on its free toolbar at toolbar.google.com. Internet Explorer also has an "autofill" option.

•**Always read the rules.** Sweepstakes disqualify entries that vary from their guidelines.

Common mistakes: You're ineligible to win because of location or demographic restrictions …you enter too early or too late…your address is incomplete, or it's a PO box, which many contests won't accept.

•**Set up a separate e-mail address exclusively for sweepstakes** entries at a free site, such as Gmail.com, Yahoo.com or Hotmail.com. While different sweepstakes offer different degrees of privacy, you're still going to be deluged with junk e-mail.

Smart: When you enter an on-line contest, read the entry form carefully. Uncheck any boxes that give your consent to be contacted by a third party, advertisers, licensees or partners.

•**Keep records for taxes.** You are expected to report any sweepstakes winnings to the IRS if the amount you win is a total of $600 or more—but you don't have to list the sweepstake sponsor's estimated value of your prize. You are allowed to make a fair-market adjustment.

Example: I won an iPod that the sweepstakes sponsor valued at $300, but I found an ad for the same iPod for $215. I kept the ad and used the lower figure on my tax forms.

•**Follow the requirements exactly when you claim your prize.** Otherwise, your win can be invalidated. Typically, you must fill out an affidavit and mail it back within 14 days from the date on the win-notification letter.

Caution: A legitimate sweepstakes will never ask for credit card information or require paying any taxes or shipping charges as a condition of claiming your prize. You may need to provide your Social Security number. If you're not sure if the request is legitimate, call the company that is sponsoring the contest.

FAVORITE SITES FOR SWEEPSTAKES

•**Sweepsadvantage.com.** The Web's largest sweepstakes directory. Contests are divided into daily, weekly, monthly and one-time categories. Free.

•**Sweepstakestoday.com.** In addition to contest listings, this site provides a popular forum where sweepstakes players can pose questions, exchange tips, etc. Free.

•**Bestsweepstakes.com,** publishes a 12-page newsletter that recommends sweepstakes, such as those offering the best odds. 12 issues. $27.50/yr.* Free three-day trial subscription. Best Publications, 763-537-4037.

*Price subject to change.

Golf Course Discounts

For discounts at golf courses, go to TeeTimes America.com, which offers from 10% to 40% off on last-minute reservations,* primarily in the southern and western regions of the country… LastMinuteGolfer.com offers discounts on your next-day reservations, available at hundreds of courses, mainly in the central and eastern US… Click4TeeTimes.com offers various discounts for southern California golf courses.

Arthur Frommer's Budget Travel, 530 Seventh Ave., New York City 10018, *www.frommers.com*.

*Rates subject to change.

Easy Way to Become A Better Putter

Improve your putting game with weights. It makes sense that golfers will be able to hit the ball farther after they increase their strength by weight training. But a recent study that confirmed this fact found that they become better putters as well.

Finding: Putting distance control improved 30% for male golfers who participated in an 11-week supervised strength, power and flexibility training program.

Maj. Brandon K. Doan, PhD, The Human Performance Laboratory, Air Force Academy, Colorado.

Vegetables Anyone Can Grow

Eric Morgan, collections manager for Bartlett Arboretum & Gardens in Stamford, Connecticut, *www.bartlettar boretum.org*. The 91-acre facility includes a 3,000-square-foot vegetable garden.

Y ou don't need a green thumb to successfully grow these vegetables. Just provide lots of sun and water regularly (mulch can help retain moisture). Any of these can be grown in containers.

• **Roma tomato.** Romas have few seeds, taste good and are great sliced or in a tomato sauce. Their above-average resistance to disease makes them easier to grow than other tomatoes. Roma tomatoes benefit from a light, phosphorus-rich fertilizer, such as 5-10-5 (5% nitrogen, 10% phosphorus and 5% potassium)—follow directions on the label. Purchase young plants at the local garden store, and plant them after the last frost.

• **Boston or Bibb lettuce (also known as butterhead lettuce).** Boston lettuce and the slightly smaller Bibb lettuce have looser, softer leaves and a butterier flavor than iceberg lettuce, and they are easier to grow. Plant the seeds one-quarter inch deep and five to seven inches apart at any time after the last frost, then water every other day. In six to eight weeks, you'll have lettuce. Lettuce likes sun but will tolerate some shade.

• **Classic or Ichiban eggplant.** Classic eggplants are the large, dark purple variety. Ichiban are long and slender and appropriate for grilling or stir-frying. Both varieties produce significantly more fruits per plant than other eggplant varieties. Eggplants benefit from 5-10-5 fertilization every two weeks. Space young eggplant plants two feet apart in the garden.

• **Kirby cucumber.** These small cucumbers often are used for pickling, but they taste fine in salads and other recipes. Kirby cucumbers are more manageable than other cucumber varieties and need to be spaced only 2.5 to three feet apart. Other cucumbers can grow into sprawling vines that can envelop a garden. Cucumbers can be planted as seed in late April or in May (after

the last frost), one-quarter inch deep. They don't require fertilizer except in the poorest of soil.

• **Green zucchini.** There isn't a huge difference among zucchini varieties, but green zucchini does tend to produce the most fruit. Seeds can be planted in April or May (after the last frost). Space them two to 2.5 feet apart so they have room to grow, and bury the seeds one-quarter inch deep. Zucchini benefit from fertilization (5-10-5) every two weeks.

Free Audiobooks

F or free audiobooks, go to LibriVox.org.* You can download classic adult and children's books, short stories and poems to your iPod or burn them onto a CD. Titles include *Pride and Prejudice…A Little Princess…*and *The Call of the Wild*. All titles are in the public domain and are read by volunteers.

*Offer subject to change.

Find a Book Club You Love—or Start One

Bottom Line/Retirement interviewed Norman Hicks, executive director of Reader's Circle, a nonprofit organization located in Gardena, California, that helps people connect with reading groups and assists those who want to start their own book clubs, *www.readerscircle.org*.

W here can you experience the pleasure of exchanging views and thoughts with people who are genuinely interested in hearing what you have to say? And where can you socialize without feeling that you have to impress people, as you often do at parties and other gatherings?

Book clubs can be the answer. And despite today's often-hectic lifestyle, book clubs are burgeoning throughout the country.

Usually with fewer than one dozen members, book clubs are essentially smallish groups of friends (or friends-to-be) who all read the same books and meet periodically to discuss them. While the elements of book clubs—also called reading groups—are simple, the benefits can be far-reaching. *Members are attracted by the opportunity to...*

- **Discover and talk about new ideas.**
- **Meet new people,** including authors who increasingly speak to even small groups.
- **Talk about important topics** with people who are genuinely interested in them. Today, television seems to set the agenda for many topics people discuss—and it's not always an impressive list—talent contests, celebrity scandals, bargain shopping, etc.

At a book club, you can talk about subjects that spark your curiosity or even your passion. Like events in real life, the ideas presented in books—both serious and humorous—often inspire readers to make changes in their lives. By discussing these books, you often gain valuable perspectives on these ideas.

HOW TO FIND A CLUB

Local bookstores almost always have names of people who head book groups or who are members. Other good information sources are public libraries, local chapters of alumni associations, religious groups and social clubs.

Several Web sites also have information about book clubs—including the site of my own organization, Reader's Circle, at *www.readerscircle. org*—the area where members live, the types of books that they read and how to contact them, usually by e-mail and/or telephone.

Helpful Web sites: Reading Group Choices at *www.readinggroupchoices.com...*Reading Group Guides, *www.readinggroupguides.com...* The Book Report Network, *www.tbrnetwork.com* ...Meetup, *www.meetup.com...*The Great Books Foundation, *www.greatbooks.org.*

Most book clubs fall into one of two categories—those that concentrate on a specific genre, such as mysteries, and those that are more mainstream that generate general discussion and socializing. When you contact a club, find out if it's the type of club that will hold your interest.

Clubs you contact may invite you to sit in on a meeting or two. That gives you and club members a chance to see if everyone is compatible in discussions and interested in the same type of books. Don't be surprised, however, if a club you contact doesn't currently have room for new members, in which case you may be put on a waiting list.

HOW TO START A CLUB

Book clubs are informal groups in which the members make their own rules as to the size of the club, books to read and the schedule of meetings.

How many members? There's no single ideal size for clubs, but experience shows that those with the greatest longevity are relatively small—usually from four to eight members who are interested in the same general topics. With larger groups, meetings can be tricky to schedule, and it is frequently difficult for every member to be heard.

Start by asking friends if they would like to form a book club. If you can't find enough people who are interested, ask your friends to ask their friends, and tell bookstores to put you on their list of those who are forming clubs. Make sure you indicate what type of books the club will read.

Backups needed: Regardless of the size of the group, members do periodically drop out, so it's smart to have the names of several potential members whom you can invite to join. And by posting your reading group on one of the book club Web sites, you're likely to get a steady stream of inquiries.

Book selection: Since most disagreements in clubs are over the selection of books, make sure that all members are comfortable with the method that's chosen. *The best systems...*

- **Giving every member, in rotation, the chance to choose the next book.**
- **A random drawing of books submitted by each member.**
- **Majority vote.**

No method is clearly the best. The important point in starting a club is to make sure that every member is in agreement on the system. If, after a few months, you notice that the original selection system causes disagreement, consider changing it.

INVITE AUTHORS

Get listed on a book club–oriented Web site. This gives authors an easy way to contact you with an offer to speak to the group. Don't expect best-selling writers to make any offers, but there's a chance that a little-known author may one day be world famous.

But you don't have to wait for authors to initiate the contact. Issue invitations to authors whom members would like to meet. In today's competitive book market, more authors are looking to speak to reading groups whose members might spread the word about their latest books.

Example: If a new mystery is set in Chicago, the author might look forward to speaking to groups in the Midwest.

You can usually reach authors through their publishers, but today, many writers have their own Web sites. To find such sites, enter the author's name into Google or another search engine. Or, at Reader's Circle, just click on "Meet the Author" for authors who speak to clubs.

Free Videos on the Web

Suranga Chandratillake, CEO and founder of blinkx, the Internet's most extensive video search engine, *www. blinkx.com.*

Network TV programs, video how-to segments and daily newscasts are all now available on the Internet, many of them for free.

In December 2007, US Internet users watched a record 10 billion videos on-line, according to the research firm comScore. It does not take a great amount of computer skill to watch video on-line—anyone who surfs the Internet can do it. You will need a broadband (not a "dial-up") connection for Internet, and if the computer is more than a few years old, you might have to download some free software. (Most sites offering video can steer you through the download process.)

Among the best video Web sites today...

• **Television sites.** All of the major broadcast networks now make many of their shows available for free on the Internet, including a limited number of back episodes. Log on to ABC.com, CBS.com, NBC.com or Fox.com, then click the button labeled "Watch Full Episodes" or "Watch

Video." Expect to sit through a short advertisement before the program begins.

Most cable channels feature some video on their Web sites, but few offer a wide range of episodes. Discovery Channel now has a handful of its shows on-line (*www.discoverychannel.com*).

Other cable sites providing free video include Comedy Central (*www.comedycentral.com*), MTV (*www.mtv.com*) and VH1 (*www.vh1.com*).

• **How-to video sites.** A huge number of informational and educational videos are available for free on the Internet. Videojug.com is a great place to start. The site offers thousands of well-made how-to videos, most two or three minutes long. Subjects range from how to tie a bowtie to how to improve a golf swing. The site is well-organized, making it easy to find what you want. Epicurious (*www.epicurious.com*) is a great site for videos about food preparation.

• **News sites.** Watch news channel feeds or video feeds of the day's top news stories for free from CNN (*www.cnn.com/video)* or Bloomberg Television (*http://Bloomberg.com/news/av*).

• **Sports.** Fans of obscure sports often can find news and highlights on official league Web sites or through my site, *www.blinkx.com.*

Examples: Open-wheel racing fans can find highlights, press conferences and other free clips on Indycar.com. Bike-racing fans can find a wide range of videos on Cycling.tv, some for free.

The World's Libraries At Your Fingertips

Worldcat.org enables you to locate library materials—books, music, videos, articles, etc.—in more than 10,000 libraries throughout the world. Once you have found something that you want, you can access it on-line or have it sent to you or reserved at a local library. How you access the material will vary depending on the library.

David Boyer, a research editor and resident computer guru, *Bottom Line/Personal*, Boardroom Inc., 281 Tresser Blvd., Stamford, Connecticut 06901.

16

Hit the Road

Save at the Pump! Tricks To Conserve Gas

Despite all the technological know-how automakers have amassed, most cars, trucks and SUVs remain incredibly inefficient today. In fact, most vehicles extract only about 20% of the available energy from a gallon of gas.

There are plenty of ways, however, for you to increase your vehicle's efficiency and reduce your costs at the pump. *This is especially important as gas prices top $4 per gallon*...*

PAMPER YOUR CAR

• **Use synthetic oil.** Synthetic lubricants can give you twice the bang for your buck. By reducing friction among your engine's moving parts, synthetic lubricants improve gas mileage—and the life span of your engine. Though they seem expensive, synthetic oils last three to five times longer than petroleum-based oils,

*Prices subject to change.

allowing longer intervals between oil changes and saving you money in the long run. Prices for synthetics range from $6 to $13 per quart, compared with $1.50 to $4 per quart for regular oil.

Best brands: Amsoil...Castrol...Mobil 1...and Red Line.

• **Pay attention to your tires.** You will get higher fuel mileage if you check your tire pressure weekly. If tires are just 20% underinflated, which is five to seven pounds of air per square inch, your fuel mileage can drop by 10% to 15%. That's the equivalent of two to three miles per gallon. What's more, underinflation can reduce a tire's tread life by 15%.

• **Check your gas cap.** A defective seal on your gas cap could allow 30 gallons of gas to evaporate every year, especially if you live in a warm climate. If your gas cap is missing, you can lose even more. Plus, each leaky gas cap is

Ron Hollenbeck, coauthor of The Gas Mileage Bible (Infinity), which includes 45 suggested ways to improve fuel efficiency, www.gasmileagebible.com. He lives in Austin, Texas.

responsible for at least 200 pounds of pollutants released into the air over one year.

What to do: If the rubber seal around the gas cap is worn, replace the whole cap. A new cap at an auto parts store costs $5 to $20.

•**Clean out your car.** The federal Department of Energy estimates that you gain a 1% to 2% improvement in fuel economy for every 100 pounds your vehicle sheds. That's the equivalent of paying three to six cents per gallon less for gasoline.

Example: Take off an unneeded luggage or bike rack or car-top carrier when you are not using it. Remove stuff from your trunk, such as golf clubs and tools—your car makes an expensive closet!

IMPROVE YOUR DRIVING HABITS

•**Stop idling.** If you are tempted to let your car idle for more than one minute, don't. Idling reduces gas mileage. On cold mornings, warm up your car for only 15 to 45 seconds—that is plenty of time for the engine to get lubricated. Both the engine and catalytic converter warm up much faster when you're driving rather than when you're sitting still.

•**Avoid pedal to the metal.** Accelerating aggressively is a notorious energy waster. To avoid the lead-foot phenomenon, drive as if there is an egg under the gas pedal. Pretend that the egg will break if you press too hard or too fast.

•**Use cruise control wisely.** Cruise control is best on long, flat stretches of road. In this kind of terrain, cruise control saves gas by maintaining a consistent speed. That is tough to do on your own. Drop cruise control when driving on hills or steep grades. Cruise control doesn't know when you are going downhill, so it can't take advantage of downhill momentum as well as you can—and is also likely to accelerate more quickly than you need (thus wasting gas) when going back uphill.

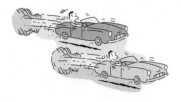

Proven Ways to Make Your Car Last 300,000 Miles

David Solomon, a certified master auto mechanic, is chairman of MotorWatch, an automotive safety watchdog organization, and editor of *MotorWatch*, Box 123, Butler, Maryland 21023, *www.motorwatch.com*.

Some drivers appear to have a lot of luck in keeping their vehicles free of trouble for many years—even decades. Others do not even make it past 60,000 miles without major problems. The longevity of your vehicle can depend on what type you own, but driving and maintenance habits also are crucial. A few proven techniques can help keep your vehicle running beyond the 300,000-mile mark.

DRIVING TECHNIQUES

•**Coast as much as possible.** Plan your approach to red lights, stop signs and turns long before you reach them. Don't accelerate unnecessarily and then step on the brake at the last moment—that wears down brakes quickly.

•**Accelerate slowly.** Avoid jackrabbit starts. Flooring the gas pedal when the engine is cold is a major reason for blown head gaskets, which are expensive to fix. Drive as though you have an egg between your foot and the gas pedal. Reserve rapid acceleration for emergencies.

•**Allow the engine to get hot.** To help flush contaminants, such as fuel and moisture, from the motor oil, drive at highway speeds for 30 minutes at least once a month.

•**Delay heating or cooling.** To prevent adding an extra load on the engine, allow it to run for a minute so that it is lubricated before you turn on the defroster or air conditioner.

•**Run the air conditioner or windshield defroster at least once per month** (even in cooler weather) for about a minute to circulate oil through the heating and cooling system. Otherwise, oil may settle in the compressor, causing the system to stop operating.

•**Use the parking brake.** If you don't use it at least once per week while parked—even if you are not parked on an incline—the parking brake can freeze up and fail to release.

•**Wind down turbocharged engines.** The engine should be allowed to idle a few minutes before you shut it down. This allows the turbo to stop spinning while it is still being lubricated with motor oil. (Don't close the garage door until the engine is off.)

•**Avoid two-footed driving.** Using the left foot to brake can lead to unconscious riding of the brakes, which wears them out and confuses the engine control computer, possibly leading to stalling, surging and high emissions.

With manual transmissions, use your brakes and not the gears to slow down since brakes are cheaper to replace than your transmission. For most manual transmission vehicles, aim to operate the engine between 2,000 and 3,000 revolutions per minute (RPM) to avoid overworking or over-revving the engine. Do not keep the clutch pedal pressed any more than necessary. Keep your hand off of the gear shift when driving to avoid excess strain on the transmission. Do not necessarily park in gear—if another car bumps into yours while yours is in gear, the transmission could be damaged.

Exception: Park in gear for extra traction on inclines.

With automatic transmissions, shift into park when idling for extended periods to allow the transmission to cool down. Do not idle for long periods in neutral, because some bearings are not lubricated in neutral.

FUEL CHOICES

•**Try to use a gas additive** with every fill-up because modern gasoline does not contain enough detergents to keep the fuel system clean. Avoid additives that contain methanol, methyl, alcohol, xylene, toluene or acetone—these can damage the fuel system hoses and pump.

Best: Red Line SI-1 or Chevron Techron (usually $7 to $9 per bottle*).

Use the octane called for in the vehicle's owner's manual. Putting premium fuel in an engine designed for regular fuel, or vice versa, won't deliver better mileage, and it can cause a buildup of carbon in the combustion chambers, which hurts driving performance.

*Prices subject to change.

•**Don't let the fuel level drop below one-quarter tank.** A low tank promotes condensation, which can damage the fuel pump.

Don't fill the tank to the top of the filler neck. Topping off after the gas hose clicks can damage your evaporative emission canister, which will cause the "check engine" light to come on. Repairs could cost more than $500.

ROUTINE MAINTENANCE

•**Determine the normal life expectancy for major parts** so that you can replace them before they fail.

Example: Most people never think to replace their radiator, but a radiator needs to be changed every 10 years or 150,000 miles, even sooner, depending on your driving conditions.

A list of the normal life expectancies for most parts is at *www.motorwatch.com* (click on "Automotive Bible," "Service Charts," then on "Depart Parts Chart").

•**Rotate tires every 7,500 miles to extend tire life and improve gas mileage.** (Some vehicles have tires that cannot be swapped from front to back or side to side.) It is also a good opportunity for your technician to check the vehicle for any potential problems, such as leaks or parts that are about to fail.

•**Have the battery tested annually at an auto shop that uses a "conductance" tester,** which can predict battery life. When the battery wears out, replace it with an Absorbent Glass Mat (AGM) battery, which lasts at least twice as long as an ordinary battery, offers more cranking power, recharges faster and increases starter and alternator life. AGM batteries are sealed and don't vent explosive gases or cause corrosion of the cables or nearby electrical components, as conventional batteries do.

Examples of AGM batteries: Optima, Odyssey (prices start at $130).

If the battery can be opened up, you can top off the electrolyte (fluid). Use only distilled water for this.

•**Clean the throttle body and fuel injectors every 30,000 miles**—unless a gas additive is used regularly.

•**Change spark plugs every 60,000 miles.** Replace plug wires, if applicable, every 100,000 to 120,000 miles.

OTHER HELPFUL STEPS

• **Keep only a few keys on your ignition key ring.** The extra weight from a fistful of keys will wear out the ignition switch prematurely in some vehicles.

• **Use a car cover if you don't garage your vehicle.** It reduces environmental damage to the paint and sun damage to the interior.

Best: Covers ranging from $80 to $400 available at *www.autochic.com* (800-351-0605).

Use a windshield sunshade or a dashboard cover to preserve the dash vinyl when parked in the sun.

More from David Solomon...

When to Change the Oil, Brake Fluid...

The owner's manual often does not include recommendations for the change intervals for important fluids and filters, or the recommended intervals may be too far apart. *Use the guidelines below unless the manufacturer recommends shorter intervals...*

• **Oil.** The old rule of thumb for oil changes is every three months or 3,000 miles, but if you drive in a mild climate or use synthetic oil, this may be too frequent. If you drive in more severe conditions, it might not be frequent enough.

Better: Follow the oil change guidelines posted on my Web site, *www.motorwatch.com* (click on "Automotive Bible," then "Service Charts").

Also: Have your oil analyzed every few years with a test kit (available from Oil Analyzers Inc., 800-956-5695, *www.oaitesting.com*, $22.55, postage prepaid*). This tells you whether you change the oil often enough for your kind of driving, and it will warn you of potential problems.

Example: Finding trace amounts of coolant or sand (silica) in the oil allows you to take corrective action before the engine is damaged.

• **Brake fluid.** Every two years or 24,000 miles, whichever comes first, for vehicles with an antilock braking system (ABS). Every three years or 36,000 miles for those without ABS. Use DOT 5.1 synthetic brake fluid, which has good corrosion inhibitors.

*Price subject to change.

260

• **Power steering fluid.** Every two years or 24,000 miles.

• **Long-life radiator coolant.** Every three years or 36,000 miles. Buy a premixed coolant, or mix it yourself with distilled water, not tap water, which can cause mineral deposits to plug up the radiator.

• **Transmission fluid for automatic transmissions.** Every three years or 36,000 miles in front-wheel-drive vehicles...every five years or 50,000 miles in rear-wheel-drive vehicles. Synthetic transmission fluid extends the interval by one year or 10,000 miles.

• **Transmission fluid for manual transmissions.** Every 60,000 miles, or 100,000 miles when using synthetic transmission fluid.

• **Fuel filter.** At least every 50,000 miles. A partially blocked fuel filter can cause premature failure of the fuel pump.

Best: Use the same brand of filter that the factory supplied.

Basics of Replacing Car Tires

To test the treads on your tires, insert a penny, with the top of Lincoln's head facing into the treads of each tire. If you can see the top of his head, it is time to replace this tire. Another check is to see if the tire-wear bars are flush with the treads. These bars are black patches of rubber between the treads that become more prominent when treads wear down. Tires wear unevenly, so check the outside, middle and inside of the treads.

If one tire needs replacement, it's usually best to replace them in pairs (fronts or backs) for better braking and handling. For the same reason, make sure to use the same brand and model.

Lauren Fix, spokesperson for Car Care Council, a not-for-profit consumer education organization of 6,200 automobile industry companies in Bethesda, Maryland, www. carcare.org.

Hidden Hazards
At the Car Wash

Eric Peters, a Washington, DC–based automotive columnist and author of *Automotive Atrocities! The Cars We Love to Hate* (MBI). His Web site is *www.ericpetersautos. com.*

Washing your car regularly helps maintain its appearance and resale value. Getting bird droppings, tar and road salt off quickly prevents the paint from spotting so badly that the car loses 10% to 20% of its eventual resale value.

A good automatic car wash is convenient and can be much safer for your car's finish than washing the car yourself. Some do-it-yourselfers use too harsh a soap, which can remove protective wax and leave a chalky residue. Or they end up just rubbing abrasives into the car's finish rather than removing abrasives. Or they wash the car while it is sitting in direct sunlight, which can turn water into a magnifying glass, focusing the sun's rays and burning spots into the paint.

All that makes the $10 to $15 for a basic full-service car wash seem like a bargain if you pick the right place and the right options.

HOW OFTEN?

Washing a car once a month or even less often might be enough—particularly if the car is not driven much and is kept in a garage. Some cars, however, will need a bath as often as once a week. That's especially true if the car is parked outdoors and it is driven in areas where there is lots of dust and dirt or where the winters are long and severe and corrosive road salt is used. There's no harm in frequent washes as long as they are done properly.

WHAT TO DO

•**Make sure the car wash is "brushless."** Some older car washes still use brushes, which leave small scratches in a car's finish. On older cars with "single stage" paint jobs, light scratches often can be buffed out, but modern cars all use a "base/clear" system, with a thin, transparent layer of clear coat to provide the shine on top of the underlying color coat. Once the thin clear coat is damaged, often the only way to restore the shine is to repaint the damaged area. So be certain your automatic car wash uses felt or another type of cloth—not brushes.

Even better: "Touchless" car washes use only high-pressure water jets and detergents to clean the car. There is almost no chance of your vehicle suffering any cosmetic damage this way.

•**Skip most extras.** A "works" and "super-works" version of the car wash—which may include machine-sprayed wax, air freshener and squirting "tire shine" on tires—can cost twice as much as a basic wash without adding much value.

Some car washes provide undercarriage rust-proofing, which is usually unnecessary. Before a car is put together, rustproofing is applied to the brand-new metal to help protect it from corrosives, particularly road salt. Additionally, most new cars now are extensively rustproofed at the factory during the assembly process.

On the other hand, if the car wash offers an undercarriage wash, it might be worth the additional cost. Jets of water sprayed directly underneath the car can break loose accumulated crud that would be difficult for you to remove by hand—especially with a simple garden hose. The undercarriage bath also clears the drainage holes and prevents buildup of moisture, which could accelerate rust or lead to the formation of mold in the car's air-conditioning system.

Caution: A few car washes provide engine cleaning. Don't opt for this. High-pressure water could cause problems in a modern car's engine compartment.

Some other extras are worth it. The powerful but safe cleaners utilized for wheels by most car washes—often just several dollars extra—do a great job of removing dirt, brake dust, etc. This would be a tough job if you did it yourself using over-the-counter cleaners, a hand brush and a hose. It's especially important to keep aluminum alloy wheels clean because brake dust can permanently stain them.

•**Don't equate spray-on wax with hand-applied wax.** The car wash's machine-sprayed option is just a glaze that adds some shine and restores some water beading but does not protect like hand-applied wax. Hand-applied paste wax provides a UV-protective film, plus restores oils to the paint. Hand-applied wax costs more but is worth it.

• **Beware the wipe down.** Most automatic car washes use strong jets of heated air to blow off some water after the car is soaped up and rinsed. Then attendants typically hand-wipe the car. That's fine as long as they use fresh, clean, dry, soft towels. If you see them using wet (and therefore probably dirty) old rags, stop them and go somewhere else next time.

• **Check your car thoroughly before leaving the car wash.** Make sure the wash has done a good job of cleaning the vehicle and has not caused any damage. Although many car washes post a disclaimer saying they are not responsible for damage, this does not necessarily absolve them of damage their equipment or personnel may have caused. If you notice something, ask to see the manager and point it out. The manager should offer to fix the problem in the interest of customer relations, whether or not the car wash is legally liable.

If the manager balks, pursue the matter with someone higher up, possibly by contacting headquarters if the car wash is part of a chain. If you have a camera or a cell phone with a camera, take a photo of the damage to support your claim.

More from Eric Peters...

Car-Buying Tip

Don't say you plan to pay cash for a car until you have negotiated the best price with the salesperson. Dealerships profit by financing cars and may be willing to bring down a price if they believe they will make up the difference on the financing side.

Best: First get the best price you can—in writing, if possible—and then say you plan to pay with cash.

Car Loan Smarts

Car loans have stretched to as long as seven years. This decreases monthly payments but can cause a problem for buyers. Cars depreciate

to 50% of the original price in about three years, and most people trade cars in after three or four years. With a seven-year loan, a buyer will owe more money than the car is worth for almost the entire length of the loan. The problem is magnified by trading in the car before the end of the loan and rolling the balance into a new loan.

Self-defense: Restrict a car loan's term to no longer than four years.

Kevin Tynan, the auto industry analyst at Argus Research in New York City.

Get a Great Deal On a Used Car

A new way to save on a used car is to buy one from your employer. More companies are selling their cars to employees once the cars come off lease.

Typical savings: $300 to $1,900 off dealer prices.*

Other pluses: Availability of the car's maintenance history and the ability to talk with the original driver.

Sign of the times: One-quarter to one-third of company cars coming off lease are sold to employees or their friends and family members.

The Wall Street Journal, 200 Liberty St., New York City 10281, *online.wsj.com.*

*Rates subject to change.

Want to Get Out of Your Lease?

Get out of a car lease by going on the Web to sites that help businesses and consumers with unwanted leases find others willing to pick them up. Among these sites are *www.leasetrader.com* and *www.swapalease.com.* The sites charge sellers and buyers up to $130 each* to arrange a lease transfer—and the seller pays an extra $0 to $650 to transfer the car title.

*Prices subject to change.

Caution: If you are planning to take over a lease, read it carefully—mileage allowances and fees vary widely.

James Bragg, founder of FightingChance.com, which provides consumers with information on car buying and leasing, Long Beach, California.

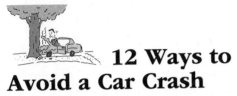

12 Ways to Avoid a Car Crash

William Van Tassel, PhD, manager of driver-training operations at the American Automobile Association's national office in Heathrow, Florida, *www.aaa.com.*

There are more than six million police-reported auto collisions in the US each year. Nearly three million people are injured in these crashes and about 40,000 die.

Even an excellent driver can make a mistake and cause a car crash—or become involved in a collision if an inattentive, inexperienced or inebriated driver makes a mistake. *Wise ways to reduce the risk of auto crashes...*

DRIVING STRATEGIES

1. Stay off the roads between midnight and 3 am on Saturday and Sunday mornings. Drunk-driving collisions are most common then. The safest time to drive on weekend nights is between 9 pm and midnight, when most heavy drinkers are still at bars and parties.

Most weekday crashes occur during the morning and evening rush hours, but these tend to be less severe crashes, not the frequently fatal smashups caused by drunk drivers.

2. Choose routes with intersections that have left-turn green arrows—in particular if you are over age 70 or live in a region with lots of older drivers. Turning left in front of the oncoming vehicles at an intersection is one common driving mistake among those over 70 because age often impairs our ability to judge the speed of approaching traffic. Such collisions are much less common where traffic lights have green arrows that let drivers know when to turn.

3. Brake and accelerate in a straight line on slick roads. When roads are wet or icy, try to complete your braking before you enter a turn and begin accelerating only after you have come out of it. This reduces the odds of a skid.

Keep headlights on, even during the day if you don't have daytime running lights. This increases the odds that other drivers will see you.

4. Look through the car ahead of you. Most drivers focus on the back of the vehicle in front of them when they are on crowded roads. But, if that driver brakes or swerves suddenly, you might have little time to react. It is better to look through the rear window and front windshield of the car you are trailing to keep an eye on the vehicle ahead of it (assuming that tinted windows or some other elements of the vehicle's design do not block your view). This will provide more warning if there is a problem on the road ahead.

5. Use your brake lights to be more visible to those behind you. If there is a vehicle behind you when you need to slow down, tap on your brake pedal very slightly a few seconds before braking, assuming there is time to do so safely. When stopped in traffic or at a light, tap your brake a few times as another vehicle approaches from behind. This is particularly helpful if the drivers behind you are looking into the sun.

6. Drive with one hand between 8 o'clock and 9 o'clock...and the other between 3 o'clock and 4 o'clock on the wheel. The traditional 10 and 2 o'clock positions cause unnecessary arm fatigue on long drives, leading to less-than-optimal driver reaction time in emergencies. It also increases the odds that one of your arms will hit you in the face if your air bag deploys, causing lost teeth or a broken jaw.

DANGEROUS DRIVERS/VEHICLES

7. Avoid driving next to or in front of passenger vehicles towing trailers. If these drivers are inexperienced at towing, they might underestimate the time it takes to stop their vehicles with the extra weight of the trailer, causing them to rear-end the car in front of them...take a turn too fast and lose control of their trailer...or momentarily forget that they are towing a trailer and attempt to merge in front of another car before the trailer has cleared it.

8. Let an aggressive driver pass. If the driver right behind you tailgates, flashes his headlights or makes numerous lane changes, get out of his way as soon as possible. This aggressive driver could cause a collision, and you do not want to be anywhere near him.

If you're in the left lane, ease into the right lane as soon as you can safely do so to let him pass. If it's a two-lane highway, maintain your speed until you can safely pull off. It's generally safer to pull off into a parking lot or driveway than onto the shoulder of the road.

Helpful: Certain types of vehicles offer hints that their owners might be more aggressive or negligent on the roads. These include cars that have extra-wide tires or loud mufflers...numerous dents...or are covered in dirt and grime.

Try to give such vehicles a wide berth or at least your close attention.

9. Be extra careful in reverse. Many minor collisions occur when drivers back up, most often in parking lots. Even very experienced drivers aren't accustomed to driving backward, and our visibility is limited when we do so.

When you put your car in reverse, turn your upper body and your head to the right so that you can look directly out of your rear window, rather than depending on your rearview mirror. Turning provides a wider view.

10. Keep an eye on the drivers to your sides, not just their cars. If a driver just ahead of you in the next lane keeps glancing in your direction, he might soon merge in front of you. Give this driver room, or at least stay out of his blind spot. If a driver next to you appears to be speaking on a cell phone, adjust your speed to distance yourself from that vehicle.

11. Avoid driving near trucks. Crashes involving large trucks often are fatal. When following a truck, stay far enough back so that you can see the truck's side mirrors.

12. To pass a truck on a multilane road, wait for all other vehicles to clear the truck, then pass as rapidly as conditions and the speed limit safely allow. Be well past a truck before pulling in front of it.

Cell Phone Warning

Drivers' cell phone use triples crash risk. This is comparable to the risk of driving with a blood alcohol level at the legal limit. It doesn't matter if you use the hands-free device or hold your cell phone.

Reason: Drivers on the phone are paying attention to their conversations, so reactions are delayed.

Frank Drews, PhD, assistant professor of psychology, University of Utah, Salt Lake City, and the coauthor of a study of 40 drivers, published in *Human Factors.*

Safer Seating

In a recent study of fatal auto accidents, backseat occupants were 59% to 86% safer than front seat occupants, with the middle backseat 25% safer than the window seats on either side of it.

Why: There is a much bigger "crush zone" around the middle seat that can absorb an impact without injuring the passenger, compared to the window seats. Also, in rollover car accidents middle-seat passengers are subject to lower rotational forces and so incur fewer injuries.

Dietrich Jehle, MD, associate professor of emergency medicine, and lead author of a study conducted at the Center for Transportation Injury Research, State University of New York at Buffalo.

Better Fuel Efficiency Costs Lives

For every 100-pound reduction in automobile weight to achieve government fuel-economy standards, there have been 2,200 to 3,900 additional lives lost in accidents annually.

Reason: On average, when safety features are equal, lighter vehicles are less safe than heavier ones in collisions.

H. Sterling Burnett, PhD, senior fellow, National Center for Policy Analysis, Dallas.

17

At Home

Home Improvements That Pay Off Big Now... And When You Sell Your House

Instead of focusing on building houses bigger and bigger, home owners today are stressing more useful features when it comes to renovating or building.

The right elements will make your home safer, more enjoyable and more energy-efficient. They also can increase the home's appeal to potential buyers when it comes time to sell—particularly in the tremendously difficult real estate market we have today.

Kitchens and baths are the rooms most likely to be renovated—and the rooms most likely to take away from a home's selling price if they appear out-of-date. However, home owners are now rethinking many other areas of the home as well.

Below, Kermit Baker, chief economist at the American Institute of Architects (AIA), identifies the most desired features for homes today...

KITCHEN ENHANCEMENTS

• **Kitchen recycling centers.** As more towns offer (or insist on) recycling in addition to trash removal, more home owners desire a dedicated but inconspicuous space in or near their kitchens for recycling bins. This is typically a concealed area under a kitchen countertop or in a mudroom or laundry room.

• **Natural stone (such as granite) or concrete countertops.** Solid, attractive and durable, these countertops continue to be in great demand—with natural soapstone increasing in popularity as an alternative to granite. It has a warmer feel, with soft, subtle blue-gray colors, and deep scratches can be sanded away.

Kermit Baker, PhD, chief economist for the American Institute of Architects (AIA), Washington, DC, *www.aia. org*, and senior research fellow, Harvard University's Joint Center for Housing Studies, Cambridge, Massachusetts. The AIA questions approximately 500 residential architectural firms quarterly to identify trends in remodeling and home construction.

• **Restaurant-look appliances.** The large, expensive, stainless steel–trimmed cooking areas, refrigerators and other appliances are becoming more and more popular for residences.

• **Wine fridges.** More Americans are drinking wine and installing wine fridges. They're still a specialty item, but one that's rapidly becoming common.

BATH AMENITIES

• **Two of everything in the master bath.** Couples with more money than time to spare are no longer willing to wait for their partner to be finished in the bathroom. They're installing two vanities…two sinks…even two shower stalls in the master bath.

• **Radiant heat in bathroom floors.** This comfort feature, which uses embedded systems with heated water or electricity to warm up the floor, is rapidly gaining popularity, though it is not yet mainstream.

On the decline…

• **Whirlpool tubs.** Once a mainstay of American master baths, whirlpool tubs are rapidly losing popularity. Home owners say that they take up too much space in the bathroom, are difficult to clean and that the whirlpool feature is rarely used.

BACKYARD LIVING

Home owners increasingly wish to enjoy time outside without losing all the comforts of home. *Popular features now…*

• **High-end backyard landscaping.** There was a time when home owners sank their landscape budgets into their front yards so that their homes would look nice from the street. Now they are just as likely to pour dollars into their backyards, to create beautiful, private outdoor places for the family.

• **Large decks and patios.** A deck or patio large enough for the whole family, rather than just a smallish add-on, is becoming an essential part of the home. Gazebos and courtyards also are gaining popularity.

• **Outdoor cooking stations.** These upscale, outdoor kitchens—some of which include sinks and even refrigerators—are replacing the traditional backyard barbecue.

• **Privacy screening.** Americans are spending more time in their backyards, but the average yard size has decreased. This makes fences, walls and hedges that provide additional backyard privacy more valuable.

GREENER HOMES

Environmentally friendly homes are finally finding favor with mainstream Americans.

Higher energy costs for heating and cooling mean that an energy-efficient home makes even better financial sense than before…and Americans are increasingly interested in protecting the environment even when it does not lower their bills.

Below are some of the more popular green-home design features…

• **Bamboo floors.** Home owners who select bamboo can have the look and durability of traditional hardwood flooring without contributing to deforestation.

Most hardwood floors come from forests that can take decades to regrow once cut down. But bamboo is not a tree at all—it's a type of grass that regrows very quickly.

• **Triple-glazed windows.** Three panes of glass can add $4 to $7 per square foot* to the price of a new window but can cut energy consumption by an extra 10% to 11% compared to typical double-paned windows.

• **Decreased home size in the high-end market.** The luxury homes have grown steadily larger in recent decades, until just last year, when the biggest high-end homes suddenly lost much of their allure, in part because of the high cost of heating and cooling massive residences. Should this trend continue, 3,500- to 4,500-square-foot homes might hold their value better than huge 6,000-square-foot mansions.

Smaller is not better at the lower end of the housing market, however—most people living in homes with less than 3,000 square feet still would like to live in larger spaces.

On the decline…

• **The two-story entrance foyer.** With more houses being built with nine-foot-high or even 10-foot-high first-floor ceilings, the energy-and-space–hogging two-story entrance foyer is not seen as the necessity it once was in mid-level and upper-end homes.

*Prices subject to change.

INCREASED ACCESSIBILITY

Older home owners tend to prefer residences that are easy to get around. It's no surprise that we're seeing increasing demand for accessibility features now that the baby boom generation is reaching retirement age. *These include…*

•**No-threshold showers.** Stepping over the high tub wall onto a slick surface can be dangerous for aging home owners with hip, leg or balance problems. Easy-access showers that don't require this big step are now becoming a popular choice.

Other shower features gaining momentum: Handheld showerheads…doorless shower stalls…and even two-person showers.

•**Residential ramps and elevators.** These are no longer just for public buildings. Elderly home owners are adding on ramps to their entryways, and they even are installing in-home elevators when the stairs become too much of a physical challenge.

•**Single-level layouts.** Stairs and elevators are not necessary when all the rooms in a home are on one level. When a small lot size makes a single-story layout impractical, today's home owners still like to locate the master bedroom on the first floor, with all of the other bedrooms upstairs.

ADDITIONAL FEATURES

A few more already popular home design features that are gaining momentum today…

•**Home offices.** There has been a huge increase in the demand for home work spaces in recent years.

Flexible office hours that let employees work from home one or two days per week and high gas prices that make commuting expensive appear to be driving the trend. Home offices differ from spare bedrooms mainly in that they tend to be located in the quietest corners of the home, away from children's bedrooms, television rooms and kitchens. They also might have additional electrical outlets or specialized telecom wiring.

•**Three-car (or larger) garages.** Americans own more vehicles than in the past and prefer homes that have space for all of them.

•**Open floor plans.** Home owners increasingly believe that having a big "great room" is preferable to separate living, dining and family rooms. Many of today's homes, in fact, are being built without a "living room" at all, and formal dining rooms are losing popularity.

•**Locations close to urban centers.** Living near cities, employers and train stations is becoming more popular. Many home owners like these locales because they trim commute times and gas expenses. Other home owners prefer the engaged, active lifestyles offered by urban centers to the "get away from it all" advantages of gated communities and more isolated suburban properties.

The Best Place to Live

The best place to reside in the US is Gainesville, Florida. Their ranking is based on 50 criteria in 10 categories, with the most weight given to cost of living, climate and overall quality of life. Bellingham, Washington, was rated second, and the Portland-Vancouver (Washington)-Beaverton (Oregon) metro area was third. And, the lowest-rated city of the 375 measured was Modesto, California.

Go to *www.bestplaces.net* to compare cities.

Bert Sperling and Peter Sanders, coauthors of *Cities Ranked & Rated* (Wiley).

"I Might Need It One Day"…and Other Common Excuses for Clutter

Peter Walsh, an organizational consultant who's based in Los Angeles and featured on the TLC program *Clean Sweep*. He is author of *It's All Too Much: An Easy Plan for Living a Richer Life with Less Stuff* (Free Press). His Web site is *www.peterwalshdesign.com*.

Most people desire to eliminate clutter, but many never quite manage to get the job done. They know that throwing away the stuff they no longer use would make it easier to find the things they do need...that decluttered lives can be more focused and less anxiety-ridden...and that less clutter can mean lower levels of dust and allergens in the home. But, they simply cannot convince themselves to take action.

The most common excuses for not getting rid of clutter and how to move beyond them...

"I MIGHT NEED IT ONE DAY"

Some people are unable to throw anything away out of fear that they might need it later. In truth, the vast majority of items saved because "I might need it one day" are never needed. They just pile up and get in our way.

Example: Your sister gave you a new electric coffeepot as a present. You hold on to your old one "just in case."

This might-need-it mentality sometimes stems from a subconscious fear regarding the future. Those who were raised in poverty or who lived through the Depression are especially prone to such thinking.

What to do: Establish a "one-in, one-out" routine. When a new magazine arrives in your home, throw away an old issue. When you purchase one new piece of clothing, choose an old piece of clothing to discard.

"IT'S TOO IMPORTANT TO LET GO"

Some possessions can become intermingled with our memories. We assign sentimental value to items linked to events of our past, then find it psychologically difficult to discard them.

Some of these objects are related to our family's history, creating a sense that we have been "entrusted" with them and are obliged to keep them. Others, such as sports trophies and term papers, are related to accomplishments that required considerable effort on our part or that of our children.

What to do: Consider where items that have "sentimental value" have been stored. If these objects have spent many years untouched in boxes in the attic or gathering dust in the back of a dark closet, they may not be as important as we think. Truly important possessions are kept in more prominent locations. If you are not willing to put an item on display somewhere in your home, throw it away. (If this object is a piece of

family history, first ask other family members if they wish to take it off your hands.)

Your memories and sense of accomplishment will not be diminished by the loss of a physical item related to the event—nor is it an insult to your dear, departed grandma to get rid of the porcelain figurines that she once loved, but you do not.

"IT'S WORTH A LOT OF MONEY"

Do not confuse the amount that something costs with what it is worth to you. The fact that you paid $3,000 for a massage chair or a pool table is irrelevant if this item is never used. In fact, an unused item has negative value to you—not only do you derive no enjoyment from it, but it takes up valuable space in your home.

What to do: Try to sell unused "valuables" on an on-line auction site, such as eBay, or through consignment stores. Recovering any portion of your costs will mitigate the psychological pain of getting rid of something expensive.

"MY HOUSE IS TOO SMALL"

Some people claim that they don't have too much stuff—they simply have insufficient space. In reality, the size of your home is the least flexible factor in the clutter equation. If your small home is bursting at the seams, it is much easier to get rid of some things than it is to move into a larger space. Until you declutter, your possessions will just make your small home feel much smaller.

What to do: Understand that the size of your home provides a limit to what you can acquire. Don't rent a storage locker or waste living space on unnecessary things.

"I DON'T HAVE TIME TO GET ORGANIZED"

Organizing can be a major chore, taking several days or longer.

What to do: Think of getting organized as a way to save time. In the long run, organization makes it easier to find things and eliminates "panic cleaning" before guests visit.

Also, divide big jobs into more manageable tasks.

Example: Every day, set aside 10 minutes to walk around your home filling one trash bag with trash and another bag with items to give to charity. Do this for one week, and you'll see what a big impact this has on clutter.

"IT'S NOT THE PROBLEM MY SPOUSE THINKS IT IS"

Perhaps your clutter and disorganization don't bother you—but wouldn't doing away with it be easier than arguing with your spouse about it? Clutter can cause tension in relationships.

What to do: Ask your spouse for his/her vision for a room, then share your own vision. Perhaps you see your living room as a comfortably cluttered space where you watch the ballgame, but your spouse views it as a place to entertain guests. One solution could be to move the TV to another room and keep the living room neat for guests.

"IT'S NOT MY STUFF"

Do friends and family members treat your home like a storage facility? Do your grown children still keep childhood possessions in their old rooms?

What to do: Decide if it is okay that your home is used by others for storage. If it is, you must learn to live with the clutter. If not, politely ask these other people to come and claim their things by a certain date.

Heloise's Unexpected Uses for Everyday Items

Heloise, a columnist and contributing editor to *Good Housekeeping* magazine. Located in San Antonio, she is author of numerous books on household hints and organization, including *All-New Hints from Heloise* (Perigee). Her legendary mother, the first Heloise, began writing her column, "Hints from Heloise," in 1959. Her Web site is *www.heloise.com*.

Famed household hints guru Heloise has discovered hundreds of alternative uses for everyday products. *Here, she discusses all her favorites...*

MOUSE PADS

Companies sometimes give away free foam mouse pads as advertisements.

- **Jar opener.** Use the grippy underside of it to open stubborn jar lids.
- **Kneeling pad** for gardening or home-improvement projects.
- **Pedicure spot.** Place a mouse pad under your foot when you give yourself a pedicure to catch any drips.

PLASTIC GALLON JUGS

Water, milk and orange juice often come in plastic gallon jugs. *When empty, these jugs have many uses...*

- **Scooper.** Slice a capped jug in half on the diagonal to scoop ice-melting granules or dirt for the garden.
- **Funnel.** Turn the jug upside down, cut it in half horizontally and use as a funnel for liquids or dry material, such as dog food or bird seed.
- **Fishing buoy.** Use a capped jug to mark where you've placed a fishing line.

MAYONNAISE

Be sure to use real mayonnaise, not diet mayonnaise or salad dressing.

- **White mark remover for wood furniture.** If you see a cloudy white mark on a wood table where a coffee mug or some other hot item recently stood, put a dab of mayonnaise on your finger and rub the stained area in the direction of the wood grain until your finger feels a bit warm and the oil from the mayo gets absorbed into the wood. Let the mayo sit overnight, then wipe it off and buff the surface. A little mayo also can hide light scratches on dark wood.
- **Plant shiner.** Apply a light coating of mayonnaise to plant leaves, and buff gently using a paper towel. Use mayo only on the tops of leaves—it might interfere with plants' ability to breathe if applied to the underside, too.
- **Hair conditioner.** Rub one to two tablespoons of mayonnaise into the bottom inch or two of your hair. Pin the hair up (if it is long enough to do so), put on a plastic shower cap, then wrap your head in a bath towel and leave the towel on for at least 30 minutes, preferably an hour. Be sure to rinse thoroughly afterward.

NAIL POLISH

- **Organizer helper.** Use nail polish of different colors to differentiate similar items.

Example: I put a dot of pink nail polish on the end of my tools so that my husband will not think they are his and move them into his toolbox.

• **Contact lens case marker.** Place a dot of red nail polish on the right side of your contact lens case. This will make it simple to tell which lens is stored on which side, even when you do not have your contacts in. And, both "right" and "red" start with the letter R.

• **Childproof medication bottles.** Use any brightly colored nail polish to mark up both the bottle and bottle cap of your childproof medication bottles where the top must be correctly lined up to open. The bright marks will be easy to see and align (of course, do this only if you don't have young children in the house).

Helpful: If you take several medications, also use nail polish to write the first letter or two of each medication on its bottle in large print so that you do not have to squint at labels to figure out which is which.

• **Rust preventer.** Use colorless nail polish to provide invisible protection.

Example: If there is rust on the screws holding your toilet seat or lid in place, remove the screws, soak them in vinegar to clear off the rust, dry them, put the screws back, and then apply a coat of clear nail polish to ward off future rust.

• **Button saver.** Apply one layer of clear nail polish to the threads on top of dress-shirt buttons. The nail polish will help the threads endure the heat of laundering, keeping the buttons on the shirt longer.

HAIR SPRAY

• **Panty hose run stopper.** Spray a small amount of hair spray on minor snags in panty hose to prevent them from turning into longer runs. (Clear nail polish also works.)

• **Needle threader.** Spray the end of a piece of thread if you are having trouble threading a needle. Let the hair spray dry for 10 seconds, then try threading the needle again. The spray will stiffen the end of the thread and make it easier to thread the needle.

PANTY HOSE

There might be more uses for old, clean panty hose than any other household product...

• **Item finder.** When you drop a small object on the floor and can't find it, stretch a piece of older panty hose over the end of your vacuum hose, secure with a rubber band, then vacuum the area. The vacuum will suck up the lost item, but the panty hose filter will prevent it from being sucked past the nozzle. Shut off the vacuum to release the item.

• **Plant ties.** Use strips of panty hose to tie garden plants in place. Unlike rope and plastic ties, panty hose will not cut into the plants, and its natural shade will blend unobtrusively into your garden. You also can put a piece of panty hose across the bottom of the inside of a pot to keep soil from falling out through the drainage holes.

• **Shoe bags.** Slide a pair of shoes into the snipped-off leg of old panty hose before packing the shoes in a suitcase. It keeps the pair together and prevents the shoes from coming in contact with other clothes.

• **Onion and potato storage.** Keep potatoes and onions fresh longer by snipping the legs off panty hose and storing these vegetables in the legs. Put in one onion (or a potato), tie a knot, followed by another onion and another knot for the length of the leg, then hang the leg inside a pantry door. Onions and potatoes will last longer because they will have better air circulation than they would have had in a bag. When you need an onion, just take a pair of scissors and clip off the bottom section, leaving the rest of the panty-hose leg in place.

Recipe Substitutions

Family Circle, 110 Fifth Ave., New York City 10011, *www.familycircle.com.*

D id you run out of an important ingredient for a favorite recipe? *Here are a few common substitutions so you can keep on cooking...*

• **Corn syrup.** For one cup corn syrup, use one cup sugar plus an additional quarter cup liquid used in the recipe.

• **Mustard.** Use one teaspoon of dry mustard plus one tablespoon water to replace one tablespoon prepared mustard.

• **Flour.** Use one tablespoon cornstarch for every two tablespoons flour when flour is used as a thickener.

• **Lemon juice.** One-quarter teaspoon white vinegar can sub for one teaspoon lemon juice.

• **Unsweetened chocolate.** Use three tablespoons unsweetened cocoa powder plus one tablespoon butter as a substitute for a one-ounce square of unsweetened chocolate.

• **Buttermilk.** Replace one cup of buttermilk with one tablespoon vinegar or lemon juice plus milk to equal one cup.

• **Brown sugar.** One cup of firmly packed brown sugar can be replaced by one cup sugar plus two tablespoons molasses.

• **Cake flour.** You can use one cup less two tablespoons all-purpose flour instead of one cup cake flour.

• **Tomato sauce.** One three-quarter cup tomato paste plus one cup water equals two cups tomato sauce.

How to Find Broken Glass

The easiest way to detect small shards of broken glass is to get a flashlight and turn off the overhead lights. Use the flashlight at an angle low to the floor so the shards will sparkle, making them easy to find and dispose of.

The Family Handyman, 2915 Commers Dr., Eagan, Minnesota 55121. *www.familyhandyman.com.*

Bacteria-Free Towels

For germ–free towels, wash towels after two uses so dirt and perspiration don't build up.

Load the washer to half its capacity, so towels have room to agitate. Select the longest, hottest cycle. As soon as the cycle finishes, move towels to the dryer.

Steve Boorstein, a national dry cleaning consultant in Boulder, Colorado, *www.clothingdoctor.com.* He is coauthor of *The Clothing Doctor's 99 Secrets to Cleaning and Clothing Care* (Fashion Media Group).

Is "Green" Cleaning Really Better?

A "green" cleaning product might not be any better for you or the environment than other cleaners. Products advertised as environmentally friendly leave out certain chemicals thought to harm human health or the environment, such as *glycol* and *phthalates*—but they may contain other volatile organic chemicals whose effects are not known, such as *acetones*.

Self-defense: Avoid packaged products altogether. Almost all home cleaning can be done with white vinegar or baking soda. For example, clean windows with vinegar and crumpled newspaper, or make a paste of baking soda to remove counter stains.

Tom Natan, PhD, research director and chemical engineer, National Environmental Trust, a nonprofit organization that provides information on environmental issues of concern, Washington, DC.

Let the Air In

Air out your home regularly. Homes built after 1970 are well insulated—which means they are less drafty and less expensive to heat and cool than older houses, but also more likely to retain chemical vapors from building materials and household products.

Result: Indoor air may be 100 times more toxic than outdoor air.

Self-defense: Opening up windows can help with ventilation, but it may not be enough. More reliable is mechanical ventilation, as can be provided by bathroom exhaust fans or a dedicated whole-house ventilation system.

Also helpful: Use low- or no-VOC (volatile organic compound) paints and buy low-formaldehyde cabinets and furniture.

Alex Wilson, author of *Your Green Home* (New Society) and executive editor, *Environmental Building News.*

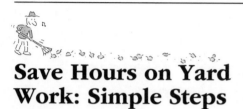

Save Hours on Yard Work: Simple Steps

Catriona Tudor Erler, author of nine books about gardening and landscaping, including *New Complete Home Landscaping* (Creative Homeowner). Based in Charlottesville, Virginia, she has gardened on both coasts and has written about gardening for more than 25 years.

If you don't like yard work and if you would like to avoid or cut down on the expense of hiring a gardener, consider these strategies that give your yard a beautiful look without all the work...

• **Use more mulch.** The more of your property you cover in mulch, the less there is to mow, weed and fertilize. An "island" of mulch around a tree or shrub looks great, and it eliminates the tricky, time-consuming mowing and edging often required around these areas. Mulch also provides nutrients, reducing the time you must spend fertilizing.

If there are several shrubs or trees in the same general area in your lawn, group them into one large mulch island, rather than creating separate islands for each.

To create a mulch island: Lay about six layers of newspaper on top of the existing grass and weeds. Then cover this with three to four inches of organic mulch, such as shredded bark (different kinds are available at most nurseries). The newspaper helps kill the grass and weeds. Over time, the newspaper will decompose, adding additional nutrients to the soil.

Remulch once a year—just put fresh mulch on top of the old. You don't need to add more newspaper. The fastest way to mulch perennial beds is to do it in early spring, before the plants send up their shoots.

Important: Leave a few inches of open space between mulch and tree trunks to allow airflow. But, you can safely mulch right up to the base of most other plants.

• **Choose a ground cover other than grass.** Replace all or part of your lawn with an attractive, low-lying ground cover that requires little or no maintenance once established.

Appropriate ground covers vary regionally, so ask a local garden store for advice. (Garden store employees will usually have more time to talk if you visit on a weekday.)

Options: Sedum, creeping thyme, daylilies, low-growing hostas, Korean grass, pachysandra, certain varieties of clover or moss and more.

Be aware that many ground covers cannot be walked on without damaging the plants. If you enjoy the feel of grass under your feet or have young kids who play on your lawn, maintain a small lawn and use ground cover for the rest of your property.

Or plant Stepables, a line of ground covers designed to withstand foot traffic (503-581-8915, *www.stepables.com*).

There also are some grasses that require very little mowing, but these vary by region. Check in with the Lawn Institute for more information (800-405-8873, *www.thelawninstitute.org*).

• **Place plants where they will get what they need without your help.** Ask your garden store what type of soil...how much sun... and how much moisture a particular plant likes before you purchase it.

Position water-loving plants near the wettest sections of your lawn and sun-loving plants in exposed locations. Group all plants with similar needs together so that you do not have to tend to each individually.

Also, select native plants. Plants indigenous to your region are likely to thrive in your yard with little attention from you. Your local garden store can suggest appropriate native options.

• **Plant evergreen trees rather than deciduous trees.** If you add trees to your property, avoid unnecessary autumn raking by selecting coniferous trees, such as pine trees, which do not shed needles.

If there already are deciduous trees on your property, create large islands of mulch around them. Leaves that fall on this mulch do not need to be raked.

Do keep in mind that well-placed deciduous trees can cut your home's energy use by providing cool shade in summer and letting the sun hit the house in winter.

• **Favor flowering shrubs over other flowers.** Flowering shrubs usually require much less care than other flowers. Popular options include camellia, lilac, abelia and azalea. Ask your garden store to recommend the flowering shrubs most appropriate for your region. Plant a selection of shrubs that flower at different times of year so that your yard is colorful during most of the year.

Examples: Encore azaleas bloom in both spring and fall...Glacier azaleas bloom sporadically throughout the summer...and witch hazel blooms in winter or early spring.

• **Select a slow-growth shrub for a low-maintenance, tailored-hedge look.** The fast-growing shrubs, including Leyland Cyprus, are very popular with home owners because they quickly turn into substantial privacy-providing barriers.

Problem: Fast-growing shrubs will continue to grow quickly even when we want them to stop, which means frequent and time-consuming trimming is necessary for them to appear well-groomed.

If you want a tailored-hedge look, it is better to choose a slow-growing shrub, such as boxwood, yew or hornbeam. These will take longer to provide full privacy but require far less care to remain neat and tailored once they do. (If you like a loose look, they don't have to be pruned at all.)

Important: Make sure that the mature size of the shrubs and other plants you select is appropriate for the locations you choose for them. If a plant is too big for its location, you will spend the rest of the plant's life trimming it back as it tries to expand. The nursery can provide a mature size estimate, or look for a tag on the plant when you purchase it.

• **Divide big yards into "rooms."** If you have several acres of property, do not try to tend to it all. Divide the property into "rooms," and devote your yard-work hours only to the rooms closest to your home or the road.

Use hedges, stone walls or other borders to divide these rooms from the rest of the property, and allow more distant rooms to take on a relaxed and natural appearance. This can look perfectly appropriate, assuming that the property is relatively rural and not surrounded by manicured lawns on all sides.

Best Time to Fertilize

Fertilize your lawn in the fall—three weeks before the final mowing of the season. This gives both energy and nutrients to grass roots throughout the winter, and it makes your lawn strong and healthy. Choose a fertilizer that is four parts nitrogen to one part phosphorus and two parts potassium (called 4-1-2). Or ask a clerk at your local garden center what fertilizer is best for your type of grass and soil.

The Family Handyman, 2915 Commers Dr., Eagan, Minnesota 55121, *www.familyhandyman.com.*

How You and Your Partner Can Be Wonderfully Happy Again

Susan Page, MDiv, a couples and singles workshop leader since 1980, based in San Miguel de Allende, Mexico, *www.susanpage.com.* She is author of *Why Talking Is Not Enough: 8 Loving Actions That Will Transform Your Marriage* (Jossey-Bass) and *If I'm So Wonderful, Why Am I Still Single?* (Three Rivers).

Time after time, books about relationships urge us to communicate better with our spouses or partners. In my experience as a couples workshop leader and counselor, however, I've seen that talking often fails to solve relationship problems and may even make things worse.

What does work: Taking a completely different, action-oriented approach—something I call spiritual partnership.

BECOME A SPIRITUAL PARTNER

A spiritual partnership is a relationship that is guided by the universal principles of connection, authenticity and love…

• **Connection.** Anything that can move you away from isolation and separation moves you toward connection.

• **Authenticity.** We all have layers of behaviors that hide our actual selves. Authenticity is anything that moves you toward who you really are.

• **Love.** We all possess fears that stop us. By getting past our fears, we let love move freely through our lives.

Talking doesn't accomplish these things. Action does.

What to do: Ask yourself, repeatedly throughout the day, "If I were to behave in accord with my highest spiritual values right now, what exactly would I do?"

When you decide to become a spiritual partner, the focus is no longer on your relationship's problems or on "fixing" your partner, it's on your own actions, which, in turn, will also make an impact on your relationship.

TAKE LOVING ACTIONS

To be a spiritual partner and improve your relationship, you need to take loving actions. *A loving action is…*

• **Driven by the need for spiritual growth,** not for personal gain or "scoring points."

• **Unilateral.** You take it on your own, not because someone wants you to or forces you to.

• **Disciplined.** It's an act of will, not just a response to your emotions.

• **Experimental.** You're willing to try a new behavior or action even though you don't know what the result will be.

What happens when you take loving actions instead of just talking? Your focal point shifts from your partner and your relationship to your own spiritual path. Instead of trying to change your partner, you work to become a more spiritually developed person who can accept and honor your partner for who he/she is as an individual.

GOODWILL

When I was interviewing happy couples for my book *The 8 Essential Traits of Couples Who Thrive* (Dell), I discovered one outstanding thing they all have in common—a spirit of goodwill. Goodwill is an overall feeling of generosity toward your partner. It's the attitude, "I am on your side. I am your ally, not your adversary."

Having the spirit of goodwill is the first and most important loving action you can take, as it will help you to focus on the good parts of your relationship and let you make a genuine effort to diminish the amount of time and energy you devote to the things that are bothering you. It's amazing how many problems in a relationship simply disappear when you bring the characteristics of goodwill—acceptance, thoughtfulness, tolerance, generosity—to them.

OTHER LOVING ACTIONS

By taking other loving actions, you can develop your spirit of goodwill and help it grow…

• **Give up problem solving.** Problems are like goldfish—the more you feed them, the bigger they get. In most instances, it's an illusion to think that you "work on," or solve, a relationship problem. So-called problem solving will simply make you focus in on the problem and not on what you love about the other person or what's good in your relationship.

Experiment: Make a pact with yourself that for a few days you will not focus on or do anything to try to solve a relationship problem you are having. In fact, don't even think of it as a "problem"—think of it as a fact of life, because this lets you learn how to accept it and adapt and live with it.

• **Act "as if."** You can feel angry inside, and admit this to yourself, but still act as if you're not angry. You can choose to behave in a loving way. If you deliberately behave in a way that you know is going to create more harmony, more connection and more love, then you're acting on your spiritual values. It's not a deception or denial, but a deliberate spiritual choice to behave in a way that might bring more positive results than if you behave in exactly the way you feel. You can't control your emotions or order your feelings around, but you have a great deal of choice in the way you behave.

• **Practice restraint.** Make an agreement with yourself that for a given period of time—a day, a week—you will not say anything negative, demanding or critical to your partner.

When you refrain from making such a comment, you open the possibility in yourself that you are going to become more accepting, more compassionate and more forgiving of your partner. You'll probably see the impact of your behavior immediately as the atmosphere around your house becomes much calmer.

Restraint is probably the single most effective loving action.

• **Balance giving and taking.** The old way of looking at the give and take of a relationship is when we disagree about something, "we both have to give 50%" to keep things fair. That does not work very well, because you have no control over what your partner gives. What you do have control over is how much you give and how much you take in a relationship.

If you think you're giving too much and not taking care of your own needs, you can find ways to help yourself without depending on your partner. If you're taking too much, find ways to give to your partner. Never again can you say to yourself, This relationship is unbalanced and my partner isn't giving enough—because you now have the control over that.

Example: You feel that you get stuck with all the housework, and endless discussion about it is getting you nowhere except angry with each other. Accept that talking won't change the situation—but do not stop giving. Instead, take one evening a week for yourself. See a movie, have dinner with friends, enjoy a bubble bath. Let all the housework wait, and let your partner accept your decision—or not.

• **Acting on your own.** To make a spiritual partnership work, you have to be willing to recognize that some relationship problems are the result of your own issues and that you need to handle those issues on your own. Be open but firm with your partner, making it clear that this is something you need to do for yourself.

Example: If control of money is a source of conflict, suggest a way to handle some of your money independently, perhaps with a separate account.

• **Practice acceptance and compassion.** They are the ultimate goal of what you're seeking to do with loving actions and spiritual partnership. People change, not in an atmosphere of criticism, complaining or demanding, but in one of love and support.

Once you start viewing your relationship as a spiritual partnership and begin consciously taking loving actions, it's easy to stay on the new track. Loving actions are so effective that once you see how well they work, you won't want to go back.

Life After Infidelity

Joy Browne, PhD, a clinical psychologist located in New York City. Her internationally syndicated call-in radio show, *The Dr. Joy Browne Show*, is the longest-running of its kind, *www.drjoy.com*. Dr. Browne is the author of many books, including *Getting Unstuck: 8 Simple Steps to Solving Any Problem* (Hay House).

No woman in her right mind would suggest that adultery can strengthen a marriage. *But a relationship can survive and even thrive afterward if the wounded partner finds the courage to demand answers to three questions...*

• **Why did this happen?** Claiming, "I was drunk" or "It just happened" doesn't cut it. If it "just happened" once, then it could just happen again—so there's no basis for resurrecting trust. The unfaithful partner must figure out the real reason—"I felt old and was trying to feel young again" or "I miss the way we used to make love." Once the problem is acknowledged, it can be worked on.

• **How can you promise it will not happen again?** A fidelity plan identifies the lesson learned ("A fling is not worth endangering our marriage")...puts constraints in place ("I will be home by 6 pm every night")...and offers options ("I'll go with you for counseling or do whatever you want to show how sorry I am").

• **What's in it for me if you cheat again?** This idea came about when a caller to my radio show said her cheating husband wanted another chance. He adored his boat—so I said, "If he'll sign a document saying that if he cheats, you get the boat, then you've got a shot. Before he's unfaithful again, he'll think, 'Bimbo? Or boat?' If he won't sign, he's not willing to put his heart into fidelity."

Grown-Up Kids Need Your Love More Than Ever...Even If They Don't Think They Do

Bernie Siegel, MD, the founder of Exceptional Cancer Patients, a form of individual and group therapy, *www. ecap-online.org*. He is the author of the best-selling *Love, Medicine and Miracles* (Rider). His most recent book is *Love, Magic and Mudpies* (Rodale). Based in Connecticut, he retired from general and pediatric surgery in 1989.

The love we give to our children in their early years has a powerful effect on their behavior, life choices and self-esteem. But parents sometimes forget that older children, including teens and those who have already left home, need just as much love.

With love comes self-esteem, the ability to live with criticism and the avoidance of self-destructive behavior. It can even keep kids healthy. In one Harvard University study, nearly 90% of the participants who did not feel loved as teenagers experienced a serious illness by midlife, while only 25% of those who had felt loved had a serious illness.

Lessons I've learned from my experience as a pediatric surgeon, father of five and grandfather of eight...

BE THERE

It is not enough merely to be present with your children—you need to give them your full energy and attention.

Young children yearn for parental attention. Grown-up children are more likely to push their parents away. At the same time, they crave understanding and kindness. It's crucial for parents to reach out even when they're faced with apparent rejection.

Ask all your kids what's happening in their lives—do this often. Do not try to resolve their problems for them. You do not even need to agree with what they're saying. There were lots of times when I didn't always approve of things our children were doing. When I didn't approve, I let them know it. You can love your children and not like things they are doing. Simply show them that you take them seriously and that their thoughts and feelings matter.

LET THEM GROW UP

Parents want more than anything to keep the kids safe. It is tempting to supervise their every move...bail them out of every difficulty...and try to protect them from the consequences of their own (sometimes immature) decisions.

But safety isn't all there is to life. We should encourage kids to take chances and experience new things. That does not mean we should let children risk their lives, but they can't grow up until we stop being so overprotective and allow them to make their own mistakes.

Example: One of our kids did brilliantly in school. I wanted him to attend university and have an incredible career. One day, he told me he wanted to go to an auto mechanic school. It wasn't what I had imagined at all, but you can't make your child go to college. So, after serious thought, I said, "Go ahead."

As it turned out, he later went into law enforcement and ultimately graduated from law school. Today, he restores cars on his own time as a hobby. I learned an important lesson. If your kids have an interest, encourage them to go all the way—even if it isn't something that you wish they would do. There's no telling where they'll wind up eventually.

DEFINE FAILURE

I've heard parents say to their kids things like, "You don't do anything right." I've seen cancer patients who grew up with so much criticism as a child that they were afraid to draw pictures as part of their therapy.

Failure is a word with many different meanings, depending on the way a person experiences it. It can be a disaster or an opportunity—or at the very least, the source of some great stories.

Always tell your children that there's a huge difference between experiencing a setback and being a failure as a person. They will never live fully if they're always worried about failure.

Help your children understand that mistakes are part of growth and that it's possible to succeed even when things don't go as planned.

It also is important to realize that there's immense pressure on kids to succeed in terms of money, job status, etc. But what about the more important kinds of success, such as generosity, honesty and happiness? Without these, all the money in the universe doesn't add up to very much. If you are happy, you are successful.

LIGHTEN UP

Why are so many parents so serious all the time? One of the best ways to stay close to your kids—and have fun—is to stay young at heart. Identify with your kids, rather than feeling you have to be "grown up."

When something goes wrong in your children's lives, find ways to help them laugh at the situation (without embarrassing them). Share a similar story from your own life. Tell them about all your mistakes…how ridiculous you felt…and how it now makes you laugh. At the same time, tell them how you resolved your difficulty and learned to do better.

Every so often, devote a few days to growing young with your kids. Do something they enjoy. Depending on their ages, it could be going to an amusement park or a concert. Enjoy their young adulthood with them. You can always take a catnap when you get home.

Thinking of Adopting a Child?

Benefits for employees who adopt are now offered by nearly half of employers. Among the benefits are cash reimbursement for adoption costs…adoption-related legal services…paid time off…and more. Ask an employer what benefits it offers or plans to offer—more companies are adding adoption benefits all the time.

Randall K. Abbott, senior consultant and practice leader, group benefits and health-care practice, Watson Wyatt Worldwide, Boston.

Natural Cough Remedy for Kids

An FDA review of over-the-counter (OTC) pediatric cough medications found that they posed more risk than benefit to children under age six. Side effects of these medications can include mild sedation or hyperactivity and, in the case of an overdose, death.

Recent finding: A teaspoon or two of honey before bedtime reduces coughing more than the OTC cough suppressant *dextromethorphan* or no treatment. Further research is required to determine if specific types of honey are more effective than others.

Caution: Honey should not be given to children under age one because of a rare but serious risk of botulism.

Ian Paul, MD, associate professor of pediatrics, Public Health Sciences, Pennsylvania State Children's Hospital, Hershey, and author of a study of 105 children, published in Archives of Pediatrics & Adolescent Medicine.

A Mother's Tip

Help your child swallow bad-tasting medicine by first giving him/her a sticky food, such as applesauce or pudding. The food helps prevent the bad taste from coming through.

Alternative: Give the child a drop of honey or a chocolate chip before the medicine.

Deborah Kristeller Moed, an early childhood teacher, the mother of two children and a Bottom Line/Personal subscriber.

Does Your Child Really Need Antibiotics?

Ear infections usually clear up on their own—without antibiotics.

Recent study: As many as two-thirds of the parents of children with ear infections who went

48 hours without filling a prescription for antibiotics never filled their prescriptions. The children who did not receive antibiotics recovered at the same rate as children who started taking them immediately.

David Spiro, MD, an assistant professor of emergency medicine and pediatrics, Oregon Health & Science University, Portland, and leader of a study published in *The Journal of the American Medical Association.*

Antibiotic Alert

Infants given broad-spectrum antibiotics for respiratory tract and ear infections may be more likely to develop asthma later in childhood.

Recent study: A child who got four or more courses of such antibiotics during the first year of life was 50% more likely to develop asthma by age seven than a child who received no antibiotics. The reason is unknown.

Self-defense: Avoid the use of broad-spectrum antibiotics in a child's first year unless necessary.

Anita Kozyrskyj, PhD, an associate professor, faculty of pharmacy, University of Manitoba, Winnipeg, Canada, and leader of an analysis of data on more than 13,000 children, published in *Chest.*

Flu Nasal Spray

Flu nasal spray is more effective than flu shots for young children. According to one recent study, the spray is 55% more effective in protecting children under age five than the shots are.

Likely reason: The weakened but live viruses in the nasal spray (influenza shots contain dead viruses) stimulate an extra immune reaction in the nose and throat.

The spray has been approved for use in children ages two to five. Research has not shown a similar boost in effectiveness among adults.

Samuel Katz, MD, Wilburt C. Davison professor and chairman of pediatrics at Duke University Medical Center, Durham, North Carolina, and former president of the American Pediatrics Society.

Did Your Child Get the Meningitis Vaccine?

The meningitis vaccine is now recommended for children from ages 11 to 18 and may be given to children as young as age two who are at high risk for bacterial meningitis or have been exposed to the disease. The meningococcal vaccine protects against bacterial meningitis and a related bloodstream infection—rare conditions in the US, but ones whose symptoms (stiff neck, fever, low blood pressure and rash) can develop quickly and may lead to death within just hours. Meningitis can be spread by coughing, sneezing and kissing. And, living in a communal setting increases the risk.

The vaccine costs about $89* and is usually covered by insurance.

Jon S. Abramson, MD, past chairman, Advisory Committee on Immunization Practices of the Centers for Disease Control and Prevention (CDC), Atlanta, and professor, department of pediatrics, Wake Forest University School of Medicine, Winston-Salem, North Carolina.

*Price subject to change.

 # If Your Child Is In the Hospital...

Most drugs given to children in hospitals are not approved for use in pediatric patients. In fact, very few medications have gone through testing to prove that they are safe and effective for children.

Result: Nearly 80% of hospitalized children get drugs not specifically approved for people their age. This sort of off-label use is most common with central nervous system drugs, such as morphine.

Self-defense: Parents should always inquire about the interactions with other medications and what is known about the effects of any medicine given to their children.

Samir S. Shah, MD, an infectious diseases physician, at the Children's Hospital of Philadelphia, and leader of an analysis of the medical records of more than 355,000 children, ages 18 or younger, admitted to 31 US hospitals during 2004, published in *Archives of Pediatrics & Adolescent Medicine.*

Before Your Child Gets Glasses

Nearly one in five children wears glasses that he or she doesn't need.

Reason: Optometrists and ophthalmologists who usually treat adults may diagnose children as farsighted, but many children outgrow their farsightedness without glasses.

Best: Take children to a pediatric ophthalmologist, who will be more familiar with children's eye problems.

Sean P. Donahue, MD, PhD, an associate professor of ophthalmology, pediatrics and neurology at Vanderbilt University School of Medicine, Nashville, and the lead author of a study of 102,508 preschoolers, published in *Journal of the American Association of Pediatric Ophthalmology and Strabismus.*

Zinc Is Good for Kids' Brains

In a recent study, seventh-grade students who took 20 milligrams (mg) of zinc daily (twice the recommended daily allowance) for 12 weeks significantly improved their scores on visual and verbal memory tests, as well as their attention when performing tasks.

Increasing zinc intake also has been shown to improve memory in adults.

Best sources for zinc: Lean red meat, fish and grains. With the exception of oysters, beef is the richest source of zinc. A six-ounce serving of lean ground beef contains almost 12 mg of zinc, while a cup of Cheerios contains approximately 4.5 mg and a single slice of toast contains about 0.5 mg.

Caution: Don't give your children zinc supplements without a doctor's supervision.

James Penland, PhD, Agricultural Research Service, US Department of Agriculture, Washington, DC.

What Kids Really Want from Parents

Children wish their parents would relax. In surveys of 600 parents and 1,000 children in grades three through 12, children were asked if they had one wish to change how their parents' work affected them, what would it be? The parents guessed that their children would wish for more parent time.

Reality: The children wished their parents were less stressed and tired.

Advice: Set aside some "unwind" time after work so that your mood doesn't adversely affect your family.

Ellen Galinsky, president, Families and Work Institute, New York City, and leader of the nationally representative study "Ask the Children," presented to the American Psychoanalytic Association.

Depressed Mothers, Troubled Kids

Children whose mothers are depressed are three times more likely to develop anxiety, behavioral disorders and depression than kids whose mothers are not depressed.

Good news: Children do improve when their mothers' treatment for depression is successful.

Myrna Weissman, PhD, professor of epidemiology and psychiatry at the College of Physicians and Surgeons of Columbia University in New York City, and leader of a study of 151 mother-child pairs, published in *The Journal of the American Medical Association.*

A Better Way to Praise Your Kids

In a recent finding, children who were praised for being intelligent ("You're so smart") were less likely to take risks...were highly sensitive to failure...and were more likely to give up when faced with a difficult challenge.

Better: Parents should be sure to give children *specific* praise for their effort, concentration and strategies.

Example: "You must have studied really hard."

Carol Dweck, PhD, professor of psychology, department of psychology, Stanford University, California, and lead researcher of a study of 128 fifth-graders, published in *Journal of Personality and Social Psychology.* She is author of *Mindset* (Random).

 # Turn Off the TV

Too much TV is linked to attention problems in kids.

A recent finding: Children ages five to 11 who watched more than two hours of TV a day were 40% more likely to have attention problems as teenagers.

Possible reasons: TV watching might take the place of concentration-promoting activities, such as reading and games and the rapid scene changes in TV programs may overstimulate developing brains, making it harder to focus on slower-paced reality.

Caution: The study does not prove that TV watching causes attention problems—it may be that children prone to attention problems are attracted to television.

Carl Erik Landhuis, assistant research fellow, University of Otago, Dunedin, New Zealand, and leader of a long-term study of more than 1,000 children, published in *Pediatrics.*

Sex Offenders in Your Neighborhood?

Marjory Abrams, publisher, *Bottom Line* newsletters, Boardroom Inc., 281 Tresser Blvd., Stamford, Connecticut 06901.

Prompted by an item in my local paper, I entered my zip code into the US Department of Justice's Web site at *www.nsopr. gov* to see whether any convicted sex offenders live near me. I got seven "hits," but I wasn't sure how dangerous these offenders were or what I should do with the information.

Law professor Bill Chamberlin, PhD, director of the University of Florida's Citizen Access Project (*www.citizenaccess.org*), informed me that states disseminate this information to alert families that persons convicted of sexually oriented crimes live nearby. But, he explained, on-line information about sex offenders varies considerably by state.

For example, Connecticut provides offenders' names, addresses, birth dates, physical descriptions, head shots, and dates and types of conviction. New York law requires not only a photo of the offender but also the posting of more details about the actual crimes—including the nature of the offenses. California law requires the posting of information about only "sexually violent predators," which it explicitly defines. New Hampshire requires posting convicts with lesser crimes, such as indecent exposure, in addition to more dangerous individuals.

I could probably obtain more information regarding sex offenders in my community (one of them resides only two blocks away!)…but then what? Nancy McBride, national safety director for the National Center for Missing & Exploited Children (*www.missingkids.com*), explains that simply knowing a past offender lives nearby will keep you on alert against potentially dangerous situations. Most crimes against kids are committed by people they know, and surveys show that almost 70% of rape victims know their assailants.

Should I warn my children about the nearby offenders? "You can advise older children about the sex offender, but it is still up to the parent or guardian to supervise his/her kids," said McBride. "Practicing different types of scenarios is most important."

Examples: What if someone asked your child to help search for a lost puppy? Whom could he/she go to for help if he became lost?

Of course, if anyone—a friend or stranger—does anything that makes a child feel scared, uncomfortable or confused, the child should get out of the situation and tell a trusted adult.

If You Have a Teen...

Nearly half of US teens mutilate themselves. Forty-six percent admit to cutting or burning their bodies...biting themselves...or picking at their skin to draw blood. Self-injury is glorified in some movies, songs and Web sites. Teens who do it say it gives them a sense of control over their lives...or that the physical pain distracts them from mental or emotional distress.

More information: Go to Selfinjury.com, or call 800-DONT-CUT.

Elizabeth E. Lloyd-Richardson, PhD, assistant professor of psychiatry and human behavior, Brown Medical School and The Miriam Hospital, both in Providence, and leader of a survey of 633 high school students, published in *Psychological Medicine*.

Better College Visits

If you and your child are in the process of visiting colleges, here's how to get the most from your time...

•**Ask how the school supports its freshmen** as they make the big transition.

•**Check campus security,** including whether escorts and shuttle buses are available late at night.

•**Find out how the college cares** for students who become ill.

•**Visit the local community to find out about shopping and dining** and to see how welcome students are.

•**Sit in on a lecture,** preferably in a subject your child is considering, to evaluate class size and student participation.

•**Eat a meal in the dining hall** to observe the quality and variety of foods offered.

•**Read the student newspaper,** and look at the bulletin board postings to get a sense of campus life.

Arthur Mullaney, publisher, *College Impressions,* a newsletter for secondary-school counselors, and a former high school director of guidance to college admissions in Kingston, Massachusetts.

How to Care for Loved Ones from a Distance

Majd Alwan, PhD, executive director, Center for Aging Services Technologies, Washington, DC, *www.agingtech.org.*

Big electronics companies, such as Philips and Honeywell, have now created high-tech devices for the home that caregivers can use to monitor the activities of their loved ones. With the help of these systems, seniors can now live independently in their homes for longer, forestalling the need for care in facilities.

You may be able to rent these systems from home-care agencies. Also, check with your insurance company to see if the cost is covered.

ACTIVITIES OF DAILY LIVING

With the eNeighbor Auto-PERS, small, wireless electronic sensors are placed in strategic areas of a senior's home to monitor activities of daily living (when someone gets out of bed, moves from room to room, etc.). The sensors communicate with a base station located in the senior's home. If abnormal activity or lack of activity is detected, the base station sends an alert via phone and e-mail to you or someone appointed by you to be on call, such as a health-care provider. There is also a pendant with an emergency call button that can be worn by the senior.

Example: If the shower runs for several hours, the system calls the senior to ask if he/she is OK. If there is no response, the system calls or sends an e-mail alert to someone else, such as a health-care provider or an adult child.

Best for: Seniors capable of taking care of themselves, including taking medications, but who might be prone to falls.

Cost: From $699, plus $59.95 to $89.95 each month for the monitoring service.*

Where to buy: Healthsense (800-576-1779, *www.healthsense.com*).

Also good for independent-living seniors, but without some of eNeighbor's specialized sensors, such as the bed pad that detects presence in bed, the QuietCare system consists of wireless sensors that detect motion, heat or sound. Placed in frequently used areas of the home—

*Prices subject to change.

bathroom, bedroom and kitchen—the sensors transmit data to a book-sized base station located in the senior's home. The station is plugged into an electrical outlet and a phone jack. Data is sent via the phone line to a call center. Caregivers get daily e-mails or can go on-line to a Web site to check on a loved one's typical behavior, when he wakes up, uses the bathroom, eats, etc.

When abnormalities in behavior are detected, the call center sends an alert by e-mail, pager or voice or text message to the caregiver. In certain instances—for example, no morning activity detected—the call center will call the caregiver.

The base station also detects nonemergencies that may require medical attention. For example, if a person usually uses the bathroom once at night but suddenly starts using it much more.

Best for: Seniors who don't require the vigilance of the e-Neighbor system, or who require continual monitoring but whose care is supplemented by home health care part of the day.

Cost: From $199 for the hardware (the base station including heat-sensing antenna to detect home temperature plus six monitoring sensors) and about $99 per month (varies by region) for monitoring data and alerting the caregiver.

Where to buy: QuietCare Systems (800-658-6939, *www.quietcaresystems.com*).

VITAL SIGNS

Viterion Link lets a patient with a chronic disease, such as diabetes, send vital information, such as blood sugar levels, heart rate and blood pressure, to health-care providers and caregivers through the phone line to an Internet server. The patient's health-care provider can access the server through a secure site on the Internet. The server is able to connect to 20 different personal measuring devices from other companies, such as glucose meters from LifeScan and Bayer.

The even more sophisticated Viterion 100 Tele-Health Monitor is designed for home-care use by seniors following a serious episode that required hospitalization. It supplements in-home visits by health-care professionals with frequent vital-sign monitoring and communication with the patient. A display on the screen guides patients through their self-checkup. Patients can measure blood pressure, blood oxygen, blood sugar, weight and temperature. The caregiver (usually a doctor's of-

fice) can send out health-related questions, such as "Did you sleep well?" and "Are you tired today?" and advice messages.

Viterion products are available only through health-care providers, and the cost may be covered by Medicare or other insurance. Discuss it with your loved one's doctor.

Cost: Viterion Link starts at less than $200, and service fees start at less than $50 per month. The Viterion 100 is leased, starting at about $100 per month, including service.

More information: Viterion TeleHealthcare (800-866-0133, *www.viterion.com*).

How to Find A Lost Pet

To locate a lost cat or dog, first search your property—cats and small dogs can get into tight places. Then walk around the neighborhood. Talk to everyone about your pet, and give out your phone number. Try making a noise that your animal is familiar with while walking—animals can hear you from a long way off. Stop often and listen for a response. Also, put personal items with a strong scent outside your home to attract your pet—dirty clothes work well.

Call local veterinarians and emergency clinics, and ask if an unidentified animal has been brought in. And, visit local animal shelters and animal-control agencies. Be sure to post flyers within a one-mile radius of where you last saw your pet. Give a phone number, but no name or address and offer a reward. If possible, put a color photo of your pet on each flyer.

PetRescue.com.

Toxic Fruit

As few as seven grapes or raisins can cause vomiting, diarrhea, shaking and potentially fatal kidney failure in dogs. Never use raisins or grapes as dog treats, and keep the fruits where dogs cannot get to them.

Laurinda Morris, DVM, Danville Veterinary Clinic, Danville, Ohio.

18

Better Ways

Secret to Making a Great First Impression

 e all desire to make an admirable first impression. But to do so, we must understand that there are six different personality types.

Each basic personality type has a unique way of talking and looking at the world. To achieve rapid rapport with a new acquaintance, quickly identify which personality group he/she belongs to, then speak in terms that he is comfortable with. If you do this successfully, everyone you meet will walk away from your initial encounters thinking, "I like that guy—he really understands me."

HOW TO DO IT

When people speak, pay close attention. Hidden in their words and gestures are clues to their personality types. (Each of us has elements of all six personality types within us, but only one

is predominant.) If you cannot determine which category someone falls into, just take your best guess, say something appropriate, then measure the results. There usually is still enough time for a course correction if you sense that this initial guess is incorrect.

Best handshake: When you meet someone for the first time, maintain eye contact and offer your hand for a handshake with the palm pointing directly to the left. A slightly downward-facing palm sends the message that you think there is something wrong with this person...while a slightly upturned palm sends the message that you are a victim. Press your palm to the other person's—a gap between palms during a handshake conveys a lack of trust or closeness.

Taibi Kahler, PhD, president of Kahler Communications, Inc., a management training and consulting organization based in Little Rock, Arkansas, *www.taibikahlerassociates. com.* He is an award-winning clinical psychologist who has been a consultant for NASA and served as communication adviser to former President Clinton. He is author of several books, including *The Mastery of Management* (Kahler).

People do pick up on these subtle signals and form opinions about us without even realizing that they are doing so.

The six personality groups…

THINKERS

Thinkers are responsible and organized. They value facts and logic, and they tend to identify and categorize people and things. According to our research, about 25% of the US population falls into this group. The vast majority of thinkers are men.

Identifying a thinker: Thinkers like to ask questions to gather information. They tend to use phrases such as "How much is…," "What is the difference between…," "What options…," "Does that mean…," and words such as "facts," "information" and "data."

To establish rapport with a thinker: Use phrases such as "I'm here to give you all the information that I can," "Here are your options…," "The three advantages are…" or "The key facts are…" Explain the logic behind your decisions, and encourage questions.

Example: A salesman believes a potential client is a thinker. The salesman might say, "I'm happy to provide all the information I can. We offer four product options. Here are the key facts that you need to know to choose."

FEELERS

All feelers are warm and sensitive. Family, friendship and compassion are very important to them. Feelers perceive the world primarily through their feelings about people and situations. Approximately 30% of the US population falls into this category. The vast majority of feelers are women.

Identifying a feeler: Feelers often talk about comfort levels and personal relationships. They tend to use phrases such as "I feel…," "In my heart…," "I'm comfortable with…," "I care…," "I love…," and words such as "my family," "happy" and "sad."

To establish rapport with a feeler: Use phrases such as "I'd love to hear all about your family," "I can just imagine how you're feeling," "I'm here to be your personal representative" or "You're very welcome here." Use first names, offer compliments and strive to become this person's friend.

Example: A voter tells a political candidate that she "feels terrible" because she lost her job and cannot find a new one. Rather than describe a policy that is meant to spur the economy, the politician says, "I can imagine how much you are suffering. I share your pain."

FUNSTERS

Funsters are lively and playful. They appreciate spontaneity, creativity and humor. Their view of the world is shaped by their strong likes and dislikes for people and situations. About 20% of the US population falls into this group.

Identifying a funster: These people tend to use phrases such as "I like/love…," "I don't like/hate…" or "I want/don't want…" They often use popular words and phrases, such as "wow," "hanging out," "chillin' " and "What's up?"

To establish rapport with a funster: Show that you are fun, too. Be friendly and jokey. Speak with enthusiasm, and use casual terms.

Example: "Hi, Bob! C'mon in and grab a seat! What's up?"

BELIEVERS

All believers are observant, conscientious and dedicated. They value dependability, loyalty and integrity, and perceive the world through this value system. Approximately 10% of people in the US are believers.

Identifying a believer: Believers often use phrases such as "In my opinion…" and "I believe…" and words such as "safe," "trust," "respect," "values," "commitment" and "dedication."

To establish rapport with a believer: Use phrases such as "I'm here to earn your trust and respect," "Your trust is valued" or "We believe in service." Provide references to vouch for you. Admit to any potential problems at the start to show your honesty and integrity. If you are not sure what to say to a believer, tell the truth and trust that this person will value your honesty.

Example: The potential car buyer who responds to your used-car-for-sale classified ad is a believer. Mention your car's minor flaws before the buyer spots them. Explain that you wouldn't want to take advantage of him.

DREAMERS

Dreamers are calm and introspective. They have active imaginations but would rather reflect on what is happening than make a decision or take action. They appreciate privacy and dislike small talk. They often avoid close relationships with business associates. Approximately 10% of the US population falls into this category.

Identifying the dreamer: Dreamers might say "I need time to reflect…," "I'm not sure what to do…" or "I don't want to rock the boat."

To establish rapport with a dreamer: Be calm and deliberate. Take charge of the situation, but give this person time to absorb and reflect upon the information you provide. Use phrases such as "I'm here to help you" and "Let me give you some advice."

Example: Tell a dreamer, "Let me tell you what I think you need to do." Once you have made your proposal, finish with, "You think about that, and we'll talk again later."

DOERS

Doers are charismatic and persuasive. They value initiative, action, adaptability, self-sufficiency and charm. They make things happen. Only 5% of the US population falls into this category.

Identifying a doer: Doers use phrases such as, "Make it happen" or "I'll go for it."

To establish rapport with a doer: Show that you are bottom-line–oriented and can get things done. Use phrases such as "I'm here to make you the best deal I can," or "Let me know what I can do to help you get what you want."

Example: The president of your company is a doer whom you have never met in person. If she calls you into her office and asks you if you can take on a project, do not equivocate. Say, "Absolutely, I can get that done. I need two weeks and access to the latest marketing data."

Great Icebreakers

Marjory Abrams, publisher, *Bottom Line* newsletters, Boardroom Inc., 281 Tresser Blvd., Stamford, Connecticut 06901.

A major part of my job is getting people to talk, so I'm always looking for provocative questions to break the ice. My friend Joe Polish, the brilliant marketer whose company—Piranha Marketing (*www.joepolish. com*)—teaches entrepreneurs how to "rip their opponents to shreds," is the master at getting people to open up. Joe regularly advises business tycoons, top sports personalities and other celebrities.

Joe revealed several of his "secret questions" that anyone can use to get clients, interviewees and even first dates to open up about themselves. A personal favorite of his is, "If you could have superpowers, what would they be?" The question takes the other person by surprise and gets him/her to chuckle, opening up a friendly conversation quickly.

According to Joe, questions used in social settings should focus on the positive, while business settings may lend themselves to discussing problems and challenges. Good in any setting—"What's the most profound book you have ever read…and why?"

A particularly provocative question is, "Who are six people, dead or alive, who have had a positive impact on you?" Some good follow-up questions are, "What three qualities of each person do you admire? Is it loyalty? Commitment to work, family or social justice?" These questions can even help a person determine what he wants in his own life by recognizing the qualities he admires in others.

Joe doesn't like being bored. He favors questions that elicit excitement, and sometimes even friction. He told me about a guest at a dinner party who asked the other guests to share how old they were when they had their first sexual experience. It is not a question I would ever ask—but it certainly broke the ice!

Best Ways to Ask For a Favor

If you need a favor, try leaving a voice message first, so that your request can be considered. Don't sound desperate—be direct, and offer to perform an equivalent good deed in return. If someone helps you, let him/her know about any results. Don't forget to say thanks when he says he will grant the favor...while he is doing it... and again once the favor has been completed. Write a note, send flowers or drop off a gift.

Laurie Puhn, JD, relationship communications expert, New York City.

"People Skills" Are More Important Than IQ

Daniel Goleman, PhD, a co-chairman of The Consortium for Research on Emotional Intelligence in Organizations at Rutgers University, Piscataway, New Jersey, and author of *Social Intelligence: The New Science of Human Relationships* (Bantam). He is also producer of *Wired to Connect,* a downloadable conversation series with experts in the field of social intelligence. His Web site is *www. danielgoleman.info.*

Psychologist and journalist Daniel Goleman, PhD, achieved widespread recognition during 1995 with his groundbreaking book *Emotional Intelligence,* which showed how success in life and work is founded on much more than IQ.

In his most recent book, *Social Intelligence,* he explains that all human beings are wired to connect with one another. When we meet other people face-to-face, our brains search for subtle clues in their facial expressions to deduce what they are feeling—then our minds adjust our own feelings to match. The better you are at this, the more in sync you will be with those around you, increasing your chances of success in personal relationships and the workplace.

Below, Dr. Goleman answers questions about social intelligence...

•**Exactly what is "social intelligence?"** Social intelligence is interpersonal skills. It's our empathic ability to understand what other people are thinking and to feel what other people are feeling. It also is having the willingness and ability to know what to do with this information in order to create smooth interactions with other people and achieve our goals.

•**Are these social-interaction skills something we're born with or something we can develop?** Both. About 15% of children are born with a tendency to shyness, but these children will not end up to be shy grown-ups if they are

encouraged to be more outgoing while they are still young. We are not prisoners of our genetics where social intelligence is concerned. The social wiring in our brains is not even fully formed until our mid-20s, and experiments have shown that we can continue to develop our social intelligence throughout our lives.

•**What's the best way to learn to relate better to other people?** One way is to become a better listener. Do you really hear what people are saying when they talk to you...or do you leap to conclusions about what they mean based on what you are thinking? It takes a concerted effort to become a better listener, but it can be done...

Pay close attention to good listeners you know when they are engaged in conversations. Think back to these skilled listeners during your own conversations.

Make a contract with yourself to never respond until you are certain you understand what has been said. If you're not sure what the other person means, restate what he/she said and ask if that is what he meant.

Use every conversation as an opportunity to develop your listening skills, even in exchanges that are not particularly important to you.

I also recommend the MicroExpression Training Tools (METT) created by facial expression and gesture expert Paul Ekman, PhD ($49* from *www.mettonline.com*). This interactive Internet training tool can dramatically improve your ability to identify those quick flashes of expression that betray people's true emotions.

•**You write that humans do not just identify emotions in others. We actually adopt their emotions as if they were our own. How is this done?** Neurologists have discovered that our brains contain "mirror neurons" that activate the emotions we sense in the brains of those around us. This often occurs without us even realizing it is happening. To a lesser extent, we even pick up emotions from actors on television or in the movies.

This ability to absorb the emotions of those around us makes it easier for us all to work and live together harmoniously in groups, but it also means that we can catch other people's emotions as easily as we catch their colds. You might be having a great day, but if you interact with people

* Prices subject to change.

who are fearful or angry, you could become fearful or angry yourself without knowing why. Or you could walk away suddenly happy from a brief encounter with someone who is upbeat.

• **If we are susceptible to the emotions of others, can it be damaging to spend time with negative people?** If there is someone in your life who is "emotionally toxic," you might want to spend less time with him/her for your own good. If you cannot get these toxic people out of your life—or if you have a job that regularly exposes you to negative emotions, such as an emergency room nurse or police officer—you need to inoculate yourself against negative emotions and learn to be more emotionally resilient. Staying positive may even have a positive effect on toxic people.

I recommend using Jon Kabat-Zinn's books and CDs about mindfulness meditation, a stress-reduction technique taught in many hospitals. His *Mindfulness for Beginners* CD (Sounds True, $19.95) is available at bookstores and on-line at Amazon.com.

• **Is there a way to convey criticism that does not cause bad feelings?** The emotional content of our messages can be important. Studies have shown that two leaders can deliver exactly the same message with completely different results, depending on their emotions when the words are spoken—the team will perform well if the leader is upbeat, poorly if the leader is downbeat.

A boss even can criticize his underling and have that underling walk away feeling good, but only if the boss truly feels positive and supportive when he offers the criticism. If the boss feels anger or exasperation, the employee will more likely become angry or depressed.

When you want to let someone down easy, convey positive emotions and bracket your "no" between two upbeat statements. You can say something like, "It really is great working with you. You always bring me quality ideas. I'm going to have to say no this time—I just don't have room in the budget. Keep up the good work, and we'll talk again in a few months."

• **Are men and women different when it comes to social intelligence?** There are statistically significant differences. In general, most women tend to be more emotionally empathic than men—that is, better able to pick up the emotions of others. Women also tend to be more socially skilled—better able to do the right thing to keep a relationship running smoothly. Men tend to be better at returning to normal after experiencing distressing emotions. Men also tend to have more self-confidence in social situations.

What's Holding You Back? Habits That Sabotage Success

Marshall Goldsmith, PhD, cofounder of Marshall Goldsmith Partners LLC, a network of management and behavioral consultants who work with Fortune 500 CEOs. The American Management Association chose Dr. Goldsmith as one of 50 great thinkers in the field of management in the past century. Located in Rancho Santa Fe, California, he is author of 22 books, including the best-selling *What Got You Here Won't Get You There* (Hyperion). His Web site is *www.marshallgoldsmithlibrary.com.*

What is holding you back from more success in your career and in personal relationships?

The answer might surprise you. I have counseled thousands of high-potential executives and managers and found that it's not lack of talent or intelligence that thwarts success. It's inadequate "people" skills. *Here are the five most common interpersonal habits that hold people back...*

NEEDING TO BE RIGHT ALL THE TIME

You go to lunch with your colleague. He takes you to restaurant X even though you tell him that restaurant Y is better. The experience confirms all your misgivings—restaurant X is terrible. You now have two choices. You could either smugly point out how wrong your colleague is or keep quiet about it and make the best of lunch.

Whenever I give seminars, 75% of the attendees say that they would point out how wrong the colleague is. But a relationship with a colleague is more important than winning a trivial argument. *Strategies...*

• **Do a quick cost/benefit analysis.** Ask yourself, "Is it worth it?" Criticizing your colleague will just make him feel resentful. Conversely, if you act more diplomatically, there is a greater chance that he'll listen to your advice next time.

It's important to win when it counts, but when it doesn't, you often gain more by not winning.

• **Avoid using the words "no," "but" or "however."** You use all these words when you want to pay lip service to the opinions of others, but you really just want to prove them wrong.

Example: You say to your colleague, "The restaurant you chose was highly rated, *but* the food and service were not very good." Trigger words such as these often lead to rebuttals and arguments.

NOT LISTENING

People will tolerate all sorts of rudeness, but not paying attention is especially disrespectful, perhaps because paying attention is something all of us should be able to do with relative ease. *Strategy…*

• **Make the person you are speaking with feel like the only individual in the room.** It's the skill that separates great executives from the merely competent leaders. Former president Bill Clinton was a real master at making everyone he spoke with feel special. He locked in on your eyes and mouth whenever you talked with him. He never interrupted. He made a point of knowing something positive about you, and without making a big show of it, he would say something to let you know he knew it. In essence, he was bragging about you to you.

• **Eliminate the physical affects of impatience.** Don't fidget…glance at your watch…reply before others are done speaking…or respond with robotic verbal ticks ("uh-huh, uh-huh").

MAKING EXCUSES

When you commit a mistake, excuses rarely provide the explanatory, mollifying effect you hope they'll have.

Example: You're late meeting a friend for dinner. When you arrive you say, "It's my kids' fault. They were acting up." What you're conveying to the other person is your insincerity. You're telling him, "I'll make a show of apologizing to you, but it's not my fault."

Also, don't make an apology that blames the mistake on some genetic flaw. You say, "I'm always late. I'm terrible at time management." This makes me think, "So why do I have to suffer for it? And why aren't you trying to get better at it?" *Strategy…*

• **Take responsibility for all your behavior** without trying to rationalize it. Say, "I'm sorry. It won't happen again." Then stop talking about it.

PASSING JUDGMENT ON THOSE WHO TRY TO HELP YOU

Many of the individuals I coach don't know how to respond whenever people around them make a suggestion or offer advice. Their instinct is to dispute the advice.

Example: You seek a colleague's opinion about your marketing plan. He gives you his honest criticism. You respond, "What are you talking about? Everyone else likes it."

This response will push a person away. Next time, he's not going to stick his neck out and might withhold valuable information. You have now created a problem where none should exist. *Strategy…*

• **Use the default response "thank you"** if you have nothing nice to say. "Thank you" is a magical supergesture. It makes people see you as agreeable, even when you are not agreeing with them.

GETTING ANGRY

Anger can make people do what you want, but the price you pay over the long run is steep. Once you get a reputation for being a hothead, it becomes your defining characteristic to the people around you. They're uncomfortable, always waiting for you to blow up and lose control. They fear you, but don't respect you. *Strategies…*

• **Impose a small monetary penalty.** Most bad communication habits can be stopped with careful self-monitoring, but taming a bad temper can require much stronger incentives. I fine executives with hair-trigger tempers $20 every time they blow up. You can do this for yourself. One friend of mine fines himself when he blows up, and the money is sent to charity. Money penalties work well because they provide a very clear challenge and risk/reward scenario that competitive people can relate to.

• **Get yourself a coach,** maybe a sibling, a colleague or a friend who checks in with you a few times a week to see how you are coming with your personal anger-management program. Just knowing you must update another person on your progress strengthens your resolve.

Positive Ways to Deal With Complainers, Pessimists and Other Negative People

Jack Canfield, coauthor of the *Chicken Soup for the Soul* book series, which has sold more than 100 million copies. He holds the Guinness World Record for having the most books (seven) on *The New York Times* best-seller list simultaneously. Located in Santa Barbara, California, he is author of *The Success Principles: How to Get from Where You Are to Where You Want to Be* (Collins). His Web site is *www.jackcanfield.com.*

The world is full with cynics, whiners and naysayers. It's best to weed out the negative individuals from our lives and spend time with people who uplift and encourage us, but some negative people aren't easy to avoid. They could be coworkers, neighbors, spouses, parents, siblings, even our children. *Strategies to deal with negative people...*

- **Concede a negative person's point very quickly and completely.** Whatever he/she complains about, tell him that you agree, then take his argument even further. This leaves the complainer with nowhere to go on the subject, and it might shut him up or elicit an admission that the situation is not really that bad.

    Example: My mother used to tell me that I was a horrible son because I didn't call her often enough. Arguing got me nowhere. Finally I told her, "You're right. I am a horrible son. If I had a son like me, I would think he was horrible, too." She responded, "Oh, you're not that bad."

- **Set up conversational boundaries.** Some people become negative only when certain topics are broached. Tell them that you do not wish to discuss these topics with them in the future, and ask them to agree that this is okay. (You may need to provide an occasional reminder of this agreement in the future.) Do not tell them that their poor attitudes are the reason you want this restriction—that might lead to arguments. Just say that you feel very uncomfortable talking about these topics.

    Example: A man might tell his brother, "Let's not talk about our careers anymore. I feel uncomfortable because our opinions about the workplace are different, and I don't like to argue with you."

- **Share inspirational stories.** Some negative people truly believe that success is impossible. Sharing stories about the victories of others might open them up to the possibility of success in their own lives. Use stories from your own experience, or find material in biographies, memoirs and articles about successful people.

- **Turn complaining sessions into strategy sessions.** Sometimes negativity can be transformed into a mandate for action. Tell the negative person that his complaints have merit—so let's find a way to improve the situation.

    Example: A neighbor complains endlessly about the stupidity of local government. Encourage him to circulate a petition or write an editorial for the local newspaper.

    Complainers often respond to calls to action with some variation of "What's the point? I can't change anything." Explain that if they just sit around complaining, things are guaranteed not to change. If they take action, at least they have a chance.

- **Use humor.** A joke can help lift the dark clouds that a negative person can bring down upon a room. Just make sure that your jokes are about yourself or the situation and never about the negative person. Making jokes at a negative person's expense will worsen his mood.

- **Separate the past from the future.** Negative people often are negative because they have suffered past defeats. These people tend to shoot down ideas with statements such as "We tried that five years ago. It didn't work." Respond that while past experience is worth considering, it is not always a guarantee of what will happen in the future. The world has changed...the economy has changed...technology has changed...and the people involved have new skills. An idea that failed five years ago might succeed today.

- **Press for solutions.** Negative people are good at telling us why our ideas will not work, but they are very bad at telling us how to overcome these problems. Whenever a negative person mentions a perceived problem, immediately ask him (and anyone else present) to come up with three potential solutions. This encourages people to focus in on a solution rather than the problem. Over time, this can become a new way of thinking for them.

• **Cross out all the problems.** Draw a line down the middle of a dry-erase board or a piece of paper. On one side write, "Ways that we can make this plan work" and on the other, "Reasons this plan will not work." Ask for suggestions for both columns. You can do this with your spouse, children, even coworkers. When all the thoughts are in, draw a big X through the second column and say, "Let's focus in on what we can accomplish." This approach allows negative people to express themselves and then move on.

Example: A businessman I know wanted to stage a fund-raiser for the victims of a natural disaster just days after the disaster occurred. The negative people in his group protested that it takes weeks to get such a project off the ground. The businessman wrote up all of their reservations, then he crossed them out and encouraged the group to focus on what could be done. He ended up raising $3 million in three days.

How to Avoid Getting Caught In the Games People Play

The late Martin Groder, MD, a business consultant and psychiatrist in Chapel Hill, North Carolina, and adviser to *Bottom Line/Personal* since 1976. He died in 2007.

W hen we want attention, we behave in a manner that we think will produce desired reactions in others. But when such behavior goes too far, the desired result often is not just attention but also manipulation. When people repeatedly manipulate others, they eventually are met with resistance and other negative reactions.

Psychologists refer to these behavior patterns as the games people play. Once we understand the reasons behind these games, we can take steps to avoid them in others and ourselves.

IMPORTANT DISCOVERY

Psychiatrist Eric Berne, MD, first reported on this "game" behavior in 1964, in his best-selling book *Games People Play.* He explained that people play games to get attention and fill up time if intimacy or productivity is not available. Even stirring up negative attention like anger, outrage and hurt is more gratifying than being ignored or feeling bored or useless, he pointed out.

In my own research, I have explored the very important role that games play in the workplace, where people use them to exercise power, deal with risk and manage interpersonal relations. It has become clear to me that spotting the games others play—and those we ourselves play—can be crucial to our mental health and often our economic survival.

THE GAMES

• **"See what you made me do."** With this game, a manager who is failing and/or has lost the motivation to succeed asks subordinates for suggestions on how to execute a project or solve a problem. Then, when the suggestions fail, the manager blames the subordinates.

In the family, a parent or spouse becomes irritated at being interrupted while performing a task, such as cooking or balancing the checkbook. Then, when a mistake is made, the parent or spouse blows up at the family member who made him/her slip up.

Why the game is played: Feeling victimized puts the player in a morally superior position of power—as opposed to having to recognize the failure.

What you can do to stop it: Instead of falling into the trap, firmly refuse to provide suggestions unless you are empowered to act on them.

• **"Now I've got you"** is played by someone who seems engaged in meaningful activity but whose real aim is to trap others when they slip up. The player is often heard to proclaim that no one does anything right around here.

Why the game is played: It allows the player to feel justified. The player can "righteously" vent his anger.

What you can do to stop it: Make rules and obligations explicit—who is responsible for what and by when—and strictly adhere to them.

• **"Kick me."** In this game, the player behaves in a way that others find obnoxious, irritating and arrogant.

The negative response from others will always arouse a hostile reaction from the player, often followed by an injured wail of, "Why does this always happen to me?" The player is like a person wearing a sign that says, "Kick me."

Why the game is played: The player enjoys watching others lose control while he remains very calm. He likes being victimized while feeling superior.

What you can do to stop it: Don't rise to the bait. Instead, point out the unnecessary provocation and indicate a willingness to work with him—or don't work with him further.

• **"I'm always late—but that's too bad for you."** Workers who are constantly late for work or meetings, miss deadlines or take forever to return phone calls may be playing this game. They always do what they're supposed to but insist on being irritatingly late.

Why this game is played: The player is seeking control and resents being controlled by others. He takes the upper hand by determining the pace of his life and yours without open rebellion.

What you can do to stop it: Discuss the problem openly, making it clear why promptness is vital to the company. Negotiate mutually acceptable limits—and hold the player to them.

• **"What do you think? Thanks, but I disagree."** In this game, the player complains about a problem and fends off every suggested solution by explaining why it won't work.

Why the game is played: It provides the player with reassurance. The player assumes the role of a child, and his listeners are transformed into sage parents giving him their wisdom. And he can feel superior to his failed "rescuers."

What you can do to stop it: Remember that the player isn't looking for a real solution. React with sympathy, not advice. Offer suggestions such as, "That is a difficult problem. What will you do about it?" or simply, "That's too bad."

Dr. Joy Browne's Simple Steps to Solving Any Relationship Problem

Joy Browne, PhD, a clinical psychologist located in New York City. Her internationally syndicated call-in radio show, *The Joy Browne Show*, is the longest-running of its kind, *www.drjoy.com*. Dr. Browne is the author of many books, including *Getting Unstuck: 8 Simple Steps to Solving Any Problem* (Hay House).

Over many years, most people who have called my radio program are unhappy, seeking my help to convince someone else to stop making them miserable. The work I do is based on my conviction that we are all capable of change. But we can only change our own behavior, not that of someone else. I believe this as fundamentally as that the sun will rise tomorrow. *Ways to break free…*

IDENTIFY PATTERNS

When counting or recounting your woes, listen to the words you use. If "always," "usually/tends to," "never" or "everyone" recurs, a pattern may be at work. *Listen to yourself…*

"Aunt Tish never liked me." "My friend Leslie has always put me down." "The people next door avoid me." (Did you hear "usually" in the last one?)

Is everybody else really that stuck? Or could it be you?

Danger: If you notice yourself feeling good about feeling bad and trying to win sympathy, beware—you're on the wrong track.

Solution: Try to determine why someone "always" and "never" does things to or for you. Aunt Tish may be unskilled at demonstrating affection…Leslie may not realize how harsh she sounds…your neighbors may have their own issues unconnected to you—they may be busy or even assume that you are avoiding them.

TURN A NEGATIVE INTO A POSITIVE

When you feel mired in a negative pattern, apply to the situation the positive patterns that have helped you succeed in other areas of your life.

Example: Marvin yells at members of his family, who then get upset. He formerly prided himself on keeping his head during difficult situations at work. Recalling the tools he used to remain cool at the office before his recent retirement—taking deep breaths, waiting 10 minutes to respond when angry, talking about problems, striving to see others' points of view—he can learn to adapt those patterns to his home life.

OLD WOUNDS, NEW TRICKS

In many cases, callers to my show have made an unconscious decision to dwell on injustices of the past instead of working creatively toward a more rewarding future. As a result, they perpetuate their own unhappiness.

Examples: Shelley's husband had affairs, but, despite feeling lonely, she hasn't dated since the divorce…Margo avoids family get-togethers because she believes her daughter-in-law doesn't like her…George, eyeing a pile of rejection slips, stops writing poetry and misses it.

See my point? Yet the "stuck" quality that was clearly holding them back had to be pointed out to them. The next step—accepting the past and moving toward the present—became obvious.

IT'S CONTAGIOUS

You may find that the past in which you are stuck is someone else's.

Example: Sal called my radio show and said, "The woman I love is mourning her lover of 15 years who died three years ago. She says she's not ready for another committed relationship. She's 77. I'm 84 and running out of time. Should we break up?" Sal's love is stuck in her past, a place he doesn't want to go.

Compromise: You can't rush someone else's love (or life) for your own reasons. I suggested that Sal should consider his girlfriend more of a friend and less of a mate and begin to see other women.

DOORS OPEN, DOORS CLOSE

Resistance to change can be disruptive, as can change itself. Admittedly, accepting the inevitable isn't always easy. Shifting family dynamics, for example, can be rough.

One woman's stepdaughter-to-be upset her family by refusing to face the closing of a door. Grace, age 74, a widow of 16 years, called to say, "I am engaged to Bill, who's 81. Our families are happy for us, except Bill's daughter Jane, who is having a hard time celebrating. After assisting

with her dad's physical problems since her mother died six years ago, she resents me. Shouldn't Jane rejoice at her father's new life?"

Many grown children would happily give up caregiving tasks, I told Grace, but Jane may feel that having you on the scene will reduce her significance as the favored child…or see you as a rival, stealing her nurturing role.

Solution: Grace and Bill need to convince Jane that she'll always be important and loved. I recommended inviting Jane to participate in the wedding in a special way…treating her to a lavish meal…giving her a token of their appreciation. "But don't wait for her blessing before getting married," I warned. "Make her feel appreciated, and she'll probably come around in time."

If only Jane had called me.

THE LOSE–LOSE GAME

The relationships between siblings can remain stuck in their childhood dynamics. Those connections fare best without constant criticism. *A classic example…*

Maggie told me, "My younger brother, Bob, is about to move in with our 80-year-old mother. His two marriages and a long-term relationship ended because he accused all three women of cheating on him. Mother and I have repeatedly explained that the real problem is his jealousy. He doesn't listen. She's worried that they'll fight after he moves in. What should we do?"

I told Maggie: "If you violently disagreed with Bob about politics, your best approach would be not to discuss it. Do the same about this issue.

"Give up the notion that you and your mother must convince your brother that you're correct. Your mother can tell Bob, 'I'm looking forward to having you come. Let's agree that we're not going to discuss your marriages because those conversations make us both unhappy.'"

ABANDON GENERALITIES

The more specific you can be about what is irking you, the better equipped you'll be to find a solution. For a jump-start, pose your problem as a question.

Reason: The moment you can formulate a specific question or state a need, you'll have begun to take charge of your present and your future—and refuse to carry the bulky baggage of the past.

More from Dr. Joy Browne...

Say No with a Smile

Many women have trouble saying no. Perhaps deep down, we still believe we must be good little girls, compliant and charming, so people will love us. But when we're pushovers, others take us for granted—and we feel resentful. Here's how to stop being a martyr without giving offense.

● **Sleep on it.** Your nephew asks for a loan. If you are not sure how to respond, instead of agreeing now and kicking yourself later, say, "I'll get back to you." Take time to decide whether you have the means and the desire to comply, then give your answer.

● **Suggest an alternative.** Suppose a friend invites you over for her holiday cookie-baking marathon. A lame excuse ("Sorry, I...um...have to bathe the cat") may insult her. Instead, be honest—"I'd love to see you, but I am dieting. Can we take a walk together instead?"

● **Set limits.** If work for charity eats up family time, for instance, resolve to volunteer only a certain number of hours. Once those hours are booked, decline all additional requests.

Remember that yes rhymes with stress. If you agree to a task and then can't follow through, it's worse for everyone than if you had just said no from the get-go. It's far harder to change a yes to a no than it is to change a no to a yes.

Also from Dr. Joy Browne...

Letting Go of Hurt

Anyone over age four has had someone "do dirt" to him/her at some point—by betraying a confidence, being insulting or abandoning him in a time of need. When this happens, you must get past the hurt to regain happiness.

● **Stop seeing yourself as a victim.** A "poor me" attitude leaves you feeling defensive—and defenseless. A plan of action helps you to overcome the victim mentality.

● **Analyze how the hurt happened.** Were there warning signs that you ignored? For instance, if your cash-strapped brother often expresses concern about money, it is no wonder he was snide when you showed off your fancy new SUV.

● **Recognize your own role in it, however small, rather than blaming the event 100% on the rat fink.** Did a coworker broadcast a nasty rumor about your boss, which eventually was traced back to you? It is easier to change your own behavior than anyone else's—so resolve henceforth not to gossip.

● **Try role reversal.** Imagining yourself in another person's shoes makes it easier to excuse a transgression.

● **Decide if the relationship is worth saving.** If a casual pal is repeatedly insensitive, cut off contact. But if the conflict is with a lifelong friend, try and try again to make things right.

● **Forgive.** Letting go of anger is an investment in your happiness.

How Not to Catch Other People's Stress

Redford Williams, MD, director, Behavioral Medicine Research Center at Duke University, Durham, North Carolina. He is coauthor of *In Control* (Rodale) and *Lifeskills* (Three Rivers). His Web site is *www.williamslifeskills.com*.

Most women can be empathetic, excellent listeners, as well as masterful interpreters of other people's emotional signals. These are admirable qualities—yet they can make a woman vulnerable to feeling another person's stress so acutely that she becomes stressed herself. Thus, she falls prey to "contagious stress."

Like secondhand smoke, secondhand stress is harmful. Chronic stress weakens immunity... contributes to heart disease, depression and other health problems...and even kills brain cells.

To determine if you are prone to taking on other people's stress, consider the four following scenarios...

● **The couple in the checkout line in front of you is arguing.** You begin to feel anxious.

● **Your friend is always running in 50 different directions at once.** After seeing her, you feel frazzled.

● **Your husband gripes incessantly about his tennis team's lackluster performance.**

Whenever he starts to mention it, your whole body tenses up.

• **Your coworker is panicking about a big team project.** Even though your portion of the project is finished—and has been amply praised by the boss—you start to panic, too.

If any of these examples sounds familiar, consider these easy and effective ways to inoculate yourself against contagious stress.

THE FOUR-QUESTION TEST

Whenever you notice that you are beginning to feel tense in the company of someone who is stressed, just ask yourself the following four questions…

1. Is this situation important to me?

2. Is my level of anxiety appropriate, given the facts?

3. Is the situation modifiable?

4. Considering the effort involved, is taking action worth it?

To remember these questions when you are under pressure, use the phrase "I am worth it"—a partial acronym for Important…Appropriate…Modifiable…and Worth It.

IF ANY ANSWER IS NO…

Often, simply answering no to the first question is enough to put the matter in perspective. You may quickly realize that the situation does not involve you personally—as in the case of the feuding couple in the checkout line, whom you don't even know.

If the answer to any of the other questions above is no—because your feelings are out of proportion to the problem, or because you cannot, or choose not to, change the situation—you need a strategy that deflects contagious stress. *Practical techniques you can use anywhere…*

• **Change what you say to yourself.** Cognitive therapists have discovered that it is possible to reason yourself out of anxiety. Take one of the "I am worth it" questions to which you answered no, and turn it into a statement that you repeat silently to yourself.

How this might work: You realize that a situation is not modifiable, so you say to yourself, "I cannot change the fact that my friend is overscheduled. I have suggested that she drop some of her activities, and she has chosen not

to. Maybe she gets an adrenaline rush from multitasking—but this doesn't have to stress me."

• **Use thought-stopping.** This technique can prevent you from reacting automatically or to an inappropriate degree. Every time you find yourself getting pulled into someone's stress—for instance, when you tense up over a trivial matter, such as your husband's tennis team complaints—silently tell yourself to, "Stop!" *If that alone is not enough to change your train of thought, also use one of these strategies…*

• Add in a physical cue. Place a rubber band around your wrist, and snap it as you repeat the "stop" cue. The physical sensation helps to short-circuit persistent thoughts.

• Distract yourself. Hum your favorite song… read an interesting article in a magazine…phone a friend…or make detailed plans for an activity that you're looking forward to, such as your next vacation or planting a new garden.

• Relax. Close your eyes and take four slow, deep breaths. On your initial inhalation, squeeze your hands into fists…then let them go limp as you breathe out and silently say, "relax." On the next deep breath, shrug your shoulders as high as you can…then let them drop as you exhale slowly and focus your mind on the word relax. On the third inhalation, tilt your head to the right as far as you can…and on the fourth breath, tilt it to the left…each time repeating the silent mantra to relax as you exhale. This technique takes only a few moments. Practice it when you are not feeling stressed, to improve your ability to relax at will.

IF ALL ANSWERS ARE YES…

When the answer to all four of these "I Am Worth It" questions is yes, you are affirming that the situation is important to you…your feelings are justified…it is within your power to improve the situation…and the rewards for doing so outweigh the effort involved. In that case, the key to reducing contagious stress is to help the other person solve her problem.

First: Make sure that the stressed-out person wants your assistance. If you just spout advice, she is likely to resist it.

Simple problem-solving techniques are effective in most situations. *The steps…*

• **Brainstorm together.** Write down all the ideas that each of you comes up with, no matter how wacky.

• **Select the best approach.** Once you have got an uncensored list of ideas, winnow them, choosing the options most likely to succeed.

• **Put the plan into action.** Periodically evaluate your progress, and make adjustments to the plan as necessary.

Example: You can't just tune out your co-worker's panic, because the project's overall success is important to you, too. Say to her, "Perhaps it would be helpful to write down every task this project requires of you, prioritize them and then set a manageable schedule for accomplishing each one. Would you like me to work with you on that?" Once your coworker feels more in control and sure of her role in the project, her panic will subside...and you will recover from your case of contagious stress.

Take My Hand

Holding your spouse's hand can help to reduce stress.

Recent finding: Women threatened with electric shock had reduced activity in the brain's stress-responsive regions when they held their husbands' hands. Stress increased when holding strangers' hands or not holding hands at all.

James Coan, PhD, an assistant professor, department of psychology, University of Virginia, Charlottesville, and the leader of a study published in *Psychological Science.*

Forgive for Your Health

Forgive others for the benefit of your health. Forgiving others eliminates the toxic effects of stress that result from anger at being wronged. And it increases your ability to become close to other people, which is also important to physical and mental health in many ways.

Edward Hallowell, MD, director, The Hallowell Center, Sudbury, Massachusetts, *www.drhallowell.com.* He is also author of *Dare to Forgive: The Power of Letting Go and Moving On* (HCI).

A Benefit of Anger?

Anger is thought to trigger irrational behavior, but studies show that sometimes people think more clearly when they are angry.

Possible reason: Anger motivates people to resolve what is making them feel upset and protect themselves from threats.

Wesley G. Moons, PhD candidate, department of psychology, University of California, Santa Barbara, and co-author of a study of 550 people, published in *Personality and Social Psychology Bulletin.*

Self-Help for the Winter Blues

Tamara Eberlein, editor, *Bottom Line/Women's Health,* Boardroom Inc., 281 Tresser Blvd., Stamford, Connecticut 06901.

Every winter, I try to fight the urge to eat and sleep too much and mope around indoors feeling irritable and unmotivated. Research shows that lack of sunlight may disrupt the internal body clock...increase production of melatonin, a sleep-related hormone that's linked to seasonal depression...and reduce serotonin, a mood-regulating chemical in the brain.

The "winter blues"—and its more serious form, seasonal affective disorder (aptly acronymed SAD)—affect three times as many women as men. The blues are more common in the North but also strike Southerners. *Based on advice from SAD experts, here's how we can ease the cold-weather doldrums...*

• **Start an indoor project.** Learn to paint, read all of Jane Austen's novels or dust off the old clarinet.

• **Socialize.** Plan a party, join a club or eat out. When stuck inside, phone or e-mail a friend.

• **Find cold-weather fun.** If it snows, ride a sled, build a snowman or ski. In the South, hike or bike—you'll survive the 40°F cold snap.

• **Simulate spring.** Buy cut flowers, or paint a room sunny yellow.

• **Avoid downers.** Don't pick this time to write a will or visit pessimistic people.

• **Ask a doctor about light therapy.** Sitting in front of a portable light box (which provides an intense light) can trigger a mood-lifting biochemical change in the brain. Light boxes are sold on-line and in some major drugstores without a prescription ($200 and over*). I have used one—and it helps.

*Price subject to change.

How to Overcome Life's Disappointments

Rabbi Harold S. Kushner, Rabbi Laureate of Temple Israel in Natick, Massachusetts. He is author of numerous best-selling books, including *When Bad Things Happen to Good People* and *Overcoming Life's Disappointments* (both from Anchor).

Most of us must face the disappointment of not having all of our dreams come true. The fact that we experience failure does not make us failures—although the manner in which we respond to these failures could do exactly that. *Here is what to do when you have trouble getting past life's disappointments…*

• **Remember for whom you are working— you.** The promotion you had hoped for went to someone else…your family doesn't appreciate the many things you do for them. It is natural to feel disappointment when things like this occur, but our mistake is to rely on others for validation. We should work hard because to do any less would be letting ourselves down. We should work hard for the sake of our own sense of integrity and knowing we have done our best.

• **Understand that those who have never been disappointed are really the failures.** People who achieve everything they set out to achieve in life obviously have set their bars too low. We achieve more if we aim high—though this also means that we will be disappointed more often, because lofty goals are difficult to reach. Understand that disappointments are inevitable when we strive for greatness, and consider your

life successful if you accomplish just a fraction of your goals.

• **Escape the isolation of disappointment.** We feel alone when we lose a loved one…suffer a life-threatening illness…or experience a major financial setback. Our loneliness then drives us further into despair.

Example: My wife and I saw only happy families around us when one of our children became seriously ill. Not until after our child had died did we discover that some other families we knew had gone through similar ordeals.

A tragedy does not separate us from everyone else. Sharing our grief only brings us closer to the brotherhood of the afflicted, a huge club consisting of everyone who has ever endured pain or inequity. Our misfortune even makes us qualified to help other grieving people. Assisting others can get us past the sense of helplessness that often comes with major disappointments.

• **Keep disappointments in perspective.** Try to remember what was worrying you two weeks prior. Many people cannot. Most disappointments are less consequential than we feel they are at that time. Psychiatrist George Vaillant, MD, director of the Harvard Study of Adult Development, which followed 800 men for five decades, found that it is not the bad things that happen to us that stay with us in life—it is the good people we run into along the way. People who handle misfortune best are the ones who focus not on what happened to them but on all the people who rallied around them when it happened.

• **Fashion a new dream.** There's no reason to let the failure of one dream keep you from dreaming—and trying. The experience you have gained can help you create a new, more realistic and achievable dream.

Example: When Al Gore lost the presidential election, he recast his dream. He moved from politics to environmentalism, producing a highly acclaimed documentary on global warming called *An Inconvenient Truth.* His success and influence have been tremendous since his "failure."

• **Get angry with God.** Some people consider it wrong to get angry with God. I believe that if we cannot get angry with God, then we have a constrained, artificial relationship with God.

When the world disappoints you, go ahead and blame God. Vent your anger, and bemoan the inequity. Voicing an unhappiness with life's disappointments can bring you closer to moving beyond them. God does not mind. He will continue to stand by you no matter how angry you become. God understands that you really are getting mad at your misfortune, not at Him.

All the friends, coworkers and loved ones on whom we depend sometimes will disappoint us. *Two ways to forgive them...*

• **Don't focus on the mistake.** Before ending any relationship based on a single failure—however terrible—consider this person in total. Think about who he/she has been in the past and who he can become in the future.

Example: A husband cheats on his wife. The wife might choose to end the relationship, but she also might choose to view this as a single error from a loving but flawed partner.

• **Consider forgiveness a favor that you do for yourself.** People often believe that if they forgive those who have wronged them, the transgressors "get away with" the misdeeds. But forgiveness benefits you more than the transgressor. Offering forgiveness removes the heavy burden that you have been carrying around. It cleanses your soul and eases your pain. The sooner you forgive, the sooner you can move on from your disappointment.

How to Feel More At Peace When a Loved One Dies

Alice Aspen Marsh, motivational speaker and author based in Los Angeles.

Many people have unresolved feelings of hurt and guilt when a loved one dies. It is important to find closure for yourself—otherwise, you'll carry these lingering troubled feelings into relationships throughout your life and even may pass them on to your own children. *What to do...*

• **Write a letter to your loved one telling him/her what you needed and what you got and didn't get from him.**

Examples: I felt left out...I never got the respect I needed...you never really saw me for who I was.

• **Then create an action so that the letter gets "sent."**

Examples: Read it at the cemetery...tear it up or burn it...take it to the ocean, read it, then tear it up and let the pieces float away.

• **Talk to others.** If you have siblings or other relatives who knew your loved one well, ask if they would be willing to talk with you. Supportive listeners can be vital to healing.

How to Stop Memory Loss Before It's Too Late: Recent Research

Gary Small, MD, professor of psychiatry and biobehavioral sciences, director of the UCLA Center on Aging and one of the world's leading physician/scientists in the fields of memory and longevity. Dr. Small has authored more than 500 scientific papers and was named one of the world's top innovators in science and technology by *Scientific American*. He is author of *The Memory Bible, The Memory Prescription* and *The Longevity Bible* (all are from Hyperion). His Web site is *www.drgarysmall.com.*

Nearly half of all people age 50 or above complain of minor, age-related memory problems.

Good news: Studies show that 65% of aging's effects—including memory-erasing aging of the brain—are not caused by genes but by lifestyle. That means you can take action to prevent memory loss.

A brain-healthy diet, regular exercise, stress reduction and memory-boosting techniques are four effective ways to keep your memory sharp.

Recent finding: Combining these lifestyle strategies can strengthen your brain and improve your memory immediately. Scientists at the UCLA Center on Aging conducted a study of 17 people, average age 53, with mild memory complaints typical of middle age. Eight participants went on a 14-day program consisting of a brain-healthy diet, aerobic conditioning, relaxation exercises and memory training...nine did not.

Before and after the program, all 17 participants were tested for memory and mental ability. They also had brain positron emission tomography (PET) scans to observe blood flow in their brains. After the 14 days, subjects on the brain-healthy program exhibited an average 20% improvement on a test of mental ability, and their scans showed an average 5% greater efficiency in a brain area that regulates memory. The control group showed no significant changes.

Here is what to do to preserve and improve your memory, starting today...

DIET THAT FIGHTS MEMORY LOSS

Healthful dietary strategies can nourish the brain...

•**Limit your calorie intake.** A high body mass index (BMI) is a risk factor for Alzheimer's and other forms of dementia. Being overweight also increases risk for high blood pressure and diabetes, which can lead to a stroke (death of brain tissue), as well as resulting memory loss or dementia.

•**Eat low glycemic index carbohydrates.** Fast-digesting carbohydrates, such as sugar and white flour, cause spikes in blood sugar levels, which can lead to diabetes—a disease that reduces circulation to the brain.

Recent finding: People who have "borderline diabetes"—slightly higher-than-normal blood sugar levels—have almost a 70% higher risk for developing Alzheimer's than those with normal levels, reported Swedish researchers at the 2006 International Conference on Alzheimer's Disease and Related Disorders.

The glycemic index (GI) is used to measure how quickly the carbohydrates metabolize. Slow-digesting foods that are low on the GI include most whole grains, beans, legumes, fruits, vegetables, nuts, seeds and low-fat dairy products. Make these the bulk of your diet.

•**Keep blood sugar levels steady.** Eating three smallish meals and two snacks a day helps keep blood sugar levels even. For snacks, try mixtures of healthy carbohydrates and protein, such as raisins and almonds...or fresh fruit and low-fat cottage cheese.

•**Consume ample quantities of omega-3 fatty acids, and reduce omega-6 fatty acids.** Omega-3 fatty acids—in fatty fish, such as salmon, mackerel, lake trout, herring and albacore tuna, and in walnuts, flaxseeds and their oils—keep brain-cell membranes soft and flexible.

Recent finding: Dutch researchers tested the mental sharpness of 210 healthy men between ages 70 and 89 over five years. The researchers reported in the April 2007 issue of *The American Journal of Clinical Nutrition* that those who regularly ate fish rich in omega-3s had a slower decline in mental function than those who didn't eat fish.

Omega-6 fatty acids, found in margarine, mayonnaise, most processed foods and fried foods, may contribute to chronic brain inflammation.

•**Favor antioxidant-rich foods.** Oxidative stress—basically, the internal rust from everyday cellular wear and tear—accelerates brain aging. Antioxidants slow that process. Fruits and vegetables are high in antioxidants.

Best fruits: Berries of all varieties, cherries, kiwi, oranges, plums and red grapes, as well as prunes and raisins.

Best vegetables: Avocados, beets, broccoli, brussels sprouts, corn, eggplant, onions and red bell peppers.

Recent finding: In one study of 1,800 older people, published in the September 2006 issue of *The American Journal of Medicine*, researchers at Vanderbilt University School of Medicine reported that drinking three or more four- to six-ounce servings per week of antioxidant-rich fruit or vegetable juice cuts the risk of Alzheimer's by 76%.

THE 10-MINUTE REMEDY

Exercise improves the flow of oxygen and nutrients to brain tissues and may promote growth of brain cells. Studies show that people who are active between the ages of 20 and 60 are three times less likely to develop Alzheimer's.

Recent finding: Walking for as little as 10 minutes a day decreases the risk of developing Alzheimer's by 32%, according to a study in the May 2006 issue of *Annals of Internal Medicine*.

Try doing several forms of aerobic exercise—walking, swimming, biking and/or other activities that comfortably raise your heart rate—and choose those that you enjoy most and that you can fit into your day. Thirty minutes of aerobic exercise most days of the week is a good prescription for brain health.

SELF-HYPNOSIS

Laboratory research shows that animals subjected to continuing stress have fewer cells in the hippocampus, a brain structure involved in memory and learning. In human studies, even just several days of exposure to high levels of stress decreases memory performance.

Ways to reduce stress include getting plenty of sleep and not having too much to do. *Also, practice stress-reduction techniques, such as the following self-hypnosis exercise...*

Sit in a comfortable position...take three long, deep breaths...and try to relax all your muscles. Focus your attention on a spot on the wall or on a piece of furniture. Try to empty your mind of any thoughts. Concentrate on your focus spot, and breathe slowly. Repeatedly tell yourself that the longer you pay full attention to the spot, the deeper your sense of relaxation will be. Do this for five minutes. Build up to 10-minute sessions twice a day.

More from Dr. Gary Small...

Memory Tricks

Three basic skills are the foundation of an effective memory-training program...

• **Look.** The biggest reason that people don't remember is that they do not pay attention. By making a conscious decision to absorb information—by looking or listening carefully—you can fix information in your memory.

• **Snap.** Transforming information into vivid mental snapshots that have movement, dimension and detail is one of the most effective techniques for long-term memory storage.

Example: If you park your car on level 3B of a parking garage, visualize three giant bumblebees over your car and you'll remember the spot.

• **Connect.** Try to associate two or more snaps so you can remember the connection later, a skill that will help you connect the name to the face.

Example: If Mrs. Beatty has full lips, focus on her mouth to create a memorable face snap.

If you are a movie buff, her name snap is easy—you'll see the actor/director Warren Beatty. Connect the two snaps with the image of Warren Beatty kissing her lips. Next time you see this woman, you'll likely remember her name.

Anemia Impairs Brain Function in Women

In a recent study, researchers gave 354 women from ages 70 to 80 cognitive tests as well as blood tests to check for anemia (a deficiency in hemoglobin, the oxygen-carrying molecule in blood).

Result: Women with mild anemia scored up to five times worse on the cognitive tests than those who did not have anemia.

Theory: When hemoglobin levels are extra low, blood carries less oxygen to the brain, leading to cognitive decline.

Self-defense: If you have symptoms of anemia, such as fatigue, muscle weakness or dizziness, see your doctor.

Paulo H.M. Chaves, MD, PhD, assistant professor of medicine and epidemiology, Johns Hopkins University, Baltimore.

Pour Another Cup of Coffee

Caffeine may keep memory problems at bay in women, according to new research. In a study, women age 65 and older who drank three cups of coffee per day had 30% less risk for memory decline than women who drank one cup or less. Coffee drinkers over age 80 had 70% less risk.

Karen Ritchie, PhD, lead researcher, INSERM, French National Institute for Health and Medical Research, Montpellier, France.

What to Eat for Better Memory

Consuming foods with *epicatechin,* such as black or green tea, cocoa, blueberries and grapes, may improve memory. Epicatechin is an antioxidant, which reduces damage caused by harmful molecules called free radicals.

Recent finding: Epicatechin helps increase the size of blood vessels in an area of the brain that is important for memory.

For a bigger boost: Exercise increases epicatechin's effect on memory.

Fred Gage, PhD, professor, laboratory of genetics at the Salk Institute for Biological Studies, La Jolla, California, and leader of a study of the effects of epicatechin on mice, published in *The Journal of Neuroscience.*

Simple Steps to Control "Spam" E-Mail

Patricia Robison, president, Computing Independence, Box 2031, New York City 10011. She is a technology security specialist and gives seminars on using computers and technology safely and efficiently.

Junk e-mail, or "spam," is impossible to avoid. But it is easy to manage so that it becomes only a minor bother. *Simple steps...*

• **Have multiple addresses.** If you give your e-mail address to businesses or post it on-line in discussion groups or on blogs, it is sure to draw a flood of spam.

In that case, set up two addresses—one you keep only for use by family and close associates, and another you make available to the public. Then, set-up a "spam trap" (see next bullet). Free e-mail accounts are available from many providers, including Gmail.com, Yahoo.com and Hotmail.com.

• **Create a "spam trap."** Nearly all the e-mail programs today provide filter systems that can sort mail as it arrives into mailboxes you set up. These filters focus on such items as the names of the sender and recipient. Using them, you can set a simple "spam trap" that will catch the great majority of the junk e-mail.

How: E-mail has three address lines—"To," "CC" (for copies of a message) and "BCC" (blind copies).

The To and CC address lines are visible to the message recipient, but the BCC line is not. Mass mailers use the BCC line to hold long lists of message recipients. If such a long list were visible, it would make the message huge.

Key: Since most spam is mass-addressed on the BCC line, create a spam trap by setting a filter that simply catches all mail that is not addressed to you on either the To or CC line and sends it into the trash. This will catch the bulk of the spam sent to you so you need never see it. For instructions, check under "help" for your e-mail.

Note: It's possible that a legitimate party will send you messages addressed on the BCC line. To account for this, you can set a filter to catch all mail from that sender and sort it into your regular in-box.

Best: Use a spam trap and two e-mail addresses. You'll keep your private e-mail free of spam (or nearly so) while making it easier to retrieve genuine messages from your "public address" in-box, after the trap deletes most of the spam sent to it.

You need only occasionally review your "public address" in-box to find real messages from people newly trying to reach you. And most of the spam sent to you will never be seen.

19

Business Success

How to Never Get Fired

Do your job well, and your organization will consider you a valuable member of the team, correct? Unfortunately, it does not always work that way. Employees who desire to earn stellar performance reviews, promotions and raises—or even just hang on to their jobs during periods of layoffs—must do more than fulfill their job objectives. *They must take extra steps to be seen as especially valuable...*

GET CLOSER TO THE MONEY

To increase your value, decrease the distance between you and your employer's major sources of revenue. If you're in sales or account management, you probably are close to your company's revenue. But if you're in the legal department... or human resources...or technical support, you might not have anything to do with corporate revenue directly. If so, you're missing an opportunity to become more valued.

See if you can...

• **Provide support to your organization's salespeople in the field.** If the top salespeople consider you to be indispensable, then you are indispensable.

• **Join a team that works directly with a big client.** Go out of your way to assist this client in any way possible, even if it goes beyond the official limits of your job description. If a big client loves you, your employer will, too.

Example: If you work in the information technology (IT) department, solve your largest client's IT problems, even if the problems have nothing directly to do with your company.

Keep your work team and your boss informed about what you're doing so that you don't blindside them or create unpleasant surprises. Test out your riskier ideas or approaches with a trusted coworker before trying new approaches with a real customer.

Peter Uher, PhD, partner in the Atlanta office of Traversa Consulting, Inc., a consulting firm that specializes in leadership development, *www.traversaconsulting.com*.

• **Find ways to help your employer slash costs if you can't get close to your company's revenue.** This, too, directly improves the bottom line and your value to the company.

HELP THE BOSS

Find out how your boss's job performance is evaluated, then help him/her achieve his goals. Your value to your company is determined not so much by your job performance as by your boss's perception of your job performance. One great way to improve that perception is to accept your boss's career goals and job objectives as your own. Assist your boss even in areas that are not your direct responsibility, and you will be considered a valuable asset.

Ask your boss if there's any goal or objective that is of particular concern to him, then find a way to help him in this area.

If your relationship with your boss is not close enough to ask this, strive to make it that close—having a tight personal relationship with your boss will help your perceived value. If your boss isn't the chummy sort, at least have a quick "clarification discussion" about how your goals mesh with the company's goals. That should help you better understand the big picture.

Example: A junior lawyer with a large corporation learned that her boss's job evaluation depended on the success of upcoming meetings with difficult government regulators. The junior lawyer had dealt with the same regulators in a previous job and was able to give her boss useful details about each regulator's personality and style.

SHOW A WILLINGNESS TO LEARN

Employees who are eager to learn new things tend to be valued beyond their current contributions to their companies. Such employees are labeled "high potential" and frequently land on the fast-track for promotion. Employers see their ability to absorb new skills as a sign that their job performance will continue to improve...that they could become the future company leaders ...and that they are adaptable enough to remain useful even if the marketplace or the company changes.

To show a willingness to learn, enroll in night classes that are relevant to your career. Review trade journal articles about new techniques in your field, and discuss them with your boss. Volunteer for cross-departmental teams, and take an interest in the workings of the company outside your area.

Example: A salesman might spend time talking with his company's engineers so that he understands the product line better than anyone else in the sales department.

BE A FIXER

Something always goes wrong in a business, throwing budgets and schedules into jeopardy. Many employees try to dodge the chore of fixing such mini disasters, but that's a mistake. An employee who earns the reputation as a fixer of blowups will be among the most valued. A fixer takes problems off of his boss's desk and is loved for it. His job usually is safe even when the company hits a rough stretch, because he's seen as someone skilled at steering through the rough stretches.

Example: A large corporation new to the cosmetics business finds out that some antiaging claims it is making about its soon-to-be-released product could run afoul of the Food and Drug Administration. Though it isn't in his job description, a midlevel executive who has dealt with the FDA in the past volunteers to help with the problem.

SPEAK UP WITHOUT HOGGING THE SPOTLIGHT

Overlooked often means undervalued in the workplace. The employees who keep their heads down and quietly do their work seldom get as much recognition as those who toot their own horns. Inform your boss in person or via e-mail whenever you accomplish one of your job objectives or reach a milestone on a long-term project. Contribute during meetings in ways that show you are prepared and add value. It's not enough just to agree with what other people say.

The trick is to speak up and get noticed without going too far and coming off as overbearing. Ask a trusted colleague to let you know how you're perceived and to cut you off when you're talking too much. Offer to do the same for him.

STAY ONE STEP AHEAD OF YOUR COMPANY

Is your employer about to launch a new product line? Expand into a new country? As soon as you hear rumors about a new corporate direction or major project, position yourself to be an asset in that area. Read up on business practices in the country that your company will be entering, or start learning the language. Research the new product area by reading articles in business publications or by networking with those in the sector. You'll always be valued if you're always where your company is heading.

Helpful: Try to get assigned to the core team evaluating a major acquisition or a high-profile product launch. Even if you are just a small part of this team, you'll be perfectly placed to play a role in your company's future. You'll also have a chance to interact with some of your company's most trusted people.

If the project fails, the risk of "going down with the ship" in this kind of circumstance is pretty minimal because in new product innovation, "failure" is expected more often than major success. For every iPod-like hit, Apple has a bunch of products that are barely noticed by the consumer. Most companies realize that innovation is a game of averages, much like baseball. You strike out more often than you have a hit. To succeed in the long run, you need to keep swinging the bat and keep innovating.

"I Didn't See It Coming": Warning Signs That You Might Lose Your Job

Amy Dorn Kopelan, president of the conference management organization Bedlam Entertainment, Inc. in New York City, and a coauthor of *I Didn't See It Coming: The Only Book You'll Ever Need to Avoid Being Blindsided in Business* (Wiley, *www.ididntseeitcomingthebook.com*). Her 20-year career at ABC included nine years as the programming manager for *Good Morning America*.

Even the most secure-seeming job is never completely safe. Changes in a company's direction…petty office politics…a strained relationship with one's boss…or any of a host of other factors can cost even the most competent worker his/her job.

Amy Dorn Kopelan lost her position as head of morning programming at ABC in 1995, when Capital Cities Communications acquired the network. She had thought her job was safe because of the high ratings of their morning programs. She failed to consider that Capital Cities already had a skilled morning programmer and had no need for two.

Kopelan, along with two other high-powered executives who lost their jobs, decided to write a book on warning signs of workplace trouble. *Here are six career-threatening events and what to do about them…*

1. Your company merges or is acquired. Top-performing employees often just assume they'll survive the layoffs that follow a merger or an acquisition, but an entire division might be eliminated, taking the stars out the door along with everyone else…or the acquiring company might already have someone in your role. Do not feel completely secure even if your boss "guarantees" you that your job is safe—in the new company, your boss might not have the power to make the final decision.

What to do: Consider how your skills and talents could be applied elsewhere in your organization, and discuss this with executives in those divisions. This increases your odds of finding a safe haven should your current division or position be eliminated. Also prepare an exit strategy, which would include networking with others in the industry, updating your résumé, contacting headhunters and trying to quickly acquire any important skills you lack. This way you're all set to look for a job if you need to.

2. Your boss loses power. If your boss falls out of favor with the company's top brass, his career is not the only one at risk—yours could be threatened as well. Your whole department might be viewed negatively, stalling the careers of all assigned to it…your boss's favorable opinion of you will have very little weight, making it harder for you to advance…and your boss's fall from grace could mean a new leader will soon take over, which could create its own problems (see below).

Signs a boss is losing power…

• His demands become uncharacteristically unrealistic as the pressure to produce forces him to ask the impossible of underlings.

• A consultant is brought in to study your department.

• The departmental budget is slashed.

• Your boss suddenly has trouble getting access to top executives.

What to do: The safest strategy is to attempt to transfer to a different department offering a more highly regarded leader. The more aggressive strategy is to put yourself forward for your boss's job. You could talk to a division head you know or someone you have befriended in human resources to decide how best to go about this. Attempt it only if you have specific ideas for improving the department and a track record that suggests that such a promotion is merited.

3. You get a new boss. It's just not enough to show your new boss that you are intelligent and hardworking. To make certain that your career path remains on course, you also need to match your style to that of your boss. Does he like to receive daily e-mails from people who report to him or just the occasional verbal update? Does he encourage an informal atmosphere or a buttoned-down workplace? Does he like hard-driving go-getters or easygoing team players?

What to do: New bosses often form lasting opinions of their employees within minutes of meeting them, so it is best to get the answers to these questions before the boss walks through the door. As soon as you learn your new boss's name, start tracking down any employees, clients and colleagues from his previous positions who can fill you in. Be aware that word might get back to the new boss, so frame your queries in a very positive way.

Example: "I'm really excited about working with John and want to make a good impression. What can you tell me about him?"

4. A coach is brought in. If your organization brings in a coach to help you improve your communications or conflict-resolution skills, the appropriate response is to fear for your job. These coaches typically are hired to spend time with executives whom companies intend to let go. A report from an outside coach stating that an executive was unwilling or unable to address his serious communication problems will make it more difficult for this executive to sue the company for wrongful termination later.

What to do: Listen to the coach, and implement his advice even if you consider it silly or unnecessary. Your company might have hired this coach to push you out the door, but if you show improvement and maintain a positive attitude, management might let you keep your job.

Exception: Consider it a very positive sign if a coach is hired to help you with your marketing skills. Marketing skills coaches generally are hired when companies think an executive has excellent ideas but needs to learn how to present them better. (If you are not sure whether a coach hired to work with you is a positive or negative omen, find out which department is paying the coach's bill. Your career could be in danger if it is the human resources department.)

5. You remind your boss of someone he is/was fond of. It can seem like a huge career boost when a boss takes a liking to you based on a perceived similarity with someone else, such as a son or daughter, spouse, protégé or even himself at your age.

In the long run, however, this is more likely to harm your career than help it. Your colleagues could come to resent your seemingly undeserved special treatment, making it difficult for you to work with them. Or your boss could start to base his evaluations of you on the abilities and actions of someone else, taking your future out of your control and possibly hindering your career.

What to do: Consider whether there is something in particular about your behavior or appearance that triggers the association with this other individual. Take steps to alter this similarity.

Example: If your boss treats you like a son and you find yourself being deferential toward him, reposition yourself. Say something such as, "I've been thinking about what we discussed last week, and I have a very different approach."

Also, establish boundaries if the boss seems to be trying to get too close. If you are asked to join your boss for drinks or dinner more often than your colleagues, thank him for the invitation but say that you have previous plans.

And, keep your colleagues on your side by standing up for their interests with the boss.

6. You are promoted ahead of all your peers. Being promoted in your department bodes very well for your future—but if mishandled, it could derail your career. Some of your colleagues will resent you for getting the promotion that they had hoped for. Others might have trouble treating a former equal as the boss. If you cannot convince the entire team to treat you with respect, you lose effectiveness as a manager and your career could stall.

What to do: Do not celebrate your promotion in front of your colleagues. This will only deepen any animosities. *Also...*

• Meet with each member of your new team one-on-one, and reassure each individual that you respect his talents.

• Let team members take the glory when your team has success. You should claim credit primarily for leading your troops.

• If any member of your group cannot adjust to your new role, try to find the person another position elsewhere in the company.

Should You Take a Job Buyout Offer?

Robert Barry, president of Barry Capital Management, a financial-planning firm located in Hackettstown, New Jersey and in Wauwatosa, Wisconsin, *www.barrycapital. com.* He is also a past president of the Financial Planning Association.

Some of the big automakers have offered as much as $140,000 to tens of thousands of workers willing to give up their jobs. Automakers aren't the only ones paying employees to not show up. Many other organizations have "bribed" employees to quit in recent years. And the pace of such offers may pick up if the faltering economy doesn't. Companies provide these "buyout offers" and "early retirement packages" to trim their payroll, pension and health-care obligations without resorting to layoffs. *How to decide whether to accept...*

EVALUATE YOURSELF

Even before you analyze the financial details of the buyout offer, ask yourself...

• **What do I want to do with the rest of my life?** Have you always dreamed of trying a different career...working for a different company...

moving to a different part of the country...or retiring early? Getting the buyout offer might be a great opportunity to do so.

• **How employable am I?** If you're confident that you could find a good job fast, accepting the buyout probably makes financial sense. But if it appears that finding an equally or more attractive new job will take a long time or require a relocation that you and/or your spouse would dread, you may want to reject the offer.

• **Am I financially ready to retire in the manner I desire?** If you consider a buyout your ticket to early retirement, first make sure that you have enough money saved to never work again.

EVALUATE RISKS OF STAYING

• **How financially secure is my company?** If there's a significant chance that your employer might soon go out of business or be forced to implement large-scale layoffs, the buyout might be a smart way to exit the sinking ship. Consider what may happen to your job.

• **Will there be future buyout offers?** And if so, might their terms be less attractive?

• **Will your job change?** A shrunken workforce may mean a lot more work or less desirable work.

EVALUATE THE OFFER

Not all buyout offers are created equal. *Important considerations...*

• **Do I get to keep my health insurance?** This is a vital factor unless you are eligible for Medicare or have access to an affordable insurance plan through some other source, such as a spouse's employer. Individual health insurance policies can be prohibitively expensive. This may be enough reason to reject the buyout.

• **How will my pension be impacted?** If you have a defined benefit pension plan, which promises specific monthly benefits at retirement, the size of your pension is likely determined in part by the number of years you have been employed by the company. With some buyouts, the employers agree to add several years to service time in pension calculations. If not, it may pay to stick around.

Important: If you have a defined contribution pension plan, such as a 401(k), your pension should not be a major issue. You can simply roll over your retirement savings to a new employer's retirement plan or into an IRA.

• **Is there a lump-sum option,** instead of a series of smaller payments over the coming years, and if so, should I take it? The lump-sum option might push you into a higher tax bracket in the year of the payout and thus create a larger total lifetime tax bill—but the option may be the prudent choice if there's any chance that the company could go bankrupt before you receive the last of the deferred payments.

Lost Your Job?

If you are out of a job, don't accept a severance package too quickly. By law, you can take 21 days to think it over. And, don't sue your former employer unless your attorney says you have a very strong case. When interviewing, don't bad-mouth your former employer. Do expect to take up to 18 months to find a new job.

Career Opportunities News, 132 W. 31 St., New York City 10001.

How to Get Your On-Line Résumé Noticed

Margaret Dikel, a consultant in Rockville, Maryland, who helps college career offices, outplacement firms and other organizations improve their use of the Internet as a job search tool. She is coauthor of *The Guide to Internet Job Searching* (McGraw-Hill). Her Web site is *www.rileyguide.com*.

Job openings posted on major employment Web sites can attract thousands of responses. Many firms have turned to résumé analysis software and other high-tech tricks to cut candidate pools down to manageable numbers. *Here's how to help your résumé survive the culling process...*

INCLUDE KEY PHRASES

Make sure that each job requirement is addressed in your résumé.

Example: If an employer asks for "management experience," somewhere in your résumé should appear the exact phrase "management experience."

Anticipate other keywords and phrases that employers might stress by checking which terms appear repeatedly in job listings in your field.

Example: If job listings for your profession often request "problem-solving skills" or "project management experience," find a permanent place for these phrases in your résumé.

SELECT A SMART FORMAT

Format your résumé as a text-only (also called "plain text") document before you submit it on-line. (Go to my Web site at *www.rileyguide.com*, or check in the help section of your word-processing program for instructions.) This reduces the odds that the résumé will become garbled in transmission.

Use a familiar font—Arial or Times New Roman—and select a conventional résumé layout.

Example: The work-experience portion of your résumé should be arranged with your most recent job first.

TRY THE SMALLER JOB SITES

The biggest employment Web sites are Monster.com and CareerBuilder.com. Jobs posted to these popular sites generally receive the largest number of responses. Devote more of your online job-search time to smaller sites. The Web sites of professional associations, trade journals and recruiters specializing in your industry or profession typically list job openings.

Or search for jobs in your region through local newspaper Web sites, chamber of commerce Web sites and state job boards (go to *www.jobboardinfo.com*, click the "State Job Boards" link, then select your state).

Many employers also post job openings on their corporate Web sites. *To submit a résumé via e-mail...*

• **Get the name and e-mail address of a specific person to send it to.**

• **Mention your job function and interest in job openings in the subject line.**

Example: "Structural engineer interested in employment opportunities."

• **Start the e-mail with a short introduction explaining who you are** in three or four sentences.

• **Put your résumé in the e-mail—don't attach a file.** Attachments often go unread, due to the effort it takes to open them and risk of computer viruses.

The Most Satisfying Jobs

Job satisfaction is highest among people whose work involves helping others. Among members of the clergy, 87% say they are very satisfied with what they do. Among firefighters, 80% report being highly satisfied...physical therapists, 78%...teachers, 69%. Jobs such as waitress (27%) and clothing salesperson (24%) provide the least satisfaction.

Tom W. Smith, senior fellow and director for General Social Survey at the National Opinion Research Center, University of Chicago.

The Best Careers

The best careers for the next decade are in the areas of health care, education and financial services. Avoid careers in manufacturing, which will decline by more than 5% as the US shifts production overseas and changes from a goods-producing to a services-producing economy.

Also: Despite advances in the computer industry, the need for computer programmers in the US will slow by 2% due to outsourcing.

Forbes, 60 Fifth Ave., New York City 10011, www.forbes.com.

Considering an MBA?

On-line MBA programs, designed to accommodate busy schedules, are offered by 152 schools, including Duke University, University of Massachusetts and Indiana University. Choose a program that is regionally accredited and recognized by the Association to Advance Collegiate Schools of Business (*www.aacsb.edu*). On-line MBA programs require 12 to 15 courses, and the cost averages from $6,000 to $21,000.* (Comparable campus-based degrees often cost more than $100,000.) Programs require participation in on-line discussions, and 40% of programs require some on-campus time. On-line programs have the same admissions standards as the schools' regular admissions.

Vicky Phillips, CEO, GetEducated.com, which surveys the top programs across the US every two years and offers a free report of the "Top 25 Best Buys" according to cost at its Web site, www.geteducated.com.

**Prices subject to change.*

Never Eat Alone...and Other Networking Secrets

Keith Ferrazzi, founder and CEO of FerrazziGreenlight, a marketing and sales consulting company based in Los Angeles. He is the author of Never Eat Alone: And Other Secrets of Success, One Relationship at a Time (Currency, www.nevereatalone.com).

Getting ahead can have just as much to do with whom we know as what we know. There is much more to building relationships than trading business cards. *Here, networking secrets...*

• **Engage in a conversation.** It is better to have one or two meaningful conversations per conference than dozens of quick handshake exchanges. Search for topics that will interest both you and the people you meet, then speak with passion on those subjects. While you are speaking with someone, don't let your eyes wander around the room, looking for other people you want to meet.

• **Discover the power of vulnerability.** The cardinal "rule" of all small talk—avoid the overly personal, the potentially unpleasant and the controversial when speaking with people you do not know well—is exactly wrong. True, you won't offend if you engage only in pleasant banalities, but you also will not make much of an impression.

If you want to be remembered, confound expectations and raise topics that show who you are and what you think.

Example: I once apologized for my sullenness to the woman sitting next to me at a conference. I explained that my long-term relationship had just ended. My admission inspired everyone at the table to speak up about their own failed relationships. We bonded on a much deeper level than people usually do at business conferences.

• **Build your network before you need it.** The time to make contact with potential employers, employees and clients is *before* you need them. If you wait to reach out until you need something, your attempt will seem desperate.

To make valuable contacts for the future, take leadership positions in organizations and associations…join your college alumni club and attend its events…or angle for a position with your current employer that lets you interact with decision makers in your company or industry.

• **Never eat alone.** Attend events and conferences whenever possible, and keep your social calendar filled. Consider whom you could eat with before you head to lunch…whom you could exercise with before you go for a jog or to the gym…whom in the area you could meet with while you are traveling on business.

• **Invest the required time.** Years ago, I hired temps to send holiday cards to the thousands of people in my contact database. A friend wrote back to say how nice it was to receive not one but three cards from me, all with different signatures. I learned my lesson. When it comes to maintenance of relationships, sincerity matters more than efficiency. Mass e-mails and form letters send only the message that you don't think someone really is worth your time.

• **Remember health, wealth and children.** *The three most reliable ways to turn an acquaintance into an ally…*

• Help him/her get through a difficult health situation. *Examples:* Listen to a client's health concerns…share the diet plan that worked for you.

• Find a way to make him money. *Example:* Pass along a lead on a job to an acquaintance who is out of work.

• Take a genuine interest in his kids. *Example:* Help an acquaintance's child get an internship.

• "Ping" all of the time. You must reach someone at least two to three times each year by e-mail, phone or in person to avoid being forgotten. Great pinging opportunities include when you come across an article that might be useful to this person…when you're visiting his region and have time to meet…and his birthday.

Better Meetings In Less Time

Stuart R. Levine, former CEO of Dale Carnegie & Associates, Inc., and current chairman and CEO of Stuart Levine & Associates LLC, a consulting and leadership-development company based in Jericho, New York, *www. stuartlevine.com*. He is the author of several best sellers, including *Cut to the Chase: And 99 Other Rules to Liberate Yourself and Gain Back the Gift of Time* (Currency).

Meetings can be big time wasters. Whether it is a meeting of family members, work colleagues or a volunteer group, here is how to get more out of a meeting in less time…

• **Define the end time.** Setting a firm end time keeps a meeting on track. When the pace lags, remind those present how much time is left. "Let's move along—we have only 30 minutes left."

If you're not in charge of the meeting, tell the person who is in charge that you have to leave at a certain time and then alert him/her when you have, say, 30 minutes left.

• **Match up the message to the audience.** Don't explain things the way you would want them explained, explain them the way that your listeners need to hear them. Consider your audience's priorities, level of expertise and familiarity with industry jargon before you speak.

Example: A client probably doesn't want a long-winded explanation about why his delivery is late—he just wants to know when his order will arrive. Add the explanation only if one is requested.

•**Forget consensus.** If you wait for everyone in a group to agree on a course of action, you might be waiting forever. Before you even ask for opinions, explain how the decision will be made. Will you move forward when there is a majority? Or will you consider all input but pick whatever direction you think best?

•**Opt out when you're not needed.** Does a two-hour meeting involve you only peripherally? Ask another participant to call you when you're needed. In the meantime, do something more productive nearby.

•**Use a story to illustrate a point.** Busy people often omit an anecdote to speed things along, but most listeners do understand and remember stories better than they do instructions, facts or figures. Just make sure the story is engrossing, focused and relevant.

A good time to use a story is to show a human face when you are presenting a lot of data.

Example: If you are explaining the importance of quality outcomes in a hospital setting, it would be helpful to tell the story of a specific patient who benefited from increased quality of care.

•**Say "I got it" if you've heard enough.** If you ask a question, as soon as you understand the answer, tell the speaker "Thanks, I got it," so he/she knows to move on. Ask those you deal with regularly to do the same with you. It will help save time and keep everyone's mind clear. When we sit through explanations of things we already understand, we tune out and lose our mental edge.

•**Don't get bogged down in details when negotiating.** One of the secrets of negotiation is to know when to stop. Unless you're negotiating an international peace treaty, once you get past the two or three most important issues, the rest is just details that can be worked out at a different time. If you continue to debate these minor points, you'll waste time—and you might put big issues at risk for the sake of small ones.

•**Debrief yourself after meetings, presentations and events.** Your personal two-to-five-minute debriefing session immediately after the meeting can save hours later. *While events are still fresh in your mind, ask yourself…*

•What did I/we do right?

•What did I/we do wrong?

•What is the next step I/we need to take? Schedule another meeting? Send a memo? Do a particular task?

The No-Cost Way to Publicize Your Business

Alan Caruba, president of The Caruba Organization, a public relations firm based in South Orange, New Jersey, serving both national and international clients, *www.caruba.com*. He has more than 40 years of experience in public relations.

So-called "news releases" are article ideas sent to media outlets in hopes of generating press coverage. They can be the best way for smaller businesses, self-employed professionals and community and charity organizations to receive a lot of publicity without paying for advertising or direct mailings.

An effective news release typically doesn't just tout the organization or a product. It provides insight into a newsworthy topic related to one's field.

Strategy: "Piggyback" your news releases onto stories currently in the headlines. Distribute the news release to the local media explaining how a national or international news story will affect your community or providing some other insight or perspective on the topic that the original reports lacked. "Piggybacked" news releases should be sent out within 24 to 48 hours of when the initial reports appeared.

Example: A doctor might issue a news release commenting on the possibility that a recent disease outbreak in Asia will reach his region.

Consult *The News Media Yellow Book* to find contact information for journalists, and e-mail your press release. *The Yellow Book* is available in libraries or by subscription (it's $452 for four quarterly editions,* 212-627-4140, *www.leadership directories.com*).

*Prices subject to change.

COMMON MISTAKES

With so much competition for journalists' attention, it's vital to avoid these common errors…

•**Omitting the headline.** Busy journalists won't read your news release if there's no headline to grab their attention. Timely headlines are best.

Example: A New York restaurant's rodent problems make national news. The next day, an exterminator in a different city puts out a release with the headline, "Rats a Major Problem in Local Restaurants."

•**Dull opening paragraph.** The first paragraph of your news release should briefly explain what's happening and why it's important. Include a compelling fact, statistic or a quotation from yourself (in the third person). Save the extended details about you and your company for later in the news release.

•**Too much hyperbole.** Your press release should read like a news story, not ad copy. Use facts to establish your qualifications. Mention the number of years you have been in this industry…your advanced degrees…or that your company is the leader in its field.

Example: Replace "John Jones, Johnsonville's best dry cleaner" with "John Jones, who has operated a dry-cleaning business in Johnsonville for 34 years."

•**Failing to cite evidence.** When possible, attribute facts to recognized, respected outside sources.

Example: "The US Department of Energy estimates that replacing a clogged air filter can save drivers as much as 10% on their gas bills. Larry Walters, owner of Larry's Auto Parts in Thomaston, says that many drivers are wasting money on gas by not maintaining their cars properly."

•**Going on too long.** Long press releases are less likely to be read. Keep yours between 750 and 1,000 words.

•**Spelling, punctuation and grammar errors.** Ask a friend to proofread your news release …or find a retired reporter in your region who is willing to edit your news releases for perhaps $20 to $50 apiece.

•**Being hard to reach.** If journalists cannot reach you by their deadlines, your release accomplished nothing. Include your phone number and e-mail address, and remain accessible at all hours.

How to Design A Winning Web Site

Mark Wachen, cofounder and CEO of Optimost, New York City, a technology company that specializes in marketing for e-commerce Web sites, *www.optimost.com.*

With a little bit of technical assistance, anybody can develop a Web site that will attract potential customers…

LAUNCHING A WEB SITE

There are two options…

•**A Web design company can create a basic site for you for perhaps $500 to $700,*** then keep it updated for a few hundred dollars per year. Web site hosting (which is, in essence, renting space on a company's computer server for your site) and domain name registration may add an additional $150 or so to your annual bill.

Some Web hosting companies worth considering: FatCow (*www.fatcow.com*)…Homestead (*www.homestead.com*)…or Yahoo Small Business (at *http://smallbusiness.yahoo.com*, click on "Web Hosting").

•**Create your own site using design software.** Leading programs include Microsoft Expression (*www.microsoft.com*, $199 to $999) and Adobe Dreamweaver (*www.adobe.com*, $400).

WHAT TO INCLUDE AND OMIT

•**Include your company's hours, policies, purpose, contact information and location.** Also include a "virtual shopping cart" for online buying, if applicable, or at least a list of products.

•**Don't make your site too large or complex.** It's best to have more than one page, but

*Prices subject to change.

dozens of screens aren't needed. Think quality over quantity.

- **Make the site easy to navigate.** If visitors can't find what they want within seconds of clicking onto a site, they are likely to leave and never return.

- **Include only three bullet points describing what's great about your product or service,** not five or six.

- **Do not go overboard with assurances that a Web site is secure for e-commerce.** Some companies post logos of security systems and promise that "we won't ever spam you," but this can backfire. The customer probably wasn't even thinking about security issues, and now you have made him/her fearful.

- **Display prominently a guarantee or special offer** that might convince the customer to buy your product or service.

- **Include as few lines as possible in any on-line form you use for customers to place an order or sign up for your service.** You can lose a potential customer by asking him to fill in too many fields or lines of information.

- **Make your "submit" button red.** Many companies are reluctant to use red because they equate the color with "stop," but our research indicates that red means "pay attention." Be very clear when designing the "submit" procedure. Many companies think that marking a button "submit" or "click here" is too boring, but it is a safe, effective way to get the customer to click.

Take It to the Next Level

Take your business to the next level with a "mastermind group." The four to eight advisers on this board—each of whom has his/her own business—serve as a combination cheering section and accountability tool for one another.

Create a mastermind group by inviting people you meet at networking organizations, etc. The members should have similar goals, such as locally focused or global business ambitions. The group should meet for two to three hours each month. At each meeting, discuss any accomplishments and successes in the past month...current problems and concerns...and goals for the next month. Members must be willing to let others in on their business plans. Have a confidentiality agreement—a verbal one is fine.

Jane Pollak, professional speaker specializing in entrepreneurship; a coach for creative professionals, Westport, Connecticut and author of Soul Proprietor (Crossing).

Mental Illness in The Workplace

Serious mental illness is more common in the workplace than most people realize.

Recent finding: One worker in every 12 has a debilitating mental illness, such as depression or an anxiety disorder.

Consult your doctor if you develop symptoms such as confused thought, persistent sadness or anger, or a general inability to cope. If you observe these symptoms in a coworker, notify the human resources department.

Geoff Birkett, president and CEO, NARSAD, the world's leading charity dedicated to mental health research, Great Neck, New York.

Plan for the Avian Flu

Plan for an avian flu pandemic so that you will be able to keep your business running if the flu strikes and much of your workforce is ill or won't come to work because of fear of contagion. Consult with local government officials about public plans to see how yours will work with the government's, and let an official know about your organization's ability to provide essential services or facilities in case of a pandemic.

Amy Kao, consultant in global corporate citizenship and coauthor of a report on preparation for an avian flu pandemic by The Conference Board, a research organization, New York City.

Dumb Mistakes That Kill Small Businesses...and What You Can Do Instead

Ruth King, founder of ProfitabilityChannel.com, a provider of Web-based business-improvement videos in Norcross, Georgia. She's also author of *The Ugly Truth About Small Business: 50 Never-Saw-It-Coming Things That Can Go Wrong And What You Can Do About It* (Sourcebooks).

You have a strong work ethic, a solid business plan and a great reputation in your field. Your small business ought to be a success. Yet a single seemingly minor mistake might be all it takes to make a thriving young company go belly up.

Fatal small business mistakes often can be avoided, but only by business owners who recognize the danger in time. *Common errors that can doom small companies...*

Mistake 1: Relying too much on one customer. New businesses will sometimes start out with just one or two clients. When these clients provide all the work the business can handle, the customer list doesn't expand. After all, why search for new clients when the dance card is already full? However, short client lists increase the odds of disaster. Small companies often collapse when one customer that accounts for 50% to 100% of their income decides to use another supplier...eliminate a product line...or handle a previously outsourced function in-house.

What to do: Continue to search for additional customers even if one or two big clients already give you all the work you can handle. If necessary, add an employee. Avoid letting any customer make up more than 25% of your revenue.

Mistake 2: Losing key employees to competitors. A small business might have only a few employees. It can be a crippling blow if one or two of your best leave to join a rival. Not only are the company's most productive people now working for the other team, but the owner often must do the work that these former employees would have done. On top of that, he/she has to hire and train replacements, all of which could distract him from leading the company. The departed employees even might take some of the company's best customers with them.

Example: Several top-producing employees of one small Nevada mortgage brokerage company were hired away by a new rival that was attempting to enter this sector. The mortgage brokerage owner could not find adequate replacements and was forced to scale back his operations despite surging demand.

What to do: To keep your employees loyal, do everything in your power to keep them happy. Remember to praise employees and thank them for their efforts. Keep the attitude of the office positive. An enjoyable working environment is at least as important for employee retention as hefty salaries.

Mistake 3: Trusting a bookkeeper too much. Even an honest-seeming bookkeeper could be an embezzler.

Example: A Georgia contracting company hired a grandmotherly bookkeeper whom everyone loved—until they learned that she had forged $100,000 in checks.

What to do: Maintain personal control over your company's money whenever possible. Do not give a bookkeeper check-signing privileges. Have bank statements sent to your home so you see them before your employees do. Each quarter, print out lists of receivables and payables and scan them for unusual entries. Divide any financial tasks that you cannot handle yourself among several employees so no one employee can steal without another noticing a problem.

Mistake 4: Turning a hobby into a business without understanding what is involved. Coin collectors often dream of owning coin shops... skilled amateur photographers hope to open up their own studios. Unfortunately, many people turn their hobbies into small businesses without first considering the time and money required, all the risks and their lack of practical business skills.

Example: A woman interested in Native American jewelry opened two jewelry stores— one in Colorado, the other in Arizona. She had a great eye for jewelry, but she had no knowledge of the local markets...didn't know how to write a business plan...and had never worked in retail. Both shops failed.

What to do: Before launching your business, work for someone who has a comparable business so you can learn about the field. (This business either should be a few towns removed from where you intend to start your business or have a slightly different focus so that you won't later be in direct competition.) Try to master all mundane back-office tasks that are unfamiliar to you, such as balancing the books and negotiating with distributors and suppliers.

To reduce your risk, try to launch your business part-time before leaving your current job. This means working very hard for a while, but it is better than taking the leap without a safety net.

Mistake 5: Having a relationship with just one bank. Most small businesses do depend on loans and lines of credit to help get them off of the ground and to avoid cash-flow shortfalls. When a business builds a relationship with only one bank, that credit can dry up if the bank's policies or management change.

What to do: Try to do business with at least two local banks so they get to know you and believe in your company.

Mistake 6: Thinking you'll never get sick. A long-term health problem, even if it is not life-threatening, could mean the demise of your business, particularly if it is a sole proprietorship.

Example: A Georgia hairdresser broke his arm in a motorcycle accident and could not cut hair for more than a month. He contracted with another hairdresser to cut his clients' hair for the time his arm was in a cast. Had his customers gone elsewhere, his business might never have recovered.

What to do: Do not work yourself so hard that your health deteriorates. Stop doing risky hobbies. Consider signing an agreement with a friendly and respected competitor to look after each other's businesses in the event of extended health problems. Make sure this agreement includes a promise not to poach customers. If you can afford it, buy disability insurance.

Mistake 7: Failing to share your workload with employees or partners. Some small business owners find it psychologically difficult to give anyone but themselves important assignments. Their unwillingness to accept assistance limits their companies' growth, and eventually they burn out.

What to do: If your current employees can't handle the work, hire or train employees who can.

Mistake 8: Working with unstable suppliers or distributors. When a small business's supplier or distributor has problems, the small business itself has problems.

Example: A California writer lost her stream of income and her full inventory of books when her book distributor went bankrupt.

What to do: Work with multiple suppliers or distributors whenever it's possible. Watch out for signs of financial problems in these companies, such as bounced checks or slow-to-arrive payments. Ask your lawyer to look over your contracts with distributors to make sure that you'll still own all of your products if the distributor goes bankrupt.

For more information about protecting your small business: www.smallbusinessadvo cate.com…www.sbresources.com…www.startup nation.com.

Tax Breaks from Uncle Sam for Starting a Business

Martin S. Kaplan, CPA, 11 Penn Plaza, New York City 10001, *www.irsmaven.com.* He is a frequent guest speaker at insurance, banking and financial planning seminars and is author of *What the IRS Doesn't Want You to Know* (Villard).

Many people dream of starting their own businesses—to become their own bosses…earn extra income…turn a favorite hobby into a career…or have a rewarding second career after retiring from a current job.

The IRS will subsidize the start-up of your business—and after you start it, you can obtain deductions and legal tax-sheltered breaks from it that you'll get no other way.

This is all true even if your business is only a sideline, and is an activity that you enjoy—and even if it loses money. *What you need to know…*

SMALL-BUSINESS FUNDAMENTALS

The key to obtaining business status and deductions for an activity is to have a profit motive for engaging in it—you must intend to make money from it.

But there is no requirement that you actually do make a profit from it—nor does the fact that you enjoy the activity disqualify it from being a business.

Business status has been allowed for part-time collectors, songwriters, musicians, artists, writers, farmers, breeders, sports competitors, car racers and many others in activities they enjoyed.

Of course, neither the IRS nor Tax Court can read your mind to determine whether you have a profit motive for an activity, so they deduce whether you do from your actions, by looking to see whether you operate in a businesslike manner. *They look to see if you...*

•**Obtain business licenses and registrations** required under local law.

•**Keep business bank accounts** that are segregated from personal accounts.

•**Keep business books/records—**such as cash-flow statements, invoices and inventories.

•**Actively advertise and market to obtain customers.**

•**Have a plan that explains how you intend to make a profit—**and revise it periodically in light of business results.

•**Consult with an expert in your field** to learn ways to make your business successful.

Other businesslike actions may be considered as well.

No one factor is determinative, but the more of these conditions you meet, the more likely it is that you will be deemed to have a profit motive—even if your business in fact loses money.

Example: A longtime stamp collector tried to deduct his collecting costs as sideline business expenses. The IRS and Tax Court both said no, ruling that he had only a hobby. Then the collector obtained a business license, acquired a business credit card, organized formal inventory and other business records—and deducted his collecting as a business again. This time, the Tax Court granted business status, even though his collecting lost him $5,000 (*Eugene Feistman*, TC Memo 1982-306).

The tax subsidy: The typical business loses money during its start-up stage. When a business you own does so, you can deduct its loss against your regular income from other sources—such as income from a job. Thus, the business can serve as a legal tax shelter, with the cash-saving value of the loss deduction helping to pay its start-up costs.

You may be able to obtain these subsidy deductions many years in a row.

Example: An advertising executive bought a run-down farm and worked on it on weekends, desiring to make it profitable 10 years in the future and, later, to make farming his second career. He was challenged by the IRS, but the Court of Appeals said his profit motive enabled him to deduct the losses he incurred while improving the farm (*Melvin Nickerson*, CA-7, No. 82-1323, 700 F2d 402).

TAX-FREE PROFITS

Once your business turns profitable, you may be able to shelter much or even all of its profits from tax.

Examples...

•**With a solo 401(k) retirement plan, the self-employed person can deduct a contribution of $15,500** ($20,500 if older than age 50) plus 20% of total self-employment profits up to set limits. (See Publication 560, *Retirement Plans for Small Business.*)

•**Far bigger tax-deductible contributions can now be made to a defined-benefit plan** for an older business owner, say, older than age 50. There is no cap on the size of contributions—any amount needed (as determined by an actuary) can be contributed to fund the plan benefit by retirement age. The maximum benefit is $185,000 in 2008—for such a benefit, annual contributions may exceed $100,000.

Many other retirement plan options exist for small businesses. Consult an expert about what's best in your case.

FAMILY SALARIES AND BENEFITS

You can give salaries to children and other low-tax-bracket family members who work for your business, deducting them at your high tax rate while they are taxed at the recipients' low or zero rate.

No FICA tax is owed on salaries paid to children younger than age 18 by a parent's unincorporated business.

The "kiddie tax" that taxes a child's investment income at the tax rate of the child's parents does not apply to all earned income. And, after 2007, with the kiddie tax extended to children up to 24 years old who are in school, lower tax rates that remain available for a child's earned income are even more valuable.

Children as young as seven years old have had deductible salaries upheld by the Tax Court for such work as cleaning up, taking messages and other office tasks.

Family-member employees also qualify to get tax-deductible benefits, that include retirement accounts and medical expense reimbursement plans.

DEDUCTIBLE TRAVEL

When you travel within the US on a trip primarily motivated by business, you can deduct the cost of travel to and from your destination and the cost of lodging there, even if the trip includes significant pleasure elements—such as visiting friends or taking in theatrical or sporting events.

Moreover, if you travel with someone (such as your spouse or a friend), you may be able to deduct most of your combined costs instead of only half. This is because having a companion along may increase many costs only slightly.

Examples: The cost of a double hotel room may be only slightly more than that of a single room...the cost of a rental car is no more than you would have paid if you were traveling alone.

HOME DEDUCTIONS

Having your own business can enable you to have a qualified home office—and deduct expenses for your home that otherwise would be nondeductible.

Examples: Depreciation, insurance, maintenance, repairs and utilities allocable to the portion part of your home used as an office.

The office must be a part of your home that you utilize exclusively for business on a regular basis. It must be either your principal place of business or needed for essential business record keeping.

Strategy: Take photos or a video of your office space to show how it is used, to be available

in case you are ever audited—even after you may have sold the home. And see IRS Publication 587, *Business Use of Your Home.*

INCOME SHIFTING

If your business becomes decidedly profitable, you may be able to reduce tax on its profits by giving share interests in it to children or other family members in a lower tax bracket than you.

By adopting the business structure of a limited partnership or a limited liability company, you can retain operating control of the business and set your own compensation at the level you want even after giving majority ownership of the business away through such income-shifting gifts. Consult a tax expert or an expert on your state's business organization laws—such as an accountant or lawyer.

BAILING OUT

When you truly want to retire, if your business is an activity that can be performed by someone else, you can sell your business and reap the value you have built up in it as a tax-favored, long-term capital gain.

Tax Strategies to Help Your Company Ride Out a Recession

Barbara Weltman, Esq., an attorney located in Millwood, New York, and author of *J.K. Lasser's Small Business Taxes* (Wiley). She is publisher of the free monthly on-line newsletter *Big Ideas for Small Business* at *www.barbaraweltman.com.*

Whether we are in an actual recession (defined as two consecutive quarters of declining gross domestic product) or simply an economic slowdown, tough times are here for many businesses. The impact of a downturn doesn't have to be traumatic—you can use tax breaks and smart business practices to help see you through.

INVENTORY

Keep tight control over your merchandise to help cut the cost of carrying inventory at a time when sales may well be down. *How...*

• **Offer slow-moving inventory for sale.** If your inventory has decreased in value, you can deduct the decline as a tax loss as long as you offer to sell the inventory at a lower price. Even if the merchandise doesn't sell, you'll be entitled to deduct the loss. Put the items up for sale for at least 30 days after taking a physical inventory and then carefully document the sales attempts you make.

• **Deduct shrinkage.** The losses due to theft, breakage, bookkeeping errors and similar occurrences is called shrinkage. Shrinkage can be deducted even if a physical inventory is not taken at year-end but, instead, at some time during the year (to determine the extent of shrinkage). You merely have to estimate inventory on December 31 to claim shrinkage.

• **Donate inventory.** Can't sell it? Donate it to charity. Usually, the deduction for the donation is based on the item's fair market value on the date of the contribution, reduced by any gain that would have been realized if it had been sold instead of donated.

Example: An item that cost you $20, but today is worth $15, would create a tax deduction of $15.

Some items donated by C corporations are eligible for an enhanced deduction. For instance, the deduction for inventory that will be used for the care of the ill, the needy, or infants can be increased by 50% of the difference between the items' basis (cost) and their fair market value. But in no event may the write-off exceed 200% of the items' basis.

Important: After donating the items, remove them from your opening inventory account (how you value your inventory at the start of the year). If the inventory was manufactured by you (instead of purchased), also remove from the cost of goods sold your materials, labor and other indirect costs that were included in the cost of production (essentially, cost of inventory).

SELL AGGRESSIVELY

Offer discounts and promotions to generate sales. You can't deduct price reductions—they simply reduce the income that you collect and are taxed on. Hopefully, however, you will see greater revenue from your marketing efforts.

THE BARTER OPTION

Using barter to obtain the goods and services that your business needs will help you preserve precious cash. Bartering may be especially helpful in disposing of excess inventory. You can accrue barter credits through a bartering group or association that can be used later on.

For tax purposes, bartering does not let your business avoid income—you must include in income the value of goods or services you receive in exchange for your goods or services.

Example: If a carpenter builds shelves for a clothing store in exchange for several of the items in the store, the carpenter reports income based on the value of the clothing he received.

Barter transactions are reported to the IRS on Form 1099-B, *Proceeds from Broker and Barter Exchange Transactions.*

Barter transactions are subject to sales taxes, just as if you had paid cash for the item. Therefore, you have to use cash to pay the sales tax.

BAD DEBTS

A business can experience bad debts because of sales to customers that go unpaid, or because of loans to suppliers, employees or other business connections that are not repaid. If these business bad debts become partially or wholly worthless, the business may be entitled to a bad debt deduction on its tax return. You must show that the debt has become worthless (for example, the buyer has permanently left the country or died without any money, or there is an uncollectible judgment against him/her). But you don't have to wait until a debt actually becomes worthless if you know there is no hope of recovery (for instance, a loan to a business that's received a discharge in bankruptcy).

Don't let your accounts receivable age without smart collection efforts. Stay on top of slow-paying customers, limit credit to buyers with questionable credit histories, and, if it's necessary, use professional assistance (an attorney or collection agency) to collect outstanding receivables.

Accrual-basis businesses can use the "specific charge-off method" to deduct losses related to receivables to offset the income that they accrued when they completed the initial sales transaction. No bad debt deduction can be claimed for estimated losses, only for actual losses.

Cash-basis businesses, such as professionals who perform services, cannot deduct bad debts that arise when clients or customers fail to pay their bills—since the businesses never reported the income, they cannot take a deduction.

Note: If you deduct a bad debt that you recover in a later year, you may have to report the recovery as income in the year you receive it.

BENEFITS OF ABANDONMENT

If you own property—equipment or inventory —that has lost all of its value to you, consider abandoning it to claim a tax loss.

If the property is depreciable, abandonment allows you to deduct the remaining basis (the part of the property's cost that has not yet been depreciated). This is then treated as an ordinary loss.

If you abandon inventory, you do not take a deduction. Instead, you adjust your inventory valuation to reflect the actual value, which may be scrap value or zero.

Abandonment requires a physical action, such as trashing the item or removing it from your premises. You can't take an abandonment loss by merely making the notation in your books while retaining the item.

LOSS CARRYBACKS

When expenses exceed your revenues for the year, you may have a net operating loss. If you had a loss last year, you can use it to get an immediate infusion of cash. You can carry back a net operating loss for two years (longer periods in special situations, such as for Hurricane Katrina victims). The loss carryback will offset your income in those years so that you can get a tax refund.

More from Barbara Weltman, Esq....

Embezzlement Precautions

Small businesses can minimize embezzlement risk by having all checks signed by the owner personally—don't use a signature stamp, because an employee can use it to make checks out to himself/herself...doing background checks on all employees who handle company finances...and not assuming that longtime employees can be trusted—use the same security precautions with them as with new hires.

Also: The business owners should personally open and review bank statements. It is generally safe to let an employee pay for business expenses with a corporate credit card, as long as credit limits are established and the owner opens and reviews the monthly statements.

Six Tax Breaks For Companies That "Go Green"

Carolyn R. Turnbull, CPA, MST, senior tax manager at Grant Thornton LLP in Atlanta, *www.grantthornton.com*, and a member of *The Tax Adviser* editorial board, American Institute of Certified Public Accountants. She has also been named to the IRS Advisory Council.

Companies gain multiple benefits for being green. In addition to helping the environment, they save money on fuel and energy consumption...gain a marketing edge by promoting their environmentally responsible behavior...and become eligible to get tax breaks at the federal and/or state levels. *Here are six ways companies can go green and gain tax breaks...*

1. Allow staff to telecommute.

A recent survey: Just one day of telecommuting by one employee can save, on average, an amount of energy equivalent to 12 hours of electricity (measured as equal to 12 hours of an average household's electricity use).

Note: The amount of electricity utilized was based on energy used for transportation (aside from gasoline) and energy associated with use of commercial office space.

Tax savings: A company does not currently receive a federal tax break for allowing its employees to telecommute, but Georgia implemented a tax credit for companies whose employees agree to telecommute. Other states may follow this example.

Permitting workers to telecommute can also help them qualify for the home-office income tax deduction on their personal returns—which may help with a business's labor expenses and employee retention.

Helpful support for the employee deduction: A formal written agreement between the company and the employees at the time the telecommuting arrangement goes into effect stating that the arrangement is for the convenience of the company.

Note: Be aware that if any of your employees telecommute from any state other than the state where your company is physically located, you need to check what taxes you might owe the other state.

2. Encourage the use of public transit. Workers can help the environment by taking public transportation rather than driving to work. Companies can encourage this practice by offering monthly transit passes as an employee benefit. Payment for these passes can be set up so that employees either pay for them on a pretax basis using an arrangement similar to making pretax contributions to a 401(k) plan, or the company pays for them as a tax-free fringe benefit.

Tax break: The following two income tax savings are available to either employees or the company, depending on who pays for monthly transit passes…

• If an employee pays for his/her transit passes on a pretax basis, the portion of wages used to pay for the passes is not subject to income tax.

• If a company pays for the passes, the company can deduct the cost of the passes. Furthermore, a company can save on employment taxes because employment taxes are not imposed on tax-free transit passes (up to $115 monthly in 2008).

States may offer additional tax incentives.

Example: Maryland gives employers a 50% tax credit for providing transit passes on top of the deduction for paying for the passes.

Alternative break: Commuting in a company-provided "commuter highway vehicle" (a vehicle that seats at least six adults, not including the driver) is also tax free up to $115 per employee per month in 2008. At least 80% of the vehicle's mileage must be used for transporting employees between home and work, and on those trips, at least half of the adult seating capacity of the vehicle (excluding the driver) must be occupied by employees.

3. Use hybrids. A company can purchase a vehicle that runs on alternative fuel, such as the Honda Civic GX, which operates on compressed natural gas, or a hybrid vehicle (a vehicle that combines gasoline and electric power).

Tax break: The federal government offers a tax credit for purchasing a hybrid vehicle. The amount of the credit is determined by the IRS.

A 2008 Ford Escape two-wheel-drive hybrid, for example, qualifies for a $3,000 credit.

For a complete listing of available credits, go to the IRS newsroom page at *www.irs.gov/newsroom/article/0,,id=157557,00.html*. State breaks (exemption from sales tax on qualified purchases, for example) may also be available.

Caution: Because of their popularity, Toyota hybrid vehicles are no longer eligible for credits, and the credits for Honda hybrids have been reduced for 2008.

4. Buy energy-efficient equipment. Use computers, office machines, etc., that meet energy-saving standards—they are less costly to run.

Information: Energy Star, *www.energystar.gov*, and click on "Office Equipment."

Tax breaks: There are no special tax breaks for energy-efficient office equipment, but small businesses can choose to fully expense the cost of up to $128,000 of equipment purchases for 2008. If total equipment purchases for the year exceed $510,000, then the $128,000 is reduced dollar for dollar by each one dollar of excess purchases (i.e., no deduction once the purchases exceed $638,000). If a business doesn't qualify for expensing or chooses not to use it, the business can depreciate the cost of equipment over a five-year, seven-year, or longer period fixed by law.

5. Make commercial spaces energy efficient. Energy usage in commercial buildings accounts for 40% of US global warming emissions (excessive amounts of carbon dioxide introduced into the atmosphere). Making buildings more energy efficient can contribute significantly to conservation efforts.

Tax breaks: Companies that own their facilities (buildings, factories, etc.) can qualify for a special tax deduction if their space meets certain federal energy standards. The deduction is $1.80 per square foot of space for a building that achieves a 50% energy reduction from the target for that type of building (60¢ per square foot for more modest improvements in energy-efficiency).

You get a tax deduction for being energy efficient—it does not matter how much it cost to achieve that efficiency. See *IRS Notice* 2006-52 for the rules for qualifying for this break.

There may also be state tax breaks and other incentives (loan programs, property tax exemptions) available. In Maine, there is a utility rebate program for half the installation costs and a portion of the equipment costs for energy-efficient water heaters, building insulation and specified other equipment in buildings.

6. Convert to solar energy. It can cost thousands to millions of dollars to convert to solar energy, depending on the size of the facility, but it may take only seven years before savings start to materialize.

Tax breaks: There is a 30% federal tax credit for converting to solar power that applies to equipment used to generate electricity, or heat or cool a building, as well as to equipment that uses solar energy to illuminate the inside of a structure using fiber-optic distributed sunlight.

Details: See the instructions to Form 3468, *Investment Tax Credit.*

There may also be significant state-level tax breaks. In California, there is a utility rebate program for installing solar units (also called photovoltaic cells) to convert sunlight into electricity in commercial and residential property.

Details: EcoBusinessLinks, provides links to solar energy retailers by state, *www.ecobusiness links.com/solar_wind_power.htm.*

How to Avoid Tax Traps for Unreasonable Compensation

John W. Morrisset, CPA, a principal in the accounting firm of Damitz, Brooks, Nightingale, Turner & Morrisset at 200 E. Carrillo St., Santa Barbara, California 93101. Past president of the Channel Counties chapter of the California Society of Certified Public Accountants, Morrisset has also been a visiting lecturer at the University of California at Santa Barbara.

If you're a decision-maker at a small or midsized company, be careful how you set your compensation. Missteps can be costly.

The too-high trap: At regular C corporations, the IRS looks for indications that compensation is unreasonably excessive.

In such situations, some of your compensation will be recast as a dividend. This dividend will be doubly taxed, to you as well as to your corporation.

The too-low trap: If you elect S corporation status, you generally won't have to worry about the corporate income tax because all corporate income is reported on the shareholders' personal tax returns.

However, the IRS may charge S corporation owners with trying to avoid the payroll tax by taking too little compensation. Reported profits may be recast as compensation, forcing you to pay more Medicare tax and possibly more Social Security tax.

Strategy: To avoid either trap, carefully decide upon and document the amount of compensation that you and all other decision-makers receive.

C CORPORATIONS

If you run your business as a C corporation, you will want to avoid double taxation of your income.

Crucial: To the IRS, "compensation" includes not only your salary but also your bonus, retirement plan contributions and executive benefits. You must justify the total package to avoid double taxation.

Situation: Bob Smith is the 100% owner of a C corporation. Including all the elements mentioned above, the IRS finds that Bob's total compensation in a recent year was $500,000.

Problem: Only $200,000 is considered by the IRS to be reasonable pay for someone in Bob's position.

In this situation, $200,000 is characterized by the IRS as Bob's compensation and $300,000 is deemed to be a dividend—a distribution of corporate earnings.

Result: Bob's corporation will owe tax on an extra $300,000 worth of income because it can't deduct the dividend payment. Bob will owe tax on that $300,000 dividend as well as tax on his $200,000 in compensation. Even if your company's dividend payment qualifies for the 15% tax rate, a combined tax bill for the corporation and owner-employee still can be substantial. Some basic planning can avert this double taxation.

To rebut such an IRS attack and justify your compensation…

• **Pay some dividends.** A C corporation that never pays dividends to shareholders is especially vulnerable to the charge of unreasonable compensation. Paying even a smallish dividend each year (and paying double tax on those dividends) may convince the IRS that you're playing by the rules.

• **Build up your base pay.** IRS challenges in this area generally focus in on bonuses and other forms of incentive pay. If your company has a $100,000 operating profit and then pays $100,000 in "bonuses" to shareholders, bringing corporate income down to zero, that might look like a $100,000 dividend.

The higher your salary, which the company is obligated to pay each year, the less likely the IRS will claim that you're juggling compensation to soak up profits.

• **Be smart about bonuses.** Say your corporation has two 50% shareholders. If the annual bonus is divided 50-50 between the two owners, that will look like a division of the profits (a dividend) to the IRS.

Alternatively, the bonuses should be tied to performance. For example, the shareholder who brings in more business during the year might get a larger bonus.

Tactic: Pay bonuses to nonshareholders, too. This will make bonus payments to shareholders look less like dividends.

• **Follow a formula.** Use your corporate minutes to describe how bonuses will be awarded. If these outlays are linked to preset performance goals, there will be demonstrable standards for determining executive bonuses.

Once this formula is in place, apply it consistently, year after year. This can show that these payouts were not calculated to disguise distributions of profits.

S CORPORATIONS

If you operate your business as an S corporation, no corporate income taxes will be due, so double taxation is not an issue. Therefore, some S corp owners attempt to hold down compensation to minimize payroll taxes.

Generally, once a valid S election is in effect, a corporation is not subject to tax at the corporate level (assuming no accumulated earnings and/or profits). The S corporation, with certain modifications, computes income as an individual.

Situation: Jessica Jones is the 100% owner of an S corporation. This year, she takes $50,000 in salary.

She also receives $150,000 in profits from her S corporation. All $200,000 is reported on her personal tax return.

Benefit: Jessica will pay Social Security and Medicare tax on only $50,000 worth of earned income. In 2008, only $102,000 is subject to Social Security tax—there is no earnings ceiling for the Medicare tax.

At a 15.3% rate (employer and employee contributions), she saves $6,762 in tax by paying Social Security and Medicare taxes on a $50,000 salary, rather than on $102,000.

In addition, she saves 2.9% on earnings over $102,000 by not paying Medicare tax.

IRS position: The IRS might claim that her earned income really is higher than $50,000—as high as $200,000. If so, she'll owe the additional payroll tax.

Strategy: In your corporate minutes, provide reasons for keeping executive salaries at low levels. There might be a need to keep a cushion in case of business downturns, for example.

Follow up by keeping some cash in the company. Thus, it won't seem as though you're trying to avoid payroll taxation by paying yourself compensation disguised as corporate profits.

HELP WANTED

Regardless of the type of business entity, the more evidence you can provide that your compensation is reasonable, the less exposure you'll have to an IRS challenge to your compensation. The reasonableness of an employee's salary is determined by comparing the amount of compensation paid with the value of the services performed.

How to do it…

• **Depend on your directors.** Have your company's executive compensation structure set by a board of directors that includes outsiders. The board should produce a written compensation policy relating to such things as length of service with the business, previous levels of compensation, compensation at other companies in the industry and individual performance goals.

Even better: Go with a pro. Instead of asking your directors to put together the compensation package, hire an independent professional or a consulting firm.

Either way, you'll be less vulnerable to an IRS challenge if you don't set your own pay.

• **Don't give in.** If the IRS attempts to reduce or increase your reported compensation, you'll have an opportunity to appeal. Gather data to illustrate that your compensation was reasonable, based on your qualifications, corporate performance and surveys showing comparable executive compensation in your industry.

Your trade association may be able to provide you with industry compensation information.

Tax Loopholes for Business Travel

Edward Mendlowitz, CPA, partner in the CPA firm of WithumSmith+Brown at One Spring St., New Brunswick, New Jersey 08901. He's also author of *The Adviser's Guide to Family Business Succession Planning* (American Institute of Certified Public Accountants).

Business travelers who plan carefully can trim the costs of their trips. Generally, "ordinary and necessary" business expenses are tax deductible while you're traveling, if you keep proper records.

Examples: Costs for transportation…hotels and lodging…tips…meals…the laundry and dry cleaning…baggage handling…trip insurance and other related costs.

For starters: An employee who is fully reimbursed for business travel expenses by his/her employer does not need to account for all these payments on his tax return. However, if you receive an expense allowance for which you don't need to account to your employer, the amounts paid must be reported to you on your W-2 wage statement as income. You then can claim your business travel expenses on your tax return on Schedule A as a miscellaneous deduction. The total of your miscellaneous deductions is tax deductible to the extent that it exceeds 2% of your adjusted gross income.

Here are some travel tax-savers…

Loophole: **You do not need receipts for the IRS for expenses (other than lodging) of $75 or less if the expenses are properly recorded in a business diary contemporaneous with the activity.**

Required information: Business purpose …time…place and date…names of people involved…what was purchased…how much was paid.

Exception: A receipt is required for lodging costing any amount.

Loophole: **For out-of-town travel (or outside the country), ask your employer to give you the standard IRS meal allowance rather than to reimburse your actual expenses.** These amounts are not taxable income even if you spend less than the total allowance—so, if you keep your meal expenses low, you'll actually be earning extra tax-free income. The rates, which are set by the IRS, vary by area. Domestic travel per diem rates are listed in IRS Publication 1542, *Per Diem Rates*, available on-line from *www.irs.gov*. Foreign travel per diem rates are available from *www.gsa.gov*.

Note: Cruise ship travel deductions are limited to twice the domestic per diem rate.

Loophole: **Consider attending a business conference on a cruise ship.** You can deduct up to $2,000 annually for such conferences if all the ports are in the US and the ship is registered in the US—the per diem rules (see above) don't apply to conferences. But, strict tax reporting requirements apply, so check with your tax adviser before embarking.

Loophole: **Out-of-town "commuting" costs are fully deductible.** While commuting costs generally are not deductible, business travelers can deduct such expenses (including car rental, cab fare, limo, and mass transit) as the cost of "commuting" from a hotel to their place of business.

Loophole: **Consider establishing an official "tax home" if you regularly travel to work in multiple locations.** Your tax home is the location of your principal place of business.

Without one, you cannot deduct any travel and meal costs.

Note: A "tax home" cannot be merely a mailing address or the local library or Starbucks—it must be a legitimate location where you conduct business.

Loophole: **Even if you work at a temporary business location for many months, if the period is less than a year, all travel and lodging costs are deducted by the business and aren't taxed to the employee.** After one year, the government considers this a "permanent" business location and travel costs are not deductible...or alternatively, they are deducted by the business and taxed to the employee.

Loophole: **Married couples who work in different cities during the workweek could maintain separate "tax homes" for travel deduction purposes.** However, once the one-year threshold is exceeded, even legitimate expenses are not tax deductible.

Loophole: **Meal costs, which generally are not deductible by employees, are fully deductible on trips of at least one overnight stay.** The deduction for meals is limited to 50% of their cost.

Loophole: **Domestic business travel combined with some vacation activities is deductible if business is the primary purpose of the travel.** If the primary purpose is vacation, but you do some incidental business, you can deduct the business costs, but not transportation and lodging.

Strategy: Extending a business trip into the weekend to benefit from lower airfares, and using the time for vacation, does not alter the primary business nature of the trip.

Loophole: **Business travel outside the US plus vacation activities may be deductible.** The primary purpose of the travel must be for business. And, as opposed to the domestic travel rules, you also must have no control over the purpose or timing of the trip.

Loophole: **Expenses of spouses who help entertain business associates on a trip can be fully deducted.** The entertainment must be immediately before, during or after the business meeting or activity. You also must demonstrate

that your spouse was helpful to your business relationship.

Loophole: **Frequent-flier miles received for business travel but used for personal travel are not taxed.**

Exception: Miles that are converted into cash are taxed as compensation.

Deduct a Convention in Aruba...or the Bahamas

Expenses of attending a convention or seminar outside of "North America" are generally disallowed according to Section 274(h) of the Tax Code. But the definition of North America has recently been changed (see *Revenue Ruling* 2007-28). The US, its possessions, the trust territories of the Pacific Islands and Canada and Mexico are all acceptable destinations. The Bahamas, Aruba and the Netherlands Antilles have been added to the list. St. Lucia was dropped as of April 4, 2007, because its government failed to enact legislation to exchange financial information with the US.

Note: The Cayman Islands and the British Virgin Islands are not included on the list of acceptable destinations because those governments have limited the scope of financial information that may be exchanged with the US.

Ms. X, Esq., a former agent with the IRS who is still well connected.

IRS Loses: Playing Slots Qualifies as a Business

Linda Myers had a full-time job but also spent 40 hours per week playing casino slot machines. She lost money and deducted her losses as a business expense, but the IRS denied her deduction, claiming that "playing slots" is not a business.

Tax Court: Myers spent full-time hours gambling, had a record of her activity (through her casino card), had a "system" for watching machines to determine which were most likely to pay off, modified the system in light of results and had hit enough jackpots to show it was possible for her to have a profit. All this indicated she had a profit motive, so her gambling was a business and her losses were deductible.

Linda M. Myers, TC Summary Opinion 2007-194.

Hottest Audit Targets Today

Frederick W. Daily, Esq., a tax attorney based in St. Pete Beach, Florida, and the author of several tax books, including *Stand Up to the IRS* and *Tax Savvy for Small Business* (both from Nolo.com).

IRS audit rates are rising now. Moreover, the IRS is targeting its audits more effectively after conducting a national research program on taxpayer behavior.

Here are the most dangerous areas of audit risk now—*and how to minimize the danger they pose to you*...

SELF-EMPLOYMENT

The IRS's clear number-one audit priority is examining the tax returns of people who own sole proprietorship small businesses and who file Schedule C with their tax returns.

Why: IRS research shows sole proprietors underpay their taxes by far more than any other group.

Example: Small-business sole proprietors underpaid their taxes by a total of $68 billion, compared with only $30 billion for all large corporations, in 2001 (the year that the national research program examined), says the IRS.

Former IRS Commissioner Mark Everson has publicly stated: "Our increased focus will be on those individuals who are filing 1040s and are running businesses that are not incorporated...Typically, that's individuals who are filing Schedule C."

The highest audit risk is faced by those who report net losses from their businesses. *The IRS believes that many such people...*

- **Underreport income and inflate deductions to manufacture deductible losses.**

- **Aren't running legitimate businesses at all,** but only hobbies or sidelines that have no real profit motive behind them.

Danger: If the IRS chooses such a business loss for audit, the audit can spread to become a full examination of the individual's entire tax return—even if the loss was only a small-dollar amount reported from a sideline business.

Example: A doctor client of mine with a successful high-income hospital practice as an employee set up a sideline solo practice close to year-end as a proprietorship. Start-up costs created a perfectly legitimate small business loss for it. Even though the loss was insignificant relative to the doctor's total income, the IRS selected it for audit—and the audit spread to become a full examination of three years of his returns.

Self-defense: If you report a loss on Schedule C...

- Be able to show that your business is legitimate, not a mere hobby, by showing that it has a profit motive. *How:* Have a written business plan that explains how you intend to make a profit... keep a diary showing the amount of work you put into the business to render it profitable...operate the activity in a "businesslike manner" by having segregated business bank accounts, keeping full accounting records, obtaining all the required local business licenses and so on.

- Be aware that the loss might be examined by the IRS, and keep full records documenting how it was actually incurred.

Also, if a loss will be small and not important to you—as in the case of my doctor client—try to avoid incurring it (and the heightened audit risk it involves) by steps such as postponing deductible expenditures until after year-end. (Perhaps in the following year, your business will turn a net profit.)

PROFITABLE PROPRIETORSHIPS

All Schedule C filings that report profits incur a heightened audit risk as well. The key to the degree of audit risk is whether deductible expenses reported on the Schedule C are so large as to be out of line with industry averages. The more by which such deductions exceed the averages, the more likely it is that the IRS will select a return for audit.

Helpful: The IRS does not publish such tax deduction averages. However, the Government Accountability Office (GAO) has published data obtained from the IRS about the average deductible expenditures of proprietorships in different industries by size of the business and how they operate (such as with or without a home office). The data is from 2000, but probably still provides a generally accurate picture.

Details: Check out *Information on Expenses Claimed by Small Business Sole Proprietorships,* report #GAO-04-304, available at *www.gao.gov.*

If your business's deductions are unusual or unusually large for its industry, be prepared to defend them to a tax examiner.

PRIVATE CORPORATIONS

The IRS says that it is also targeting for examination the compensation of top executives of private corporations who set their own pay. *Key issues…*

•**Level of salary.** The salary of an owner-executive of a private corporation must be "reasonable" for the work that's done in order for a corporation to deduct it. *However, the IRS claims that many…*

•S corporation owner-executives set their salaries at zero to avoid employment taxes and receive all of their income as corporate profits that "pass through" to their personal tax returns.

•Regular (C) corporation owner-executives set their salaries too high to help eliminate corporate profits that otherwise would be subject to double taxation (first as corporate income and then as dividend income).

Caution: Zero salary for any S corporation owner is an audit red flag. Salary that varies annually to consume all of each year's profits of a C corporation is a red flag, too.

"Reasonable" salary may cover a wide range, but it falls within these audit-risk extremes. To learn a "reasonable" salary range for your business, consult with your tax adviser.

•**Noncash compensation.** The IRS is suspicious of top executives who arrange high-value noncash compensation, such as stock and perquisites, for themselves.

For details of what to beware of, see the audit technique guide on the subject, as described below.

AUDIT TECHNIQUE GUIDE TARGETS

The IRS has published more than 40 audit technique guides that its tax examiners follow when conducting examinations of audit targets.

These guides cover audits of specific kinds of small businesses (such as automobile repair, construction and veterinary medicine), as well as items on tax returns that draw special audit attention (such as lawsuit awards, executive compensation and passive losses from real estate investments).

To find these audit guides, go to the IRS Web site, *www.irs.gov.* Enter "audit technique guides" in the search box.

Look to see if any of these audit guides are relevant to you. *If so…*

•**Be warned that the IRS has a special audit interest** in the subject and that increases your audit risk.

•**Use the audit guides to learn in advance what the IRS will look for in an audit,** and to arrange your records and affairs to audit-proof your return against an IRS examiner.

20

Safe and Sound

Hidden Dangers In Your Home

Though it might be hard to believe, your home can be among the greatest threats to your health. According to the National Safety Council, a deadly injury occurs in someone's home in the US every 14 minutes and a disabling injury occurs every four seconds. *Here's a checklist of ways to protect yourself from some of the leading causes of home injuries and deaths...*

•**Install bars and railings.** Preventing falls and slips should be your number-one priority. Falls are the leading reason for injuries in the home. Make sure there are bars in showers or tubs, next to low toilets and even next to a sink where someone may stand. Put secure banisters on each side of stairways. Install grab bars on walls next to any steps (even if there are only one or two) leading out a door. If you have a ramp, make sure you install a secure railing on each side. Grab bars typically cost $25 to $100, including installation.*

•**Move or get rid of furniture.** Be sure you can move from room to room without bumping into furniture. Remove bulky, unused furniture or rearrange it so that it is pushed against walls, rather than blocking pathways. If you or a family member has difficulty getting up from a chair or couch, look for new furniture with seats that are 20 inches off the floor, and that have long, secure armrests. This makes rising from a seated position less risky.

•**Minimize bending and reaching.** Many people lose their balance and fall while reaching overhead or bending down. Start by replacing cabinet knobs with handles (handles are easier

*Prices subject to change.

Charles B. Inlander, a consumer advocate and health-care consultant, located in Fogelsville, Pennsylvania. He was the founding president of the nonprofit People's Medical Society, the consumer advocacy organization credited with key improvements in the quality of US health care in the 1980s and 1990s, and is the author of 20 books, including *Take This Book to the Hospital with You: A Consumer Guide to Surviving Your Hospital Stay* (St. Martin's).

to grasp) and mounting them low on high cabinets and high on low cabinets. Buy inexpensive "grabbing" tools, available at home-goods stores and from the on-line retailers (such as Amazon.com), that allow a person to reach up or down more easily. If possible, install pull-out shelves in kitchen and bathroom cabinets, so you don't have to reach in too deeply.

• **Make your house slip-free.** Get rid of any mats or area rugs that are not skid-free. Take castors off chairs and replace them with skid-proof pads, which typically are made of rubber. Place nonskid tape on the edges of all noncarpeted steps to help prevent falls.

• **Install and check out safety equipment.** Make sure you have smoke alarms on every floor of your home, including your basement. Having a carbon monoxide detector on every floor is a smart move as well, as nearly 500 Americans die each year from this deadly gas. And, of course, change the batteries in detectors every six months. You should have at least two small fire extinguishers, one in your kitchen and one within easy access in another location in your home. Nightlights that go on automatically as a room darkens are an inexpensive (about $5) and a smart investment that helps prevent falls during the night. Having a flashlight with fresh batteries in a drawer in each room of your home can prevent injuries during a power failure. And make sure that the outdoor lighting by the entrances to your home is bright enough to illuminate all steps and handles.

 Lightning Self-Defense

When you see a lightning flash, count the seconds until you hear the thunder. If the number is less than 30, the storm is less than six miles away and you should seek shelter immediately—a house, barn, office building or cave. Avoid open areas, such as patios, tents, baseball dugouts and carports. Never stand near tall trees or powerlines. If you are in the open and cannot get to shelter, crouch down with your feet together and stay twice as far from the nearest tree as the tree is tall—stay 100 feet away from a 50-foot tree. Lightning can strike indoors, too.

The leading cause of indoor lightning injuries is the fixed-wire telephone. Use a cordless or cell phone during storms.

Information: National Oceanic and Atmospheric Administration (NOAA) National Weather Service, *www.lightningsafety.noaa.gov.*

What Would You Do If Your Home Caught Fire?

Marjory Abrams, publisher, *Bottom Line* newsletters, Boardroom Inc., 281 Tresser Blvd., Stamford, Connecticut 06901.

Last Christmas, a friend's oven caught on fire, probably ignited by food that spilled over. Fortunately, no one was hurt, and the fire was contained by keeping the oven door closed. But the smoke that poured from the oven spread ash throughout the house. Their insurance company sent in a cleaning crew. But the oven was not salvageable, and some furniture needed to be replaced.

This fire was relatively small. *But Chief Steven Westermann, president of the International Association of Fire Chiefs, says that the incident has lessons for us all...*

• **Develop an escape plan for fires.** If you don't already have one, the City of Phoenix has a good guide on its Web site, *http://phoenix.gov/fire/escfire.html.* Get everyone out of the house immediately if a kitchen fire spreads beyond a pot or pan. Do not try to extinguish the fire.

• **Call 911 even if a fire seems minor.** A fire can double in size every minute and may take only three or four minutes to spread throughout a house.

• **Know where the fire extinguisher is—** and how to work it. This sounds obvious, but many people do forget after not having to use it for many years. Instructions are clearly marked. Review them regularly so that you're ready.

• **Contain flames.** When using the oven, put cookie sheets under the bakeware so that spills stay off of the heating elements. If something starts flaming, turn off the oven and keep the oven door closed.

Most kitchen fires start on top of the stove, especially when frying in deep fat. If a grease fire occurs, immediately cover the pan with a lid to shut off the oxygen supply. It's old advice to never leave the stove unattended when a burner is on, yet far too many people still do—while simmering soups or stews, for example.

• **Install smoke alarms on every level of your home**—typically, at the top and bottom of staircases. Replace batteries every six months. A sprinkler system is highly recommended. If you are building a new house, have a sprinkler system installed at the start.

Unfortunately, a home owner's problems usually don't end once the fire is put out. "Cleanup is tricky," says Peter Duncanson, director of training and technical support for disaster restoration at ServiceMaster Clean (*www.servicemaster clean.com*). "Wiping up ashes with a wet cloth will create even more of a mess. And all fires give off a gas that damages stainless steel, glass, marble and other substances."

To prevent contamination of the entire house after any fire in the home, Peter suggests putting cheesecloth or other filters over all air vents and keeping the room where the fire started closed off for as long as possible. The actual cleanup is best done by restoration professionals. They will pretreat certain materials, test various chemicals to see what works and deodorize the home. Immediate cleanup is critical to prevent permanent damage and protect your health. Your insurance carrier can provide more information to help you minimize your loss.

How to Prevent a Chimney Fire

Mark McSweeney, executive director of the Chimney Safety Institute of America (CSIA) in Plainfield, Indiana. He is CSIA's representative to the US Environmental Protection Agency's Great American Woodstove Changeout Program.

The beauty of burning logs in the fireplace can be mesmerizing—but if you don't inspect and maintain your fireplace properly, the result could be carbon monoxide leaking into your home or even a raging chimney fire. *How to avoid problems…*

CHIMNEY CLEANING

Creosote is the dark residue that sticks to chimney walls when wood is burned. This buildup can lead to a chimney fire that's hot enough to melt mortar, crack tiles, collapse a chimney liner and rapidly spread to the rest of the house.

A blockage in the chimney—from a buildup of creosote and debris—could lead to the spread of fumes, including carbon monoxide.

Your chimney needs to be inspected annually and cleaned when there is one-quarter-inch buildup of creosote or sooner if the creosote has formed a shiny glaze, which means it is more flammable.

Note: If you're switching your wood-burning fireplace to gas, the chimney needs to be thoroughly cleaned first. With gas, the creosote does not build up as quickly, but annual inspection is still needed to check for cracks.

Check my organization's Web site, *www.csia. org*, for certified chimney sweeps in your area. Also, ask friends for recommendations on which chimney-cleaning firm to hire.

Cost: $130 to $300 for the typical inspection and cleaning.*

PREVENTING BUILDUP

• **Use dry wood.** Fresh-cut wood can contain up to 45% water, and that produces more creosote. Well-seasoned firewood contains only 20% to 25% water. Look for wood that has been split and allowed to age for six months to a year.

Alternatives: Duraflame is an artificial log made of dry wood sawdust. It produces no creosote. Java-Log—made of used coffee grounds, not wood fiber—releases 86% less creosote than wood.

• **Don't start a fire with newspaper**—the ink creates additional creosote—and do not use gift-wrapping paper, because it might contain cadmium, lead and other materials that can create toxic fumes. Instead, use kindling or one of the commercially available solid-fuel fire starters —commonly made of compressed wood chips and wax.

*Prices subject to change.

• **Do not restrict airflow.** Closing the glass doors or neglecting to open the damper wide enough may restrict the air supply to the fire, slowing the movement of smoke through the chimney and increasing the amount of creosote created.

Home Security Doesn't Have to Cost a Lot

Paul Shotlander, a recently retired 30-year veteran of the security consulting industry. He was a consultant to large department stores, including Macy's, and owned PJG Security Systems, Ltd., in the Toronto region.

If you reside in a low-crime area and do not keep large amounts of jewelry, cash, art or other valuables in your home, paying $25 to $50 a month for monitored security may be more than you need to spend. Also, monitored security systems are not always so effective—thieves might get in and out before police or a security guard can reach your home in response to the alarm. Unmonitored home-security devices offer a lower-cost alternative. They will not scare off every intruder, but the good systems will deter many of them, and there are no monthly fees.

Advantages and drawbacks of each type…

LIGHTS AND SOUNDS

• **Motion-activated outdoor floodlights.** Purchase a few of these for as little as $20 a piece* at a home-supply or hardware store. Mount them on any side of your home that is not otherwise lit at night. These scare away most prowlers.

Drawbacks: They might not wake you if you are asleep, and they are not effective during the day. They can be activated by animals or even tree branches blowing in a strong wind.

• **Wireless indoor motion-detector systems** use wall-mounted sensors and bedside monitors to alert you with a beeper or alarm and, in some models, lights. With one version, you can link up the monitor to four battery-powered sensors, each of which covers motion over a range of 40

*Prices subject to change.

feet. Install these sensors in your kitchen, living room, main hallway or wherever intruders are likely to pass. The door to the basement should be within range of one of the sensors.

Drawback: Pets can trigger false alarms. Use pet barriers to keep pets out of areas with sensors at night…and turn off your monitor when you get up.

Example: The Household Motion Alert System (includes one sensor), $33 at The Home Depot…$30 from *www.smarthome.com*, plus $20 for each additional sensor or monitor.

DIALERS

• **Full-fledged wireless security systems** come in versions that will dial your cell phone or other numbers you select when motion detectors or door/window sensors are triggered.

These easily installed systems will usually include a wall-mounted control panel, a siren and several sensors. Some of the advanced motion detectors can be programmed to ignore movement below a certain height, so pets don't trigger false alarms unless they jump high enough.

Though ineffective as independent units (see below, these systems' door/window sensors are useful with a larger wireless security system.

Expect to spend $100 to $400, depending on the number of components included. The systems are available at Web sites, including *www.homesecuritystore.com* or *www.smarthome.com*, and at home-supply stores.

Example: Protector Plus Voice Dialer X-10 Wireless Home Security Alarm System, which includes a 95-decible alarm, the voice-alert dialer that calls up to four phone numbers, a motion sensor, two door/window sensors, plus remote controls and a lamp module that causes lights to flash on and off when the alarm is triggered. $100 at *www.x10securitysystems.net*.

PICTURE-TAKING ALTERNATIVE

• **A small security camera that takes digital pictures or records video** will not necessarily stop someone from vandalizing your home, but it will show you—and the police—who was responsible. Some models provide infrared night vision, allowing them to record intruders in the dark. Those without infrared will be of limited use at night. If you want to deter criminals rather than catch a culprit, choose a camera that is designed to be obvious, not one designed to be covert.

Examples: Swann Bulldog Security Camera comes in a metal casing and has night vision, $89 on Amazon.com. Swann Night Hawk wireless outdoor camera kit includes one video camera with night vision that can connect wirelessly to either a DVR, VCR or television, $82 on Amazon.com.

• **Fake security cameras** are inexpensive and mounted outside of your home. They can be a crime deterrent, as long as they are not obvious fakes and are easily seen by potential thieves.

Example: The SVAT ISC200 Outdoor Imitation Security Camera, $30 on Amazon.com.

ALARMS TO AVOID

• **Independent door and window alarms** are inexpensive but not very useful if they are not part of the housewide security system (see above). These small devices mount on the inside of your home's potential entry points and make noise when their magnets sense that the door or window has been opened.

Unfortunately, if they are not wired into a larger security system, they make noise only at the point of entry. Also, experienced thieves know that these alarms can be disabled quickly.

• **Glass-break alarms.** These do not sense burglars who cut through the glass, rather than smashing it. They often miss the noise from a small pane of glass breaking, and they are prone to false alarms from large trucks rumbling past.

Do Alarm Company Signs Deter Burglars?

Alarm company signs and stickers actually help thieves choose targets. Thieves assume that houses with these signs have things worth stealing. A determined thief might deliberately trigger an alarm and then wait close by to see how long it takes the police to respond. Then the thief can return sometime later, with a good idea of how long it might take the police to get there.

The worst of signs identify the burglar-alarm company—a thief usually can get a schematic of the type of system and figure out how to bypass the alarm. Generic signs, which let thieves know that the house is monitored but don't name a company, are better.

Better than stickers or alarms: Closed-circuit monitors at entrances and around the house. No thief wants to be caught on camera—even wearing a mask. Be aware that nonfunctioning cameras can deter thieves, too.

Walter Shaw, security consultant in Fort Lauderdale, Florida—and a former cat burglar.

Better Locks

Most household pin tumbler (key) locks can be opened by "bump" keys. A bump key is one that has been modified so that its grooves are cut to the deepest allowable position. When the key is inserted, then tapped, the bottom pins are bumped upward, opening the lock.

Best: "Bump-proof" locks, such as Medeco High Security.

Barry Wels, The Open Organisation of Lockpickers, Amsterdam, the Netherlands, www.toool.nl.

Self-Defense Made Simple

Master John G. Townsend, founder of the Tao-Zen Ryo Shindo system of martial arts, designed for women and other smaller defenders, www.tao-zen.com. He is the head instructor at the Tao-Zen Academy of Traditional Martial Arts in Poulsbo, Washington, and author of Self-Defense for Peaceable People (Blue Snake).

Sixty percent of American women are victims of violence at least once in their adult lives. Easy, effective martial arts moves that you can learn at home may give you a fighting chance of thwarting an attacker long enough to run away and yell for help. While imagining an assailant in various positions and aiming for his vulnerable spots, practice these techniques until they feel automatic. Remember, your goal is not to beat up the attacker, just to stun him for a few seconds so you can escape. Strike and run!

- **Palm heel strike.** With your hand held in front of you, palm facing forward, tilt your hand back at the wrist and curl your fingers slightly. Drive the heel of your hand upward into an attacker's chin or nose, or forward into his breastbone, stomach or ribs.

- **Sword hand ("karate chop").** Raise your arm with elbow bent and fingers together and extended. To strike, straighten the elbow and hit the assailant with the side edge of your hand, using the fleshy area between the little finger and wrist. With your palm facing the floor, strike at the throat, nose or right above the upper lip.

Alternatives: With the palm facing sideways, strike the collarbone or (if the attacker is beside or behind you) the groin.

- **Side hammer.** With a traditional forward punch that strikes with the knuckles, there's a high risk of breaking bones in your hand or wrist.

Safer: Clench your hand, thumb on the outside of the fingers, and strike with the little-finger side of your fist. Use a downward blow to the bridge of the nose or collarbone, or a sideways blow to the temple, cheek or ribs.

- **Elbow strike.** A bent elbow swung forcefully can produce a powerful blow when the attacker is at close range. Raising one arm, bring your elbow down on his nose or collarbone, or swing it out to the side to strike at his throat or breastbone, or thrust it rearward if he is behind you.

- **Cobra kick.** This pushing/shoving kick can easily break an attacker's knee. Raise one leg, with your knee bent, and plant the sole or ball of your foot on the front of the assailant's knee, just above the joint. Then straighten your leg, pushing quickly and forcefully with your foot.

Self-defense illustrations by Shawn Banner.

- **Stomp.** At close range, stomp your heel down on the attacker's instep. This works well if you're being held from behind.

- **Knee strike.** A time-honored and effective technique is a good old-fashioned knee to the groin. But most men expect this maneuver—so distract him first by trying to poke your fingers in his eyes. While he is focused on protecting his face, knee him hard where it hurts the most.

In Case of Emergency

Key an "in case of emergency" (ICE) contact name and phone number into your cell phone. If you are disabled in an accident or by a medical event, emergency medical workers will look at your phone, see the "ICE" entry in its directory, and know whom to contact. This could be vital if such a contact is needed to quickly obtain your medical history.

Also: Have other family members key "ICE" numbers into their phones.

UC Berkeley Wellness Letter, 6 Trowbridge Dr., Bethel, Connecticut 06801, www.berkeleywellness.com.

Scammed! Don't Let What Happened To These Victims Happen to You

Audri Lanford, PhD, cofounder/coeditor of Internet ScamBusters, a Web site based in Boone, North Carolina, that reports on scams, *www.scambusters.org.*

Con artists are constantly coming up with creative new ways to scam unsuspecting people out of their money. *Here are true stories of scam victims and the lessons we can learn from them…*

GIFT CARD FRAUD
Lisa, a senior citizen in the Midwest, purchased several Walmart gift cards for her grandchildren

last Christmas. When her grandkids tried to use them, they were told that the cards had little or no balance remaining. Lisa returned to the store and demanded that the mistake be corrected, but she was told there was no mistake—the money on the gift cards had already been spent. Only after an hour of arguing with Walmart managers was her money refunded.

Lisa learned later that in the weeks before the holidays, criminals snuck handheld gadgets known as "skimmers" into stores and used them to scan the unique ID codes from gift cards' magnetic strips. The thieves then called the gift card toll-free number to determine which cards had been purchased—and thus activated. They also could have checked on the balances of the cards and then used the stolen codes to shop on-line. They even could have purchased other gift cards for $5 each and then used simple technology to reprogram them with the stolen unique ID numbers and spent the balances.

Lesson: In any store, don't buy the gift cards displayed on store racks. Ask at the customer service desk whether there are any cards behind the counter, out of all customers'—and criminals'—reach. Make sure any packaging has not been tampered with. Keep your receipt, and tell the recipients of your gift cards that they should let you know if there's a problem using the cards.

LATEST LOTTERY CON

Roger, an educated man in his 40s, knew all about the "lottery scam," an old con in which victims are told that they've won a foreign lottery, but to receive their money, they first must pay taxes or fees. (Victims who pay these fees find that their "winnings" never arrive.) So Roger was skeptical when he received an e-mail telling him that he had won the equivalent of thousands of dollars in the British lottery.

He also was intrigued. This wasn't the usual sloppily written spam mail. It seemed very professional and included the names and phone numbers of the lottery representatives he could contact. When Roger called, he was convinced that this was not a scam. The lottery representative promised Roger that he would not have to pay any taxes or money out of his own pocket. Instead, Roger could pay the fees and taxes out of the first installment of his winnings after he received them.

A British cashier's check for $7,600 soon arrived in Roger's mail. Roger deposited the check into his bank account...waited one week for his bank to make the funds available...then mailed in a check for $5,500 to cover taxes and fees, as directed. Roger was sure it couldn't be a scam of any kind—after all, he was $2,100 ahead, even if the rest of the money never arrived.

But the check had never cleared, and several weeks later, Roger's bank informed him that the $7,600 cashier's check had bounced. Now he was out $5,500 of his own money.

Lesson: Be suspicious whenever you're asked for money, even if you have already been paid a larger amount in the form of a check. It can take many weeks for a bank to determine whether a foreign or cashier's check is valid. The check could bounce even after your bank has made the funds available to you, leaving you on the hook to return the entire amount to the bank.

Winning a lottery you did not enter is always too good to be true, even if the con artist does spin a plausible tale about how you came to win and his/her country's unique lottery rules.

Also, according to the Federal Trade Commission, it is illegal for US citizens to play in a foreign lottery.

ON-LINE DATING

Chad, a single man in his mid 50s, started an on-line relationship with a young woman in her 20s named Eileen through a popular dating Internet site. Chad and Eileen e-mailed frequently during a period of many months and exchanged photos via e-mail. Chad was flattered that this attractive, younger woman was interested in him. When Eileen needed $1,500 for a plane ticket to visit a dying relative, Chad was more than happy to comply.

Eileen's hard-luck stories and money requests continued. Eventually, Chad gave Eileen money to get a plane ticket so she could visit him. She claimed to reside hundreds of miles away. That was the last he heard from her. He had been scammed out of more than $4,000.

Lesson: A scam artist might spend months building rapport on-line before asking for a dime. Even if you think you know this person well, consider that you really don't know anyone from your communications over the Internet—you just know the way he/she chooses to present himself in e-mail.

HIT MAN CON

Steve, a financially successful Massachusetts man in his 30s, received an e-mail that sent him into a panic. The writer claimed to be a hit man hired to kill Steve. The hit man offered to call off the job if Steve gave him $75,000—$15,000 more than he said he had been paid for the hit.

This hit man seemed to have done some research on Steve. He knew Steve worked in the financial services industry and that he could afford the $75,000 price.

Steve was given a phone number to call…four days to raise the money…and a warning not to contact the police. But Steve did go to the police, who had seen similar e-mails and explained to him that this was only a scam and that his life was not in danger. The con artist had probably found Steve's e-mail address in a work-related database, which told him Steve's profession. The lucrative nature of that profession suggested that Steve could afford the $75,000 price.

Lesson: Con men know that making victims fear for their lives is a great way to encourage them to hand over their money. Good con artists learn a few details about their intended victims to make their threats more credible. When you are told not to go to the authorities, that's when you should be sure to go to the police.

More from Dr. Audri Lanford…

Phone Scam Targets Military Families

In a new scam, callers pretending to be from the Red Cross call people who have a family member overseas in the military, say that he/she has been injured, and then go on to say that personal information (such as Social Security number, date of birth, etc.) is needed before medical help can be provided to him. Spouses and close family members are particularly vulnerable to the scam.

Safety: The Red Cross does not report casualty information to family members—the Department of Defense contacts families directly. People with family members in the military are warned not to provide any information to such callers.

Don't Lose Twice To Scammers

Thieves maintain lists of victims and may call a second time, claiming to be able to help get back the stolen money.

Example: The caller may purport to be a law-enforcement officer and say that the money has been seized and will be returned for a small fee…or might claim to be a legitimate firm that has bought out another company that had promised prizes that were never sent and now wants to send the prizes if the recipients pay some related costs.

These follow-up scams (called "reloading") are designed to steal additional money. Law-enforcement personnel will never ask victims for money after seizing stolen assets, nor will an honest company that is fulfilling legitimate claims against a firm that it has purchased.

Mark Huffman, contributing editor, *ConsumerAffairs. com*, a free consumer news publication, Washington, DC.

More from Mark Huffman…

Tax Scam Targets Seniors

Seniors seeking tax help are being scammed. Victims are told that they overpaid past income taxes and are instructed to obtain 1099s (income statements) from the Social Security Administration for the past three years. The scammer prepares three "amended" returns for a fee of $40 to $100. The victim files these returns and receives a refund. Later scrutiny by the IRS uncovers the error, the funds must be returned—and the scammer has disappeared.

No Free Anything

In recent examinations, the SEC and state securities regulators found that virtually all free-dinner "investment seminars" for seniors were actually sales presentations. If attendees weren't asked to buy something then and there, they were lined up for a future appointment, perhaps with the pretext of preparing a financial plan.

Some elderly victims winded up signing away huge amounts of their life savings without realizing it. Regulators found everything from misleading and vastly exaggerated claims to clearly unsuitable recommendations to outright fraud.

Julie Jason, president, Jackson Grant Investment Advisers, Two High Ridge Park, Stamford, Connecticut 06905, www.juliejason.com.

Beware Fake Calls And E-Mails "From the IRS"

The IRS warns that scams invoking its name and targeting individuals, businesses and tax-exempt organizations are multiplying. The scams take the form of phone calls and e-mails that try to trick recipients into revealing confidential information (such as bank account or Social Security numbers) that can be used to commit theft.

Alert: The IRS never asks for such information through unsolicited contacts in this manner.

Scams That Catch Young Adults—and Other People, Too

Marjory Abrams, publisher, *Bottom Line* newsletters, Boardroom Inc., 281 Tresser Blvd., Stamford, Connecticut 06901.

The other week, my college-aged daughter picked up an automated call on her cell phone. The recording asked her to enter her card number, press # and enter it yet again. While the voice did not specify which card, my daughter entered her credit card number. When she told me about it, I immediately assumed it was a scam.

"Many scams rope in people who are not yet wise to the ways of the world," says scam tracker Audri Lanford, PhD, codirector of ScamBusters.

Here is her advice for young adults that may benefit us all...

• **If it's spam, it's probably a scam.** Don't respond to it. Don't even open it, because spam may corrupt your computer and could lead to identity theft. If you receive any e-mail, phone call or text message about an account that needs to be "verified," contact the company or bank independently.

• **Don't display your full name in on-line profiles on social networking sites,** and be very cautious about entering your street address. Spammers troll the Internet for personal information. Also, avoid all e-mail surveys that ask for detailed information. When posting the résumé, leave out your address and phone number. Instead, note that the information is available upon request.

COMMON SCAMS TODAY

• **Overpayment scams** involve transactions in which people receive checks for more than they are due.

Example: A college graduate advertises—say, on Craigslist.org—for his roommate. One respondent seems perfect, and the two agree on terms. The prospective roommate sends a check for a larger amount than the required deposit, then explains that he made a mistake and asks for a refund for the overpayment. He gets his refund, but eventually the bank informs the victim that the original check was fraudulent.

Smart advice: Accept only a cashier's check from a local bank for the exact amount you are due. Make sure that these funds have not only cleared but also have been collected by the bank. And don't assume that having a stranger's phone number means that you can track him/her down. Scammers often use disposable cell phones.

• **The Nigerian e-mail scam** is still alive and well. Targets receive messages from foreigners (not necessarily in Nigeria, though that's where the scam started) who supposedly have access to an inheritance or other assets in their homeland that they will share with the right person in exchange for helping them gain access to it. As the scam plays itself out, money is requested to pay fees, taxes, etc.—but the anticipated payout never materializes.

• **Lottery scams** with e-mails promising that huge prizes will be yours after you pay various fees and "taxes." The victims pay, but the prizes never arrive.

Fortunately, my daughter didn't lose any money. She called her credit card company and, to be safe, her bank to cancel all her old accounts and receive new cards. She now is a little wiser in the ways of the world. May your loved ones grow wiser as well.

ID Theft at the Auto Dealership

D on't let a new car test drive lead to identity theft. Before a test drive, the car salesperson will ask to make a photocopy of your driver's license. That's OK because the dealership needs to know you are licensed and needs to have a record in case an accident happens during the drive. But when the test drive is over, be sure to get the copy of your license back—a crooked car salesperson can provide the information on it to scammers who commit ID theft.

Linda Foley, founder and executive director, Identity Theft Resource Center, San Diego, *www.idtheftcenter.org.*

Before You Post Your Résumé On-Line

I f you post your résumé to an on-line employment Web site, you may be targeted by scammers. "Employers" that express interest in your résumé actually might be criminals trying to get your bank account information, credit card information or Social Security number. No legitimate employer will ask for your bank account or credit card data during the hiring process. A legitimate employer will need your Social Security number, but in general this is not required

until you have been through a lengthy interview process and received a job offer.

Margaret Dikel, a Rockville, Maryland–located consultant, who helps organizations improve their use of the Internet as a job search tool. She is a coauthor of *The Guide to Internet Job Searching* (McGraw-Hill). Her Web site is *www.rileyguide.com.*

Airport Alert

T rying to use wireless (Wi-Fi) networks at airports can pose a computer privacy danger. High-tech scammers create what appear to be legitimate airport Wi-Fi systems, which show up when you search for access on your laptop. The con men steal passwords and other confidential information or transmit viruses or spyware.

Self-defense: Download connection management software from a wireless service provider, such as T-Mobile (*client.hotspot.t-mobile.com*) or AT&T (*www.att.com*), before your trip, and then connect only to that provider's hotspots.

Rick Farina, a security researcher with AirTight Networks, Inc., a wireless intrusion-prevention systems company, Mountain View, California, *www.airtightnetworks.net.*

When Not to Give Away A Cell Phone

David Goldschlag, executive vice president and chief technology officer at Trust Digital, a McLean, Virginia, security company that assists companies and government agencies with data protection, *www.trustdigital.com.*

A lthough you think that you've "erased" the data in your old cell phone before selling or otherwise disposing of it, you probably haven't.

Such "erased" information generally remains stored in the phone's memory while being removed only from the indexes in the phone's operating system. But people with the right software can still recover it.

Scary: A security company recently bought 10 used cell phones on eBay. From the phones, they have recovered bank account numbers and their passwords, confidential corporate business plans, private pictures, messages between a married man and his lover and thousands of pages of other private messages.

What to do: Some phones have special instructions for a "full" reset that erases everything in memory. Consult the manual or contact the manufacturer.

If you cannot eliminate your private information, consider destroying the phone instead of selling it...giving the phone to a child or another family member (who doesn't have the tools to recover your private information) to keep it from hackers...keeping the phone in your car or home for emergency use—deactivated phones can still call 911.

ATM Theft Scams

Michael Brown, president of CardCops, Inc., Malibu, California, *www.cardcops.com.*

There are plenty of gadgets out there that help scammers steal your money at the ATM...

• **Blocking devices.** These are installed in the ATM card slot to capture cards—or a thin sleeve is put in the cash slot to prevent money from coming out. Thieves wait for you to go into the bank to report the problem, then steal your card or cash.

• **Card skimmers.** Attached to the ATM to read your card's information, this device is often mounted near the ATM with a label such as "card cleaner." Some skimmers have signs on them telling ATM users to slide their cards through the skimmer first. Skimmers can collect data on 200 cards before thieves need to remove them.

• **Wireless video cameras.** These are mounted inside the ATM area to steal PINs. Magnetic strips and fake ATM cards are easy to make. Thieves then use the PIN information with phony cards.

Self-defense: Look for any signs of tampering or unusual devices when using an ATM...shield the keypad with your hand when entering your PIN...change your PIN at least every six months.

Protect Your Credit Card

Instead of signing the back of your credit card, write "ask for photo ID." This will prevent someone who steals your credit card from using it by copying your signature.

Note: Be sure to carry your driver's license or state ID card to prove your identity.

Kirk M. Herath, chief privacy officer and associate general counsel, Nationwide Insurance, Columbus, Ohio, *www.nationwide.com.*

An Obituary May Lead To Identity Theft

Identity thieves often take the identities of the dead.

Safety: In a published obituary, do not give the exact birth date of the deceased or a married woman's maiden name. Also, upon the death of a family member, immediately notify the Social Security Administration and state Department of Motor Vehicles to prevent the deceased's Social Security number and driver's license from being used by wrongdoers.

Kiplinger's Retirement Report, 1729 H St. NW, Washington, DC 20006, *www.kiplinger.com.*

Safer Passwords

The most commonly utilized passwords and personal identification numbers (or PINs) for computers, e-mail accounts, bank accounts and other password-protected information are *password...123456...qwerty...abc123...letmein...*and the user's first name. There is no foolproof way to create a secure password, but the safest ones meet the following criteria—they contain eight or more characters...combine parts of two unusual words...mix both upper- and lower-case letters with symbols and numbers…and/or combine a foreign and English word.

Sid Kirchheimer, investigative reporter, Audubon, Pennsylvania, and author of *Scam-Proof Your Life* (Sterling).

If Your Identity Is Stolen…

Asa Aarons, an Emmy award–winning consumer reporter who writes a consumer column with his wife, reporter Noreen Seebacher, for the *New York Daily News*.

It's not uncommon for victims of ID theft to feel shock, anger, embarrassment and helplessness. *To regain your balance and retake control…*

•**Contact the security or fraud department** at each of the compromised credit card companies or banks.

•**Place a fraud alert on your credit files,** which can make it difficult for an ID thief to open any credit accounts in your name. You just have to telephone one of the three major consumer reporting agencies—call Equifax (888-766-0008) …Experian (888-397-3742)…or TransUnion (800-680-7289). The company you call is required to notify the other two on your behalf.

•**File a report with your local police** or the police in the community where the fraud took place. Get a copy of the police report in case any creditors request proof of the crime.

•**Follow up your calls to your credit card issuers and banks with a letter** outlining the fraudulent activity. You can use a company's fraud dispute form (contact the company to get one) or download the ID Theft Affidavit from the Federal Trade Commission at *www.ftc.gov/bcp/conline/ pubs/credit/affidavit.pdf*. Mail in the letter, along with supporting information, such as a copy of the police report, to the address on the company's form or the address listed on your monthly statements for "billing inquiries." Send the material by certified mail, return receipt requested.

Copy Your Wallet

Copying your wallet is a simple and effective way to protect the valuable information you carry. Every six months or so put the contents of your wallet on a copying machine and copy the front and back of every significant paper. Then store the copies somewhere secure. If you lose your wallet, you still have all the information—account numbers, business cards, receipts, addresses, telephone numbers and everything else you stashed in it for future reference.

Martin Shenkman, CPA and attorney who specializes in trusts and estates in New York City and Teaneck, New Jersey. He is also the author of many books. His Web site, *www.laweasy.com*, provides sample forms.

Keep Your Computer Safe from Hackers

Databreaker will automatically turn off your Internet connection when it detects that your monitor has entered sleep mode, which will help keep hackers away. Plug the Databreaker into a standard outlet, and then plug your modem cable and monitor's power cord into it and turn on your computer. Works with PCs and Macs, as well as with cable and DSL modems. The cost is $29.95.*

Information: Databreaker, *www.databreaker. com*. Also available at Circuit City.

David Boyer, a research editor and resident computer guru, *Bottom Line/Personal*, Boardroom Inc., 281 Tresser Blvd., Stamford, Connecticut 06901.

*Price subject to change.

Index